Phonologies of Asia and Africa

Phonologies of Asia and Africa

(Including the Caucasus)

Volume 1

edited by

Alan S. Kaye

Technical Advisor

Peter T. Daniels

Winona Lake, Indiana
EISENBRAUNS
1997

© Copyright 1997 Eisenbrauns

All rights reserved
Printed in the United States of America.

Library of Congress Cataloging in Publication Data

Phonologies of Asia and Africa : (including the Caucasus) / edited by
Alan S. Kaye ; technical advisor, Peter T. Daniels.
   p.   cm.
   Includes bibliographical references.
   ISBN 1-57506-017-5 (vol. 1: cloth : alk. paper). — ISBN 1-57506-018-3
(vol. 2: cloth : alk. paper). — ISBN 1-57506-019-1 (2-vol. set: cloth : alk.
paper)
   1. Asia—Languages—Phonology. 2. Africa—Languages—
Phonology. I. Kaye, Alan S. II. Daniels, Peter T.
P381.A75P48   1997
414—dc21   97-4964
                                                                           CIP

The paper used in this publication meets the minimum requirements of the American National Standard for Information Sciences—Permanence of Paper for Printed Library Materials, ANSI Z39.48-1984. ∞

Contents

Volume 1

List of Maps ix
List of Tables ix
Preface xiii
Introduction xv

1 Afroasiatic Languages
Semitic Languages
  Ancient and Medieval
East Semitic
1 *Akkadian and Amorite Phonology* 3
   Giorgio Buccellati
2 *Eblaite Phonology* 39
   Cyrus H. Gordon
Central Semitic
3 *Ugaritic Phonology* 49
   Cyrus H. Gordon
Northwest Semitic
4 *Phoenician and Punic Phonology* 55
   Stanislav Segert
5 *Ancient Hebrew Phonology* 65
   Gary A. Rendsburg
6 *Tiberian Hebrew Phonology* 85
   Geoffrey Khan
7 *Jewish Palestinian Aramaic Phonology* 103
   Geoffrey Khan
8 *Old Aramaic Phonology* 115
   Stanislav Segert
9 *Classical Syriac Phonology* 127
   Peter T. Daniels

v

10 *Modern and Classical Mandaic Phonology* 141
    Joseph L. Malone

South Semitic

11 *Old South Arabian Phonology* 161
    Gene Gragg
12 *Ge'ez Phonology* 169
    Gene Gragg

Modern

Central Semitic

13 *Arabic Phonology* 187
    Alan S. Kaye
14 *Moroccan Arabic Phonology* 205
    Jeffrey Heath
15 *Cypriot Arabic Phonology* 219
    Alexander Borg
16 *Maltese Phonology* 245
    Alexander Borg

Northwest Semitic

17 *Israeli Hebrew Phonology* 287
    Shmuel Bolozky
18 *Modern Aramaic Phonology* 313
    Robert D. Hoberman

South Semitic

19 *La phonologie des langues sudarabiques modernes* 337
    Antoine Lonnet et Marie-Claude Simeone-Senelle
20 *Chaha (Gurage) Phonology* 373
    Wolf Leslau
21 *Amharic Phonology* 399
    Wolf Leslau

Egyptian Sub-branch

22 *Egyptian and Coptic Phonology* 431
    Antonio Loprieno

Berber Languages

23 *Berber Phonology* 461
    Maarten G. Kossmann and Harry J. Stroomer

Cushitic Languages

24 *Awngi Phonology* 477
    Robert Hetzron

25 *Oromo Phonology* 493
   Maria-Rosa Lloret
26 *Somali Phonology* 521
   Annarita Puglielli

Chadic Languages

27 *Hausa Phonology* 537
   Paul Newman

Volume 2

2 **Indo-European Languages**
  Ancient and Medieval
    Anatolian Languages
28 *Hittite Phonology* 555
   H. Craig Melchert
    Iranian Languages
29 *Old Persian and Avestan Phonology* 569
   David Testen
30 *Pahlavi Phonology* 601
   Dieter Weber
  Modern
    Indo-Aryan Languages
31 *Hindi-Urdu Phonology* 637
   Alan S. Kaye
32 *Gujarati Phonology* 653
   P. J. Mistry
    Iranian Languages
33 *Persian Phonology* 675
   Gernot L. Windfuhr
34 *Kurdish Phonology* 691
   Ernest N. McCarus
35 *Ossetic Phonology* 707
   David Testen
36 *Pashto Phonology* 733
   Josef Elfenbein
37 *Balochi Phonology* 761
   Josef Elfenbein

Armenian Sub-branch
  38 *Armenian Phonology* 777
      John A. C. Greppin

3 **Dravidian Languages**
  39 *Brahui Phonology* 797
      Josef Elfenbein

4 **Nilo-Saharan Languages**
  40 *Nilo-Saharan Phonology* 815
      M. Lionel Bender

5 **Niger-Congo Languages**
  41 *Swahili Phonology* 841
      Ellen Contini-Morava
  42 *Sango Phonology* 861
      James A. Walker and William J. Samarin

6 **Altaic Languages**
  Turkic Languages
  43 *Turkish Phonology* 883
      Bernard Comrie
  44 *Tatar (Volga Tatar, Kazan Tatar) Phonology* 899
      Bernard Comrie
  45 *Uyghur Phonology* 913
      Bernard Comrie

7 **Caucasian Languages**
  46 *Georgian Phonology* 929
      Howard I. Aronson
  47 *Chechen Phonology* 941
      Johanna Nichols
  48 *Lak Phonology* 973
      Gregory D. S. Anderson

8 **Unaffiliated Languages (Language Isolates)**
  49 *Sumerian Phonology* 1001
      John Hayes
  50 *Burushaski Phonology* 1021
      Gregory D. S. Anderson

List of Maps

1. Geo-Chronological Distribution of Akkadian Dialects and of Amorite 8
2. Les langues sudarabiques modernes 338
3. Nilo-Saharan Locations 818
4. The Swahili-Speaking Area 843
5. Ubanguian Languages 862

List of Tables

1-1. Synopsis of Consonants and Glides (semivowels) for Amorite, Old Akkadian, and Later Akkadian Dialects (OB+) 16
1-2. Correspondences among Laryngeals and Pharyngeals 18
1-3. Graphemic Sets and Modern Phonemic Notations for Sibilants with Divergent Realizations 20
1-4. Phonemic and Graphemic Correspondences for Sibilants with Divergent Realizations 20
1-5. Akkadian Vowels 22
1-6. Amorite Vowels 23
4-1. Phoenician Consonants 59
4-2. Phoenician Vocalic System 60
6-1. Tiberian Hebrew Vowels 91
7-1. Jewish Palestinian Aramaic Consonants 105
8-1. Old Aramaic Consonants 119
9-1. Syriac Consonants 132
10-1. Mandaic Segments 142
11-1. Old South Arabian Consonants 163
11-2. Semitic Consonant Correspondences 166
12-1. Ge'ez Consonant Correspondences 173
12-2. Ge'ez Consonant Articulation 174
12-3. Ge'ez Vowels 177

13-1.	Comparison of the Major Semitic Languages	188
13-2.	Modern Standard Arabic Consonants	192
14-1.	Primary Moroccan Colloquial Arabic Consonants	208
15-1.	The Cypriot Arabic Segmental Paradigm	222
15-2.	Cypriot Arabic Dental Stop Contrasts	233
16-1.	Maltese Consonants	249
16-2.	Maltese Short Vowels	264
16-3.	Maltese Long Vowels	268
16-4.	Maltese Diphthongs	270
17-1.	Israeli Hebrew Consonants	287
18-1.	Amadiya Aramaic Consonants	315
19-1.	Correspondances consonantiques en sémitique méridional	346
19-2.	Système consonantique du sudarabique moderne commun	349
20-1.	Chaha Vowels	395
21-1.	Amharic Consonants	400
21-2.	Amharic Vowels	419
22-1.	Early Egyptian Consonants	437
22-2.	Early Egyptian Vowels	440
22-3.	Early Egyptian Syllabic Structures	441
22-4.	Later Egyptian Vowels	444
22-5.	Later Egyptian Syllabic Structures	445
22-6.	Coptic Consonants	447
22-7.	Sahidic Coptic Vowels	452
22-8.	Sahidic Coptic Syllabic Structures	455
23-1.	Tashelhit Consonant Inventory	467
24-1.	Awngi Consonants	478
24-2.	Awngi Vowels	482
25-1.	Oromo Vowels	494
25-2.	Oromo Consonants	495
25-3.	Oromo Transcriptions	495
26-1.	Somali Consonants	522
26-2.	Somali Vowels	524
26-3.	Somali Sandhi	532
27-1.	Hausa Consonants	538
27-2.	Hausa Vowels	541
28-1.	Hittite Consonants	559
29-1.	Iranian Languages	570
29-2.	Common Iranian Phonemes	574

29-3.	The Old Persian Writing System	578
29-4.	Old Persian Phonemes	580
29-5.	The Avestan Writing System	587
30-1.	Pahlavi Phonemes	611
31-1.	Hindi-Urdu Consonants	642
31-2.	Hindi-Urdu Vowels	642
31-3.	Comparative Indo-Aryan Phonology	647
32-1.	Gujarati Consonants	656
32-2.	Gujarati Vowels	657
33-1.	Persian Consonants	677
33-2.	Persian Vowels	678
33-3.	Persian Consonant Classification	678
33-4.	Persian Glides and Vowels	678
34-1.	Consonant Phonemes	692
34-2.	Vowel Phonemes	696
35-1.	Consonantal Phonemes	710
35-2.	Semivocalic Phonemes	711
35-3.	Vocalic Phonemes	711
35-4.	Transitive Past Tense	714
35-5.	Intransitive Past Tense	715
35-6.	Vowel Alternations in Verb Stems	726
36-1.	Pashto Consonants	741
37-1.	Balochi Consonants	771
38-1.	Classical Armenian Consonants	783
39-1.	Brahui Consonants	800
40-1.	Proposed Genetic Structure of Nilo-Saharan	815
40-2.	Nilo-Saharan Segments Overall	823
40-3.	Common Nilo-Saharan Segments	832
40-4.	Proto-Nilo-Saharan Segmental Phonemes	836
41-1.	Standard Swahili Consonants	844
41-2.	Standard Swahili Vowels	850
41-3.	Proto-Sabaki Segments	857
42-1.	Pidgin Sango Vowels	864
42-2.	Sango Consonants	866
42-3.	Contractions of Particles	872
42-4.	Urban and Rural Features	878
43-1.	Turkish Vowels	884
43-2.	Turkish Consonants	885

44-1.	Tatar Vowels	900
44-2.	Tatar Consonants	902
45-1.	Uyghur Vowels	914
45-2.	Uyghur Morphophonemic Vowel Qualities	914
45-3.	Uyghur Consonants	915
46-1.	Georgian Stops	929
46-2.	Georgian Fricatives	930
46-3.	Georgian Liquids, Nasals, and Glides	930
46-4.	Georgian Postvelars	931
46-5.	Georgian Vowels	931
46-6.	Georgian Vocalic Distinctive Features	932
46-7.	Georgian Phonemic System	932
47-1.	Chechen Consonants	943
47-2.	Chechen Vowels	945
47-3.	Chechen Umlaut	948
47-4.	Chechen Umlaut: *i*-Verbs	948
47-5.	Chechen Dialect Vowels	956
47-6.	Chechen Dialect Umlaut Processes	959
47-7.	Chechen Consonant Frequencies	966
47-8.	Proto-Nakh Consonant Cognate Sets	969
48-1.	Lak Vowels	974
48-2.	Lak Consonants	978
49-1.	Sumerian Consonants	1008
49-2.	Sumerian Vowels	1011
49-3.	Possible Sumerian Five-Vowel System	1012
49-4.	Possible Sumerian Eight-Vowel System	1012
50-1.	Burushaski Consonants	1023
50-2.	Burushaski Vowels	1027

Preface

This work has evolved over the course of the past few years and has involved the cooperation of 39 distinguished linguists. As such, uniformity in methodology and terminology has not been a desideratum, nor would it have been possible to attain. The achievements, nevertheless, have, in my opinion, proved to be remarkable. The goal of this publication is to provide a summary of what is currently known about the phonology of selected Asian and African languages. In addition, three languages of the Caucasus are included. What I, as editor, have strived to do here is to give each author enough leeway to allow for the presentation of interesting facts in an informative way, while paying strict attention to what is most significant about the language(s) under investigation. Of course, the readership will ultimately have to take it upon itself to decide the extent to which I have succeeded. I would like to express my sincere thanks to all the contributors for their efforts, and above all, for their extraordinary patience while the book was in production. These collaborative projects often take much more time to complete than was originally envisaged, as I found out once before with the two volumes containing approximately 1,800 pages by 134 scholars I edited in 1991: *Semitic Studies in Honor of Wolf Leslau on the Occasion of His Eighty-Fifth Birthday*.

One contributor deserves special commendation. Peter T. Daniels has served admirably as the technical advisor to this collection. His service has proven to be exemplary and far beyond the call of duty. Let me briefly elaborate. Peter has been influential in the final product in three crucial ways. First, he performed many copy-editing tasks and was responsible, along with his Abjad Press, for the typesetting of the articles, often corresponding with authors on both technical and scientific matters. All the contributions are better off as a direct result of Peter's personal intervention. His commitment to excellence is obvious on each page which follows (and can also be seen in *The World's Writing Systems*, which he co-edited with William Bright and single-handedly typeset). Second, it was Peter who first suggested to me the idea that Tiberian Hebrew should be covered in a separate undertaking, in addition to the commissioned chapter on Biblical Hebrew. Readers could thus compare and contrast both these treatments. He further recommended that since the Aramaic coverage was to be so extensive among all the Semitic languages discussed in the book, a special effort should be made to treat Palestinian Jewish Aramaic in an entire article by itself. As it turned out, both of his proposals came to fruition. Third, Peter recruited his colleagues at the University of Chicago, Howard Aronson, David Testen, and Gregory D. S. Anderson, to contribute to this reference by writing on their specializations, and also secured the services of Johanna Nichols to prepare the article on Chechen. These particular chapters have given this work, already a hefty tome prior to the arrival of this new material, an even greater appeal and strength by virtue of the variety of the additions, thus unquestionably justifying the larger size. Although I, as editor, bear full responsibility for the final selection of languages treated herein, it is Peter who must be credited for his insight that the volume should delve somewhat more into the heart of Africa than was originally contemplated, and offer as wide a coverage as possible, given our original framework of the prospective title, *Phonologies of Asia and Africa*.

Finally, I wish to express my gratitude to Wolf Leslau and Franz Müller-Gotama, who made a number of useful suggestions concerning the introduction.

Alan S. Kaye
Fullerton, California
December 1995

Introduction

Why yet another book on phonology when, apparently, there are already so many published volumes of every conceivable size, shape, orientation, theory, and methodology imaginable that deal with this subject? I hope to convince the reader that this book is unique, and furthermore, that it yields valuable insights to anyone interested in any type of descriptive phonology. In offering both introductory undergraduate as well as graduate courses in this field for almost 30 years, I have had the opportunity to use a variety of books and other materials. Most enjoyable for me and for the great majority of my students (as they have confided to me) have been articles (from a wide assortment of journals) that are devoted to specific languages. These include works by such notables as Edward Sapir, John Rupert Firth, Roman Jakobson, Zellig Sabbetai Harris, and numerous other outstanding scholars. These linguists have all had one thing in common—vast personal experience working on many languages and dialects, often via fieldwork and active language learning, be it in coursework or through independent study. All have introduced the reader to a large assortment of different perspectives—a virtual smorgasbord of aromas and tastes—everything from the Prague or London Schools (prosodic analysis) to the Copenhagen School of glossematics, structural or Bloomfieldian and Neo-Bloomfieldian to stratificational approaches, generative phonology of all persuasions including natural generative phonology, natural phonology, lexical phonology, autosegmental phonology, CV phonology, particle phonology, atomic phonology, dependency phonology, metrical phonology, experimental phonology, moraic phonology, and so on. While the dominant paradigms within phonology and phonological theory have been developing and, as seems only too obvious to report, rapidly changing over the past few years and even decades, the data-oriented discussions by the linguists of yesteryear seem to have held their own. Here we may cite some of the classic papers in the field, such as Leonard Bloomfield's "Menomini Morphophonemics" (1939), or Edward Sapir's "La réalité psychologique des phonèmes" (1933), available in English since 1949. Like good wine, they have all mellowed with age; like a good movie from the 1930s or 1940s, they are still enjoyable; and like a good book from bygone days, one can still profit from them, while noting beauty, care in their preparation, and refinement, not to mention a superb elegance of phraseology and in the handling of minute details. In my view, they still have something worthwhile to say, and their contents are, even after all these years, germane. As many have claimed, not everything new or newer is necessarily better, and data-oriented linguistics (and one may add philology in general) can still contribute to the larger picture of the complicated workings of *parole*, *langue*, and even *langage*—to the grand synthesis or syntheses, if you will. There have been many other data-oriented articles which have appeared over the years. However, nothing similar to the compilation of articles I wanted to assemble and edit for the general linguist as well as the specialist has ever, to my knowledge, appeared until now.

The idea for this volume came about as I searched in vain for a book which would enable my students to gain a concrete familiarity of solid phonological work by subjecting them to the exposure of many of today's (hard-)working linguists who would concisely describe and comment on the phonological processes in and structures of languages which they have carefully scrutinized, both ancient or medieval and modern. In many cases, the authors chosen are the leading specialists on these languages (and often the language families to which they belong as well). As I have repeatedly emphasized in some writings and especially in my classes over the years at California State University, Fullerton, linguistics to me is, first and foremost, about languages—real, natural languages with all their messy details, including exceptions to this rule or that. Let me reiterate this very position here. This philosophy of science—or, perhaps better stated, this philosophy of how to do science—is a premise about how to do linguistics and about what linguistics is (and, invariably, is not), or, at least, this type or genre of linguistics. My *Weltanschauung* has been that linguists research languages and study structures—a simple enough supposition, or so it would appear (contra Noam Chomsky, who has repeatedly stated that "linguistics is *part of* psychology"; cf., e.g., his *Language and Responsibility*, p. 43). This seems even truer when one talks specifically about phonetics and phonology (rather than linguistics as a whole, which, I readily admit, is, *mutatis mutandis*, an interdisciplinary and multidisciplinary science). Phonology has, in fact, over the years continuously seen a steady stream of textbooks, handbooks, reference works, chrestomathies, and "surveys" of varying length and quality. Indeed our library shelves seem to be bulging to the breaking point with reprinted works and commmentaries thereon, even commentaries on the commentaries, on the various schools of phonology, phonologists, and phonological scope, analysis, explication, interfacing, etc. Moreover, numerous new books regularly appear promising what jacket blurbs usually push as new universal insights into phonological structure, phonological typology, phonological universals, or some such arena. As illustrative of the two aforementioned points, let me make mention of *Readings in Linguistics I and II*, edited by Eric P. Hamp, Martin Joos, Fred W. Householder, and Robert Austerlitz; while Bruce Hayes's *Metrical Stress Theory* is a current exploration of this popular phonological theory. Furthermore, Michael Kenstowicz's *Phonology in Generative Grammar* is a 700-page encyclopedic discussion of various theoretical concerns, and John Clark and Colin Yallop and John Goldsmith satisfactorily survey more or less the entire field (Clark and Yallop, *An Introduction to Phonetics and Phonology*; Goldsmith, ed., *The Handbook of Phonological Theory*). What the entire field of phonology has always lacked and is still lacking until now is a book with the present focus and scope, in which the subject matter is thoroughly packaged, consumed, and digested as a data-oriented, descriptive discipline, and does not merely serve as a hotplate for a rehash of rules of various types and layouts with assorted labels and devices reflectant of different premises, styles, interests, or parameters.

The only volume known to me which, at least in part, attempted to cover the phonetics and phonologies of various languages is *Manual of Phonetics*, edited by Louise Kaiser, although there are brief phonological discussions in other works dealing with numerous languages, such as *The World's Major Languages*, edited by Bernard Comrie; George L. Campbell's two-volume *Compendium of the World's Languages*; or *International Encyclopedia of Linguistics*, edited by William Bright. Part D.b of the aforementioned Kaiser tome, however, dealt exclusively with language data, and one author therein (Wolf Leslau writing on the Semitic languages) has managed to contribute two articles in the same general area of specialization for this volume. The profound difference between the earlier study by this celebrated linguist and the present essays herein is one of detail(s), since the former was severely limited in space (pp. 325–29), and the author had little choice but to deal in generalities only.

The other coverages in the Kaiser *Manual* were devoted to Romance, Germanic, Slavonic, Finno-Ugrian, and African tone languages (this is the terminology employed in that work). The paper on the tonal languages of Africa was allotted a total of six pages (pp. 330–35, by A. Burssens). Unfortunately, that important section of the volume on specific languages was removed in the book's second edition, which, according to the new editor, Bertil Malmberg, was a completely revised and expanded version of the prior *Manual* edited by Kaiser. Malmberg justified this decision to excise this material (after "a long discussion between the publisher" and himself, p. v) stating that the information devoted to "particular languages ... in a book of this kind seems to be of little interest, firstly because the choice of languages described is completely arbitrary, secondly because the space admitted for each language or language family does not permit any real presentation of its particularities" (ibid.). The present work is meant to alter, at least somewhat, this lamentable state of affairs which has existed far too long.

I have always wanted my students to come away from their courses in phonology with dual experiences. First and most important, they should have gained expertise with the phonological structure of real languages, both synchronically and, to a lesser extent, diachronically. Theory comes and goes, yet the facts of Arabic phonology, e.g., have not changed very much over the past half century or more. One still needs, even after all these years, to make reference to the problem of "emphasis" (pharyngealization or velarization) and the "emphatics," no matter what labels are *au courant*, what terms are trendy or in vogue, or what types of rules are fashionable or conventions in bloom. On the other hand, general phonology is hardly recognizable from the days in which Charles F. Hockett, Kenneth L. Pike, André Martinet, and Zellig S. Harris were among the household names of the 1940s or 1950s. Secondly, students should have become familiar with competing analyses while, at the same time, also being sensitive to different approaches to linguistic explications. This tome has been designed to allow readers, including seasoned veterans in the field, the opportunity to come to grips with the phonologies of many non-European languages. All the articles which follow, the collaborative efforts of several different phonological traditions, are written by experts who have considerable *savoir-faire* with languages. All of these linguists enjoy national and international reputations.

Let me now devote a few words to the difficulty encountered in the selection of languages. Reviewers will inevitably point out that this language should have been included or that that one was unnecessary, and thus could have been omitted. Since my own forte as a Semitist and an Afroasiaticist has been in the languages of parts of Asia and Africa, these geographical areas have, of necessity, been emphasized (see below for further details). It must be admitted that I at one time toyed with the idea of entitling this manual *The Phonology of Oriental Languages*. That idea had eventually to be abandoned because the designation "Orient" as currently used is inexact, and colleagues, especially those in the humanities or social sciences, would not be receptive to the idea that it did not, in fact, deal with Chinese, Japanese, Korean, etc., certainly considered "Oriental" according to any current sense of the term. The present title is also somewhat ambiguous, I confess; yet no promise was ever intended by this choice that all languages of this region would be covered. Rather, the implication was and still is that we would be dealing with selected languages. A further more pragmatic factor had to do with the availability of certain authors who could meet our time frame.

Let me now turn to the specifics about which languages and dialects have been chosen for inclusion. The reader will surely have become aware of the extensive coverage given to the Semitic languages. Since some Arabic dialects (so-called) are, in my opinion, better designated separate and distinct Semitic languages in their own right, I made a special endeavor to recruit the leading authorities on Moroccan and Cypriot Arabic so that the contrasts would be noticeable when one compared these with the phonological facts discussed in the articles dealing with Maltese and Arabic (Modern Standard and Egyptian [Cairene]). The other modern Semitic languages treated herein include some of the most interesting (and most involved) of the diachronic developments from the Proto-Semitic stage. These are: Modern Israeli Hebrew, Modern (or Neo-) Aramaic, really a conglomeration of different languages (not dialects), six Modern South Arabian languages, Chaha (one of several distinct Gurage [Ethio-Semitic] languages), and Amharic, the national language of Ethiopia.

The ancient (including medieval) Semitic languages include: Akkadian (Assyro-Babylonian) and Amorite, Eblaite, Ugaritic, Phoenician and Punic, Biblical and Tiberian Hebrew, Palestinian Jewish Aramaic, Old and Biblical Aramaic, Syriac, Mandaic, Old (Epigraphic) South Arabian (also known as Epigraphic South Arabic), and Ge'ez (Classical Ethiopic).

The related Afroasiatic (Hamito-Semitic or Afrasian) languages include: Ancient Egyptian and Coptic, the Berber languages (not dialects), the Cushitic languages—Awngi, Oromo, and Somali—and the Chadic language, Hausa.

The culturally and geographically related (to the above) languages include: Sumerian (an isolate), Hittite, Avestan and Old Persian (Old Iranian), Pahlavi (Middle Persian), Persian, Ossetic, Kurdish, Pashto, Balochi,

Armenian (all Indo-European), Brahui (Dravidian), Turkish, Tatar, and Uyghur (Turkic sub-branch of Altaic).

Finally, there is a section of languages (the first two of which continue the aforementioned grouping) of interest to phonological typologists, which includes: Hindi-Urdu (Hindustani) and Gujarati (Indo-Aryan sub-branch of Indo-European), Burushaski (an isolate), Swahili (the Bantu sub-branch of Niger-Congo), Sang(h)o (a creole based on Ngbandi, which is Niger-Congo), Nilo-Saharan languages, and Georgian, Chechen, and Lak (South, North Central, and Northeast Caucasian respectively).

It should be noted that a serious attempt has been made from the outset to ensure that the chapters would be both understandable and useful to a linguist of any persuasion, while simultaneously anticipating that anthropologists, sociologists, historians, and other researchers could utilize the pages which follow for their own scholarly pursuits. For any shortcomings in this regard, it is I, as editor, who must assume full responsibility for the articles, including both of mine. In other words, the usual disclaimers apply.

Finally, there is one last item—a request of the readership. It would be greatly appreciated if comments could be sent directly to me suggesting improvements on any of the selections for the book's planned subsequent editions.

Alan S. Kaye
Linguistics Program
California State University, Fullerton
Fullerton, California 92634-9480
e-mail: akaye@fullerton.edu
Fax: 714-449-5954

References

Bloomfield, Leonard. 1939. "Menomini Morphophonemics." *Travaux du cercle linquistique de Prague* 8: 105–15.
Bright, William, ed. 1992. *International Encyclopedia of Linguistics.* New York: Oxford University Press.
Campbell, George L. 1991. *Compendium of the World's Languages.* London: Routledge.
Chomsky, Noam. 1979. *Language and Responsibility.* New York: Pantheon.

Clark, George, and Colin Yallop. 1995. *An Introduction to Phonetics and Phonology*, 2nd ed. Oxford: Blackwell.
Comrie, Bernard, ed. 1987. *The World's Major Languages*. London: Croom Helm; New York: Oxford University Press.
Daniels, Peter T., and William Bright, eds. 1996. *The World's Writing Systems*. New York: Oxford University Press.
Goldsmith, John, ed. 1995. *The Handbook of Phonological Theory*. Oxford: Blackwell.
Hamp, Eric P., Martin Joos, Fred W. Householder, and Robert Austerlitz, eds. 1995. *Readings in Linguistics I and II* (abridged edition). Chicago: University of Chicago Press.
Hayes, Bruce. 1995. *Metrical Stress Theory*. Chicago: University of Chicago Press.
Kaiser, Louise, ed. 1957. *Manual of Phonetics*. Amsterdam: North Holland.
Kaye, Alan S., ed. 1991. *Semitic Studies in Honor of Wolf Leslau on the Occasion of His Eighty-Fifth Birthday*. 2 vols. Wiesbaden: Harrassowitz.
Kenstowicz, Michael. 1994. *Phonology in Generative Grammar*. Oxford: Blackwell.
Malmberg, Bertil, ed. 1968. *Manual of Phonetics*. Amsterdam: North Holland.
Sapir, Edward. 1933. "La réalité psychologique des phonèmes." *Journal de psychologie normale et pathologique* 30: 247–65. English orig. in *Selected Writings of Edward Sapir in Language, Culture, and Personality*, ed. David G. Mandelbaum. Berkeley and Los Angeles: University of California Press, pp. 46–60.

1 Afroasiatic Languages

Chapter 1
Akkadian and Amorite Phonology
Giorgio Buccellati
University of California, Los Angeles

1.1. The graphemic base

1.1.1. The writing medium

Akkadian and Amorite are dead languages, in the specific sense that their speakers died out around 1600 B.C. (for Amorite) and 600 B.C. (for Akkadian). Our reconstruction of both languages is thus based exclusively on the written record, except for the inferences that may be drawn from the fact that they are related to other Semitic languages for which there are informants. The written medium, though rich in information, presents considerable limitations which must be taken into account. In addition, two other filters must be reckoned with, particularly in any discussion of phonology.

(A) The writing system was not originally developed for a Semitic language, but rather for Sumerian. The process of adaptation to Semitic was gradual and organic, and was not governed by a-priori linguistic considerations. Especially in the early periods, the scribes, who were conversant with Sumerian, maintained the basic graphemic oppositions which were best suited for Sumerian and subsumed under them a variety of Semitic oppositions. For instance, it has been suggested (Gelb 1961: 31–33) that Sumerian had an opposition between stops (without distinction of voice) and aspirates; this two-way graphemic opposition was used to render a three-way opposition, in Akkadian, between voiced, voiceless, and emphatics. (An interesting

AUTHOR'S NOTE: I wish to thank the editor of this volume, Alan S. Kaye, for his thoughtful comments on the first version of my manuscript, and for various substantive and bibliographical suggestions. ABBREVIATIONS: Am, Amorite; Ar, Arabic; OA, Old Assyrian; OAkk, Old Akkadian; OB, Old Babylonian; OB+, Old Babylonian and later dialects; PS or *, Proto-Semitic.—Standard symbols used in Assyriological literature: $'_1$ = $'$; $'_2$ = $ḥ$; $'_3$ = $ḫ$; $'_4$ = $ʿ$; $'_5$ = $ġ$; $'_6$ = w; $'_7$ = y. Note also: $\underline{t}$ = $θ$. For $ś$, $š$, and $ṣ̌$, see § 1.3.5. Square brackets are occasionally used in Assyriological literature to indicate the graphemic transliteration. This however generates confusion with the more common linguistic use of square brackets for phonetic transcription. Accordingly, where an explicit graphemic notation is needed, I either render transliterated cuneiform signs in small capitals (DA), or else I enclose them in angle brackets (<da>). Small capitals are also used to render logograms (generally, in their Sumerian reading).

parallel with a modern situation is found in Polomé 1981, concerning the influence on the phonology of hitherto unwritten languages of "educated" transcriptions introduced by non-native speakers.)

(B) A second major filter affects Amorite. It seems certain that Amorite was never written down as such, i.e., there was no Amorite scribal tradition and accordingly, no Amorite texts. We only have Amorite personal names (plus a few technical terms), which were written down by Sumerian and Akkadian scribes, who developed their own conventions for rendering in writing the sounds of a language they did not normally speak, though presumably they did understand it (the existence of Amorite "interpreters" is presumably applicable only to the Sumerian south, at a time when Amorite was still something of a novelty).

1.1.2. *The writing system*

Inasmuch as we are dealing with a dead language, considerations about phonology are fundamentally affected by our understanding of the cuneiform writing system. Here are some of the most significant.

(A) There is a heavy reliance on various LOGOGRAPHIC subsystems, which apply especially to certain nouns and numerals, and exhibit considerable differences depending on time periods and text types (in modern transliterations, logograms are generally rendered in small capitals with their Sumerian value, e.g., URU for *ālum* 'city'). Logograms are of no value for phonological reconstruction—so much so that one might question whether they are graphemes at all (see § 1.1.4). This, however, does not seriously affect our overall understanding of phonology since there are sufficient syllabic correspondences of words as lexical items to compensate for the widespread use of logograms as textual items.

(B) The use of HISTORICAL WRITINGS is more problematic, and it affects especially our ability to determine the time period at which a certain phonological change first occurred. For instance, the loss of final short vowels begins to be attested towards the end of the second millennium, but vowels in this position continue to be marked in the writing all the way down to the end of the documentation. In such cases we may assume that the linguistic phenomenon (as distinct from its graphemic representation) became operative across the board when first attested—a conclusion which is confirmed, in the particular case mentioned, by the fact that a short vowel in word-final position, written to indicate a presumed case ending, is often incorrect by morphological standards (e.g. *ālu*, *āla*, or *āli* are used indiscriminately for *āl*), which indicates that the proper vowel was no longer supplied by any active linguistic competence.

(C) ORTHOGRAPHIC CONVENTIONS correspond to certain phonological regularities which we must define inferentially. For instance, while there are cuneiform signs used to render the presence of glottal stop, they do not normally occur in word-initial position; thus the word for 'city' may be written with the two signs <a-lum>, but not with the signs *<'a-lum>. If we do nevertheless assume that Akkadian words did not begin with plain vowel (hence regularly /'ālum/, rather than */ālum/, see § 1.3.8) it is because (a) we recognize graphemic rules next to graphemic values (see § 1.1.4), (b) we have very few examples of sandhi across word boundary (e.g. *libbālim* for *libbi 'ālim* 'heart of the city'), and (c) we postulate a fundamental similarity with other Semitic languages.

1.1.3. Phonology and graphemics

The theory and application of GRAPHEMICS[1] is fundamental for an understanding of Akkadian phonology. This point needs to be stressed here in a special way because linguists who approach the Mesopotamian documentation without a proper understanding of the writing system can easily be misled into deriving false conclusions from what are presumed to be safe data. (Conversely, philologists are found sometimes to pay lip service to linguistic jargon, in that terms like "grapheme" or "phoneme" are used simply because they are perceived as more sophisticated than traditional terms like "sign" or "sound"; the consequent lack of proper definition makes for confusion rather than clarity.) I adhere to a narrower understanding of graphemics than usual. What phonemics is to meaning, graphemics is to sound. In other words, graphemics is the systemic correlation between graphic symbols and phonemes. Hence it is neither paleography (which deals with the shape of the symbols) nor orthography (which deals with the stylistic choice of alternative symbols from the same repertory). If every phoneme were represented by a single graphic symbol, the graphemic system would simply be a graphic overlay of the phonemic inventory. The alphabet (first invented in northeastern Syria towards the end of the second millennium—though some would push it back to the end of the third, Mendenhall 1985) comes close to this ideal, and it is, in this respect, a profoundly abstract linguistic accom-

---

1. What follows is based on my understanding of graphemic theory, as articulated in Buccellati 1979, 1982, 1984, 1990a. For an antithetic view, which calls into question the very notion of graphemics, see Daniels 1993.

plishment, besides serving as a very significant socioeconomic innovation. But unfortunately the cuneiform graphemic system is not quite as transparent. It is, in fact, a much more complex organism which includes multiple values and clustering laws.

Except for logograms, numerals written as digits, and semantic indicators (determinatives), all cuneiform signs are syllabic in nature. Each syllabic sign can render a variety of GRAPHEMIC VALUES, only some of which are made explicit in our modern system of sign-by-sign transliteration. For instance, in Old Babylonian any sign corresponding to a syllable with initial voiced stop may stand for a syllable with a homologous emphatic—i.e. the sign DA can stand for either /da/ or /ṭa/, though not for /ta/. GRAPHEMIC LAWS refer essentially to the clustering of values (hence they may be considered grapho-tactic in nature); for example, consonantal length may or may not be shown overtly, or else aleph may be marked by a simple vowel sign in word-initial position (e.g., <a-lum> for /ʾālum/) or in medial position after a sign ending in a consonant (e.g., <iš-al> for /ʾišʾal/), but not necessarily after a sign ending in a vowel (e.g., <ba-a-bum> for /bābum/, not */baʾabum/, but <ša-a-lum> for /šaʾālum/).

In the American tradition of Assyriology (following I. J. Gelb), one uses the term "transliteration" to refer to the sign-by-sign rendering of graphemes (e.g., *i-il-la-ak*), and "transcription" to refer to the normalized rendering of their phonemic realization (e.g., *illak*).

1.1.4. Graphemic analysis

It is important to stress that not all writing systems, or subsystems, are equally graphemic in their import. In other words, not every written sign is a grapheme, nor is every grapheme fully explicit in terms of its correlation to phonemics. Ideograms, for instance, are not graphemic, and logograms are only minimally graphemic. Thus Akkadian numerals are for the most part written as digits: were it not for the very few instances of syllabic writing and for comparative inferences, these digits would be pure ideograms which would only convey the notion, but not the word, of the pertinent numerals (e.g., the notion of 'one' but not the word *ištēn*); and it is only to the extent that we can make the correlation between the digit 1 and the word *ištēn* that the sign acquires the status of a logogram. The graphemic value of a logogram is minimal, however, as it does not indicate, for instance, morphological variations, which must be interpolated from the context, through rules which are not properly graphemic, but rather grammatical. This is the problem that affects much of third-millennium cuneiform, especially

Eblaite. The reason is that the texts are set, by virtue of their content, within the Sumerian scribal tradition, and so logographic writing (based on Sumerian) is prevalent. Text categories which are less formulaic in nature (such as letters), and thus more likely to depart from logography, are unfortunately not well represented for the third millennium (and they are of course altogether missing for Amorite). Accordingly, the area which preserves the most explicit graphemic record for Old Akkadian is that of onomastics.

The Assyriological tradition has dealt all along with graphemic issues and has resulted in what must be recognized as an exemplary control of the data—the major achievement being the build-up of a cumulative list of sign values, culminating in von Soden 1948a (and von Soden and Röllig 1967). Gelb 1952 (2nd ed., 1961) and Huehnergard 1988 provide a model implementation of graphemics to individual dialects. But the development of a specific theoretical model for graphemic analysis is in its initial stages (Buccellati 1979, 1982, 1984, 1990a; Gaebelein 1976; Gelb 1961, 1970a; Kobayashi 1975; Lieberman 1977: 96–117; Platt 1993; Prosecky 1986; Reiner 1973a).

Two special considerations affect our understanding of Amorite graphemics. (1) Given our general assumption that there were no proper Amorite scribes (at least, no real Amorite scribal tradition, see § 1.2.3), the rendering of Amorite phonemes is to be understood through Akkadian graphemic practice. (2) Even though Amorite is typologically contemporary with Old Akkadian, for the most part it is preserved through the graphemic understanding of the later scribes; hence we must reckon with three different systems: third-millennium phonemes rendered by third-millennium graphemes (Old Akkadian); third-millennium phonemes surviving into the early second and rendered by second-millennium graphemes; second-millennium phonemes rendered by second-millennium graphemes.

1.2. Akkadian and Amorite

1.2.1. Geographical and chronological distribution

Akkadian is known from cuneiform texts dating from about 2500 B.C. to about the time of Christ, and Amorite from personal names (some 4000 text occurrences) preserved in cuneiform texts dating from about 2400 B.C. to about 1600 B.C.

In the third and early second millennium there is a substantial linguistic, and cultural, unity across the regions that correspond to modern-day Iraq and Syria: to this world we give the name Syro-Mesopotamia (see Map 1 for

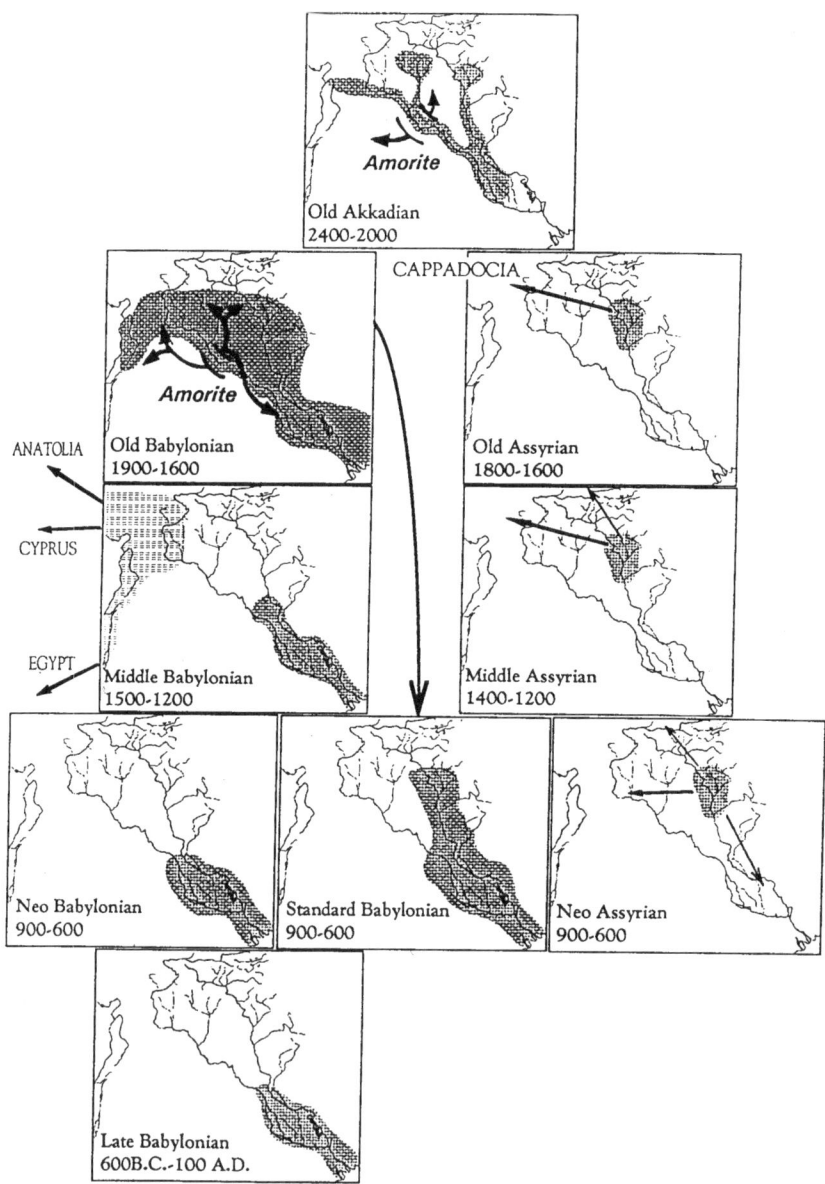

Map 1. Geo-Chronological Distribution of Akkadian Dialects and of Amorite

a diagrammatic rendering of the dialects across this area). Akkadian (with Eblaite) is the language common to all city-states in this region; in other words, we are assuming the presence of native speakers of Akkadian from the Gulf to the Mediterranean. The term "Akkadian," which continues to be used for the language as a whole, is taken from the name of the political entity which controlled most of Syro-Mesopotamia in the third quarter of the third millennium. Amorite is originally the language of the rural classes of the Middle Euphrates (see § 1.2.2), which extended originally to the steppe and began towards the end of the third millennium to migrate towards southern Mesopotamia. The term "Amorite" is derived from the Hebrew rendering of an original Amorite term, which is rendered as *Mardu* in Sumerian and *Amurru* in Akkadian, by which these people identified themselves as an ethnic group.

In the early second millennium there begins a marked differentiation between Babylonian and Assyrian, an innovation which mirrors the political development which resulted in the establishment of vast macro-regional states. (Obviously, the names of the two languages are derived from those of the political capitals.) Babylonian covers the entire area of Syro-Mesopotamia, while Assyrian is limited to a small enclave in the northeast (at least in terms of native speakers, excluding merchant colonies which are established as far west as central Anatolia). Individuals bearing Amorite names are now found over the whole of Syro-Mesopotamia, and we may assume that they were becoming more and more assimilated in the urban (Akkadian) setting; we presume that their competence as native speakers decreased as they became assimilated, until we lose all trace of even their names by the middle of the second millennium. (The political entity known as the kingdom of Amurru in the later second millennium may in fact be an efflorescence of earlier Amorite migrations, but it has no direct linguistic connection with Amorite.)

In the latter part of the second millennium, the geographical domain where we can expect native speakers becomes progressively restricted to the core areas corresponding to present-day southern and northern Iraq, respectively; Babylonian and Assyrian spoken (or often just written) outside these areas are juxtaposed to distinct local languages. (Of these, the most important is Aramaic, which may be seen as analogous to Amorite in its development from a rural base, except that it was protected by independent political institutions and it acquired the status of scribal language—hence it was preserved through textual evidence and not only through onomastics.) The peripheral dialects, especially western Akkadian as found in the letters written in the local Syro-Palestinian courts of the late second millennium, are more properly to be considered as "bastardized" scribal adaptations than as genuine linguistic developments. Akkadian (in its Middle Babylonian variety) is used as the lingua franca for diplomatic exchanges among the contemporary world powers, including Egyptians and Hittites, but there is no evidence that it was ever used as a native language there.

From circumstantial evidence, it would appear that beginning at least with the 7th century Akkadian was no longer spoken, even though it continued to flourish in its written form all the way down to Seleucid times. The dialects of the first millennium come to be more and more closely associated with the scribal setting of the school than with the competence of native speakers. The "dialect" known as Standard Babylonian is specifically a literary hybrid, which harks back with a certain degree of almost archaeological awareness to Old Babylonian perceived as a model. The "dialect" known as Late Babylonian refers to the language of the periods after the loss of political autonomy (i.e., after the fall of Babylon), when Aramaic had become the prevailing language, under the political tutelage of the Persians, the Greeks, and the Parthians.

Comparative Semitics tends to consider Akkadian as a monolith, and to ignore Amorite altogether. The discovery of the archives of Ebla has redirected attention to the third millennium, yet often within the wrong perspective. Eblaite is a third-millennium language, while Akkadian continues to be seen as a second-millennium one and Amorite continues to be ignored. I think that one should instead take bolder steps in redrawing our perceptual map of early Semitic. Old Akkadian–Eblaite (or urban third-millennium Semitic) and Amorite (or rural third-millennium Semitic) should be studied on their own as reflecting the earliest documented phase of Semitic. Geographically speaking, they overlap with each other over the entire Syro-Mesopotamian area. Later Akkadian (though partly overlapping, in terms of the scribal documentation, with Amorite) is essentially a second-millennium language, the native base of which becomes progressively restricted to Babylonia and Assyria. The Akkadian of the first millennium is much less significant in terms of genuine linguistic development, because it is questionable how closely identified it might have been with the competence of native speakers.

1.2.2. *Sociolinguistic position of Amorite*
Amorite is universally regarded as a WEST SEMITIC LANGUAGE, and this is understood in a specific geo-historical sense. It is assumed, in other words, that

the carriers of this language were nomads who came to Mesopotamia from the Syrian steppe. This is not the place to dwell on the socio-historical details as to the nature of this "nomadism," described in the literature through such categories as enclosed, full, or semi-nomadism. What matters, in our present context, is the overwhelming consensus that Amorite is West Semitic not just typologically, but also geographically and sociolinguistically. From this perspective, it would have to be treated as a separate chapter.

If I choose, instead, to present Amorite together with Akkadian[2] it is because I view Amorite and Akkadian as two closely related SOCIOLECTS, i.e., Amorite as the rural, and Akkadian as the urban, Semitic dialect of Syro-Mesopotamia in the third millennium (Buccellati 1992). This view is supported by socio-historical considerations which are not directly pertinent to our present discussion. But one should consider at least the following points. There is no indication of any movement from the West towards Mesopotamia, but only from the middle Euphrates, which is geographically at the very center of Syro-Mesopotamia. The typological similarity with later West Semitic may be explained by assuming a derivation of the latter, Aramaic in particular, from Amorite (Zadok 1993; but see Knudsen 1991: 883). The sequence would then be as follows. Amorite and Old Akkadian are the rural and urban counterparts of the same branch of Semitic in the third millennium, with Akkadian being, predictably, more innovative on account of the social context of its speakers. In second-millennium Mesopotamia, Akkadian continues its evolution independently. Amorite influence is practically nonexistent, since most probably all individuals with Amorite names spoke or at least understood Akkadian, and there were no new urban centers established by Amorites. In western Syria, on the other hand, Amorite speakers retained and developed their autonomous characteristics, especially following the fall of the kingdom of Khana (with its capitals Mari and Terqa, Buccellati 1990), which resulted in an urban vacuum on the Middle Euphrates and thus in the loss of a direct urban base for the Amorite speakers.

Regardless of how one may wish to view this overall reconstruction, the description of Amorite phonology given below stands on its own. The significance of Amorite in general has not been sufficiently appreciated for the study of early Semitic, and it is hoped that the treatment given here may help

---

2. The question has been posed by Garbini (1972: 151–54). His treatment is, however, different from the one proposed here.

to correct this situation. An important reason is the archaic nature of Amorite which places it, in my view, at an earlier stage of development than either Old Akkadian or Eblaite. Garbini (as early as 1960: 175–77) is one of the scholars who have emphasized the importance of Amorite, though he views it as being more innovative than I do.

The considerations I have adduced above are in support of my choice to consider Amorite together with Akkadian. If one objects to my understanding of linguistic correlations, one may simply wish to raise the discussion of Amorite to the status of a separate chapter. It should be noted in this connection that such distinctions are often heavily influenced by extra-linguistic considerations. Thus, Amorite is ignored because there is no literary tradition associated with it. On the other hand, an important reason why Eblaite is often considered a separate language (as in this volume), rather than an early dialect of Akkadian, is to be found in the geo-historical significance of the single archive which documents its existence; yet Eblaite and Old Akkadian are more closely linked to each other than, for example, Old Akkadian is to Neo-Babylonian.

1.2.3. Phonological studies of Akkadian

The year 1952 marked the beginning of a new era in the study of Akkadian grammar in general, and phonology in particular. It was then that both Gelb's *Grammar*[3] and von Soden's *Grundriss* were published in their first editions. The latter is a monumental achievement, as to comprehensiveness of coverage (it includes all Akkadian dialects) and degree of philological control; methodologically it remains within a generic Neogrammarian mold. The former brings a whole new degree of theoretical sophistication to a proper linguistic study of Akkadian; in particular, its treatment of graphemics as the foundation for a proper understanding of phonology remains unmatched. Von Soden's grammar was to have a profound influence in the field, so that every other grammar that followed (with the exception of Reiner 1966; Huehnergard 1988; Izre'el 1991) was written strictly within the framework he had established (Aro 1955; Finet 1956; De Meyer 1962;

---

3. A very sharp criticism of Gelb's phonological reconstruction, especially with regard to the Old Akkadian sibilants, is found in Garbini 1972: 147–51. His objections concern especially the nature of graphemic correspondences and of the pronominal system. While recognizing the merit of some of his criticism, particularly with regard to broader methodological issues, a fuller philological analysis than Garbini's seems to me to ultimately validate Gelb's position, which is the one I essentially follow here.

Salonen 1962; Jucquois 1966; Hecker 1968; Giakumakis 1970; Wilhelm 1970; Mayer 1971).

Of fundamental importance for phonology is the study of the cuneiform syllabary, of which von Soden and Röllig 1967 represents the culmination. But it almost looks as though the two fields (grammar and syllabary) are conceived apart from each other, so that the full implications for phonology are not adequately articulated. Note how the major work on Neo-Assyrian "Lautlehre" (Deller 1959) is in fact primarily concerned with orthography rather than with phonology. It is in this respect that Gelb's contribution stands out as a major methodological undertaking. In his work more than in any other scholar's the accurate study of the syllabary is merged with a sensitive understanding of phonology, resulting in the most exemplary treatment of this topic.

Several studies on Eblaite (see elsewhere in this volume) touch on questions pertaining to Old Akkadian, but an in-depth comprehensive new study of Old Akkadian phonology remains a desideratum, especially considering that for Old Akkadian itself the documentary database has increased since Gelb's groundbreaking work. Diakonoff 1985, 1991–92 and Faber 1985 represent a major step in this direction in terms of linguistic analysis, but they do not attempt to provide any systematic documentation.

In terms of a general treatment of phonology, a special place must be accorded Reiner 1966 and Diakonoff 1991–92. Reiner's remains to date the most sophisticated linguistic analysis of Akkadian phonology; in particular it should be noted that she presented the first, and so far only, generative treatment of Akkadian phonology. Diakonoff is far-reaching in his implications, though his very strength (the correlation of Akkadian with Afro-Asiatic) limits the range and effectiveness of his Assyriological documentation and often obscures his elaboration of Akkadian phenomena.

1.2.4. *Phonological studies of Amorite*

The first modern treatment of Amorite phonology is Gelb 1958. Ironically, this remains also the only major work to provide a systematic treatment of the subject. Garbini has dealt with problems of Amorite phonology (1960: 19–80, 175–77; 1965; 1972: 23–96, 141–54), but from the point of view of specific comparative concerns. Neither Buccellati 1966 nor Huffmon 1965 covers phonology in any systematic way. While the last work by Gelb on Amorite (1980) is based on a rigorous understanding of phonology and provides all the essential data for a full discussion of the topic, it does not articulate any of the details, for which the reader is referred to a forthcoming volume on Amorite Grammar that unfortunately Gelb did not live to complete; still, the volume is extremely significant not only because of the exhaustive database it provides, but also because important phonemic decisions are presented, particularly with regard to the establishment of the phonemic inventory (especially pp. 8f., 538f.).

Knudsen (1991; see also 1982a: 4–7) is of great import in that it proposes explicit criteria for assessing the relative degree to which Amorite consonants may be attributed full phonemic status (pp. 874f.), and divides the consonantal phonemes into three classes ranked in descending order of probability; unfortunately, Knudsen's contribution is only a summary which, by virtue of its self-imposed limitations, can neither develop a full articulation of its own argument, nor provide an adequate documentation for its conclusions.

1.3. Phonemics

1.3.1. Phonemic inventory

That we are able to reconstruct a plausible phonemic inventory for these languages is due to the essentially graphemic nature of the cuneiform writing system. For the most part, the scribal tradition was sensitive to the phonemic, rather than phonetic, dimension of Akkadian (Greenstein 1980; but see Diakonoff 1991–92: 3) and, though perhaps to a lesser extent, of Amorite. (It is due to this sensitivity that the invention of the alphabet was eventually possible.) The oppositions that are marked in the graphemic system correlate well to what we otherwise know, on the basis of living Semitic languages, about phonemic oppositions. It is for this reason that we can presume to draw up a phonemic inventory for dead languages on the basis of articulatory categories, a procedure which may appear at first bizarre considering that we have no record at all, acoustic(!) or descriptive, about the nature of such articulation. The exact articulatory nature of a group of consonants considered bilabial may well remain hypothetical, but its structural contrast with another category (which we will call, say, also hypothetically, dental) is beyond doubt. A simplistic way of expressing the net result of this procedure is to say that, were we to meet a living Akkadian-speaking informant and were we to try to speak Akkadian to him or her, we might be deemed to have an accent, but would not be incomprehensible, for the most part.

For Amorite, there is the additional filter of non-Amorite scribal transmission, which is especially critical in the rendering of phonological values. But just as Old Akkadian graphemics (though not paleography) was accurately preserved by Old Babylonian scribes, so it is to the credit of Mesopotamian scribes that they preserved many of the Amorite phonemic oppositions, even when they did not introduce any new graphic symbols.

One problem should be pointed out. In terms of their structural oppositions, the accuracy of the presumed articulatory identifications is not crucial. Such phonetic labels may serve just as such, i.e., as tags which approximate phonetic reality and are more convenient than non-descriptive labels (e.g., "labial" instead of "category A"). As with the reconstruction of proto-languages, emphasis tends to be on phonemic rather than specific phonetic identifications. Accordingly, we must be careful about raising articulatory terms, used as descriptive labels, to the status of real phonetic phenomena without the benefit of thorough critical analysis. To have done the latter is the merit of Diakonoff (1981; 1991–92: 1–4). A particular warning should be voiced against charting historical processes of change on the basis of definitions that have been introduced as labels. Change presupposes real sounds, not just labels. The case has been made recently for Proto-Semitic (Bomhard 1988), but it obtains of course for Akkadian and Amorite as well.

There are considerable difficulties in establishing a complete phonemic inventory for the third-millennium languages, and for second-millennium Amorite. This is due in part to the nature of the graphemic documentation, as mentioned above. But, considering the sizable amount of textual data available, the difficulty may also be attributed to the lack of in-depth studies on the subject. This is all the more remarkable in view of the widespread attention that has been lavished in recent years on the language evidenced by the texts of Ebla. It would seem that a proper understanding of Ebla phonology would be greatly enhanced by a detailed study of Amorite and Old Akkadian. This remains to be accomplished.

1.3.2. *Consonants and semivowels*

Besides giving an overall synopsis of the phonemic inventory (Table 1-1), I will deal with phonemic classes which present special problems and which have been the object of important recent contributions, especially the Old Akkadian sibilants.[4] For comparative purposes I will refer to proto-forms or

---

4. This term is retained here because of its widespread use even though it describes improperly the acoustic, rather than articulatory, nature of the phoneme.

Table 1-1. Synopsis of Consonants and Glides (semivowels) for Amorite, Old Akkadian, and Later Akkadian Dialects (OB+)

			Labial	Dental	Interdental	Denti-alveolar	Alveolar	Palato-alveolar	Velar	Pharyngeal	Laryngeal
Stops	Unvoiced	Am	p	t					k	ʿ	ʾ
		OAkk	p	t					k	ʿ	ʾ
		OB+	p	t					k		ʾ
	Voiced	Am	b	d					g		
		OAkk	b	d					g		
		OB+	b	d					g		
	Emphatic	Am		ṭ					q		
		OAkk		ṭ					q		
		OB+		ṭ					q		
Fricatives	Unvoiced	Am		s		ŝ	š	ḫ?		ḥ	h
		OAkk		s	ṯ		š	ḫ			
		OB+		s			š	ḫ			
	Voiced	Am		z	ḏ						
		OAkk		z			[ž]				
		OB+		z							
	Emphatic	Am		ṣ							
		OAkk		ṣ							
		OB+		ṣ							
Sonants	Nasal	Am	m	n							
		OAkk	m	n							
		OB+	m	n							
	Lateral	Am					l				
		OAkk					l				
		OB+					l				
	Trill	Am					r				
		OAkk					r				
		OB+					r				
	Glide	Am	w						y		
		OAkk	w						y		
		OB+	w						y		

to Proto-Semitic, but I use these terms cautiously. We must remember that the validity of these forms is only proportional to the comparative basis from which they are derived, and that the posited proto-forms from which a historical derivation is assumed are in the first place projected back through a logical process. A proto-form is actuarial, as it were, rather than actual; it is an index for a set of correspondences, and should strictly be considered as such.

The inventory given here is in the form of a synopsis that offers a complete list for the consonants from each of the three major language groups. The listing should not be understood as describing historical development; the superposition of phonemes within the same cell is rather to be viewed as some sort of three-dimensional array which simply describes the phonemic attestations for the same type of articulation.

1.3.3. Special problems concerning Amorite

In the consonantal inventory of Amorite given here I use the list found in Gelb 1980: 9, which corresponds to the first two classes of Knudsen 1991: 874 ("established positive consonants," i.e., consonants whose phonemic status is based on both unequivocal comparative and graphemic considerations, and "established neutral consonants," based only on unequivocal comparative considerations, without graphemic support).

A questionable phoneme in Amorite is the unvoiced fricative palato-alveolar *ḫ*. While it is attributed specific phonemic status in Gelb 1980: 8, 538, most of the entries given to support its existence are followed by a question mark. In Knudsen 1991: 874, *ḫ* is considered a "non-established neutral" phoneme (i.e., a phoneme for which neither comparative nor graphemic criteria can be applied in a unequivocal way). I include it here in the inventory, but with a question mark.

Three additional consonantal phonemes have been proposed for Amorite,[5] namely *ḍ*, *ẓ*,[6] and *ġ*.[7] They are best considered, however, as historical reconstructions since there is no real evidence for their independent phonemic status. Gelb 1980: 8, 538 does not include them in his inventory, and Knudsen 1991: 874 defines them correctly as "non-estabished neutral" consonants. Accordingly, they are omitted in the inventory.

5. Gelb 1958 § 2.7.2; Knudsen 1991: 874.
6. Knudsen 1991: 874 uses the symbol *t* for this phoneme; but this must be a typographical error for *ṭ*, which is analogous to Gelb's *ẓ*. The example *ṭabū* 'gazelle' (written *ṭabū* in Knudsen 1991: 874) corresponds to graphemic *ṣa-bu-um*, see Knudsen 1982a: 15.
7. Knudsen uses the symbol *y* to render this phoneme.

1.3.4. Laryngeals and pharyngeals

Laryngeals are distinguished graphemically in Amorite but not in Akkadian, where *h* is subsumed under *ʾ*. The pharyngeals are distinguished graphemically as a set, but it cannot be determined whether they are further distinguished from each other. In Amorite, they are rendered by signs with *ḫ*. In Akkadian there is no overt graphemic marker, but we can infer that they were still present in Old Akkadian, because of the way in which they affect the vocalism of the word in which they appear: in Old Akkadian the vowel in contact is *a*, except in closed syllables beginning with pharyngeal, where it becomes *e*,[8] while in the later dialects all *a* vowels in the core of the word become for the most part *e* (see § 1.4.2). Table 1-2 lists the correspondences for laryngeals and pharyngeals among the various dialects and their posited Proto-Semitic equivalent.

Table 1-2. Correspondences among Laryngeals and Pharyngeals

*	Am	OAkk	OB+	Am	OAkk	OB+	Gloss
ʾ	ʾ A	ʾ A	ʾ A	ʾabu	ʾabu	ʾabu	'father'
h	h ḪA	ʾ A	ʾ E	haddu	ʾadad	ʾadad	'storm god'
ʿ	ʿ ḪA	ʿ A	ʾ E	ʿzb	ʿzb	ʿzb^a	'to leave'
ḥ	ḥ ḪA	ʿ A	ʾ E	bḥr	bʿr	bʾr^b	'to choose'
ġ	? ḪA	ʿ A	ʾ E	?	ʾrb	ʾrb^c	'to enter'

a. Babylonian *ezēbu*, Assyrian *ezābu*.
b. Babylonian *bēru*, Assyrian *beʾāru*.
c. Babylonian *erēbu*, Assyrian *erābu*. Knudsen 1991: 874 gives *purġušu* 'flea' as an Amorite example for *ġ*. See Diakonoff 1985: 20 for an Eblaite equivalent.

1.3.5. Sibilants

The treatment of the sibilants (see notes 4 and 5) presents us with severe problems. (A) The graphemic rendering, while relatively consistent within each dialect, appears to us confusing when comparing different dialects. (B) The phonetic realization of some of the phonemes is in part uncertain. (C) The notations used in the literature are often ambiguous.

It is regrettable that Gelb, while distinguishing clearly the various categories on the theoretical level, does not carry this over to either the text of his *Grammar* (1961) or the entries of his *Glossary* (1957); rather, he uses capital *Š* to subsume without differentiation *š, ś, ž*, and *ṭ*. In their edition of Old

---

8. For a fuller statement of the pertinent rules see Gelb 1961: 123–25.

Akkadian royal inscriptions, on the other hand, Gelb and Kienast (1990) use a hybrid system whereby the phoneme ś is marked in the transliteration (e.g., *u-śa-am-qí-it*), even though the value is not recognized in the standard syllabaries. Von Soden (1965–81) uses the same symbol ś to render both *ś (he writes śiāmu s.v. šiāmu 'to set') and *ṯ (wasábu s.v. wašābu 'to dwell').

Diakonoff 1985, 1991–92 and Faber 1985 present a divergent interpretation whereby they assume an affricate realization for the sibilants (see already Steiner 1977: 144–48, 159; 1982: 70–74). Their theory is of great interest and is all the more noteworthy since they arrived at it independently of each other (Diakonoff 1991–92: 55, n. 61) and from different points of departure. While it affects especially phonetic realization[9] rather than phonemic distribution, it is important in that it proposes new possibilities for historical derivation and for morphophonemic alternations, though not without difficulties (see § 1.4.3). I will not follow their theory here because I feel that more reflection is needed before their results may be accepted. As already noted in the case of Gelb, it is regrettable that Diakonoff himself does not carry through his notation consistently: generally he uses the traditional notation š (e.g., *šin-a* 'two', 1991–92: 17), and only occasionally the notation he proposes (e.g., *sawxat* for traditional *šamḫat*, 1991–92: 114; *'uč:ič* for traditional *uššiš*, 1991–92: 52).

Here I will attempt to clarify the situation by comparing various aspects of the problem. Table 1-3 summarizes the terms of the problem with regard to graphemic rendering and divergent modern notations. Graphemes are grouped in sets which share the same consonantal realization, and have a different vowel for each sign. (It should be noted that accent marks and subscripts have no phonemic implication, but simply serve as standard Assyriological indices for the identification of homophonous cuneiform signs.) For each graphemic set I show the variant modern notations used to render the phonemic value of the consonant in question for different dialects and periods. It must be stressed that this table establishes only a synopsis of graphemic correspondences; in other words, the chart should not be understood to say that Old Akkadian š corresponds to Old Babylonian s, but only that graphemes of the class sá are used to render š in Old Akkadian and s in Old Babylonian.

Table 1-4 singles out those phonemes which present divergent realizations in the different dialects and periods, and it shows their correspondence with

---

9. Diakonoff 1991–92: 39–41 goes into great detail as to the precise phonetic "pronunciation" of this series.

20 Giorgio Buccellati

Table 1-3. Graphemic Sets and Modern Phonemic Notations for Sibilants with Divergent Realizations[a]

	Amorite			OAkk					OB+	
Graphemes	G	K	B	G	GK	D	F	B	c	D
SA SE₁₁ SI SU	ś	ś	š̬	{š, š₁ / ś, š₂}	š	c	s	š	s	c
SÁ SU₄ ŠÈ	ž	ḍ	ḏ	ž, š₄	š	c	s	š	s	c
ŠA ŠI ŠU	š	š	š	ṭ, š₃	ś	č	ṭ	ṭ	š	{s / č}
ZA ZI ZU	{ s / ṣ / z	s / ṣ / z	s / ṣ / z }	s / ṣ / ʒ	s / ṣ / z	c / ç / ʒ	ts[b] / ts' / ds	s / ṣ / z	(s) / ṣ / z	c / ç / ʒ

a. B, Buccellati; c, common use; D, Diakonoff; F, Faber; G, Gelb; GK, Gelb–Kienast; K, Knudsen.

b. Digraphs of the type *ts* stand for single (affricate) phonemes; similarly, *ts'* stands for a single phoneme which Faber defines as a glottalic pressure affricate. Note that Faber 1985: 105 considers *ts*, *ts'*, and *ds* to be phonetic realizations of one and the same phoneme *z*.

Table 1-4. Phonemic and Graphemic Correspondences for Sibilants with Divergent Realizations

*	Am	OAkk	OB+	Ar	Am	OAkk	OB+	Ar	Gloss
š	} š̬ SA	š	SA	} š	s	šumu	šumu	šumu	'ism	'name'
ś					SA	š	šym	šym	šym	(šym)	'to place'
ṭ	š ŠA	ṭ	ŠA		ṭ	yšb	wṭb	wšb	(wṭb)	'to dwell'
ḏ	ḏ SÁ	z	ZA	z	ZA	ḏ	ʾḫḏ	ʾḫz	ʾḫz	ʾḫḏ	'to take'

regard to a posited proto-form, and, for ease of reference, with Arabic (or South Semitic) as well. I give here only the phonemic notation that I have chosen to use, plus the graphemic rendering with only one sign for each of the sets given in Table 1-3. I also add representative word examples.

Following are comments on each of the phonemes listed in Table 1-4. I relate in some detail the definitions given by various scholars, because they are often presented cryptically in the literature, and it is difficult to correlate opinions about what should be simple facts.

ś   is the symbol for a lateral that is reconstructed for Proto-Semitic,[10] but is not preserved as such in either Amorite or Akkadian.[11] Even though it is used often in the Assyriological literature, this notation should be avoided when dealing with those two languages.

š̬   is a symbol I am using to render what I assume to be a distinctive Amorite phoneme, at least in terms of its derivation. The Amorite phoneme corresponds to "Proto-Semitic" *š* and *ś*. Though it is often transliterated as *ś*, it does not appear to be a lateral,[12] because of the writing with signs of the class ꜱᴀ. It seems possible to postulate a phonetic development similar to Arabic, i.e., a change in the direction of *s*,[13] with place of articulation shifting toward the dental position. But that it could not simply have merged with *s* is also indicated by graphemic considerations.[14] Hence I am postulating, on a purely indicative basis, that this phoneme may have been realized as a denti-alveolar fricative. At any rate, the phoneme is distinct from any other in terms of its correspondences (i.e., it corresponds to *š* and *ś*, but not to *ṯ*), and this by itself is sufficient to justify the use of a different symbol.

ṯ   is the symbol used for the voiceless interdental fricative (θ) in the posited proto-form. The Old Akkadian correspondence is generally transcribed as *ś* in the literature, but, since there is no reason to assume a lateral realization for this phoneme in Old Akkadian, I prefer to retain consistently the notation *ṯ* on the assumption that the original interdental realization was preserved.[15]

---

10. The autonomy of this phoneme for "Proto-Semitic" is controversial, but it can at least be safely postulated as an antecedent to Amorite and Old Akkadian (Gelb 1961: 34f.).

11. Except possibly in Old Akkadian, see Reiner 1966: 110; Greenstein 1980, with review of previous literature; also Diakonoff 1985: 22, where the notation *ḏ* is used. The strongest indication in its favor is based on the explanation of the assimilation *š+š > ss* as presupposing a second consonant *ś*, see § 1.4.3, where I also give reasons why it seems nevertheless better not to include it in the standard phonemic inventory.

12. As Greenfield 1969: 94 seems to suggest, on the assumption that *š coalesced with *ś, so that both came to pronounced *ś*.

13. Knudsen 1982a: 5 says that its phonetic realization is "similar to Old Babylonian *s*." Gelb does not address the issue of articulation for this phoneme.

14. To render *š̬*, signs of the ꜱᴀ class are used next to signs of the šᴀ class, and only signs of the ᴀš class are used. To render *s*, only signs of the ꜱᴀ and ᴀꜱ classes are used.

15. "Possible pronunciation in the direction of Arabic *ṯ*, perhaps not in Mesopotamia proper but in an outlying region" (Gelb 1961: 37). In the chart in ibid. p. 39, the "sound" of this phoneme is indicated as *t'*, which, according to the discussion on p. 33, would seem to stand for an aspirated correlative of *ṯ*.

š   is the standard symbol for the voiceless palatal or alveo-palatal fricative. It continues in OAkk and OB+ (where it comes to subsume other phonemes as well). Amorite š, on the other hand, corresponds to PS *ṯ*, and is presumed to be phonetically the same as Akkadian š,[16] because the graphemes used to render it are those used to render š in contemporary Old Babylonian.

z   is the standard symbol for the voiced denti-alveolar fricative. It corresponds in OAkk and OB+ to PS *ð*. In addition, z is also the normal Am, OAkk, and OB+ correspondence for PS z (not shown in the chart above).

ð   is the voiced interdental, which has a correspondence in Amorite.[17] Gelb also thinks that there may be an archaic ž in OAkk, derived from PS *ð*.[18] Since this is, however, uncertain, I omit it from the phonemic inventory given above.

1.3.6. Vowels

Both Old Akkadian and later Akkadian share the same inventory of four vowels (Table 1-5).[19]

Table 1-5. Akkadian Vowels

	Front	Back
High	i	u
Low	e	a

---

16. "Probabilmente una sibilante š piuttosto che una dentale fricativa *ṯ*" (Gelb 1958 § 2.7.9). "Similar to Old Babylonian s" (Knudsen 1982a: 5); "one of the two Amorite phonemes [ś and š] probably represented the palatal groove spirant š" (Knudsen 1982a: 6).

17. "Voiced interdental spirant" (Knudsen 1982a: 4; he uses the symbol *d* to render this phoneme). "Support in favor of [a pronunciation as ẓ] is to be found in the phonemic analysis of Old Akkadian ..., Amorite and Ugaritic" (Gelb 1980: 8b).

18. "Signs of the š₄ class are to be considered as leftovers from a period in which Akkadian recognized a phoneme ẓ (=š₄) < *d*" (Gelb 1961: 38). In the chart in ibid. p. 39 the "sound" of this phoneme is indicated as *ṯ*, i.e. the non-aspirated member of the pair discussed on p. 33. This phoneme is omitted from the list given on p. 119.

19. Diakonoff 1991–92: 68 has noted that in Akkadian primary nouns, the vocalic system essentially excludes *u*, and that *e* is used only in Sumerian loanwords, while conversely in verbal roots the vocalic system excludes *e* except as allophone of *a* (on the phonemic status of *e* see also p. 123). This interesting observation pertains more to the study of word formation than of phonology per se. On the phonemic status of *e* see Izre'el 1987.

Diakonoff (1991–92: 123–25), following a suggestion by Lieberman (1979), concludes that at least from OB on Akkadian had a phoneme *o* (and, with corresponding length, *ō*). He argues in part from the observation that the presence of a phoneme *e* causes the system to be asymmetrical, and therefore unstable. However, the phoneme *o* (and *ō*) is in fact understood by him as a phonetic realization of *u* (and *ū*), so that the asymmetry noted is simply shifted to another plane. Accordingly, I prefer to retain the traditional scheme as given above.

The situation in Amorite seems to be limited to three vowels (Table 1-6).

Table 1-6. Amorite Vowels

	Front	Back
High	i	u
Low		a

The vowel *e* does appear in the writing of Amorite, but, given the absence of contrasting minimal pairs, it may more properly be understood as an allophone of *i* or *a* (Knudsen 1991: 870). Gelb 1958 § 2.1.1–4 assumes the existence of a phoneme *ē*, and Knudsen 1991 : 870 the existence of both *ē* and *ō*, i.e., long vowels without a corresponding short vowel. For neither vowel, however, can one adduce a convincing minimal pair. Thus *ē* and *ō* are considered here as special phonetic realizations deriving from the contraction of diphthongs.

1.3.7. Suprasegmentals

All consonants and vowels can be lengthened in Akkadian and Amorite. Considering certain practices which are current in standard Assyriological tradition, and which are misleading for a proper understanding of length, it bears mentioning that this phenomenon is to be understood as the holding of the articulation for a fraction of time. (1) One speaks of "doubling" of consonants (so much so that the derived verbal stem with lengthening of the middle radical is labeled with D for doubling): but there is obviously no reason to suppose that the articulation was repeated twice, only that it was held longer. (2) One uses a two-tiered notation for long vowels, e.g., *ā* and *â*, but there is no conclusive evidence that this corresponds to a phonemic distinction; in other words, there are no minimal pairs to show that there were two contrasting degrees of length. The distinction made in standard Assyriological notation between *ā* and *â* is etymological rather than phonemic (circumflex is used to mark derivation from contraction). It also leads to confusing and contradictory applications, so that it should best be ignored.

It is possible that the phenomenon behind the dual notation of length envisaged by our modern grammatical tradition may, instead, have something to do with stress (on this see Sarauw 1939; Knudsen 1980; Greenstein 1984: 24–27; Diakonoff 1991–92: 104–15). Consider the following: *'panū* 'face' vs. *pa'nū* 'first'. If there is in fact a contrast based on stress (thus also Diakonoff 1991–92: 111), it is because the second word derives by contraction from *pan-ī-u*. The traditional view about Akkadian stress is that it falls on the first long syllable from the end of the word, except that morphemic length in final position is disregarded (as with *'panū*). A possible case for an alternative theory has been made by Reiner (1966: 38, following a suggestion of Poebel 1939: 60): she thinks it probable that in Assyrian, at least, primary (non-phonemic) stress would fall on the first syllable of the word. Diakonoff (1991–92: 104–15) has argued convincingly in favor of the traditional view, which is retained here.

1.3.8. *Phonotactics*

A number of distributional limitations affect the actual cooccurrence of phonemes in a variety of ways. I will describe them here as functions of word boundaries, clustering, and syllabic structure.

1.3.8.1. *Word-initial position*

Any simple consonant may occur in word-initial position in both Amorite and Akkadian; of the semivowels, only *y* may occur in Amorite, and only *w*[20] in Old Akkadian and Old Babylonian/Old Assyrian (in the later Akkadian dialects initial *w* is also excluded). The exclusion of initial long consonant or consonantal cluster is no surprise, since it is a common Semitic feature. Only two additional comments are in order. (1) We assume that vowels are not allowed in word-initial position on account of comparative and (to some extent) graphemic considerations. The alternation in the writing of forms like <i-il-la-ak> and <il-la-ak> 'he goes' suggests that in the first instance ' was overtly indicated (one could transliterate <'i-il-la-ak>), while in the second the notation was omitted because its presence was assumed as automatic. In modern transcription, ' is regularly omitted, for the same reason (hence our writing *illak* really means *'illak*); see also § 1.1.2. (2) The con-

---

20. For the exclusion of initial *y* in Akkadian see Reiner 1964; Gelb 1970a: 536–43.

trast between ʿy in Amorite and ʿw in Akkadian is particularly significant because the Amorite situation is universally assumed to be an innovation that closely links it with West Semitic.

1.3.8.2. Word-final position
Any simple vowel (short or long), and any simple consonant, may occur in word-final position. Specifically, no semivowel, long consonant, or consonantal cluster may occur in this position. These rules apply equally to Amorite and Akkadian.

1.3.8.3. Clusters
Consonantal clusters of two, but not more, consonants occur in word-medial position. Vocalic clusters occur in Amorite, Old Akkadian, and Old Babylonian/Assyrian when a morphemic boundary intervenes between them, e.g., *rabī+at* 'she is great' (with but few exceptions, e.g., *ʾiqīaš* 'he donates', without morphemic boundary). It is likely that in these cases a glide was present (*rabīyat*, *ʾiqīyaš*). In some cases, both graphemics and word structure suggest the presence of a long glide, e.g., *dayyānum* 'judge'. Vocalic clusters do not occur in later Akkadian.

1.3.8.4. Syllabic structure
(See especially Greenstein 1984 with the reviews Edzard 1986; Knudsen 1986.) The following distributional rules apply: the components of a cluster are always separated by syllabic boundary; long consonants are treated like a cluster, as if we had reduplicated consonants with syllable boundary between them, even though there is no reason to assume double articulation (see § 1.3.7); no syllable begins with a vowel, except as second element of a vocalic cluster; no long vowel occurs in front of either a consonantal cluster or long consonant. These rules apply equally to Amorite and Akkadian.

Vowel harmony is a very distinctive Assyrian phenomenon: *a* in a short medial syllable which follows a stressed syllable assumes the quality of the following vowel, e.g., OB *ʾiṣbatū* ~ OA *ʾiṣbutū*. (One may consider the possibility that in OB short *a* may have been used in writing to render ə, see § 1.3.9; if so, *iṣbatū* and *iṣbutū* may be understood as graphemic equivalents rendering one and the same form *iṣbətū*. In other words, vowel harmony would be a graphemic rather than a specifically phonemic feature, in the sense that both Babylonian signs with *a* and Assyrian signs with *a/e/i/u* would stand for a purely phonetic ə.)

Reiner's suggestion (1966 § 4.1.2.5) of an equivalence between V:C and VC: is applicable only in prosodic terms, and should not be taken to mean (as seems to be the case in Diakonoff 1991–92: 116) that no phonological opposition exists. An opposition is clearly apparent in such morphemically diverse minimal pairs as *šūma* 'he himself' vs. *šumma* 'if'; *dānum* 'judge' vs. *dannum* 'powerful'; *'ikūnū* 'they stood firm' vs. *'ikunnū* 'they stand firm'.

1.3.9. *Phonetic realizations*
While the cuneiform writing is essentially phonemic in nature, there are clues to abnormal phonetic realizations which, as far as we can tell, fall outside the phonemic range. Some of the more interesting pertain to vocalic quality (*ö*, *ü*, von Soden 1948b; *ə*, Buccellati forthcoming §§ 14.1, 55; see also § 1.3.6, and § 1.4.2 herein); nonemphatic realization of velar emphatic (*k* for *q*, Knudsen 1961); spirantization of stops (*p*, *b*, *t*, *d*, *k*, *g*, von Soden 1968); realization of *m* as *w* from OB on (Diakonoff 1991–92: 125); stress (Aro 1953). All these phenomena have been observed for the dialects later than Old Akkadian. For an affricate realization of the sibilants see § 1.3.5.

1.4. Phonological change

1.4.1. *Historical changes affecting individual phonemes*
The correspondences which have been noted above for laryngeals and pharyngeals (§ 1.3.4), sibilants (§ 1.3.5), and vowels (§ 1.3.6) are the most significant in terms of a presumed derivation from a common proto-form. Amorite and Old Akkadian are, in different ways, relatively close to the posited proto-forms.

Amorite appears to be the most archaic. It preserves (1) the laryngeals and pharyngeals, presumably in their differentiated form; (2) *ð*; and (3) a restricted vocalism with only *i*, *a*, *u*. The major innovations in terms of the inventory are the change of **ṭ* to *š*, and of *š* and *ś* to *s̀*. The former is in common with later Akkadian and with other Semitic languages, while the latter seems to be peculiar to Amorite.

Old Akkadian occupies an intermediate position. It is more archaic than Amorite only in its preservation of *ṭ*, while the other sibilants appear already in the same form as in later Akkadian. Both laryngeals appear as '; as in later Akkadian. The pharyngeals appear to have merged in a common consonant, for the quality of which we have no indication in the writing, but which we assume to be ʿ.

By the beginning of the second millennium, Akkadian has undergone radical changes, in particular the reduction of Old Akkadian ' and ʿ to '; and the reduction of Old Akkadian *š* and *ṭ* to *š*. As a result, the later phonemic inventory of Akkadian, though still quite ancient in terms of chronology (about 1900 B.C.!), is to be considered very recent in terms of typology.

1.4.2. Historical changes affecting phonotactics
A great variety of phonotactic phenomena can be identified over the long history of Akkadian. Here I will only mention a few that seem particularly characteristic of each major period.

The alternation between Akkadian ʿw and Amorite ʿy is generally explained as Akkadian conservatism and Amorite innovation, respectively, vis-à-vis a presumed proto-form ʿw.

Diphthongs (understood as vowel+semivowel in closed syllable) have been posited for proto-forms such as **mawtum* from which Akkadian *mūtum* would have derived. Such proto-forms, however, may reflect an undue emphasis on consonantal triradicalism; if we assume that length may function as a radical (Buccellati forthcoming § 39.1), then forms like *mūtum* may in fact be archaic, and those with *w* recent (introduced to fit a triconsonantal scheme).

The reduction of Old Akkadian ʿ (corresponding to ʾ, *ḥ*, and *ġ*) to ʾ was compensated for by a change in vocalic quality from *a* to *e*. This change is partly morphophonemic (see § 1.4.4), because the change occurs only within the core of a word that is not affected by external inflection; e.g., OB ʾ*ezēb-am* (not **ʾezēb-em*) 'to abandon' with accusative ending (contrast ʾ*alāk-am* 'to go', also with accusative ending). In Assyrian, only the vowel in contact with ʾ shifts to *e*, i.e., ʾ*ezāb-am*, ʾ*iltanaqqē* 'he repeatedly took' (contrast OB ʾ*ilteneqqē*).

In Middle Babylonian the consonantal clusters formed by *š* plus a dental stop or an alveolar fricative, *š* shifts to *l*; e.g., OB ʾ*ištakan* ~ MB ʾ*iltakan* 'he then placed'.[21]

The loss of short vowel in final position is a phenomenon which is found in the major Northwest Semitic languages of the first millennium, with important consequences for morphology (case endings) and syntax (determina-

---

21. No phonetic explanation has been offered for this shift. Very tentatively, one may entertain the following conjecture: dental lateral *ś* may have been preserved in early Aramaic dialects (for Akkadian, see Diakonoff 1985: 22), and the shift to a liquid lateral *l* may have started with clusters of the type *śt* and then spread to *št* and others. The evidence for *ś* in Ancient Aramaic is controversial (Degen 1969 § 13; Segert 1975 §§ 3.2.3.5.3, 3.2.8.3–6), but note for instance how the Masoretic rendering *Kaśdîm* (Hebrew) / *Kaśdāy* (Aramaic) corresponds to later Babylonian *Kaldu*. For suggestions of *ś* in Akkadian see § 1.3.5.

tion). It is interesting to note how Northwest Semitic syntax compensates through the introduction of the article, which was never introduced in Akkadian: this is one of the important indications that first-millennium changes within Akkadian, minimal as they are, no longer take place within the context of a living language.

1.4.3. A note on morphophonemic alternations

Many of the phonological changes which are discussed in standard treatments of Akkadian and Amorite phonology are in fact alternations conditioned by morphemic factors (Reiner 1966: 104–12). Since they presuppose an understanding of morphology, they cannot be taken up here, particularly because a fully coherent statement along those lines entails that the entire system of the so-called weak verbs be presented as part of morphophonemics, and this is clearly beyond our present scope (an extensive section is devoted to this topic in Buccellati forthcoming). I will only mention here four rules which are of particular interest because they apply only in Akkadian, and not in Amorite. (1) It is generally (but improperly) stated that in a sequence of three short vowels the middle vowel is dropped. The full conditions may be stated instead as follows: a word resulting, through internal inflection, in a sequence of three syllables of which the first two are short[22] is realized with the elision of the vowel in the middle syllable; e.g., Akk. {damiq-um} /damqum/ 'good', contrast Am. *malak-a* 'he has ruled' (see Huffmon 1965: 89).[23] (2) The pattern MAPRAS is realized in Akkadian with initial *n* if any of the radicals is a labial, whereas initial *m* is retained in Amorite, e.g., Akk. *našparum* 'envoy', contrast Am. *mašparum*. (3) Two emphatic radicals are found to cooccur in Amorite, whereas in the Akkadian correspondence one of the radicals is realized as unvoiced (Geers 1965); e.g., Am.

---

22. This formulation implies that at least the consonant of the third syllable be part of internal inflection, as in {damiq+um}. The rule so stated excludes (1) a case like {iṣbat+u+šu} (/iṣbatušu/, not /iṣbassu/) 'that he seized him', where only the sequence /bat/ properly belongs to internal inflection; (2) primary nouns, e.g., *išar+um* (not *išrum*) 'normal' (see Goetze 1946, 1947); (3) loanwords, e.g., *Uruk+ī+u* (not *Urkūm*) 'Urukean', *gabadibb+u* (not *gabdibbu*) 'parapet'; sequences derived (4) through external inflection, e.g., *šarra+šunū* (not *šarrašnū*) 'their king' or (5) through onomastic name composition, e.g., *Abu-ṭāb* (not *Abṭāb*) 'Father-is-good'.

23. A related case is seen in the formation of certain feminines where Akk. opts for a plain -*t*- marker, whereas Am. uses -*at*-, e.g. , Akk. *watar-t-um* 'exceeding', contrast Am. *yatar-at-um*. Occasional exceptions in Amorite, which are explained as orthographic in nature, are quoted by Knudsen 1991: 872f.

qṣr; Akk. *kṣr* 'to bind'. All these statements are applicable in Old Akkadian as well as in late Akkadian.

(4) A case of particular interest is the Akkadian realization of {š+š} as /ss/ where the first *š* is part of a nominal or verbal base[24] and the second *š* stands for the first consonant of the pronominal suffixes of the third person. The dental realization is baffling, because it seems to imply a different phonetic status for suffixal *š*. It has in fact been suggested that suffixal *š* may have been a distinct phoneme *ś*, which would continue the *ś* of the PS pronominal suffix.[25] If so, the dental realization as /ss/ may be explained on the basis of an original cluster *š+ś*, e.g., *ēpuš-śunūšim* /epussunūšim/ 'do it to them!'. However, this would be the only evidence for a phoneme *ś* in later Akkadian. Hence, rather than positing *ś* as a distinct phoneme, it is generally preferred, e.g., Reiner 1966: 110, to posit instead a special morphophonemic rule. This particular phenomenon is all the more remarkable since suffixation is very productive even with neologisms in later periods, e.g., Neo-Babylonian *išag-giš+šu* /išaggissu/ 'he will kill him' (von Soden 1965–81: 1126b).

It should be noted here that the affricate interpretation of the sibilants (see § 1.3.5) seems at first to account well for some analogous instances where a similar assimilation occurs. Thus, if, e.g., *māt+šu* 'his land' is interpreted as *māt+su*, the resulting phonetic realization would indeed be /mācu/. But all is not as simple as it seems at first. For instance, the affricate realization /mācu/ yields a short consonant, whereas graphemic considerations suggest that the consonant in question was long; how then would we explain the realization /maccu/ from /mat+su/, since [ts] is /c/ and not /cc/? More importantly, how does a cluster of two identical dental sibilants (e.g., *epus+sunūsim* in Diakonoff's transcription for *epuš+šunūšim* in the standard transcription) yield a long affricate (/epuccunūsim/, again in Diakonoff's transcription)?

---

24. This formulation excludes, for instance, *'ašar-iš+šu* 'to his place', since the affix *-iš* is not a nominal or verbal base. The affix *-iš* may in fact go back to *-iś* (Rabin 1969: 192). Such exclusion, too, casts doubt on an interpretation of suffixal *š* as *ś*, but see Reiner 1966: 110. Reiner reports as an additional exception the realization /šš/ when the final radical *š* derives from PS *š*, as with the root *q:š* 'to donate'. However, forms with such a realization (e.g., {iqīš+ši} /iqišši/ 'he donated her') are late; OB forms generally show a realization /ss/ (e.g., {lūqīš+šim} /lūqissim/ 'let me donate to her'). Note that long *š* is otherwise well attested in a variety of other environments, e.g., *kaš-kašš-u* 'very powerful' from the root *kšš*.

25. See above, n. 12. Note that no such environment may occur in Amorite given the lack of suffixes beginning with *š*.

1.4.4. Free variation

Alternations which cannot be explained with any degree of plausibility are best considered simply as free variants. Two examples may be mentioned here. (1) Vocalic alternations, e.g., Akkadian *'ušakniš ~ 'ušekniš* 'he subdued'. (2) Contraction across word boundary (sandhi), e.g., Akkadian *libbālim ~ libbi 'ālim* 'within the city', or Amorite *yarkibaddu ~ yarkib Haddu* 'Adad rides' (Knudsen 1980: 7f.).

1.4.5. Historical development

From the descriptive presentation of inventories and changes, two important points emerge. (A) Akkadian, already at the stage of Old Akkadian, presents more innovations than Amorite. Two concurrent explanations may account for this. On the one hand, Akkadian was subject to the direct influence of Sumerian—something which has long since been recognized. On the other hand, if I am correct in viewing Amorite as the rural counterpart of Akkadian (see § 1.2.3), we can easily accept the conservative nature of its documentation, even if chronologically later in terms of scribal attestation.

(B) Within Akkadian itself, the major changes occur at the level of phonotactics, whereas the inventory as such undergoes only relatively minor changes after Old Akkadian (and fewer changes yet if one accepts the reconstruction of the sibilants by Diakonoff 1985, see § 1.3.2). In particular, no substantial change can be identified within the first millennium. Again, two concurrent explanations may be given. The first is that, within the second millennium, the scribal tradition acted both as a filter in the transmission of the evidence and, to a more limited extent, as a brake to change. Phonotactic changes are the ones that are more difficult to hide with standard scribal mechanisms. The second explanation is more complex. Within the first millennium, the influence of Aramaic was so pervasive that, in effect, it hardly showed at all. By this I mean that it was a social rather than a linguistic influence: somewhere in the early centuries of the millennium, speakers were at best bilingual, and soon afterwards (probably by the eighth/seventh century) Aramaic took over as the only spoken language, while Akkadian continued merely as a literary medium. Hence it is that the linguistic influence on Akkadian is essentially limited to the lexical and syntactic spheres.

Bibliography

Aro, Jussi. 1953. "Abnormal Plene Writings in Akkadian Texts." *Studia Orientalia* 19/11. Helsinki: Societas Orientalis Fennica.

———. 1955. *Studien zur mittelbabylonischen Grammatik. Studia Orientalia* 20. Helsinki: Societas Orientalis Fennica.

———. 1959. "Die semitische Zischläute *(ṭ)*, š, ś und s und ihre Vertretung im Akkadischen." *Orientalia* 28: 321–35.

Berkooz, Moshé. 1937. *The Nuzi Dialect of Akkadian: Orthography and Phonology* (Language Dissertations 23). Philadelphia: University of Pennsylvania.

Bomhard, Allan R. 1988. "The Reconstruction of the Proto-Semitic Consonant System." In *Fucus: A Semitic/Afrasian Gathering in Remembrance of Albert Ehrman*, ed. Yoël L. Arbeitman (Current Issues in Linguistic Theory 58), pp. 113–40. Amsterdam: Benjamins.

Buccellati, Giorgio. 1966. *The Amorites of the the Ur III Period* (Ricerche 1). Naples: Istituto Orientale di Napoli.

———. 1971. Review of Jucquois 1966. *Oriens Antiquus* 10: 79–83.

———. 1979. "Comparative Graphemic Analysis of Old Babylonian and Western Akkadian." *Ugarit-Forschungen* 11: 89–100.

———. 1982. "Studies in Ebla Graphemics, 1." *Studi Eblaiti* 5: 39–74.

———. 1984. "Introduction." In *Graphemic Categorization, 2: The Middle Assyrian Laws*, by Claudio Saporetti, pp. 1–20. Malibu, Calif.: Undena.

———. 1990a. "The Ebla Electronic Corpus: Graphemic Analysis." *Annales Archéologiques Arabes Syriennes* 40: 8–26.

———. 1990b. "From Khana to Laqê: The End of Syro-Mesopotamia." In *De la Babylonie à la Syrie, en passant par Mari (Mélanges Kupper)*, ed. Ö. Tunca, pp. 229–53. Liège: Université de Liège.

———. 1990c. "'River Bank,' 'High Country' and 'Pasture Land': The Growth of Nomadism on the Middle Euphrates and the Khabur." In *Tall al-Hamidiyah 2*, ed. S. Eichler, M. Wäfler, and D. Warbuton, pp. 87–117. Göttingen: Vandenhoek & Ruprecht.

———. 1992. "Ebla and the Amorites." *Eblaitica* 3: 85–106.

———. forthcoming. *A Structural Grammar of Babylonian*. Wiesbaden: Harrassowitz.

Cantineau, Jean. 1951–52. "Le consonantisme du sémitique." *Semitica* 4: 79–94.

Daniels, Peter T. 1993. "Is a Structural Graphemics Possible?" *Eighteenth LACUS Forum* 528–37.

Degen, Rainer. 1969. *Altaramäische Grammatik der Inschriften des 10.–8. Jh. v. Chr.* (Abhandlungen für die Kunde des Morgenlandes 38/3). Wiesbaden: Steiner.

Deller, Karlheinz. 1959. "Lautlehre des Neuassyrischen." Ph.D. dissertation, University of Vienna.
———. 1962a. "Studien zur neuassyrischen Orthographie." *Orientalia* 31: 186–96.
———. 1962b. "Zweisilbige Lautwerte des Typs KVKV im Neuassyrischen." *Orientalia* 31: 7–26.
De Meyer, Leon. 1962. *L'Accadien des contrats de Suse* (Suppléments Iranica Antiqua 1). Leiden: Brill.
Diakonoff, Igor M. 1981. "Towards the Pronunciation of a Dead Language." *Assyriological Miscellanies* (Copenhagen) 1: 7–12.
———. 1985. "The Importance of Ebla for History and Linguistics." *Eblaitica* 2 (1990): 3–29.
———. 1991–92. "Proto-Afrasian and Old Akkadian: A Study in Historical Phonetics," with Contributions by Olga Stolbova and Alexander Militarëv. *Journal of Afroasiatic Languages* 4: 1–133.
Edzard, Dietz Otto. 1986. Review of Greenstein 1984. *Journal of the American Oriental Society* 106: 359–62.
Faber, Alice. 1985. "Akkadian Evidence for Proto-Semitic Affricates." *Journal of Cuneiform Studies* 37: 101–07.
Finet, André. 1956. *L'Accadien des lettres de Mari* (Classe des lettres et des sciences morales et politiques, Mémoires 81). Brussels: Académie royale de Belgique.
Gaebelein, Paul W. 1976. "Graphemic Analysis of Old Babylonian Letters from Mari." Ph. D. dissertation, University of California, Los Angeles.
Garbini, Giovanni. 1960. *Il semitico di Nord-Ovest* (Quaderni della Sezione Linguistica degli Annali 1). Naples: Istituto Universitario Orientale di Napoli.
———. 1965. "Configurazione dell'unità linguistica semitica." In *Le "Protolingue": Atti del IV convegno internazionale di linguisti tenuto a Milano nei giorni 2–6 settembre 1963, presso il Sodalizio Glottologico Milanese* (Atti del Sodalizio glottologico milanese, Supplemento 16). Milan and Brescia: Paideia.
———. 1972. *Le lingue semitiche* (Studi di storia linguistica, Ricerche 9). Naples: Istituto Orientale di Napoli.
Geers, Frederic W. 1965. "The Treatment of Emphatics in Akkadian." *Journal of Near Eastern Studies* 4: 65–67.
Gelb, I. J. 1952. *Old Akkadian Writing and Grammar* (Materials for the Assyrian Dictionary 2). Chicago: University of Chicago Press (See Gelb 1961).

———. 1957. *Glossary of Old Akkadian* (Materials for the Assyrian Dictionary 3). Chicago: University of Chicago Press.

———. 1958. "La lingua degli Amoriti." *Atti della Accademia nazionale dei Lincei: Rendiconti della Classe di scienze morali, storiche e filologiche*, ser. 8, vol. 13, no. 3–4: 143–64.

———. 1961. *Old Akkadian Writing and Grammar* (Materials for the Assyrian Dictionary 2), 2nd ed., pp. 24–43, 119–27. Chicago: University of Chicago Press.

———. 1970a. "Comments on the Akkadian Syllabary." *Orientalia* 39: 516–46.

———. 1970b. "A Note on Morphographemics." In *Mélanges Marcel Cohen*, ed. D. Cohen (Janua Linguarum Series Major 27), pp. 73–77. The Hague: Mouton.

———. 1980. *Computer-aided Analysis of Amorite*, with the assistance of J. Bartels, S.-M. Vance, and R. M. Whiting (Assyriological Studies 21). Chicago: Oriental Institute.

Gelb, I. J., and Burkhart Kienast. 1990. *Die altakkadischen Königsinschriften des dritten Jahrtausends v. Chr.* (Freiburger Altorientalische Studien 7). Stuttgart: Steiner.

Giakumakis, George, Jr. 1970. *The Akkadian of Alalaḫ* (Janua Linguarum Series Practica 59). The Hague: Mouton.

Goetze, Albrecht. 1937. "The Sibilant in Old Babylonian *naẓārum*." *Orientalia* 6: 12–18.

———. 1946. "Sequence of Two Short Syllables in Akkadian." *Orientalia* 15: 233–38.

———. 1947. "Short or Long *ā*?" *Orientalia* 16: 239–50.

———. 1958. "The Sibilants of Old Babylonian." *Revue d'Assyriologie* 52: 137–49.

Greenfield, Jonas C. 1969. "Amurrite, Ugaritic and Canaanite." In *Proceedings of the International Conference on Semitic Studies Held in Jerusalem 19–23 July 1965*, pp. 92–101. Jerusalem: Israel Academy of Sciences and Humanities.

Greenstein, Edward L. 1977. "Phonological Studies in Akkadian." Ph.D. dissertation, Columbia University.

———. 1980. "The Assimilation of Dentals and Sibilants with Pronominal *š* in Akkadian." *Journal of the Ancient Near Eastern Society* 12: 51–64.

———. 1984. "The Phonology of Akkadian Syllable Structure." *Afroasiatic Linguistics* 9/1: 1–71.

Haupt, Paul. 1884–85. "Assyrian Phonology, with Special Reference to Hebrew." *Hebraica* 1: 175–81.

———. 1887. "The Assyrian E-Vowel: A Contribution to the Comparative Phonology of the Assyro-Babylonian Language." *American Journal of Philology* 8: 261–91.

———. 1887. "Über den Halbvocal *w* im Assyrischen." *Zeitschrift für Assyriologie* 2: 259–86.

———. 1890. "Über die beiden Halbvocale *w* und *y*." *Beiträge zur Assyriologie* 1: 293–300.

Hecker, Karl. 1968. *Grammatik der Kültepe-Texte* (Analecta Orientalia 44). Rome: Pontificium Institutum Biblicum.

Huehnergard, John. 1988. *The Akkadian of Ugarit* (Harvard Semitic Studies 34), pp. 23–122. Atlanta: Scholars Press.

Huffmon, Herbert B. 1965. *Amorite Personal Names in the Mari Texts: A Structural and Lexical Study*. Baltimore: The Johns Hopkins University Press.

Hyatt, James Philip. 1941. *The Treatment of Final Vowels in Early Neo-Babylonian* (Yale Oriental Series, Researches 23). New Haven: Yale University Press.

Izre'el, Shlomo. 1987. "The Complementary Distribution of the Vowels *e* and *i* in the Peripheral Akkadian Dialect of Amurru: A Further Step towards Our Understanding of the Development of the Amarna Jargon." In *Proceedings of the Fourth International Hamito-Semitic Congress (Marburg, 20–22 September 1983)*, ed. H. Jungraithmayr and W. W. Müller (Current Issues in Linguistic Theory 44), pp. 525–41. Amsterdam: Benjamins.

———. 1991. *Amurru Akkadian: A Linguistic Study*, with an appendix on the history of Amurru by Itamar Singer, 2 vols. (Harvard Semitic Studies 40–41). Atlanta: Scholars Press [esp. 1:26–94].

Jäger, M. 1890a. "Der Halbvokal *y* im Assyrischen." *Beiträge zur Assyriologie* 1: 443–91.

———. 1890b. "Das babylonische Hauchlautszeichen." *Beiträge zur Assyriologie* 1: 589–92.

Jucqouis, Guy. 1966. *Phonétique comparée des dialects moyen-babyloniennes du nord et de l'ouest* (Biliothèque du Muséon 53). Louvain: Institut Orientaliste.

Kinnier Wilson, J. V. 1968. "'Desonance' in Accadian." *Journal of Semitic Studies* 13: 93–103.

Knudsen, Ebbe E. 1961. "Cases of Free Variants in the Akkadian *q* phoneme." *Journal of Cuneiform Studies* 15: 84–90.
———. 1969. "Spirantization of Velars in Akkadian." In *Lišān mitḫurti: Festschrift von Soden*, ed. W. Röllig (Alter Orient und Altes Testament 1), pp. 147–56. Neukirchen-Vluyn: Neukirchener Verlag.
———. 1980. "Stress in Akkadian." *Journal of Cuneiform Studies* 32: 3–16.
———. 1982a. "An Analysis of Amorite." *Journal of Cuneiform Studies* 34: 1–18 [review of Gelb 1980].
———. 1982b. "The Mari Akkadian Shift *ia* > *ê* and the Treatment of ל"ה Formations in Biblical Hebrew." *Journal of Near Eastern Studies* 41: 35–43.
———. 1986. Review of Greenstein 1984. *Bibliotheca Orientalis* 43: 723–32.
———. 1991. "Amorite Grammar: A Comparative Statement." In *Semitic Studies in Honor of Wolf Leslau on the Occasion of his Eighty-fifth Birthday, November 14th, 1991*, ed. Alan S. Kaye, pp. 866–85. Wiesbaden: Harrassowitz.
Kobayashi, Yoshitaka. 1975. "Graphemic Analysis of Old Babylonian Letters from South Babylonia." Ph.D. dissertation, University of California, Los Angeles.
Labat, René. 1946. "Le système phonétique de l'akkadien: Observations préliminaires à une étude phonologique." *Comptes Rendues du Groupe Linguistique des Etudes Chamito-Sémitiques* 4: 9–12.
Lieberman, Stephen J. 1977. *The Sumerian Loanwords in Old-Babylonian Akkadian*, vol. 1: *Prolegomena and Evidence*. Missoula, Mont.: Scholars Press.
———. 1979. "The Phoneme /o/ in Sumerian." In *Studies in Honor of Tom B. Jones*, ed. M. A. Powell and R. H. Sack, pp. 21–28. Neukirchen-Vluyn: Neukirchener Verlag.
Mayer, Walter. 1971. *Untersuchungen zur Grammatik des Mittelassyrischen* (Alter Orient und Altes Testament Sonderreihe 2). Neukirchen: Neukirchener Verlag.
Mendenhall, George E. 1985. *The Syllabic Inscriptions from Byblos*. Beirut: American University of Beirut.
Murtonen, A. 1966. "The Semitic Sibilants." *Journal of Semitic Studies* 11: 135–50 [esp. pp. 149f.].
Platt, James H. 1993. "Eblaite Scribal Schools: Graphemics and Orthography." Ph.D. dissertation, University of California, Los Angeles.

Poebel, Arno. 1939. *Studies in Akkadian Grammar* (Assyriological Studies 9). Chicago: University of Chicago Press.

Polomé, Edgar C. 1981. "Can Graphemic Change Cause Phonemic Change?" In *Bono Homini Donum: Essays in Historical Linguistics in Memory of J. Alexander Kerns*, ed. Yoël L. Arbeitman and Allan R. Bomhard (Current Issues in Linguistic Theory 16), vol. 2, pp. 881–88. Amsterdam: Benjamins.

Prosecky, Jiri. 1986. "L'analyse graphémique de la version paléobabylonienne du mythe d'Atramhasis: Contribution à la méthode de l'analyse graphémique des textes cunéiformes akkadiens." *Archiv Orientalní* 54: 61–76.

Rabin, Chaim. 1969. "The Structure of the Semitic System of Case Endings." In *Proceedings of the International Conference on Semitic Studies Held in Jerusalem 19–23 July 1965*, pp. 190–204. Jerusalem: Israel Academy of Sciences and Humanities.

Ravn, Otto Emil. 1939. "The Substitution of -ss- for -šš- in Babylonian." *Acta Orientalia* 17: 318–28.

Reiner, Erica. 1964. "The Phonological Interpretation of a Subsystem in the Akkadian Syllabary." In *Studies Presented to A. Leo Oppenheim*, pp. 167–80. Chicago: Oriental Institute.

———. 1966. *A Linguistic Analysis of Akkadian* (Janua Linguarum Series Practica 21). The Hague: Mouton.

———. 1970. "Akkadian." In *Current Trends in Linguistics*, ed. Thomas A. Sebeok, vol. 6, *Linguistics in South West Asia and North Africa*, pp. 274–303. The Hague: Mouton.

———. 1973a. "How We Read Cuneiform Texts." *Journal of Cuneiform Studies* 25: 3–58.

———. 1973b. "New Cases of Morphophonemic Spellings." *Orientalia* 42: 35–38.

———. 1985. "The Uses of Astrology." *Journal of the American Oriental Society* 105: 589–95.

Riemschneider, Kaspar K. 1976. "Compound Graphemic Units in Standard Babylonian Writing." *Journal of Cuneiform Studies* 28: 65–71.

Rimalt, E. S. 1933–34. "Zur Lautlehre des Neubabylonischen." *Archiv für Orientforschung* 9: 124–26.

Salonen, Erkki. 1962. *Untersuchungen zur Schrift und Sprache des altbabylonischen von Susa* (Studia Orientalia 27/1). Helsinki: Societas Orientalis Fennica.

Sarauw, Chr. 1939. *Über Akzent und Silbenbildung in den älteren semitischen Sprachen*. Copenhagen.
Segert, Stanislav. 1975. *Altaramäische Grammatik mit Bibliographie, Chrestomathie und Glossar*. Leipzig: VEB Verlag Enzyklopädie.
Shehadeh, Lamia R. 1987. "Some Observations on the Sibilants in the Second Millennium B.C." In *Working with No Data: Semitic and Egyptian Studies Presented to Thomas O. Lambdin*, ed. David M. Golomb, pp. 229–46. Winona Lake, Ind.: Eisenbrauns.
Steiner, Richard. 1977. *The Case for Fricative-Laterals in Proto-Semitic* (American Oriental Series 59). New Haven: American Oriental Society [esp. pp. 144–48, 159].
———. 1982. *Affricated Ṣade in the Semitic Languages* (American Academy for Jewish Research Monograph Series 3). New York: American Academy for Jewish Research [esp. pp. 70–74].
von Soden, Wolfram. 1948a. *Das akkadische Syllabar* (Analecta Orientalia 27). Rome: Pontificium Institutum Biblicum.
———. 1948b. "Vokalfärbungen im Akkadischen." *Journal of Cuneiform Studies* 2: 291–303.
———. 1952. *Grundriss der akkadischen Grammatik* (Analecta Orientalia 33). Rome: Pontificium Institutum Biblicum.
———. 1965–81. *Akkadisches Handwörterbuch*. Wiesbaden: Harrassowitz.
———. 1968. "Die Spirantisierung von Verschlussläuten im Akkadischen: Ein Zwischenbericht." *Journal of Near Eastern Studies* 27: 214–20.
———. 1969. *Grundriss der akkadischen Grammatik samt Ergänzungsheft* (Analecta Orientalia 33/47). Rome: Pontificium Institutum Biblicum.
von Soden, Wolfram, and Wolfgang Röllig. 1967. *Das akkadische Syllabar*, 2nd ed. (Analecta Orientalia 42). Rome: Pontificium Institutum Biblicum.
Westenholz, Aage. 1978. "Some Notes on the Orthography and Grammar of the Recently Published Texts from Mari." *Bibliotheca Orientalis* 35: 160–69 [esp. pp. 161–64].
Wilhelm, Gernot. 1970. *Untersuchungen zum Ḫurro-Akkadischen von Nuzi* (Alter Orient und Altes Testament 9). Neukirchen-Vluyn: Neukirchener Verlag.
———. 1983. "Reconstructing the Phonology of Dead Languages." In *Writing in Focus*, ed. F. Coulmas and K. Ehlich (Trends in Linguistics, Studies and Monographs 24), pp. 157–66. Berlin: Mouton de Gruyter.

Zadok, Ran. 1993. "On the Amorite Material from Mesopotamia." In *The Tablet and the Scroll: Near Eastern Studies in Honor of William W. Hallo*, ed. M. E. Cohen, D. C. Snell, and D. B. Weisberg, pp. 315–33. Bethesda, Md.: CDL Press.

Zimmern, Heinrich. 1890. "Zur assyrischen und vergleichende semitischen Lautlehre." *Zeitschrift für Assyriologie* 5: 367–98.

Chapter 2
Eblaite Phonology
Cyrus H. Gordon
New York University

Eblaite designates the language of the largest archives known from anywhere in the world during the Early Bronze Age (3000–2000 B.C.E.). The inscriptions of the Ebla archives already unearthed number about 15,000, many on large, well-preserved clay tablets. They have been excavated by an Italian expedition at the ancient site of Ebla, a little over thirty miles south of Aleppo, Syria. The archives were written during a period of about fifty years during the 23rd century.

Eblaite is a Semitic language embodying East and West Semitic features. Texts in the same language have been found at Mesopotamian sites such as Mari, Tell Abū-Ṣalābīḫ, and Kish. Eblaite is essentially a written lingua franca used by scribes, merchants, and diplomats. It was not limited to Ebla, nor was it the spoken language of Ebla.

Scribes, and some of their employers, could probably converse in it, but it is most unlikely that the scribes, merchants, diplomats, or anyone else spoke Eblaite at home.

The Eblaite texts are written in the cuneiform system of Mesopotamia, developed by the Sumerians and adopted by the Semitic Akkadians. The system has ideograms in addition to syllabic signs. It also employs determinatives to fix the semantic category of a word. So many Sumerograms are used that it is often possible for an Assyriologist to sense the meaning of a passage, or even of an entire tablet, without knowing how to pronounce it in Eblaite. The ends of words are sometimes added syllabically to the Sumerograms so that we can deduce the case endings of nouns and the modal suffixes of verbs, as well as the suffixed personal pronouns and conjugational suffixes. Particles (conjunctions, prepositions, and the like) and names are usually spelled out phonetically. There are also extensive bilingual school texts giving us the Eblaite translations of Sumerograms.

AUTHOR'S NOTE: Abbreviations: DN, divine name; GN: geographical name; PN, personal name.

However, much of that vocabulary is highly specialized and not as applicable as we might wish to the other tablets found by the excavators.

In the Ebla archives, the Sumerograms do not follow Sumerian word order, but instead are placed in accordance with the rules of Eblaite syntax. We can thus learn much about Eblaite phrase and sentence structure even when we cannot pronounce the Eblaite words for which the Sumerograms stand.

The reconstruction of Eblaite does not involve the decipherment of a script, nor essentially the interpretation of the texts. It is rather the extracting, analyzing, classifying, and assembling of seemingly endless linguistic details with the aim of enabling us to compose a grammar and glossary of the Eblaite language. For the on-going process, see Archi (1987), Diakonoff (1990), and Gordon (1987, 1990, 1992).

Eblaite is written in the Mesopotamian cuneiform system which was not designed for, and hence is not well suited for, recording Semitic languages. In spite of nearly a century and a half of linguistic scholarship devoted to Akkadian, many details of the phonology remain controversial. The script is characterized by the two opposing (and confusing) principles of polyphony and homophony. Polyphony means that a sign may have several (often many) different phonetic values; e.g., there is a common sign that is to be pronounced *ur*, or *taš*, or *lik* (along with several other values) depending on context. Homophony means that the same sound may be represented by several (often many) entirely different signs.

When whole, phonetically spelled Eblaite texts will have come to light, no seasoned Semitist should experience insuperable trouble in reading, translating, and describing them linguistically in detail. This will be the case no matter whether the script is syllabic or alphabetic. Our main present obstacle is simply that there is no sizable Eblaite prose or poetic literature spelled out phonetically without a plethora of Sumerograms and proper names. Names are often unconnected with the language of the people who bear them. My name (Cyrus) is Persian and my wife's name (Constance) is Latin (Constantia). Neither of us is Iranian or Italic and our language is English.

The Eblaite system of writing is inherited from Sumerian proto-writing of Early Dynastic II. Semitic phonology includes a threefold repertoire of dental and palatal stops and sibilants, namely surd (voiceless), sonant (voiced), and emphatic. Thus we find *t/d/ṭ*, *k/g/q*, and *s/z/ṣ*. Sumerian lacks the emphatic; so that DA covers *da* and *ṭa*, GA covers *ga* and *qa*, and ZA covers *za* and *ṣa*. However, in Eblaite all three grades are lumped together so that DA covers *ta/da/ṭa*, GU covers *ku/gu/qu*, and SA covers *sa/za/ṣa*. Neither the doubling of consonants nor the length of vowels is normally indicated.

It follows that normalization and etymology cannot be ascertained mechanically. The process requires an extensive and systematic knowledge of the Semitic languages.

In the bilinguals, šu-tur (literally 'little hand') designates 'finger', and its Eblaite form corresponds to the Common Semitic word that appears as 'eṣba' 'finger, toe' in Hebrew. The Eblaite is written two ways: *i-sa-ba-um* tur and *iš-ba-um* tur. Note the open-syllable spelling with *sa* for vowelless [ṣ] in the first form, and also note the *š* for *ṣ* in the second form.

Eblaite is often written in open-syllable orthography (like Linear A and B, or Japanese). A word beginning ['aṣmi-] is spelled either *a-za-mi-* or *a-zi-me-*; note that the vowelless [ṣ] is written either *za*, reflecting the vowel of the preceding syllable, or *zi*, reflecting the *i* of the following syllable. This open-syllable orthography often gives the illusion that there are no closed syllables in Eblaite, which is not at all the case.[1]

The mixed character of Eblaite is reflected in the words designating the large numbers: *mi-at* '100' is Common Semitic, *li-im* '1,000' is East Semitic, *rí-bab* '10,000' is West Semitic, and *ma-i-at* '100,000' goes its own way in a new direction.

It is interesting to note the Eblaite forms of Sumerian names: ^{d}EN-LIL > *I-li-lu*, ^{d}NIN-KAR-DU > *Ni-ka-ra-du*, ^{d}SUMUQAN > *Sa-ma-gan*, ^{d}AŠNAN > *A-sa-ma-an*.

The bilingual equation baḫar 'potter' = *wa-ṣí-lu-um* (cognate with Hebrew *yôṣēr* 'potter') illustrates that (1) unlike in Northwest Semitic, initial [*w-] remains in Eblaite (as in Akkadian and Arabic) without shifting to [y-]; and (2) [r] may change to [l]. The change of [r] to [l] (which is quite common) is not reversible, for [l] never shifts to [r]. The falling together of [r] and [l] (in the [r > l] shift) reflects a common phenomenon. In Linear A and B, and in hieroglyphic Egyptian, [r] and [l] fall together, at least in the orthography. In Chinese and Japanese, they definitely fall together in the spoken language as well.

The GN *Ar-ga*^{ki} ['arqa] has lost the final *-t* of the singular feminine suffix *-at*. In the Amarna letters this GN is called *Arqat*. Cf. the GN *É-ma*^{ki} = *Ḥămāt*

---

1. Gimbutas (1991) has shown that the Linear A graphs are derived from the Old European graphs of about 5300–4300 b.c.e. See chap. 8, "The Sacred Script" (esp. p. 320, fig. 8-22). She attributes the disappearance of the Old European script toward the end of the fifth millennium to the Indo-Europeanization of Central Europe at that time. The people who had fostered the Old European script were forced into the Aegean area, carrying that script to Crete and Cyprus, where it survived for millennia. Her discovery will have a major impact on the reconstruction of ancient history, in several different ways.

(modern Hama). In the *status absolutus* the final [-t] of the singular feminine suffix is generally dropped in Hebrew, and regularly in spoken Arabic. Final [-t] begins to be dropped in Egyptian already in the third millennium.

The GN *Máš-a*^{ki} is to be compared with the GN *Maśśā'*(Prov. 30:1, 31:1). The *-a* accordingly does not reflect the feminine suffix (which would be written with a final *-h* in Hebrew), but final *-'*.

Etymology indicates that [l] frequently loses its normal consonantal character in Eblaite and is not represented in the script. E.g., *a-bi-nu-u(m) i-a-ba-nu* SIG$_4$-GAR [ābinū yabānū libitta] 'brickmakers will make the brick'. The root of the first two words is **lbn* although no [l] appears in the orthography. We must reckon with vocalic [ḷ] (and also vocalic [ṛ]) in the Semitic languages. In Akkadian, the second radical of all quadriconsonantal verbs is either [l] or [r]. This may explain the Arabic IIIrd conjugation (*qātala*; cf. Heb. *pôlēl* with a long vowel representing the absorption of vocalic [ḷ] or [ṛ]).

Initial [w-] does not undergo the Northwest Semitic shift to [y-]. Eblaite retains [w-] like Akkadian, Arabic, and Ethiopic. In addition to [w-] (discussed above), note (the dual) *wa-ti-a* [wādi-a] 'the two wadis'.

The script reflects four vowels: *a, i, u/o,* and *e*. However, *e* may well be non-phonemic but only positionally conditioned by contact with *ḫ* or *'*.

The diphthongs [ay], [aw], and [ue] can all be reduced to [ā]. In the case of [ay > ā] and [aw > ā], the shift can be explained as "falling" diphthongs (with the accent on the [a]) as distinct from "rising" diphthongs (with the accent on the [y/w]) whereby **bayt* yields *bīt* 'house' and **mawt* yields *mūt* 'death' in Akkadian. While we find many Eblaite examples of [ay > ā] and several of [aw > ā], there is only one of [ue > ā]: the Akkadian *Suen* (which comes into Babylonian and Assyrian as *Sin*) is reduced to *San* 'Moon' in *San-Ugāru* 'Moon of the Field' (an epithet of the Moon) in an incantation where the reference to the Moon is fixed by duplicate passages which have ITI 'month, moon' instead. San also appears instead of Sin (the Moon god) in the Hebrew form of the Mesopotamian names *San-ḫērīb* (Sennacherib) and *San-ballaṭ*. In the Palestinian GN 'Beth-shean' the second element (Shan) designates the Moon god. Examples of [ay > a] in Eblaite: *ba-du* [bāt-] 'house'; *a-na* and *a-na-a* ['anā] 'eyes' (dual); *ba-nu* [bān-] 'tamarisk' (vs. Akkadian *bīn-* with rising diphthong); *ma-sa-lu-u(m)* [masalu] 'justice, uprightness' from **yšr* (note Hebrew *mêšārîm*) and from the Št stem of the same root *uš-da-ši-ir* [uštašir] 'he prepared, released (lit. caused to be right)'. There are fewer examples of [aw > ā]: [*'aw > 'ā] 'or'; and the PN *Mu-ša-ra-du* (Š participle of ** wrd* 'to bring down gods with gifts' = 'to propitiate them successfully'; cf. Arabic and especially Ugaritic).

Cryptic writings were meant to be read by the initiated. We know from a bilingual tablet that ᵈMUL = *Kab-kab* 'Star'; however, in an incantation it is written *ga : ga : ba : bù* [kabkabu] (ending in nominative *-u*). A similar cryptograph is *ga : ga : li : la*, which calls to mind *galgal* 'wheel'; if correct, note that *li* stands for vowelless [l].

The name *Da-gu-nu* corresponds to Heb. *Dāgôn* (< *Dagān*) with ā > ō, which is frequent in Canaanite. Cf. also Minoan *Da-gu-na*.

[-dk-] is assimilated to [-kk-] in *a-za-me-ga* ['aṣmikka < *'aṣmid-ka] 'I bind thee'.

*Sum-ar-rum*ᵏⁱ 'Sumer' comes into Hebrew as *Šinʿār* 'Babylonia'. Note that AR = *ʿar* and begins a new syllable. Another change in syllabification is inherent in Eblaite and Old Akkadian *en-ma* (> standard Akkadian *um-ma*) and Hebrew [nm̥]—all meaning 'so says' (followed by direct discourse). The initial *n-* is properly vocalic [n̥], which is written either *en-* or *um-* according to the rules of the Mesopotamian syllabary, and נְ (*ně*) according to the orthographic rules of Masoretic pointing.

Vocalic nasals and liquids include [r̥]. The tree called the ᵍⁱˢ̌ŠU-ME is bilingually rendered in Eblaite as either *šì-rí-mi-nu* or *ša-mi-nu*. Expressed alphabetically, the choice is between *šrmn* and *šmn*. The [r̥] is vocalic and not represented in the latter.

Philippi's law ([i > a] in an originally closed accented syllable) is operative in Northwest Semitic (Canaanite, Aramaic, Ugaritic). It does not take place in Akkadian, Arabic, etc. Since Eblaite is a border language between East and Northwest Semitic, it is not surprising that it occurs sporadically. Thus in Eblaite both *libittu* and *libattu* (spelled *li-bi-tum* and *li-ba-tum*) 'brick' occur.

The following independent personal pronouns are attested and bring out the difference between the orthography and probable phonetic pronunciation. In the case of *a-na/an-na* 'I', ['anna] is preferred (vs. the pronoun in the other Semitic languages) because in normal Mesopotamian orthography, doubling a consonant means phonetic doubling, while writing a single consonant can stand for either a single or a double consonant in the pronunciation.

sg. 1 comm.nom.	*an-na, a-na* ['anna] 'I'
sg. 2 masc.nom.	*an-da* ['anta] 'thou'
acc.	*gu-wa-ti* [kuwāti] 'thee'
dat.	*gu-wa-si* [kuwāši(m)] 'to thee'

sg. 3 masc.nom.	*su-wa* [šuwa] 'he'
acc.	*su-wa-ti* [šuwati] 'him'
dat.	*su-wa-si* [šuwāši(m)] 'to him'
sg. 3 fem. nom.	*si-a* [šiya] 'she'
du. 1 comm.dat.	*ne-si-in* [nešin] 'to both of us'
pl. 2 masc.nom.	*an-da-nu* ['antanu] 'ye, you'
pl. 3 masc.nom.	*su-nu* [šunū] 'they'

The following suffixed personal pronouns are attested:

sg. 1 comm.gen.	*-i* [-ī], or (postvocalic) *-a* [-(y)a] 'my'
acc.	*-ni* [-ni] 'me'
sg. 2 masc.gen./acc.	*-ga* [-ka] 'thy, thee'
dat.	*-kum* [-kum] 'to thee'
sg. fem. gen./acc.	*-gi* [-ki] 'thy, thee'
sg. 3 masc.gen./acc.	*-sù*, *-su* [-šu] 'his, him'
dat.	*-su-um* [-šum] 'to him'
sg. fem. gen.	*-sa* [-ša] 'her'
pl. 1 comm.gen.	*-na* [-nā], *-nu* [-nū] 'our'
pl. 2 masc.acc.	*-gu-nu* [-kunū] 'you'
pl. 3 masc.gen./acc.	*-su-nu* [-šunū] 'their, them'
pl.3 fem. gen.	*-si-na* [-šina] 'their'
acc.	*-si-na-at* [-šināt] 'them'

The lone occurrence of an unusual pronominal suffix calls for special notice. The meaning of *ši-ne-mu* [šinn-êmo] 'his teeth' is fixed by context. That all three vowels are to be pronounced is indicated by the difference among [i, e, u], which rules out zero-grade vowels disguised by open-syllable orthography. The ending *-êmō*, known from biblical Hebrew poetry, is a general possessive suffix that can be applied regardless of person. Here it means 'his teeth' but in another context it could mean 'their teeth' and so forth. An exact (though admittedly clumsy) translation is 'thereof'.

The six case endings are: nominative *-u(m)*, genitive *-i(m)*, accusative *-a(m)*, dative-locative *-iš*, locative-adverbial *-u(m)*, absolute *-a/-∅*. The three commonest cases (nom., gen., acc.) are often confused. There are some indeclinables in *-a*, especially among the PNs such as *Ra-ba*, *Ba-ga-ma*, *Tab-rí-sá* and the DN ᵈ*Ba-ra-ma*. While a bilingual renders the name of the Sumerian god EN-KI as *É-um* [Ḥayyum] 'The Living One' in Eblaite, the other Eblaite texts regularly render the name *É-a* [Ḥayya] ending in *-a*. Other DNs in *-a* are: *É-da* [Hadda] and *Qu-ra* [Qūra].

The absolute in [-∅] (zero) is common in some proper names; e.g., the DNs ᵈ*Ga-mi-iš*, ᵈ*Ra-sa-ap*; the GNs *A-da-bi-ik*^(ki), *A-da-ti-ik*^(ki), and month names such as ITI *za-é-na-at*.

The construct state is not always expressed in writing; e.g., it is not expressed in *ḫa-za-nu* GN 'the mayor of X', while it is in *ma-lik* GN 'the advisor of Y'.

The suffix marking the dual is *casus rectus* -ā(n), *obliquus* -ay(n) (which can shift to -ā(n) in accordance with the reduction of the diphthong [ay > a]); e.g., *tal-da-an* [daltān] 'double doors' and *su-lu-la-a* 'the two horns'. The following citation has the dual suffix in the word designating a pair of deified rivers and a dual noun in apposition with them: 2 ᵈ*Ba-li-ḫa wa-ti-a* [Baliḫa wādia] 'the two divine Baliḫ rivers, the two streams'.

There is one pair of words that raises fundamental questions. The nouns *ḫrd* 'child' and *ms* 'son, child' have long been known only from Egyptian. Then both turned up in Ugaritic of the Late Bronze Age, and now in Eblaite of the Early Bronze Age. Ebla had connections with Egypt; alabaster vessels with the names of Chefren (4th Dynasty) and Pepi I (6th Dynasty) have been found at Ebla in the archeological stratum that yielded the archives. The meaning of Eblaite *ḫar-da-du* [ḫardātu] in the sense of 'young women' is fixed by context; the same form with the same sense occurs in Old Kingdom Egypt. The situation with Eblaite *maš* (= Egyptian *ms*) is more complex and tantalizing. It is common in all periods of Egyptian from start to finish. But it also may occur in Sumerian (MÁŠ) with the meaning of 'kid, young goat'. Words for young animals are often applied to children.

The adjective has long been known to be inflected like the noun except for the feminine plural, *status absolutus* in Syro-Aramaic. Now Ebla shares that exception with Syro-Aramaic. In Hebrew *mĕlāḵîm/n* 'kings' has its feminine counterpart in *mĕlāḵôt* 'queens'. But in Aramaic the phonetic equivalent of Hebrew feminine plural construct *malḵôt* מַלְכֹת 'queens (of)', namely *malḵāt* מַלְכָת 'queens (of)', can only serve as the construct. The Aramaic absolute (corresponding in meaning to Hebrew *mĕlāḵîm/n* 'kings') is *malḵān* מַלְכָן 'queens'. Thus Eblaite *du-na-an* [dunnān] 'mighty (females)' has the suffix -*ān* for the adjective plural feminine absolute.

There are two principal tenses: (1) the so-called imperfect with prefixes and some suffixes, and (2) the so-called perfect with suffixes but no prefixes. Verbs are usually classified as strong (with a root of three stable consonants) or weak (with a semivowel: *w* or *y*, functioning as one of the root consonants; or with only two consonants in the root with the second one repeated). A root can be treated within the matrix of several conjugations, all familiar from the other Semitic languages; e.g., G, Gt, D, Š, ŠD, ŠDt. Like Aramaic, Eblaite has no N conjugation. The imperfect has modal suffixes; thus -*u* is the sign of the indicative. In the perfect, the singular 3rd masculine ends in -*a*. In Akkadian the perfect is for stative or intransitive verbs; in West Semitic the perfect is used for transitive as well as intransitive verbs; here, Eblaite goes with West Semitic.

The imperfect has *a*, *i*, or *u* as the thematic vowel between the last two consonants of the root:

> *u*-class: *Iq-bu-ul-(Ma-lik)* is a PN meaning '(The Divine King) has accepted (the propitiatory offerings of the parents and granted the child who bears the PN)'.
>
> *i*-class: *Ig-ri-iš-(Li-im)* is a PN meaning '(God) has driven out (the forces of evil)'.
>
> *a*-class: *Ir-kab-(Ar)* is a PN meaning ' (The deity Ar) rides'.

The prefix vowel gives the impression that there is an isogloss with East Semitic, in which we find Akkadian *iprus, iddin, iṣbat*, vs. West Semitic, where we find Arabic *yaqtul, yajlis, yasmaʻ*. Little weight can be attributed to the loss of the *y*- in Akkadian because of the vocalization of the Hebrew in the LXX (Septuagint Greek) tradition and some living traditions like the Arabic. Note LXX ΙΣΑΑΚ 'Isaac' (vs. Masoretic *Yiṣḥāq*) and Arabic *'Isḥāq*; and vs. Masoretic *Yiśrā'ēl* 'Israel', note Arabic *'Isrā'īl*. However, *ya*- is preserved in both the LXX and Arabic traditions: Masoretic *Ya'aqōḇ*, LXX IAKOB-, Arabic *Ya'qūb*.

The attested morphs of the imperfect tense are: sg. 1st comm. *'a*-CCvC, sg. 2nd masc. *ta*-CCvC, sg. 3rd masc. *i*-CCvC, sg. 3rd fem. *ta*-CCvC, pl. 3rd masc. *i*-CCvC-*ū*.

The perfect (3rd masc. sg. = CaCvCa) is used in PNs such as *Ra-ga-ma-Il* 'God has spoken' (with *rgm 'to speak' as in Ugaritic) or *Qá-ba-Lum* 'God has spoken' and *Qa-ba-Da-mu* '(The god) Damu has spoken' (where the verb is familiar from Akkadian *qabū* 'to speak'). East Semitic restricts the perfect to intransitive verbs, whereas Eblaite, like West Semitic, uses it for transitive as well as intransitive verbs. In addition to the above transitive perfects, note also *ba-na-a* 'he has built'.

The following is a D imperfect intensified by an infinitive absolute ending in adverbial -*u* (as in Ugaritic and Akkadian): *i-na-é-áš na-é-su* [*'inaḥḥaš naḥāšu*] 'I shall verily perform magic'. Note that the D prefix does not go with Arabic and Akkadian *'u*-.

The infinitive absolute in -*u* appears in the *figura etymologica*: *ḫu-mu-zu ḫa-ma-zi, bù-ru₁₂ ba-ra-ru₁₁* (**brr*).

The ŠD participle *muška"inum* is of interest because it explains Akkadian *muškēnum* 'helot, plebeian', which survives into modern Hebrew *miskēn* and Arabic *miskīn* 'poor'; and French *mesquin* 'shabby, mean'.

The composite, interregional nature of Eblaite precluded the modicum of consistency and uniformity that more natural languages have developed through analogic leveling. We thus find the same root (**hlk*) with two treatments of the G infinitive in the bilinguals: É-*a-gu-um* [hākum] and É-*la-gum* [halākum] 'to go'. There would be little merit in our striving to create a consistency that is not there.

The Early Bronze Age date of the Ebla archives provides an abundance of Semitic documents in Syria a millennium earlier than the Ugaritic tablets and half a millennium earlier than Minoan Linear A.

Bibliography

Sources

ARET: *Archivi Reali di Ebla—Testi*, Rome (the chief publication of the Ebla tablets; eight volumes have appeared).

Eblaitica: *Eblaitica: Essays on the Ebla Archives and Eblaite Language* (Publications of the Center for Ebla Research at New York University), ed. C. H. Gordon and Gary Rendsburg. Winona Lake, Ind.: Eisenbrauns. 1, 1987; 2, 1990; 3, 1992.

MEE: *Materiali Epigrafici di Ebla*, Naples (four volumes have appeared, including Giovanni Pettinato's vol. 4 (two parts, 1982) on the bilinguals, which is very important).

SEb: *Studi Eblaiti*, University of Rome (the journal of the Ebla Expedition, headed by Paolo Matthiae; valuable articles have appeared in it).

UT: C. H. Gordon, *Ugaritic Textbook*. Rome: Pontifical Biblical Institute, 1967.

References

Archi, Alfonso. 1987. "Ebla and Eblaite." *Eblaitica* 1: 7–17.
Diakonoff, I. M. 1990. "The Importance of Ebla for History and Linguistics." *Eblaitica* 2: 3–29.

Gimbutas, Marija. 1991. *The Civilisation of the Goddess*. San Francisco: HarperCollins.
Gordon, C. H. 1987. "Eblaitica." *Eblaitica* 1: 19-28.
———. 1990. "Eblaite and Northwest Semitic." *Eblaitica* 2: 127–39.
———. 1992. "The Ebla Exorcisms." *Eblaitica* 3: 117–37.

Chapter 3
Ugaritic Phonology
Cyrus H. Gordon
New York University

Ugaritic preserves Semitic phonetic structure better than any known language except North and South Arabic. Our topic is complicated by the fact that Ugaritic is not a single dialect recorded in a single script. Although the Ugaritic texts date from a restricted period (ca. 1400–ca. 1185 B.C.E.) and most of them come from a restricted area (a small city-state along the coast of Syria north of Latakia), they are not in one homogeneous dialect. Prose and poetry often operate according to different rules, and there are within each of those two categories texts that deviate from their own norm in various ways, including phonetically.

Most of the Ugaritic tablets are written in an alphabet of thirty letters which, however, reflect only twenty-seven different consonantal phonemes; for three of the 30 letters have been tacked on to an earlier 27 without adding any new consonants. Instead of one alef there are three depending on the vowel that follows it; and the 30th letter (ś) duplicates the 19th (s) phonetically, for calendrical reasons. It is remarkable that the ABC which has come down to us had multiple uses, such as numerical and calendrical (to keep track of the days in a lunar month) as well as phonetic spelling. There was also a shorter ABC in which the falling together of consonants yielded the 22-letter ABC of the Arameans/Hebrews/Phoenicians in which some of the Ugaritic tablets are written. And, especially in lexical tablets, Ugaritic words

AUTHOR'S NOTE: The references are (except where stated otherwise) from *UT* (Gordon 1967), because it is the only extensive corpus of texts with a detailed grammar and full glossary. *KTU* (Dietrich, Loretz, & Sanmartín 1976) is valuable insofar as it keeps adding the new texts. However, like *CTA* (Herdner 1963) that preceded it, *KTU* has changed the text numbers, injecting chaos in a field that instead needs order. The system of numbering in *UT* was designed to accommodate future discoveries and at the same time to facilitate checking with the *editio princeps*. This has not been understood by the authors of *CTA* and *KTU*, who apparently regard their disconcerting renumbering of the tablets as part of their scholarly contribution.

The spate of important publications on Ugarit goes on unabated. The most comprehensive and useful is Pardee 1988.

are sometimes inscribed in the Mesopotamian syllabary. And finally we may note that individual scribes have written tablets which confront us with phonetic solecisms.

The alef (ʾ) appears in three different forms which are transliterated *a*, *i*, and *u* respectively. Their normalization, however, calls for a consonantal alef: [ʔa], [ʔi], [ʔu]. The vowel inherent in an alef letter reflects the vowel following the alef; in the case of a vowelless alef, it usually reflects the preceding vowel.

Semitic [b], [g], and [d] normally come into Ugaritic unchanged as *b*, *g*, and *d*. However, Semitic *b* may interchange with *p* in the same word; thus *šbḥ* and *špḥ* 'family' occur (Heb. מִשְׁפָּחָה) and similarly *nbk* and *npk*.

The phoneme [ḏ] is preserved only sporadically in Ugaritic (i.e., represented by the letter *ḏ*); normally it shifts to [d] as in standard Syro-Aramaic.

Semitic [h], [w], and [z] come into Ugaritic unchanged and are written *h*, *w*, and *z*.

Semitic [ḥ] (which falls together with [ḫ] in Hebrew and Aramaic) is preserved in Ugaritic and written *ḥ*. It should also be observed that one of the words for 'young man' in Ugaritic is *ḫrd*. (That it is not a loanword in Ugaritic is indicated by its presence in Eblaite, a millennium before Ugaritic.) The word is common in Egyptian, where it is written *ḫrd* (with *ḫ* rather than *ḥ*). Since Ugaritic is Egypto-Semitic, we may accordingly note that Egypto-Semitic [ḫ] converges with [ḥ] in Semitic.

Semitic [ṭ], [y], [k], [l], [m], [n], [s] and [ʕ] come into Ugaritic unchanged and are written with the letters *ṭ*, *y*, *k*, *l*, *m*, *n*, *s*, and *ʿ*.

Semitic [ġ] is preserved in Ugaritic and is represented by the letter *ġ*. However, there are several words in which Arabic [ẓ] corresponds to *ġ* in Ugaritic. Ordinarily, Arabic *ẓ* corresponds to *ẓ* in Ugaritic. It has been tentatively suggested that the correspondence of Ugaritic *ġ* with Arabic *ẓ* may reflect a hitherto unknown Semitic phoneme.

Semitic [p] comes into Ugaritic unchanged and is indicated by the letter *p*. But occassionally, as noted above, *p* and *b* are interchanged in variant spellings of the same word.

When we find [s] in all the other Semitic languages, it is also written with the letter *s* in Ugaritic. Usually Semitic [ḍ] falls together with [ṣ] and appears as the letter *ṣ* in Ugaritic However, in text 75, Semitic [ḍ] appears as the letter *ẓ*. Dialectically, classical Arabic *ḍ* is pronounced *ẓ*; e.g., in Iraq.

In text 77, Semitic [t] appears as the letter *ẓ*.

Usually Ugaritic *q* corresponds to Semitic [q]. However, Ugaritic *q* interchanges with Ugaritic *g* in the variants *ṯqt* (Krt:223) 'bellowing' // *ṯgt*

(Krt:120) (Heb. שָׁאֲגָה 'roar'). (In Bedouin and in Iraqi Arabic, [q] is commonly pronounced [g].)

Semitic [r] remains *r* in Ugaritic but final [-r] may be dropped. The name of the god Kōṯar appears as *kṯ in* ('nt:VI:18) and the jussive *yaṯbur* is written *yṯb* (1 Aqht:108, 123) 'may he break', as shown in duplicate passages (*yṯbr* in lines 137, 149).

Both [š] and [ś] fall together as *š* in Ugaritic. The same thing happens in unpointed Heb. and yet שׁ [š] and שׂ [ś] have been sharply distinguished since Masoretic times down to the present. The causative prefix (*š-*) of the Shaf'el conjugation shifts (by assimilation) to [t] in roots where the first consonant is [t].

Semitic [ṭ] regularly comes into Ugaritic as *ṭ*.

The vowels inherent in the three alefs do not indicate that any of the three main Semitic vowels [a, i, u], long or short, have been altered or dropped in Ugaritic in any position, except for (1) the conditioned shift of [aʔ] to [eʔ] at the end of a syllable, and (2) vowel harmony.

The shift of [aʔ-] to [eʔ-] is illustrated by words like *[raʔš-] 'head' (Arabic [raʔs-]), which developed from *[raʔš-] into *[rā(ʔ)š-] and finally with the Canaanite shift of accented long *ā* to *ō* into Hebrew [rō(ʔ)š-]. But in Ugaritic it is [reʔš-] (written *riš*); cf. Akkadian and Aramaic [rēš-] 'head'. Similarly, Semitic *[daʔn-] 'small cattle' = 'sheep and goats' appears as [ṣēn-] in Ugaritic (but as [ṣō(ʔ)n] in Hebrew). Note that this shift cuts across East and West Semitic. It appears selectively in Hebrew, starting with the first word in the Old Testament: *(bĕ)-rē(')šīt* < *[raʔšīt].

The Canaanite shift of long *ā* to *ō* does not take place in Ugaritic. Thus the feminine plural suffix [-āt] does not shift to [-ōt]; *ksat* 'thrones' (vs. Hebrew כסאות). Similarly, *šmal* [šimʔāl-] 'left' (vs. Hebrew שְׂמֹאול). The preservation of the *ā* cannot be attributed solely to the early date for Ugaritic, for the shift to *ō* is already attested in Canaanite words spelled syllabically in the Amarna tablets.

Vowel harmony is apparent in Ugaritic words such as *'ullūp* 'prince, chief' (Hebrew אַלּוּף), *udm* 'Edom' (Hebrew אֱדֹם), *urbt* 'window' (Hebrew אֲרֻבָּה), etc. For a suggested formulation of the conditions under which vowel harmony takes place in Ugaritic, see UT § 5.19.

The final *-m* of mimation is dropped except in a few adverbial accusatives such as *gm* 'aloud (lit. 'with voice')' and *bkm* 'weepingly, tearfully'.

Initial *[w-] shifts to [y-] in Ugaritic, as in Northwest Semitic (Canaanite and Aramaic). The פ"י verbs provide many examples; e.g., *ybl* 'to bring', *ydd* 'to love', *yld* 'to bear (a child)', *yṣ* 'to go out', *yrd* 'to go down', *yṯb* 'to sit'.

Note also *yrḫ* (9:11) [yarḫ-] 'month' (Hebrew יֶרַח) and *yrḫ* (77:4) '(the moon-god) Yariḫ-' = Hebrew יָרֵחַ 'moon' (vs. Akkadian [warḫ-] 'month').

The assimilation of [n] to a directly following consonant is normal in Ugaritic. Thus *at* for masculine [ʔatta < *ʔanta] or feminine [ʔatti < *ʔanti] 'thou', *mṣb* [maṣṣab- < *manṣab-] 'stand or beam (of scales)', *gt* [*gint-] 'wine or oil press' like *bt* [*bint-] 'daughter'. This assimilation does not take place with third radical [n] in verbal forms like *ytnt, mgntm*. Cf. all Hebrew final-*n* verbs, except *ntn* in which the final radical is (unlike the [n] in Ugaritic *ytn*) assimilated; thus Hebrew נָתַתָּ [natatta] 'thou hast given'. Note that the [-n] of the preposition *min* 'from' (which is exceedingly rare in Ugaritic) is assimilated to the following alef in *mab* (1015:11) = מֵאָב 'from father'.

The [l-] of *lqḥ* 'to take' is assimilated to the directly following [q], as in *iqḥ* 'I shall take' (like Hebrew אֶקַּח).

In reduplicated biconsonantals, a final radical [n] may or may not be assimilated. Note *knkn* beside *kkn(t)*.

As in Hebrew, so too in Ugaritic, [-nh-] may or may not be assimilated to [-nn-]. Thus 'I shall bury him' appears interchangeably as *aqbrn* (1 Aqht:126) or *aqbrnh* (1 Aqht:111) in otherwise identical contexts. Cf. the accusative suffix in Hebrew 'he will guard him' with assimilation (יִשְׁמְרֶנּוּ) or without it (יִשְׁמְרֶנְהוּ).

The diphthongs [ay] (certainly) and [aw] (probably) are at least sometimes reduced to [a] instead of to [ē] and [ō], respectively. The presence of the reduction of [ay] to [a] in Ugaritic was demonstrated in an unusual and unexpected way. A Minoan wine jar from Knossos was labeled by the Linear A syllables *ya-na*, which I identified as meaning 'wine' even though in Northwest Semitic the word was then expected to appear as [yayn-] or [yēn-]. Subsequently, the name of a village in the Ugaritic realm was brought into the discussion. The village is spelled *yn* in the Ugaritic alphabet, but in Akkadian texts from Ugarit it is written ^{āl}*ya-na* or ^{āl}GEŠTIN^{na}. The latter spellings show that the name *Ya-na* means GEŠTIN 'wine' in Ugaritic. Accordingly, the diphthong [ay] has been reduced, not to [ē], but to [a]. This has many broad ramifications. To cite only one: in Hebrew inscriptions such as the Samaria ostraca the word for 'wine' is written *yn*, which, for all we know, is to be normalized [yan] rather than [yēn]. Hitherto, all Semitists regarded [yēn] as the only possibility (see Rendsburg 1990).

The voiced dental stop [d] is assimilated to the corresponding emphatic [ṭ] in the personal name *Ṣdqšlm* (under the influence of the emphatics [ṣ] and [q]) by the scribe of text 1005:4, 10, 14, who spells the name *Ṣṭqšlm*.

Ugaritic Phonology

The second [ʕ] in the personal name *ʕbdʕnt ('Servant of the goddess 'Anat') is dissimilated to zero in the atypical tablet 1045:4, 8, where the name is written ʕbdnt [ʕabdanat] < *[ʕabd-ʕanat].

The dissimilation of [m – m] to [l – m] takes place in lḥmd [laḥmad] (51:V:101) for mḥmd [maḥmad] (lines 78, 94) 'pleasantness, choiceness' = 'the best of …'.

The [t] of ttb '(the god) Teshub' is partially assimilated to the voiced [d] of the preceding [g] in the Hurrian personal name agdtb [ag(i)deṭub].

The scribe of the atypical text 1045 spells the names usually written tlmyn as ṭlmyn (with emphatic [ṭ] for unvoiced [t]) in 1045:7; and conversely spells the personal name yplṭn as ypltn in 1045:4.

Thrice in 1045, voiced [ġ] occurs for unvoiced [ḫ]; to wit, in the personal names ʕbdyrġ (:2), ġyrn (:3), and ṣġr (:13), which are elsewhere spelled ʕbdyrḫ, ḫyrn and ṣḫr. Note that [r] occurs in all three, and also that the letter [ḫ] does not appear anywhere in 1045.

The voiced [d] of the root ṣdq 'righteous' in the personal name ṣdqn is changed to voiceless [t], atypically, in ṣtqn (in 1153:2, 3; 1154:4, 6, 7). Moreover, the emphatic [q] is dissimilated to unvoiced [k] atypically in ṣdkn (1045:6) under the influence of the emphatic [ṣ].

The labials [b] (voiced stop) and [m] (bilabial nasal) occasionally interchange. Thus bbqr (Krt:113) = bmqr (Krt:216f.) 'in the well', where the [m] has been assimilated to the preceding [b]. Conversely, the [b] of ybmt in Anat's familar epithet ybmt . limm (. represents the word divider character) appears as ymmt . limm in 'nt:III:9. It is interesting to compare the personal name יְמִימָה, Job's second daughter, in English *Jemimah*.

As in Hebrew אַחַת, the feminine of the numeral '1' also in Ugaritic is aḥt (i.e., masc. aḥd + fem. -t) [ʔaḥ(ḥ)att- < *ʔaḥ(ḥ)adt-] with [-dt-] assimilated to [-tt-]. The same assimilation takes place in the conjugation of verbs where the third radical [d] is followed by a suffix beginning with [t]; e.g., ylt [yalattā] 'they (3rd fem. dual) have borne' from yld.

The loss of the 1st common sing. preformative [ʔa-] before [ʕ] in sandhi: ʕdbk (3 Aqht:'obv':22) 'I shall set thee'; wank . ʕny (137:28) [wa-ʔanakuʕniyu] 'and I shall answer'. Note that this phenomenon is indicated in the Masoretic treatment of פ״ע verbs (where the א is historic—not phonetic: וָאעֱנֶה (1Kgs. 11:39), וָאעֱשֹׂר (Zech. 11:5).

Note [ṭṭ] for [ṭ] in ṭṭl 'dew' (1 Aqht:200); elsewhere it regularly is written ṭl. That this is not a scribal error is indicated by the name of Baal's daughter Ṭly, which is spelled Ṭṭly in 67:V:11.

Ḫkpt 'Aigyptos/Egypt' (originally the designation the Memphis area, now the Cairo area) is once written ḥqkpt ('nt:VI:13) reflecting a vacillation between representing the palatal stop as *k* or *q*. Note that the Old Testament word for 'helmet' (in modern Hebrew it means 'hat') is written either קוֹבַע or כּוֹבַע.

References

Dietrich, Manfred; Oswald Loretz; & J. Sanmartín. 1976. *Die keilalphabetischen Texte aus Ugarit einschließlich der keilalphabetischen Texte außerhalb Ugarit*, part 1. *Transkription*. Kevelaer: Butzon & Bercker; Neukirchen-Vluyn: Neukirchener Verlag (Alter Orient und Altes Testament 24).

Gordon, Cyrus H. 1967. *Ugaritic Textbook*. Rome: Pontifical Biblical Institute (Analecta Orientalia 38).

Herdner, Andrée. 1963. *Corpus des tablettes en cunéiformes alphabétiques découvertes à Ras Shamra–Ugarit de 1929 à 1939*. Paris: Imprimerie Nationale; Geuthner (Bibliothèque archéologique et historique 79, Mission de Ras Shamra 10).

Pardee, Dennis. 1988. *Les textes para-mythologiques de la 24e campagne (1961)*. Paris: Éditions Recherche sur les Civilisations (Mémoires 77, Ras Shamra–Ougarit 4).

Rendsburg, Gary. 1990. "Monophthongization of *aw/ay* > *ā* in Eblaite and in Northwest Semitic." *Eblaitica* 2: 91–126.

Chapter 4
Phoenician and Punic Phonology
Stanislav Segert
University of California, Los Angeles

4.1. Terms and problems

The term "phonology" can be applied to Phoenician and Punic materials in its most narrow sense: dealing with reconstructed phonemes and their relationships.

Phonological evidence for Phoenician is preserved only in written records from antiquity, in various scripts. Data and also analogies from other languages have to be used for reconstruction and characterization of Phoenician and Punic phonemes. These attempts to introduce necessary phonetic criteria are in many respects uncertain, due to both the variety and inconsistency of the written sources, to dialectal differences and developments not clearly attested, and to an assorted range of problems having to do with the cognate languages.

It is possible to establish a fairly uniform phonological system for Phoenician used in its older period, during the first half of the first millennium B.C., at the eastern shore of the Mediterranean Sea. But the later extension of colonies toward the west, and then the influence of other languages, some of them non-Semitic, led to various changes. Some of them are difficult to trace, due to uncertainties and inconsistencies in various graphemic systems used for recording later Phoenician and Punic words.

Phoenicians are credited with the invention of the alphabetic script, in which phonemes are consistently indicated by appropriate graphemes. As this system was limited to indicating only consonants in the Phoenician period, it is necessary to search for the data about vowels in records in other scripts and in analogical phenomena in cognate Semitic languages. In Punic gradually some vowels became indicated by consonant letters, but this incomplete evidence has to be supplied by information from sources in other scripts.

AUTHOR'S NOTE: Abbreviations: DN, divine name; NL, place name; PN, personal name.

While for source materials presented below, an exact rendering from the preserved documents is presented, many reconstructions should be provided with a question mark due to circumstances mentioned above.

4.2. Sources

The number of Phoenician texts accessible now is about ten thousand, but most of them repeat one votive formula, with various personal names. As the number of connected texts is very limited, a large amount of data is contained in personal names, of which more than one thousand are preserved.

These texts are written in the Phoenician alphabet, which contains 22 letters for consonants. In Punic, especially in later texts, inconsistencies in expressing consonantal phonemes may be observed.

In later Punic inscriptions some consonant graphemes were used for the indicating of several vowels. A system was developed on this basis.

Another system imitated the model of Roman vowel letters, which was itself based on Phoenician letters, accepted via Greek and Etruscan intermediation. E.g. ʾ = a: tḥt /taht/; h = e: bhrm /bērīm/.

Punic conversation is recorded in Roman letters in the comedy *Poenulus* by Plautus. Both consonants and vowels are rendered in these samples.

As Phoenician was used in many countries over a period of many centuries, various dialects developed.

In the Eastern Mediterranean, the Old Byblian dialect is attested in inscriptions from about 1000 B.C. More inscriptions are preserved from the later periods of the first millennium B.C.; most of them were found in the Phoenician cities on the eastern Mediterranean shore, some farther to the North, in Syria and Cilicia.

Specific dialectal features can be observed in the texts from the Phoenician colonies on Cyprus.

Phoenician texts from the western Mediterranean written during the first half of the first millennium B.C. follow their eastern models.

Some changes appear in the texts from Carthage and other colonies in the second half of the first millennium B.C.; their dialect is called Punic.

Texts written after the destruction of Carthage in 146 B.C. are called Late Punic. They were exposed to the influence of Latin and Berber languages.

In Egyptian texts some Phoenician words, mostly names, are attested; their rendering in the Egyptian mostly consonantal script does not always exactly express the Phoenician consonants; cf. e.g. *k-p-n* for /g-b-l/ 'Byblos'.

Babylonian and Assyrian texts in syllabic cuneiform do not render all the consonants exactly enough, but are valuable for expressing all vowels of Phoenician words, especially names.

Similarly the Cypriot syllabic script indicates Phoenician vowels within the Greek context.

Consonantal writing of Phoenician names in the Hebrew Bible corresponds to Phoenician practice, but the indication of vowels can reflect later traditions.

Phoenician names and words are contained in ancient Greek inscriptions from various areas and also in works by ancient Greek authors.

Many Punic names are preserved in Latin inscriptions from North Africa. Punic names and words appear in books by Roman authors.

This variety of sources, different in script type and manner of preservation, is reflected in the system of transliteration and transcription used here. As a matter of principle, only words from Latin sources are rendered by usual Roman letters, while all other scripts are rendered by italics. In transcriptions from syllabic scripts, cuneiform and Cypriot, syllables are separated by hyphens. Words from ancient Greek and Roman inscriptions are given in capital letters, those quoted from literary works transmitted by copying in lower case letters. Reconstructed words are given in Roman letters within slant brackets.

> Phoenician: italics, with further indication of the dialect: O(ld) By(blian); Ph(oenician) in Western Asia; Cy(prus dialect); Pu(nic), in North Africa; L(ate) Pu(nic), after 146 B.C. E.g. *ḥrm* OBy; *ṣpnbʻl* Pu.
> Hebrew: *ḥīrām* and *ḥyrwm* (H) /ḥīrōm/
> Egyptian: *k-p-n-* (Eg), for Ph /gubl-/ NL 'Byblos'
> Babylonian and Assyrian: *ḫi-ru-um-mu* (cuneiform syllabary) for /ḥīrōm/
> Cypriote syllabary: *mi-li-ki-ya-no-to-se* (Cy syll.), for /milki-/
> Greek epigraphic: *ThENNEITh* (Gr), DN 'Tanit'
> Greek text: *amilchar*
> Latin epigraphic: ANNIBAL
> Latin text: hannibal
> Reconstructed forms: /ḥīrōm/
> Hypothetic forms: *ʼaḥat-milk

4.3. Kinds of phonological data

While all direct evidence about Phoenician phonological phenomena is contained in texts written in antiquity, for phonological reconstructions phonetic observations of languages preserved from antiquity by oral tradition, such as Hebrew, or even modern languages, such as Arabic, are necessary.

Knowledge of ancient phonological features is limited to the signs and graphical devices used in the ancient scripts.

The evidence about consonants is adequately provided by the Phoenician alphabet of 22 consonant graphemes. In the cuneiform syllabary some consonants are not clearly distinguished. Not all Phoenician or Punic consonantal phonemes can be directly rendered in the Greek and Roman alphabets.

No vowels are indicated in Phoenician inscriptions. The indication of vowels in Punic texts by consonant letters is not always complete and often inconsistent. Special vocalic signs in the Phoenician names quoted in the Hebrew Bible reflect a later tradition of pronunciation. Vocalic elements of cuneiform syllabic signs indicate Phoenician vowels, but not always exactly. There is no specific manner to distinguish /o/; it is indicated by the same sign element as /u/. The Greek alphabet accurately expresses Phoenician vowels. In the Latin alphabet the basic vocalic values are indicated.

For the quantity of vowels there are no specific signs in the Phoenician alphabet. In some Punic texts some long vowels are marked by phonologically related consonant signs. Reduced vowels are not indicated as such in the Phoenician script. Long /ē/ and /ō/ can be clearly indicated in the Greek alphabet, while the reduced vowels may be suggested by *y*. The length of vowels is sometimes indicated by repetition of vocalic elements in the syllabic cuneiform.

While doubling of consonants is not indicated in Phoenician script, it is marked by the repetition of Greek and Roman letters and sometimes of consonantal elements in syllabic cuneiform.

In no ancient script used for recording Phoenician words are graphical signs for word stress attested. Accent marks in some Greek manuscripts were added later.

The use of analogy cannot be avoided, due to the incomplete attestation of Phoenician in the ancient written texts.

The close relationship of Phoenician to another Canaanite language, Hebrew, makes it possible to use the phonetic tradition transmitted in the reading of the Hebrew Bible. For consonants this comparison is reliable; for vowels it is necessary to take into consideration both the specific differences between Hebrew and Phoenician and the relatively late time for the fixation of the Hebrew vowel signs.

Another Canaanite language, Ugaritic, may be used for some reconstructions. This archaic language from the late Bronze age, before 1200 B.C., was written in an alphabetic cuneiform script in which some vowels were indicated.

Both literary Arabic and the contemporary Arabic dialects of Lebanon and Syria can be used as help for a better understanding of Phoenician phonology. The basic values of consonants in modern Semitic languages are based on phonetic recordings and observations of the Arabic pronunciations.

4.4. Consonantal phonemes: Inventory and systemic changes

The Phoenician consonant inventory (Table 4-1) can be reconstructed with help of Hebrew and Arabic. The partial disintegration of this system in Punic does not allow presentation of a corresponding table.

Table 4-1. Phoenician Consonants

				Linguals	Nasals	Semivowels
Laryngeals		ʾ	h			
Pharyngeals		ʿ	ḥ			
Velars	q	g	k			
Palatals			š			y
Sibilants	ṣ	z	s	l		
Dentals	ṭ	d	t	r	n	
Labials		b	p		m	w
	Emphatic	Voiced	Unvoiced			

It is possible that Phoenician in its oldest period, at the beginning of the Iron age about 1200 B.C., had more consonant phonemes (as had Ugaritic), but inscriptions on arrowheads do not provide sufficient evidence to prove this.

The weakening and elision of some consonants and the apparent confusion of some consonant signs were influenced and accelerated by the close contact of Punic in North Africa with non-Semitic languages, viz., Berber and Latin.

The laryngeal /'/, from phonetic viewpoint glottal stop, was no longer used in writing to indicate a specific phoneme; e.g. *mlkt*—instead of original *ml'kt*—'work'.

Weakening of the pharyngeal /ʿ/ can be observed: *šmʿ* 'he heard', then *šm*ʾ, SAMŌ.

Laryngeal /h/ and pharyngeal /ḥ/ seem to have persisted relatively longer. They could be indicated by the Latin letter *h*. For /h/ cf. *mhrbl*, maharbal (PN), but a-elichot 'the hospitality', *ha-he-; for /ḥ/ cf. *ḥnbʿl*, hannibal, but also ANNIBAL; use of letter for weakened voiced pharyngeal ʿ: *ʿym* for older *ḥym* 'life'. (Names are transliterated from Greek and Latin without capital letters at the beginning, in accordance with the ancient writing practice.)

Oppositions between voiced and unvoiced and between emphatic and non-emphatic consonants were disregarded, especially in Punic, more frequently in its later stages. This confusion affected mostly sibilants. E.g. *mls* instead of *mlṣ* 'interpret'; demonstrative pronouns *s*, *st*, sith 'this' instead of *z-*; *mšl* instead of *mzl* 'fate'.

4.5. Vocalic phonemes: Inventory and systemic changes

Unlike for consonants, the evidence for Phoenician vowels is scanty. Data from words, mostly in not always adequate non-Phoenician writing systems, have to be supplemented by often hypothetic information from the corresponding features in related Semitic languages.

An attempt to reconstruct the Phoenician vocalic system is in Table 4-2.

Table 4-2. Phoenician Vocalic System

Short vowels	i	a	u
Long vowels	ī	ō	ū
Long vowels		ē (<*ai)	ō (<*au)

This system corresponds with that of the archaic Canaanite language, Ugaritic, and with that of the conservative Classical Arabic.

The monophthongization of diphthongs occurred early, as no *y* or *w* letters used in related languages for the indication of diphthongs are attested. Cf. *bt* /bēt/ 'house', Greek name of letter *bēta* (but *baitylon* in Sanchuniaton); *mōt* 'death'.

The Canaanite vowel shift of *$ā$ > /ō/ can be explained as conditioned by phonetic behavior: if the mouth is not sufficiently opened, pure long $ā$ cannot be produced, the sound tends toward $ō$. Cf. PN /ḥīrōm/, ḥi-ru-um-ma, ḥyrwm and ḥīrōm (Hebrew), eirōmos; /-yatōn/ 'he gave' in PNN mi-li-ki-ya-to-no-se (Cypriot), BALIATON; /-malōk/ 'he reigned' in PN ba-al-ma-lu-ka; NADŌR 'he vowed'; /-milkōt/ 'queen' in PN ab-di-mil-ku-ut-ti.

It seems that this Canaanite change *$ā$ > $ō$ affected not only the originally long $ā$-vowels, but also vowels lengthened secondarily through word stress: *milkát > *milkāt > /milkōt/; perfects like *yatán > *yatān > /yatōn/; *'adám > *'adām > ADOM 'man'.

The change in this direction continued in Phoenician (unlike in Hebrew) all the way toward /ū/. It affected both ō-vowels originated by monophthongization from *au; e.g. *qaul > *qōl > /qūl/, KOULŌ 'his voice'—and those which resulted from original *$ā$: ADOUN 'lord' (cf. Hebrew 'ādōn < *-ān), salus /šalūš/ 'three', SANUTH /šanūt/ 'years'.

The vowel /e/ in other than Phoenician script can be considered an allophone of /i/; cf. ers and chirs 'shard'. This may be valid also for some instances of /ē/: abdēlimos PN 'Servant of gods'. ("Servant" with capital S, since in English proper names are written so.) Similarly /o/ is related as allophone to /u/; cf. MOTTHUN and MUTTHUN PN 'Gift'.

For vowels outside of the system the letter y could be used in Greek and subsequently in Latin texts: for *ü: cf. chyl and chil 'all', probably /kül/; for reduced vowel: ys, ys, sy 'which', by-marob /b^e-/ 'by protection'.

4.6. Conditioned consonant changes

These changes were caused either by position of the consonant within the word or the syllable or by contact with other phonemes, consonantal or vocalic.

In later Punic, consonants articulated in the dental area, /d/, /t/, /l/, could be eliminated from the end of a word or a syllable. Cf. ḥmlkt ~ HIMILCO PN 'Son of the queen', mlk 'mr, MOLCHOMOR ~ MOCHOMOR 'offering of lamb'.

The consonant /y/ at the beginning of a word or its element could be submitted to elision: yqdš ~ 'yqdš 'he consecrated', mlkytn ~ mlktn, MILCATON PN 'Milk gave'.

The semivowel /y/ was elided between vowels; cf. bny /banaya/ in Old Byblian and Phoenician bn /banā/ 'he built'; ybrky'/-kiya/ and Punic ybrk'/-kā/ 'may they bless her'.

New consonants can be inserted to avoid hiatus between vowels; cf. the later form of the suffixed pronoun of the 3rd person pl. masc. -*nm* /-nom/ against older -*m* /-om/, e.g. *ḥbrnm* /-ēnom/ 'their colleagues' (against BUNOM 'their son'). An additional consonant /m/ appears in late Punic: *bnm*, BINIM 'his son'.

Regressive assimilation of /n/ is amply attested in Phoenician; e.g. *št* /šatt-/ < *šant- 'year', *kt* /kattī/ 'I was' from the verb /k-w-n/. In later Punic, however, forms with non-assimilated /n/ reappear, e.g. *mnṣbt* beside *mṣbt* 'stela'.

Some unusual forms can be explained by dissimilative tendencies. Cf. *n'spt*, against *m'spt* 'assembly', by the dissimilation of labials at a distance.

The consonant /h/ can be assimilated to a preceding or following /i/ into /y/. Cf. Old Byblian '*bh* /-ihu/ and Cypriot '*by* /-iyu/ 'his father'.

4.7. Conditioned vocalic changes

Since most of the evidence for vowels and their changes is based on records in scripts which did not render them consistently, the presentation is hypothetical.

Changes caused by word stress are discussed below. Short *á was lengthened by the impact of stress into **ā́* which was changed into /ṓ/, through a systemic change, the Canaanite vowel shift.

Even as there are no specific signs for reduced vowels in the Phoenician script, they can be traced if they are rendered by the Greek and subsequently Roman letter y or if there is uncertainty in their rendering. For examples see § 4.5, also *bynuthi* 'my daughters'. Variety of forms in Greek letters of the plural in construct state 'face(s) (of)', *PhANE* and *PhENĒ* can point to a reduced vowel in the first syllable. The quality of the original vowel before its reduction cannot always be traced with certainty.

Vowels in the initial syllable were often omitted after the glottal stop /'/ preceding them was no longer respected. Cf. *ḥrm* < '*ḥrm* /'aḥī-/ PN 'My brother ...', *bb'l* and '*bb'l* PN 'My father ...', *donni* 'my lord' ~ '*dn*; in particles: *t*, *Th* (originally '*t*) nota accusativi introducing object, perhaps *p* (cf. '*p*) 'also'.

4.7.1. The development of secondary vowels

Prothetic vowels indicated in writing by ' ('aleph): '*ršp* /aršap/, cf. *ršp* DN; Cypriot '*z* (cf. *z*) 'this', YMU '(what) > which'; before a preposition: '*bbt* /'ab-bēt/ 'in house'.

Anaptyctic vowels: in segolate nouns: *qbʾr* /qabar/ (cf. *qbr* /qabr/) 'grave', *ʾsʾr* 'ten', *syris* (cf. *šrš*) 'root'.

Assimilation to vowels: u-ulech < *(h)a-(h)ū-* 'the visitor'; perhaps *ui* < *ʾuḥuya* 'my brother'.

Assimilation to consonants: to labials, in direction to /u/: *moutinas*, MUT-TUN, *muttines* (cf. *mattēn*, MITUN, *ma-ta-an-*) PN 'Gift'; perhaps *BYN*, *byn* /bün/ 'son' (cf. Ugaritic *bun-*).

4.8. Other phonological features

Only one suprasegmental feature can be observed, word stress, but only by indirect suppositions. Syllabic structures have to be mentioned in a survey of phonology.

No graphic signs or direct information about word stress is available. But by observation of the change *$á$ > *$\bar{á}$ > /ō/ the position of word stress can be determined on the last syllable in most instances.

Open syllables appear both with short (CV) and long vowels (CV̄). Closed syllables had probably only short vowels in the center (CVC). Also closed syllables with the cluster of two consonants on the end can be observed (CVCC): OTMILC <*ʾaḥāt-milk* PN fem. 'Sister of the king'; *qrtḥdšt* /qart-ḥadašt/ NL 'New City', cf. derived adjectives *carthadati* and *KARKhA-DONION*, cf. Latin CARTHAGO and Greek *karchēdōn* from shortened form *karthadō*.

For the dropping of syllables in the middle of a word, cf. BONCAR and BODMILKAR, *bdmlqrt* PN 'In hand of Melqart'.

Selective Bibliography

Benz, Frank L. 1972. *Personal Names in the Phoenician and Punic Inscriptions*. Rome: Biblical Institute Press.

Dothan, Aron 1976. "Stress Position and Vowel Shift in Phoenician and Punic." *Israel Oriental Studies* 6: 71–121.

Friedrich, Johannes, and Wolfgang Röllig. 1970. *Phönizisch-punische Grammatik*, 2nd ed. Rome: Pontificium Institutum Biblicum.

Fuentes Estañol, María José. 1980. *Vocabulario Fenicio*. Barcelona: Biblioteca Fenica.

Harris, Zellig S. 1936. *A Grammar of the Phoenician Language*. New Haven: American Oriental Society.

Jean, Charles-F., and Jacob Hoftijzer. 1965. *Dictionnaire des inscriptions sémitiques de l'Ouest*. Leiden: Brill.

Moscati, Sabatino, ed. 1988. *The Phoenicians*. New York: Abbeville.

Segert, Stanislav. 1955. "Zum Übergang $\bar{a} > \bar{o}$ in den kanaanäischen Dialekten." *Archiv Orientální* 23: 478.

———. 1976. *A Grammar of Phoenician and Punic*. Munich: Beck.

———. forthcoming. "113b, Semitic: Phoenician and Punic." In *Namengebung – Proper Names*. Berlin: de Gruyter.

———. forthcoming. "Phoenician and Eastern Canaanite Languages." In *The Semitic Languages*, ed. Robert Hetzron. London: Routledge.

Veenhof, K. R. 1973. "Phoenician-Punic." In *A Basic Bibliography for the Study of the Semitic Languages*, ed. J. H. Hospers, vol. 1, pp. 146–71. Leiden: Brill.

Chapter 5
Ancient Hebrew Phonology
Gary A. Rendsburg
Cornell University

5.1. Hebrew and the Semitic languages

Hebrew is a Semitic language, attested since ca. 1100 B.C.E. as the language of the Israelites (the Bible also uses the ethnonym Hebrews, and later the term Jews becomes more common). Ancient Hebrew died out as a spoken language in the third century C.E., though it was retained in an unbroken chain for liturgical and literary purposes unto the modern era. In the late 19th and early 20th centuries, Hebrew was revived as a spoken language. It is used today as the national language of Israel. Not surprisingly, during its history of more than three millennia, the language has undergone various changes, especially in the realm of phonology. This chapter is devoted to ancient Hebrew, defined here as the period of ca. 1100 B.C.E. to ca. 250 C.E., with a particular emphasis on historical matters. Occasionally, later developments in the medieval period also will be noted. For the phonology of Modern Hebrew, see Chapter 17.

Semitists continue to debate the classification of the individual Semitic languages, but all agree that Hebrew falls within the Northwest Semitic group. The languages of this group are Amorite, Ugaritic, Canaanite, and Aramaic. According to many scholars (myself included), Ugaritic is to be subsumed under Canaanite, but the former is attested in the second millennium B.C.E. and the latter almost exclusively in the first millennium B.C.E., so for the nonce I distinguish them. An additional Northwest Semitic language may be Eblaite, though a majority of scholars holds that it is more closely linked to Akkadian (East Semitic).

In essence Hebrew is but a dialect of Canaanite. The other dialects of this language are Phoenician, Ammonite, Moabite, Edomite, and Deir 'Alla (referring to the epigraphic remains found at Tell Deir 'Alla a few miles east of

---

AUTHOR'S NOTE: I am grateful to Alan Kaye and Saul Levin for their comments on an earlier version of this essay. We do not agree on all the points raised, and I alone am responsible for the views expressed. I also extend thanks to my graduate students Scott Noegel and Richard Wright for their critical reading.

the Jordan River, though other opinions hold that Deir 'Alla is a dialect of Aramaic or an independent branch of Northwest Semitic altogether). These dialects of Canaanite, attested mainly in the first millennium b.c.e., were all mutually intelligible, and probably were differentiated no more than, say, the geographical varieties of Modern German or Modern English.

Phoenician, Ammonite, Moabite, Edomite, and Deir 'Alla are known primarily through inscriptions found in archaeological excavations in the Levant (Phoenician is an exception in two regards: [a] epigraphic remains have been found throughout the Mediterranean region, and [b] occasional classical writers, especially Plautus, preserve material). The total amount of known material would fill only a slender volume. The corpus of ancient Hebrew, by contrast, is quite large. The sources are the Hebrew Bible (Old Testament), the book of Ben Sira (one of the Apocrypha), the Dead Sea Scrolls found at Qumran, the Mishnah and other works authored by the rabbis of late antiquity, and various inscriptions (some of considerable length, but hundreds are very short, often consisting of only personal names).

Much of the following discussion concerning Hebrew phonology also may hold for the other Canaanite dialects, but our knowledge of these dialects is limited. On the other hand, we know that some of the other varieties of Canaanite were differentiated specifically in the realm of phonology (see the above comparison with German and English dialects, and see below for an occasional point of contrast).

5.2. Variation within Ancient Hebrew

Until now I have spoken of Hebrew as if it were a unified dialect within Canaanite, but this is an oversimplification. In fact, ancient Hebrew may be distinguished in various ways.

A) Based on differences visible in the Bible, diachronically we can distinguish Archaic Biblical Hebrew (ca. 1100–1000 b.c.e.), Standard Biblical Hebrew (ca. 1000–550 b.c.e.), and Late Biblical Hebrew (ca. 550–200 b.c.e.). The Hebrew of the Dead Sea Scrolls, known also as Qumran Hebrew (after Qumran, the site of discovery of these documents), is a continuation of Late Biblical Hebrew, and is attested ca. 200 b.c.e. – ca. 70 c.e.

B) Ancient Hebrew had various regional varieties. This finding also is based on various differences visible in the Hebrew Bible, and is confirmed in some instances by the epigraphic remains. Here we may distinguish Judahite

Hebrew, i.e., the regional dialect used specifically in Judah and its capital of Jerusalem, versus Israelian Hebrew, i.e., the dialect bundle of all other areas of traditional Israelite territory (areas such as Samaria, Galilee, and Transjordan). The vast majority, about 80%, of the Bible is written in Judahite Hebrew, and the remaining sections are written in Israelian Hebrew. I refer to Israelian Hebrew as a dialect bundle, because almost certainly there were minor differences between, for example, Transjordanian Israelian Hebrew and Galilean or Samarian Israelian Hebrew. The Transjordanian variety no doubt shared many features with Ammonite, Moabite, and Deir 'Alla; while the Galilean variety no doubt shared many features with Phoenician (and with Aramaic too). However, the available data generally do not allow us to isolate such minor differences, and for the most part it suffices to speak of Israelian Hebrew as a unified group of local varieties which, as a whole, contrasts with Judahite Hebrew.

C) Ancient Hebrew also was characterized by diglossia. The Bible, Ben Sira, and the Dead Sea Scrolls are written in the literary standard. But everyday speech differed considerably, as can be determined by occasional departures from the classical norm in these texts, especially when these phenomena parallel colloquial developments known from other spoken varieties of Semitic (e.g., colloquial Arabic). In late antiquity, the colloquial dialect was utilized to record texts such as the Mishnah and related works, so that the term Mishnaic Hebrew is used. The data at our disposal which allow us to posit diglossia in ancient Hebrew are mainly in the realm of morphology. Differences in phonology are more difficult to demonstrate.

In presenting the phonology of ancient Hebrew, in the main we refer to Standard Judahite literary Hebrew, i.e., the literary variety utilized in Judah ca. 1000–586 B.C.E. But where the data permit us to witness distinct usages in other varieties of ancient Hebrew, these will be noted.

5.3. Orthography

The Israelites utilized the 22-letter alphabet typically called the Canaanite alphabet (invented by the Phoenicians, according to the standard view). This alphabet represents only consonants, not vowels. Moreover, ancient Hebrew possessed more than 22 consonantal phonemes, so that some of the graphemes (letters) served double duty.

In the earliest Hebrew orthography, vowels were not indicated at all. According to the standard theory, in time, scribal practice led to the adoption of three letters, <h>, <w>, and <y>, to indicate final vowels. Eventually, this system was expanded to indicate medial vowels as well, though this practice was not carried out consistently. When <h>, <w>, and <y> are utilized in this fashion, they are called *matres lectionis* or vowel letters (see further § 5.6.4, where another, non-standard view of the vowel letters is presented also).

These problems of both consonants and vowels, but especially the vowels, created a certain ambiguity in the reading of ancient Hebrew. The extent to which such ambiguities caused readers problems cannot be determined, but probably in general usage no undue hardship arose. However, because the biblical books achieved a level of sanctity in Judaism, no amount of ambiguity could be tolerated in the reading of sacred literature. An official reading tradition existed, in which the reader of the Bible (for example, in the synagogue for liturgical purposes) read the text in its traditional manner.

In time, a system of vowel markings and other diacritic marks was developed to record the official reading tradition. The people responsible for this notation system are called the Masoretes (tradents) who were active ca. 850 C.E. My reconstruction of the history here is actually a bit too simplistic; in reality there was more than one official reading tradition (the Jews of Israel had one main tradition, the Jews of Babylonia another, etc.), and the Masoretic activity actually led to different notation systems too. The normative Masoretic system in use among Jews for the past millennium has been the Tiberian one, named for the city of Tiberias (on the Sea of Galilee) where it developed. Our discussion of the phonology will be based on this system.

The question remains as to how accurately the reading tradition of the biblical text and the Masoretic transcription thereof reflects ancient Hebrew. That is to say, the Masoretic Text (that is, the traditional text of the Bible) dates to ca. 850 C.E. and reflects the manner in which Biblical Hebrew was pronounced at that time. But how traditional, i.e., how ancient, was the reading tradition of the readers for the centuries before ca. 850 C.E.? In other words, does the Masoretic Text reflect Hebrew as it was pronounced five hundred years earlier, one thousand years earlier, even fifteen hundred years earlier? In some cases, we can answer this question, but no definitive conclusion can be reached.

Nevertheless, we will base ourselves on the assumption that the readers of the first millennium C.E. were extremely conservative in their biblical reading tradition, and that the Masoretic Text more or less accurately reflects the pronunciation (or at least one pronunciation) of ancient Hebrew in the first millennium B.C.E., i.e., the time of the composition of the biblical books. I say "more or less" because, among other points, (a) in some instances we know that the Masoretes no longer recognized consonantal phonemes which were distinguished in ancient Hebrew but which merged only later on, and (b) the system of vowels according to the Masoretic notation has an exceedingly large number of allophones, some or many of which may have developed only after the ancient Hebrew period.

The picture presented in the above outline is further complicated by the fact that there exists an important non-Masoretic reading tradition. The Samaritans, who developed as an offshoot of Judaism ca. 400 B.C.E., also possess the first five books of the Hebrew Bible (the Torah or Pentateuch) as canonical. They have an independent reading tradition for their Scripture, but in this essay we refrain from entering into these differences.

5.4. Phonology of the consonants

At least 29 consonantal phonemes are traceable to Proto-Semitic (comparison with other families in the Afroasiatic phylum suggests the possibility of still other phonemes). The most ancient Hebrew attested retained 25 of these; one local variety of Israelian Hebrew retained one other phoneme; and the remaining three phonemes merged with other phonemes (though one cannot discount the possibility that any or all of these three may have been retained in some restricted geographical locale, lack of evidence notwithstanding). As noted above, the Hebrew (Phoenician) alphabet has only 22 signs, so the recovery of the additional three or four phonemes requires special comment (see below for the individual cases).

Below I list the consonantal phonemes of ancient Hebrew, grouped according to place and/or manner of articulation. Transliteration is based on the standard system utilized in Semitics. Where the IPA symbol differs, it is noted as well. I also note the letter of the alphabet used to render each phoneme.

5.4.1. Bilabial plosives
/p/ – פ.
/b/ – ב.

5.4.2. Interdentals
/t/ (IPA [θ]). In virtually all dialects of Hebrew, this phoneme shifted to /š/, indicated by שׁ. However, in the Hebrew of Transjordan (specifically Gilead),

as well as in the neighboring Canaanite dialect of Ammonite, this phoneme was retained. The evidence for this comes from the famous passage in Judges 12:6 known as the "shibboleth incident." The story relates how the Gileadites controlled the fords of the Jordan River. When retreating Ephraimites (from Cisjordan) sought to cross, the guards at the fords asked them to pronounce the word *ṯibbōlet* [ṯibbōlet], which in Hebrew means 'stream, torrent', a fitting password for the crossing of the Jordan River. Since most Israelites did not possess this sound in their phonetic inventory, the Ephraimites would say [sibbōlet], thus revealing the fact that they were not Gileadites. (Compare the manner in which various foreign speakers of English [Germans, for example] pronounce English /ṯ/ as [s], or the manner in which Persians and other non-Arab Muslims pronounce Arabic /ṯ/ as [s].) Since standard Hebrew (and the dialect of Canaanite for which the alphabet was invented) did not possess this phoneme, there was no special grapheme for representing this sound. In the passage just mentioned, Judges 12:6, the letter שׁ = <š> is used.

For the secondary development of /ṯ/ = [θ] as the fricativized form of /t/, see § 5.5.4.

On the two remaining interdentals of Proto-Semitic, see § 5.4.13.

5.4.3. Dental plosives
/t/ – ת.
/d/ – ד.
/ṭ/ – a voiceless emphatic dental plosive, indicated by ט. On the nature of the "emphatics," see § 5.4.14.

5.4.4. Nasals
/m/ – מ.
/n/ – נ.

5.4.5. Rolled
/r/ – either a rolled dental or a rolled uvular (its exact articulation is unknown), indicated by ר.

5.4.6. Sibilants
/s/ – ס.
/z/ – ז.

/ṣ/ – a voiceless emphatic sibilant (according to most opinions it is a fricative, others hold it to be an affricate), indicated by צ. On the nature of the "emphatics," see § 5.4.14.
/š/ (IPA [ʃ]) – ש. Since this letter represented more than one sound relatively late in the history of Hebrew, a diacritical mark was added by the Masoretes on the right side to produce the grapheme שׁ. See further § 5.5.1.

5.4.7. Laterals
/l/ – ל.
/ś/ (IPA [ɬ]) – ש. Since this letter represented more than one sound relatively late in the history of Hebrew, a diacritical mark was added by the Masoretes on the left side to produce the grapheme שׂ. See further § 5.5.1.
　On the one remaining lateral of Proto-Semitic, see § 5.4.13.

5.4.8. Velar plosives
/k/ – כ.
/g/ – ג.
/q/ – a voiceless emphatic velar plosive, indicated by ק. On the nature of the "emphatics," see § 5.4.14.

5.4.9. Velar fricatives
/ḫ/ (IPA [x]) – ח. This sign was also used to represent /ḥ/. We are able to postulate the existence of both phonemes in the ancient period on the basis of transcriptions of Hebrew words (mainly proper names) in the Septuagint (the ancient Greek translation of the Bible) of the Pentateuch (ca. 250 B.C.E.). When Proto-Semitic comparisons indicate that the consonant /ḫ/ is present in the Hebrew word, the Septuagint transcription uses χ (see § 5.4.10 for the practice of transcribing /ḥ/). For the eventual merger of /ḫ/ and /ḥ/, see § 5.5.2. For the secondary development of /k̠/ = [x] as the fricativized form of /k/, see § 5.5.4.
/ġ/ (IPA [ɣ]) – ע. This sign was also used to represent /ʕ/. We are able to postulate the existence of both phonemes in the ancient period on the basis of transcriptions of Hebrew words (mainly proper names) in the Septuagint of the Pentateuch (ca. 250 B.C.E.). When Proto-Semitic comparisons indicate that the consonant /ġ/ is present in the Hebrew word, the Septuagint transcription uses γ (see § 5.4.10 for the practice of transcribing /ʕ/). For the eventual merger of /ġ/ and /ʕ/, see § 5.5.2. For the secondary development of /ḡ/ = [ɣ] as the fricativized form of /g/, see § 5.5.4.

5.4.10. Pharyngeal fricatives

/ḥ/ (IPA [ħ]) – ח. This sign was also used to represent /ḫ/. We are able to postulate the existence of both phonemes in the ancient period on the basis of transcriptions of Hebrew words (mainly proper names) in the Septuagint of the Pentateuch (ca. 250 B.C.E.). When Proto-Semitic comparisons indicate that the consonant /ḫ/ is present in the Hebrew word, the Septuagint transcription shows no consonant (see § 5.4.9 for the practice of transcribing /ḫ/). For the eventual merger of /ḫ/ and /ḥ/, see § 5.5.2.

/ʿ/ (IPA [ʕ]) – ע. This sign was also used to represent /ġ/. We are able to postulate the existence of both phonemes in the ancient period on the basis of transcriptions of Hebrew words (mainly proper names) in the Septuagint of the Pentateuch (ca. 250 B.C.E.). When Proto-Semitic comparisons indicate that the consonant /ʿ/ is present in the Hebrew word, the Septuagint transcription shows no consonant (see § 5.4.9, for the practice of transcribing /ġ/). For the eventual merger of /ġ/ and /ʿ/, see § 5.5.2.

5.4.11. Laryngeals
/ʾ/ (IPA [ʔ]) – א.
/h/ – ה.

5.4.12. Glides (semivowels)
/w/ – ו.
/y/ (IPA [j]) – י.

5.4.13. The remaining Proto-Semitic phonemes

There are three remaining traceable Proto-Semitic phonemes: /ḏ/ (IPA [ð]), /ẓ/ or /ṯ̣/ (IPA [ð']), and /ḍ/ [IPA [ɫ']). There is no evidence for the preservation of these sounds in ancient Hebrew. Instead, in most regional dialects of ancient Hebrew, /ḏ/ shifted to /z/ (in some Israelian dialects it shifted to /d/); and both /ẓ/ and /ḍ/ shifted to /ṣ/ (in some Israelian dialects the former shifted to /ṯ/ and the latter shifted to /q/ or later to /ʿ/). At the same time, scholars recognize that any one, two, or three of these phonemes may have been preserved in some locales. But since the Hebrew alphabet does not have special signs to represent these sounds, it is difficult to ascertain if and where such phonemes may have been retained. Were it not for the story in Judges 12:6 (see § 5.4.2), we would not know that Gileadite Hebrew retained the voiceless interdental /ṯ/, so it is conceivable that elsewhere in ancient Hebrew /ḏ/, /ẓ/, and /ḍ/ existed.

Ancient Hebrew Phonology 73

5.4.14. *The nature of the emphatics*
The exact nature of the emphatic consonants /ṭ/, /ṣ/, and /q/ cannot be determined. The corresponding consonants in Arabic are velarized/ pharyngealized; in Ethiopic and Modern South Arabian they are glottalized. Most likely the glottalization is the original Proto-Semitic manner of articulation, so that this can be postulated for ancient Hebrew.

5.5. Historical changes in the consonantal phonology
The consonantal phonology described above is correct for Hebrew in its most anciently attested phase. But already in the biblical period there is evidence for various changes, and in the post-biblical period still more changes are evident. These historical developments will be presented here.

5.5.1. *The shift of /ś/ to /s/*
In the course of time the voiceless lateral fricative /ś/ shifted to a sibilant and merged with /s/. This is indicated by the numerous interchanges between שׁ and ס in the spelling of ancient Hebrew. This tendency is less acute in the pre-exilic (pre–586 B.C.E.) books of the Bible, but becomes quite common in the exilic and post-exilic (post–586 B.C.E.) books. Thus, we may conclude that the merger of /ś/ and /s/ occurred in Late Biblical Hebrew and continued in still later phases of the language. This shift may be the result of Aramaic influence.

In the centuries after the merger occurred, copyists of the Bible remained faithful to the received text. Accordingly, even though /ś/ now was pronounced the same as /s/, in the great majority of cases the biblical manuscripts continued to represent this sound with שׁ. When the Masoretes devised their system of marking all phonetic distinctions in the received text, diacritic marks were invented to distinguish the two sounds represented by שׁ. With the dot placed over the upper left hand corner, the grapheme שׂ represented the former lateral fricative /ś/, though now pronounced [s]. With the dot placed over the upper right hand corner, the grapheme שׁ represented /š/.

5.5.2. *Merger of /ḫ/ and /ḥ/ and merger of /ġ/ and /ʻ/*
In ca. 200 B.C.E., the phoneme /ḫ/ merged with the phoneme /ḥ/, and the phoneme /ġ/ merged with the phoneme /ʻ/. This can be determined from the following. In the Septuagint of the Pentateuch, accomplished ca. 250 B.C.E.,

these phonemes all are represented differently in the Greek transcription of proper names and occasional common nouns (see §§ 5.4.9, 5.4.10). But in the Septuagint of the other books of the Bible, which was accomplished several decades or perhaps even a century later, this consistency disappears. Accordingly, we confidently can fix this phonological development to ca. 200 B.C.E.

5.5.3. Weakening of the pharyngeals and laryngeals

In the preceding paragraph we observed that ca. 200 B.C.E. the velar fricatives /ḫ/ and /ġ/ merged with the corresponding pharyngeals /ḥ/ and /ʿ/. As time passed, there is evidence for an overall weakening of the pronunciation of the pharyngeals and laryngeals. This can be determined from the Masoretic vocalization system which indicates (a) that the consonants /ḥ/, /ʿ/, /h/, and /ʾ/ cannot be geminated (this holds for /r/ as well); (b) that they cannot be vocalized with the vowel shwa, but instead require an auxiliary vowel; and (c) that in final position an anaptyctic vowel is required for all except /ʾ/, e.g., /rûḥ/ > [rûaḥ] 'wind'.

In time, in certain locales, this process became extreme. Post-biblical writings (e.g., the Talmud) describe situations in which all the pharyngeals and laryngeals merged. The cities which specifically are mentioned in this regard are Beth Shean, Haifa, and Tivon, all in the Lower Galilee region. Presumably this is due to Greek influence (we know, for example, that Greek influence was strong in Beth Shean). One amusing story records how a certain individual requested a particular item, but the storekeeper could not determine whether he desired ʾimmar 'lamb', ḥămār 'donkey', ḥĕmar 'wine', or ʿĕmar 'wool'. These forms are Aramaic, which was the dominant language in the Galilee ca. 300 C.E., but the story no doubt reflects the situation in Hebrew as well. On the other hand, we have the testimony of Jerome (ca. 400 C.E.) that the Jews mocked the Christians for their inability properly to pronounce the pharyngeals and laryngeals. Accordingly, we may conclude that in some communities Jews retained the original pronunciation of the pharyngeals and laryngeals, while in others they were weakly pronounced or disappeared altogether.

5.5.4. Fricativization (spirantization) of non-emphatic plosives

At some point in ancient Hebrew, the six non-emphatic plosives: /p/, /b/, /t/, /d/, /k/, /g/, developed a twofold realization. In post-vocalic position they came to be pronounced as fricatives (spirants); otherwise they retained their original plosive character. The corresponding fricative (spirantized) pronunciations are, respectively: /f/, /v/, /t̠/ (IPA [θ]), /d̠/ (IPA [ð]), /k̠/ (IPA [x]), /ḡ/ (IPA [ɣ]). Almost without exception, these sounds are allophones. Only in rare instances, due to other factors, did phonemic differences arise.

Exactly when the fricativization of the non-emphatic plosives in post-vocalic position occurred cannot be determined. According to one theory, it is due to Hurrian influence, in which case it must have occurred quite early (ca. 1000 B.C.E. [?]). However, most scholars date the fricativization of the non-emphatic plosives in post-vocalic position to a later period, say, ca. 400 B.C.E., perhaps under Aramaic influence.

The reader already has noted that several of these allophones are equivalent to other phonemes in the language. For example, /k̠/ is the same as /ḥ/ (both IPA [x]), and /ḡ/ is the same as /ġ/ (both IPA [ɣ]). Assuming, as most scholars do, that the fricativization of /k/ to /k̠/ [x] and of /g/ to /ḡ/ [ɣ] occurred ca. 400 B.C.E., and that /ḥ/ [x] and /ġ/ [ɣ] were distinguished as late as ca. 200 B.C.E. (see § 5.5.2), then we may posit the coexistence for about two centuries of two sets of one phoneme and one allophone each, phonetically identical (or almost identical).

Similarly, the fricativization of /t/ to /t̠/ may have resulted in another such case, if we assume that at the same time at least one Hebrew dialect retained the original phoneme /t̠/ (see § 5.4.2).

Clearly these sounds were pronounced by all (?) Jews ca. 850 C.E. when the Tiberian system of the Masorah was developed. In time, however, the ability to pronounce some of these sounds was lost by various Jewish communities, especially those in Europe.

The three sounds which remained most stable were /v/, /k̠/, and /f/. Among most European Jews, however, /t̠/ was realized as [s] (compare the shibboleth incident described in § 5.4.2, though there is no direct connection between the two phenomena). In the two remaining cases, /ḡ/ and /d̠/, fricativization disappeared and /g/ and /d/ were pronounced as [g] and [d] in all environments. On the other hand, Jews in Arab lands retained most if not all of the fricativized allophones into the 20th century. The Jews of Yemen are an example of a community whose pronunciation of Hebrew included the proper realization of all six allophones.

5.5.5. *Velarization of the emphatics*

Above (§ 5.4.14) we discussed the nature of the emphatics, with the conclusion that originally they most likely were glottalized. Because the corresponding consonants in Arabic are velarized/pharyngealized, and because the majority of Jews in the world ca. 1000 lived in an Arabic-speaking milieu and themselves spoke Arabic as their native language, in time the emphatic consonants in Hebrew became velarized/pharyngealized as well. This pronunciation remains to the present among the Jewish communities of North Africa and the Middle East.

Jews in Europe, on the other hand, lost the ability to pronounce the emphatic consonants altogether. Thus, in time, /ṭ/ > [t], so that it merged with /t/; /q/ > [k], so that it merged with /k/; and /ṣ/ > [ts], a phoneme common in many European languages, e.g., German.

5.6. Phonology of the vowels

The exact pronunciation of the vowels of ancient Hebrew cannot be recovered. However, we may assume that the classical pattern of Semitic (illustrated best in Classical Arabic) was operative in Hebrew in its earliest historical period. Thus we can reconstruct three basic vowels, either short or long: /a/, /i/, /u/, /â/, /î/, /û/. I utilize herein the circumflex to indicate long vowels which are "pure long" or "etymologically long"—that is, they correspond to long vowels in cognates. By contrast, the macron will be used in the transliteration scheme to indicate short vowels which have been lengthened due to stress—that is, they are "tone long" vowels (see § 5.6.2).

The Masoretic notation system, as noted above (§ 5.3), dates to ca. 850 C.E., and most accurately reflects the pronunciation of Hebrew in the early medieval period. By this time, the classic triangular vowel system had broken down, and numerous allophones had developed, based on a complex system of syllabification and accentuation. Again, exactly when the shift from the basic three vowels, short or long, to the system to be described below occurred, is unknown. But it is apposite to quote the view of Jerome (ca. 400 C.E.): "It is of no consequence whether [the word Shalem] is pronounced Salem or Salim, because Hebrew very rarely uses vowel letters in the course of words, and according to the discretion of readers and the different regions the same word is pronounced with different sounds and accents." In other words, there was much local variation in the realization of the vowels. One may wish to compare the situation in colloquial Arabic, where slight changes in vowels are noticeable in its various dialects (for example, the definite article can be [al], [el], [il], [əl], or [l]).

Below we present the vowel system according to the Tiberian Masoretic system. We begin with the long vowels, which are far simpler in their historical development, then move to the short vowels, and conclude with a treatment of the diphthongs.

5.6.1. Long vowels

Typically, the Proto-Semitic long vowels retain their basic pronunciation in all environments. Thus, /î/ is always [î], and /û/ is always [û]. The only area of fluctuation is with /â/. When Semitic cognates indicate /â/, the Hebrew reflex typically will be /ô/, though sometimes the /â/ is retained. Thus, for example, Arabic *lâ* = Hebrew *lô* 'no'; Arabic *salâm* = Hebrew *šālôm* 'peace'; etc., but Arabic *ṭabbâḫ* = Hebrew *ṭabbâḫ* 'cook'; etc.

5.6.2. Short vowels

The above discussion (§ 5.6) about the numerous vowel allophones refers most importantly to the short vowels. The Tiberian Masoretic notation system reflects different realizations of the three original vowels /a/, /i/, and /u/, depending on the kind of syllable in which the vowel occurs and depending on the accent.

If the short vowel occurs in an accented syllable, or in an unaccented open syllable immediately preceding the accent, the following developments occur (I include the name of the Hebrew vowel, its Tiberian symbol in parentheses, and the traditional transliteration in italics):

/a/ > [ɔ] *qameṣ* (ָ) *ā*
/i/ > [e] *ṣere* (ֵ) *ē*
/u/ > [o] *ḥolem* (ׄ) *ō*

If the short vowel occurs in an unaccented closed syllable, typically the original pronunciation is not affected, but with two of the vowels there is the possibility of an allophone. Thus:

/a/ > [a] *pataḥ* (ַ) *a*
/i/ > [i] *ḥiriq* (ִ) *i*
   or
/i/ > [ɛ] *segol* (ֶ) *e*
/u/ > [u] *šureq* (ֻ) *u*
   or
/u/ > [ɔ] *qameṣ* (ָ) *o*

Different environments usually will determine whether /i/ > [ɛ] as opposed to [i], and whether /u/ > [ɔ] as opposed to [u]. For example, if the vowel is followed by a geminated consonant, one can expect /i/ > [i], e.g., *libbî* 'my heart', and /u/ > [u], e.g., *kullām* 'all of them'; by contrast witness /i/ > [ɛ] in *leb-yām* 'heart of the sea', and /u/ > [ɔ] in *kol-ʾîš* 'every man'.

If the short vowel occurs in an open syllable more than one syllable before the accent, then the vowel is reduced to shwa [ə] (noted by ְ). If, however, the consonant involved is a pharyngeal or a laryngeal, then an auxiliary vowel is necessary (often called "compound vowel," due to its orthographic representation in the Masoretic system) (see § 5.5.3). The auxiliary vowel is halfway between a true shwa and the corresponding short vowel. Thus, using the traditional transliteration of Hebrew grammarians, /a/ > ă (̆), /i/ > ĕ (̆), and /u/ > ŏ (̆).

We illustrate this whole process with one example. The word for 'word' in Hebrew is [dɔvɔ́r], with original short vowel /a/ in both syllables. The first [ɔ] occurs because it appears in an unaccented open syllable immediately preceding the accent; the second [ɔ] occurs because it appears in an accented syllable. In the expression 'the word of Esther' [dəvar-ʾɛstér], the two words together have only the one accent, at the end of the expression. The first /a/ vowel now appears in an unaccented open syllable more than one syllable before the accent, and thus is reduced to shwa. The second /a/ vowel now appears in an unaccented closed syllable and thus is realized as [a].

Note that one Hebrew vowel sign, the *qameṣ* (̣), is transliterated as *a* when it derives from an /a/ vowel, but is transliterated as *o* when it derives from an /u/ vowel. This reflects the realization of this vowel according to the Jews of most Arab lands and according to standard Israeli pronunciation today. However, the Masoretic notation clearly demonstrates a single pronunciation for this vowel, which most accurately is [ɔ] and which is realized thus by the Jews of Europe and of Yemen. This demonstrates that the short vowel /a/, when it was accented and when it appeared in an open syllable immediately preceding the accent, was raised to a quality approaching the short vowel /o/. Such a process is in fact clearly indicated for Phoenician, and was no doubt true of ancient Hebrew as well, at least in the pronunciation tradition which emerged among the Tiberian Masoretes. It parallels the case of the long vowel /â/ shifting to /ô/; thus we may wish to postulate a general drift in this direction in ancient Hebrew and Phoenician.

It is important to note that the above charting of rules governing the short vowels is not to be taken as hard and fast. As in most languages, also in Hebrew, /a/ is the most stable vowel. When an /i/ vowel or an /u/ vowel is present, often the above rules will be violated. For example, ** burâš* > [bərôš] 'juniper, cypress' shows reduction of the /u/ vowel to shwa, even though the open syllable in which it occurs immediately precedes the accent. By contrast, of similar nominal pattern is ** šalâš* > [šɔlôš] 'three', with the /a/ vowel retaining its character (actually, with raising to [ɔ], as discussed in the preceding paragraph).

Similarly, auxiliary vowels can arise after consonants which are not pharyngeals or laryngeals. For example, /u/ does not reduce to *shwa* in the word *haggŏrānôt* 'the threshing floors'; rather it appears as *ŏ*. This is due to the circumstance of back vowel /u/ following the velar consonant /g/. Instead of reducing fully to *shwa*, as normally would be expected in the case of an unaccented open syllable more than one syllable before the accent, /u/ retains part of its original quality (i.e., as a back vowel) following a consonant pronounced in the back of the mouth (i.e., the velar /g/).

5.6.3. Diphthongs

Two diphthongs are reconstructed for ancient Hebrew in its earliest stage: [aw] and [ay]. In some cases, for example, in final position, these diphthongs remain unchanged, e.g., *qāw* 'line', *ḥay* 'alive' (though with the former note again the raising of the vowel to *ā* = [ɔ]). Typically, however, one of two changes occurs. Either an anaptyctic vowel is inserted, thus, e.g., *mawt* > [mɔwet] 'death' (or [mɔweṯ] showing fricativization), *bayt* > [bayit] 'house' (or [bayiṯ] showing fricativization) (again note the raising of the vowel in the former example); or monophthongization occurs.

Monophthongization in Hebrew almost always means [aw] > [o] (traditionally transliterated as *ô*), and [ay] > [e] (traditionally transliterated as *ê*), e.g., *yawm* > [yom] 'day', *bayḏa* > [beṣɔ] 'egg'. However, in a small number of instances, these two diphthongs monophthongize to [ɔ] (traditionally transliterated as *ā*). Examples of this latter process may be localized to two geographical regions in Israel: the northern part of the country (Galilee) and a small pocket in southern Judah (northern Negev).

5.6.4. Vowel letters

While a treatment of the vowel letters more properly belongs to a discussion of orthography rather than of phonology, a brief mention of them is appropriate. First, however, a basic overview of the problem is necessary. The oldest Hebrew inscriptions do not indicate the vowels; instead the 22-letter alphabet represents only the consonants. From the 8th century B.C.E. onward, according to the standard view, the practice arose to utilize certain letters, namely, <h>, <w>, and <y>, to indicate vowels (first only final vowels were indicated, later the practice was extended to mark medial vowels as well). When used in this manner, these letters (as already has been mentioned, see § 5.3) are known as *matres lectionis* or "vowel letters." By the 1st century B.C.E., this practice had increased so greatly, that in some of the Dead Sea Scrolls from this period virtually all vowels are marked by the aforementioned letters.

The Masoretic text presents a middle ground. Even though our earliest Masoretic manuscripts are from the early Middle Ages, they must go back to much older prototypes, because generally they are much more conservative in their use of the vowel letters than are the Dead Sea Scrolls of a millennium earlier. Two examples will suffice: in the Bible [loʼ] 'no, not' is spelled regularly <l> and more rarely <lw>; in the Dead Sea Scrolls there are about 400 cases of <lw> and about 100 cases of <l>. Similarly, in the Bible [kol] ~ [kɔl] is spelled regularly <kl> and in only one case <kwl>; in the Dead Sea Scrolls there are about 700 cases of <kwl> and only about three dozen cases of <kl>.

Most scholars have concluded that the use of the vowel letters in the Masoretic text is arbitrary, i.e., they have no phonetic significance. According to this theory, whether a given word is spelled with vowel letter or without indicates nothing about the pronunciation of the word. However, close analysis often reveals a remarkable degree of consistency in spelling variation, and this consistency, it has been argued, indicates that the vowel letters indeed do tell us something about the actual pronunciation of the Hebrew word. According to this view, the vowel letters <w> and <y> indicate an offglide. For example, <qwl> 'voice' would have been pronounced [qoʷl], with the allophonic off-glide, but <hql> 'the voice' would have been pronounced [haqqol]. The majority view has so dominated the field of Hebrew linguistics that little regard has been paid to the minority view. Further research on this issue remains a desideratum, but an open mind should be kept once the idea of allophonic off-glides is countenanced.

5.7. Historical changes concerning the vowels

5.7.1. /i/ > /a/ *in an originally closed accented syllable*
This law is known as Philippi's Law. An original /i/ vowel shifts to /a/ in an originally closed accented syllable (that is, a syllable that was closed even in its proto-form [as opposed to a closed syllable brought about by some other historical development]). Thus, for example, Proto-Semitic **gint* > **gitt* (via assimilation, see § 5.8.2) > **git* (with surrendering of word-final gemination) > [gat] 'winepress, olivepress'. In Akkadian transcriptions of the city in Canaan by this name, dating to as late as ca. 720 B.C.E., the form is still *Gint* (or *Gimt* [with partial dissimilation]). In the Septuagint of ca. 200 B.C.E., the rendering reflects [gɛt], and in the Masoretic text the pronunciation is [gat]. Accordingly, we are able to trace the historical development of this shift,

though the Septuagint rendering is too equivocal ([gɛt] apparently halfway between earlier [git] and later [gat]) to allow us to pinpoint the century in which Philippi's Law occurred.

5.7.2. /a/ > /i/ in an originally closed unaccented syllable
This law does not have an official name, but it may be called the corollary to Philippi's Law. An original /a/ vowel shifts to /i/ in an originally closed unaccented syllable (again, that is, a syllable that was closed even in its protoform [as opposed to a closed syllable due to some other historical development]). Thus, for example, *magdal > [migdal] 'tower' (also a toponym 'Migdal'); *šamšôn > [šimšôn] 'Samson'; etc. In the Septuagint and the New Testament (1st century C.E.), the Greek renderings of proper names reflect the original /a/ vowel (witness our English Samson, Mary Magdalene, etc.). Jerome (ca. 400 C.E.) still has *Magdal* in his Latin translation of the Bible. The Masoretic text reflects the shift to /i/ at some point within the following four and a half centuries. Thus, we may date this shift to sometime between 400 C.E. and 850 C.E.

5.8. Varia

5.8.1. Metathesis
The most consistent case of metathesis occurs in the Hitpaʻel form of the verb, when the first root consonant is any of the sibilants, /s/, /z/, /ṣ/, /š/, or the lateral fricative /ś/. In such cases, the /t/, which forms part of the morphology of this verbal stem and which normally precedes the first root consonant, interchanges with the above consonants. For example, *ʼetšammer > [ʼeštammer] 'I guard myself'.

Other examples of metathesis are the word pairs [kɛvɛś] ~ [kɛśɛv] 'sheep', and [śimlɔ] ~ [śalmɔ] 'article of clothing', both of which interestingly contain the lateral fricative /ś/.

5.8.2. Assimilation
Regressive assimilation occurs with vowelless /n/, except before pharyngeals and laryngeals. Thus, for example, to use an item noted earlier, *gint > *gitt (eventually shifting to [gat]) 'winepress, olivepress'. Similarly, *yandur eventually emerges as [yiddor] 'he vows'. Note also the same phenomenon with vowelless /l/ in various forms of the verb lqḥ 'take' (e.g., *yilqaḥ > yiqqaḥ 'he takes'); and with vowelless /d/ preceding its voiceless counterpart /t/. A

regular example of the latter is *'aḥadt > ['aḥat] 'one' (fem.). Another unique example occurs in *lalidt > *laladt (via Philippi's Law) > *lalatt > [lɔlat] (with surrendering of final gemination) 'to give birth', a form which occurs only once in the Bible (the normal form is [lɔlɛdɛt], or with fricativization [lɔlɛḏɛt], arrived at through different means).

Partial progressive assimilation occurs in the Hitpaʻel form of the verb, when the first root consonant is /z/ or /ṣ/ and it precedes /t/ (see also § 5.8.1). No examples with /z/ occur in the Bible, but from post-biblical Hebrew we may cite *hiztayyef > [hizdayyef] 'be forged', in which /t/ shifts to /d/ because of the preceding /z/. One example with /ṣ/ occurs in the Bible: *niṣtaddaq > [niṣtaddaq] '(how) shall we justify ourselves', in which /t/ shifts to /ṭ/ because of the preceding /ṣ/.

5.8.3. Prothetic vowel
The pronunciation of initial consonant clusters is assisted by the placement of a prothetic vowel. The best example is the attestation of both [zəroaʻ] and [ʻɛzroaʻ] 'arm', though the latter may be limited to specific regional dialects. Another example is [ʻɛṣbaʻ] 'finger', which from the cognate evidence (especially Egyptian ḏbʻ) can be shown to be originally without the initial [ʻɛ-].

5.8.4. Anaptyxis
The presence of anaptyctic vowels has been noted on several occasions above (see §§ 5.5.3, 5.6.3). One further example occurs in the creation of the "segolate" nouns, e.g., *dalt > dalet (attested in Hebrew in sentence positions requiring a pause, e.g., at the end of a verse) > delet [dɛlɛt] (with vowel harmony) 'door'. Greek and Latin transliterations of such words tend to show the forms without anaptyxis, though they do so inconsistently. In any case, this development most likely occurred in the 1st millennium C.E.

5.8.5. Stress
Stress in Hebrew at times is phonemic, e.g., [rɔḥel bɔ'ɔ́] 'Rachel is coming' vs. [rɔḥel bɔ́'ɔ] 'Rachel came'.

Bibliography

Blau, Joshua. 1970. *On Pseudo-Corrections in Some Semitic Languages*. Jerusalem: Israel Academy of Sciences and Humanities.

———. 1982. *On Polyphony in Biblical Hebrew.* Proceedings of the Israel Academy of Sciences and Humanities 6/2. Jerusalem: Israel Academy of Sciences and Humanities.

Garr, W. Randall. 1990. "Interpreting Orthography." In W. H. Propp, B. Halpern, and D. N. Freedman, eds., *The Hebrew Bible and Its Interpreters*, pp. 53–80. Winona Lake, Ind.: Eisenbrauns.

Kutscher, E. Y. 1982. *A History of the Hebrew Language*, ed. Raphael Kutscher. Jerusalem: Magnes; Leiden: Brill.

Levin, Saul. 1988. "The Hebrew of the Pentateuch." In Y. L. Arbeitman, ed., *Fucus: A Semitic/Afrasian Gathering in Remembrance of Albert Ehrman*, pp. 291–323. Amsterdam: Benjamins.

Moscati, Sabatino, et al. 1964. *An Introduction to the Comparative Grammar of the Semitic Languages.* Wiesbaden: Harrassowitz.

Qimron, Elisha. 1986. *The Hebrew of the Dead Sea Scrolls.* Atlanta: Scholars Press.

Rendsburg, Gary. A. 1990a. *Linguistic Evidence for the Northern Origin of Selected Psalms.* Atlanta: Scholars Press.

———. 1990b. "Monophthongization of *aw/ay* > *ā* in Eblaite and in Northwest Semitic." *Eblaitica* 2: 91–126.

Segal, M. H. 1927. *A Grammar of Mishnaic Hebrew.* Oxford: Clarendon.

Steiner, Richard. C. 1977. *The Case for Fricative-Laterals in Proto-Semitic.* New Haven: American Oriental Society.

———. 1982. *Affricated Ṣade in the Semitic Languages.* New York: American Academy for Jewish Research.

Waldman, Nahum M. 1989. *The Recent Study of Hebrew.* Cincinnati: Hebrew Union College Press; Winona Lake, Ind.: Eisenbrauns.

Zevit, Ziony. 1980. Matres Lectionis *in Ancient Hebrew Epigraphs.* Cambridge, Mass.: American Schools of Oriental Research.

Chapter 6
Tiberian Hebrew Phonology
Geoffrey Khan
University of Cambridge

Until the second half of the first millennium A.D., the text of the Hebrew Bible was transmitted in a form of writing that represented the consonantal phonemes but left the majority of the vowels and also consonantal gemination without graphic expression. When the Bible was read aloud, the reader followed a tradition of pronunciation that was transmitted orally and changed with the passage of time. At some period between the seventh and ninth centuries A.D., a circle of scholars in Tiberias known as Masoretes recorded in written form many of the missing details of the pronunciation of Biblical Hebrew, including the vowels, consonantal gemination, and even the distinction between the allophones of some of the consonantal phonemes. They also recorded the musical cantillation of the reading tradition. The system of signs created by the Tiberian Masoretes to represent these details is known as the Tiberian vocalization system. During the Middle Ages other vocalization systems were developed, which used different signs. The Tiberian system, however, became standardized and gradually replaced the others.

We must distinguish the Tiberian vocalization system from the original Tiberian Hebrew pronunciation, which it was designed to represent. This was the pronunciation of Hebrew which was used in the traditional reading of the Bible in the region of Tiberias during the seventh–ninth centuries A.D. Whereas the Tiberian vocalization tradition has survived in written form, the Tiberian pronunciation of Hebrew, which was an orally transmitted tradition, is extinct. None of the pronunciation traditions of the Hebrew Bible that are in use among Jewish communities today derive from the Tiberian pronunciation.

The original Tiberian pronunciation that lies behind the vocalization signs can be reconstructed from several sources. These include:

1. Masoretic and grammatical texts. Of primary importance are the texts from Palestine, especially the work *Hidāyat al-qāri* 'Guide for the reader'. The grammarians from medieval Spain sometimes describe the articulation

of a sound in greater detail than the Eastern sources. Their descriptions have to be treated with caution, however, since they could in some cases reflect a local type of pronunciation that differed from the Tiberian.

2. Transcriptions of the Tiberian pronunciation tradition into Arabic script which are found in medieval manuscripts written by Karaites (a medieval sect of Judaism).

3. The use of Hebrew letters and Tiberian vocalization signs to represent other languages. Of particular importance are medieval texts that represent Arabic in this way.

In this chapter an attempt is made to present the main features of the Tiberian pronunciation tradition based on the latest research on the aforementioned medieval sources.

6.1. Consonants

The letters are discussed in alphabetical order.
'Alep̄ (א). /ʔ/
   Phonetic realization: Glottal plosive [ʔ].
Bet /b/
   Phonetic realization: Two allophones: (1) (בּ) Voiced bilabial stop [b] and (2) (ב) voiced labiodental [v].
   Hidāyat al-qāri describes the [b] allophone as primary (*'aṣl*) and the [v] allophone as secondary (*far'*) (fols. 8b, 10a; cf. Eldar 1980-81: 254 n. 58).
Gimel /g/
   Phonetic realization: Two allophones: (1) (גּ) Voiced velar stop [g] and (2) (ג) voiced uvular fricative [ʁ].
   Hidāyat al-qāri describes the [g] allophone as primary (*'aṣl*) and the [ʁ] allophone as secondary (*far'*) (fol. 8b; cf. Eldar 1980–81: 254 n. 58).
Dalet /d/
   Phonetic realization: Two allophones: (1) (דּ) Voiced post-dental stop [d] and (ד) voiced post-dental fricative [ð].
   The *Hidāyat al-qāri* describes the [d] allophone as primary (*'aṣl*) and the [ð] allophone as secondary (*far'*) (fol. 8b; cf. Eldar 1980–81: 254 n. 58).
   The medieval scholar Isaac Israeli (9th–10th centuries A.D.), who had expert knowledge of the Tiberian reading tradition, is said to have pronounced [ð] with a secondary "emphatic" (i.e. velarized or uvularized) articulation [ð̣] in two words, viz. [ʔappað̣noː] 'his palace' (Dan. 11:45) and [ˌvaːjjað̣raˈχuː] 'and they have bent' (Jer. 9:2) (cf. Schreiner 1886: 221; Mann 1931–35, 1: 670 n. 106; Dukes 1845–46: 9, 73; Grossberg 1902: 24).

He (ה) /h/
Phonetic realization: Glottal fricative [h].
Waw (ו) /w/
Phonetic realization: Two allophones: (1) Labiodental [v] and (2) labiovelar semivowel [w].
The usual realization of /w/ was [v]. The allophone [w] occurred when the letter was preceded or followed by a *u* vowel, e.g. [ufuwˈwɔː] 'and Puwwa' (proper name) (Gen. 46:13), [vajjiʃtaːhaˈwuː] 'and they prostrated themselves' (Deut. 29:25), [tɔːˈwuː] 'they span' (Ex. 35:26) (see David ben Abraham al-Fāsī 1936, 1:451–52; Mishael ben Uzziel 1965: 20; Eldar 1978, 1:85, 1980–81: 259, 1984: 10–11).
Zayin (ז) /z/
Phonetic realization: Voiced alveolar sibilant [z].
The *Hidāyat al-qāri* mentions a variant of the letter *zayin* which is referred to by the Tiberian scholars as *zāy*[1] *makrūḵ* (Eldar 1984–85: 32).[2] The epithet *makrūḵ* was used by the Tiberian scholars to describe also a variant type of *reš*. It apparently referred to an emphatic (i.e. velarized or uvularized) articulation of the letter (cf. Khan to appear a). It appears, therefore, that *zayin* had an emphatic allophone [ẓ], though its distribution is unknown.
Ḥet (ח) /ḥ/
Phonetic realization: Unvoiced pharyngeal fricative [ħ].
Ṭet (ט) /ṭ/
Phonetic realization: emphatic (i.e. velarized or uvularized) unvoiced alveolar plosive [ṭ].
Yod (י) /j/
Phonetic realization: palatal unrounded semivowel [j].
According to one medieval source (Saadya Gaon 1891: 42–43), the Tiberians pronounced geminated *yod* like Arabic *jīm*, i.e. as a voiced palatal stop [ɟ] (cf. Roman 1983: 101–6, 218), which had the same place of articulation as *yod* [j]. This was the result of strengthening the articulation of [j] to a stop.
Kap̄ /k/
Phonetic realization: Two allophones: (1) (כ) Unvoiced velar stop [k] and (2) (כ) unvoiced uvular fricative [χ].

---

1. The *Hidāya* uses the Arabic letter name.
2. The Yemenite orthoepic treatise known as the Hebrew *Maḥberet ha-Tījān*, which was based on the long version of the *Hidāya*, contains a similar statement (1870: 81, cf. Morag 1959–60: 219 n. 45): *wkn yš lhm zyn nqrʾ mkrwk vʾynw ydwʿ ʾṣlynw* 'They (i.e. the Jews of Palestine) have a *zayin* called *makrūḵ*, but it is unfamiliar to us (i.e. the Jews of Yemen)'.

We know from Greek transcriptions that in the first half of the first millennium A.D., plosive *kap̄* was pronounced with aspiration [kʰ] (cf. Kutscher 1965: 24–35). This was likely to be the case also in the Tiberian pronunciation tradition.

Hidāyat al-qāri describes the [k] allophone as primary (*'aṣl*) and the [χ] allophone as secondary (*farʿ*) (fols. 8b, 10a; cf. Eldar 1980–81: 254 n. 58).

Lamed (ל) /l/

Phonetic realization: Voiced alveolar lateral continuant [l].

Mem (מ) /m/

Phonetic realization: Voiced bilabial nasal [m].

Nun (נ) /n/

Phonetic realization: Voiced alveolar nasal [n].

Samek (ס) /s/

Phonetic realization: Unvoiced alveolar sibilant [s].

ʿAyin (ע) /ʿ/

Phonetic realization: Voiced pharyngeal fricative [ʕ].

Pe /p/

Phonetic realization: Two allophones: (1) (פּ) Unvoiced bilabial stop [p] and (2) (פ) unvoiced labiodental fricative [f].

The *Hidāyat al-qāri* describes the [p] allophone as primary (*'aṣl*) and the [f] allophone as secondary (*farʿ*) (fol. 8b; cf. Eldar 1980–81: 254 n. 58).

Saadya refers to the existence of a "hard" *pe* in the word [ʔappað'no:] 'his palace' (Daniel 11:45), which he describes as between plosive *bet̄* and plosive *pe* (1891: 42). This appears to be referring to an unaspirated, fortis realization of [p]. One may infer from this that the voiced stop *bet̄* was unaspirated whereas the normal unvoiced stop *pe* was aspirated. We know from Greek transcriptions that in the first half of the first millennium A.D. plosive *pe* was pronounced with aspiration (cf. Kutscher 1965: 24–35). This appears also to have been the case in the Tiberian pronunciation tradition. Dunash ben Tamim reports that the scholar Isaac Israeli (9th–10th centuries), who was "an expert in the reading of the Tiberians," pronounced the *dalet̄* in the word [ʔappað'no:] as the emphatic (velarized or uvularized) Arabic letter *ẓā'* (cf. Schreiner 1886: 221; Mann 1972: 670 n. 106; Dukes 1845–46: 9, 73; Grossberg 1902: 24). This implies that the 'hard' *pe* was also emphatic [p̣] (cf. Steiner: 1993: 551–61).

Ṣade (צ) /ṣ/

Phonetic realization: Unvoiced emphatic (velarized or uvularized) alveolar sibilant [ṣ].

Ibn Kaldūn refers to a voiced allophone of *ṣade* [z̧] in the pronunciation of the name אֲמַצְיָ֫הוּ, i.e. [ʔamaẓ'jɔːhuː] (cf. Schreiner 1886: 254).

Qup̄ (ק) /q/

Phonetic realization: Unvoiced uvular plosive [q].

According to the *Hidāyat al-qāri*, it was articulated with the middle of the tongue (*wasṭ al-lisān*), i.e. somewhere on the tongue between the back third and the tip (fols. 10a–10b, ed. Eldar 1980–81, lines 61–72). This was further forward than fricative *kap̄* and *gimel*, which were articulated with the back third of the tongue.

Reš (ר) /r/

Phonetic realization: Two allophones: (1) Voiced uvular roll [ʀ] or frictionless continuant [ʁ] and (2) emphatic (velarized or uvularized) linguo-alveolar roll [r̩].

The basic articulation of the Tiberian *reš* was an uvular roll [ʀ] or frictionless continuant [ʁ]. It was realized as the allophone [r̩] in the environment of the alveolar consonants /d/, /z/, /ṣ/, /t/, /ṭ/, /s/, /l/, /n/. The precise rule given in the medieval sources is that [r̩] occurred when preceded by /d/, /z/, /ṣ/, /t/, /ṭ/, /s/, /l/, /n/ or followed by /l/, /n/ and when the *reš* was either in contact with these letters or at least in the same syllable, e.g. [dar'koː] 'his way' (Gen. 24:21), [jizˈroːq] 'he scatters' (Isa. 28:25), [lirḥoːṣ] 'to wash' (Gen. 24:32), [sar'neː] 'rulers' (Josh. 13:3). This allophone of *reš* was alveolar, by assimilation to the adjacent alveolar consonants. It can be established from medieval sources that it was also emphatic (velarized or uvularized) (see Khan to appear a).

Sin (שׂ) /s/

Phonetic realization: Unvoiced alveolar sibilant [s].

This had the same pronunciation as *samek̄* in the Tiberian pronunciation tradition.

At an earlier historical period, *sin* and *samek̄* were distinct in pronunciation and represented separate phonemes, as is shown by minimal pairs such as סַר [saːr] 'stubborn' and שַׂר [saːr] 'rule, captain'.

Šin (שׁ) /š/

Phonetic realization: Unvoiced palato-alveolar fricative [ʃ].

Taw /t/

Phonetic realization: Two allophones: (1) (ת) Unvoiced alveolar stop [t] and (2) (ת) unvoiced alveolar fricative [θ].

The *Hidāyat al-qāri* describes the [t] allophone as primary (*ʾaṣl*) and the [θ] allophone as secondary (*farʿ*) (fol. 8b; cf. Eldar 1980–81: 254 n. 58).

We know from Greek transcriptions that in the first half of the first millennium A.D. plosive *taw* was pronounced with aspiration (cf. Kutscher 1965: 24–35). This was likely to be the case also in the Tiberian pronunciation tradition.

6.1.1. Distribution of the allophones of /b/, /g/, /d/, /k/, /p/, /t/

In general the fricative allophones of these letters (i.e. [v], [ʁ], [ð], [χ], [f], and [θ] respectively) occurred after a vowel when the letter was not geminated, e.g. [ʀɑːv] 'much', [ʃɔːˈvaːʀ] 'he broke', [jiʃkaˈvuː] 'they lie down'. In many cases, however, the preceding vowel had been elided some time in the history of the language before the period of the Masoretes but the letter nevertheless remained a fricative, e.g. [baʃɔχˈvoː] < *bašukuˈbō 'when he lies down', [malˈχeː] < *malaˈkē 'kings', [ʃɔːχˈvuː] < *šākaˈbū 'they lay down'. In a few such cases a plosive and a fricative are in free variation, e.g. [ʀiʃˈfeː] and [ʀiʃˈpeː] 'flames'. The distribution of the plosive and fricative allophones, therefore, is not completely predictable from the phonetic context in Tiberian Hebrew, since it is an alternation that was inherited from an earlier stage of the language.[3]

In theory the phonetic processes described above could have given rise to a phonemic opposition between the plosive and fricative forms of the letters. However, no certain minimal pair that proves this opposition is attested in the corpus of the Hebrew Bible. Z. Harris (1941: 143–67) proposed the hypothetical minimal pair [ʔalˈfeː] 'thousands' vs. [ʔalˈpeː] 'two thousand'. The form of the second word in the pair is deduced from what we know about Hebrew morphology but is not attested.

6.1.2. Consonant gemination

This is marked in the Hebrew script by placing a dot in the letter known as *dageš*. According to the *Hidāyat al-qāri*, "*dageš* makes the letter heavy." This "heaviness" of letters is brought about by increased muscular pressure of speech organs (*Hidāyat al-qāri* fol. 9a–9b, ed. Eldar 1980–81, lines 15–16, 37–38). A geminated consonant, therefore, was pronounced with greater pressure than its ungeminated counterpart. Some consonants could not be geminated. These included the laryngeals (/ʔ/, /h/) and pharyngeals (/ʕ/, /ḥ/) and also /r/, except in a few isolated cases.

---

3. This is a simplified account of the distribution of the allophones of /b/, /g/, /d/, /k/, /p/, /t/. For a more detailed description see Yeivin 1980: 285–96.

6.2. Vowels

Tiberian Hebrew had the vowel system shown in Table 6-1.

Table 6-1. Tiberian Hebrew Vowels

i	u
e	o
ɛ	ɔ
a	

Pataḥ (_̞) /a/
Phonetic realization: Open, unrounded. There was no phonemic opposition between front and back vowels in the open position, so the allophonic scatter of /a/ is likely to have included both front [a] and back [ɑ] qualities. Evidence for this can be found in Judaeo-Arabic texts with Tiberian vocalization.[4]

Segol (_̤) /ɛ/
Phonetic realization: front, half-open unrounded [ɛ].

Qameṣ (_̞) /ɔ/
Phonetic realization: back, half-open rounded [ɔ].

Ṣere (_̈) /e/
Phonetic realization: front, half-close unrounded [e].

Ḥolem (וֹ) /o/
Phonetic realization: back, half-close rounded [o].

Ḥireq (_̣) /i/
Phonetic realization: front, close, unrounded [i].

Šureq (וּ), **qibbuṣ** (_̤)[5] /u/
Phonetic realization: back, close, rounded [u].

6.2.1. Vowel length

Vowel length is in most cases predictable from syllable structure and the placement of stress. Meaningful contrasts between words were not usually

---

4. In one text (T-S Ar. 8.3), for instance, which uses both *pataḥ* and *qameṣ* signs, *pataḥ* is used to represent Arabic *fatḥa* both in the environment of emphatic consonants, where it would be expected to have had a back quality [ɑ] (e.g. [ʔaʕẓɑm]), and also in the environment of non-emphatics, where a front quality [a] would have been expected (e.g. [watafī]). The *qameṣ* sign is used in this text to represent a back vowel somewhere in the region of mid vowels [ɔ] and [o] which resulted from the contraction of the diphthong [aw], e.g. [foːq].

5. These are orthographic variants of the same vowel.

made by differences in vowel length alone. Differences in length are in virtually all cases relatable to differences in syllable structure or stress placement. Length was not an independent contrastive feature of vowels. The vowel *qameṣ* may have been an exception, since pairs of words can be found in which a contrast of meaning appears to have been made only by a difference in length of the vowel, e.g. [ʔɔχ'lɔ:] 'food' vs. [ʔɔ:χlɔ:] 'she ate'. Possible other minimal pairs are words such as [dɔ'mi:] 'silence' and [dɔ:'mi:] 'my blood'. The validity of both such minimal pairs, however, is not completely certain (see below).

The basic contexts for the occurrence of a long vowel are (1) a stressed syllable or (2) an open unstressed syllable. Examples: ['mɛ:lɛχ] 'king', [jiʃ'ma:ʕ] 'he hears', [ha:'hu:] 'that'. Many words carry a secondary stress in addition to the main stress, e.g. [ˌhɔ:ʔɔ:'ðɔ:m] 'the man', [ˌni:θhakka'mɔ:] 'let us deal wisely' (Ex. 1:10).

As has been remarked, a vowel in an unstressed closed syllable was, on principle, short. If, however, it was followed by a series of contiguous consonants of relatively weak articulation (e.g. /ʔ/, /h/, /ʕ/, /ḥ/, /j/, /n/, /l/), then the vowel was sometimes lengthened even when not stressed. This occurred in certain prefixes of the verbs [hɔ:'jɔ:] 'he was' and [ḥɔ:'jɔ:] 'he lived', namely the [i] of prefixes before [h]/[ḥ], e.g. [ji:h'jɛ:] 'he will be', and the [a] of the conjunctive prefix [va] before [j], e.g. [va:jhi:] 'and it was'. It is occasionally found elsewhere, e.g. [ha'ʃɔ:ma:ʕ ʕɔ:m] 'did any people hear?' (Deut. 4:33).

The duration of long vowels varied considerably. From the medieval sources we are able to infer the existence of several different degrees in the relative duration of long vowels. Most of these were conditioned by differences in stress, vowel height, or consonantal strength. We shall mention here some of the conditions of these variations that are known in the present state of research.[6] This list does not include all the variations that we have evidence for. There were likely to have been, moreover, a number of other variations for which we have no evidence from the extant sources.

1. Stressed long vowels were longer than unstressed long vowels, e.g. in the word [ha:'hu:] 'that' the [u:] was longer than the [a:].

2. A long vowel with secondary stress was longer than a long vowel in an unstressed syllable, e.g. in the word [ˌhɔ:ʔɔ:'ðɔ:m] 'the man' the second [ɔ:] was shorter than the other two.

3. A close vowel [i, u] in a closed syllable with secondary stress was shorter than an open vowel [a] in the same conditions, e.g. in the words [ˌni:θhak-

---

6. For the evidence for these variations see Khan 1987, 1989, 1994b.

ka'mɔː] 'let us deal wisely' (Ex. 1:10) and [ˌvaːttiṣpa'neːhuː] 'and she hid him' (Ex. 2:2), the [ˌiː] vowel of the first was shorter than the [ˌaː] of the second.

4. The close vowel [i] of prefixes of the verbs [hɔːjɔ] 'he was' and [ḥɔːjɔː] 'he lived' was shorter than the open vowel [a] in prefixes of these verbs, e.g. in the words [jiːhjɛː] 'he will be' and [vaːjhiː] 'and he was' the [iː] of the first was shorter than the [aː] of the second.

5. The close vowel [iː] of the prefixes of the verbs [hɔːjɔː] 'he was' and [ḥɔːjɔː] 'he lived' was shorter than [iː] in a stressed syllable or an unstressed open syllable but longer than [iː] in a closed syllable with secondary stress, e.g. in the words ['ʔiːm] 'if', [jiːhjɛː] 'he will be', and [ˌniːθḥakka'mɔː] 'let us deal wisely' the three [iː] vowels were of decreasing degrees of length.

6. The [aː] vowel in prefixes of the verbs [hɔːjɔː] 'he was' and [ḥɔːjɔː] 'he lived' (e.g. [vaːjhiː] 'and he was') and in other words before two weak consonants (e.g. [ha'ʃɔːmaːʕ 'ʕɔːm] 'did any people hear?' Deut. 4:33) was longer than an [aː] vowel in a closed syllable with secondary stress (e.g. in [ˌvaːttiṣ-pa'neːhuː] 'and she hid him' Ex. 2:2).

6.2.2. Syllable structure and the šewa

In the Tiberian pronunciation tradition, many short vowels occurred in open syllables, e.g. [jiʃma'ʀuː] 'they guard', [jaːʕa'sɛː] 'he does'. These were represented in the vocalization system by the *šewa* sign or one of the *ḥaṭep̄* signs. These were different from the regular vowel signs. From the Masoretic sources and Judaeo-Arabic texts with Tiberian vocalization, we know that these vowels were equivalent in length to short vowels in unstressed closed syllables (see Khan 1987: 37–39, 1992: 105–11). Does the occurrence of these short vowels in apparently open syllables contradict the vowel length principle stated above?

According to the medieval Masoretic sources, a consonant with one of these vowels did not constitute a syllable. In a word such as [tispa'ʀuː] 'you count', the syllable structure would be, according to the medieval sources, [tis-pa'ʀuː]. This concept of the syllable reflects the phonotactic rules of Tiberian Hebrew and corresponds to the phonotactic definition of syllables espoused in modern times by linguists such as Pulgram (1970: 40ff.). The basic principle of Pulgram's definition is that a sequence of consonant and vowel segments has the status of a syllable only if the onset of the sequence can stand in word-initial position and the coda (i.e. closure) can stand in word-final position. There is no structural reason why it cannot stand by itself as a word. In the medieval Tiberian reading tradition of Biblical

Hebrew, a short vowel did not occur in word-final position. According to this definition, therefore, the sequence consonant + short (CV) vowel did not have the status of a syllable. Only consonants and long vowels could occur in word-final position, and so only these could constitute permissible codas of syllables.[7] The sequence CV occurred in word-initial position. It could, therefore, form the onset of a syllable. This allowed it to be attached to the beginning of a sequence which had a permissible coda and so had the status of a syllable, viz. CV+CVC or CV+CV̄. The sequences CVCVC and CVCV̄, therefore, were regarded by the Masoretes as single syllables.

Rather than denying the status of syllable completely to a CV sequence on the basis of this phonotactic definition, it is helpful to distinguish between principal and dependent syllables. Principal syllables are those that can stand independently, since they have onsets and codas that can open or close an independent word. A dependent syllable is one that cannot stand independently, but only in combination with a following principal syllable. The aforementioned distribution of vowel length, therefore, refers to principal syllables. Any open syllable with a short vowel must be a dependent syllable. This is a phonotactic distinction. It is not usually taken account of by the accent system of Tiberian Hebrew, which counts beats on syllable nuclei between accents without distinguishing between dependent and principal syllables.

The reality of the phonotactic distinction between dependent and principal syllables is reflected by the concept of the syllable that is expressed in the medieval Masoretic literature. It is also reflected by the vocalization system, which represents the vowel nuclei of dependent syllables with signs (*šewa* and *ḥaṭepīm*) that are different from those representing the nuclei of principal syllables. Furthermore, some features of Tiberian Hebrew phonology are sensitive to the distinction. The occurrence pattern of the allophones of Tiberian /r/ is a clear example of this. The apico-alveolar allophone of /r/, i.e. [r̺], occurred when it was preceded by one of the dental/alveolar consonants /d/, /z/, /ṭ/, /s/, /ṣ/, /t/, /l/, /n/ and when either (a) the *reš* was in direct contact with one of these letters or (b) the *reš* occurred together with one of them in the same syllable, e.g. [dar̺kamo:'ni:m] 'drachmas', [vɔ:ʔɛzˈr̺e:m] 'and I winnowed them' (Jer. 15:7) [bamizˈr̺e:] 'with a pitchfork' (Jer. 15:7), [ṣar̺uːˈfɔ:] 'smelted',

---

7. The only possible exceptions are words ending in a consonantal cluster such as וַיַּשְׁקְ 'and he watered', נֵרְדְּ 'nard'. Some medieval sources state that the second *šewa* in these words was vocalic (e.g. David Qimḥi 1952: 16–17). Most sources, however, state that both *šewa*s were silent (e.g. Ibn Janāḥ 1880: 275, Abraham ibn Ezra 1791: 3).

[limˈtˁaːr] 'through the rain'. When the dental/alveolar was followed by a full vowel the /r/ was realized with the uvular allophone [ʀ], e.g. in [tɔːˈʀuːsˁ] 'you run'. How did words such as [limˈtˁaːr] and [sˁaruːˈfɔː] differ from [tɔːˈʀuːsˁ]? The most obvious answer is that in [limˈtˁaːr] and [sˁaruːˈfɔː] the *reš* was in the same syllable as the dental/alveolar, whereas in [tɔːˈʀuːsˁ] it was in a different syllable.

We may, therefore, elaborate the description of the contexts for the occurrence of a long vowel as follows: A vowel is long if it occurs in a stressed syllable or in an open principal syllable.

There are no phonological oppositions between the vowel of a dependent open syllable CV (represented by vocalic *šewa* or a *ḥaṭep* sign) on the one hand and zero (represented by silent *šewa*) on the other. The vowel in the syllable CV, therefore, can be regarded as an allophone of zero. It is no doubt for this reason that the Masoretes did not consider vocalic *šewa* to be a vowel and represented it with the same sign as they represented zero. A word such as [ʃaˈvuː] 'sit! (pl.)', therefore, should be represented phonologically as /šbu/. There are phonological oppositions, on the other hand, between the vowel of the dependent syllable CV and that of the principal syllable CVː, e.g. [ʃaˈvuː] 'sit!' (imperative pl.) vs. [ʃɔːˈvuː] 'they captured'.

In the Tiberian reading tradition, a short vowel in the dependent syllable CV, which was represented by the *šewa* sign, was usually pronounced with the quality of [a]. Where, however, *šewa* preceded a guttural consonant it took the quality of the vowel after the guttural and where it preceded [j] it had the quality of a short [i], e.g. בְּאֵר [beˈʔeːr] 'well', מְאֹד [moˈʔoːð] 'very', בְּיוֹם [biˈjoːm] 'on the day' (Baer and Strack 1879: 12–15; Yeivin 1980: 281–82). In places the Masoretes considered that the reader may be uncertain whether to pronounce the *šewa* as vocalic or silent and may have been unsure about the pronunciation of *šewa* where its quality differed from the norm. In such circumstances, the Masoretes added a vowel sign to the *šewa* sign creating a composite sign known as a *ḥaṭep* sign. The marking of the *ḥaṭep* signs under the gutturals was fixed in the Tiberian Masoretic tradition, and the Tiberian model codices do not exhibit significant differences. The marking of these signs under the non-gutturals, however, was not fixed, and considerable differences are found in the manuscripts.

Some scholars have claimed that the quality of the *ḥaṭep* vowels was phonemic on the basis of pairs such as אֲנִיָּה [ʔanijˈjɔː] 'mourning' vs. אֳנִיָּה [ʔɔnijˈjɔː] 'ship'; חֲלִי [ħaˈliː] 'ornament' vs. חֳלִי [ħɔˈliː] 'illness'; עֲלִי [ʕaˈliː] 'go up!' (imperative fem.sg.) vs. עֱלִי [ʕɛˈliː] 'pestle' (cf. Cantineau 1950: 114–16, Garbell 1958–59: 154). If this is the case, they could not be interpreted as

96   Geoffrey Khan

allophones of zero. It will be shown below, however, that the validity of these minimal pairs is doubtful.

Although vowel length is in general predictable from the syllabic context, it would appear that the syllable structure was determined by the length of the vowels. This is because a sequence containing vowels of unspecified length could have been syllabified in various ways, e.g. *tisparu* 'you count' could be [tis-paː-ʀuː] or [tis-paʀuː]. The correct syllabification [tis-paʀuː] could only have been achieved if the length of the vowels had already been fixed.

The length of vowels in the Tiberian pronunciation tradition was determined by the earlier history of the language or by phonetic processes that were operative during the masoretic period. Some long vowels were originally long, e.g. [koː'heːn] 'priest' < *kāhin*. Others were lengthened through phonetic processes that took place at various periods, e.g. lengthening of a vowel in an open syllable before the stress (pretonic lengthening), e.g. [jɔː'quːm] 'he rises' < *yaʾqūm*; the lengthening of stressed vowels, e.g. [mið'bɔːʀ] 'desert' < *midʾbar*; lengthening of vowel as compensation for the loss or absence of gemination in the following consonant, e.g. [javɔː'ʀeːχ] 'he blesses' < *yabarrik*, [haː'huː] 'that' < *hahhū*. Most of the phonetic processes had ceased to operate by the time of the Tiberian Masoretes. For instance, pretonic short vowels in open syllables were not lengthened ([ʃɔːma'ruː] 'they guarded' did not shift to [ʃɔːmaː'ruː]). In such cases, and also in the case of originally long vowels, vowel length was an inherited feature of the language. Some phonetic processes seem to have been still active in the masoretic period. One such process is the general lengthening of all stressed vowels. We know this was a relatively late process (see Khan 1987, 1994a: 133–44).

As a result of the historical background of the Tiberian pronunciation tradition, the vowels *ṣere* /e/ and *ḥolem* /o/ were always realized as long. The other vowels were realized as either long or short.

In some circumstances there appear to have been differences in duration between stressed vowels that were historically long and those that were historically short. The term "historically long" here refers to vowels that were originally long or that were lengthened by phonetic processes that took place before the masoretic period. "Historically short" refers to vowels that were short or were lengthened by phonetic processes that took place during the masoretic period. In the Tiberian pronunciation tradition, a *šewa* on a letter coming after a historically long vowel was usually silent, e.g. [ʃoːmʀiːm] 'guards'. Such a closed syllable before the main stress could take secondary stress in the form of an accent: שׁוֹמְרִים [ˌʃoːmˈʀiːm]. This implies that the vowel was long enough to accommodate the musical melisma of the accent associated with the secondary stress. Normally, secondary stress was separated from the main stress by an unstressed, buffer syllable, so that the two stress beats did not come together. In a form such as [ˌʃoːmˈʀiːm] it appears that the first vowel was lengthened to the extent that it included both the beat of the secondary stress and the unstressed buffer. This would mean that it contained two syllabic peaks: [ʃóːŏmʀíːm]. Historically short vowels, on the other hand, could not take the secondary stress in the form of a regular musical accent. When they took secondary stress it was marked by a sign known as a minor *ga'ya*, e.g. [niθhakkaˈmɔː] > [ˌniːθhakkaˈmɔː] (נִתְחַכְּמָה) 'let us deal wisely'. Such cases of *ga'ya* rarely occur immediately before the syllable bearing the main stress since they were not long enough to accommodate both the beat and buffer in contrast to the first vowel in [ʃóːŏmʀíːm]. The Arabic transcriptions, moreover, indicate that a vowel with the so-called minor *ga'ya* (i.e. the type found in closed syllables with a historically short vowel) was shorter than one that could take secondary stress in the form of a regular accent (i.e. syllables with a historically long vowel as in [ʃóːŏmʀíːm], [ˌhɔːʔɔːˈðɔːm] 'the man').

A vocalic *šewa*, which was a historically short vowel, was sometimes lengthened by secondary stress marked by *ga'ya*, e.g. [banaːhaˈlɔː] > [ˌbaːnaːhaˈlɔː] (בְּנַחֲלָה) 'as an inheritance' (Josh. 13:6). There is evidence that also these vowels were not as long as a historically long vowel in an open syllable with secondary stress, e.g. [hɔːʔɔːˈðɔːm] > [ˌhɔːʔɔːˈðɔːm] 'the man' (see Khan to appear b).

The analysis of the historically long vowel in a closed syllable with secondary stress as having two peaks has implications for the phonemic status of *qameṣ*. It was remarked above that pairs such as [ʔɔχˈlɔː] (אָכְלָה) 'food' vs. [ˌʔɔːχˈlɔː] (אָכְלָה) 'she ate' seem to require us to identify short and long *qameṣ* as two separate phonemes. If the syllable structure of the second word was in fact [ˌʔɔːɔχˈlɔː], then this would not be a minimal pair proving the phonemic status of the length of *qameṣ*.

There was ambiguity in the syllabic status of some short vowels in open syllables, notably [ɔ] (represented by the *ḥaṭep qameṣ* sign) in words such as דֳּמִי [dɔˈmiː] 'silence', צֳרִי [sɔˈʀiː] 'balsam', צִפֳּרִים [sippɔˈʀiːm] 'birds', כֻּתֳּנֹת [kuttɔˈnoːθ] 'tunics' (Ex. 28:40), הַגֳּרָנוֹת [haggɔʀɔːˈnoːθ] 'the threshing floors' (Joel 2:24). The vowel [ɔ] in these words was the reflex of an originally short [o] or [u]. The syllable with the short [ɔ] vowel sometimes took secondary stress and the *ḥaṭep̄* sign was replaced by an ordinary *qameṣ* in the model Tiberian manuscripts, e.g. [qɔðɔːˈʃiːm] (קֳדָשִׁים) > [ˌqɔːðɔːˈʃiːm] (קָדָשִׁים) 'holy things'. This differs from the occurrence of secondary stress marked by *gaʿya* on a vocalic *šewa* sign, which was not replaced by a full vowel sign, e.g. [banaħaˈlɔː] > [ˌbaːnaħaˈlɔː] (בְּנַחֲלָה) 'as an inheritance' (Josh. 13:6).

Moreover, the writing of ordinary *qameṣ* in place of *ḥaṭep̄ qameṣ* is found in some model Tiberian manuscripts also in a pretonic syllable. The medieval grammarian Ibn Janāḥ refers to the vocalic *šewa* being "lighter" than *ḥaṭep̄ qameṣ* in such words. This implies that there was a difference in length. According to Saadya Gaon (1891: 79), the rules for the occurrence of the apical-alveolar allophone of the Tiberian *reš* treated the word [sɔˈʀiː] 'balsam' as having two syllables. As we have seen, these rules treat a consonant with vocalic *šewa* as belonging to the following syllable.

There is reason to believe, therefore, that in words such as [sɔˈʀiː], [dɔˈmiː] the *ḥaṭep̄ qameṣ* vowel was longer than a vocalic *šewa*. This applies both to cases where the syllable was unstressed and those in which it had secondary stress. This difference in length was sufficient to give the consonant + vowel sequence the status of a independent syllable as reflected by the rules for the distribution of the allophones of Tiberian /r/. We may describe these vowels as half long (CV·), lying in between short vowels (CV) and long vowels (CV:). It appears that a half long vowel could act as a coda of a principal syllable, whereas a short vowel could not.

If the *ḥaṭep̄ qameṣ* was a principal syllable nucleus, then the long and short *qameṣ* in minimal pairs such as [dɔ·ˈmiː] 'silence' and [dɔːˈmiː] 'my blood' would have to be identified as separate phonemes, since vowel length is the only feature that contrasts them. Since the phonemic contrast is between only two degrees of length, the phonemes could be represented as short /ɔ̆/ vs. long /ɔ/.

This could apply in general to cases of *ḥaṭep̄* vowels that have not been leveled to the normal quality of *šewa* but have a quality close to that of the original short vowel from which they developed. If this is correct, the validity of the aforementioned pairs as proof of phonemic contrasts of short vowels in open syllables would be in doubt, viz. [ʔanijˈjɔː] 'mourning' vs. [ʔɔnijˈjɔː] 'ship', [ħaˈliː] 'ornament' vs. [ħɔˈliː] 'illness', [ʕaˈliː] 'go up!' (imperative fem.sg.) vs. [ʕɛˈliː] 'pestle'. This is because the two members of each pair would have had a different syllable structure. The syllables with [ɔ] and [ɛ] had a quality close to that of the original vowel:[8] [ʔɔ·nijˈjɔː] < *ʾoniyyā

---

8. The original quality is preserved in the Babylonian tradition of Hebrew; cf. Yeivin 1985, 2: 876–79.

vs. [ʔanij-'jɔː] 'mourning', [hɔˑ-'liː] 'illness' < *ḥuly vs. [ħa'liː] 'ornament', [ʕɛ+-'liː] 'pestle' < *ʕily vs. [ʕa'liː] 'go up!' (fem.sg.).

6.3. Summary of the phoneme inventory with the known allophones

6.3.1. Consonants
6.3.1.1. Labials
/b/ [b], [v]
/m/ [m]
/p/ [pʰ], [f], [p̪]
/w/ [v], [w]

6.3.1.2. Dentals/alveolars
/t/ [tʰ], [θ]
/d/ [d], [ð], [ḏ]
/ṭ/ [ṭ]
/s/ [s]
/z/ [z], [ẓ](?)
/ṣ/ [ṣ], [ẓ]
/š/ /ʃ/
/n/ [n]
/l/ [l]

6.3.1.3. Palatal
/j/ [j], [ɟ]

6.3.1.4. Velars and uvulars
/k/ [kʰ], [χ]
/g/ [g], [ʁ]
/q/ [q]
/ʀ/ [ʀ], [ɾ]

6.3.1.5. Laryngeals and Pharyngeals
/h/ [h]
/ʔ/ [ʔ]
/ḥ/ [ḥ]
/ʕ/ [ʕ]

6.3.2. Vowels

(In the following phonemic notation, /V/ is a phoneme unspecified for length, /V̆/ and /V̄/ are phonemes which contain length as a component feature.)

/a/ [a], [aː], [ɑ], [ɑː]
/ɛ/ [ɛ], [ɛː]
/ɔ̆/(?) [ɔ], [ɔˑ]
/ɔ̄/(?) [ɔː]
/e/ [eː]
/o/ [oː]
/u/ [u], [uː]
/i/ [i], [uː]
/Ø/ [Ø], [a], [ɛ], [ɔ], [e], [o], [i], [u]

References

Abraham ibn Ezra. 1791. *Sep̄er ha-Moznayim*, ed. Wolf Heidenheim. Offenbach.

Baer, Seligman, and Hermann L. Strack, eds. 1879. *Die Dikduke Ha-Tᵉamim des Ahron ben Moscheh ben Ascher*, Leipzig.

Cantineau, Jean. 1950. "Essai d'une phonologie de l'hébreu biblique." *Bulletin de la Société de Linguistique de Paris* 46: 82–122.

David ben Abraham al-Fāsī. 1936–45. *The Hebrew–Arabic Dictionary of the Bible Known as Kitāb Jāmi' al-Alfāẓ (Agrōn)*. 2 vols. (Yale Oriental Series, Researches 20–21), ed. Solomon L. Skoss. New Haven: Yale University Press.

David Qimḥi. 1952. *David Ḳimḥi's Hebrew Grammar (Mikhlol) Systematically Presented and Critically Annotated by William Chomsky*. New York: Bloch.

Dukes, Leopold. 1845–46. *Qunṭras ha-masoret*. Tübingen.

Eldar, Ilan. 1978. *The Hebrew Langugage Tradition in Medieval Ashkenaz (ca. 950–1350 C.E.)*, vol. 1: *Phonology and Vocalization* (in Hebrew). Jerusalem: Hebrew University.

———. 1980–81. "Hidāyat al-Qāri (the longer Arabic version): A Specimen Text, Critically Edited, with Hebrew Translation, Commentary and Introduction" (in Hebrew). *Lĕšonénu* 45: 233–59.

———. 1984. "The Law of אוי״ה and בגדכפ״ת" (in Hebrew). *Hebrew Union College Annual* 55: א-יד.

———. 1984–85. "The Two Pronunciations of Tiberian *rêš*" (in Hebrew). *Lĕšonénu* 48–49: 22–34.

Garbell, Irene. 1958–59. "The Phonemic State of the šwa, the Ḥăṭéfim and Spirantal ב ג ד כ פ ת in Masoretic Hebrew" (in Hebrew). *Lĕšonénu* 23: 152–55.

Grossberg, Menasseh. 1902. *Sefer Yezirah Ascribed to the Patriarch Abraham, with Commentary by Dunash ben Tamim.* London.

Harris, Zellig. 1941. "The Linguistic Structure of Hebrew." *Journal of the American Oriental Society* 61: 143–67.

Ibn Janāḥ. 1880. "Kitāb at-taḵrîb wat-tashîl."In *Opuscules et traités d'Abou 'l-Walîd Merwan Ibn Djanah*, ed. Joseph and Hartwig Dérenbourg, pp. 268–342. Paris: Imprimerie Nationale.

Khan, Geoffrey. 1987. "Vowel Length and Syllable Structure in the Tiberian Tradition of Biblical Hebrew." *Journal of Semitic Studies* 32: 23–82.

———. 1989. "The Pronunciation of מַה־ before *dageš* in the Medieval Tiberian Hebrew Reading Tradition." *Journal of Semitic Studies* 34: 433–41.

———. 1992. "The Function of the Shewa Sign in Judaeo-Arabic Texts." In *Genizah Research after Ninety Years: The Case of Judaeo-Arabic*, ed. Joshua Blau and S. C. Reif, pp. 105–11. Cambridge.

———. 1994a. "The Historical Background of the Vowel *ṣere* in some Hebrew Verbal and Nominal Forms." *Bulletin of the School of Oriental and African Studies* 57: 133–44.

———. 1994b. "The Pronunciation of the Verbs היה and חיה in the Tiberian Tradition of Biblical Hebrew." In *Semitic and Cushitic Studies*, ed. Gideon Goldenberg and Shlomo Raz, pp. 133–44.Wiesbaden: Harrassowitz.

———. to appear a. "The Pronunciation of *reš* in the Tiberian Tradition of Biblical Hebrew." *Hebrew Union College Annual*.

———. to appear b. "The Pronunciation of *šewa* with *ga'ya* in the Tiberian Tradition of Biblical Hebrew." *Vetus Testamentum*.

Kutscher, Eduard Yehezkiel. 1965. "Contemporary Studies in North-western Semitic." *Journal of Semitic Studies* 10: 21–51.

Maḥberet ha-Tījān. 1870. *Manuel du lecteur*, ed. Joseph Dérenbourg. Paris.

Mann, J. 1931–35. *Texts and Studies in Jewish History and Literature.* 2 vols. Cincinnati: Hebrew Union College Press.

Mishael ben Uzziel. 1965. *Kitāb al-Ḵilāf* (in Hebrew), ed. Lazar Lipschütz. Jerusalem: Hebrew University.

Morag, Shlomo. 1959–60. "'The Seven Double Letters בג״ד כפר״ת'" (in Hebrew). In *Studies in Honour of N. H. Tur-Sinai* (Publications of the Israel Society for Biblical Research 8), pp. 207–42. Jerusalem.

Pulgram, Ernst. 1970. *Syllable, Word, Nexus, Cursus* (Janua Linguarum series minor 81). The Hague: Mouton.

Roman, André. 1983. *Étude de la phonologie et de la morphologie de la koinè arabe*. 2 vols. Aix-en-Provence: Université de Provence.

Saadya Gaon. 1891. *Commentaire sur le Séfer Yesira ou Livre de la création, par le Gaon Saadya de Fayyoum*, ed. Mayer Lambert. Paris: Bouillon.

Schreiner, M. 1886. "Zur Geschichte der Aussprache des Hebräischen." *Zeitschrift für die alttestamentliche Wissenschaft* 6: 213–59.

Steiner, Richard C. 1993. "Emphatic *p* in the Massoretic pronunciation of *'appad̲no* (Dan 11:45)." In *Hebrew and Arabic Studies in Honour of Joshua Blau*, ed. M. Bar Asher, Z. Ben-Hayyim, M. J. Kister, A. Levin, S. Shaked, and A. Tal, pp. 551–61. Jerusalem: Tel Aviv University and The Hebrew University of Jerusalem.

Yeivin, Israel. 1980. *Introduction to the Tiberian Masorah*, trans. and ed. E. J. Revell. Missoula, Mont.: Scholars Press.

———. 1985. *The Hebrew Language Tradition as Reflected in the Babylonian Vocalization* (Texts and Studies 12). 2 vols. Jerusalem: Academy of the Hebrew Language.

Chapter 7
Jewish Palestinian Aramaic Phonology
Geoffrey Khan
University of Cambridge

Jewish Palestinian Aramaic (JPA) is the dialect of Aramaic that was spoken and written by Jews in Palestine during the Byzantine period (3rd-7th centuries A.D.) and during the beginning of the Arab period (7th century onwards). By the tenth century it appears that Arabic had replaced Aramaic as vernacular of the Jews of Palestine (Goitein 1966: 198, Friedman 1980: 50–51). By the third century A.D., clear dialectal divisions emerge in Aramaic according to geographical area and confessional community. Among scholars of Aramaic this period is known either as Middle Aramaic (Rosenthal 1939: 104–72) or Late Aramaic (Fitzmyer 1966: 19). JPA is classified as a Western Aramaic dialect, together with the contemporary Aramaic dialects of the Christians and Samaritans.

JPA has been preserved in a number of written sources. These include (i) the Palestinian Talmud, (ii) Palestinian Midrashim (exegetical discussions of the Bible), (iii) texts discussing Jewish Law (*halakha*), (iv) inscriptions, (v) Targums (interpretive translations of the Bible) that were written in Palestine during the Byzantine period, (vi) poetry, (vii) letters and documents preserved on papyrus in Egypt datable to the 5th century, (viii) marriage contracts (*ketubbot*) following the Palestinian tradition of Jewish law written in the Arab period, (ix) magical texts, and (x) marginal notes written in medieval Tiberian Bible codices by the Masoretes. For the bibliography relating to these sources see Sokoloff (1990: 19–28).

One can find minor linguistic differences among some of these sources. It has been customary to refer to the dialect of some of the aforementioned texts, especially types (i)–(iv), as Galilean Aramaic. It would be misleading to assume, however, that there was a geographical dialectal cleavage between the Jewish Aramaic of southern Palestine and that of the Galilee further north. Although the centers of learning and literary activity during the Amoraic period (A.D. 200–500) were in Galilee, where the Rabbinic texts were produced, the inscriptions in JPA datable to this period, the language of which is very close to that of the Rabbinic texts, have been found throughout Palestine (Sokoloff 1978: 161). In the present state of research it now seems that much of the linguistic variation can be attributed to other factors, such as differences in the chronological period in which the texts were written (Tal 1979) and varying degrees of linguistic conservatism according to the different stylistic registers in which they were written (Greenfield 1974, Yahalom 1993: 332–33).

The language of many of the Rabbinic texts and Targums that were originally written in JPA was corrupted in later mansuscripts and printed editions. The late copyists harmonized the language with the Eastern Aramaic of the Babylonian Talmud and the Aramaic of Targum Onkelos (originally written in Palestine but influenced by Babylonian Aramaic in its transmission), with which they were more familiar. For this reason a linguistic description of these must be based on manuscripts which contain the early, uncorrupted form of the text (Kutscher 1976, Sokoloff 1978). Reliable manuscripts of the Rabbinic and Targum texts as well as many of the other aforementioned sources of JPA have been preserved in manuscripts from the Cairo Genizah. This was a medieval repository for discarded manuscripts that was discovered in the Ben-Ezra synagogue of Old Cairo (*al-Fusṭāṭ*). Of particular importance for a study of the phonology of JPA are manuscripts with vocalization. Most of these are fragments of a Palestinian Targum that have been discovered in the Cairo Genziah. They are vocalized with either Tiberian or Palestinian vowel signs. Sporadic vocalization is found also in Genizah manuscripts of the Palestinian Talmud and of Aramaic poetry.

7.1. Consonants

The inventory of consonant phonemes (based on Fassberg 1991: 24–25) is seen in Table 7-1.

Each of these phonemes is represented by a separate letter of the Hebrew alphabet. It is not clear whether the primary articulation of /r/ was as an alveolar or a uvular (see below).

7.1.1. /bgdkpt/

The vocalized texts of the Palestinian Targums indicate that the phonemes /bgdkpt/ had both a plosive and a fricative allophone. In manuscripts with Tiberian vocalization, the plosive allophones are marked by the sign *dageš* and the fricative allophone by the absence of *dageš* and sometimes by the sign *rap̄e* (Fassberg 1991: 25).

Table 7-1. Jewish Palestinian Aramaic Consonants

Labials	/b/, /p/, /m/, /w/
Dentals/alveolars	/t/, /d/, /s/, /z/, /š/, /n/, /ṭ/, /ṣ/, /l/, /r/ (?)
Palatal	/y/
Velars	/k/, /g/
Uvular	/q/, /r/ (?)
Pharyngeals	/ʕ/, /ḥ/
Laryngeals	/ʔ/, /h/

There is no direct evidence for the precise phonetic realization of the fricative allophones of /bgdkpt/, though it is likely that they were the same as, or close to, their counterparts in the Tiberian pronunciation tradition of Biblical Hebrew and Aramaic, viz. [v], [ʁ], [ð], [χ], [f], [θ] respectively (see chapter 6). The occurrence of the fricative allophones was originally conditioned by the existence of a preceding vowel. As in Tiberian Hebrew, however, due to further phonetic processes that took place before the period in which the vocalized manuscripts were produced (10th–11th centuries A.D.), the fricative allophones are sometimes found also after a consonant, e.g. ʾayṯi 'he brought' (Fassberg 1991: 25).

Many JPA texts exhibit the interchange in their orthography of the letters *beth*, which normally represents /b/, and *waw*, which normally represents /w/. When this occurs, either *beth* represents consonantal /w/ or *waw* represents the fricative allophone of /b/. The first of these is far more common than the second. When representing a consonant, the letter *waw* is often written twice to distinguish it from its use as a *mater lectionis* for the vowel /o/. Examples: *lgb* 'inside' (= *lgww*, Kutscher 1976: 16), *wrbh* 'and he became intoxicated' (= *wrwwh*, ibid.), *lmhby* 'to be' (= *lmhwy*, Friedman 1980: 56), *sytbh* 'winter' (= *sytwh*, Naveh and Shaked 1993: 43), *wdlwwyy* 'and of plane-tree' (= *wdlbyy*, Fassberg 1991: 25). This demonstrates that the fricative allophone of /b/ had the same phonetic realization as the consonant /w/. This may have been [v] or [w]. It was most likely [v], since this was the realization in the Biblical reading traditions in Palestine (see chapter 6).

7.1.2. /s/

The phoneme /s/ is represented either by the letter *sin* or by the letter *samek̠*, reflecting the merger of the former with the latter, e.g. שָׂהֵיד/סָהֵיד *sahed* 'witness' (Fassberg 1991: 26; Dalman 1894: 53, 104).

7.1.3. /n/

Final /n/ is often elided after the diphthong /ay/, e.g. *myy* 'water' (< *myyn*, Kutscher 1976: 46), *tryy* 'two' (< *tryyn*, ibid. 26, Svedlund 1974: 31), *bʿyy* 'asking' (masc.pl. participle < *bʿyyn*, Kutscher 1976: 44, Svedlund 1974: 31), *ḥmyy* 'seeing' (masc.pl. participle < *ḥmyyn*, Kutscher 1976: 44).

There is a tendency to append a final *n* to indeclinable words ending in a vowel, reflecting a form of nasalization. Such an addition of final *n* is optional. This is clearly shown by an inscription from Jaffa (Klein 1939: 80, no. 1), where a man is called Ἰουδα in Greek but *ywdn* in Hebrew. In the Greek Septuagint translation of the Bible, the earliest parts of which are datable to the 3rd century B.C., a final *n* is sometimes added to proper names ending in a vowel, e.g. Σαλωμων 'Solomon' (< Hebrew *šlmh*). This may be evidence that this phonetic process already existed in the vernacular of the Jews of Palestine and Egypt at that period. Due to the existence of this appended *n* in JPA and its optional omission, an original final *n* in some indeclinable words is dropped. This is attested in a number of proper names, e.g. *ywḥnh* < *ywḥnn* 'Joḥanan' (Kutscher 1976: 62).

A final *n* is added also to other words. These include, e.g., *sgyn* 'much' (< *sgy*, Dalman 1894: 72), *kdwn* 'now' (< *kdw*, ibid. 73), *ʾntyn* 'you (fem.sg.)' (< *ʾnty*, Friedman 1980: 57), *pwtḥwn* 'open' plural imperative (< *ptwḥw*, Yahalom 1993: 334), *patḥun* 'they opened' (< *ptaḥu*, ibid. 339). Rather than through nasalization of the final vowel, the final *n* in many of these may have a different origin, e.g., by the process of analogy with other words with final *n*. The extent to which the appended *n* occurs, both by final nasalization and by grammatical anology, depends on the date and literary register of the text. It is less widespread in texts that reflect an earlier phase of JPA than in those reflecting later phases (Tal 1979, Yahalom 1993, Fassberg 1991: 73–74).

In JPA there was a tendency for word-final *m* to shift to *n*. This is attested in proper names, e.g. the place name *Mrwn* (< Biblical *Mrwm* 'Marom', Kutscher 1976: 63), and occasionally elsewhere, e.g. *ḥkyn* 'clever' (< *ḥkym*, Ginsberg 1933: 422). By the phonetic process described in the preceding paragraph the final *n* is sometimes elided, e.g. *Mrw* (< *Mrwn* < *Mrwm*, Kutscher 1976: 61), *Mryh* 'Maria' (< *Mryn* < *Mrym* 'Miriam', ibid.). The shift of final *m* > *n* may have been more extensive in JPA than is revealed by the orthography of the extant texts. It is attested in a number of Hebrew words in texts from Palestine written during the JPA period (Kutscher 1976: 58–60). It is also attested in the modern spoken Arabic dialects of the Levant, e.g. the personal name *Maryen* < *Maryam* (Feghali 1919: 70).

7.1.4. Pharyngeals /ḥ/, /ʿ/

There is evidence that the pharyngeals /ḥ/ and /ʿ/ were weakened in JPA spoken in some regions of Palestine to the extent that they were pronounced as the laryngeals *h* and *ʾ* or even completely reduced to zero. The weakening was apparently brought about by the influence of Greek, particularly in the Hellenized urban centers. In many areas, however, the pronunciation of the pharyngeals was retained. There is no evidence for their weakening in the Palestinian Targum fragments from the Cairo Genizah (Fassberg 1991: 27). Furthermore, scores of place names that were in use in Byzantine Palestine contain to this day the original pharyngeal consonants, e.g. *Ḵirbet Jaʿṭūn* < *Gʿtwn*, *Yānūḥ* < *Ynwḥ* (Kutscher 1976: 85–86). In modern spoken Western Aramaic, the pharyngeals have been retained.

The shift of the pharyngeal *ḥ* to *ʿ* is attested in several words in the Palestinian Talmud and Midrashim, e.g. *ʿwyh* 'snake' (< *ḥwyh*, Kutscher 1976: 71, Svedlund 1974: 35), *ʿyyb* 'guilty' (< *ḥyybʾ*, Kutscher 1976: 71), and in one instance in the Targum fragments from the Genizah (Fassberg 1991: 65). This shift of the unvoiced pharyngeal *ḥ* to the voiced pharyngeal *ʿ* no doubt reflects a lenition in the articulation, since unvoiced sounds are generally pronounced more fortis than their voiced counterparts. It was, therefore, the first stage in the loss of the pharyngeals.

7.1.5. /r/

We have no direct evidence for the precise phonetic realization of /r/. It should be noted, however, that *a* sometimes shifts to the back vowel *u/o* before /r/, e.g. *šwry* 'he began' (< *šari*, Svedlund 1974: 31), *bquryekon* 'in your cities' (< *bqaryekon*, Fassberg 1991: 69). This could have resulted from an uvular articulation of /r/ or from a secondary velarization of an alveolar articulation. These are the two phonetic realizations of /r/ in Tiberian Hebrew.

7.2. Vowels

The main source for our knowledge of the vowels of JPA is constituted by the Palestinian Targum fragments from the Cairo Genizah that are vocalized with Tiberian or Palestinian vowel signs (Fassberg 1991: 28–57). The other Palestinian Targums, viz. Targum Pseudo-Jonathan and the Fragment Targum, have Tiberian vocalization in their printed editions, but this is heavily influenced by the vocalization of Biblical Aramaic and Targum Onqelos and does not represent the original vowel system of JPA. Even the vocalization of the Targum fragments from the Genizah imitates that of the Tiberian tradition of Biblical Aramaic, and so caution is necessary when interpreting the data.

Although the vocalization in the Targum fragments from the Genizah was influenced by the standard Tiberian tradition of Biblical Aramaic, the vowel system of the language of the Targum fragments differed from that of the Tiberian pronunciation tradition. The vocalization of the Targum fragments appears to reflect the existence of five vowel phonemes: /a/, /e/, /i/, /o/, /u/ (Fassberg 1991: 30) and *šewa* vowels, which should perhaps be assigned to the phoneme /∅/. There are no phonemic contrasts of vowel length.

7.2.1. /a/

In manuscripts with Tiberian vocalization, /a/ is represented by either the vowel sign *qameṣ* or the sign *pataḥ*. Likewise, in those with Palestinian vocalization it is represented by two vowel signs, corresponding to Tiberian *qameṣ* and *pataḥ*. Tiberian *pataḥ* and its Palestinian equivalent predominates. This suggests that the phonetic realization of /a/ was closest to that of Tiberian *pataḥ*, i.e. an open front [a]. The confusion of *pataḥ* and *qameṣ* is attested also in the sporadic vocalizations of the Aramaic of Targum Neophyti and of the Palestinian Talmud (Fassberg 1991: 52).

7.2.2. /e/

In Targum manuscripts from the Genizah with Tiberian vocalization, /e/ is represented by one of the three signs *segol*, *ṣere*, or *ḥireq* (Fassberg 1991: 34–38). The most frequently used sign in most contexts is *segol*, suggesting that the phonetic realization was close to that of *segol* in the Tiberian pronunciation tradition, i.e. a half-open front [ɛ]. In non-final, open, stressed syllables, however, only *ṣere* is used, which implies that in this environment the realization was a higher vowel [e] corresponding to the quality of Tiberian *ṣere*.

In the Targum fragments from the Genizah, short [i] has shifted to a lower quality and has merged with the phoneme /e/, e.g. ʾ*ennun* 'they' (< ʾ*innun*, Fassberg 1991: 35), *lebbeh* 'his heart' (< *libbeh*, ibid.). The occasional vocalization with Tiberian *ḥireq* in unstressed closed syallables with an original [i] may reflect a fluctuation in the phonetic realization between [i] and [ɛ]. Alternatively it could be due to the influence of the standard Tiberian tradition of Biblical Aramaic, where short [i] is preserved. The [i] > [ɛ] shift is attested also in the sporadic vocalizations of the Aramaic of Targum Neophyti and of the Palestinian Talmud (Fassberg 1991: 52, Kutscher 1968: 233). Greek and Latin transcriptions of proper nouns and Hebrew words from the Septuagint (3rd century B.C.) until Jerome (4th–5th century A.D.) reflect the shift [i] > [ɛ] in closed unstressed syllables. This demonstrates that the shift had taken place in the pronunciation of Aramaic and the sub-standard pronunciation of Hebrew at this period among the Jews of Palestine. In the standard reading tradition of the Bible, these shifts were resisted to a greater extent (Kutscher 1968: 219–27).

In some cases /e/ in an unstressed closed syllable is the reflex of an original short *a* vowel. These can be divided into (i) those that are paralleled by an *a* > *i/e* shift in the equivalent word in a wide range of other Aramaic dialects and represent a shift that took place early in the history of Aramaic, e.g. *dekrin* 'males' (< *dakrin*, Fassberg 1991: 35), and (ii) those that are particular to JPA (and occasionally to some other Aramaic dialects of Syria-Palestine) and represent a later extension of this phonetic process to a wider range of words, e.g. *yemma* 'the sea' (< *yamma*, ibid. 66), *kepna* 'the famine' (< *kapna*, ibid.).

In late texts written in the Arab period, long *ā* is occasionally represented by the *mater lectionis y*, which reflects the raising of the vowel to the region of [ē], e.g. *dmšmšyn* 'who serve (fem.pl.)' and *ṣny'yth* 'modest (fem.pl.)' (Friedman 1980: 58) in place of the expected fem. pl. endings -*ān*, -*ātā*. This shift took place most likely under the influence of Arabic, where long [ā] was raised towards [ē] by a process known as *'imāla*. It is attested also Christian Palestinian Aramaic texts from the same period (Müller-Kessler 1991: 60).

/e/ in the Targum fragments from the Genizah is sometimes the reflex of an original diphthong *ay*, e.g. *millekon* 'your words' (< *millaykon*, Fassberg 1991: 36).

7.2.3. /i/

/i/ is the reflex of [ī] vowels that were long at the time of the [i] > [ɛ] shift, e.g. *mitu* 'they died', *qṭila* 'the dead one' (Fassberg 1991: 38).

7.2.4. /o/

The vocalized Targum fragments appear to reflect a general shift of short [u] to [o], e.g. *qorbanak* 'your sacrifice' (< *qurbanak*, Fassberg 1991: 40), *yeqṭol* 'he will kill' (< *yiqṭul*, ibid. 41). The vowel /o/ (< [u]) is occasionally represented with Tiberian *šureq*, *qameṣ* and even *pataḥ*. Most of these cases, however, can be explained as arising through the influence of the standard

Tiberian vocalization of Biblical Aramaic (ibid. 40–42). Greek and Latin transcriptions of proper nouns and Hebrew words from the Septuagint (3rd century B.C.) until Jerome (4th–5th century A.D.) reflect the shift [u] > [o] in closed unstressed syllables (Kutscher 1968: 219–27).

/o/ before a labial consonant is sometimes the reflex of an original short *a*. This is represented by the *mater lectionis w*, e.g. *šwbh* 'Sabbath' (< *šabbā*, Kutscher 1976: 17), *'wp* 'also' (< *'ap̄*, ibid.), *šwb'yn* 'seventy' (< *šab'īn*, Friedman 1980: 57), *rwbyn* 'large (masc.pl.)' (< *rabbīn*, ibid.). In the vocalized fragments of the Targum from the Genizah this vowel is [o] or [u], which are both allophones of /o/ (see above), e.g. *gobrin* 'men' (< *gabrin*, Fassberg 1991: 69), *šub'a* 'seven' (< *šab'a*, Fassberg 1991: 69). This shift occurs occasionally before *r* and *l*, e.g. *pwlg* 'half' (< *palga* Friedman 1980: 58), *šwry* 'he began' (< *šari*, Svedlund 1974: 31), *bquryekon* 'in your cities' (< *bqaryekon*, Fassberg 1991: 69).

In some cases /o/ is the reflex of an original diphthong [aw], e.g. *tora* 'the ox' (< *tawra*, Fassberg 1991: 41), *'oledt* 'you begat' (< *'awledt*, ibid.).

7.2.5. /u/

/u/ is the reflex of [ū] vowels that were long at the time of the [u] > [o] shift, e.g. *ydunun* 'they will judge', *sebu* 'old age' (Fassberg 1991: 42).

7.2.6. /∅/ ? (Šewa)

Short vowels in open unstressed syllables after a non-guttural consonant are generally represented by the *šewa* sign in Targum fragments with Tiberian vocalization. We have little external evidence for vowel length differences in JPA. Let us assume, however, that vowels in open syllables that are regularly represented by vowel signs rather than the *šewa* sign (e.g. *napeq* 'going forth') were long, as was the case in Tiberian Hebrew. If this were the case, then vowels marked by the *šewa* sign would be distinguished from other vowels in open syllables by their shortness. It seems, moreover, that such short vowels in open syllables would not contrast phonemically with zero, so perhaps they should be analyzed as allophones of the phoneme /∅/, as is the case with *šewa* vowels in Tiberian Hebrew phonology. Occasionally the *pataḥ* [a] sign is used where one would expect *šewa*, suggesting that vocalic *šewa* was pronounced with the quality of [a], which was its normal phonetic realization in the Tiberian pronunciation tradition (Fassberg 1991: 47) and is attested also in some Hebrew manuscripts with Palestinian vocalization.

The interchange of the Tiberian signs *šewa* and *pataḥ* is found also in the vocalization of poetry written in JPA (Yahalom and Sokoloff 1995 Introduction). Furthermore, when two vocalic *šewa*s follow one another in the Targum manuscripts from the Genizah, the second *šewa* is elided and the first is represented by an *a* vowel sign, e.g. *labsar* 'to the flesh of' (Fassberg 1991: 107). Conversely, the *šewa* sign is sporadically used to represent an [a] in a closed syllable (ibid. 33). Before /y/ vocalic *šewa* is often represented by *ḥireq* [i], which also corresponds to the Tiberian pronunciation tradition. In manuscripts with Palestinian vocalization an *e* vowel sign is often used where vocalic *šewa* would occur in Tiberian vocalization (ibid. 46). The practice of representing vocalic *šewa* with an *e* vowel sign is found also in Hebrew manuscripts with Palestinian vocalization. It is possible, therefore, that the Tiberian and Palestinian reading traditions of Hebrew influenced the scribes who vocalized the Aramaic texts, and it is difficult to establish with any certainty the authentic quality of the vocalic *šewa* in the Aramaic.

Vocalic *šewa* is, occasionally, represented by a *mater lectionis*. In Targum texts with Palestinian vocalization, *mater lectionis yod* is found in this function (Fassberg 1991: 63). In some amulets and inscriptions in JPA, vocalic *šewa* before a labial is represented by *mater lectionis waw*. This is attested in the word *šwmyh* 'heaven' (< *šamayya*, Naveh 1978: 40–42, 106–9; Naveh and Shaked 1985: 50–54, 82–85). The [a] > [o] shift before labials, therefore, operated on short vowels in closed and open syllables alike. The existence of the vowel [o] shows that the quality of the vowel before the shift must have been [a], i.e., that of the Tiberian *šewa*. It is not clear whether this can be taken as evidence that short vowels in open unstressed syllables in general were leveled to the quality of [a], as in the Tiberian tradition.

7.3. Diphthongs

In most environments, the diphthong /ay/ does not contract. In unvocalized texts the existence of the diphthong is shown by the many cases where the [y] is spelled with double *yy*, which indicated that the letter was to be pronounced as consonantal /y/ and not as a vowel: *byyty* 'my house', *'yynh* 'the eye'), *ḥyylh* 'the strength' (Kutscher 1976: 19). /ay/ contracts to /e/ before pronominal suffixes on masc. plural and dual nouns, e.g. *bnek* 'your children' (Fassberg 1991: 58).

The reflex of an original diphthong *aw*, on the other hand, is generally /o/ in JPA, e.g. *tor* 'ox' (< *tawr*, Fassberg 1991: 58).

References

Dalman, Gustaf. 1894. *Grammatik des Jüdisch-Palästinischen Aramäisch.* Leipzig: Hinrichs.

Fassberg, Steven E. 1991. *A Grammar of the Palestinian Targum Fragments from the Cairo Genizah* (Harvard Semitic Series 38). Atlanta: Scholars Press.

Feghali, Michel T. 1919. *Le parler de Kfar ʿAbîda (Liban–Syrie).* Paris: Geuthner.

Fitzmyer, Joseph A. 1966. *The Genesis Apocryphon of Qumran Cave I: A Commentary* (Biblica et Orientalia 18). Rome: Biblical Institute Press.

Friedman, Mordechai A. 1980. *Jewish Marriage in Palestine.* Tel-Aviv: Tel-Aviv University.

Ginsberg, H. Louis. 1933. "Zu den Dialekten des Talmudischen-Hebräischen." *Monatsschrift für Geschichte und Wissenschaft des Judentums* 77: 413–29.

Goitein, Shlomo D. 1966. "Four Old Marriage Contracts from the Cairo Genizah" (in Hebrew). *Lěšonénu* 30: 197–216.

Greenfield, Jonas C. 1974. "Standard Literary Aramaic." In *Actes du premier congrès international de linguistique sémitique et chamito-sémitique* (Janua Linguarum Series Practica 159), ed. André Caquot and David Cohen, pp. 280–89. The Hague: Mouton.

Klein, Samuel. 1939. *Sep̄er ha-Yiššuv*, vol. 1. Jerusalem: Dvir.

Kutscher, Eduard Y. 1976. *Studies in Galilean Aramaic*, trans. Michael Sokoloff. Ramat-Gan: Bar-Ilan University.

———. 1968. "Articulation of the Vowels *u, i* in Transcriptions of Biblical Hebrew, in Galilean Aramaic, and in Mishnaic Hebrew" (in Hebrew). In *Benjamin de Vries Memorial Volume*, ed. E. Melamad, pp. 218–51. Jerusalem: Tel-Aviv University and Stichting Fronika Sander Fonds.

Müller-Kessler, Christa. 1991. *Grammatik des Christlich-Palästinisch-Aramäischen*, part 1. Hildesheim: Olms.

Naveh, Joseph. 1978. *On Stone and Mosaic: The Aramaic and Hebrew Inscriptions from Ancient Synagogues* (in Hebrew). Tel-Aviv: Israel Exploration Society.

Naveh, Joseph, and Shaul Shaked. 1985. *Amulets and Magic Bowls: Aramaic Incantations of Late Antiquity.* Jerusalem: Magnes.

———. 1993. *Magic Spells and Formulae: Aramaic Incantations of Late Antiquity.* Jerusalem: Magnes.

Rosenthal, Franz. 1939. *Die aramaistische Forschung seit Th. Nöldekes Veröffentlichungen*. Leiden: Brill.

Sokoloff, Michael. 1978. "The Current State of Research on Galilean Aramaic." *Journal of Near Eastern Studies* 37: 161–67.

———. 1990. *A Dictionary of Jewish Palestinian Aramaic of the Byzantine Period*. Ramat-Gan: Bar-Ilan University.

Svedlund, Gerhard. 1974. *The Aramaic Portions of the Pesiqta de Rab Kahana* (Acta Universitatis Upsaliensis). Uppsala.

Tal, Abraham. 1979. "Layers in Jewish Palestinian Aramaic" (in Hebrew). *Lěšonénu* 43: 165–84.

Yahalom, Joseph. 1993. "Verbal Suffixes in Jewish Palestinian Aramaic" (in Hebrew). In *Hebrew and Jewish Studies in Honour of Joshua Blau*, ed. M. Bar Asher, Z. Ben-Hayyim, M. J. Kister, A. Levin, S. Shaked, and A. Tal, pp. 331–40. Jerusalem: Tel-Aviv University and the Hebrew University of Jerusalem.

Yahalom, Joseph, and Michael Sokoloff. 1995. *Aramaic Poetry of the Byzantine Period from Eretz Israel* (in Hebrew). Jerusalem: Israel Academy of Sciences and Humanities.

Chapter 8
Old Aramaic Phonology
Stanislav Segert
University of California, Los Angeles

8.1. Terms and problems

Under the heading "Old Aramaic" the basically uniform, but not monolithic language preserved in sources composed in the first millennium B.C. is dealt with here. "Biblical Aramaic," the language of texts mostly from the 6th, 5th and 2nd centuries B.C., is one part of Old Aramaic.

The terminology for stages and dialects of Old Aramaic is not uniform. Here the term "Old Aramaic" is used for the entire first millennium B.C. In some other publications this term is applied only to the older stage, until 612 B.C. approximately; for this stage the term "Early Aramaic" is used here.

The use of Aramaic as the official language in a great part of the Persian Empire is expressed in the terms "Imperial Aramaic," calqued from German *Reichsaramäisch*, or more generally, "Official Aramaic." From a linguistic viewpoint "Biblical Aramaic" is a part of this stage. As the Aramaic texts from the second half of the first millennium B.C. reflect mostly the uniform language of the Persian Empire even after its termination in the 4th century B.C., the period of "Imperial Aramaic" can be extended to the 2nd century B.C., before the splitting of the Aramaic languages into Western and Eastern groups.

The notion of "phonology" in its narrower sense is applicable for the written documents, the phonemes of which have to be reconstructed. But the pronunciation of the Aramaic passages of the Bible has been preserved also by oral tradition, which could be influenced by the later development of Aramaic and its related languages. Thus some phonetic observations can be made in this survey.

The overwhelming majority of Old Aramaic texts are written in an alphabet taken over from Phoenician. A few texts and some words are attested in

ABBREVIATIONS: BA, Biblical Aramaic; DP, Demotic Papyrus; EA, Early Aramaic; IA, Imperial (Official) Aramaic; OA, Old Aramaic; SA, Samalian Aramaic.

the Mesopotamian cuneiform syllabary. An important manuscript on papyrus, Amherst Egyptian 63 (containing mostly poetry), is written in Egyptian demotic script. This important text is being edited by Richard C. Steiner; he kindly provided relevant data which are incorporated in the text of this chapter.

Aramaic was used for communication between peoples of different language backgrounds, and also in areas where other languages were more common. In the Assyrian and Babylonian Empires Aramaic connected the ruling class speaking Akkadian with the common Aramaic people. For contact with Hebrew speakers cf. 2 Kings 18:26. Judeans returning from the Babylonian exile brought with them the Aramaic language. In the multilingual Persian Empire Aramaic was introduced as official language in large areas of Western Asia and also in Egypt. After the demise of the Persian Empire in the 4th century B.C., Aramaic was still used in many countries.

The combination of data from Aramaic texts along with the traditional pronunciation, and some features of other Aramaic and related languages, make it possible to reconstruct Old Aramaic phonology, even if this is not always perfectly reliable.

8.2. Sources

When Emil Kautzsch published his German grammar of BA in 1884, very few other Old Aramaic texts were known. Since that time hundreds of inscriptions and papyri have been found, mostly by excavations in various Near Eastern countries.

Aramaic biblical texts in the books of Ezra and Daniel represent about 1% of the Old Testament canon. Comparison of complete Masoretic texts written around 1000 A.D. with fragments from the Qumran area near Jericho shows that for 1,000 years these texts were transmitted with few changes in the consonantal writing. Vowel signs were added in the last centuries of the first millennium A.D.; they are completely accessible according to the Tiberian system, with some sections also in the older Babylonian vocalization.

The archaic dialect of the kingdom of Sam'al ('North') is represented by three inscriptions from the 8th century B.C. found in the ruins of the capital of Ya'udi (near Zincirli in southern Turkey).

Early or Ancient Aramaic texts on stone, from the 9th–7th century B.C., were preserved in Syria. Texts from the later part of this period were written on clay tablets and ostraca (sherds) in Assyria (northern Iraq).

Texts from the Imperial Aramaic stage, about the 7th–2nd century B.C., were found in many countries, from western Asia Minor to the Indus Valley, from the Caucasus to Upper Egypt. They were written on stone and sherds. A great number of papyri were preserved in Egypt, mostly from the Jewish military colony on the Nile island Jeb (Elephantine) near Seven (Aswan).

The clay tablet in syllabic cuneiform script found in Uruk in Lower Mesopotamia shows, like some other texts from Mesopotamia, some features of the Eastern Imperial Aramaic dialect.

A large collection of Aramaic texts written in Egyptian demotic script is preserved on Papyrus Amherst Egyptian 63 in the Pierpont Morgan Library in New York. After short samples were published by Raymond Bowman in 1944, Charles F. Nims and Richard C. Steiner have published since 1983 several cultic poetic texts. Steiner is now preparing a complete edition of the papyrus. This papyrus scroll found at Thebes in Egypt was written probably in the early Ptolemaic period, in the third century B.C., but many poems, like that parallel to biblical Psalm 20 or that on an Assyrian king, point to older traditions. This Upper Egyptian text exhibits features of Western Aramaic, including some which were previously thought to be Late Aramaic innovations.

Quotation from sources in the alphabetic script are presented here in italics, those from cuneiform syllabaries also in italics, with dashes between transcriptions of syllabic signs. The quotations from the text in the demotic script are marked DP (Demotic Papyrus).

8.3. Kinds of phonological data

Ancient phonological features are represented by phonemic signs and graphic devices in ancient and medieval texts. This evidence is supplemented by phonetic observations on the traditional pronunciation patterns of Biblical Aramaic.

The alphabetic script of Phoenician origin has 22 graphemes. In principle each of them indicated one consonant phoneme.

As in Early Aramaic the number of consonant phonemes was more than 22, some letters had to indicate more than one consonant. E.g., the letter *z* was used both for the sibilant /z/ and interdental /d̠/; cf. § 8.4.1.

Since the 9th century B.C. some consonant letters were used also for indication of vocalic phonemes. The letter *w* could indicate the bilabial consonant /w/, the long vowel /ū/, or the diphthong /au/. Similarly the letter *y* served to indicate the consonant /y/, the long vowel /ī/, or the diphthong /ai/. Also the letters *h* and *'* were used for indicating vowels, mostly long /ā/.

In the late centuries of the first millennium A.D. specific graphic signs for vowels—and accents—were introduced into Biblical Aramaic texts. The older Babylonian system used signs above consonant letters; the Tiberian system put most signs beneath the letters.

The gemination of consonants is marked only in the Biblical Aramaic of the Tiberian tradition.

The cuneiform syllabary indicated by its vocalic components vowels—except /o/, often also their length. However, the rendering of consonant phonemes by consonant components is not always exact.

The demotic script is able to distinguish some phonemes which in the Aramaic alphabet are rendered by a common grapheme. The uvular *ḫ* is distinguished from pharyngeal *ḥ*, e.g in *ḫ.mr^m* 'wine' versus *ḥ.m.^{m}* 'venom' (cf. Ugaritic *ḫmr* 'wine', *ḥmt* 'venom'). The voiced uvular *ġ* is indicated in DP by *ḫ* or *ḥ*, e.g. *.rḫ.^{m}* /'arġ-/ 'earth'.

The uninterrupted tradition of reading Biblical Aramaic texts provided by vocalic and accentual signs in the late first millennium B.C. allows phonetic observation about the pronunciation of sounds indicated by graphemes and additional signs. The older Babylonian tradition was preserved only in Yemen; the younger tradition fixed in Tiberias is commonly employed.

These traditions as well as their graphic bases were influenced by later commonly spoken Aramaic dialects and by the traditional pronunciation of Biblical Hebrew.

8.4. Consonantal phonemes: Inventory and systemic changes

The number of consonant phonemes in EA was larger than in IA. Several allophones developed in BA.

In Table 8-1 this situation is indicated by different graphics: graphemes are in angle brackets, their reconstructed pronunciation within slants, the traditional pronunciation presently observed within square brackets.

8.4.1. Interdentals

The interdentals were in the Early Aramaic texts indicated by letters corresponding to the equivalent words in Canaanite languages, Phoenician and Hebrew: /t̯/ by *š*, e.g. *šlš* /t̯-l-t̯/ 'three', cf. Hebrew *šlš*; /d̯/ by *z*, e.g. *zhb* /d̯-h-b/ 'gold', cf. Hebrew *zhb*; /z̯/ (/ṭ̯/) by *ṣ*, e.g. *ṣby* 'gazelle', cf. Hebrew *ṣby*.

Table 8-1. Old Aramaic Consonants

	Early Aramaic			Imperial Aramaic			Biblical Aramaic allophones		
	Emphatic	Voiced	Unvoiced	Emphatic	Voiced	Unvoiced	Emphatic	Voiced	Unvoiced
Laryngeals		<'>	<h>		<'>	<h>			
Pharyngeals		<'>	<ḥ>		<'>	<ḥ>			
Uvulars		/ġ/	/ḫ/					[ġ]	[ḵ]
Velars	<q>	<g>	<k>	<q>	<g>	<k>			
Palatovelars			<š>			<š>			
Sibilants	<ṣ>	<z>	<s>	<ṣ>	<z>	<s>			[ś]
Interdentals	/ẓ (ṭ)/	/ḏ/	/ṯ/					[ḏ]	[ṯ]
Dentals	<ṭ>	<d>	<t>	<ṭ>	<d>	<t>			
Labials		<b>	<p>		<b>	<p>			
Bilabials								[b̄]	[p̄]
Linguals		<l r>			<l r>				
Nasals		<n m>			<n m>				
Semivowels		<y w>			<y w>				

In the Tell Fekheriye inscription (9th century B.C.) the interdental /ṯ/ is indicated by the phonetically close sibilant letter s, e.g. y-s-b /y-ṯ-b/ 'to sit', while this word is written in other Early Aramaic texts as y-š-b, cf. Hebrew and Phoenician y-š-b.

The consonant going back to Proto-Semitic *ḍ—or perhaps originally lateralized *ḍˡ—is indicated in EA by the letter q which is by its place of articulation close to /ġ/; e.g. 'rq /'-r-ġ/ 'earth' (cf. Arab. '-r-ḍ, Phoen. and Hebr. '-r-ṣ), qmr /ġ-m-r/ 'wool' (cf. Hebr. ṣ-m-r).

In IA this consonant indicated in EA by q changed into the pharyngeal '; e.g. 'r', 'mr. For another interpretation of these facts, based on the demotic text, see Steiner (1991a: 1499–1501).

The interdentals changed in IA into dentals; new forms of words listed above were written tlt, DP t.rt.ᵐ; dhb, DP t.h.bᵐ; ṭby.

8.4.2. Other consonants

After vowels some simple plosive consonants, /t/, /b/, /p/, developed in later BA tradition spirant position variants (allophones), [ḡ] (cf. /ǵ/), [k̲] (cf. Arab. ḫ), [d̲] (cf. /ḏ/), [t̲] (cf./ṯ/), [b̲] (cf. English [v]), [p̄] (cf. Arab. f).

The dot above the left side of the letter š in BA texts with Tiberian signs indicates the pronunciation as [ś] (śīn).

8.5. Vocalic phonemes: Inventory and systemic changes

All vowels are indicated in BA texts from about 1000 A.D. These traditions reflect to a large extent the IA pronunciation, but they were affected by later commonly spoken Aramaic dialects and by the traditional pronunciation of Biblical Hebrew. For reconstruction of EA vocalism, indication of vowels by consonant letters and evidence from non-alphabetic sources can be used.

The Tiberian vocalization system is exact, but it applies the patterns of the traditional pronunciation of Hebrew to Aramaic.

The Babylonian vocalization system is simpler and closer to the original BA pronunciation.

The consonant letters *y*, *w*, *h*, and *'* were used for long vowels.

In the following survey the vowels according to Babylonian and Tiberian systems are presented:

Babylonian system: *i e a o u* short and long; reduced mixed vowel ^{ə}
Tiberian system: the same vowels, minus long /ā/, and additional vowels: æ and å, short, long, reduced; reduced ^{a}

Vowel signs are identical for short and long vowels. Long vowels are often indicated by consonant letters which were introduced already in EA and IA stages.

In the Uruk incantation text, which probably reflects the pronunciation of the early IA stage, qualities and quantities of vowels are indicated by vocalic components of cuneiform syllabic signs.

The vowel /o/ is indicated by -*u*- components; cf. *ti-ḫu-ú-tú* /tiḫōt-/, cf. BA *t^{ə}ḥōt* 'below'.

Length is indicated, but not consistently, by repeating vocalic elements; *qu-ú-mi-* /qūmī-/ 'stand up!' (fem.); but *ša-am-lat* /šamlat/, cf. Arab. *šamlat-*, Hebr. *śimlat* < *śam-* 'cloak, clothing'.

The most reliable indicators of vowels in the demotic papyrus are the signs for /w/ and /y/ (including multiconsonantal signs like *sw* and *ty*). In addition to their consonantal value, these signs also have vocalic value, being used to represent high back and high front vowels, respectively.

It can be supposed that the inventory of vowels was smaller in EA and older stages of IA.

Long vowels /ō/ and /ē/ developed mostly as diphthongs /aw/ and /ai/ were monophthongized (cf. § 8.7.2).

Long /ā/ remained basically unchanged also in the Babylonian tradition of BA. In the late Tiberian tradition of BA it is pronounced like Hebrew more closed *ā̊*.

8.6. Conditioned consonant changes

8.6.1. By position in word or syllable

The glottal stop ' was elided at the end of words and syllables; e.g. IA *śgy'*, BA *śaggi(')*, and IA *śgy* /śaggī/ < *-*i*'*; IA *(-)m'mr, (-)mmr*; BA *mē(')mar, mēmar* /mēmar/ < *mi'm-* 'to say'. In the demotic papyrus, elision of ' is also attested as a sandhi phenomenon, e.g., $\overline{mn}.n.nty^m\ ety^m$ [manantī 'attī].

If the postpositive article /-ā/ developed from an original deictic element *-'ā, the elision of final glottal stop could be supposed: *-'ā > *-á' > /-ā̊/. But the letter ' can be considered a device for indicating the long vowel /-ā/.

The elision of *h* sporadically attested for suffixed pronouns in IA is rather common in the DP, e.g. $mšhtn^m$ 'their sin'. The feminine marker *-t* is elided in the absolute state: *millat-* (cf. construct state *millat*) > *millā(h)* /millā/ 'word'; *malkūt-* (cf. constr. *malkūt*) > *malkū* 'kingdom'.

The final consonant of pronouns and perfect forms of 2nd and 3rd person pl. masc. was -*m* in IA and Ezra, but -*n* in the younger BA, in Daniel.

In the DP, final *n* preceded by the diphthong *ay* may be deleted as later in Galilean Aramaic, e.g., $k.py^m$ 'overturned' (masc. pl.) and $b.y.^m$ 'among'.

8.6.2. By combination of consonants

Assimilation and dissimilation occur mostly at nasals and liquids.

Regressive total assimilation of the nasal /n/ to the immediately following consonant is very frequent, but forms without assimilation are attested. Cf. DP $\overline{in}p.kw$ 'take out', EA *ypq* 'he goes out', and IA *tnpq* 'she goes out'; BA *yippel* 'he falls down'; IA *ttn* and *tntn*, BA *tintēn* 'you give' (2nd person sg. masc.). Such assimilation can be observed on the verb *l-q-ḥ* 'to take': EA *yqḥ* and *ylqḥ* 'he takes', IA *'lqḥ* 'I take'.

Progressive assimilation is attested for the verb *s-l-q* 'to get up': EA *ysq* 'he gets up', BA *hassíqū* 'they brought up'.

Geminated consonants can be dissolved into *n* + simple consonant: *hassāqā > IA *hnsqh*, BA *hansāqā* 'to bring up'; *ha"ālā (inf. Haf'el of *'-l-l*; cf.

hæ'ālā BA) > han'ālā 'to introduce'; DP hnḫ.rw hnǵlw 'they were brought in'. Some forms with n + consonant in late IA and in BA may be the result of this dissimilation; cf. ttn, tntn, tinten.

Dissimilative tendencies were active in replacing consonants close in their articulation place by consonants more distant. Instead of original *b-n, preserved in plural bnn (cf. Hebr. and Phoen. bn), Aram. has br in EA and IA, bar in BA for 'son'; also brh 'daughter', pl. bnt. Original *n, preserved in the ordinal numeral IA tnyn, BA tinyānā(h) (fem.) 'second' (cf. Ugar. ṯn, Hebr. šny(m), Phoen. šnm 'two' was replaced by r in the cardinal numeral 'two'; IA tryn, BA tartēn (fem.) DP tīry.^{m}.

Liquids also participate in metathesis. Cf. IA (and BA) tr' 'gate'; the original sequence is preserved in Ugar. ṯǵr and Hebr. and Phoen. š'r; cf. SA lgry (du. constr.) 'feet', DP r.krȳk.^{m} (lgryk) 'your feet' and IA rgly 'my foot'.

If two emphatic consonants are together in one root, one of them can be dissimilated: IA kṣph 'his anger', original q preserved in BA q^{ə}ṣap; q-t-l 'to kill' in SA and RA, q-ṭ-l in RA and IA.

8.6.3. By contacts with vowels

The semivowel y can be elided between two long vowels; cf. IA qym /qāyēm/ and BA qā'ēm 'standing up'.

8.7. Conditioned vowel changes

Short vowels in open syllables were reduced or elided in later IA and BA. The transition can be observed in the cuneiform Uruk text: ga-ba-ri-e and ga-ab-ri-e 'men'. Cf. š^{ə}nat (constr.) < *šanat 'year (of)'; malk^{ə}tā < *malkatā 'the queen'; kāt^{ə}bā 'writing' (fem. partic.) < *kātibat; yišk^{ə}nūn 'they dwell'; elision: ḥatmah < *ḥatam-ah- 'he sealed it (fem.)'.

Primary vowels change into secondary ones in closed syllables: i – e, e.g. BA s^{ə}gid 'he did homage' – š^{ə}leṭ 'he ruled'; ī – ē, e.g. BA h^{a}qīm and h^{a}qēm 'he set up'; u – o, cf. BA gubbā (determinate) and gōb (absolute) '(the) pit'.

In BA the vowel /a/ in a closed unstressed syllable can change into /i/, e.g. *baśrā (cf. Hebr. bāśār) > biśrā 'the flesh'.

New vowels are inserted to avoid clusters of consonants: in the segolate nouns, e.g. *malk- > mælæk 'king', *-lm- > ṣ^{ə}lem 'statue'; in the 1st person sg. masc. of perfect: *šam't- > šim'eṯ 'I heard'.

Similar vowels in adjacent syllables can be dissimilated: *'abū-hū > 'abū́hī 'his father'.

Laryngeals, pharyngeals, and *r* tend to change the adjacent vowels in the direction toward /a/: **sāpir > sāpar* 'writing (partic.), scribe'; **kāhin-ā > kāhᵃnā* 'the priest'; **i – æ* in the infinitive of the *miqtal* pattern (cf. *mišbaq* 'to let') *mæʽbaḏ* 'to make'. In the Tiberian tradition *a* is inserted between long vowel and the final pharyngeal: *rūaḥ* 'spirit', *tērōaʽ* 'she crushes'.

8.7.1. Compensatory lengthening
Vowels are lengthened as compensation for loss of "weak" consonants.

Compensatory vowel lengthening occurs after the loss of glottal stop: **riʼš > BA rē(ʼ)š*, cf. IA *rš* '(the) head'; **ba-ʼtar > BA bā(ʼ)ṯar* 'after', BA *bāṯᵊrāḵ* 'after you'.

As compensation for simplification of the doubled consonant the preceding vowel is lengthened: **min-ʼarʽā > miʼ-ʼarʽā > BA mēʼarʽā* 'from the earth'; **-hh- > BA mitbāhal* 'frightened'; **-rr- BA > bārik* 'he blessed', BA *tārāʽ-* 'gate-keeper'.

8.7.2. Monophthongization
Diphthongs /aw/ and /ai/ were monophthongized in IA and BA, into /ō/ and /ē/ respectively: **yawm > IA ywm* and *ym*, BA *yōm*; IA *byt*, BA *baytā* 'the house'; IA *byt*, BA *bē(y)ṯ* (constr.) 'house (of)'.

8.8. Other phonological features

8.8.1. Word stress
This suprasegmental feature can be observed directly in BA texts provided with accent signs and in their traditional pronunciation. For older stages only inferences supported by reconstructions and analogies can be delivered.

In the Masoretic accentuation of BA (corresponding apparently to Hebrew accentuation) most words have stress on the last syllable. The following types of words have accent on the last but one syllable: segolate nouns and verbal forms with anaptyctic vowel in the last syllable, e.g. *mǽlæk < *malk-* 'king', *śǽmæṯ < *śāmt(u)* 'I set'; verbal forms with afformatives ending on long vowel, e.g. *ᵃkúlī* 'eat!' (fem.), *yē(ʼ)báḏū* 'may they perish', *šᵊʼélnā* 'we asked'; weak verbs with long vowel in the 3rd sg. fem. perfect, *sápaṯ* 'she was fulfilled'; words going back to (adverbial) accusatives: *ʽéllā* 'above'; words provided with suffixed pronouns consisting of consonant + vowel, e.g. *ʽaḇḏṓhī* 'his servants', *haʽélnī* 'bring me in!'.

Most of the types just given point to original accentuation on the last but one syllable. After short end vowels indicating cases or persons, perhaps partially still preserved in earlier IA—cf. (*mi-in*) *ig-ga-ri* '(from) wall', *ḫa-al-li-tú* /ʾallítu/ 'I entered', in the Uruk text—the originally last but one syllable became the last one, but the accent remained on it.

8.8.2. Syllables

Quantities of vowels and accents can be exactly observed only in the Tiberian tradition of BA. Some of these features are the results of a relatively late development.

Open syllables with long vowels (C$\bar{\text{V}}$) appear as stressed and unstressed. Only rarely open syllables with short vowels (CV) are attested. They changed into syllables with reduced vowels (C^v).

Closed syllables with short vowels (CVC) occur with or without stress, those with long vowels (C$\bar{\text{V}}$C) with stress, thus mostly at the end of words.

These observations may be applied for ostensible consonant clusters at the end of words: cf. "^{a}|*baḏ*|*t^ə* 'you made' (sg. masc.)

Selective Bibliography

Abou-Assaf, Ali, Pierre Bordreuil, and Alan R. Millard. 1982. *La statue de Tell Fekherye et son inscription bilingue assyro-araméenne*. Paris: Recherche sur les civilisations.

Bauer, Hans, and Pontus Leander. 1927. *Grammatik des Biblisch-Aramäischen*. Halle/Saale: Niemeyer.

———. 1929. *Kurzgefasste biblisch-aramäische Grammatik*. Halle/Saale: Niemeyer.

Degen, Rainer. 1969. *Altaramäische Grammatik der Inschriften des 10.–8. Jh. v. Chr.* Wiesbaden: Deutsche Morgenländische Gesellschaft.

Dion, Paul-Eugène. 1974. *La langue de Ya'udi*. Waterloo, Ontario: Corporation for the Publication of Academic Studies in Religion in Canada.

Drijvers, H. J. W. 1973. "Aramaic." In *A Basic Bibliography for the Study of the Semitic Languages*, ed. J. A. Hospers, vol. 1, pp. 290–335. Leiden: Brill.

Fitzmyer, Joseph A., and Kaufman, Stephen A., eds. 1992. *An Aramaic Bibliography*, part 1, *Old, Official, and Biblical Aramaic*. Baltimore: The Johns Hopkins University Press.

Kautzsch, Emil. 1884. *Grammatik des Biblisch-Aramäischen*. Leipzig: Vogel.

Kutscher, Eduard Yechezkel. 1970. "Aramaic." In *Current Trends in Linguistics*, ed. Thomas A. Sebeok, vol. 6, *Linguistics in South West Asia and North Africa*, pp. 347–412. The Hague: Mouton.

Leander, Pontus. 1928. *Laut- und Formenlehre des Ägyptisch-Aramäischen*. Göteborg (repr. Hildesheim: Olms, 1966.).

Rosenthal, Franz 1939. *Die aramaistische Forschung*. Leiden: Brill (repr. 1964).

———. 1961. *A Grammar of Biblical Aramaic*. Wiesbaden: Harrassowitz.

Segert, Stanislav 1956. "Mluvnice aramejštiny" (A grammar of Aramaic). In Otakar Klíma and Stanislav Segert, *Mluvnice hebrejštiny a aramejštiny* (A grammar of Hebrew and Aramaic), pp. 12–17, 20–21, 237–302. Prague: Nakladatelství Československé akademie věd.

———. 1975. *Altaramäische Grammatik*. Leipzig: Enzyklopädie (repr. 1990).

Steiner, Richard C. 1991a. "Addenda to *The Case for Fricative-Laterals in Proto-Semitic*." In *Semitic Studies in Honor of Wolf Leslau*, ed. Alan S. Kaye, pp. 1499–1513. Wiesbaden: Harrassowitz.

———. 1991b. "The Aramaic Text in Demotic Script: The Liturgy of a New Year's Festival Imported from Bethel to Syene by Exiles from Rash." *Journal of the American Oriental Society* 111: 362–63 [bibliography in note 1].

Strack, Hermann L. 1911. *Grammatik des Biblisch-Aramäischen*, 5th ed. Munich: Beck.

Chapter 9
Classical Syriac Phonology
Peter T. Daniels
University of Chicago

9.1. Introduction

9.1.1. *The Syriac language*

The astute eighteenth-century Orientalist Johann David Michaelis recommended that those who would undertake the study of Semitic languages begin with Aramaic, because it is the simplest and most familiar—its syntax and vocabulary have been considerably influenced by Greek—but still embodies the main characteristics of the Semitic type; next proceed to Arabic, for it is the most elaborately developed yet also the most regular; and only then turn to Hebrew, the most important and attractive yet also the most difficult (1786: 21–26). This observation holds especially for the great literary language of the Aramaic group: Syriac.

Syriac is the liturgical language of many Eastern churches, founded on the dialect of Edessa (modern Urfa), seat of one of the first Christian kingdoms, Osrhoëne. Besides the standard Bible translation called the Peshitta and several earlier and later versions, an enormous devotional literature exists (preserved in manuscripts in monasteries throughout the Syrian desert, ranging from modern Turkey to Iran; Brock 1994), the creation of which was not interrupted by the Islamic Conquest of the 7th century C.E.; the last and perhaps greatest writer of Classical Syriac, Gregorius Bar Hebraeus, whose versatility rivaled that of Aristotle, lived in the 13th century.

There was a change, though, in the spoken language of the region following the Conquest: the Muslim majority spoke Arabic, with Aramaic-speaking Jewish and Christian minorities found in villages isolated in the mountainous terrain of Kurdistan. The written Aramaic languages continued in use in these communities, with relatively little influence from the spoken dialects. Moreover, as is often still observed in polycultural societies,

ACKNOWLEDGMENT: I am, as always in matters Aramaic, indebted to Robert D. Hoberman—who was my first teacher of Semitic linguistics, when we were fellow undergraduates.

there seems to have been little interaction among the Muslim, Christian, and Jewish populations and hence little convergence or mutual influence of their languages—so not much of an Arabic element can be found in Classical Syriac.

The literature in Syriac is periodized into a Golden Age, before the Conquest, and a Silver Age, afterward. The territory was partitioned between the Persian and Roman empires. During the Golden Age there came about a schism in the Syrian church, on Christological grounds, with the Persian (East) Syrians becoming Nestorian Christians and the Roman (West) Syrians Monophysite (or Jacobite) Christians. From the fifth century, these two communities had nothing to do with each other, and separate reading traditions, with distinct phonologies, grew up. The West Syrians maintained the Academy at Edessa and the East Syrians established their at Nisibis. The former seem to have maintained the historic forms more consistently (Nöldeke 1904: xxxi–xxxiv).

None of the Aramaic languages currently spoken seems to be a direct descendant of Syriac, though they use its script; but it remains the language of congregations as widely dispersed as the Martomite Christians of Madras, India (who take their name from the Apostle Thomas, whom legend names as the first missionary to the East), and the Aramaic-speaking diaspora of Flint, Michigan; Chicago, Illinois; Modesto, California; and, most recently, Western Europe, especially Sweden.

9.1.2. The study of Syriac

Our knowledge of the phonology of Syriac derives from four sources: from statements of Classical Syriac grammarians (Bar Hebraeus not least among them); from the notations in the texts prepared by the Syriac Masoretes; from the reading tradition as preserved by liturgical scholars; and from consideration of related languages and of loanwords to and from Syriac.

9.1.2.1. Syriac grammarians

The Syriac grammarians can be catalogued from the index entries in Baumstark 1922. Wright 1889 includes more information about the authors, but the generation between the two histories was notably productive in Syriac studies. Duval 1907, though less detailed than the other two histories, is arranged thematically rather than chronologically.

After some authors known only from mentions by later chroniclers, the earliest to write a grammar of which portions survive and have been published is Jacob of Edessa (d. 708; ed. Phillips 1869, Wright 1871), representing the Jacobite tradition. (Mingana 1933: 251f. describes ms. 104—dated ca. 1840—as containing two works of Jacob; it seems not to be known to the earlier editors.) Richard Gottheil (1893) discovered fragments of a grammar by Davidh bar Paulos of Beth Rabban, from the late 8th century. Two Nestorians, contemporaries, are Elias of Tirhan (d. 1049; ed. Baethgen 1880) and Elias bar Shinaya (975–after 1049; ed. Gottheil 1887); and Joseph bar Malkon and Johannes bar Zoʻbi (both early 13th century) wrote major grammars that remain unpublished. Jacob of Tagrit (= Severus bar Shakko, d. 1241) composed a grammar (ed. Merx 1889) and a treatise on accentuation (ed. Martin 1879). Gregory Abu-l-Faraj, called Bar Hebraeus (1225/6–1286), composed a large prose grammar, the "Book of Rays" (latest ed. Moberg 1922 [apparatus in French], German trans. Moberg 1907–13; this is what is cited below), a shorter grammar in verse (ed. Bertheau 1843; Martin 1872, vol. 2), and at his death left unfinished a third, the "Book of Sparks." The scholars most associated with study of the Syriac grammarians are the Abbé Paulin Martin (whose work tends to be deprecated by subsequent scholars, e.g. Nöldeke 1872), Adalbert Merx (his *Historia* is the only extended treatment), and J. B. Segal (his 1953 and 1989 studies of specific points of orthography consult both the manuscript tradition and the testimony of the grammarians). The Syriac grammatical tradition is dependent, first, on the Greek (specifically Dionysius Thrax, see Matthews 1994), and, later, on the Arab. A chapter on it—the first in any modern reference work—has been announced for the *Geschichte der Sprachwissenschaften* to be published by Walter de Gruyter; Kees Versteegh is the responsible editor.

9.1.2.2. Liturgical tradition
The received tradition among one of the churches that preserve Syriac liturgy has recently been studied by Hoberman (in press). He transcribes and analyzes the pronunciation of two expatriate Chaldean Catholic clergymen: tape recordings of a Chicago resident, and didactic materials prepared by a Californian. Mingana (1905) is regarded as a codification of the normative rules for the pronunciation of Syriac.

9.1.2.3. Modern linguistic investigation
Sokoloff (1978: 161) observed that the amount of work devoted to each of the Aramaic languages is in inverse proportion to the quantity of materials

preserved in each. While in recent years growing attention has been paid to contemporary spoken Aramaic (see Hoberman, this volume), it remains true that Syriac is the most neglected of the classical Semitic languages. The only full-scale grammar of modern times remains that of Duval (1881), which is exhaustive but betrays a premodern mindset. The standard reference is Nöldeke 1904 [1898], by the greatest of all scholars of Aramaic (and of much else Oriental). Crichton's translation includes some corrections and notes, but many fewer than his edition of Dillmann (1907). The marginalia in Nöldeke's copy of the book were transcribed (and lightly supplemented) by Schall (1966: 313–46) as an appendix to the reprint. The grammar is in fact, however, *Kurzgefaßte* (or *Compendious*—condensed, or abridged).

Study grammars of Syriac—textbooks—are in slightly fuller supply. The convenient Porta Linguarum Orientalium has included two avatars, Nestle (1889) and Brockelmann (1960; first edition, 1899). Nestle's has a more linguistic feel, and includes a very comprehensive bibliography both of the literature and of grammatical studies to date; Brockelmann's was reprinted as recently as 1976. The rival series Clavis Linguarum Semiticarum (which boasts the same general editor, Hermann L. Strack) includes Ungnad (1913), another manual informed by contemporary linguistics. All three of these contain reading selections and a glossary; Brockelmann's is made available to the English-speaking student by Goshen-Gottstein (1970).

The textbook most likely to be encountered by the student is Robinson 1962 (which follows the English model of lessons with translation exercises both out of and into Syriac but does not include a chrestomathy); it has been superseded by Healey (1986), using the inductive method. Kiraz (1994) includes a glossary of words occurring 10 or more times in the New Testament, verb paradigms, indexes, and a "skeleton grammar" by Sebastian P. Brock. Muraoka (1987) addresses the student whose teachers do not heed the advice of Michaelis. More than half of Eaton 1980 concerns Syriac studies; Brock (1980: 14–18) describes additional pedagogical materials.

There are two desk dictionaries, J. Payne Smith 1903 and Brockelmann 1928; the former is based on R. Payne Smith and Margoliouth 1879–1901 (supplemented, Margoliouth 1927). Brockelmann's etymological indications remain the fullest and most reliable available for Semitic. His and the large *Thesaurus*'s definitions are in Latin; J. Payne Smith's are in English.

An unwonted, welcome appearance of Syriac and other classical Aramaic data in the theoretical linguistic literature is found in Aronoff 1994.

9.2. Orthography

9.2.1. Consonants

The Syriac alphabet provides for the same 22 consonants as the Hebrew alphabet: <' b g d h w z ḥ ṭ y k l m n s ' p ṣ q r š t>. There are three different forms of the script (akin to the difference between, say, Roman type, the Fraktur formerly used for German, and the Irish alphabet): the older Estrangelo, the Serto of the Jacobites, and the Nestorian. They look different—a few of the letters even exhibit different basic forms—but the consonantal inventories are the same and orthographic principles do not vary (Daniels 1996).

9.2.2. Vowels

Syriac makes greater, more regular use of *matres lectionis* (vowel letters, i.e., consonant letters indicating vowels) than earlier forms of Aramaic. Virtually all long vowels other than $\bar{a}$ are indicated within the consonantal text, as well as every occurrence of *o* and *u* (except in the two words *kul* 'all' and *meṭul* 'because').

There are in addition two different sets of optional vowel marks. The Nestorian script can be vocalized with a set of characters (developed from the diacritic point described in § 9.2.3) built from dots above and below the line of consonants: <a ā e ē i o u>. The Serto script can be vocalized ("pointed," the term used in Hebrew studies) with a set of characters derived from the Greek vowel letters: <a e i o u>. These are placed above or below the line of consonants, with specific positioning depending on esthetic considerations. (Modern publications tend to mix the styles of vowel and consonant, probably according to the fonts of type available to a particular printer.)

9.2.3. Diacritics

The Syriac script provides for diacritics on the orthographic, phonological, and morphological levels. Consonants that are not pronounced but are retained as part of historical orthography can be "canceled" with an overscore. Spirantized pronunciation of the six stops can be marked by a small dot under the letter, and plosive pronunciation by a dot above (Segal 1989).

Plural nouns are marked by a horizontal pair of dots above the word. Single dots above or below words otherwise spelled alike (but vocalized differently) distinguish various verb inflections. These two kinds of morphological markers tend to be used even in otherwise unpointed texts. The evolution of the second kind from dots originally indicating broad vocalic categories (full/reduced, high/low) can be followed in the manuscripts (Segal 1953).

9.3. Segmental phonology

9.3.1. Consonants

The phonological change in Semitic that characterizes all (except the earliest) and only the Aramaic languages is the shift of the interdentals to stops (in Hebrew and Akkadian they became sibilants, and in South Semitic they survived). The reconstructed segment *ẓ, whose reflexes vary in earlier Aramaic, is realized as ʕ in Syriac. [Examples hereinafter are generally taken from Nöldeke.]

The consonants shown in Table 9-1 are those notated in the Syriac script. The characterizing phrases in the list that follows are Bar Hebraeus's descriptions. On the phonemic status of the fricatives, see § 9.4.1.

Table 9-1. Syriac Consonants

p b	t d		k g		ʔ
(f v)	θ ð		x ɣ		h
	ṭ		q		
	s z	š		ḥ ʕ	
	ṣ				
w		y			
	r				
	l				
m	n				

9.3.1.1. Labials
b ܒ Voiced bilabial stop
p ܦ Voiceless bilabial stop
m ܡ Bilabial nasal

There was an additional voiceless labial, answering to Greek π, presumably completely unaspirated, discernible only in carefully pointed texts; in the absence of a symbol for an emphatic labial stop, ordinary ܦ was used (cf. ܛ for τ and ܩ for κ).

9.3.1.2. Dentals

d ܕ   Voiced dental stop
t ܬ   Voiceless dental stop
ṭ ܛ   Emphatic dental stop
n ܢ   Dental nasal

Bar Hebraeus (Tractate IV, chap. 1, sec. 3) describes these as apico-dental.

9.3.1.3. Velars

g ܓ   Voiced velar stop
k ܟ   Voiceless velar stop
q ܩ   Voiceless uvular stop

9.3.1.4. Laryngeals

ʔ ܐ   Glottal stop
h ܗ   Glottal fricative

Etymological (orthographic) ʔ is virtually never pronounced. Words spelled with initial ʔ are pronounced with initial vowel instead (#ʔC > #eC, #ʔi > #i, etc.) Intervocalically, ʔ is [j].

9.3.1.5. Pharyngeals

ʕ ܥ   Voiced laryngeal fricative
ḥ ܚ   Voiceless laryngeal fricative

Bar Hebraeus does not distinguish the pharyngeals from the laryngeals in terms of place of articulation; he includes h with the fricatives and ḥ with the sibilants as regards interruption of the airstream (loc.cit., sec. 4). Hoberman reports the pronunciation of Classical ḥ and ʕ as [ħ] and [ʕ] by speakers of Colloquial Aramaic who use [x] and [ʔ] in corresponding vernacular words. He recognizes that "this fact ... suggests that these sounds existed continuously in the speech repertoire of the community even as they were changing to [ʔ], zero, or [x] in the vernacular (and were not merely reintroduced subsequently in borrowings from Arabic). Before the change the word for 'life' was [ˈħaːje] in both literary and colloquial registers. After the change it was [ˈxaːje] in the colloquial language but remained [ˈħaːje] in contexts that marked it as belonging to the literary register" (ms. p. 7, transcription adjusted).

9.3.1.6. Emphatics

Bar Hebraeus does not group the three emphatics ṭ, q, and ṣ in his lists of places or manners of articulation. According to Hoberman (pers. comm.),

134   Peter T. Daniels

they are realized as [tˤ, sˤ, q] in the modern Classical tradition and tend to affect neighboring segments, as in Arabic. Duval (1881: 42) and Nöldeke (1904: 39) suggest that the phenomenon of "flat" vs. "plain" words found in Modern Aramaic was operative or at least incipient in Syriac, but there is no orthographic evidence.

9.3.1.7. Sibilants

z	ܙ	Voiced apico-dental sibilant
s	ܣ	Voiceless apico-dental sibilant
ṣ	ܨ	Emphatic apico-dental sibilant
š	ܫ	Palatal sibilant

9.3.1.8. Resonants

l	ܠ	Lateral
r	ܪ	Apico-dental vibrant(?)

9.3.1.9. Semivowels

w	ܘ	Bilabial approximant
y	ܝ	Palatal approximant

Postvocalically, *w* and *y* enter into diphthongs. Initial radical *w shares in the Northwest Semitic change to *y*: *yeldat̲* 'she bore', cf. Arabic *waladat*, but (causative) *awlad̲* 'he begot'. (The third person imperfect subject prefix is *n*- rather than *y-, cf. *l*- in other varieties of Aramaic. This does not have a phonological explanation.)

9.3.2. Vowels

The distinction between East and West Syriac is seen in the respective vocalic systems. Hoberman (1992: 99) reconstructs an Early Syriac vowel system *ī ẹ̄ ē ā ō ū ɛ a ʊ* (*ẹ̄* merges with *ē* in the east and with *ī* in the west; see Blau 1969 on the "extra" *ẹ̄*). The East Syriac more closely reflects the inherited Aramaic pattern; the West Syriac seems to reflect an areal phenomenon that has persisted from ancient Canaanite through modern Arabic dialects: *ā* > *ō*.

9.3.2.1. East Syriac vowels

In its most elaborated form, the East Syriac vowel notation system (using combinations of dots) denotes the seven segments customarily transliterated as follows: *ă, ā, ĕ/ĭ, ē, ī, ŭ, ŏ*. As in transliterations of Masoretic Hebrew, the use of breves and macrons is misleading; not quantity, but quality is distinguished (Nöldeke 1904: 9). Likely phonetic equivalents would be respectively [a, ɒ, ɛ~ɪ, e, i, u/ʊ, o/ɔ]. Quantity is taken to depend on syllable structure.

9.3.2.2. West Syriac vowels
The West Syriac vowel notation system (using Greek letters) denotes the following five segments: *a, ō < ā, e, ī* (partly < *ē*), *u* (partly < *o*). Note the historical tendency to vowel raising: WS *nīmar*, ES *nēmar* 'he says', WS *ṣlūṯō*, ES *ṣlōṯā* 'prayer'. This is the style of vocalization and pronunciation that first came to European attention, so the Syriac Bible in early works is called the "Peshitto."

9.3.2.3. Shwa
Whether to claim the existence of shwa in Syriac depends on the phonological theory espoused. There are no symbols for notating shwa, so Bar Hebraeus is unable to describe it. But spirantization patterns (see immediately below) require the presence of some sort of vowel in many circumstances where none is written. For those who operate in terms of underlying representations, this may be a hypothetical vowel that is deleted in the process of deriving surface forms; for those—including Nöldeke—who wish to interpret Syriac as though it were Biblical Hebrew (or, at least, Biblical Aramaic), there is much talk of "vocal shwa" or "*shwa mobile*"; and for those who place Syriac in the context of the entire history of Aramaic, the evidence of the orthography is taken literally, and Syriac is transliterated without shwa (so Hoberman, after Kaufman 1984, followed by Daniels 1996). Evidence for the absence of shwa is voicing assimilation affecting consonants originally separated by a shwa (Nöldeke 1904: 15). In Hoberman's corpus, only in a sequence of three or more consonants is an epenthetic shwa inserted, and that before the next to last consonant (without regard for etymology): [ummaːrəɬˈhoːn] 'and he said to them', = *wmar lhon*.

9.4. Phonological processes

9.4.1. Spirantization
Characteristic of all of Aramaic (and probably borrowed thence into Hebrew) is the fricativization, or lenition, of any non-lengthened non-emphatic postvocalic stop, a process traditionally called spirantization and usually transliterated either with a barred letter (*ḇ ḡ ḏ*) or with *h* (*bh gh dh*). Because

it is predictable from syllabic structure, one might suppose that spirantization need not be noticed in transcription or in linguistic work—except for the fact that it constitutes the only distinction between the first person singular and the second person masculine singular in the perfect tense of so-called "third weak" verbs: *rmīṯ* 'I threw' vs. *rmīt* 'thou (m.) threwest'. (Further examples, with a historical account and noting of exceptions, may be found in Nöldeke 1904 § 23.) Spirantization is thus "phonemic," and so long as it is consistently marked, it serves to indicate the underlying, or historical, vocalic patterns of Syriac words, and shwa need not be marked.

The spirantized version of *ḇ* is not [v], but [w]. East Syriac *p̄* is given a spirantized pronunciation in only a handful of words; and in those few words, it is not [f] as might be expected, but [w]. (Hoberman states that Maronite Aramaic uses [b] for *b* and *ḇ*, and [f] for *p* and *p̄*, presumably as in Arabic.)

9.4.2. Assimilation

Consonant clusters tend to exhibit regressive assimilation: *nezke* [neske] 'conquers', *dazḵaryā* [dasxarja:] 'of Zacharias', *ḥesdā* [ħezda:] 'disgrace'; even *š* [ʒ] as in *ḥušbānā* [ħuʒba:na:] 'an account'.

The *t* of the reflexive(-passive) prefix *et-* assimilates in emphasis or voice to a following dental first radical (cf. *etqṭal* 'was killed'): *eṭṭasse* 'was concealed', *neddaḵrāḵ* 'remembers thee', but *ettḵar* 'remembered'.

Similarly, a final dental stop radical coalesces with *t* of the feminine suffix *-tā*: *pšīṭṭā* [pʃiṭa:] 'simple', *ḥadtā* [ħaθa:] 'new'.

Nearly every preconsonantal *n* assimilates to the following consonant.

Final radical ʕ, *h*, *ḥ*, and *r*, when closing a syllable, change preceding *e* to *a*: *dabbaḥ* 'sacrificed', cf. *qaṭṭel* 'murdered'.

9.4.3. Metathesis

The *t* of the aforementioned reflexive prefix metathesizes with an initial radical sibilant: *estḇar* 'was thought' (cf. *sḇar* 'thought'), *eštḇī* 'was taken prisoner', *eṣṭleb* 'was crucified', *ezdakkī* 'was justified'.

9.4.4. Dissimilation

Within a root, ʕ followed by another ʕ becomes ʔ and is treated accordingly (this normally arose when one or the other ʕ < *ẓ), as in *(ʔ)elʕā* 'rib' < *ʕelʕā* (so Jewish Aramaic; cf. Hebrew *ṣelaʕ*, Arabic *ḍil(a)ʕ*). In West Syriac only, ʕ dissimilated to ʔ before *h* as well, as is sometimes indicated by spelling variants like *ʔhyr* for *ʕhyr* 'to be in heat'.

9.5. Stress

Nöldeke reports (1904: 40) that among Nestorians, stress is always on the penult; but among the Maronites, stress is on a final closed syllable, otherwise on the penult. Hoberman reports the latter pattern as normative today among Chaldeans, noting that the final vowel is short unless stressed—i.e., the only final long vowels are in monosyllables, e.g. ['laː] 'not', ['biː] 'in me'.

9.6. Intonation

One might not expect to be able to recover information as to intonation patterns in a language that has not been in current use for nearly a millennium and a third, but fully pointed Syriac texts are provided with a series of "accents" that are intended to resolve syntactic ambiguities (Bar Hebraeus's introductory passage is translated by Segal 1953: 61–62); and from Bar Hebraeus's detailed account (loc.cit. chap. 6), it just *may* be possible to extract some information about the intonation of the affected clauses.

References

Aronoff, Mark. 1994. *Morphology by Itself: Stems and Inflectional Classes* (Linguistic Inquiry Monograph 22). Cambridge: MIT Press.

Baethgen, Friedrich. 1880. ܟܬܒܐ ܕܡܠܬ ܐܢܫܐ *oder syrische Grammatik des Mar Elias von Tirhan*. Leipzig: Hinrichs.

Baumstark, Anton. 1922. *Geschichte der syrishen Literatur*. Bonn: Marcus & Weber.

Bertheau, Ernestus. 1843. *Gregorii bar Hebraei qui et Abulpharag grammatica linguae syriacae in metro Ephraemo*. Göttingen: Vandenhoeck & Ruprecht.

Blau, Joshua. 1969. "The Origins of Open and Closed e in Proto-Syriac." *Bulletin of the School of Oriental and African Studies* 32: 1–9.

Brock, Sebastian. 1980. "An Introduction to Syriac Studies." In Eaton 1980: viii, 1–33.

———. 1994. "The Development of Syriac Studies." In *The Edward Hincks Bicentenary Lectures*, ed. Kevin J. Cathcart, pp. 94–113. Dublin: University College, Department of Near Eastern Studies.

Brockelmann, Carl. 1928. *Lexicon syriacum*, 2nd ed. Halle: Niemeyer. Repr. Hildesheim: Olms, 1966.

———. 1960. *Syrische Grammatik mit Paradigmen, Literatur, Chrestomathie und Glossar*, 12th ed. Repr. Leipzig: VEB Verlag Enzyklopädie, 1976.

Daniels, Peter T. 1996. "Aramaic Scripts for Aramaic Languages: Classical Syriac," in *The World's Writing Systems*, ed. Peter T. Daniels and William Bright, pp. 499–504. New York: Oxford University Press.

Dillmann, August. 1907. *Ethiopic Grammar*, 2nd ed., enlarged and improved, ed. Carl Bezold, trans., with additions, James A. Crichton. London: Williams and Norgate. Repr. Amsterdam: Philo, 1974.

Duval, Rubens. 1881. *Traité de grammaire syriaque*. Paris: Vieweg.

———. 1907. *La littérature syriaque des origines jusqu'à la fin de cette littérature après la conquête par les arabes au XIIIe siècle*, 3rd ed. Paris. Repr. Amsterdam: Philo, 1970.

Eaton, John, ed. 1980. *Horizons in Semitic Studies: Articles for the Student* (University Semitics Study Aids 8). Birmingham, England: University of Birmingham, Department of Theology.

Goshen-Gottstein, Moshe. 1970. *A Syriac–English Glossary with Etymological Notes Based on Brockelmann's Syriac Chrestomathy*. Wiesbaden: Harrassowitz.

Gottheil, Richard J. H. 1887. *A Treatise on Syriac Grammar by Mâr(i) Eliâ of Ṣôbhâ*. Leipzig: Drugulin.

———. 1893. "Dawidh bar Paulos, a Syriac Grammarian." *Journal of the American Oriental Society* 15 (1893) cxi–cxviii.

Healey, John F. 1986. *First Studies in Syriac*, corrected repr. ([Birmingham] University Semitics Study Aids 6). Sheffield: Sheffield Academic Press.

Hoberman, Robert D. 1992. "Aramaic." In *International Encyclopedia of Linguistics*, ed. William Bright, pp. 98–102. New York: Oxford University Press.

———. in press. "The Modern Chaldean Pronunciation of Classical Syriac." In *Humanism, Culture, and Language in the Near East: Studies in Honor of Georg Krotkoff*, ed. Asma Asfaruddin and A. H. Mathias Zahniser. Winona Lake, Ind.: Eisenbrauns.

Kaufman, Stephen A. 1984. "On Vowel Reduction in Aramaic." *Journal of the American Oriental Society* 104: 87–95.

Kiraz, George Anton. 1994. *Lexical Tools to the Syriac New Testament* (*Journal for the Study of the Old Testament* Manual 7). Sheffield: Sheffield Academic Press.

Margoliouth, J[essie] P[ayne Smith]. 1927. *Supplement to the Thesaurus of R. Payne Smith.* Oxford: Clarendon.

Martin, Abbé [Paulin]. 1872. *Oeuvres grammaticales d'Abou 'lfaradj dit Bar Hebreus.* 2 vols. Paris: Maisonneuve.

———. 1879. *De la métrique chez les Syriens* (Abhandlungen für die Kunde des Morgenlandes 7/2). Leipzig: Brockhaus.

Matthews, P. H. 1994. "Greek and Latin Linguistics." In *History of Linguistics*, ed. Giulio Lepschy, vol. 2: *Classical and Medieval Linguistics*, pp. 1–133. London: Longmans.

Merx, Adalbert. 1889. *Historia artis grammaticae apud Syros* (Abhandlungen für die Kunde des Morgenlandes 9/2). Leipzig. Repr. Nendeln, Liechtenstein: Kraus, 1966.

Michaelis, Johann David. 1786. *Abhandlung von der syrischen Sprache, und ihrem Gebrauch*, 2nd ed. Göttingen: Vandenhock.

Mingana, Alphonse. 1905. *Clef de la langue araméenne ou grammaire complète et pratique des deux dialectes syriaques occidental et oriental.* Mosul: Imprimerie des Pères Dominicains.

———. 1933. *Catalogue of the Mingana Collection of Manuscripts Now in the Possession of the Trustees of the Woodbrooke Settlement, Selly Oak, Birmingham*, vol. 1: *Syriac and Garshūni Manuscripts.* Cambridge: Heffer.

Moberg, Axel. 1907–13. *Buch der Strahlen: Die grössere Grammatik des Barhebräus.* Leipzig: Harrassowitz [*Einleitung und Zweiter Teil*, 1907; *Erster Teil und Stellenregister*, 1913].

———.1922. *Le livre des splendeurs: La grande grammaire de Grégoire barhebraeus* (Acta Reg. Societatis Humaniorum Litterarum Lundensis 4). Lund: Gleerup.

Muraoka, T. 1987. *Classical Syriac for Hebraists.* Wiesbaden: Harrassowitz.

Nestle, Eberhard. 1889. *Syriac Grammar with Bibliography, Chrestomathy and Glossary*, 2nd ed., trans. Archibald R. S. Kennedy (Porta Linguarum Orientalium 5). Berlin: Reuther.

Nöldeke, Theodor. 1872. [Review of Martin 1872]. *Zeitschrift der Deutschen Morgenländischen Gesellschaft* 26: 828–35.

———. 1904. *Compendious Syriac Grammar.* Translated by James Crichton. London: Williams & Norgate.

Payne Smith (Mrs. Margoliouth), Jessie. 1903. *A Compendious Syriac Dictionary.* Oxford: Clarendon.

Payne Smith, R., and D. S. Margoliouth. 1879–1901. *Thesaurus syriacus*. Oxford: Clarendon.

Phillips, George. 1869. *A Letter of Mār Jacob, Bishop of Edessa, on Syriac Orthography* .... London: Williams and Norgate.

Robinson, Theodore H. 1962. *Paradigms and Exercises in Syriac Grammar*, 4th ed., rev. L. H. Brockington. Oxford: Clarendon.

Schall, Anton, ed. 1966. "Die handschriftlichen Ergänzungen in dem Handexemplar Theodor Nöldekes und Register der Belegstellen." In Theodor Nöldeke, *Kurzgefaßte syrische Grammatik*, 2nd ed. (1898), repr. Darmstadt: Wissenschaftliche Buchgesellschaft, pp. 307–401.

Segal, J. B. 1953. *The Diacritical Point and the Accents in Syriac* (School of Oriental and African Studies, London Oriental Series 2). London: Oxford University Press.

———1989. "*Quššaya* and *Rukkaka*: A Historical Introduction." *Journal of Semitic Studies* 34: 483–91.

Sokoloff, Michael. 1978. "The Current State of Research on Galilean Aramaic." *Journal of Near Eastern Studies* 37: 161–67.

Ungnad, Arthur. 1913. *Syrische Grammatik mit Übungsbuch* (Clavis Linguarum Semiticarum 7). Munich: Beck.

Wright, William. 1871. *Fragments of the Syriac Grammar ... of Jacob of Edessa*. London(?): privately printed in an edition of 50 copies; reproduced [apparently not in facsimile] in Merx 1889: ܡܟܬܒ [73–84].

———. 1889. "Syriac Literature." *Encyclopædia Britannica*, 9th ed., 22: 824–56. Repr. separatim.

Chapter 10
Modern and Classical Mandaic Phonology
Joseph L. Malone
Barnard College and Columbia University

10.1. Introduction

This chapter deals with two types of Mandaic, a Northwest Semitic language of the Eastern Aramaic subfamily: Modern Mandaic (MM), still spoken residually in southern Iran and not long ago in southern Iraq as well; and Classical Mandaic (CM), which flourished over roughly the same terrain for several centuries up to the Islamic ascendancy, leaving a rich heritage of sacred texts still used by the Mandean religious community. An intermediate form of the language, Postclassical Mandaic, will be occasionally mentioned but not treated in its own right.

The following pages depend crucially on the work of Rudolf Macuch: Drower & Macuch 1963 (D), Macuch 1965 (H) (of which the Vocabulary of the Vernacular, pp. 489–526, will be tagged as VV), and Macuch 1989 (C).

(This may be a suitable spot for listing some other abbreviations to be employed throughout: # = word or clitic boundary; C = consonant (when not tagging Macuch 1989); G = 'ghost consonant' (§ 10.4); V̆, V̇, V̄ = reduced (§ 10.2.2), short, long vowel respectively; V = V of any length; V́ = stressed V (most often not indicated); √ = root, radical (Semitic internal-flective, non-concatenative lexeme or segment thereof); <X>, t[Y] = X is orthographic, Y is a traditional pronunciation of CM (§ 10.3.0); in rules iA, jB, kC, ... = rule i precedes j precedes k ..., as a special case of which B* marks a 'circuit' rule (§ 10.3.2); X ⌢ Y = X precedes Y (§ 10.2.4).)

MM will be treated in § 10.2, CM in § 10.3. A few theoretical matters will be briefly touched on in § 10.4 as an appendix.

Table 1 is a (broad-)phonetic chart for MM and CM segments compositely, parenthesized segments being exclusively MM.

142   Joseph L. Malone

Table 10-1. Mandaic Segments

p	t	ṭ[a]	(č)		k	q[a]	
b	d	(ḍ)	(j)		g		
	f	θ	s ṣ š		x		(ḥ)
β	ð[b]	z	(ẓ) (ž)		ɣ		(')
m	n				ŋ[c]		
	l						
	r						
w			y				
			i[d]				
			e ĕ (or ə̆)	ŏ	o		
			æ[e]	ă	ɔ		
			a				

[a] 'Emphatics'; analyzed as uvularized in Malone 1976.
[b] MM only in Arabic borrowings; otherwise exclusively CM (§ 10.2.3).
[c] Prevelar allophone of /n/.
[d] Vowels other than V̆ may appear as short or long.
[e] [æ, a, ɔ] appear to be mutual allophones, though [ɔ] and [æ] sometimes also vary with [o] and [e] respectively.

10.2. Modern Mandaic

10.2.1. Consonant groups

While MM is quite tolerant of two-member clusters in word-final position, it is quite stingy with the same word-initially. Of the 3000-odd entries in VV, this was found in only six lexemes (šβīr 'good', trēn 'two', smāla 'left', sfargəlā 'quince', drafšā 'cross', šboroxta 'life') and twice in the morphosyntactic combination durative proclitic q- plus participle (qṣāyel 'spin', qyādī 'know').

It is not clear what generalizations might be made here. For one thing, some of the items show alternatives to #CC-: in particular #CV̆C- (šə̆βīr, qə̆māyeṣ 'suck'), #CV̇C- (qabāyeṣ 'stay' [s.v. 'silent']), and #V̇CC- (ešbīr [see § 10.2.3 for the b], esmāla). Moreover, these alternations show up in other morphemes involving the same Cs (e.g. də̆rā ~ derā 'lift' (G:213), cf. drafšā).

When intervocalic in clearly word-internal position, CC is unconstrained. However, the question arises as to what bearing proclitics might have on the pertinent (prosodic) notion of 'word' involved here. Provisionally, it seems as if a proclitic forms a bond with its host word looser than that contracted between clearly word-internal morphemes, but not so loose as that across independent words. Thus though the proclitic *la-*, *læ-* 'not' most frequently (though not invariably (C:216)) combines with a past tense verb in its #CV̆C- or #CV̄C- form (*læ-dehelt* 'you didn't fear' (C:211), rather than *læ-dhelt*), the #CC- form appears in the durative (*la-qdahlā* 'she doesn't fear' vs. *qə̆dāhel* 'he fears' (for the *a* ~ *ā*, see § 10.2.5)). (The *q-* ~ *qə̆-* are themselves proclitic, by the way, as in *qṣāyel* and *qyādī* seen earlier. For more on this, see § 10.2.2 rule 1A.)

Even as there are thus organic relations among #CC-, #CV̆C-, #CV̇C- (occasionally #CV̄C-), and #V̆CC- (occasionally #V̄CC-) initially, so we find analogous relations among at least some of -CCC-, -CCV̆C-, -CCV̇C- (occasionally -CCV̄C-), and -CV̇CC- medially. To these we turn next (§ 10.2.2). Here finally be it only noted that VV contains just one instance of -CCC-, *ginztær* s.v. 'utmost', analytically 'much' plus comparative suffix *-tær* borrowed from Persian. (Perhaps this functions as an enclitic in MM, in which case *nz* might be effectively acting as (quasi) word-final.)

10.2.2. Rules for consonant groups

Pending further research, alternations of the type just considered (excluding V̇ ~ V̄ components, for which see § 10.2.5) will be tied together by three rules: **Reduction**, which either weakens a vowel or deletes it altogether; **Promotion**, which stregthens a V̆ to full-vowel status; and **Prothesis**, which resyllabifies the initial portion of a word through introduction of an anlaut vowel. Reduction must be able to precede the other two rules, since a Reduction-introduced V̆ is subject to Promotion or to loss as a byproduct of Prothesis.

(1A) **Reduction.** Most clearly in verbs (including participles) and proclitics, a non-long normally open-syllabic vowel is either deleted or weakened to V̆.

The alternatives in 1A are largely dictated by syllabic canons, deletion being mandatory when weakening would result in the impermissible sequence VCV̆CV, and weakening being mandated when deletion would entail the sequence CCC (unattested except for *ginztær* (§ 10.2.1), which however does not involve Reduction). On the one hand compare *yehem* 'he sat' (C:225), *ahaβ* 'he gave' (H:550) with their feminine counterparts, where the second schematic (stem vowel) has been deletion-Reduced upon suffixation with *-at*: *yehmat* 'she sat' (C:225), *ahβat* 'she gave' (H:550). On the other hand compare various cases of proclisis of durative *qa-*, whose *a* remains in *qambašqer* 'he recognizes' (C:207) unweakened (as normally, its syllable being closed), or in fact does weaken (a rarity except perhaps in the proclitic /qa-/, as here) as per *qəmbašqernanī* 'we recognize him' (C:207), but in neither case deletes, which would entail impermissible *qmb*—and then also, as seen in § 10.2.1, either weakens in *qəmāyeṣ* or deletes in *qṣāyel*, again however neither option entailing CCC. (In this vein, another symptom of the full-word vs. part-of-word ambivalence of proclitics discussed in § 10.2.1 may be seen in the occasional failure of open-syllabic *qa-* to reduce; e.g. *qabayeṣ* 'stays' (H:519). Such retention may be found even prevocalically (over a 'ghost' consonant (G), see appendix (§ 10.4)), e.g. *læ-eβādnī* ~ reduced *la-βādnī* 'we didn't do it' (C:47), from /la-Gəβadnī/.)

Though Reduction is formulated to introduce V̆, this does not preclude there being underived V̆s as well. In fact, assuming such V̆s whenever it can be gotten away with is one way of cutting down on arbitrary analytic choices for phonological representations. And as a case in point, we may assume that many forms whose first vowel is phonetically ə̆, like most of those seen in § 10.2.1, show the same ə̆ phonologically: thus /šə̆βīr/, /də̆rā/ (or perhaps /də̆ray/, cf. Malone 1985).

(2D) **Promotion.** Under various circumstances, a V̆ advances to full-vowel status, especially in a medial or closed syllable.

Before looking at some examples, a few words about V̆ are in order. In MM as in the classical Aramaic languages, this refers to what in German is called 'Murmelvokal', a (somewhat) midded and centralized vowel shorter in duration and laxer than its full-vowel counterparts. V̆s may be 'colored' or 'bleached', the latter seeming to be the unmarked case in MM, surfacing as [ə̆]. While in some languages (e.g. Tiberian Hebrew (Malone 1993)) full vowels reduced to V̆ may retain distinctive coloring, in MM they seem not to—though they do sometimes pick up new coloring from environing consonant positions. In fact in C (though not in H) Macuch provides special symbols for these: [a, o] in this paper retranscribed as ă, ŏ. Since underlying V̆s are assumed to be /ĕ/, ă and ŏ are derived by rule:

(3B) **Schwa Coloring.** ə̆ may labialize (ŏ) or lower (ă) under the influence of an adjacent C position.

Modern and Classical Mandaic Phonology   145

This much said, consider the derivation of three of the four allomorphs of the word for 'white', underlyingly /hə̆wārā/: (i) the null case, = [hə̆wārā]; (ii) by Schwa Coloring (due to w), → [hŏwārā]; (iii) by Schwa Coloring followed by Promotion, → hŏwārā → [howārā].

The fourth possibility is Promotion **without** Schwa Coloring, which gives [hewārā]—the default color of ə̆ being closest to unrounded front mid (cf. Chomsky & Halle 1968, Malone 1993). (All forms from C:216.)

While the 'circumstances' mentioned in 2D remain to be discovered and systematized, it seems clear that Promotion of V̆ is the unmarked choice—most notably in medial syllables. (The only forms I have found to surface with medial V̆ are *sfargə̆lā* (§ 10.2.1), *yardə̆nā* 'Jordan' (C:49), *mazgə̆dā* 'mosque' (H:511), *aβγə̆ṣī* 'stop (fem.)!' (C:204), and *ahlə̆xon* 'your (pl.) family' (C:195).)

Some further examples. From § 10.2.1: /də̆rā/ either = [də̆rā] or 2D → [derā]. From under 1A: /yə̆hem/ 2D → [yehem], /yə̆hemat/ 1A → *yə̆hmat* 2D → [yehmat] (Promotion is virtually obligatory in closed syllables; exceptions like [qə̆mbašqernanī] are rare, usually involving proclitic *qə̆-*; if 2D did apply here, [qe-] would be predicted, as in fact in [qe-mbăsqerettellī] 'you (pl.) know him' (C:182); thus [qa-] in homoparadigmatic [qambašqer] is not via 2D, but rather retains phonological /qa-/); /Gə̆haβ/ 3B → *Găhaβ* 2D → [ahaβ], /Gə̆haβat/ 1A → *Gə̆hβat* 3B → *Găhβat* 2D → [ahβat] (the shadow consonant G (§ 10.4) frequently triggers ă-coloring 3B for historical reasons, being the reflex of a lost *ʔ (as here) or *ʕ). From H(281–82): /qamə̆hambelet/ 1A → *qamhambə̆let* 2C → [qamhambelet] 'you profane': /qamə̆hambalat/ 1A → *qamhambə̆let* 2C → [qamhambelet] 'you are profaned' (note the neutralization of the opposition between these forms, still maintained in the masculine [qamhambel] vs. [qamhambal] (loc. cit.); note also the deletional Reduction (1A) of /ə̆/, relieving an impermissible sequence VCV̆CV).

(4C) **Prothesis.** An initial group #C(V̆)C may resyllabify to #V̆CC.

Though Prothesis itself is relatively rare, it appears to categorically feed Promotion (2D). Examples: /hə̆roβ/ may undergo 3B → *hăroβ* or not = *hə̆roβ*, whereupon *hăroβ* may undergo 4C → *ăhroβ* and all three alternatives undergo 2D → [heroβ], [ahroβ], [haroβ] 'he was spoiled' (H:260); /nə̆heθ/ –3B±4C → *ə̆nheθ ~ nə̆heθ* 2D → [enheθ] ~ [neheθ] 'he descended' (H:499).

The formulation in 4C states 'initial', rather than specifically 'word-initial', thus hedging on whether the rule may apply following a proclitic, cases like [qa-erqīha] analytically 'in heaven' (H:505) for default of alternations being ambiguous as to whether ← /erqīhā/, /rə̆qīhā/, or even /rqīhā/ (for the a ~ ā, see § 10.2.5). (In vein of the last possibility, note the Prothesized variant [esmāla] to [smāla] in § 10.2.1. Should the underlying representation of such #CC forms be as per null-case /smālā/ or rather /sə̆mālā/ with lexically governed deletion-Reduction (1A)? The question must be left open here.)

Mention should also be made of a special process for alleviating -CC(V̆)C- when the first two Cs constitute a geminate, a process which moreover extends to dispelling geminate -CC# in word-final position:

(5B) **Simplification.** A geminate CC simplifies to C when in word-final position (___#) or when preceding a consonant either immediately (___C) or mediately over a reduced vowel (___V̆C). In the latter case, moreover, the reduced vowel is elided.

Examples: /barrexat/ 1A → barrə̆xat 5B → [barxat] 'she blessed', cf. /barrex/ = [barrex] 'he blessed' (both H:264); /rabb/ 5B → [rab] 'large' (predicative form), cf. /rabbā/ = [rabbā] 'large' (attributive form) (both H:490). (For the inertness of ə̆ in 4C, 5B, and various other rules below, see § 10.4.)

10.2.3. Spirantization

Very little is left in MM of the venerable classical Aramaic process of postvocalic spirantization of simple non-emphatic (possibly unuvularized (Malone 1976)) stops. Putting aside for the moment certain innovations to be picked up later (q ~ x, t ~ h), the only de facto alternations I have found are these (in most cases citations are not exhaustive):

(6)			**Stops**	**Spirants**
	a.	√zbn 'transact'	zabben (C:221)	zə̆βan (C:221)
		√bGy 'want'	qa-bā (C:160)	qa-βā (C:160)
	b.	feminine gender nominal suffixes (H:206, C:59)	-tā, -tī	-θā, -θa, -θī; -aθ, -θe; -āθī, -āθ, -āθa
	c.	√sbr 'good, beautiful'	ešbīr (H:504) šbīrtær (H:498) ešbertī (H:493)	š(ə̆)βīr (H:493, 504) ešβertā (H:511)
	d.	√byṣ 'stop'	beyeṣ (C:204) abyeṣ (H:521)	aβyə̆ṣī (C:204)
	e.	√rbb 'great'	rab (H:490) rabbā (H:490)	raftī (H:3)

Clearly there are traces here of the old rule, which was by hypothesis still alive in CM (see § 10.3.3). Thus in 6a the pair *zabben* 'sold' and *zŏβan* 'bought' is unchanged from CM, where only *β* of the latter reflects spirantization of a *b* which is both postvocalic and simple (non-geminate). The alternation in *qa-bā ~ qa-βā* might likewise be tractable when the ambivalence of proclitics is taken into account (§ 10.2.1). Moreover in 6b the constancy of spirantal *θ* postvocalically in the singular construct (-*aθ*) and the plural (-*āθī*, -*āθ*, -*āθa*) also works out identically to the situation in CM. However, the overall disposition of the singular non-construct (-*tā*, -*tī*; -*θā*, -*θa*, -*θī*) can no longer be captured by a fully well-behaved phonological rule, despite the clearly persisting tendency for *θ* to occur postvocalically and *t* postconsonantally. Note e.g. -*ta* in *baratta* 'daughter' (C:204) but -*θa* in *hadaθθa* 'story' (C:214) (and -*ta* again in the VV-given variant of the latter, *hadaθta*). Note also post-consonantal -*θa* in *demehθa* 'tear' (VV). A plausible way of responding to this situation in MM is with a **lexical redundancy condition** along the following lines:

(6) The feminine nominal suffix unmarkedly subcategorizes for either of two shapes, /t/ postconsonantally and /θ/ postvocalically.

Since 7 is lexical, it may be overriden by contrary lexical stipulations; e.g., /demeh/ would subcategorize for /θa/. Similarly the alternations in the other sets of 6 are, with one exception, best interpreted as synchronically lexical—though in part fossilized residue of the once living rule (notably in 6a) and in part governed by another redundancy condition:

(6) In non-rilled non-uvularized obstruent internal-flective root consonants other than voiced apical, 1√C is unmarkedly occlusive while 2√C and 3√C are normally spirantal.

This condition is worded to exempt rilled *č, j, s, š, ṣ, z, ž, ẓ*, and uvularized *ṭ, ḍ*, as well as *d* which in MM is reflex of the merger < *d, *ð. (One other change in phonetic content, incipient *θ > *h*, clings to a tenuous synchronic existence in the dialect variation *yitem ~ yehem* 'sat' (C:41).) While 8 does not hold for 6c (where it would predict only *β*) nor the *β* of 6d, it does hold for the *β* of 6a as well as for *b* and *γ* in 6d. The *bb* in 6a, e might possibly reflect a third, overriding condition favoring occlusion of geminates (as in CM), but this is by no means certain since MM sports quite a few spirantal geminates, especially *θθ*; e.g. *hadaθθa* (seen earlier), *maθθednax* 'I'll lift you' (C:200), *aθθī* 'brought' (C:200), *eθθa* 'woman' (C:245);

but also *ff* in *affeq* 'brought out' (C:239) (for *ββ* and *xx*, see 10A, 11B). The *b* in *rab* of 6e would follow either from the possible condition favoring occlusive geminates (*rab* deriving from /rabb/ by 5B), or from lexical stipulation preempting 8.

This leaves only *raftī* in 6e uncovered. Following Macuch's lead in H:38, 56–57 I think we may be dealing with a rule here. Not knowing the precise conditions, I make bold to formulate broadly:

(7D) **Cluster Balancing.** A heterophonous cluster XY, X a nonrilled obstruent (especially *b*, *β*, *q*) and Y a stop (especially *t*), may dissimilate X in manner to become a spirant but assimilate X in voice.

Thus in 6e, /rabbtī/ 5B → *rabtī* → [raftī]; also *haβtella* → [haftella] 'you gave it' (C:38); *bedaqtī* → [bedaxtī] 'I put it' (C:42). (It is possible that the spirantization and devoicing in 9D are independent processes, that the latter may be fed by the former, and be variably conditioned by other environments than /__C: cf. [genaβ] ~ [genaf] 'steal' (VV) vs. invariant [rab] ⊬ non-occurrent [rap] 'big' (H:490); also √nsq in *nesxe-l-īd* 'kissed the hand' (C:42). On the other hand these may just reflect lexical quirks of √gnb and √nsq. Suggesting this may be occasional auslaut *t* in lieu of expected *d* (e.g. (C:193).)

Two other rules involving spirants in MM:

(8A) **Reciprocal Assimilation.** In a group *abb*, *a* may regressively labialize to *o* and *bb* progressively open (spirantize) to *ββ*.

E.g. *tabbar* → [toββar] 'break' (VV), *habbeṭ* → [hoββeṭ] 'mix' (VV). (Note that [zabben] (above) is an exception.)

(9E) **Spirant Assimilation.** *hx* may assimilate to *xx*, and *dθ* to *θθ*.

The sole examples involve the roots √ghx 'laugh' and √hdθ 'tell', but it may be that only these roots provide the sequences *hx* and *dθ* in MM: *gehxat* → [gexxat] 'she laughed' (C:208); *qa-mhaddǝ́θā* 5B → *qa-mhadθā* → [qa-mhaθθā] '(I (fem.)) tell' (C:215).

It may be noted in passing that 10A and 11B add [ββ] and [xx] to [θθ] and [ff] (see above) as permissibly geminate slit spirants in MM. Recalling that [ð] is absent from MM except in Arabic loans, this leaves unattested only [ɣɣ] (in the corpus available to me).

10.2.4. Stress

Aside from some Persian loans, which may retain their original ultimate accent (e.g. *pæšimā́n* 'sorry' H:139), my reading of Macuch (H:135–40, C:49) suggests that word stress in MM is for the most part given by this rule:

(10E) **Stress Placement.** For a full vowel V, V → [+stress] /__X#, where X contains no more than one full V.

Thus from § 10.2.1: [šβī́r] (X contains only *r*), [dráfšā] (X contains *fšā*, whose only *ā* is a full vowel), [sfárgə̆lā] (X contains *rgə̆lā*, where again only *ā* is a full vowel), [šboróxta], [ésbīr], [dérā] ~ [də̆rā́] (X is empty and *ə̆* is unstressable because not a full vowel).

Notice that [ésbīr] and [dérā] show that Stress Placement must follow both Prothesis (4C) and arguably normally Promotion (2D). The qualification 'arguably normally' is called for in the case of forms like *aθā́, aθā́n* 'he, they came' (C:49), which suggest that Stress Placement applies to such forms **before** the *a* has Promoted from *ă* (← *ə̆* by ghost consonant Schwa Coloring (3B)). If the totality of such forms should begin in vowels, it might be possible to continue the ordering 2D⌒12E and instead add to 12E the variable condition 'V is not initial' (variable in view of forms like [émar] 'he said' (H:135)). However the forms [šeβáq] 'left' (C:138) and [bená] 'constructed' (C:160) plus some remarks by Macuch at H:265 suggest that non-initial Promoted vowels may also sometimes remain unstressed. If so, the best response is perhaps to add to 12E as unmarked the following earlier ordering as a marked option:

(11D) **Stress Placement.** (Same content as 12E, but marked in application)

10.2.5. Alternations of quantity

MM evinces alternations of both consonant and vowel length in part determined by the stress. One situation is rather simple to state:

(12F) **Pretonic Shortening.** A geminate or long segment earlier in the word than the stress tends to shorten.

Thus [áθθī] 'he brought', but *aθθī́tū* → [aθī́tū] 'she brought them' (C:200); *āβdétton* → [aβdétton] 'you (pl.) do' (C:194).

Rule 13F apart, the situation with vowels is as of this writing bewilderingly unclear to me (cf. also C:47), at least a few examples being found of /V̇/ → [V̄] and /V̄/ → [V̇] in just about all positions within the word. Covert prosodic conditions may very well be at work here. However, two cases appear with sufficient frequency to warrant a provisional rule:

(13F) **Length Adjustment.** In /V́C(C)(V)/, either stressed /V̌/ may lengthen and/or unstressed /V̄/ may shorten.

Thus *át* = [át] ~ [ā́t] 'you' (C:200), ámr = [ámr] ~ [ā́mr] 'command' (C:198), *eβádyon* → [eβádyon] 'they did' (C:193), eβádnī = [eβádnī] ~ [eβā́dnī] 'we did' (C:193), *gáβrā* [gáβrā] 'man' (C:207), *árbīn* = [árbīn] ~ [ā́rbīn] ~ [ā́rbin] 'forty' (C:199), *gabbā́rā* 13F → *gabā́rā* = [gabā́rā] ~ [gabā́ra] 'hero' (C:207).

10.2.6. *Alternations of vowel quality*

One pristine rule of Aramaic may still linger in MM, though rendered moribund by exceptions:

(14A) **Assimilatory Lowering.** A short vowel may drop to *a* immediately preceding 3√r (and by prediction 3√h, though no examples could be found). That is, V̇ becomes [+low] under regressive contact with a [+low] C, as long as the latter is lexically third radical.

Thus, two antithetical examples from the /CaCCeC/ (pael, quadriconsonantal) verb: /tabber/ +15A → [tabbar] 10A⁻12E → [tóββar] 'break' (VV), but /bašqer/ −15A⁻12E → [bášqer] 'know' (C:207). (This rule has arguably already disappeared as such in MM, living on merely as the lexical quirk of certain verbs. Of the twelve 3√r verbs listed in the glossary of C (pp. 193–263), only one (√kmr) is consistently +15A, another (√tβr, above) is mixed, yet another (√dxr) is moot, and the balance are arguably or certainly −15A.)

Beyond 15A, MM contains a striking amount of variation in vowel color, especially in the verb, where moreover the variation is notably compounded by interaction with Length Adjustment (14F) and allied processes. Thus after Promotion (2D) from *gǝnon*, we have [genōn] ~ [genon] ~ [genōn] ~ [ginōn] ~ [gīnān] 'they slept' (C:210). (The 'allied process' responsible for V̇ ~ V̄ in the suffixal vowel here is provisionally lexical allomorphic.)

Whatever processes may ultimately be shown to be involved in this and a myriad other cases, it seems likely that at least part of such variation may be accounted for by a rule like this (dubbed 'vowel harmony' in Malone 1992b, but I now feel the regressive direction of the process more likely bespeaks umlaut):

(15F) **Umlaut**. Under conditions remaining to be determined, the earlier V in VC(C)V assimilates in color to the later V.

Thus [láxṭa], [lóxṭow] 'he took her, them' ← *léxṭa, léxṭow*; and while [léxṭī] 'he took him' remains unchanged (C:232), note [gínβī] 'he stole it' (C:210) ← *génβī*. Note also unumlauted [hámbel], [hambélat] 'he, she profaned' vs. umlauted [hambī́līt] 'I profaned' (H:264–65), with the long [ī́] possibly by 14F, and conversely by shortening 14F in [læ-déhlet] 'let me not fear' vs. unmarked [qɔ̆-dáhel] 'he fears' (C:211). (Rule 16F may in fact be iterative, if three-syllable stretches such as the following should be cases in point: [mahriβíllī] 'they destroy it' (C:219).)

Probably independently of 16F, there are also widespread [e ~ i] and [o ~ u] alternations (as in one form or the other common to most Northwest Semitic languages). Though one or two contributing factors are reasonably clear (such as the influence of *y* in favoring *i*, see forms under √yhm 'sit' at C:225), conditions are for the most part uncertain. However, some promising leads are adduced by Macuch at C:47.

10.3. Classical Mandaic

10.3.1. *Phonetic interpretation*

CM is written in a development of the so-called West Semitic syllabary notable as the only autochthonous Semitic orthography to have evolved from a (tendentially) consonant-only representational system to a fullblown functional alphabet bringing vowels up to parity with consonants without resorting to supernumerary diacritics. The strategy was wonderful for its simplicity. A handful of letters originally representing glides (notably ʾ, w, y, ʿ) were pressed into virtually obligatory double-duty service for presenting vowel (respectively *a, u/o, i/e, i/e*). In what follows these letters will be transcribed as <a, u, i, e>, answering to Macuch's <a, u, i, ᶜ>. Though <i> and <e> both represent *i* or *e*, <i> is the all purpose letter for this, <e> being for the most part restricted to special positions, notably anlaut. Thus <ehbit> [ehβeθ] 'I gave' while initial <i> in <iahbit> represents nonvocalic *y*, [yahβeθ], also 'I gave' (D:189).

Ironically CM orthography, by the very virtue of becoming fully alphabetic, poses certain ambiguities of phonetic interpretation to a greater degree than some at best partially alphabetic sisters and cousins like Babylonian Talmudic Aramaic (BTA) and Mishnaic Hebrew (MH). This is due to the fact that CM writing systematically fails to indicate segment length, V or C, while BTA and MH tend to use their glide letters (so-called 'matres lectionis') only (or largely) for long vowels: thus CM <basim> 'fragrant' (D:48) might represent adjectival [bassīm] or stative-participial [bāsem] and in either event would be homographic with factive [bassem] 'make fragrant' (cf. D:67).

Another pervasive ambiguity of CM orthography derives from the system's failure to indicate spirantization (§ 10.3.3 below), in that <p> may stand for [p] or [f] (let alone [pp] and maybe even [ff]), and likewise <t; k; b; d; g> vis-à-vis [t, θ; k, x; b, β; d, ð; g, ɣ].

The two widest-ranging tools for dealing with these and other cataracts of CM orthography are the panoply of comparative Semitics and the testimony of MM. A third resource, despite its apparent richness, tends to be of rather limited help. I refer to the traditional reading pronunciation of CM texts by MM-speaking priests (tarmīdī), concerning reliance on which Macuch rightly cautions care (e.g. H:104). Based on my own experience, a rule of thumb has emerged favoring credence to MM over the traditional pronunciation whenever the two conflict. Despite my reservations however, the tarmīdī's readings are not always bootless to the job of reconstruction; see e.g. § 10.3.3.

Considerable latitude of interpretation is often possible in reconstructing CM phonetics. In what might be called the **progressive mode** (p-mode), we would hypothesize CM to be as similar to MM as the overall reconstructive enterprise will allow. In the **conservative mode** (c-mode), on the other hand, we would take the opposite tack, and hypothesize CM to be as old-fashioned as possible, again subject to compatibility with the overall comparative-reconstructive frame.

In what follows, both modalities will receive some discussion, but only the conservative mode will be consistently developed.

10.3.2. Consonant groups

If we apply the bipolar reconstructive strategy mentioned in § 10.3.0 to initial C groups in CM, we may posit at the progressive pole that these distributed quite as in MM (§ 10.2.1), evincing all of [#CC-] ~ [#VCC-] ~ [#CVC-]; or alternatively at the conservative pole posit only [#V̇CC-] and [#CV̇C-] for full-blown Cs, admitting #CV̇C- only for initial ghost consonants (§ 10.4), as #GV̇C- = [#V̇C-].

For non-geminate medial and final groups, however, CM contains resolutions (virtually) absent in MM: [-CV̇CC-] and [-CV̇C#]. These aside, we would have p-modal [-CCV̆C-] (improbably also [-CCC-]), [-CCV̇C-] (~ [-CCV̄C-]), and [-CC#], as in MM; or c-modal [-CCV̆C-] and [-CC#].

The ambivalence of proclitics seen for MM (independent word? word part?) probably holds for CM as well: thus the relative autonomy of the preposition in [men lelyā] 'than (from) night' (D:274) vs. its fusion in [mellebbay] 'from my heart' (D:237).

10.3.3. Rules for consonant groups

The alternations of the type considered in § 10.3.1 are accountable, in the p-mode, by antecedents of the three corresponding MM rules considered in § 10.2.2 (Reduction, Promotion, Prothesis) plus a rule of **Epenthesis**. In the c-mode, I will present more restricted versions of Reduction and Promotion. Let us start here with the former (the significance of the star in 17B* will be explained shortly):

(16B*) **Reduction'**.
    a. A non-long open-syllabic vowel is deleted when its syllable immediately follows a vowel, and weakened to ə̆ elsewhere.
    b. Instrumentation. Regressive iterative (see also 20 below).
    c. Restriction. Does not apply to the first full vowel (i) in verbs of three or more syllables or (ii) in lexically specified nominals (Malone 1969, 1992a).

Thus *helaqā* → [helqā] 'fate' (emphatic state) (D:145), whereby regressivity dictates deletion of *a* prior to *e*, and iteration dictates that the rule scan its own output (which in this case fails to implement Reduction' of *e* since deletion has closed its syllable); *helaq* → [hə̆laq] 'fate' (absolute state) (D:145), contrast [hamar] ≠ [hə̆mar] by restriction c.

Reduction' must follow Apocope':

(17A) **Apocope'**. With certain lexical exceptions, word-final vowels are dropped.

Thus *pə̆rašū* → [pə̆raš] 'they understood' (H:348). A lexical exception is nominal -*ā*, as just seen in [helqā] 'fate'.

The CM-specific alternants [-CV̇CC-] (to [-CCV̆C-]) and [-CV̇C#] (to [-CC#]) (§ 10.3.1) arise through a rule of epenthesis (again, explanation of the star in a moment):

(18B*)**Epenthesis'**. With lexical exceptions, a group -C(V̆)C(V̆)C- or -CC# is resolved as -CV̇CC- or -CV̇C#, where V̇ is unmarkedly *e* or (lexically determined) *e* ~ *a* respectively. (For the V̇ in -C(V̆)C(V̆)C-, see § 10.4.)

Thus *pŭrašuy* 17B* → *pŭršuy* → [peršuy] 'they understood him' (D:381), *nešmoṭan* 17B* → *nešmŭṭan* 19B* → [nešemṭan] 'may he draw me forth' (D:470), *nŭsabatnnon* 19B* → *nŭšabatennon* (→ *nŭsaβaθennon* by 25B*, see § 10.3.3) → [nŭsaβθennon] 'she took them' (D:302), *malk* 19B* → *malek* (25B* → *malex*) 17B* → [mŭlex] 'king' (D:244). (The most notable lexical exception to Epenthesis' keys on the subject suffix *-t* 'you', which bonds in auslaut to a preceding consonant: [axalt] 'you ate' (D:16).)

It will be noted that in the first two examples the order of application is Reduction'⌐Epenthesis' while in the last two it is Epenthesis'⌐Reduction'. This is due to the action of the so-called **Syllable Adjustment Circuit** (for more on this, in part tacitly revised here, see Malone 1992a):

(18) **The Syllable Adjustment Circuit.** Rules tagged with *, so far Reduction' (17B*) and Epenthesis' (19B*), interact to apply regressive-iteratively until the structural descriptions of all have been exhaustively satisfied.

CM schwa coloring has (approximately) the same content as its MM reflex:

(19C) **Schwa Coloring'**. V̆ may labialize (ŏ) or lower (ă) under the influence of an adjacent C-position.

Thus *šŭmā* → [šŏmā] 'he heard' (D:469).

Rule 21C in turn feeds CM Promotion', a process (by hypothesis) considerably more restricted than its MM descendant:

(20D) **Promotion'**. Initial V̆ promotes to V̇.

Thus *Gŭxalt* 21C → *Găxalt* (for G as trigger, cf. 2D) 22D → [axalt] 'you ate' (D:16).

Like MM 2D, CM 21C and 22D are fed by a rule of prothesis:

(21B*)**Prothesis'**. An initial group #C(V̆)C- may resyllabify to #V̆CC-.

Also similarly to MM, Prothesis' is quite restricted in CM (though there is some evidence it may have been more vigorous in the interregnum Postclassical Mandaic). Example: [sŭfīhāθā] ~ [esfīhāθā] 'lips' (H:124).

Finally, CM Simplification' works out quite like its MM reflex (5B); it is ordered to follow the circuit (20):

(22C) **Simplification'**. (Same content as 5B)

Thus *šaddaran* 17B* → *šaddəran* 24C → [*šadran*] 'he sent me' (H:483). (Note that Epenthesis' (19B*) cannot preempt Simplification' to give impossible *šadedran*; see § 10.4.)

10.3.4. Spirantization

At the progressive pole, the phenomenon of spirantization in CM might approach that suggested for MM in § 10.2.3, to the extent that that situation was not catalyzed by the great influx of Persian and Arabic loans characteristic of MM.

At the conservative pole, we should have the well-known classical Northwest Semitic rule in all aspects short of its ordering with respect to the rest of CM phonology:

(23B*)**Spirantization'**. With possible lexical exceptions (notably /-t/ 'you'), a non-uvularized simplex stop (*p, t, k, b, d, g*) is spirantized (*f, θ, x, β, ð, γ*) postvocalically.

The star marks this rule as participating in the Syllable Adjustment Circuit (20), along with Reduction', Epenthesis', and Prothesis' (17B*, 19B*, 23B*). By dint of the circuit, we may expect to find Spirantization' concurrently ordered both earlier and later than other circuit rules within one and the same form: e.g. /nekdobī/ 25B* → *nekdoβī* 17B* → *nekdəβī* 19B* → *nekedβī* 25B* → *nekeðβī* 25B* → [*nexeðβī*] 'he writes it' (D:204).

The evidence justifying the ordering of Spirantization' into the circuit is wispy indeed. Since the orthography (with rare and irrelevant exceptions) gives no clue as to when a spirantizable stop is in fact spirantized, the major vehicles of potential evidence must be MM and the traditional pronunciation of CM. As may likely be gathered from § 10.2.3, analogical change has all but effaced the original patterns of spirantization in Mandaic as a phonological rule. The analogical fundaments of 8 are especially apparent, since in CM most tokens of 2√C and 3√C occurred postvocalically, particularly in the simple (qal, peal) verb, while most of 1√C failed to. This in fact provides us with a tool for teasing out a reconstruction of the ordering conditions for 25 in CM, on the basis of the precious few traditional pronunciations relevant in this regard which **defy** 8. Thus the spirantal 1√f, 1√γ in Prothesized'

(23B*) t[eftahnīn] 'we opened', t[eyṭal] 'he killed' (reading <eptahnin> H:52 and <egṭal> C:46) are plausibly interpretable to the effect that 25 could follow 23B* (pace t[eptet] 'you opened' which obeys 8, for <eptit> H:30). Since moreover 17B* must be allowed to precede 23B*, and the entire network of comparative Semitics makes it virtually foregone that 17B* must at least in some forms have followed 25 (space precludes demonstrating this here), the resulting ordering 25⁻17B*⁻23B*⁻25 invests 25 as a member of the circuit; hence the tag B*.

On the other hand the anti-8 occlusion of $2\sqrt{p}$ in t[ṣoprā] 'bird' (H:183, C:39), from ṣopparā, suggests that 25B*, and by hypothesis the whole circuit, preceded Simplification' 24, thus tagged with C: ṣopparā 17B* → ṣoppŏrā 24C → [ṣoprā].

10.3.5. Stress

While the CM stress placement rule on the p-mode hypothesis may have been like that of MM (12E), in the c-mode it would rather have been like that traditionally reconstructed for the closely related early Classical Syriac:

(24C) **Stress Placement'**. V → [+stress]/___C_0#; i.e., stress the last vowel in the word.

Thus from § 10.3.2: /helaqā/ 17B* → helqā́ 26C → [helqā́] (C_0 = ∅); /helaq/ 17B* → hŏlaq 26C → [hŏláq] (C_0 = q); /Gəkalt/ 25B* → Gə́xalt 21C, 26C → Gəxált 22D → [axált] (C_0 = lt).

10.3.6. Other alternations

Though in the p-mode alternations of quantity such as those discussed for MM in § 10.2.5 may have prevailed as early as CM, in the absence of firm evidence the c-mode position adopted in this chapter is that they did not.

Turning to alternations of vowel quality, CM indeed shows evidence for a precursor of MM 15A:

(25D) **Assimilatory Lowering'**. V̇ → [+low] /___$3\sqrt{}$[+low]. (Discursive statement as per 15A)

Thus from the /CaCCeC/ verb: tabbérʕ [tabbár] 'he broke' (D:482), bašqér → [bašqár] 'he recognized' (D:71) (contrast MM [bašqer] (§ 10.2.6)), and probably such as [šabbā́] 'he praised' (D:446) from šabbéh followed by a rule changing $\acute{V}h^ʕ$ to V̄ (cf. Malone 1985). 'Exceptions' to 27C such as [šabbehθí] 'I praised him' (D:447) and [bašqerθí] (~ [bašqarθí]) 'I recognized him' (D:71) suggest that postfocal stress may render the rule variable, thus the tag D (Stress Placement' 26 being tagged C).

There is little if any evidence for umlaut (cf. 16F) in CM, though some spelling variations adduced in H:15 may be suggestive: e.g. <birikta> ~ <burukta> 'blessing'.

Finally, the status of [e ~ i] and [o ~ u] in CM remains unclear. Interpretation at the c-pole leads me to posit consistent *e* and *o* (largely following Syriac); thus <diqna> as only [deqnā] 'beard' (D:109) despite MM [deqnā] ~ [diqna] (C:213, VV).

10.4. Appendix

For greater accessibility, the phonology fragments covered in this chapter have been largely presented in conservative conventional format. In recent years, however, great strides have been made in phonological theory, with no mean showing in Semitic. And while much of this latter work is rather directly in the tradition of John McCarthy's bellwether dissertation (1979)— e.g. Hoberman 1988—some also reflects other theoretical innovations; e.g. Lowenstamm 1991, Malone 1988, 1989a. In this appendix just a sampling of relevant Mandaic points from the body of the chapter will be touched on.

What are called above **ghost consonants** (§§ 10.2.2, 10.3.1) have been explicated as featurally empty melodic segments in Malone 1991. (The term 'ghost' is from Szpyra 1992, whither also the reader is referred for a theoretical update and review of the general literature.)

While the necessity of parenthesizing V̆ in the conventional segmental format of rules like 4C, 5B, 19B*, and 23B* ill reflects its hypothesized **inertness**, metrical phonology provides a plausibly natural account (for Tiberian Hebrew, see Churchyard 1992).

Lastly, the failure of Epenthesis' (19B*) to change forms like *šaddə̆ran* to the like of *šadedran* can be made to follow from the so-called **integrity** of geminates (see Goldsmith 1990 plus references, but note the caution sounded in Malone 1989b).

References

Chomsky, N. & M. Halle. 1968. *The Sound Pattern of English*. New York: Harper & Row.

Churchyard, Henry. 1992. "The Tiberian Hebrew Rhythm Rule in the Typology of Rhythm Rules." Meeting of the Linguistic Society of America, Philadelphia, January.

Drower, E.S. & R. Macuch. 1963. *A Mandaic Dictionary*. London: Oxford University Press.

Goldsmith, John A. 1990. *Autosegmental and Metrical Phonology*. Oxford: Blackwell.

Hoberman, Robert. 1988. "Local and Long-distance Spreading in Semitic Morphology." *Natural Language and Linguistic Theory* 6.541–49.

Lowenstamm, Jean. 1991. "Vocalic Length and Centralization in Two Branches of Semitic." *Semitic Studies in Honor of Wolf Leslau on the Occasion of his Eighty-Fifth Birthday*, ed. by Alan S. Kaye. Wiesbaden: Harrassowitz.

Macuch, Rudolf. 1965. *Handbook of Classical and Modern Mandaic*. Berlin: de Gruyter.

———. 1989. *Neumandäische Chrestomathie mit grammatischer Skizze, Kommentierter Übersetzung und Glossar*. Wiesbaden: Harrassowitz.

Malone, Joseph L. 1969. "Rules of Synchronic Analogy: A Proposal Based on Evidence from Three Semitic Languages." *Foundations of Language* 5.534–59.

———. 1976. "Messrs Sampson, Chomsky and Halle, and Hebrew Phonology." *Foundations of Language* 14.251–56.

———. 1985. "Classical Mandaic Radical Metathesis, Radical Assimilation and the Devil's Advocate." *General Linguistics* 25.92–122.

———. 1988. "Lexical Phonology and the Aramaic Verb of the Onkelos and Jonathan Targums." Meeting of the American Oriental Society, Chicago, March.

———. 1989a. "Prosodic Domains for Tiberian Hebrew Phonology." North American Conference on Afroasiatic Linguistics, New Orleans, March.

———. 1989b. "Geminates, the Obligatory Contour Principle, and Tier Conflation: The Case of Tiberian Hebrew." *General Linguistics* 29.112-30.

———. 1991. "Underspecification and Phonological Assignment of Phonetic Strings: The Case of Classical Mandaic [qen:a:] 'nest'." *Actes du XIIème Congrès International des Sciences Phonétiques*, vol. 2. Aix-en-Provence: Université de Provence. Pp.130–33.

———. 1992a. "Diachronic–Synchronic Dystony: A Case from Classical Mandaic." *General Linguistics* 32.37–58.

———. 1992b. Review of Macuch 1989. *JAOS* 112: 339–40.

———. 1993. *Tiberian Hebrew Phonology*. Winona Lake: Eisenbrauns.

McCarthy, John J. 1979. "Formal Problems in Semitic Phonology and Morphology." M.I.T. Ph.D. dissertation.

Szpyra, Jolanta. 1992. "Ghost Segments in Nonlinear Phonology: Polish yers." *Language* 68.277–312.

Chapter 11
Old South Arabian Phonology
Gene Gragg
University of Chicago

11.1. Introduction

Other chapters in this volume present detailed material on a set of Semitic languages and language subfamilies, Arabic, Modern South Arabian, and Ethiopian Semitic, which geographically occupy the southern part of the Semitic language distribution, and which are often grouped together under the rubric "South Semitic." In addition to these languages, in the core of this southern Semitic area, in the modern Republic of Yemen, from early in the first millennium B.C.E. to roughly the rise of Islam, a large number of monumental inscriptions attest to the existence of Old South Arabian (OSA), a group of closely related languages distinct from any of the other representatives of "South Semitic." There is considerable debate in the Comparative Semitic literature whether all these languages in fact constitute a sub-family of Semitic in the strict sense: a group of languages which derive from a distinct ancestral speech community, and which share a period of common development not participated in by other attested Semitic languages. The opposing hypthesis is that some or all of the similarities among these languages are the result of parallel development from Common Semitic, with tendencies toward convergence reinforced by (more or less direct) chains of (more or less continuous) contact among speech communities which have been geographically contiguous for a millennium or more.

This chapter summarizes the basic facts of OSA phonology (authoritatively presented in Beeston 1962, 1984) and situates OSA with respect to the other "South Semitic" languages.

11.2. Old South Arabian

The number of published Old South Arabian (also referred to as Epigraphic South Arabian) texts runs into the thousands, and more are being published each year. See CIASA (1977) and Avanzini (1977, vol. 1) for bibliography up to 1974; more recently note Beeston et al. (1982) and Robin (1992). The vast majority of the inscriptions are in one of four languages, corresponding to the four city-states/kingdoms located on a line running from northwest to southeast, from the Saudi Arabian border to eastern Yemen, between the inland slope of the Yemeni highlands and the Arabian desert—that is, along the southern end of the "spice route" between the Indian Ocean and the Mediterranean. These are, from north to south, the languages of: Maʿin, Sabaʾ, Qatabān (or, more properly, Qitban), and Ḥaḍramawt. Of these Sabaic, the language of Sabaʾ, is by far the best attested. After the first centuries B.C.E. the political center of Yemen shifted to the highlands (in connection with the political ascendancy of the Himyarites, and perhaps also with a shift of an important part of the spice trade to the Red Sea), and inscriptions were only drawn up in Sabaic, perhaps no longer a spoken language.

In spite of the relative abundance of documents, our knowledge of OSA is limited by a number of factors:

1. the highly stereotyped content of the monumental inscriptions;
2. a discourse style which consistently avoids using the first or second person—we know very little about the realization of these categories in the complex inflectional morphology (but see now Ryckmans et al. 1994);
3. a writing system with no indication of short vowels or consonantal gemination, no indication of /ā/, and only irregular indication of other possible long vowels, except, probably, word-final /ī/ and /ū/.

Nevertheless several things are certain. One is that the twenty-nine characters of the OSA alphabet, presented in Table 11-1 in their usual transliteration values, do seem to correspond to the twenty-nine reconstructable consonants of Proto Semitic.

11.2.1. *Comments*
11.2.1.1. *Emphatics*
On the basis of evidence from Modern South Arabian and Ethiopian Semitic (q.v.), it is likely that the "emphatics" were glottalized in OSA, and not pharyngealized, as in Arabic.

11.2.1.2. *Labial (f)*
A Latin transcription insures that the labial consonant in OSA was /f/ as in MSA and Ethiopian Semitic, not /p/ as in Canaanite, Aramaic, and Akkadian.

Old South Arabian Phonology   163

Table 11-1. Old South Arabian Consonants

	Labial	Intdnt	Dent	Palatal	Lat'ral?	Velar	Phar	Glottal
Stop								
Vceless			t			k	ʕ	ʔ
Voiced	b		d			g		
Emph			ṭ			q		
Continuant								
Vceless	f	ṯ	s³	s¹	s²	ḫ	ḥ	h
Voiced		ḏ	z			ɣ		
Emph		ẓ	ṣ		ḍ			
			r		l			
	m		n					
	w			y				

11.2.1.3. Interdental (ẓ)
Although this shows a regular correspondence with what is commonly taken to be a voiceless interdental emphatic spirant /θ̣/ in Proto-Semitic, its grapheme 𐩳 closely resembles the grapheme for /ṣ/ 𐩮, and in many texts it seems to have merged with /ṣ/ (note common modern Arabic pronunciations).

11.2.1.4. Velars (k, g, q, ḫ, ɣ)
/q/ could have been simply a voiceless glottalized velar [k']—as in Ethiopic Semitic and MSA. Note however the uvular articulation in Arabic. Note also that /ḫ, ɣ/ are post-velar spirants in both Arabic and MSA (they have not been preserved in modern Ethiopic Semitic or in the pronunciation tradition of Geʻez).

11.2.1.5. Sibilants and laterals (s¹, s², s³, ḍ)
The transcription with "s" and superscript numbers has been widely adopted for the graphemes 𐩢 = s¹, 𐩦 = s², 𐩯 = s³, largely because of the generally inconsistent and ambiguous use of the symbols "s", "š", and "ś" in the older literature. /s³/ corresponds to Proto-Semitic /*s/ in etymologies and in loanwords and /s¹/ to Proto-Semitic /*š/. /s²/ corresponds to a Proto-Semitic consonant which is preserved as a separate phoneme only in MSA, where it is realized as a voiceless lateral spirant. Elsewhere in Semitic it merges with

either /š/ or /s/, although it is preserved graphically in the Hebrew "*śin*" (see Steiner, 1977, as well as Tables 11-2 and 19-1). Historical and comparative evidence suggests that /ḍ/ was the voiced and/or "emphatic" counterpart to /s²/. Note that the occasional use of "*s¹*" for "*s³*" in the late OSA texts may indicate a merger of these two consonants at this period, as happened in Arabic. In Ḥaḍramawt /s³/ and /ṭ/ seem to have merged, with their graphemes used interchangeably.

11.2.1.6. Glides (w, y)
These occur in all positions. The graphemes "*w*", "*y*" in final position apparently can represent the, possibly long, vowels /u, ū, i, ī/, as in *s¹ṭrw* /šaṭāru/ 'they wrote', *-hw* /-hu/ 'his', *-hmw* /-hVmu/ 'their (masc.)'—note the possible writings *-h, -hm* for the latter. In medial position they can probably also represent vowels, as well as diphthongs or independent consonants: thus *kwn* 'he was' (which has *kn* as an alternate shape) is presumably /kona/, although /kawna/ cannot be absolutely excluded (for a different lexical item /ka(w)wana/ could also have been a possibility).

11.2.2. Phonological processes
Beeston (1984: 10f.) lists a number of phonological processes of the expected sort in a Semitic language: loss of laryngeals /ʔ, ʕ, h/ in certain positions; fluctuation of /w, y/; assimilation of /n/ to following consonant (not attested before /ʔ, ʕ, h, ḫ, ɣ, m/); assimilation of /d/ to following /t, ṭ/ in numerals 'one (fem.)', 'six', 'sixty' * *ʔḥdt* > *ʔḥt*, *s¹dθ* > *s¹ṭ*, *s¹dθy* > *s¹ṭy*. However, absence of real information about vocalic environment make a precise evaluation impossible. A replacement of earlier *s²lṯt* 'three' by *ṯlṯt* in later Sabaic may be an instance of assimilation at a distance.

11.2.2.1. Phonological variants in OSA grammatical forms
A well-known major morphological isogloss within Semitic involves the use of /š/ or /h, h > ʔ/ for the causative formative with verbs and the base of the third person pronoun (Akkadian: *šuprus-* 'cause to decide', *-šu* 'his'; Ugaritic: *šlḥm* 'cause to eat, feed', *-h* 'his'; Hebrew: *hiktīb* 'cause to write', *hu* 'his'). Along the same lines, chapter 19 points out a number of /š ~ h/ alternations involving these and other morphological and lexical contexts, within and between various MSA languages. Whatever is the ultimate phonological or morphological explanation of this alternation, it is interesting to note that **within** OSA, the Sabaic dialect shows the /h/ alternate for both the causative

and pronominal morphemes (*hqny* 'dedicate; cause to possess' , -*h* 'his'), while Maʻin, Qitban, and Ḥaḍramawt have *s¹* in both cases (*s¹qny*, -*s¹*).

A number of inner OSA dialect variations involve a "parasitic," non-etymological /h/, which appears in a variety of contexts in the non-Sabaic languages: in certain lexical forms in Maʻin (*bhn(t)* 'sons (daughters)', *ṯhmn*- 'eight(y)', *lhm* 'not'); as a noun suffix in construct singular and broken plural genitives, and in construct duals and external plurals in Maʻin (*bn ʔydw-h-s¹m* 'from hands-*h*-their') and occasionally in Qitban and Ḥaḍramawt; in a possible "adverbial accusative" -*h(m)* in Maʻin (*s¹lmhm* 'in peace') and Ḥaḍramawt; in a determinate singular and broken plural suffix -*hn* in Ḥaḍramawt, corresponding to -*n* in Sabaic and elsewhere. While at least some of these instances may involve phonological rather than morphological innovation not enough is known about the suprasegmental and vocalic environment to allow the formation of any coherent hypotheses.

In Qitban there is a regular alternation between a short form and a long form of the third person singular suffix pronoun: masculine -*s¹* ~ -*s¹ww*; feminine -*s¹* ~ -*s¹yw*. The short form occurs with singular and internal plural forms, the long form with dual and external plural forms. Both pre-suffix vowel length and pre-suffix stress have been suggested as a possible conditioning factor (Beeston 1962: 45 observes that this might correlate with certain of the parasitic /h/'s just noted)—but again, hard evidence is lacking. Ḥaḍramawt masculine singular pronouns seem to show the same alternation. In Maʻin an occasional masculine singular variant -*s¹w*, in place of the much more frequent -*s¹*, might also be an indication of a similar phenomenon, although these are not enough attestations to be certain.

11.3. South Semitic

In the first place it should be noted that many of the criteria used to define South Semitic are more morphological than phonological in nature. The most important are: [1] The existence of a highly developed system of internal plurals (of the kind Arabic: *bayt* ~ *buyūt*, Geʻez: *bet* ~ *abyāt*, Soqotri *beyt* ~ *íbihet* 'house ~ houses'). [2] Presence of a bi-syllabic present stem of the form CV(C)CVC, as in Geʻez *yə-qattəl* and Soqotri *yə-kʼabər* (versus CCVC as in Hebrew *yi-qṭol*). [3] Forms with /k/ in the first and second person subject suffixes of the past tense as in Geʻez -*ku*, -*ka*, -*ki* (for 1sing., 2masc.sing., 2fem.sing.) and Soqotri -*k*, -*k*, -*š* (< -*ki*) (versus forms with /t/ as in Hebrew -*ti*, -*tā*, -*t*). With respect to criterion [1], OSA clearly belongs with the rest of

"South Semitic" (Sabaic *byt* ~ *ʔbyt*). But for [2] and [3] Arabic (which shows *ya-qtul-u* and *-tu, -ta, -ti*) clearly patterns with Hebrew and Aramaic. On the other hand, for OSA, while [2] is still unknown because of lack of information about short vowels and gemination, for [3] emerging evidence (clear second person *-k* forms in Ryckmans et al. 1994; note also a possible form *rḥmk* 'thou art merciful' cited in Beeston 1984: 14) seems to indicate that OSA might pattern with MSA and Ethiopic.

Table 11-2. Semitic Consonant Correspondences

PSem	Akk	Ugar	Aram	Heb	Arab	Geʻez	OSA
*p	p	p	p	p	f	f	f
*θ	š	ṯ	t	š	ṯ	s	ṯ
*ð	z	ḏ	d	z	ḏ	z	ḏ
*θ̣	ṣ	ṭ	ṭ	ṣ	ṯ̣	ṣ	ẓ
*š	š	š	š	š	s	s	s¹
*ɬ	š	š	s	"ś" > sᵃ	š	"ś" > sᵃ	s²
*ḍ	ṣ	ṣ	ṭ	ṣ	ḍ	"ḍ" > ṣᵃ	ḍ
*ḫ	ḫ	ḫ	ḥ	ḥ	ḫ	"ḫ" > ḥᵃ	ḫ
*ɣ	Ø	ɣ	ʕ	"ʕ"ᵇ	ɣ	ʕ	ɣ

a. Earlier graphemic distinction not reflected in pronunciation tradition.
b. Evidence from transcriptions for ɣ ≠ ʕ.

The phonological evidence is summed up in Table 11-2, which gives the most common non-identity consonant correspondences for Proto-Semitic, Akkadian, Ugaritic, Aramaic, Hebrew, Arabic, Geʻez, and OSA (minus the cases where Akkadian has simply dropped a laryngeal—see chapter 19 for the sibilant correspondences in MSA). It is immediately obvious that, as already mentioned, OSA preserves intact all of the consonantal segments of Proto-Semitic, as does MSA. Arabic loses only one consonantal distinction, through a process whereby /š/ merged with /s/, after which /ɬ/, the voiceless lateral spirant, became /š/. However, apart from the shared /f/ in Arabic, OSA, and Geʻez (also in MSA), as opposed to /p/ elsewhere (frequently cited as a feature of South Semitic), there is little other evidence of the kind of shared phonological innovation that would imply a common sub-family node and a hierarchical family tree structure. One case one might point to, the common treatment of Proto-Semitic /ɬ/ and /š/ in Arabic and Geʻez, fails to lead to an unambiguous conclusion, since it is contradicted by the morphological evidence cited above.

It is in fact hard to escape the conclusion that the major phonological developments in Semitic, converging or not, took place independently in each of the major branches, and that each branch seems to have started its independent existence with the Proto-Semitic consonant system virtually intact. In this context one might note that even the "South Semitic /f/" might reflect a more complicated Pre- and Proto-Semitic situation than the postulation of a simple spirantization of Proto-Semitic /p/ might suggest (cf. widespread Afroasiatic /f/ for Semitic /p = f/: Semitic *pu- 'mouth' = Cushitic *af; Semitic *∂Vpr- 'nail, claw' = Berber a-tfər).

The upshot of all this seems to be that Ethiopian Semitic and MSA indeed form a sub-family of Semitic. It would be geographically and historically plausible that OSA would also belong to this family, and there is a small amount of linguistic evidence pointing in this direction. But this evidence is not detailed enough to tell us what the relation of OSA is to the other two, and what the resulting family substructure might be. Arabic belongs to a linguistic and cultural South Semitic contact area, whose nature still needs to be worked out. While Arabic certainly interacted with the other South Semitic language groups, in certain crucial respects Arabic seems to have followed paths of development not participated in by "South Semitic" proper.

Bibliography

Avanzini, Alessandra. 1977–80. *Glossaire des inscriptions de l'Arabie du sud 1950–1973* (Quaderni di Semitistica 3), vol. 1 *Bibliographie*, vol. 2 *Glossaire*. Florence: Istituto di Linguistica e di Lingue Orientali.

Beeston, A. F. L. 1962. *A Descriptive Grammar of Epigraphic South Arabian*. London: Luzac.

———. 1984. *Sabaic Grammar* (Journal of Semitic Studies Monograph 6). Manchester: University of Manchester.

Beeston, A. F. L., M. A. Ghul, W. W. Müller, and J. Ryckmans. 1982. *Dictionnaire Sabéen (anglais–français–arabe)*. Louvain-la-Neuve: Peeters.

Biella, Joan. 1982. *Dictionary of Old South Arabic: Sabaean Dialect* (Harvard Semitic Studies 25). Chico, Calif: Scholars Press.

CIASA. 1977–. *Corpus des inscriptions et antiquités sud-arabes*. Louvain-la-Neuve: Peeters. [Gives authoritative editions, copies, photographs, translations (usually in French or English) of more recently discovered texts. Continues several earlier series of text publications, in particular the *Corpus Inscriptionum Semiticarum* [CIS, CIH] part 4 (Paris, 1889–1929) and the *Répertoire d'Epigraphie Sémitique* [RES] vols. 5–8 (Paris, 1929–1968).]

Jamme, Albert. 1962. *Sabaean Inscriptions from Maḥram Bilqîs (Mârib)*. Baltimore: Johns Hopkins University Press.

Ricks, Stephen. 1989. *Lexicon of Inscriptional Qatabanian* (Studia Pohl 14). Rome: Editrice Pontificii Istituto Biblico.

Robin, Christian. 1992. *Inventaire des inscriptions sudarabiques*, 2 vols. Paris: Boccard.

Ryckmans, Jacques, W. W. Müller, and Y. M. Abdullah. 1994. *Textes du Yémen antique inscrits sur bois*. Louvain-La-Neuve, Belgium: Institut Orientaliste.

Steiner, Richard C. 1977. *The Case for Fricative-Laterals in Proto-Semitic* (American Oriental Series 59). New Haven: American Oriental Society.

Chapter 12
Ge'ez Phonology
Gene Gragg
University of Chicago

12.1. Introduction

Ge'ez (*gəʕəz*), a Northern Ethio-Semitic language, was the official language of the Axumite kingdom which occupied large parts of present-day highland Eritrea and the Northern Ethiopian province of Tigre during much of the first millennium A.D., reaching the height of its power and regional influence between the fourth and sixth centuries. Ge'ez is first attested in pre- and early-Axumite inscriptions from the first centuries A.D., and is seen in near-classic form in a corpus of monumental inscriptions associated with a ruler named 'Ezana, and usually dated to the fourth century. 'Ezana's inscriptions also attest to the appearance of Christianity on the Ethiopian highland; and subsequent centuries witness the appearance of a Bible translation into Ge'ez, and the nucleus of what gradually became a vast ecclesiastical, civic, and court literature, continually accumulating during the long period in which Ge'ez was the only official written language of the Ethiopian church and state. Up to the threshold of the twentieth century, some knowledge of Ge'ez was a prerequisite for both civil and ecclesiastical careers in Ethiopia; and Ge'ez is still today the liturgical language of the Ethiopian Orthodox Church. As a consequence, a characteristic feature of Ethiopian civilization has been an extensive monastery- and church-based educational tradition, formed around a curriculum leading to a mastery of Ge'ez.

Within Northern Ethio-Semitic, Ge'ez is closely related to modern Tigre (northern highlands and Red Sea coastal plain), and stands in a more or less proximate ancestral relationship to Tigrinya, which probably started to emerge as a distinct entity on the home territory of Ge'ez from around the tenth century on. The remaining Ethio-Semitic languages (a dozen or so, including Amharic) belong to a separate (Southern) group, which cannot be derived from any attested Northern Ethio-Semitic language. Northern and Southern Ethio-Semitic, however, do seem to constitute a distinct genetic node in the Semitic family tree, a node which is most closely related to a Southern group of Semitic languages that includes Epigraphic and Modern

South Arabian. The exact historical relationships among Epigraphic South Arabian, Modern South Arabian, and Ethio-Semitic, as well as the relation of these three families to (North) Arabic, have been difficult to establish because of what was until quite recently insufficient data on the Modern South Arabian languages, and because of the phonological indeterminacy and morphological poverty of the textual evidence for Epigraphic South Arabian (an extensive corpus, but written in one of the more resolutely vowelless of the Semitic writing systems, and in a discourse format which, in spite of a respectable diversity of subject matter, managed to restrict itself almost entirely to third person pronominal and verbal forms).

12.2. The evidence for Ge'ez phonology

Two lines of evidence have to be correlated in drawing any conclusions about the phonology of Ge'ez in its "classical" (i.e., pre–tenth century) form. One is the writing system itself, together with the inferences suggested by related Ethiopic and non–Ethio-Semitic linguistic evidence. The other comes from the pronunciation tradition developed in the context of the traditional educational system mentioned above.

As far as the Ethiopic writing system is concerned, its core, the representation of the consonantal inventory, is already present in the earliest pre- and early-Axumite inscriptions. This consonantal script is derived more or less directly from some version of the South Semitic writing system which also appears in the Epigraphic South Arabian inscriptions. The major missing element, the representation of the vowels, is provided by a major innovation introduced in the later inscriptions of 'Ezana. Alone among the Semitic scripts, Ethiopic represents vowels, not by a separate set of (super-linear or sub-linear) vowel signs, but by means of a more-or-less uniform modification of the basic letter-shape. The base form of the consonant sign (the so-called 'first order' form) is taken to represent the consonant followed by /ä/ [æ], and six other alterations of the basic shape are introduced to represent the consonant followed by the vowels /i u a e ə o/ (the second through seventh orders; note that the sixth order is used in addition to represent the consonant in isolation, with no following vowel). As an example, the result of this transformation for the consonant /b/ is:

ORDER:	1	2	3	4	5	6	7
SIGN:	በ	ቡ	ቢ	ባ	ቤ	ብ	ቦ
VALUE:	bä	bi	bu	ba	be	bə,b	bo

Each sign thus represents a CV sequence, and a twenty-six member alphabet is thereby transformed into a 182 member syllabary (to which are added five forms each of the consonants /k g q ḫ/ to represent the labiovelars /kʷ gʷ qʷ ḫʷ/ plus the vowels /ä i a e ə/, for a grand total of 202 signs).

The resulting writing system provided an unambiguous representation of Ge'ez words (and continues to provide the same service for Amharic and Tigrinya) except for two aspects of phonological shape—apart from stress, frequently not noted in practical orthographies in any case. These two problematic aspects are: (1) lack of a way of indicating the phonologically prominent and morphologically important feature of gemination (a two-dot diacritic, introduced to represent gemination of consonants in European grammars and dictionaries of Ethiopic since the seventeenth century, never became part of the manuscript or printed Ethiopic orthographic tradition); (2) lack of an unambiguous way of representing a consonant *not* followed by a vowel, i.e. in word- or syllable-final position (note the parallel ambiguity inherent in the Hebrew shwa symbol). As a consequence an orthographic representation <$k_1 l_6 b_6$> (where C_n is the *n*th order shape of the consonant C) might conceivably stand for any of the following values:

kälb	käləb	kälbə	käləbə	källb	källəb
källəbə	kälbb	kiäləbb	kiäləbbə	källəbb	källəbbə

(excluding values with /kk llbb/ on general phonotactic grounds).

Thus, for these missing features our only source of information is the other line of evidence, the pronunciation tradition. This tradition in its present manifestation is apparently fairly uniform, and seems to represent prestige pronunciation of Ge'ez in the central Ethiopian plateau (thus in a largely Amharic milieu) where royal residences and many centers of ecclesiastical influence have tended to be located since the decline of Axum. This pronunciation tradition is thoroughly Amharicizing in its treatment of consonantal values (but note the claim of Ullendorff 1955 about the existence of more "Tigrinya-izing" pronunciation patterns in the north). Still, the traditional pronunciation preserves stress, gemination, and syllable structure patterns which are at least in part distinct from those found either in Amharic or in Tigrinya, and as such may well reflect the state of affairs in an earlier stage of Ge'ez itself. In any case European scholarship from the seventeenth century on has been explicitly dependent directly or indirectly on information provided by a succession of Ethiopian literati who are acknowledged, usually by name, as the source of information for these aspects of lexical and grammatical representations. (On pronunciation, cf. most recently Makonnen Argaw 1984; basic earlier works are Ludoph 1661, Trumpp 1874, König 1877, Littmann 1918, Cohen 1921, and Mittwoch 1926; the fundamental reference grammar, Dillmann 1857, 1907, relies essentially on Ludolph, with corrections from Trumpp and König included in the second edition by Bezold; Lambdin 1978, the most accessible pedagogical grammar, incorporates material from the traditional pronunciation, but without much explicit discussion; note in this context the section on *säwasəw*, indigenous grammatical texts, by the Ethiopian scholar Getatchew Haile in Leslau 1987: xv–xvii.)

In the sections that follow, the representation of Ge'ez will thus be of a composite nature. Consonants and vowels (apart from the sixth order) will be given in a conventional transcription of the orthography (see the relevant sections below for interpretation or probable interpretation); representation of gemination and syllable structure (as well as stress, when indicated) will be based on what is known from the pronunciation tradition. Note that although the basic features of the pronunciation tradition are relatively clear, its scholarly investigation and evaluation is still under way. Note also, as far as the orthography is concerned, that apart from the relatively small corpus of Axumite inscriptions, apparently from the early and formative period of classical Ge'ez, almost all Ge'ez texts were either produced in a period when Ge'ez was no longer a spoken language, or are preserved in a long, poorly studied manuscript tradition, with a gap of many centuries between the period of formation of the core classical corpus (Bible translation, key liturgical, hagiographic, and monastic texts—perhaps sixth century) and the oldest extant manuscripts (rarely older than the fourteenth century). Thus the composing and transmission of texts in Ge'ez orthography are themselves aspects of the same process of cultural transmission which yields the pronunciation tradition.

12.3. Phonological segments

12.3.1. *Consonants*

In Table 12-1, row 1 gives the usual transcription value for each Ge'ez consonant, row 2 its traditional pronunciation, row 3 the corresponding consonant in Tigrinya, row 4 the most usual corresponding consonant, if present, in Arabic, and row 5 the first order shape of the corresponding consonant sign.

Table 12-1. Ge'ez Consonant Correspondences

p	ṗ	b	t	ṭ	d	k	q	g	f	s	ś	ṣ	ḍ	z	ḫ	ḥ	h	ʕ	ʔ	m	n	r	l	w	y
p	p'	b	t	t'	d	k	k'	g	f	s	s	s	ṣ	z	h	h	h	ʔ	ʔ	m	n	r	l	w	y
p	p'	b	t	t'	d	k	k'	g	f	s	s	s	ṣ	ṣ	z	h	ḥ	h	ʕ	ʔ	m	n	r	l	w	y
-	-	b	t	ṭ	d	k	q	g	f	s,θ	š	ṣ	ḍ,ẓ	z,ð	ḫ	ḥ	h	ʕ,γ	ʔ	m	n	r	l	w	y
ፐ	ጰ	በ	ተ	ጠ	ደ	ከ	ቀ	ገ	ፈ	ሰ	ሠ	ጸ	ፀ	ዘ	ኀ	ሐ	ሀ	ዐ	አ	መ	ነ	ረ	ለ	ወ	የ

Details of interpretation are given below, but it is important to note the following: The traditional pronunciation gives essentially their Amharic value to the consonantal signs—pharyngeals /ʕ/ and /ḥ/ merge with /ʔ/ and /h/ respectively, <ṣ> and <ḍ> are both pronounced /ṣ/, and <s> and <ś> are both pronounced /s/. Tigrinya (as well as Tigre) preserves the distinction between /ʔ/ and /ʕ/ and between /ḥ/ and /h/. But *no Ethiopic language* and *no element of the pronunciation tradition* provides the least bit of information about the pronunciation of the graphemes /ś/, /ḍ/, and /ḫ/. Nevertheless, since the earliest pre-Axumite writing system did adopt these consonant signs from the parent South Semitic alphabet, while excluding a number of other signs representing consonants which had already merged in Ethiopic, they must have represented distinct consonants in early and classical Ge'ez. It is not clear when the mergers took place. The graphemes seem to be used consistently in the 'Ezana inscriptions, and in some strands of the manuscript tradition (recall, however, what was already said concerning the primitive state of the study of this tradition). However, variant writings of the same word with <ḥ> and <ḫ> begin to appear already in some late monumental inscriptions, and in the low end of the manuscript tradition, <ḥ/ḫ> (and sometimes <h>), <ḍ/ṣ>, and <ś/s> are used as virtual allographs. In Table 12-2, the consonants corresponding to <ś>, <ḍ>, and <ḫ> are interpreted with the help of data from cognate languages (note Arabic correspondences in Table 12-1).

With the foregoing reservations, the articulatory features of Ge'ez consonants will be interpreted as in Table 12-2.

12.3.1.1. Emphatics /ṗ, ṭ, q, qʷ, ṣ, ḍ/
As can be seen from Table 12-2, the phonological feature commonly termed "emphasis" in Semitic is implemented as glottalization in the pronunciation tradition (hence, Amharic) and Tigrinya. In fact the feature has this implementation in all Ethio-Semitic languages—and hence presumably also in Ge'ez. Since the Arabic implementation of this feature, velarization or

Table 12-2. Ge'ez Consonant Articulation

	Labial	Dental	?	?	Velar	Labio-velar	Pharyngeal	Glottal
Stop								
Voiceless	p	t			k	kʷ	ʕ	ʔ
Glottalized	ṗ	ṭ			q	qʷ		
Voiced	b	d			g	gʷ		
Continuant								
Voiceless	f	s		ś	ḫ	ḫʷ	ḥ	h
Glottalized		ṣ	ḍ					
Voiced		z						
Nasal	m	n						
Sonorant		r l						
Glide	w	y						

pharyngealization, was once thought to be representative of early Semitic, glottalization in Ethio-Semitic was thought to represent the influence of language contact with earlier Cushitic languages in Ethiopia. However, the relatively recent discovery that emphatic consonants are also glottalized in the Modern South Arabian languages makes it possible that this might be a common South Semitic feature, and perhaps even common Semitic. Note in particular that /q/, which can be a uvular stop in some varieties of Arabic, is clearly a glottalized velar in Ethiopic. Note also that, because of the well-known difficulty in building up the glottal pressure necessary for a glottalized release while articulating a continuant like /s/, /ṣ/, the glottalized version of /s/, both in the pronunciation tradition and in modern Ethio-Semitic languages, tends to be realized phonetically as an affricate [ts]. It is uncertain whether the same was true of /ḍ/. However, since it merged with the continuant /ṣ/, it is likely that it had become a continuant at least by the time of the merger.

12.3.1.2. Voiceless labials /p, ʔ, f/

Ge'ez is unique among the Semitic languages in having not only a stop and continuant voiceless labial consonant, but an emphatic labial stop as well. Akkadian, Aramaic, and Canaanite have only a /p/, while Arabic and other

South Semitic have only a /f/. Ge'ez /f/ is clearly what is cognate with the voiceless labial consonant of other Semitic, and Ge'ez thus patterns historically, as expected, with South Semitic and Arabic. A large number of the occurrences of /p/ and /ṗ/ are in loanwords, mostly from or by way of Greek: *piläs* 'temple, gate' < Greek *pylē* 'gate', *pappas* 'metropolitan, patriarch' < Greek *papās* 'father, title of priests', *päpera, päpera* 'purple' < Greek *porphyra* 'purple dye' (note that it is not always predictable when the consonant corresponding to Greek /p/ will be glottalized /ṗ/ and when simple /p/—an indeterminacy common with other voiceless stops in loanwords from Greek). However, there are a large number of other occurrences, fully integrated into the native grammar and vocabulary of Ge'ez, where the origin of the stop is much less clear: *hepä* 'strike, throw, shoot with an arrow' (a so-called middle-weak verb from a root *hyp*, with a glide as a middle radical—on possible connection with Arabic *habba* consult Leslau 1987); *häppälä* 'wash clothes' (Leslau 1987 notes Arabic *wabīl* 'stick with which one beats clothes that are being washed'), *qäläpä, qälpäpä, qärpäpä* 'chew, bite' (meanings pattern with verb *qäläbä*, which may be borrowed from Amharic *qälläbä*).

12.3.1.3. Labiovelars /kʷ, qʷ, gʷ, ḫʷ/

Ethio-Semitic is likewise unique among the Semitic languages for having developed a distinctive labiovelar series of consonants. They are already attested in the voweled 'Ezana texts (since they are represented by modifications of the basic consonant, there is no way a non-voweled text could indicate their presence). Labiovelars can occur before the non-rounded vowels /i e ä a ə/; their non-occurrence before /u o/ is undoubtedly a neutralization effect, since all consonants in the traditional pronunciation of Ge'ez (and in most modern Ethio-Semitic) have labialized allomorphs before /u, o/. Labiovelars are relatively widespread in the Ge'ez lexicon. A count of the letter G in Leslau 1987 reveals 259 entries with initial /g/, and 92 with initial /gʷ/. Where their origin can be traced, labiovelars seem to result from phonologization of labialized allomorph of a velar before a rounded vowel. Thus the verb *tärgʷämä* 'interpret, translate' is reformed from an Aramaic word *targūm* 'interpretation' (note that this form of the word is not attested in Ge'ez, where the various words for 'interpretation', *tərgʷame, tərgʷəmt, tərgʷəmənna*, are all nominalized forms of the Ge'ez verb). Likewise the labiovelar in the Ge'ez word for 'brother' *əḫʷ* is related to the fact that in many Semitic languages the word 'brother' has forms showing a stem-final /u/ or /w/ (cf. for Arabic *aḫ* 'brother', *aḫu-* 'brother of', *iḫwa, iḫwān* 'brothers'; also *uḫt*, plural *aḫawāt*, 'sister'). In many words, however, the labiovelar appears with no apparent conditioning environment: *əgʷl* 'young of an animal' (Arabic *ʕijl* 'calf', Hebrew *ʕegɛl*, Aramaic *ʕeglā*), *ḫʷälläqʷä* 'count' (Arabic *ḫalaqa* 'create; shape', Hebrew *ḫālaq* 'divide'—influence of past participle on **ḫəlluq* 'numbered' (?)). Note that the fact that the phenomenon seems limited to velars may argue in favor of /ḫ/ being a spirant in the velar region, even though it merged with the pharyngeal /ḥ/.

12.3.1.4. /š/

This consonant corresponds most often to Arabic /š/, Hebrew /š/ (and hence to Epigraphic South Arabic voiceless lateral /s₂/, whose grapheme Geʻez uses for this consonant). Out of 34 lexical items with initial <ś> in Geʻez for which cognates are cited in both Hebrew and Arabic in Leslau 1987, about half follow this pattern; the others show various combinations of Hebrew and Arabic /s ś š/. If /š/ was its phonetic value, then it merged with /s/, the only pronunciation known by the pronunciation tradition. Such a merger of the palatal(-alveolar) spirant /š/ with the alveolar /s/ could possibly be connected with the emergence of a new series of palatal(-alveolar) spirants and affricates in Ethio-Semitic (e.g., in Amharic a new series /š ž č č' ǰ ñ/ is created from /s z t ṭ d n/ before /i, e/), with the new /š/ moving into phonetic space vacated by the old. However, one cannot exclude the possibility of a development of /s₂/ in Ethiopic and South Arabic independent of that in Arabic and other Semitic sub-groups. Note in any case that on the one hand there is a great deal of inconsistency in the correspondence sets, while on the other, the manuscript tradition is very poor, variant writings are very common, and it is frequently difficult to determine whether the citation form of a lexical item should be given with <s> or with <ś>.

12.3.1.5. *Laryngeals /ʔ ʕ ḫ ḥ h/*

As noted above, in the pronunciation tradition the only correct values for these consonants are /ʔ h/. Littmann (1918) relates anecdotally that when he read aloud a Geʻez text before some learned clerics in Axum (thus in Tigrinya-speaking territory), giving the common Semitic values to these consonants, he was accused of pronouncing Geʻez "like a peasant"—i.e., a naive Tigrinya speaker who had not learned the more elegant, courtly Amharicizing pronunciation. Note also that in Geʻez, as in many varieties of Semitic, there is no phonological distinction in word-initial position between simple vocalic and glottal onset, even though the writing system has to use a glottal-stop sign to "carry" the vowel. In the following we will not indicate an initial /ʔ/ in our transcriptions, even though rule 5 in § 12.4.2 is proof of its historical, and perhaps systematic, existence.

12.3.2. Vowels
Ge'ez has the seven-vowel system shown in Table 12-3.

Table 12-3. Ge'ez Vowels

i		ə		u
	e		o	
		ä		
		a		

/ä/ represents Semitic short low(-central) /a/. Length distinctions having been replaced by position-of-articulation as a primary phonological distinction in Ethio-Semitic generally, /ä/ is low central front, higher and more forward than /a/, secondarily perhaps also shorter; approximates IPA [æ].

/i u a/ are the primary high-front, high-back, and low(-central) vowels of Ge'ez. Historically they correspond to the Semitic basic long vowels /ī ū ā/.

/e o/ can represent morphophonemically and etymologically earlier/underlying /äy äw/. See § 12.4.3.

/ə/ is pronounced as a high, central-back, unrounded vowel. It represents a merger of the Semitic short high vowels /i u/. (Note that loss of distinction between these two vowels is a common feature of the Damascus Arabic vowel system, among others.) This is also the unmarked epenthetic vowel used to resolve unacceptable or less preferred consonant clusters which can arise in the course of inflectional and derivational processes. As noted above, the Ethiopic writing system does not distinguish between a consonant followed by /ə/ and a word- or syllable-final consonant—and thus makes its presence in practice non-distinctive. The question of the "phonematicity" of /ə/ has in fact been explicitly posed for Amharic. For the traditional pronunciation of Ge'ez, however, a number of derivational, lexical, and phonological criteria point to the necessity of treating /ə/ as a true phonological vowel, at least on a systematic phonemic level of representation. Thus it occurs (stressed and unstressed) independently of considerations of consonant clustering in first and second person possessive suffixes (cf. paradigm in § 12.5). Likewise it is subject to the traditional pronunciation's stress-assignment rules like any other vowel. For example, the penultimate syllable verb stress rule (see § 12.5) affects the penultimate /ə/ in tənäggə́ri (2 f. sg. imperfective) just as it does the /ä/ in näggä́rä (3 m. sg. perfective). Finally, certain morphological patterns have a distinctive /ə/ which cannot be dropped, and which is independent of the rules for final consonant-cluster resolution given below: thus "conative" ("third derived form") jussive yəbárək 'may he bless', never **yəbárk (contrast báhr <bäḫr> 'sea') [here and in the following, double ** will be used for non-occurring forms, as opposed to single * for reconstructed forms]; likewise the so-called quadriliteral plural pattern ä ... a ... ə, as in dänagəl, plural of dəngəl 'virgin'.

12.4. Sequential constraints

12.4.1. Syllabic structure

The preferred syllable type has a single vocalic nucleus and at most a single consonantal onset and/or coda: (C)V(C). When unacceptable or less preferred syllable types arise in morphological processes or loanwords, various strategies are invoked.

12.4.1.1. Word-initial clusters

The following epenthesis rule accounts for the resolution of the vast majority of native Ge'ez initial consonant clusters:

∅ → ə / #C __ C

Thus the imperative, whose systematic form for the simple stem of the verbs ngr 'speak' and lbs 'wear' would be ngər, lbäs, become nəgər, ləbäs. There are very few exceptions to this rule, the only widely cited ones being krämt (variant kərämt) 'winter, rainy season' and krəstos 'Christ' with derivatives krəstiyan 'Christian', krəstənna 'Christianity', krəstun 'one who has become a Christian'. There is no productive rule for breaking up clusters with an initial vowel (such as exists in Arabic). There are, however, isolated lexical patterns such as əgziʔ 'lord' from the root gzʔ 'rule' (the noun occurs in the very high frequency compound word əgziʔäbḥer 'God' [literally, 'lord of the world']), əngəda 'stranger, guest' from the root ngd 'travel'. Note also the form of some common complementizers and conjunctions əsmä 'because', ənzä 'while', əskä 'until' (of uncertain etymology, although the first may be connected to səm 'name'). Fully lexicalized loanwords apparently break up unacceptable clusters not by this rule, but by more ad hoc prothesis and epenthesis processes. Note by way of example: säṭoṭira 'coin' (from Greek statēr), askären 'box' (from Greek skrinion), askema 'monastic garb' (from Greek skhēma 'dress', cf. Syriac ʔeskēmā).

12.4.1.2. Word-final clusters

Investigations of traditional pronunciation are in agreement that, as opposed to word-initial clusters, word-final clusters of two consonants are not broken up by an epenthetic vowel. Makonnen (1984) finds that all word-final clusters are subject to the rule

∅ → ə / CC __ #

and uniformly transcribes: *bahrə* 'sea', *ṭäbbäbtə* 'wise men' (m. pl. of *ṭäbib*), *yəblə* 'he says, he will say' (irregular imperfective of *bəhlä*). Cohen (1921) and Mittwoch (1926) interpret words such as these as having word-final clusters, and usually transcribe them as such (Mittwoch adds that word-final /r, l, n/ are "syllabic" when post-consonantal, but says nothing about other clusters). Thus: *bahr*, *ṭäbbäbt*, *yəbl*. Cohen does, however, note a tendency to pronounce these words with a final /ə/ when they are used in isolation, and even notes this pronunciation in context when the cluster involves a /ʔ/: *ṣərʔ* 'Greece', pronounced both *ṣərə* and *ṣərʔə*. What is at stake here is of course accuracy of facts about phonetic performance, and not systematic phonological representation. All investigators are in agreement that the /ə/ in words such as *yəbarək* and *dänagəl* are part of the word's vowel pattern, and not the result of ephenthesis.

12.4.1.3. Clusters of three consonants

Given what has been said above about the fully vocalic nature of /ə/, it is not clear whether the morphology as such ever confronts the speaker with clusters of more than two consonants—even though the reader of Ge'ez texts frequently has to face the problem of interpreting a sequence of three or more consonant graphemes in the sixth order. Thus the word written <qäṭqt> 'break!' (root *qṭqṭ*) is to be pronounced *qäṭqət* and not *qäṭəqt because the imperative vowel pattern for the quadriliteral verb is CäCCəC. Note in this context that the /t/ suffix which frequently occurs in plurals and in feminines regularly clusters with the preceding consonant, and never occurs in the shape -ət. Thus *nəgəst* 'queen' (= *nəgəs* + *t*, not *nəgs* + *t*; cf. *nəgus* 'king', also *nägäst* 'kings').

12.4.1.4. Gemination

Gemination is a widely employed inflectional and derivational process in Ge'ez, as in the rest of Ethio-Semitic. To give a few examples, it is associated with lexical classes (verbs of lexical class II have a geminated middle radical in all inflected forms: *fäṣṣämä* 'he completed' vs. *nägärä* 'he spoke'), tense inflection (gemination of middle radical in imperfective: *yənäggər* 'he speaks, will speak'), nominal derivation (*fällas* 'sojourner' from *fäläsä* 'sojourn', *ḥäqqal* 'countryman, farmer' from *ḥäql* 'field'), plural formation (*ṭäbbäbt* 'wise men' from *ṭäbib* 'wise man'), suffixation in certain environments (especially involving the "short" vowels /ä ə/: *nägäränni* 'he spoke to me' vs. *nägäruni* 'they spoke to me', *nägärätto* < *nägärät+ä-hu* 'she spoke to him' vs. *nägärätänni* 'she spoke to me', *yəngərro* 'let him speak to him' < *yəngər* 'let him speak', *nägärkənni* 'you [f. sg.] spoke to me' < *nägärki* [cf. § 12.4.5]). In the traditional pronunciation, all consonants can geminate except the laryngeals. In general, gemination seems to be limited to vowel-pattern environments in which the introduction of gemination will not give rise to problematic consonant clusters. (Mittwoch 1926, however, consistently notes some gemination patterns of which this is not the case: *nägärkä* 'you spoke' but *nägärkkänni* 'you spoke to me', and regularly *nägärkkə́mu* 'you (m. pl.) spoke', as opposed to others' *nägärkə́mu*. These cases need more investigation, possibly in connection with the problems raised in § 12.5.)

12.4.2. Laryngeal effects

A series of rules affect the vowels /ä ə/ in the vicinity of laryngeals. (In the following, H stands for the set of laryngeal consonants /ʔ ʕ ḥ h h/, and H_n is a laryngeal in the *n*th position in a root.) Although the immediate phonological environment and output of these rules is rather straightforward, the diachronic and synchronic interaction of these rules with one another and with the morphology results in a complex set of constraints on words, especially verbs, containing laryngeals. There are various ways in which these constraints could be formulated in detail, depending on theoretical framework, and analysis of morphology. The following is simply a descriptive statement of the phenomena, with some illustrative examples.

    1. ə → ä / __ Hä
    2. ä → ə / __ H [V, high] ([V, high] = /i ə u/)
    3. ä → ə / __ H_{fin} V
    4. ä → a / __ H {C, #}
    5. ä → a / H __

Examples (where the affected segment is underlined, with a corresponding non-laryngeal form in parentheses):

    1. a) *yä̱ḥärrəs* 'he plows' (*yə̱näggər* 'he speaks')
       b) *lä̱ʔäk* 'send!' (*lə̱bäs* 'wear!')
       c) *yəsämmə̱ʔäkkä* 'he hears you' (*yənäggə̱räkkä* 'he speaks to you')

d) *abagə̲ʕä* 'sheep' [acc. pl. of *bägʕ*] (*awalə̲dä* 'daughters' [acc. pl. of *wälätt*])
2. a) *rə̲ḥib* 'wide' (*ṭäbib* 'wise')
   b) *yəmə̲hər* 'he is merciful' (*yənäggər*)
   c) *yəkə̲ʕu* [root *kʕw*] 'he pours' (*yətällu* [root *tlw*] 'he follows')
   d) *lə̲h(ə)qä* 'he grew up' (*läbsä* < **läbəsä* < **läbisä* 'he wore')
   e) *täʔə̲ḥzä* 'it was held' (*tänägrä* < **tänägirä* 'it was said')
   f) *yəsmə̲ʕu* 'may they hear' (*yəlbäsu* 'may they wear')
3. a) *sämʕä* < **säməʕä* < **sämiʕä* 'he heard' (*läbsä* < **läbəsä* < **läbisä* 'he wore')
   b) *asmə̲ʕä* 'he caused to hear' (*albäsä* 'he clothed')
   c) *nässə̲ḥä* 'he repented' (*fäṣṣämä* 'he finished')
   d) *balə̲ḥä* 'he liberated' (*baräkä* 'he blessed')
   e) *baḥbə̲ḥä* 'it roared (water)' [root *bḥbḥ*] (*qäṭqäṭä* 'it burst' [root *qṭqṭ*])
4. a) *yəsmaʕ* 'may he hear' (*yəlbäs* 'may he wear')
   b) *sämaʕku* 'I heard' (*läbäsku* 'I wore')
   c) *maʔkäl* 'midst' [root *ʔkl*] (*mängäd* 'road' [root *ngd*]
5. a) *amnä* 'he believed' (*läbsä* 'he wore')
   b) *ḥaqäfä* 'he embraced' (*nägärä* 'he spoke')
   c) *läʔakä* 'he sent' (*nägärä* 'he spoke')

Rules 1 and 2 together impose what amounts to a vowel harmony constraint across laryngeals (a short vowel before a laryngeal must have the same height as a vowel which follows). However, while rule 1 applies to H_1 and H_2 verbs, as shown by 1a and 1b, 1c–d show that the constraint does not apply to H_3 triconsonantal roots (which are governed by rule 3). Examples 2a–e show that rule 2 applies to H_2, and 2f shows that it applies (redundantly with rule 3) to H_3, 2e shows that it does not apply to H_1. 2d shows that H_2 verbs tend to be of the so-called "intransitive" *läbsä* type, and behave as though there were a /ə/ between the second and third root consonant. This prevents rule 4 from operating on these verbs, which would otherwise become **lahqä (note that example 5c shows that there are a few *nägärä* type H_2 verbs. Example 3a shows that base-form H_3 triradicals are also formally assimilated to the *läbsä* class; but as examples 3b–d show, this rule also gives rise to forms which are not paralleled in non-laryngeal verbs. 3e shows that this rule also applies to the *fourth* consonant of quadriradical roots, and that rule 3 is properly formulated in terms of *root-final* laryngeal (H_{fin}), and not just H_3. The examples for rule 4 (plus 3e) show that it applies to H_1 and H_{fin}, but to H₂ only in quadriradicals. Rule 5 "lengthens" /ä/ after H (something not always reflected in the writing). A corollary of rule 5, plus the fact that graphic and systematic word-initial /ʔV/ is pronounced as word-initial /V/ in the traditional pronunciation, is that no word can begin with the vowel /ä/ (cf. 5a).

12.4.3. Glide effects

Vowels and glides interact in a number of assimilatory and dissimilatory processes. To begin with labiovelars (where K = /k q g ḫ/, Kʷ the corresponding labiovelars, and ~ is to be read 'alternates with'), note the neutralization of the distinction between a labiovelar followed by /ə ä/ and a velar followed by /u o/:

    Kʷə ~ Ku   (qʷəl ~ qul 'bunch of grapes')
    Kʷä ~ Ko   (qʷäṭiṭ ~ qoṭiṭ 'slender')

Correspondingly, as already noted, a labiovelar cannot be followed by a rounded vowel:

    **Kʷu,o

The following rules handle short-vowel glide sequences in syllable final position:

    äw → o   (fätäwkä ~ fätokä 'you loved')
    äy → e   (sätäykä [sätekä rare] 'you drank')
    əw → u   (*yəfättəw > yəfättu 'he loves')
    əy → i   (*yəsättəy > yəsätti 'he drinks')

Of these rules, the first is optional, the second is rare, while the third and fourth are obligatory. The opposite order of glide and /ə/, at least post-consonantally, is operative in:

    wə → u / C __ (cf. labiovelar rules)
    yə → i / C __   (akyəst ~ akist, plural of käysi 'serpent, dragon';
                    cf. agbərt plural of gäbr 'slave')

There is also, in a glide context, a reduction in the reverse direction:

    u → ə / ww __   (məwwut ~ məwwət 'dead', participle of mwt 'die';
                    cf. fəṣṣum 'finished' < fṣm 'finish')
    i → ë / yy __   (qäyyiḥ ~ qäyyəḥ 'red', adjective from root qyḥ; cf.
                   ḥäddis 'new', adjective from root ḥds)

Sequences of /u i/ and a following vowel are resolved by a process that in some sense is also a reverse of the glide+/ə/ rules. (The only relevant cases seem to be those of the third person object suffix pronouns -o, -a, -omu, -on < hu, ha, homu, hon 'him, her, them (m.), them (f.)'.

u → əw(w) / __ V   (qätälu+o > qätäləwwo 'they killed him', qätälu+a
                    > qätäləwwa 'they killed her')
i → əy(y) / __ V   (qätälki+o > qätälkəyyo 'you (f.) killed him',
                    qätälki+a > qätälkəyya 'you (f.) killed her')
The preceding two statements combine a glide formation and reduction process into one step. This glide formation occurs independently between the proclitic negation marker *i* 'not' and verbal forms beginning with a vowel. Thus: *i+asmäʕä > iyasməʕä* 'he did not cause to hear', *i+əsämmäʕ > iyəsämmäʕ* 'I do not hear'. Some combination of glide formation and glide+vowel reduction is probably involved in the accusative form of nouns ending in /i/. Normal accusative is marked by suffixation of /ä/: *nəgus* 'king [nom.]' *nəgusä* 'king [acc.]'. Thus we have: *bəʔsi* 'man [nom.]' and *bəʔsi+ä > bəʔsiyä > bəʕsi(ə)yä > bəʔse* 'man [acc.]'.

12.4.4. Consonant assimilation
The only productive consonantal assimilation processes involve consonant sequences which arise across morpheme boundaries in the course of affixation. There are only three consonants involved in affixation in Geʿez, /t n k/, and of these, only /t k/ are involved in assimilation. /k/, which occurs in suffixes marking first and second person subject in the verb, assimilates to a preceding (i.e., stem-final) velar stop:

k → {g, q} / {g, q} __   (ḫädäg+kä > ḫädäggä 'you left'; säräq+ku > säräqqu
                          'I stole')

/t/ occurs as a prefix marking passive-reflexive derived stems in the imperfective tense (the shape of the prefix in the perfective is *tä-*). It assimilates fully to a following dental stop or sibilant, /t ṭ d s ṣ z ś ḍ/ = D:

t → D / __ D   (yə+t+sämmäʕ > yəssämmäʕ 'he is heard'; cf.
                yətqättäl 'he is killed')

As a suffix /t/ marks feminine (and also plural) forms of nouns and participles. Here it assimilates to a preceding dental *stop*:

t → {d, ṭ} / {d, ṭ} __   (kəbud+t > kəbədd 'heavy [fem.]'; qəṭqut+t > qəṭqəṭṭ
                          'crushed [fem.]')

Note, however, idiosyncratically 'one [fem.]' *aḥatti < aḥad+ti*, 'daughter' *wälätt < wäläd+t*.

12.4.5. Vowel reduction
There are two "shortening" rules (recall that /i a u/ come from common Semitic /ī ā ū/, while /ə/ represents a merger of Semitic /i u/ and /ä/ is Semitic

/a/). One is a dissimilation rule which reduces /i/ which is part of a feminine or plural suffix before a suffix containing an /i/:

i → ə / + (C) __ + Ci

Examples: *häb+i+ni* > *häbənni* 'give [f. sg.] me!' (vs. *häbina* 'give [f. sg.] us!'); *afras+i+ki* > *afrasəki* 'your [f. sg.] horses' (vs. *afrasihu* 'his horses'); *nägär+ki+ni* > *nägärkənni* 'you [f. sg.] spoke to me' (vs. *nägärkinä* 'you [f. sg.] spoke to us'); contrast *qätaliki* 'your [f. sg.] killer', where the *-i* is part of the 'agentive' vowel pattern CäCaCi. The other rule "shortens" /u i/ (and /a/ optionally) in syllables closed by the feminine suffix *-t*.

u, i → ə / __ C+t (*kəbur+t* > *kəbərt* 'honored [f.]'; *ləhiq+t* > *ləhəqt* 'grown up [f.]')

a → ä / __ C+t (*śännayt* ~ *śännäyt* 'beautiful [f.]' vs. *śännay* 'beautiful [m.]')

12.5. Stress

All modern observers agree that the traditional pronunciation assigns stress to Geʿez words in context, although there is a certain amount of difference on the details of this stress assignment. Ethiopian experts on Geʿez themselves can point out minimal pairs such as: *yənäggə́ra* 'they [f. pl.] speak' vs. *yənäggərá* 'he speaks to her' (cf. Mittwoch 1926: 32). The following generalizations seem to be supported by the formulations and transcriptions of most modern investigations:

1. Verbs are generally stressed on the penult: *nägä́rä, tənäggə́ri* 'he spoke, you (f. sg.) speak'
    But the following have final stress:
    a) perfective, 2 f. pl. subject: *nägärkə́n* 'you spoke'
    b) verbs with 2 f. pl. object: *yənäggərä(k)kə́n, nägärä(k)kə́n* 'he speaks/spoke to you'
    c) verbs with 3 sg. and 3 f. pl. object: *nägäró, nägärón* 'he spoke to him/them'
        Except: jussive, imperative: *yəngə́rro* 'may he speak to him'
        forms with /ə/ < /u, i/: *nägärə́wwo* 'they spoke to him'
2. Nouns and pronouns have final stress: *nəgús* 'king'
    Except: When followed by the *-ä* accusative marker: *nəgúsä* 'king [acc.]'
3. Personal pronouns and possessive suffixes follow special patterns. The most common forms are stressed as follows:

	Sg	Pl	Sg	Pl
1	ánä	nə́ḥnä	-ə́yä	-ə́nä
2m	ántä	antə́mu	-ə́kä	-əkə́mu
2f	ánti	antə́n	-ə́ki	-əkə́n
3m	wəʔə́tu	əmuntú	-(h)ú, -ó	-(h)ómu
3f	yəʔə́ti	əmantú	-(h)á	-(h)ón

It cannot, however, be overemphasized that no complete analysis of stress patterns have been made for *any* Ethio-Semitic language, and that much remains to be done in this area. Cohen's intuition (1921: 230, 258[2]) was that in Ethio-Semitic factors of intensity, syllable length, gemination (and conceivably pitch, Kolmodin 1910: 250) may be interrelated in a complex metrical pattern whose key has not yet been discovered. We still need to find out whether he may have been right.

Bibliography

Cohen, Marcel. 1921. "La prononciation traditionnelle du guèze (éthiopien classique)." *Journal Asiatique* ser. 11, vol. 17: 217–69.

Dillmann, August. 1857. *Grammatik der äthiopischen Sprache*. Leipzig: Tauchnitz.

———. 1907. *Ethiopic Grammar*, 2nd ed., enlarged and improved, by Carl Bezold (1899). Trans. James Crichton. London: Williams & Norgate.

Kolmodin, Johannes. 1910. "Meine studienreise in Abessinien 1908–1910." *Le Monde Oriental* 4: 229–55.

König, Eduard. 1877. *Neue Studien über Schrift, Aussprache und allgemeine Formenlehre des Aethiopischen*. Leipzig.

Lambdin, Thomas. 1978. *Introduction to Classical Ethiopic (Ge'ez)*. Missoula, Mont.: Scholars Press.

Leslau, Wolf. 1987. *Comparative Dictionary of Ge'ez*. Wiesbaden: Harrassowitz.

Littmann, Enno. 1918. "Ge'ez-Studien I, II, III." *Nachrichten der K. Gesellschaft der Wissenschaften zu Göttingen*, Philologisch-historische Klasse, 627–702; 318–39.

Ludolf, Hiob. 1661. *Grammatica aethiopica*. London: Thomas Roycroft.

Makonnen Argaw. 1984. *Matériaux pour l'étude de la prononciation traditionnelle du guèze*. Paris: Editions Recherche sur les Civilisations.

Mittwoch, Eugen. 1926. *Die traditionelle Aussprache des äthiopischen* (Abessinische Studien 1). Berlin: de Gruyter.

Trumpp, Ernst. 1874. "Ueber den Accent im Aethiopischen." *Zeitschrift der deutschen morgenländischen Gesellschaft* 28: 515–61.

Ullendorff, Edward. 1955. *The Semitic Languages of Ethiopia: A Comparative Phonology.* London: Taylor's (Foreign) Press.

Chapter 13
Arabic Phonology
Alan S. Kaye
California State University, Fullerton

13.1. Arabic and its relationship to the other Semitic languages

The Semitic languages (part of a larger phylum generally called Afroasiatic [Afro-Asiatic], Afrasian, or Hamito-Semitic) are usually classified into East Semitic, consisting of Akkadian with its two major dialects, Assyrian and Babylonian, and West Semitic. West Semitic, in turn, consists of (1) Northwest Semitic with Hebrew, Aramaic (a complicated variety of dialects and very distinct languages by any usual definition of this term, such as Syriac, the language of the Peshitta translation of the Bible), Amorite, and Phoenician-Punic (most scholars also include here Ugaritic but not Eblaite [the latter of which seems most closely related, in all probability, to Akkadian], two ancient cuneiform languages found in Syria in the 1920s and 1970s, respectively); and (2) Southwest Semitic comprising Arabic (Epigraphic, or Old, and Modern South Arabian), and Ethiopic (a conglomerate of many different languages and dialects). Arabic is sometimes referred to as North Arabic to differentiate it from South Arabian. Despite the similarity in name, Epigraphic South Arabian, also called Epigraphic South Arabic (ESA), is not any closer to Arabic than to some other Semitic languages. ESA is known in four major dialects (Sabaean, Qatabanian, Minaean, and Ḥaḍramatic), which are closely related to the Ethio-Semitic languages. This is quite understandable since South Arabian speakers came to Ethiopia from today's Yemen bringing their language and writing system with them. The modern South Arabian languages, such as Soqotri and Shxauri (the latter is also known as Śḥeri or Jibbāli), are not so close to (North) Arabic. They are mutually unintelligible with it, even though they have borrowed many Arabic lexemes due to the influence of Islam and the languages-in-contact situation.

AUTHOR'S NOTE: I wish to record my gratitude to the following colleagues, who contributed many useful comments on a preliminary version of this chapter: Peter T. Daniels, Stuart Davis, Robert Hoberman, Jeffrey Heath, Gary A. Rendsburg, and Stanislav Segert. Needless to say, the usual disclaimers apply, especially since I have sometimes not followed the advice offered.

Table 13-1. Comparison of the Major Semitic Languages

	Akkadian	Hebrew	Aramaic	ESA-Ethiopic	CA	
1.	kalbu	kɛlɛv	kalbā	kalb	kalbun	'dog'
2.	šūru	šōr	tawrā	sōr	θawrun	'bull'
3.	rēšu	rōš	rēšā	rɛʔs	raʔsun	'head'
4.	ʔēnu	ʕayin	ʕaynā	ʕayn	ʕaynun	'eye'
5.	ʔuznu	ʔozɛn	ʔuðnā	ʔezn	ʔuð(u)nun	'ear'
6.	lišānu	ləšōn	liššānā	ləssān	lisānun	'tongue'
7.	ʔūmu	yōm	yawmā	yōm	yawmun	'day'
8.	ʔeqlu	hɛlɛqᵃ	ḥaqlā	ḥaql	ḥaqlun	'field'
9.	šalāmu	šɔlōm	šlāmā	salām	salāmun	'peace'
10.	napištu	nɛfɛš	nawšā	nafs	nafsun	'soul'

a. Not listed by Leslau (1987: 240) but listed by Köhler-Baumgartner (1958: 306).

Some Semitic languages are compared in Table 13-1, which represents data from the ancient Semitic languages: Akkadian (Assyro-Babylonian), Hebrew (Classical or Tiberian), Aramaic (Syriac), reconstructed ESA since the vowels were not written, Classical Ethiopic (Geʻez), and Classical Arabic (CA). ESA and CA are the most conservative of all the Semitic languages, phonologically speaking. Akkadian, on the other hand, the oldest attested Semitic language, has lost the pharyngeals, among other noteworthy developments. Most modern colloquial Arabic dialects use descendants not very different from the ten sample words listed above. Thus *kalb* 'dog' and *rās* 'head' still survive in the great majority of Arabic vernaculars spoken today.

The Semitic family of languages operates on the root + vocalic pattern principle, with Arabic being the most systematic representative of the famous triconsonantal system and the one usually used by linguists as typically illustrative of Semitic. The root consists of consonants only (usually three), while the vowels often express the grammatical categories. Thus, the standard root (used by many Semitists) QTL has something to do with 'killing', such as CA *qatl* 'murder', *qatala* 'he killed', *maqtūl* or *qatīl* 'killed one (m.)', *qātil* 'murderer, killer (m.)', *qitāl* 'battle', *qātala* 'he fought with', etc. The three radicals (or root letters) are not pronounceable by themselves, and often roots do not share a single semantic sphere. For example, *ʕaliqa* means 'to hang' whereas ʕallaqa is 'to comment'. Some vocalic patterns, as the latter form illustrates, also operate with gemination of one of the radicals; e.g., qattala means 'he massacred' with the gemination of the second radical (C²) of the root (the second consonant of the root is geminated in Form II of the verb, the so-called **intensive**).

The consonantal root and vocalic patterning system was probably at least partially responsible for the evolution of the Arabic script, developed out of Aramaic (Nabatean) via the "Sinaitic" script, which was molded from the West Semitic signary. ESA and Phoenician do not express any vowels at all. Thus, the Phoenician graphemes <QTL> may mean 'he killed' (= CA qatala, Hebrew qāṭal) or 'she killed' (= CA qatalat, Hebrew qāṭəlā), even though their pronunciations were distinct. The West Semitic alphabets (Hebrew, Aramaic, and Arabic) have all made use of *matres lectionis* ('mothers of reading'), a device utilizing the morphophonemically weak consonants, viz., the glottal stop and approximants (ʔ, h, w, y), to express long vowels, although there were and still are differences of usage among the various Semitic languages. The short vowels are indicated by special markings of rather late origin and are not normally used in the modern written language (Modern Standard Arabic); for CA these markings include <a>, <i>, and <u>, *shadda* or *tašdīd* (the gemination grapheme) and other graphemes for the correct recitation of texts, i.e., the *tajwīd* of the Holy Qur'an (see especially Nelson 1985: 14–31). This classical–modern situation is similar in some ways to Classical (Biblical) and Modern (Israeli) Hebrew and their intricate interrelationships.

Arabic has survived as a spoken language, whereas Akkadian and the Canaanite dialects have died out with the exception of Hebrew, if indeed Hebrew is designated as Canaanite. Aramaic (the mother tongue of Jesus) still survives as many different spoken languages in Iraq, Iran, Turkey, and Syria (and of course, countries such as Israel and the U.S.A., to which those Middle Eastern peoples have immigrated). It is known today as either Neo-Aramaic/Neo-Syriac or modern Assyrian (rarely also as Chaldean). Many Aramaic speakers, it should be noted, also speak an Arabic dialect. The various Neo-Aramaic languages have, taken all together, approximately a quarter million speakers. (In many ways, Aramaic has developed into many Neo-Aramaic languages in a fashion similar to Latin's developing into the Romance languages.) Classical Ethiopic or Geʻez has not survived except as the liturgical language of the Ethiopic Church (paralleling the situation of Coptic in Egypt), and there are many modern, spoken Ethio-Semitic languages, such as the national language of Ethiopia, Amharic, or the two northern Ethiopian languages, Tigre and Tigrinya, to which Ge'ez is closely related in a northern Ethiopic sub-branch. There are many Arabic loanwords in the Ethio-Semitic languages (see Leslau 1990).

13.2. Arabic dialectology

Arabic is the Semitic or indeed the Afroasiatic language with by far the greatest number of speakers, probably now in excess of 200 million. It is the major language throughout the Arab world—Egypt, the Sudan, Libya, the closely knit North African countries (usually referred to as the Maghrib, which includes Tunisia, Morocco, and Algeria), Mauretania, Saudi Arabia, Iraq, Lebanon, Syria, Jordan, the Gulf states, etc. It is even the major language of a non-Arab country, the Republic of Chad in central Africa (i.e., more Chadians speak Arabic as their mother tongue or as a second language than any other single language).

As a minority language, Arabic is spoken and widely studied in other nations such as Nigeria, Iran, Afghanistan, Israel (where it is an offical language), and some Inner Asian countries, although Uzbeki Arabic may now be completely extinct. Furthermore, it is in wide use throughout the Muslim world as a second language and as a learned, liturgical language (e.g., in Pakistan, India, Tanzania, or Indonesia). Indeed, among orthodox Muslims, Arabic is *lughat al-malāʔika* 'the language of the angels', and the language *par excellence* in the world since Allah himself is believed to have revealed his Holy Book, the Qur'an, in the Arabic language. One can also readily comprehend that Arabs are very proud of their (most beautiful) language by considering that there is even an Arabic verb *ʔaʕraba* 'to speak clearly and eloquently', which has come to mean 'to express' in general, a derivative of the root ʕRB, also occurring in the word *alʕarabiyyah* 'the Arabic language', or *lisān ʕarabī* 'the Arabic language' in the Qur'an.

There are, from a purely descriptive point of view, many recognizably distinct, major Arabic dialects. The peripheral Arabic dialects are, in fact, so radically different from those of the main Middle Eastern core (in which there is somewhat of a cultural solidarity) that they are better referred to as separate languages, by any satisfactory definition of what a language is (see Kaye 1994: 47). Certainly mutual unintelligibility is an overriding factor here. (I am familiar with the old adage that the major difference between a language and a dialect is that a language is a dialect with an army and a navy.) One of these deserves very special mention. Maltese is unquestionably a dialect of Arabic from the historical point of view. This historicity has produced the rather awkward designation "Maltese Arabic." Due to its isolation from the rest of the Arab world where we have noted a cultural uniformity (see above), Maltese has developed into a new Semitic language in its own right (a similar, but slightly weaker, argument could also be made for Cypriot Maronite Arabic, now probably extinct on Cyprus). The two major reasons for not regarding Maltese as a dialect of Arabic synchronically are (1) it does not have diglossia, i.e., it does not have CA as a "high" level of language (more on this important topic later); and (2) it is written in the Latin script. Both of the aforementioned points taken together would certainly make it unique as a dialect of Arabic. Furthermore, the Maltese do not consider themselves Arabs, nor do they consider their variety of English pronunciation to be part of any so-called Arabic "accent" in the widest possible sense of this term.

13.3. Arabic as Central Semitic

According to Robert Hetzron's innovative classification of the Semitic languages (1972: 16), which is not universally accepted by Semitists, Arabic shares traits of both South Semitic and Northwest Semitic. Arabic preserves Proto-Semitic (PS) phonology almost perfectly (ESA is even a bit more conservative), except for PS *p > f and *ś > š (note that PS *ṡ and *š develop into Arabic s). But it also shares features with Hebrew, Ugaritic, and Aramaic, such as the masculine plural suffix -īna/īma and the internal passive, e.g., Arabic *qatala* 'he killed' vs. *qutila* 'he was killed', Aramaic *qəṭīl* 'killed' and Arabic *qatīl* 'killed one'; furthermore consider Hebrew *hilbīš* 'he dressed someone' vs. *hulbaš* 'he was dressed (by someone)'.

The morphology of the definite article in Hebrew (*ha-* < *han* + gemination of the following consonant, where possible) and Arabic (*ʔal-*, cognate with *han* and Ugaritic /hn-/ in the demonstrative pronouns *hnd* and *hnk*, which assimilates before dentals, sibilants, or sonorants, producing a geminate) also points to a common origin. The Hebrew *ha-*, in fact, shows up, in my view, in the Arabic demonstratives: *hāðā* 'this (m.sg.)', *hāðihi* (f.), and *hāʔulāʔi* (pl., all genders). Even the broken plurals of Arabic, in which one can see the vocalic change in the stem (cf. Arabic *kilāb* 'dogs', pl. of *kalb*), may be compared with Hebrew segholate (viz., $C^1 \varepsilon C^2 \varepsilon C^3$) plurals, such as *kəlābīm* 'dogs' (cf. Hebrew singular *kɛlɛb* < *kalb* + masculine plural *-īm*).

There are some other striking morphological affinities of Arabic with Hebrew, such as the ancient dialectal Arabic relative particle ðū = Biblical Hebrew zū, while the Western form ðī occurred in Arabic ʔallaðī 'who (m.sg.)' and Aramaic dī. In all likelihood, the form with u represents the nominative while the form with i retained the oblique (i.e., genitive and accusative) marking. Some Eastern dialects also reflected Barth's Law; i.e., they had i as the imperfect preformative vowel with a of the imperfect stem, as in the Canaanite dialects.

13.4. Consonants

The consonantal segments of a fairly typical educated pronunciation of Modern Standard Arabic (MSA), identical in most respects to CA, are included in the consonant chart in Table 13-2. The symbols are modified from the International Phonetic Alphabet (IPA), as is the custom of linguists specializing in Arabic and other Semitic languages.

Table 13-2. Modern Standard Arabic Consonants

stops	b			t d	ṭ ḍ		k	q		ʔ
affricates						ǰ				
fricatives			f	θ ð	s z ṣ ẓ̌ (z̧)	š		x ɣ	ħ ʕ	h
nasals	m			n						
liquids				l r	ḷ					
approximants	w					y				

The Arabic alphabet provides an accurate depiction of the phonological facts of the standard language. However, in many dialects there are some pronunciations that differ from those presented in Table 13-2. For instance, CA /q/ is voiced in many dialects, both ancient and modern, i.e., [ɢ] (especially among various Bedouins, and this is probably indicative of its original Arabic pronunciation). Moreover, the CA ǰīm (the name of the letter represented by the grapheme <ǰ>) corresponds to many pronunciations, such as [ǰ], [ɟ], [dy], [gy], [g], [y], or [ž] stemming from PS */g/. Cairo Arabic [g] reflects a complicated chain of developments (see Kaye 1972) from Proto-Colloquial Arabic */ž/ (as preserved, say, by Damascus Arabic).

Every consonant in CA, MSA, and most Arabic dialects may be geminated, unlike Hebrew, for example, which cannot geminate the so-called "gutturals" ʔ, ʕ, h, ħ, and r—the pharyngeals and laryngeals plus r (which may have been uvular as it is mostly in Modern Israeli Hebrew, although the acrolectic pronunciation is still rolled).

CA does not have a /p/, but standard pronunciations tend to devoice a /b/ before a voiceless consonant, e.g., /ħabs/—[ħaps] 'imprisonment' or /ħibs/—[ħips] 'dam'. Some modern Arabic dialects (notably in Iraq) have both /p/ and /p̣/ (emphatic); however, the great majority of Arabic speakers produce English /p/ as /b/ through interference modification (one Arab asks another, "Which Bombay are you going on vacation to? Bombay, India, or Bombay—Pompeii—Italy?"). Incidentally, Persian, Urdu, and other languages which have /p/ have taken the grapheme for /b/ = ب and made پ by placing three dots underneath its basic configuration to = <p> (no confusion with ت <t> or ث <θ>. This grapheme, in turn, has been reborrowed by some Iraqi Arabs, who use it both in native developments as well as in Persian loanwords.

CA does not have a /v/, but phonetically a [v] often occurs through regressive assimilation as in /ħifð/—[ħivð] 'memory'. /n/ also assimilates regressively, i.e. nb > mb (/mimbar/ منبر 'mimbar' and ng > ŋk as in /bank/ > [baŋk] 'bank'.

13.4.1. The term "emphasis" as applied to Arabic

The *emphatic* consonants, often misleadingly called velarized or pharyngealized or pharyngealized-velarized, are depicted with a dot underneath the consonant. Emphatic pronounciation has little or nothing at all to do with velarization and nothing to do with what is involved in the articulation of [ħ] and [ʕ]. Perhaps nowhere else in Arabic linguistic literature is there more controversy than in this area of the emphatics—how they are to be described and how they function in a dialect and cross-dialectally. The vowels around an emphatic consonant tend to become lower, retracted, or more centralized than those around corresponding non-emphatics. The very back consonants, /q/ and sometimes /x/, /ɣ/, and /r/, have a similar effect on vowels, which is why the vowel allophonics of Arabic are much more cumbersome and intricate than the consonant allophonics. In some dialects, e.g., Cairene, vowels are lowered after /ħ/ and /ʕ/ as well: /ħub/ 'love' = [ħob], and /ʕumar/ 'Omar' = [ʕomar]. Before or after /ħ/ and /ʕ/, the short /a/ = [ɑ] rather than the common [æ] (see Harrell 1957: 50–51). /r/ also triggers the back /ɑ/ as in [mašrubɑːt] 'drinks', and there are minimal pairs indicating a phonemic difference between /r/ and /ṛ/: baṛṛi 'my land' vs. bærri 'pertaining to land', baʔaṛi 'my cows' vs. bæʔæri 'bovine', gaːṛi 'my neighbor' vs. gæːri 'running', and ṛaːmi 'Rami (p.n.m.)' vs. ræːmi 'throwing' (Harrell 1957: 72–73).

In Old Arabic, the primary emphatics were most likely voiced, i.e., the /ḍ/ < [ẓl] (lateralized) IPA [ɮˁ], or [ẓˡ]), the /ṭ/ < /ḍ/, the /ð̣/ or /ẓ/ < /ð/, and the /ṣ/ < /ẓ/. Some linguists have argued that the emphatics in Arabic and other Semitic languages were originally glottalized, as preserved in Ethio-Semitic. My own view is that glottalization in the latter case should be regarded as due to Cushitic substratum.

13.4.2. *The debate about the nature of the emphatics*

Most dialects of Arabic spoken today contain emphatic versus non-emphatic contrasts (referred to in Arabic as *ʔiṭbāq, tafxīm*, or *mufaxxama*). Thus, a word such as CA *ṣayf* 'summer' contrasts with its non-emphatic counterpart *sayf* 'sword'. The usual phonological explanation for this feature (see Gairdner 1925) lies in the opposition of the emphatic /ṣ/ and the non-emphatic or plain /s/. In a classic article on the subject, Jakobson (1957) attributed some of the phonetic characteristics of emphasis to a contraction of the upper pharynx (usually called pharyngealization). Velarization refers in essence to a decrease in the back orifice of the buccal cavity serving as a resonator. (The IPA, unfortunately in my view, indicated both features with a wavy bar, actually a tilde, through the particular consonant, i.e., [s̴]; for [ṣ]; however, the revised IPA [1989] noted velarized [tˠ] vs. pharyngealized [tˤ], whereas [ɫ] is either velarized or pharyngealized.) In addition to the above, emphasis often involves some degree of protrusion and rounding of the lips. Cf. Nigerian Arabic *aṃṃʷ* 'mother' vs. *amm* 'paternal uncle' (Owens 1993: 25). This explains why some emphatics are often perceived as labials by non-Arabs. Any phoneme in the language which is articulated with the aforementioned phonetic features is perceived by native speakers as being emphatic (although even native speakers on rare occasions refer to certain consonants as being only "slightly" emphatic, an impressionistic phonetic designation).

The description of emphasis in terms of acoustic phonetics is perhaps easier to comprehend. The emphatic phonemes are lower in pitch; i.e., the sound spectrograph has revealed that they have higher energy in the lower frequency regions. This is why Jakobson (1957) proposed to label this particular feature [+flat] (which he also used for both labials and labialized phonemes).

Depending on the analyst's point of view, vowels may also be emphatic or, at least, influenced (via assimilation) by adjacent or nearby emphatic consonants. This means that emphatic vowels are consonantally conditioned allophones and can be predicted from the surrounding emphatic consonants.

Though emphasis has been studied from a phonetic standpoint (x-ray studies go back more than half a century), the various phonological perspectives as to its role and function in the language in terms of a more abstract or underlying (morphophonemic) level remain highly controversial. One of the main reasons for this is that emphasis is never an articulatory phonetic feature of only one phoneme. The word /ṣayf/ 'summer' (cited above) is really [ṣa̱y̱f̱]. A word such as /ṭīn/ 'mud' consists of a [ṭ] followed by [ī] and [n], i.e., [ṭi̱:ṉ] or [t̫i̫:n̫]. Emphasis always affects two or more segments, a fact not represented in the orthography of CA. For this reason, an analysis of emphasis as a monovalent distinctive feature (present or absent in a single phoneme) is unsatisfactory.

According to a modern binary viewpoint, Arabic consonants are either [+emphatic] or [–emphatic]. All emphatic vowels would be emphatic by virtue of the influence of these phonologically emphatic consonants. The biggest problem with this type of analysis is that it immediately doubles the phonemic inventory of Arabic consonants. Another oddity is that one would have terribly cumbersome morphological (allomorphic) representations, i.e., the -*t* marking the first person singular perfect has an allomorph -*ṭ* after an emphatic consonant, and so on. Consider, for example, *katab* + *t* 'I wrote' but *ḍarab* + *ṭ* 'I beat/struck'.

Still other phonologists have suggested that all vowels exist in emphatic and non-emphatic pairs. This is tantamount to stating that emphasis is a redundant feature in terms of consonants. The problems with this way of looking at things are precisely the reverse of the vocalic redundancy solution. An Arabic morpheme consists (often) of a root plus a vocalic pattern. With the "normal" triconsonantal root, the discontinuous *a–a* marks the third person masculine singular of the perfect. A pair such as *katab* 'he wrote' and *ḍarab* 'he hit' (both CA pausal forms) would require the *a–a* and an allomorph *ạ–ạ*. Another difficulty is trying to explain *ḍarabat* 'she hit', for the /b̩/ of *ḍarab* 'he hit' is emphatic but the same /b/ of 'she hit' is non-emphatic.

Some Firthian linguists tried to impose a prosodic or suprasegmental approach on the Arabic phonological system (see, e.g., various papers in Mitchell 1975). This approach was apparently more satisfactory than those mentioned so far, since (as stressed earlier) emphasis never occurs as a monovalent phonemic feature. Rather, the minimum domain for emphasis in many Arabic dialects is the common syllabic type CV. Thus, emphasis can be seen as [+syllabic] or [–syllabic]. Critics of this analysis have pointed out that one must also apply this frame of reference to voicing and velic closure as also being suprasegmental, since both appear to involve features that extend over more than one segment. However, when one given example occurs over the domain of a syllable, it is a distinctive feature of consonants but a redundant feature of vowels. This can be proven by noting the non-existence of nasalized or voiceless vowels outside nasal or voiceless environments. The corresponding situation for emphasis is quite different because it is not clear if consonants influence vowels or vice versa (as in the case of velic closure or voicing). Therefore, emphasis is much more suited for suprasegmental status than are the other two features mentioned above, since the latter extend over and are distinctive in only one segment.

Lehn (1963) reviewed much of the literature on the entire subject (including Arabic grammatical thought) and concluded that, at least for Cairo Arabic, the minimum domain of emphasis is the syllable, and the maximum domain is the utterance. Lehn suggested that emphasis not be treated as a distinctive system of the consonantal or vocalic system, but as a redundant feature of both. In his later works, Lehn underscores all emphatic syllables; thus, Cairene <u>darab</u> 'he hit' but <u>darabit</u> 'she hit'. This is testimony in favor of our notation ḍa̠ra̠b vs. ḍa̠ra̠bit.

As Ferguson (1956) has demonstrated, the /l̩/ which occurs only in the name of God in CA /ʔallāh/ (but not after /i/ as in /bismillāh/ 'in the name of Allah') is a phoneme in CA. Some modern Arabic dialects, especially those spoken in the Gulf states, have many more examples of /l̩/.

13.5. Vowels

The Arabic vowel system is well known among linguists. It has the classical triangular system that preserves PS vocalism. This system is represented as:

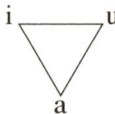

For CA and MSA, the vowels may be short or long (geminated). Many modern Arabic dialects have, however, developed other vowels such as /ə/, /e/, /o/, etc., just as the other Semitic languages did centuries and millennia earlier through a general and natural process of parallel development.

Arabic vowel allophonics are much richer than its consonant allophonics chiefly because the former take on the coloring of the adjacent emphatic and emphatic-like consonants (including /r̩/), while the non-emphatic consonants

Arabic Phonology 197

push the vowels to higher and less centralized qualities. Significantly, the pronunciation of MSA and any oral rendition of CA are all directly dependent on the nature of the speaker's colloquial dialect natively acquired. The influence of the native vernacular on MSA is most obvious in the matter of stress or consonants such as the *jiim* ([ʄ]); however, detailed studies are sorely needed in this area, neglected by specialists for far too long.

The vowel allophonics have been accurately described on the basis of sound spectrographic analysis for MSA as used in Iraq (Al-Ani 1970). Very similar rules can be formulated for other parts of the Arab world. The rules may be stated as follows (where the lack of an underscore in the environment means that the segment may occur on either side of the motivating feature or segment):

(1) /ī/ → [ɨ̄] / [+ emphatic]_ (except /l/)
         → [ī] /_ { ʕ / ɣ }_
         → [ī] / (elsewhere)

(2) /i/ → [ɨ] /_ [+emphatic]_
         → [ɪ] /_ { ʕ / ɣ }_
         → [i]   (elsewhere)

(3) /ū/ → [ʉ̄] /_ [+emphatic]_ (except /l/)
         → [ū] (elsewhere)

(4) /u/ → [ʊ] /_ [+emphatic]_
         → [u] (elsewhere)

(5) /ā/ → [ā]/ $\left[\_ \left\{ \begin{matrix} +\text{emphatic} \\ \left\{ \begin{matrix} q \\ r \end{matrix} \right\} \end{matrix} \right\} \_ \right]$
         → [ɑ̄] / $\left[\_ \left\{ \begin{matrix} ʕ \\ ɣ \end{matrix} \right\} \_ \right]$
         → [æ] (elsewhere)

(6) /a/ → [ə] / ___# (but not next to /q/, /ʕ/, /r/, and /ɣ/)
         → [a]/ $\left[\_ \left\{ \begin{matrix} +\text{emphatic} \\ \left\{ \begin{matrix} q \\ r \end{matrix} \right\} \end{matrix} \right\} \_ \right]$
         → [ʌ] / $\left[\_ \left\{ \begin{matrix} ʕ \\ ɣ \end{matrix} \right\} \_ \right]$
         → [æ] (elsewhere)

In modern Arabic dialects, the short vowels are more susceptible to change than the long vowels. Thus, CA /i/ and /u/ in Damascene merge into /ə/ (exactly as occurred centuries earlier in Geʻez—a good example of parallel development). Although /a/ is usually the most stable and conservative of the three short vowels, it too is now becoming subject to change or deletion in many dialects; e.g., Cairene /yā/ + /maḥammad/ → /ya mḥammad/ 'O Mohammed!'. Both Hebrew and Aramaic reduced the short vowels, particularly in unaccented environments. Cf. Hebrew *šəbīl* 'path' = CA *sabīl*, or Hebrew *kətabtém* 'you wrote (m. pl.)' = CA *katábtum*. CA has many doublets in its short vowel configuration such as /ḥubs/ ~ /ḥibs/ 'inalienable property the yield of which is devoted to pious purposes' or /laṣṣ/ ~ /liṣṣ/ ~ /luṣṣ/ 'thief', or /maḥǰir/ ~ /miḥǰar/ ~ /maḥǰar/ 'eye socket' (triplets!).

There are two diphthongs in CA: /aw/ and /ay/, as in /θawr/ 'bull' and /bayt/ 'house', respectively. In most of the colloquial dialects, diphthongs have monophthongized into /ē/ and /ō/, respectively /i/ and /u/ in Moroccan dialects, as had also occurred in Akkadian millennia earlier—another well-attested example of parallel development). It should, however, be kept in mind that even in dialects which generally monophthongize the CA diphthongs, they are preserved intact in some words; e.g., Cairene *mawgūd* 'present (m.sg.); here'.

13.5.1. /a/-*Raising*

ʔimāla (lit., 'inclination') refers to /a/-raising, often due to the umlauting influence of /i/. A word such as CA *ʕibād* 'slaves' could have had a dialectal pronunciation *ʕibēd* or *ʕibīd*. *ʔimāla* has produced the very distinctive high-vowel pronunciations of /a/ in many Syro-Lebanese dialects, i.e., [bēb] or [bīb], equivalent to CA /bāb/ = [bæːb] 'door' (as uttered, say, by a Cairene). Higher phonetic qualities can also be found, such as Maltese *bieb* [bɪːp] 'door', cognate with the aforementioned word. Maltese also has *kelmiet* 'words', corresponding to CA *kalimāt* and *ktieb* 'book' = CA *kitāb*. Many dialects also have final *ʔimāla* observable in the feminine ending *-a* of MSA being pronounced *-e* or even *-i*. *ʔimāla* explains why French *Michelle* is written ميشال <myšʔl> in Arabic. It is interesting to note that *ʔimāla* is especially characteristic of women's speech (along with de-emphasis), both in their native colloquials as well as their renditions of CA and MSA. One may broadly compare *sodi* in Appalachian Engish for *soda*.

13.5.2. Delabialization

ʔišmām 'delabialization' is described as "the pronunciation of *u* with a trace of *ī*" (Wehr 1974: 485). It describes the process in which /ū/ becomes /ī/ (perhaps through an intermediate stage of [ü]). This produces such alternations as *rūm ~ rīm* 'Rome' and some dialectal pronunciations of /rudda/ as [rüdda] 'it was returned' or /qūla/ for CA /qīla/ 'it was said' < a morphophonemic or underlying ||quwila||. Incidentally, some Arabic dialects have [ü] (IPA [y])—e.g., Judeo-Moroccan and Mauretanian (Ḥassaniyya) Arabic, and Cairene is noted for [ü] (Harrell 1957: 5), IPA [ʏ]. The front rounded vowel situation has yet to receive a full-length study in terms of comparative Arabic dialectology.

13.5.3. Stress

Stress is one of the most involved topics in the entire realm of Arabic phonology. Even for the Nigerian dialect of Arabic I researched firsthand in the mid-1970s, stress was the most intricate part of the variation I encountered (1982: xv). The medieval Arab grammarians never mentioned it, and modern-day stress of both MSA and CA is certainly often dependent on, and/or related to, the corresponding rules of the native colloquial dialect acquired. For instance, for the CA or MSA word <ktbtʔ>, segmentally /katabatā/ 'both of them (f.) wrote', some native speakers pronounce (1) /kátabatā/ (some Iraqis and Upper Egyptians), (2) /katabátā/ (Egyptians, especially Cairenes), (3) /katabatā́/ (most Lebanese), and (4) /katábatā/ (most Jordanians and Palestinians). It is thus possible to stress any of the four syllables and still be absolutely correct. (This would be, as far as I know, a situation difficult to match in any other language.) This is but one of the many reasons for considering MSA to be an ill-defined system of language but all colloquials, on the other hand, to be well-defined systems. This distinction is at the heart of diglossia, really therefore multiglossia, in Arabic, a sociolinguistic situation best viewed as a continuum (see Kaye 1994).

There are, however, rules of syllabicity which can be described with a greater degree of accuracy. Long vowels are shortened in closed syllables (except /ā/ in some instances), which explains why one says /yákun/ 'let him be' (jussive of /yakūnu/ 'he will be') instead of the expected (apocopated imperfect) */yakūn/. Also, only monoconsonants occur syllable-initially or -finally, rendering the borrowing of Latin *strata* 'path' as /ṣirāṭ/.

The following rules for the assignment of lexical stress in MSA apply to the varieties of many Arabic users:

(1) When a word is made up of CV syllables, the first syllable receives the primary stress, e.g., /kátaba/ 'he wrote' (but Lebanese MSA *katábahu* 'he wrote it' vs. Egyptian MSA *katabáhu*).

(2) When a word contains only one long syllable, it receives the primary stress, e.g., /kátib/ 'writer, clerk'.

(3) When a word contains two or more long syllables, the long syllable nearest to the end of the word receives the primary stress, e.g., /raʔīsuhúnna/ 'their chief (f.pl.)'.

13.6. Pausal forms in CA and MSA

The normal use of MSA and CA requires an understanding of a phenomenon traditionally known as pausal forms or pronunciations. When a pause occurs in speech (reflected in reading aloud as well), Arabic speakers drop final short vowels (case and mood markers). Furthermore, other endings are dropped or shortened. For example, Arabic marks indefiniteness by what is called *nunation* (named after the Arabic letter *nūn*): *-un* for nominative, *-in* for genitive, and *-an* for accusative (the only three cases). At the end of an utterance (i.e., sentence or breath group), a word such as /mudarrisun/ 'a teacher' → /mudarris/ and /mudarrisin/ → /mudarris/, but /mudarrisan/ → /mudarrisā/, whereas /mudarrisatun/ (nom.) or /mudarrisatin/ (gen.) or /mudarrisatan/ (acc.) → /mudarrisah/ 'a teacher (f.sg.)'. Arabic words are not usually cited with nunation (called in Arabic *tanwīn*), e.g., *kitābun* 'a book' because isolated words (e.g., *kitāb*) are associated with pause. Native vernacular influence is less obvious in word-isolated speech (single citation forms) than it is in long, connected discourse. It is important to note that, in principle, vernacular forms are based on CA pausal forms. It is important to note that no one currently speaks MSA utilizing all the CA pausal rules.

13.7. Morphophonemic changes

There are far too many morphophonemic changes to include in our discussion here. A few of the most common occurring in CA are as follows (data are cited in non-pausal forms):

(7)   awa → ā

  *qawama → qāma 'he stood up'

(8) $C^1aC^2aC^2a$ → $C^1aC^2C^2a$

  *radada → radda 'he returned'

(9) $\quad ? \begin{Bmatrix} a \\ i \\ u \end{Bmatrix} ? \rightarrow ? \begin{Bmatrix} \bar{a} \\ \bar{i} \\ \bar{u} \end{Bmatrix}$

*?a?lāmun → ?ālāmun 'pains'

(10) uw → ū

*suwdun → sūdun 'black (m.pl.)'

(11) ūy → ī

*buyḍun → bīḍun 'white (m.pl.)'
*mudarrisūya → mudarrisīya 'my teachers (m., all cases)'

(12) yw → yy

*?aywāmun → ?ayyāmun 'days'

(13) Haplology: *tataqātalūna → taqātalūna 'you are fighting each other'

(14) Dissimilation: *madīnīyun → madanīyun 'urban'

(15) āw → ā?

*qāwilun → qā?ilun 'speaker'

Arabic's basic triconsonantal root structure lends itself well to the principles and techniques of what is called "underlying" phonological analysis. Thus, rule (7) states that the root *qwm* plus the discontinous vocalic pattern a–a–a produces *qawama* (yielding eventually *qāma* 'he got up'). One can see the *w* or second radical of the root in the imperfect corresponding to this aforementioned form, viz., *yaquwmu*, in which *ya-* marks the third person and *-u* the indicative mode. Rule (10) operates on this underlying representation, yielding the surface manifestation *yaqūmu*. The root structure allows for the almost algebraic formulae which can describe various aspects of Arabic morphophonology. For instance, as one looks at the root KTB 'write', one can readily describe MSA *kataba* 'he wrote', *kātibun* 'clerk', *kitābun* 'book', *kutubun* 'books', *maktabun* 'office; desk', *maktabatun* 'library', *mukātabatun* 'correspondence', and so on. Cf. *qāla* 'he said', *qā?ilun* 'speaker', *maqālun ~ maqālatun* 'article, essay', *muqāwalatun* 'conversation', *qawl*, pl. *?aqwāl* 'saying', etc.

13.8. Some phonological rules in Cairo Arabic

Finally, no discussion of Arabic phonology would be complete without a brief look at some major phonological rules in a spoken colloquial dialect.

(It should not be forgotten that no one speaks MSA or CA as a mother tongue.) Cairo Arabic is chosen for two reasons: (1) It is relatively well researched (see Mitchell 1956, 1962, 1990, 1993; Abdel-Massih 1975; and Salib 1981); and (2) many Arabs are at least somewhat familiar with this dialect due to its political and cultural importance (particularly from the movies since Cairo is the film capital of the Arab world, and attributable to the overwhelming influence of Egyptian radio and television throughout the Middle East). Due to limitations of space, the tremendous variety of Arabic phonologies is not the main focus of this chapter. On the latter topic the reader is referred to chapters 14, 15, and 16.

13.8.1. *Anaptyxis or epenthesis*
Cairene does not allow a sequence of three consonants (including geminates, keeping in mind that any consonant can be geminated). When -CC#C- occurs (i.e., a consonant cluster at the end of a word followed by another consonant), the anaptyctic vowel /i/ is usually inserted and is pronounced as an ultrashort [ɪ] (= [ɪ]). For example, /dars/ 'lesson, class' + /ʕarabi/ 'Arabic' becomes /darsi ʕarabi/ 'Arabic class'. Some scholars have transcribed this vowel as /ĭ/ with a breve mark. Before some of the pronominal suffixes, the anaptyptic vowel can be /a/ or /u/, usually determined by vowel harmony, viz., /u/ before /-hum/ or /-kum/ (3pl. and 2pl. respectively) and /a/ before /-ha/ (3f.sg.). Thus, /gamb/ 'beside' becomes /gambuhum/ 'beside them', /gambukum/ 'beside you (pl.)', /gambaha/ 'beside her'; but note /gambina/ 'beside us', which is not vowel harmonic. The state of affairs described above is in sharp contrast with the situation of Moroccan Arabic, in which many consonants can occur adjacent to one another in clusters (see chapter 14). The facts of Moroccan Arabic phonology are to be explained by a Berber substratum, in which many consonants can occur next to one another without any audible vowel (e.g., Zuara Berber).

13.8.2. *Consonant assimilation*
Consonant assimilation in Cairene occurs quite often in rapid speech (but it may occur in careful speech as well). Examples include /dt/ → /tt/, /td/ → /dd/, and /ʔil-C/ → /ʔiC-C/. Anticipatory assimilation usually occurs at word boundaries, especially for change in voicing according to the consonant which follows: /z/ → /s/, /ɣ/ → /x/, and /ʕ/ → /ħ/. Other common assimilations include /ħh/ → /ħħ/, /ʕh/ → /ħħ/, /sš/ → /šš/, and /šs/ → /ss/. An assimilation such as /simiʕt/ → /simiħt/ 'I heard' clearly demonstrates that /ʕ/ and

/ħ/ are a structurally similar pair. One may note /simiʕ/ 'he heard' + /-ha/ 'her' → /simiħha/ 'he heard her' with a progressive assimilation of /h/ to /ħ/ (which operates after the rule which shifts /ʕ/ → /ħ/).

13.8.3. Vowel shortening

One of the most characteristic phenomena of Cairene is vowel shortening, which occurs under predictable conditions:

(1) A long vowel in a final syllable shortens if liaison with a following word causes it to be followed by -CC, e.g., /šāfū hināk/ → /šāfu hnāk/ 'they saw him there'.

(2) A long vowel shortens if another long vowel follows it, e.g., /kitāb/ 'book' + /-ēn/ (dual) → /kitabēn/ 'two books', or /kātib/ 'clerk (m.)' but /katba/ 'clerk (f.)' < /kātiba/ (some other dialects keep the long vowel in the derivative formations).

(3) A long vowel becomes short when it is followed by two consonants, e.g. /bēt/ 'house' + /-na/ 'our' → /bitna/ 'our house' (for */betna/; note /e/ → /i/ via vocalic neutralization).

(4) A long vowel shortens if suffixation puts it before the penult, e.g. /šāfit/ 'she saw' + /-u/ 'him' → /šafítu/ 'she saw him'.

13.9. Further reading

The reader is referred to five excellent works on Egyptian Colloquial Arabic (the last two deal with many other Arabic dialects as well): Harrell 1957, Mitchell 1956, 1962, 1990, 1993. The following two pedagogical works are also quite useful: Abdel-Massih 1975, Salib 1981. The following have been quoted in Table 13-1 and are most valuable for the listing of Semitic cognates: Köhler and Baumgartner 1958, Leslau 1987.

References

Abdel-Massih, Ernest T. 1975. *An Introduction to Egyptian Arabic*. Ann Arbor: University of Michigan.
Al-Ani, Salman H. 1970. *Arabic Phonology: An Acoustical and Physiological Investigation*. The Hague: Mouton.
Ferguson, Charles A. 1956. "The Emphatic *l* in Arabic." *Language* 32: 446–52.
Gairdner, W. H. T. 1925. *The Phonetics of Arabic*. London: Oxford University Press.

Harrell, Richard S. 1957. *The Phonology of Colloquial Egyptian Arabic.* New York: American Council of Learned Societies.

Hetzron, Robert. 1972. *Ethiopian Semitic: Studies in Classification* (Journal of Semitic Studies Monograph 2). Manchester: Manchester Univ. Press.

Jakobson, Roman. 1957. "Mufaxxama: The 'Emphatic' Phonemes in Arabic." In *Studies Presented to Joshua Whatmough on His Sixtieth Birthday,* ed. Ernst Pulgram, pp. 105–15. The Hague: Mouton.

Kaye, Alan S. 1972. "Arabic /žiim/: A Synchronic and Diachronic Study." *Linguistics* 79: 31–72.

———. 1982. *A Dictionary of Nigerian Arabic* (Bibliotheca Afroasiatica 1). Malibu: Undena.

———. 1994. "Formal vs. Informal Arabic: Diglossia, Triglossia, Tetraglossia, etc., Polyglossia—Multiglossia Viewed as a Continuum." *Zeitschrift für arabische Linguistik* 27: 47–66.

Köhler, Ludwig, and Walter Baumgartner. 1958. *Lexicon in Veteris Testamenti Libros.* Leiden: Brill.

Lehn, Walter. 1963. "Emphasis in Cairo Arabic." *Language* 39: 29–39.

Leslau, Wolf. 1987. *Comparative Dictionary of Ge'ez.* Wiesbaden: Harrassowitz.

———. 1990. *Arabic Loanwords in Ethiopian Semitic.* Wiesbaden: Harrassowitz.

Mitchell, T. F. 1956. *An Introduction to Egyptian Colloquial Arabic.* London: Oxford University Press.

———. 1962. *Colloquial Arabic: The Living Language of Egypt.* London: English Universities Press (Teach Yourself).

———. 1975. *Principles of Firthian Linguistics.* London: Longman.

———. 1990. *Pronouncing Arabic I.* Oxford: Oxford University Press. [This work and Mitchell 1993 deal with many Arabic dialects, Modern Standard Arabic, and Classical Arabic.]

———. 1993. *Pronouncing Arabic II.* Oxford: Oxford University Press.

Nelson, Kristina. 1985. *The Art of Reciting the Qur'an.* Austin: University of Texas Press.

Owens, Jonathan. 1993. *A Grammar of Nigerian Arabic* (Semitica Viva 10). Wiesbaden: Harrassowitz.

Salib, Maurice. 1981. *Spoken Arabic of Cairo.* Cairo: American University of Cairo Press.

Wehr, Hans. 1974. *A Dictionary of Modern Written Arabic,* ed. J Milton Cowan. Wiesbaden: Harrassowitz.

Chapter 14
Moroccan Arabic Phonology
Jeffrey Heath
University of Michigan

14.1. Introduction

Moroccan Colloquial Arabic (MCA) is one of many dialects (actually, dialect groups) that resulted from Arab military and cultural expansion shortly after the time of Muhammad. Because Arabic was overlain on various foreign languages in the course of this expansion (Persian in Iraq, Aramaic in the Levant, Coptic in Egypt), the respective colloquial vernaculars are quite different—from each other, from the modern colloquials of the Arabian peninsula, and from Classical Arabic (CA) and the modern literary Arabic based on it. Though all of the colloquials are referred to as "Arabic" and are regarded by most Arabs as low-status street-level varieties of a single literary language, they are mutually unintelligible and therefore (from the point of view of linguistic description) distinct languages.

MCA is really a collection of dialects, sharing some important features (in contrast to, say, Egyptian) but with some surprisingly important internal differences in all aspects of lexicon and grammar. The variation is, for the most part, not home grown, but rather a result of the complex settlement history of Morocco. The major components are these: (a) core dialects reflecting early Arabization of Berbers (from around 700 A.D.), (b) an invasion of "Beni Hilal" from Arabia (mid-11th century), and (c) an influx of Muslims and Jews from Spain (around 1492).

When the Arabs overran Berber-speaking Northwest Africa in the early 8th century, they established military camps, then towns, and progressively Arabized many of the Berbers. This slow Arabization process is still continuing, as the remaining Berber populations (especially those who relocate to urban centers) become bilingual and shift toward Arabic colloquials. In Morocco, unlike most of the rest of the Maghreb, the Berber languages are still doing well in the mountainous areas.

Although MCA is the unquestionably dominant vernacular in Morocco, it has many traces of Berber influence. Since Arabized Berbers must have constituted a large percentage of speakers in the formative first centuries of

MCA, it is no wonder that its pronunciation in particular is quite different from that of eastern Arabic vernaculars such as Egyptian colloquial. Two notable characteristics of MCA are the hardening of interdental fricatives (*ð, *ð̣, and *θ) to stops (*d, *ḍ, and *t), and the reduction (to shwa) or complete loss of original CA short vowels. The latter development has had far-reaching consequences for the entire phonology, prosody, and morphology.

The so-called "Beni Hilal," whose precise tribal and geographical origin in the Arabian Peninsula are not entirely clear, were unleashed onto northwest Africa by an angry Egyptian sultan. They were speakers of a "nomadic"-type dialect (the sedentary/nomadic division of dialects is an old theme in Arabic dialectology). Many of them passed through the Maghreb and kept going—into the Sahara, and beyond to Mauritania and northern Mali. Their descendants are the Moors of these two countries, and of Western Sahara (which Morocco is now attempting to annex), and their Arabic dialect (called Hassaniya) differs sharply from MCA in phonological segments, phonology (e.g. *i-žu* 'they are coming' vs. MCA *y-ži-w*), morphology (e.g. preservation of feminine plurals), and lexicon. However, some of the Beni Hilal remained in the Maghreb, north of the Sahara. They must have been partly responsible for the strongly "nomadic" features of Tunisian Arabic and of some Algerian varieties. In the settled regions of Morocco, the Beni Hilal formed smaller pockets, exacerbating the sedentary/nomadic split, but many "nomadic" features have since been leveled out. Phonological characteristics of the remaining "nomadic" dialects (best represented in the southern oases and the Saharan fringe) include retention of CA interdental fricatives *ð, *ð̣, and *θ (which become stops elsewhere in MCA), old *q reflected as *g*, and retention of (originally long) CA vowels in the final stem-syllable of broken plurals and diminutives: *brrad* 'tea kettle' has pl. *brarid* and diminutive sg. *breyrid* in the far south, versus *brar(ə)d* and *brir(ə)d* elsewhere in Morocco.

The expulsion of Jews from Spain in 1492 and the various expulsions or outmigrations of Andalusian Arabs around the same time (the last Arab kingdom, Granada, fell in 1492) had important consequences for Arabic dialects in the Maghreb, and especially in Morocco. The Andalusians, more sophisticated economically and culturally than the Moroccans, formed their own neighborhoods and networks in Moroccan cities, and in some (such as Fes) there are still distinctive elite urban dialects with Andalusian features, though dialect leveling is taking an increasing toll on them. The Jews, who came from the Christian as well as the Muslim parts of Spain (they still have family names like Toledano), spoke Judeo-Spanish. Though there have been Jewish communities in Morocco since the beginning of recorded history, the more sophisticated Spanish Jews dominated the major Jewish communities, especially in Rabat, Meknes, Fes, and Sefrou. In the far north (Tangier, Tetuan) they continued to speak Judeo-Spanish into the early 20th century. Elsewhere they shifted to MCA, specifically the then-current urban dialects of Jews and Muslims, with some Andalusian Arabic influence. When the Jews were then ghettoized in walled-off urban quarters, they became cut off from urban/rural blending among Muslims and still preserve many archaic features that even the old Muslim urban neighborhoods have since given up. Moroccan Judeo-Arabic (MJA) therefore constitutes a second dialect network, occupying essentially the same geographical space as the more visible Muslim dialects. (Because of recent migrations to Israel and consolidation of remaining Moroccan Jews chiefly in Casablanca, the old Judeo-Arabic dialects are in the process of dying out as vernaculars.)

Phonological features typical of at least the major urban MJA dialects include (a) retention of CA *q as glottalized q' or glottal stop ʔ rather than as g; (b) loss or unrounding of short *ŭ, with no transfer of rounding to neighboring back consonants; (c) loss of the alveolar/palato-alveolar distinction among sibilants (*s merges with *š, *z with *ž); and (d) spreading of pharyngealization ("emphasis") through lexical stems. However, MJA dialects occur almost throughout Morocco, and those in the far south and far east diverge from these patterns in some respects. The MJA dialect of Tafilalt, a semi-arid region in the south, is notable for its extreme reduction or loss of CA short vowels.

In what follows, unless otherwise specified the "MCA" that we are describing is the speech of Moroccans born after about 1950, living in or near the central urban belt (from Fes to Rabat) but socially mobile and with no especially prominent indicators of local birthplace. The present article, based on Heath (1987), does not pretend to be dialectologically comprehensive. A sketch of the dialectal networks is in Heath (1991); a fuller treatment is in preparation.

14.2. Consonants

The basic consonant system of MCA is as shown in Table 5-1. Found dialectally are ʔ and the fricative trio ð, ḏ, and θ. Foreign loanwords, especially from French, have introduced ǰ (affricate), v, and p into MCA.

Table 14-1. Primary Moroccan Colloquial Arabic Consonants

	(Bi-)labial	(Denti-)alveolar	Pharyngealized (denti-)alveolar	Palato-alveolar	Velar	Uvular	Pharyngeal	Laryngeal (aspiration)
Voiceless stops/affricates		t	ṭ	č	k	q		
Voiced stops/affricates	b	d	ḍ		g			
Voiceless fricatives/sibilants	f	s	ṣ	š		x	ħ	h
Voiced fricatives/sibilants		z	ẓ	ž		ɣ	ʕ	
Nasals	m	n						
Laterals		l	(ḷ)					
Rhotics		r	ṛ					
Semivowels	w			y				

All consonants may occur geminated, and gemination is a productive part of derivational ablaut: *y-bki* 'he weeps', causative *y-bkki-ha* 'he makes her (*-ha*) weep'. Definite *l-* (cf. CA *al-*) before a stem-initial coronal (alveolar or palato-alveolar) loses its own identity to form a geminate cluster: *l-brd* 'the cold', but *t-trab* 'the ground' and *ž-žbəl* 'the mountain'. The preposition *l-* 'to' (CA *li-* or *ʔilaa*) does not assimilate in this fashion: *l-ṭanža* 'to Tangiers'. Note that *ž* is treated like any other coronal in the definite assimilation rule, whereas its ancestor (CA *ǰ*) did not assimilate (*al-ǰabal* 'the mountain'). In far northern MCA dialects, a geminated *ž* is realized as [j:], so /ž-žbəl/ is [j:bəl].

14.3. Full vowels

The vowel system differs substantially from one sub-dialect to another, but the stable core of the vocalic system is the set of "full" vowels *i, a, u*. In general, these are historical reflexes of long vowels and diphthongs in CA, but since there is no longer a set of parallel short vowels it is not appropriate to consider length as part of the MCA system.

What happened to the old CA short vowels? Many have simply disappeared. Word-final short vowels were unstable even in CA, where they were omitted before e.g. a pause. In the development from CA to MCA, not only did the word-final short vowels complete their disappearing act; many other short vowels in other positions were deleted due to syncope, like the first vowel of CA *jabal* → MCA *žbəl*. Short-vowel prefixes like CA *ta-* 'you or she (imperfective)' are now typically reduced to unvocalized consonants, which may undergo assimilation to a stem-initial consonant: CA *ta-ḍrib(-u)* 'you (m. sg.)/she hits' → MCA *ḍ-ḍrb*.

14.4. Vestiges of short vowels

There are, however, some traces of the old CA short vowels. In the mainstream MCA dialect we are focusing on, old short **i* and **a* are reflected in certain positions as *ə*, while short **u* is reflected variously as shwa or as a short rounded MCA vowel that may be written *ŭ*. The position most favorable to these non-zero reflexes of old short vowels is before the final consonant (or two-consonant cluster) of a word not containing a full vowel, i.e., positions like C_CC and CC_C, where "C" represents any consonant. MCA preserves no word-final short vowels, nor are there are any clear cases of preservation word-initially.

Depending on sub-dialectal details, MCA short *ŭ* and perhaps even *ə* can be re-analysed as something other than ordinary short vowels. In the mainstream dialect, *ŭ* has a distribution like that of shwa, except that *ŭ* always seems to be in the vicinity of a velar or uvular consonant, hence *skŭt* 'shut up!', *xŭbz* 'bread', and *gŭl-t* 'I said'. This association of *ŭ* with particular consonants is an innovation in MCA. There are two other interesting facts about MCA *ŭ*. First, paradigmatic alternations between rounded and unrounded short vowels have generally been leveled out; the CA verb 'to shut up' had perfective *sakat-* vs. imperfective *-skut-*, which would normally have produced an MCA opposition **skət/skŭt*, but in fact *skŭt* has generalized to the perfective: *skŭt* 'he shut up', *skŭt-t* 'I shut up'. Second, in positions where MCA shwa undergoes syncope, as in *šəmm* 'smell! (m. sg.)' but *šmm-i* 'smell! (f. sg.)', short *ŭ* typically leaves labialization behind as a trace: *dŭqq* 'knock! (m. sg.)' but *d^wqq-i* or *dqq^w-i* 'knock! (f. sg.)'. What these facts seem to point to is the increasingly close association of rounding with the back (velar or uvular) consonant rather than with the (at best faint) short vowel. In other words, a form like [skŭt] might well have been re-analysed by Moroccans as /skʷət/, with a phonemic k^w that accounts for the rounding. Under this (re-)analysis, we can think of the vowel as an underlying shwa.

If there is only one short vowel, ə, versus three full vowels, *i a u*, it is obvious that a length opposition in the usual sense no longer exists—especially in view of the very limited set of positions where shwa can occur. At this point, one is tempted to ask whether even this restricted shwa can be "analysed out" of the system. If, for example, it occurs only in the positions C_CC and CC_C, we could consider the possibility that shwa is inserted by rule rather than being part of a lexical representation. This is probably going too far, since the very fact that CəCC and CCəC are distinct stem shapes shows that no simple shwa-insertion rule is possible. However, it may well be that this is the long-range developmental trend. In mainstream MCA, CəCC and CCəC no longer contrast when the third C is a sonorant (or when the second C is a rhotic). In some dialects of the Tafilalt area in the south, the distinction is additionally lost when the second C is any sonorant, and in the same dialects we are starting to get sporadic "crossovers" even with obstruents (*xbəz* instead of *xŭbz* or *xəbz* 'bread'). In such dialects, ə has virtually disappeared as a structurally significant phoneme, leaving *i a u* as the only vowels in the system.

14.5. Pharyngealization ("emphasis")

Kaye's article on Arabic (this volume) summarizes the debate about the phonological representation of "emphatic" consonants (or vowels, or syllables, or words). That the various dialects themselves tend toward different interpretations of this problem can be shown by a comparison between mainstream MCA and the Saharan dialects of the extreme south (and especially of Western Sahara, Mauritania, and Mali).

In the Saharan dialects, the "spreading" of pharyngealization is very narrow. Typically a pharyngealized C affects the neighboring vowel and nothing else: in *y-ăṣgăl* 'he cleans', the first vowel is backed under the influence of the pharyngealized ṣ, but the second vowel is unaffected, hence [yăṣgĕl]. In mainstream MCA, on the other hand, spreading is more substantial, especially to the "right": *ṭlb-at-u* [ṭlb-ɑt-u] 'she requested it' has a clearly backed allophone of *a*. In addition, in Saharan dialects the phonetic effect of pharyngealization on an adjoining high vowel *i u* is an evanescent velarization, marked strongly in the actual transition between the vowel and the pharyngealized C and then fading out, whereas MCA *i u* are pronounced as steady-state mid vowels [e o] next to pharyngealized Cs.

Related to this is the fact that mainstream MCA tends to avoid combinations, in the same stem, of a basic pharyngealized alveolar *ṭ ḍ ṣ ẓ ṛ* with an unpharyngealized alveolar *t d s z r*—alveolars in the same stem are either all pharyngealized or all plain. Thus CA *ṣadr* 'chest (of body)' becomes *ṣḍṛ* in some Moroccan dialects, *sdr* in others, but mixtures like *ṣdr* are rare (except in artificially re-classicized pronunciations). By contrast (leaving aside *ṛ* for the moment), Saharan Arabic seems to prefer having just one pharyngealized alveolar in a stem, and there are cases where a consonant has lost its original pharyngealization in proximity to a neighboring pharyngealized or uvular C. Thus original CA *ṣaγīr* 'small', which becomes mainstream MCA *ṣγīṛ* with pharyngealization extending to the rhotic, produces *sγir* in Saharan Arabic, the uvular fricative having prevented secondary pharyngealization of the rhotic and having actually depharyngealized the sibilant.

Because MCA spreads pharyngealization at least throughout stems to a much greater extent than Saharan (or most other Arabic vernaculars), the argument that "emphasis" is a lexical feature of stems rather than of individual consonants has more weight in MCA than elsewhere. It is even possible to experiment with radical re-interpretations—e.g. to take vocalic distinctions as primary, leading perhaps to an analysis in terms of two "vowel harmony" sets of full vowels, *i æ u* vs. *e a o*. There is no strong evidence that MCA has embraced this re-analysis, but it may be lurking in the shadows.

14.6. *r* versus *ṛ*

In CA, there appears to have been just one rhotic phoneme **r*, though it probably already had some allophonic variation depending on vocalic and consonantal environment. In the Maghrebi and Saharan (Hassaniya) dialects, a distinction between *r* and *ṛ* has now become phonemic. We can easily see how this opposition arose by considering *kbṛ* 'bigger' (comparative of *kbir* 'big') and *kbr* '(to) grow, become big'. The immediate (pre–MCA) etyma probably had the forms **kbăr* 'bigger' and **kbĭr* '(to) grow', respectively. The *a*-vocalism favored a "dark" allophone of **r*, while *i*-vocalism favored a "light" allophone. When the old short vowels merged (and were then swallowed up by the rhotic, which has become syllabic in these forms), the originally allophonic distinction became phonemic.

Although MCA has a few examples like *kbṛ/kbr*, apparently involving forms of the "same" root, such alternations are rare and it is attractive to interpret the forms as lexically distinct. Since there are only a few (about six) remaining morphological comparatives like *kbṛ*, they are probably best regarded as lexicalized (some, like *ḥsən* 'better' from *mzyan* 'good', are suppletive). In fact, the tendency has been to level out *r/ṛ* alternations, generalizing one or the other within the paradigms and derivatives of each stem. This leveling has gone farther in Morocco than elsewhere in northwest African Arabic.

In Saharan (and Tunisian) Arabic, despite some paradigm leveling there are still many telltale alternations. In particular, active participles (classical *CaaCiC) typically depharyngealize *ṛ* to *r* in C_2 or C_3 position if no other pharyngealized C is present: *mṛäg* 'he went away', participle *maarəg* (*maarig*). In mainstream MCA, by contrast, verbs with *ṛ* generalize it to participles: *šṛəb* 'he drank', *šaṛ(ə)b* (*šaarib*) 'having drunk'. Contrast the noun *šaṛ(ə)b* 'lip', which shows the regular reflex of this same *šaarib* (here a specialized nominal usage, meaning 'moustache' in CA) when not subject to analogical influence from the verb 'to drink'. (See also § 14.8.)

14.7. Derivational ablaut

Like other forms of Arabic, MCA has a system of stem-derivation whose most obvious effect is changes in vowels: *ktab* 'book', pl. *ktuba*, diminutive sg. *kʷtiyyəb*, verb *ktəb* '(to) write', active participle *katəb* 'having written' (or agentive: 'writer'), passive participle *m-ktub* 'written', etc. The early Arab grammarians, and many present-day linguists, interpret such data to mean that lexical roots are consonantal skeleta like *k-t-b*, which are interspliced with grammatically significant vowel patterns to produce actual stem shapes. In the currently most popular model, both the consonantal skeleton and the grammatical vowel sequence are linked (separately) to a third component—a "template" of consonantal and vocalic positions, such as CVCC or *m*-CCVC. In this model, a form like *katəb* 'having written' would involve a template approximately of the shape CVCC, a root skeleton *k-t-b*, and a vocalic pattern *a* (or *a–ə* if the shwa is recognized as part of the rule). Such models require a complex set of rules for linking the root consonants and grammatical vowels to C and V positions of the template.

This model radically distinguishes the morphology of Arabic from the transparently layered morphology of other languages, where an "inner" stem X is the basis for a suffixally derived stem [X]-S₁, which in turn is the source for other prefixally and/or suffixally derived stems P₁-[[X]-S₁], then [P₁-[[X]-S₁]]-S₂, etc. In an oversized English derivative like *antidisestablishmentarianism*, it is generally possible to identify a core stem (*establish*) and an ordered (bracketable) set of derivational affixes. A root/pattern analysis of MCA or other forms of Arabic would have the power to shortcut this layering, whereby each surface stem form could be directly referred to an abstract consonantal root, not to an intervening prior stem shape.

In practice, phonologists working on Arabic with the root/pattern model have had to incorporate some prior stem-shape information in their rules. In particular, the shape of singular nouns is obviously relevant to the shapes of diminutives and plurals, and at least the CV-template shapes of the singular have been allowed to play a role in generating these derivatives. However, all of the derivational patterns with well-defined templatic shapes appear to be asymmetrical, in the sense that one stem is clearly derived from another—the participles are derived from the corresponding verbs, just as the diminutive or the plural is from the singular noun. It is therefore possible in principle to trace each derived form back, directly or via intervening derivations, to a single source stem—usually a singular noun or adjective, or a simple verb.

These underived nouns, adjectives, and verbs tend to have unpredictable (and therefore, arguably, lexical) templatic shapes and vowel qualities, in contrast to the many derivatives with their rigidly prescribed vowels and templatic shapes. It seems reasonable, therefore, to analyse the underived stems as ordinary strings of consonants and vowels, just as in other languages, without the dissection into consonantal "roots," vocalic "patterns," and CV "templates." In MCA, we would represent simple stems as *xŭbz* 'bread' (or /xʷəbz/, cf. § 14.4), *ktab* 'book', and *ktəb* '(to) write'. Although suggestively similar in sound and meaning, the last two are not relatable by any productive derivational rule (CCaC as a nominal shape is uncommon and has no specific grammatical value) and so are both treated as underived; in some ancient form of pre-Arabic they may have been derivationally related. (Jewish MCA dialects typically replace *ktab*, which has scriptural associations, with *mṣḥaf*, leaving the verb *ktəb* unaffected.)

Many stems, however, are clearly derived by productive stem-formation processes that we refer to collectively as "derivational ablaut." In MCA, each derived stem is produced by the interaction between an input stem (either underived, or due to a prior derivation) and a template. Since the vowel qualities and the CV shapes are tightly fused, we may analyze the derivational templates as consisting of pre-specified vowels and blank consonantal positions (represented by "C"). For example, the active and passive participles (for verbs like *ktəb* with exactly three segments, excluding "short vowels" like shwa) are C*a*CC and *m*-CC*u*C, respectively, and they combine with *ktəb* '(to) write' to produce *kat(ə)b* 'having written' and *m-ktub* 'written'.

Derivational ablaut, like affixal derivation in other languages, can be layered, though the layering is less transparent in MCA. From *dxŭl* '(to) enter' we first create a causative/factitive *dxxəl* '(to) insert, put in'. This in turn becomes the input to affixal derivatives like participle (active or passive) *m-dxxəl*, and to further ablaut derivation, e.g., verbal noun *t-dxil* (or *t-dxal*) 'insertion' (compare verbal noun *dxul* 'entrance' from the underived verb).

Within what we may call the "stem/ablaut" model, in contrast to the root/pattern model, we (a) simplify the phonological representation of underived stems, and (b) recognize layering (derivational sequencing). In both respects, the stem/ablaut model treats MCA as not very different from other (affixing) languages. But like the root/pattern model, the stem/ablaut model does require some fairly intricate phonological subrules.

Consider what happens when an input stem and a derivational template constitute a mismatch—the input stem has too few consonants, for example. While *ktəb* is a good match for C*a*CC and *m*-CC*u*C, stems like *-akŭl* 'eat', *kun* '(to) be', and *qṛa* '(to) read, study' are not. The active participles are in fact *wakəl*, *kayən*, and *qaṛi* (feminine *qaṛy-a*). The type *wakəl* is found only with two verbs whose imperfective stems begin with *a* (in both cases a CA stem-initial *ʔ has been lost); these two stems fill the first consonantal position of all their ablaut derivatives with a *w* that may be regarded as secondary. Verbs like *kun* with imperfective C*u*C, C*i*C, or C*a*C have active participle C*ay*əC. Since we get *y* in the participle regardless of the input vowel quality (*a*, *i*, or *u*), it appears that this semivowel is inserted by rule after the initial and final input consonants are transferred to the corresponding positions of the derivative. Verbs like *qṛa* with imperfective shape CC*a*, CC*i*, or CC*u* all have the shape C*a*C*i*, which is shown to be really /C*a*Cy/ by feminine C*a*Cy-*a*. Since other ablaut derivations, including the causative, merge verb-final vowels as *i*, it is possible that this participle reflects a similar neutralization, with the *i* then being transferred to the final C position of C*a*CC and hence being desyllabified to the semivowel *y*. These examples suggest that input vowels, not just consonants, play a role in determining the output, and this is seen more transparently in cases where input stems with *u* and *i* have distinct outputs with *w* and *y*, respectively: *šuf* '(to) see', reciprocal *t-šawf-*, versus *biʕ* '(to) sell', reciprocal *t-bayʕ-*.

As these few example suggest, even when one has chosen a basic morphological model (such as the stem/ablaut model here advocated), there are a great many phonological subtleties to work out.

14.8. Loanwords

We observed in § 14.5 that MCA has added *r/ṛ* to the set of well-established plain/pharyngealized consonantal oppositions inherited from CA. We pointed out that this opposition originated in allophonic variants due chiefly to vocalic environment (**i* favoring plain *r*, back vowels favoring *ṛ*), and that the reduction or disappearance of old short vowels led to the phonemicization of the *r/ṛ* opposition, as in *kbṛ* 'bigger' vs. verb *kbr* '(to) grow'.

We pointed out that most such alternations (involving the same stem) have by now been leveled out in MCA, so that the trend is for each stem (and its associated "family" of inflected and derived forms) to generalize either *r* or *ṛ*. There is, however, one productive derivational ablaut that seems to have resisted this leveling.

The most common plural corresponding to singular nouns of the shape C*a*C is C*i*C-*an* (*wad* 'river', pl. *wid-an*). There are a number of native MCA nouns with a rhotic as final C, and here we consistently get *ṛ* in the singular versus plain *r* in the plural (the latter undoubtedly due historically to the preceding *i*-vowel): *faṛ* 'mouse', pl. *fir-an*. Only in the case of *ɣaṛ* '(mouse) hole, burrow' do we find sub-dialectal variation between pl. *ɣir-an* and *ɣiṛ-an* (about evenly distributed), and here the uvular fricative has apparently been the differential factor. One would conclude from this inspection of inherited forms that the *r/ṛ* opposition is quite stable in this singular/plural pattern.

However, loanword data show conclusively that this is not so. There are two twentieth-century loanwords, *kaṛ* 'intercity bus' and *baṛ* 'bar, tavern', which match the pattern of *faṛ* 'mouse' and lack uvulars, so we would expect plurals **kir-an* and **bir-an* with plain *r*. Instead, we get *kiṛ-an* and *biṛ-an* with pharyngealized *ṛ*. What this reveals is an otherwise hidden pressure on the *faṛ/fir-an* pattern to extend *ṛ* from singular to plural—a pressure that has heretofore been unable to actually reshape the inherited plurals, but which has succeeded in affecting new (singular) loanwords with no previously established MCA plural.

This example is typical of the subtlety of "loanword phonology" in a language like MCA with a complex and sometimes murky ablaut system. Not only must each loanword be assimilated to MCA morphology and phonology in its "foot-in-the-door" form; the borrowing is then fed into the productive ablaut processes—which in turn may require deceptively complex analytical "decisions" by MCA speakers (Heath 1989).

While the student of language contact phenomena must deal with many tricky cases like this one, involving productive derivations and fairly ordinary borrowed stems, there is also an occasional poetic jewel that comes along. Most young Moroccans are familiar with an MCA noun *xwadr-i* meaning 'brother' or 'pal, buddy', but they have no idea of its origin and it is up to the linguist to unravel it. The ingredients are (a) an ablaut pattern CCaCC-*i* forming professional nouns (*ṣabun* 'soap' → *ṣwabn-i* 'soap dealer'—note the nonlexical *w* filling the otherwise empty second C position); (b) MCA kin terms *ḅḅa* 'father', *m̩m̩-* 'mother', and *xu-* (or *xa-*) 'brother'; and (c) Spanish *padre* 'father', *madre* 'mother' (cf. *hermano* 'brother'). First, the MCA and Spanish terms for 'father' and 'mother' were playfully blended to form *pp(ʷ)aḍri* and *m̩m̩ʷaḍri*, which are still in existence (but rare, and not known to many Moroccans). These can be analyzed phonologically as /pwadr-i/ and /mwadr-i/, respectively, since initial /pw/ and /mw/ in ablaut derivatives are pronounced [ppʷ] and [m̩m̩ʷ]. The resulting forms are consistent in form with, and were probably influenced by, the CCaCC-*i* professional noun shape. In comparison with the corresponding MCA kin terms, the pattern can be taken more specifically as CCaḍr-*i*. Apparently the pharyngealization of the *ḍr* was taken as secondary (i.e., as having spread from the pharyngealized pronunciation of the initial labial clusters); alternatively, there may have been other (unrecorded) variants **pp(ʷ)adri* and **m̩m̩ʷadri* with unpharyngealized *dr*. The resulting CCadr-*i* pattern was then extended to 'brother' (MCA *xu-* or *xa-*), giving *xwadr-i*, which has gone on to have a life of its own even as *pp(ʷ)aḍri* and *m̩m̩ʷaḍri* have all but disappeared.

A form like *kir-an* 'intercity buses' reflects a complex but linguistically normal and entirely unconscious set of structural forces. A form like *xwadr-i* must have originated as a brilliant linguistic joke, among a group of young men whiling away a muggy August afternoon in a street cafe. Or perhaps it was in a certain tavern in wartime Casablanca …

References

Heath, Jeffrey. 1987. *Ablaut and Ambiguity: Phonology of a Moroccan Arabic Dialect*. Albany: State University of New York Press.

———. 1989. *From Code-Switching to Borrowing: Foreign and Diglossic Mixing in Moroccan Arabic* (Library of Arabic Linguistics 9). London and New York: Kegan Paul International.

———. 1991. "Autour des réseaux dialectaux dans l'arabe des Juifs et des Musulmans marocains," in Issachar Ben-Ami, ed., *Recherches sur la culture des Juifs d'Afrique du Nord*, pp. xlix–lvi. Jerusalem: Communauté Israélite Nord-Africaine.

Chapter 15
Cypriot Arabic Phonology
Alexander Borg
Ben-Gurion University of the Negev

15.1. Introduction

Non-standard varieties of colloquial Arabic have attracted increasing interest among linguists during the last decades. Nonetheless, peripheral vernaculars of Arabic, i.e., those spoken by non-Arabs and/or outside the Arabic-speaking countries—for instance, in southeast Anatolia (cf. Daragözü, Jastrow 1973), central Asia (Fischer 1961; Sirat and Knudsen 1973; Kieffer 1980), parts of central Africa (Roth-Laly 1969; Hagège 1973), etc.—have yet to become the object of systematic individual study. This state of affairs is largely attributable to the fact that, despite their extensive formal deviance from normative Arabic, usually entailing a break in the link of mutual intelligibility between them and native varieties of Arabic, these vernaculars generally tend to be studied almost exclusively within the narrow ambit of Arabic dialectology. With the notable exception of Maltese (see chapter 16), only rarely have these erstwhile Arabic vernaculars been examined as autonomous linguistic systems pertaining to what are today, in effect, independent languages rather than merely fossilized relics of colloquial Arabic.

Given the further fact that most of these vernaculars survive today (a) in a highly undeveloped (when not terminal) state alongside major languages with long-established literary traditions; (b) as in-languages of specific ethnic groups; and, not infrequently, (c) in situations of complex interaction with other linguistic systems, the extent of their systemic autonomy (i.e., in synchronic terms) from surrounding languages would seem to be an issue that merits individual attention.

A particularly striking instance of such a linguistic situation exists among the ethnic Ŝarap of Afghanistan (Barth 1969: 11), whose special Arabic vernacular has developed in close contact with a variety of neighboring languages. Concerning their multilingualism, Kieffer (1980: 182) notes that "tous les hommes sont plurilingues: arabe, persan, ozbaki, torkman et, dans une certaine mesure, paštō," and that they all speak Persian. A systematic description of the differential synchronic impact exercised by these languages on the Arabic of Afghanistan would no doubt yield a highly complex pattern of linguistic interference. A preliminary sketch outlining some general trends within this complex pattern of linguistic interaction in Afghani Arabic has been recently undertaken in Ingham 1994.

The focus of the present study is a specific contact-related problem within the phonology of Cy[priot] A[rabic]—a special vernacular spoken exclusively by the bilingual (Arabic/Greek) Maronite villagers of Kormakiti (northwest Cyprus). Having developed since the Middle Ages in close proximity to Cy[priot] G[reek] and in complete isolation from the normative influences of vernacular and literary Arabic, this erstwhile Arabic vernacular today represents one of the most evolved offshoots of peripheral Arabic described to date.

The special evolutionary path taken by CyA vis-à-vis colloquial Arabic—paralleled mutatis mutandis in some of the aforementioned varieties of peripheral Arabic (particularly Maltese)—has left fairly conspicuous formal traces in its present structure: in particular, a considerable degree of systemic convergence with CyG in the realms of lexicon, syntax, and especially, phonology. The Greek specialist Brian Newton, who first showed an interest in the Greek adstrate in CyA, characterized this vernacular as a "mixed language" (Newton 1964; cf. also the designation "morfosintassi mista" in Lüdtke 1977), not least on account of its highly aberrant phonology.

The early history of Arabic in Cyprus is somewhat shrouded in obscurity; however, the emigration of Arabic speakers ("Syrians") to Cyprus from the adjoining mainland at the end of the 12th century in response to an appeal by Guy de Lusignan is a well-attested fact (Jacoby 1979: 167). There is good reason to suppose that by this time CyA had already achieved a fair degree of formal distinctiveness from other varieties of Eastern Arabic. Thus though CyA has regrettably been almost completely overlooked by Western linguists and Orientalists until the middle of the present century, a reference to the existence of a Cypriot variety of Arabic occurs in a 13th century Arabic source: the *Kita:b as-Sima:t fi: asma:ʔ an-naba:t* by ʿIzz ad-Dīn Abū Isḥāq Ibrāhīm b. Muḥammad b. Tarxān as-Suwaydī (600/1204–690/1292). Summing up the contents of this work, Ullmann (1970: 291) makes the following observation, in which he mentions a number of areal varieties of Arabic recognized in as-Suwaidi's time, including Cypriot Arabic:

> As-Suwaidī gibt neben den arabischen Namen griechische (*yūnānī* und *rūmī*), syrische, persiche, kastilische (*laṭīnī*) und berberische Bezeich-

nungen an. Bei den arabischen unterscheidet er zum Teil noch die Gebrauchsweise in Ägypten, Palästina, Spanien und Cypern.

Jacoby (1979: 168) has also drawn attention to the widespread use of Arabic in 14th century Cyprus (though apparently not specifically associated with the Maronite community) reported in a travel account compiled by the Augustinian monk Frater Jacobus de Verona (1335)—edited in Röhricht (1895)—which states

> omnes de Cypro loquuntur grecum, bene tamen sciunt saracenicum et linguam francigenam, sed plus utuntur lingua greca. (p. 178)
>
> 'all Cypriots speak Greek; however, they know Arabic and French well, but they use Greek more.'

In our own century, a rare mention of CyA occurs in Storrs and O'Brien (1930: 41), where it is designated as "a bastard Arabic mixed with Cypriot Greek" spoken "by the Maronites." This lead, however, does not appear to have been taken up by subsequent research.

In Borg (1985: passim) I endeavored to show, among other things, that despite its *Sprachbund* relationship with the Greek-speaking area, CyA has, nonetheless, retained a distinctly Arabic typology inherited from a medieval Arabic colloquial displaying well-defined genetic affiliations with two fairly discrete dialect areas within contemporary Eastern Arabic:

(i) The *qētel*-group, comprising certain old sedentary Arabic dialects of north Syria and Mesopotamia which, like CyA, show the highly diagnostic Umlaut variety of the *imāla* shift (typified in Aleppine, and the *qəltu* dialects of Iraq and southeast Anatolia: CyA *klep* 'dogs' < OA *kila:b*, but CyA *nam* 'he slept' < OA *na:m*; for further details, cf. Borg 1985: 55–67; Blanc 1964: 42f.; Levin 1971; Jastrow 1978, passim).

(ii) The sedentary vernaculars spoken along the littoral of "Greater Syria" (e.g., Lebanese and Palestinian), with which it shares, for instance, the indicative verbal prefix {p-} < **b-*: /pisur/ 'he becomes'.

Thus though the historical process that yielded the present CyA sound system has been extensively activated by language contact with CyG, comparative study of CyA phonology (cf. Borg 1985: 11–74) shows that the resulting phonological system still displays numerous regular sound correspondences with Arabic—a circumstance generally indicative of gradual historical evolution in CyA rather than sudden or catastrophic change.

Nevertheless, the present chapter is less concerned with outlining the systemic regularities that CyA shares with its erstwhile congeners on the adjacent mainland than with pinpointing an area of "partial chaos" within the organization of the CyA sound pattern, specifically in the treatment of voicing in plosives. Before addressing the matter of voicing in CyA stops, it may be useful here to provide a general sketch of the CyA sound system so as to contextualize the data under examination and to account for certain trends untypical of Arabic in the surface treatment of CyA consonants.

15.2. The Cypriot Arabic sound system

The sound pattern of CyA presents the Arabic dialectologist with some of the most intriguing analytical problems in its entire structural profile. Not surprisingly, it is also in this domain of CyA that it shows the most profound systemic deviations from mainstream colloquial Arabic.

The phonological prime selected for the present analysis of the CyA sound pattern is a segmental unit closely approximating the traditional phoneme. This yields the inventory of consonants and vowels shown in Table 15-1.

Table 15-1. The Cypriot Arabic Segmental Paradigm (after Borg 1985)

Consonants							
p			t		k		
	f	θ	s	š	x		
	v	ð	z	ž		ʕ	
m			n				
			l				
			r				
				y			

Vowels				
Monophthongs:	i			u
		e	o	
		a		
Diphthongs:	ay			aw

As can be seen from this display, the sound classes of CyA present a neatly symmetrical arrangement that is more akin to the contemporary CyG sound pattern than to that of the medieval Arabic vernacular from which it evolved. Highly significant in this respect is the complete absence of an emphatic series in CyA, the O[ld] A[rabic] velarized consonants having been fused with their plain counterparts:

CyA		OA
pasal	'onions'	baṣal
kasel	'laziness'	kasal
katt	'cat'	qiṭṭ
fatt	'it was slight in quantity'	fatt
peða	'egg'	bayḍa
iðn	'ear'	uðn

The extensive impact exerted by CyG on the CyA sound system should be evident from the sketch of CyA phonology provided in Borg (1985). In effect, the systemic encroachment of CyG on CyA amounts to more than a mere case of historical language contact; it represents rather a progressive (and still ongoing) hellenization process. The potential impact of CyA on the Greek spoken by the monolingual Maronites (from Aghía Marína, Asómatos, and Karpásha) has yet to be investigated.

Highly symptomatic of the profound inroads made by Greek into CyA sound structure is the extreme contraction of the Arabic segmental paradigm actualized in the latter. Thus in contrast with the 35-odd segments typifying the sound systems of most sedentary dialects of Eastern Arabic (cf. Damascus, Cantineau and Helbaoui 1953: 14–15; Tripoli, El-Hajjé 1954: 11f.; Cairo, Selim 1967: 135; etc.), CyA has—according to my 1985 analysis—only 26 segments, a figure that closely matches the 25 segments of CyG (Newton 1972a: 22). As can be seen from the schematic display above, the selection of articulatory classes in CyA is closely modeled on that of CyG; thus, only one point of articulation, that of the CyA voiced pharyngeal fricative /ʕ/, is completely foreign to CyG. In the other direction, the CyG segments /č/ and /kʲ/ (palatalized velar stop) do not form part of the CyA segmental inventory, but are in essence present in CyA surface structure as the biphonemic sequences /tš/ and /ky/, respectively. The cumulative impact of these systemic shifts has not only rendered the surface content of CyA and CyG highly similar but, as will be seen below, it has also occasioned a notable historical restructuring of the function of voicing in obstruents; the descriptive details and wider implications relating to this change will be dealt with at length in the main section of this chapter.

15.3. Some phonological rules in Cypriot Arabic

15.3.1. Manner dissimilation
As in Cypriot and Standard Greek, biconsonantal stop clusters in CyA are subject to a manner dissimilation constraint (both diachronic and synchronic) replacing the first stop by its corresponding fricative (cf. Gk. /nixta/ < *nikta* 'night'):

/xtilt/	'you (masc.sg.) killed'	⇐ |ktilt|	< *qtilt*
/fkum/	'I get up'	⇐ |pkum|	< *baqu:m*

The unmarked character of "fricative + stop" CC clusters in CyA occasionally also yields secondary occlusivization of underlying or historical spirants: /xtir/ 'much' < *kθi:r.*

15.3.2. Palatalization and occlusivization of /y/
The CyA velar segments /k/ and /x/ undergo automatic palatalization (here indicated by an apostrophe) before the historical and/or underlying front vowels /i/ and /e/ and the palatal glide /y/:

[k'ilp]	'dog'	< *kalb*
[k'el]	'he ate'	< **ke:l* < *akal*
[x'írep]	'he left'	< **hirib*
[x'érep]	'leaving'	< *ha:rib*
[x'ar]	'cucumbers'	< *xya:r*
[pk'ut]	'houses'	< *byu:t*

The secondary velar stop in the last example is the product of a phonetic tendency in CyA (ultimately carried over from CyG) towards inserting an epenthetic velar stop [k] in dyadic clusters consisting of obstruent + palatal glide:

/pkyara/	'wells'	< **bya:ra*
/apkyað/	'white (masc.sg.)'	< *abyaḍ*
/θkyep/	'clothes'	< **θye:b*

In certain contexts, this secondary velar stop is sometimes liable to partial morphologization, as in /mišku/ 'they walked' (< **miškyu* < **mišyu*), and /ʕosk/ 'sticks' (< **ʕosky* < *ʕuṣiyy*), where the velar stop can be said to have replaced etymological /y/ as a third radical.

However, complete assimilation of the alveolar nasal and of the lateral liquid to a following /y/ is not an automatic process in CyA but appears to be restricted to certain morphological boundaries or to specific lexical items: /kayyisrok/ 'he used to steal' < **ka:n yisroq*, /teyye/ 'vine' < **da:lya*, etc.

15.3.3. Postnasal epenthesis

A fairly automatic phonetic rule in CyA requires the insertion of an auxiliary stop segment between a nasal and a following continuant or resonant, the secondary plosive agreeing with the preceding nasal in point of articulation and with the following continuant in voicing: [intsàn] 'man, husband' < *insa:n*, [kampx] 'wheat' < *qamḥ*, [x'imbl] 'load' < *ḥiml*, etc. Though no comparable sound rule has been noted for Cypriot Greek dialects in Newton (1972a, 1972b), this epenthesis rule in CyA appears to have been contracted from Greek (Johannes Niehoff, personal communication 1994).

15.4. Stop voicing in Cypriot Arabic

Stop voicing does not ordinarily present a problem area in descriptive work on mainstream varieties of spoken Arabic, where this contrast continues a formal trait inherited from OA, and ultimately, from older forms of Semitic. In Borg (1985: 12–16), I noted that special features relating to obstruent voicing in CyA arise principally from this vernacular's history of language contact with CyG, which has culminated in the high degree of Arabic/Greek bilingualism characterizing the contemporary Kormakiti community.

A concise but fairly detailed account of the surface distribution of obstruent voicing in CyA was presented in Borg (ibid.), where it was concluded that notwithstanding occasional erratic reflexes of OA obstruent voicing in CyA surface structure, the functional role of stop voicing in CyA is too negligible to be systemically significant. My purpose in resuming the discussion of this topic here is to react to critical observations that appeared in two reviews of my monograph: Hopkins (1990: 89) and Singer (1991: 408). Both scholars have suggested that recognition of a voicing opposition in CyA stops could conceivably yield a more insightful phonological analysis of the vernacular than that proposed in my aforementioned study, where this feature is assigned merely allophonic status.

In the following sections I propose to sketch some salient diachronic and synchronic trends relevant to CyA voicing and then to examine some emendations to my phonological analysis proposed in Hopkins' critique of the voicing issue, in order to determine what if anything in my original presentation requires modification.

One final remark here relates to Hopkins' view (p. 89)—echoed by Singer—alleging that my phonological analysis of CyA is "rather complicated." Hopkins, however, also recognizes the intricate character of CyA phonology when contrasted with the transparency of most other colloquial Arabic sound systems. Thus no mainstream Arabic dialect investigated so far displays a comparable degree of complexity in its phonetic treatment of underlying stop segments. As I noted in Borg (1985: 6), the complexity of CyA phonology derives simultaneously from its alignment with the CyG sound system in the realm of phonotactics and from its obvious lack of isomorphy with CyG in the domain of root structure (CyA and CyG being genetically unrelated languages). Specifically, while root morphemes in Greek, as in other Indo-European languages, comprise continuous strings displaying both consonantal and vocalic components (cf. Schwyzer 1938: 419), CyA word structure has retained the carried over mobility of Arabic radicals, with the result that phonological rules contracted from CyG, like manner dissimilation, post-nasal voicing, palatalization, etc., represent essentially historical shifts in Greek but synchronically productive processes when carried over into CyA. One example will suffice here. The aforementioned manner dissimilation rule requires the first segment in Ancient Greek stop + stop clusters to undergo spirantization in many varieties of Greek, including CyG; cf. Ancient Greek πτωχός 'poor', ὀκτώ 'eight' >CyG ftoxòs, oxtò, etc.). Observe now the morphophonemic spirantization of the velar and labial stops before /t/ in the CyA root {k-t-p} (< OA *kataba* 'he wrote'):

CyA
kitep   'he wrote'   ⇐ |kitip|
xtuft   'I wrote'   ⇐ |ktupt|
paxtop   'I write'   ⇐ |paktop|

As will be seen below, the endeavor to maintain invariant underlying representations for roots in a synchronic account of the CyA sound system introduces a certain degree of complexity into the phonological analysis of voicing in this vernacular.

15.4.1. Paradigmatic aspects of voicing in Cypriot Arabic

Voicing fulfilled a purely marginal role in the OA stop series, since, in effect, only dentals implemented this phonological opposition:

```
    –   t   k   q   ʔ
    b   d   –   –   –
```

Its functional load was greater in the OA fricative series, where four of the seven available articulatory positions within this class were occupied by voiced/voiceless pairs:

| f | θ | s | š | x | ḥ | h |
| - | ð | z | - | γ | ʕ | - |

The majority of modern Arabic dialects have generally extended and evened out the paradigmatic domain of the voicing opposition within their obstruent systems, usually by filling out the Old Arabic "empty slots" through internal change and/or integration of foreign sounds, e.g., Baghdadi Arabic (Blanc 1964: 17), the Jewish dialect of Algiers (Cohen 1912: 520–21), etc.

As shown in Table 15-1 above, CyA has, like most Arabic dialects, also developed a high degree of symmetry in its paradigmatic implementation of the voicing opposition. The impact of the CyA sound system on that of CyG has entailed for CyA both positive and negative trends, promoting internal symmetry and formal alignment with Greek in the functional contrasts implemented.

On the positive side, CyA has extensively retained the interdental articulation of *θ and *ð (< OA *ð and *ḏ̣) lost in many sedentary—principally urban—varieties of Eastern Arabic, and OA /w/ has shifted to CyA /v/; in both cases, the systemic role of voicing among CyA fricatives has been enhanced. The retention in CyA of a voiced pharyngeal fricative /ʕ/ (without a voiceless counterpart) is highly noteworthy given its complete extraneousness to the CyG consonant inventory; its survival in CyA would seem to suggest a relatively late date for intensive contact between CyA and Greek.

On the negative side, the CyA consonant paradigm shows segmental streamlining through the merger of a number of OA contrasts:

OA		CyA
ṣ, s	>	s
ḍ, ð	>	ð
ḥ, x, h	>	x
ʕ, γ	>	ʕ

The absence of the voiced uvular fricative *γ in CyA is striking given the presence of CyG /γ/. This latter factor would seem to suggest that the loss of this segment was a substratally inherited trait antedating linguistic contact with Greek.

From the specific standpoint of the voicing feature, the systemic contraction of the CyA consonant paradigm resulting from the merger of these OA fricatives has been compensated for by the aforementioned shift of *w > /v/, and of *ǧ > /ž/, both of which have voiceless counterparts in the CyA paradigm. The CyA velar fricative /x/ lacks a full-fledged voiced correlate in the inherited lexicon, but an intriguing CyA phone [γ] tends to show up in surface reflexes of certain secondary clusters: Ar. *kb, *kd > *gb, *gd > CyA [ɣb], [ɣd], respectively: CyA [ɣbiːr] 'big (masc.)' < gbiːr < Ar. kbiːr, [móɣde] 'stove' < *moːqde < OA mawqida, etc. In fact, as we shall see (in § 15.5.3), the formal interpretation of these voiced clusters in the synchronic phonology of CyA is not easily accommodated within the scope of a conventional phonological analysis.

In addition to its elimination of the voicing contrast in stops, formal restructuring within the CyA stop system has also entailed a reduction in the number of articulatory classes retained. Significantly, these latter comprise the labial, dental, and velar points of articulation—a selection that was partly dictated by the paradigmatic structure of the CyG sound system and partly by a more general naturalness factor, these being the three phonologically least marked articulatory positions along the vocal tract. (Note, for instance, the loss of the highly marked uvular position via fusion of OA *q and *k > CyA k.)

Thus, like the Greek dialect family, CyA displays the "classic" stop series, /p/, /t/, and /k/; these are voice-indifferent and derive historically in the following fashion:

CyA		OA
p	<	b
t	<	t, ṭ, d
k	<	k, q

Examples:

CyA		OA
pirek	'it flashed (lightning)'	< baraq
tute	'mulberry tree'	< tuːta
tute	'worm'	< duːda
tar	'he turned round'	< daːr
tar	'it flew'	< ṭaːr
kiser	'he broke'	< kasar
kitel	'he killed'	< qatal

The pairs of CyA homophones with dental stops provide a striking illustration of the historical loss of the voicing opposition in this vernacular.

15.4.2. Syntagmatic features of Cypriot Arabic stops

CyA utterances display both voiced and voiceless stops. As already noted in Borg (1985: 12), voiced simplex (i.e., non-geminated) stops occur most often in resonant phonetic contexts, i.e., intervocalically, and in contact with the resonant segments [m], [n], [l], and [r], or in the adjacency of /z/:

[síbel]	'stubble'	/sipel/
[k'ídel]	'he killed'	/kitel/
[tága]	'window'	/taka/
[xágle]	'field'	/xakle/
[págra]	'cow'	/pakra/
[índi]	'you (fem.sg.)'	/inti/
[ʕúrba]	'strangers'	/ʕurpa/
[várde]	'flower, rose'	/varte/
[várga]	'book'	/varka/

In contact with the voiced alveolar spirant [z], CyA stops are always voiced:

[bzáʕat]	'I feared'	/pzaʕat/
[pázga]	'spittle'	/pazka/
[nágza]	'sharp pain'	/nakza/

Outside this specific environment, CyA stops attain full phonation optimally after nasals:

/np/	⇒	[mb]
/nt/	⇒	[nd]
/nk/	⇒	[ŋg]

In other contexts potentially conducive to stop voicing, such as intervocalically and in contact with liquids, it is often difficult to distinguish with certainty between voiced stops and lax, voiceless ones. Sound spectrograms taken of CyA utterances do not always show a distinctly discernible voice bar accompanying intervocalic simplex stops. However, previous researchers of CyA have also tended to perceive phonatory activity here (e.g., Roth 1975, passim).

Voiceless realizations of CyA stops are most common pre- and post-juncturally where voicelessness is the norm for stops even in contact with a following resonant, usually with concomitant devoicing of the latter:

[pr̥úde]	'coolness'	/prute/
[kl̥ep]	'dogs'	/klep/
[kapr̥]	'grave'	/kapr/
[tipn̥]	'straw'	/tipn/

Like CyG, CyA retains historical stop gemination. The geminate clusters /pp/, /tt/, and /kk/ are always voiceless and highly aspirated; /dd/ is generally also voiceless but unaspirated. The unsymmetrical relationship between CyA simplex stops and their corresponding geminates is discussed below.

15.5. Discussion

To sum up the preceding section, laryngeal features in surface realizations of CyA labial, dental, and velar stops are generally predictable from immediate phonetic environment. Simplex CyA stops are realized:
  (a) voiceless, lax, and unaspirated in word-initial and -final positions;
  (b) lax, (usually) voiced intervocalically and after resonants, particularly nasals;
  (c) voiced in contact with /z/.

Geminated labial and velar stops are invariably tense, voiceless, and aspirated, whereas geminated dental stops can be either tense, voiceless, and aspirated; or lax, voiceless, and unaspirated.

The non-functional status of stop voicing in CyA was, incidentally, also independently postulated in Jastrow (1977) on the basis of the notational vagaries and inconsistencies in Tsiapera's (1969) descriptive sketch of this language. Arlette Roth's 1975 study of CyA verb morphology also assumes diachronic systemic loss of the voicing feature among stops in this vernacular.

As we shall see below, in the few cases where a voice contrast in stops may be ostensibly relevant from the perspective of a conventional segmental analysis, there are often good reasons for questioning the validity of this solution.

In the following sections, I shall take issue with Hopkins' argumentation in favor of a voicing opposition in CyA stops. In effect, Hopkins recognizes three sources of a potential voicing contrast in this vernacular:
  (a) post-nasal stop voicing;
  (b) the opposition of the CyA geminates /tt/ : /dd/; and
  (c) residual retention of Old Arabic voicing in certain dyadic clusters: CyA [ɣbiˑr] 'big' < Ar. *[gbiːr] < kbiːr. Let us here consider each of these points in turn.

15.5.1. Post-nasal voicing

It should be clear from the preceding sections that the oppositions $p : b$ and $k : g$ never materialize in unambiguous phonological contexts, e.g., intervocalically. That CyA reflexes of historical labial and velar stops should be voice-indifferent is hardly surprising since, as already noted, there was no historical source for these oppositions in OA. Sedentary Arabic vernaculars which have functionalized these potential contrasts have generally achieved this through the integration of lexical loans with [p] and [g]: Baghdadi /puːši/ 'veil', /parda/ 'curtain' (< Persian); for Damascene /g/, see Ferguson (1969).

By way of contrast, CyA appears to have been fairly well shielded from contact with foreign lexical influences other than those filtered through CyG.

Surface [b], [d], and [g], however, do sometimes occur post-juncturally in native CyA words, mostly verbs; here the voiced segment invariably derives from underlying bi-phonemic sequences consisting of nasal + stop, i.e., /np/, /nt/, and /nk/, respectively. Such word-initial sequences are, for instance, particularly frequent in verbs displaying the passive marker {N-}:

[pálas]	'he ran over'	
[mbálas ~ bálas]	'he got run over'	⇐ |N + palas|
[tílef]	'it leaked'	
[ndílef ~ dílef]	'it got soaked'	⇐ |N + tilef|
[k'íser]	'he broke'	
[ŋg'íser ~ gíser]	'it got broken'	⇐ |N + kiser|

Hopkins, however, contends that the initial voiced stops in the optional variants with a deleted nasal furnish a sufficient basis for setting up voiced stop phonemes in CyA:

> Borg is doubtless right in principle in saying that simple *d* and *t* no longer contrast, but there do seem to be cases where this opposition is possible. One of them is (p. 13) *tilef* "it leaked" : *dilef* "it got soaked" (~ *ndilef*). The fact that *dilef* has an alternative form should perhaps not be made to carry more than it can bear: if the form *dilef* exists and a speaker uses it, we have ipso facto a phonemic contrast between *d* and *t*. Borg himself says as much when he calls this opposition "functionally significant." (p. 89)

Hopkins' conventional reasoning is somewhat off the mark. An insightful appraisal of surface voicing must not overlook the fact that post-nasal stop voicing (with or without nasal deletion) is a quintessential hallmark of Greek phonic interference. I recall here some remarks from Hamp (1962: 641) relating to the perception of stop voicing by speakers of Greek, where, incidentally, the same analytical problem (i.e., the phonological status of voiced stops) occurs:

> One can judge from various aspects of the reactions of Greek speakers that they hear voiced stops and affricates in typical European languages as being nasal, because, for all Greek except acculturated varieties often heard in Athens, a voiced phone occurs either (i) automatically preceded by a nasal segment, or (ii) *in free variation with nasal plus voiced stop segments* ... (Hamp 1962: 641, emphasis added)

The intimate link between nasals and stop voicing in CyA can be seen in its diachronic treatment of stops, e.g., the occasional shift of Ar. *dd > CyA [nd]:

CyA	OA
[k'indám] 'before'	< *qudda:m*
[ʕánda] 'he entered'	< *ʕadda:*

If our synchronic analysis of CyA is to reflect the speaker's perception of the underlying facts, the phonological interpretation of the voiced initial stops here must surely be /n/ + voiceless stop.

Even in the event that CyA speakers were to lose the longer variants with {N-} cited above and to retain the counterparts with the initially voiced stops, there are reasons of a morphological nature why one would not want to analyze these initial voiced stops as unit phonemes. Positing the voiced stops /b/, /d/, and /g/ as underlying segments in this grammatical context would be tantamount to setting up phonological segments that harbor morphological boundaries. One would, in other words, be postulating a CyA "reflexive marker" with the odd realization [+voice]. Surely both of these features are inadmissible in a conventional linguistic analysis, particularly in the case of the CyA passive marker {N-}, which has been retained as such in phonetic environments that do not require its fusion with the stem-initial consonant:

šarat	'he ripped'	
ntšarat	'it got ripped'	⇐ |N + šarat|
faylet	'he loosened'	
mfaylet	'it got loosened'	⇐ |N + faylit|

The simplicity of the morphological analysis of CyA would thus be notably enhanced if we set up an invariant basic form of the passive morpheme {N-} which is liable to optional deletion before phonetically voiced stops thus:

Underlying form	|N + tilef| 'it got soaked'
Post-nasal voicing	[ndílef]
Optional nasal deletion	[dílef]

15.5.2. The CyA opposition /tt/ vs. /dd/

One of the special features of the CyA stop series is its differential historical treatment of single vs. geminate dentals. Whereas the present phonetic realization and distribution of CyA phones continuing the OA simplex dentals attest to the complete fusion of the OA voiced and voiceless dental series into CyA /t/, the vernacular nonetheless retains, to a certain extent, the distinction between reflexes of geminated OA /tt/ and /dd/. The phonetic basis of the latter contrast in CyA, however, is not the voicing feature, but a tense : lax opposition. Like other geminated stops, CyA /tt/ is uttered without phonation and with fairly strong aspiration; CyA /dd/, on the other hand, is voice-indifferent (generally voiceless) but never aspirated.

In fact, only a few permanently voiced reflexes of historical or secondary Ar. *dd* have been retained in CyA; as already noted in the previous subsection, these tend to show the shift Ar. *dd* > CyA *nd*, e.g., [k'indám] 'before' < Ar. *qudda:m*, etc. The special historical treatment of dental segments in CyA has yielded the following unusual patterning of phonological oppositions among plosives (the dash represents an empty paradigmatic slot for a voiced stop):

Single stop	Geminated stop
[p] : –	[pp] : –
[t] : –	[tt] : [dd]
[k] : –	[kk] : –

The phonetic bases of this three-way contrast among dentals can be tabulated as in Table 15-2:

Table 15-2. Cypriot Arabic Dental Stop Contrasts

	t	tt	dd
voice	±	–	±
aspiration	–	+	–
length	–	+	+

The oppositions between CyA dentals are optimally implemented in word-medial and -final positions:

CyA		Arabic
ʕata	'lid'	< *yita:ʔ*
ʕatta	'he covered'	< *yatta:*
ʕadda	'he bit her'	< *ʕaddha:*
mat	'he died'	< *ma:t*
fatt	'he stripped off (fruit)'	(~ ? *farat*)
madd	'he measured'	< *madd*

In word-initial position, the contrast between simplex and geminate dentals falls outside the strictly phonological sphere, since initial geminates in the native CyA lexicon generally include a morphemic or lexical boundary and tend to cooccur with certain grammatical processes, e.g., marking for definiteness by means of the article /l/, which in CyA completely assimilates to most initial consonants:

ddist	'the dish'	⇒ [tːist]
ddayn	'the debt'	⇒ [tːayn]
ttimm	'the blood'	⇒ [tʰim]
ttik	'the rooster'	⇒ [tʰiˑk]

The words just cited exemplify the analytical problem under discussion in a striking manner. Without the article, all four lexical items display an initial lax, voiceless, dental stop [t]:

[tist]	'dish'	< Ar. *dist*
[tayn]	'debt'	< Ar. *dayn*
[tim]	'blood'	< Ar. *damm*
[tiˑk]	'rooster'	< Ar. *diːk*

Once the article /l-/ is preposed, a latent contrast between CyA dentals comes to light. Within the theoretical context of a conventional phonological analysis, this is an unusual situation, since morphophonemic processes (e.g., morphologically generated consonantal gemination) do not ordinarily yield functional contrasts unattested at the purely phonological level.

One could here recognize an abstract *t : d* contrast between simplex dental stops, whose phonetic correlates are always neutralized. Since phonological neutralization as customarily understood eliminates an opposition exclusively in specific contexts (e.g., prejunctural voicing in languages such as German, Turkish, Russian, Maltese, etc.), the setting up of such an opposition in CyA would entail admitting a case of complete neutralization.

It should be clear from the last two sets of examples that the lexical distribution of the CyA geminates /tt/ and /dd/ in this morphosyntactic context corresponds only partially to the historical voice opposition between Old Arabic **t* and **d*. In fact, in the greater number of cases, historical **d* tends to yield simplex /t/ and geminate /tt/, as in the following words:

CyA			**Old Arabic**
t-tarp		'the road'	< *d-darb*
t-teyye		'the vine'	< *d-daːliya*
t-taken	< **d-daqan*	'the beard'	< *ð-ðaqan*
t-tuppane	< **d-dubbaːna*	'the fly'	< *ð-ðubbaːna*

The synchronic distribution of these CyA reflexes is, incidentally, also highly subject to idiolectal variation—possibly reflecting the terminal state of the vernacular.

From the diachronic standpoint, the phonological contrast between CyA *tt* and *dd* represents the outcome of an intriguing fusional process drawing simultaneously on both OA and CyG sound systems. Thus, while on the one hand, this functional opposition obviously continues in part the OA voicing contrast *tt* : *dd*, its phonetic implementation in CyA exploits the Greek tense : lax distinction (realized phonetically as aspirated vs. non-aspirated release) which in CyG, however, opposes simplex to geminate stops and never two different kinds of geminates. Thus the opposition *tt* : *dd* is completely foreign to CyG phonology, where only the following simplex : geminate contrasts obtain in the dental and interdental classes (Newton 1972a: 34):

CyG: *t* : *tt*   θ : θθ
              ð : ðð

The *tt* : *dd* contrast in CyA amounts to an innovation in another sense too: no other Arabic vernacular described so far utilizes phonetic aspiration as a morphological device:

Basic stem	Derived stem
šite [šíde] 'rain'	šatta [šát·ʰa] 'it rained'
kapr [kapr̥] 'grave'	kapper [káp·ʰer] 'he buried'

The analytical problem relating to the relationship between simplex and geminated dentals also shows up in another context (not discussed in Hopkins): morphologically conditioned degemination of CyA /dd/, for instance, in broken plurals of certain CyA nouns whose plural form displays two occurrences of /t/, the first realized voiceless, the second showing intervocalic voicing. One could here adopt a more abstract phonological notation than the one used in Borg (1985) in order to distinguish between simplex dentals that yield /dd/ when geminated from those that yield /tt/. The former could be indicated by means of an abstract symbol *d* and the latter by means of *t*, as in the following two lexical sets:

kiddás	'Mass'	
xdedís	'Masses'	⇒ [xtedí·s]
fiddán	'yoke of oxen'	
fdedín	'yokes of oxen'	⇒ [ftedí·n]
štume	'insult (n.)'	
šattem	'he insulted'	⇒ [šát·ʰem]
xtat	'cats'	
katt	'cat'	⇒ [kat·ʰ]

In Borg (1985) I refrained from doing so since this would have meant recognizing a *t* : *d* contrast in simplex CyA dentals for which there are no stable phonetic correlates. This would have also had the effect of obscuring the extent of historical change actualized in CyA. Above all, given the fact that voicing in simplex CyA plosives is conditioned by the immediate phonetic context, it seemed to me highly artificial to set up a genuine voicing contrast. Paradoxically, the recognition of an abstract *t* : *d* distinction (in place of the full-fledged *t* : *d* phonemic contrast suggested by Hopkins) would ideally have to ignore phonetic voicing as a criterion, since the distribution of voiced and voiceless stops in CyA is automatically predictable.

15.5.3. Voicing in dyadic clusters

A striking oddity in the synchronic behavior of CyA stops in certain words is their tendency to show up voiced (and spirantized in conformity with manner dissimilation) in immediate contact with other stops. Thus, for instance, the CyA root {k-p-r} 'big' yields the following surface forms, among others:

    (a) [k'íber]   'he grew up'
    (b) [k'íbret]   'she grew up'
    (c) [ɣbiːr]   'big (masc.sg.)'
    (d) [ɣbar]   'big (pl.)'

Voicing of /p/ in the resonant environments (a) and (b) conforms to CyA voicing norms outlined in § 15.4.2; voicing of the word-initial clusters in (c) and (d), on the other hand, represents a residual reflex of regressive voicing assimilation in Ar. **gbiːr, *gbaːr* < OA *kabiːr, kibaːr* that survived the paradigmatic loss of stop voicing in the CyA plosive class. Three voiced clusters of this kind commonly occur in CyA: [ɣb], [ɣd], and [ðb]. The dyadic clusters showing [ɣ] in first position seem to represent a "frozen" phonotactic template apparently unknown in CyG, where—assuming that the data on CyG consonant clusters provided in Newton (1972a: 29) are complete—/ɣ/ clusters exclusively with resonants: [ɣl], [ɣr], [ɣn], [ɣm]. Highly indicative here is the metathesis of stops in CyA [ɣba] 'he wept' generating this voiced cluster through regressive voicing assimilation: *[bkaː] > *[kbaː] > *[gbaː] > CyA [ɣba]. Some of these clusters also occur in the morphophonemics of verb inflection, e.g., of /rikep/ 'he rode', /páxxer/ 'he incensed', /pas/ 'he kissed', /tápax/ 'to cook':

    [ríɣbet]   'she rode'
    [piðbáxxer]   'she incenses'
    [piðbúːs]   'she kisses'
    [pittíniðbex]   'it is being cooked'

In my monograph on CyA, I analyzed voicing in such clusters as subphonemic, despite the fact that, distributionally speaking, phonological contrasts with corresponding voiceless clusters do occur, as in the following constrastive pairs:

CyA		Arabic
[ɣbar]	'big (pl.)'	kiba:r
[xpaz]	'loaves'	axba:z
[ɣdi·š]	'horse'	kadi:š
[xti·r]	'much'	kaθi:r
[móɣde]	'stove'	mawqida
[oxt]	'time'	waqt

which I transcribed phonologically: /xpar/, /xpaz/, /xtiš/, /xtil/, /moxte/, and /oxt/, respectively. Hopkins (1990: 89–90) objected to my phonological representations of the voiced clusters:

> The analysis of forms such as /xpir/ 'big' with obligatory voicing [ɣbi·r] seems to me unnecessarily complicated and abstract. If voicing of /xp/ is here obligatory, then one should think of adding either ɣ or b (or both) to the phonemic inventory. Borg, however, is unwilling to do this since he does not admit a phonemic opposition b : p, d : t, etc., and proposes instread to solve the problem by employing the ad hoc compromise device of underlining these combinations: /xp/ = [ɣb]. This is unconvincing. When Borg avers (p. 16) that the "distribution of voicing in these dyadic clusters is synchronically unpredictable" this is tantamount to saying that the proposed phonemic analysis cannot account for it.

Hopkins here adopts the viewpoint of traditional phonemics according to which phones occurring in contrasting environments are accorded systemic status. However, he overlooks other formal factors that merit consideration and which suggest, at the very least, that the CyA consonant paradigm has a gray area in its assignment of voicing:

a) CyA has extensively retained the root and scheme composition of stems typical of Arabic and other Semitic languages. This factor makes it desirable that the phonological analysis posit wherever possible invariant underlying representations for CyA root morphemes. Given the circumstance that CyA speakers perceive lexical items such as [rígep] 'he rode', [rkift] 'I rode', and [ríɣbu] 'they rode' as semantic cognates, the phonological analysis should reflect these native perceptions and assign these items identical radicals. This procedure is particularly desirable since this type of spontaneous voicing in CyA clusters is also liable to show up in morphological inflection, e.g., in the following verb forms:

CyA			Arabic
[sakʰep]	/sakkep/	'he overtook'	< *sabbaq*
[saɣbet]	/sax̱pet/	'she overtook'	< *sabbaqat*
[k'idep]	/kitep/	'he wrote'	< **kitib*
[k'íðbet]	/kiθ̱pet/	'she wrote'	< **kitbit*

Recognition of /b/, /d/, and /g/ as phonemic segments would necessarily imply an allomorphic split of these verbal roots thus: {s-k-p ~ s-ɣ-b}, {k-t-p ~ k-ð-b}, and so on throughout the CyA lexicon. The artifical nature of this "solution" can easily be inferred from the occurrence of free variants such as [rákifti] ~ [raɣbíti] 'my neck' < OA *raqabati:*, which attest to the relative automaticity and low-level status of the voiced clusters under discussion. Hopkins refers (p. 90) to my diacritical underlining of these spontaneously voiced clusters as a "cosmetic" device. However, another formal interpretation is also possible. Given the nonexistence of independently voiced segments in CyA outside the context of these dyadic consonant clusters, one could simply mark the roots that are affected by this idiosyncratic trend in preference to setting up full-fledged voiced plosives in the phonemic inventory. This treats spontaneous stop voicing in clusters as a feature pertaining to certain lexemes: in other words, a lexical rather than a purely segmental feature.

b) It is significant that the combinatory potential of these voiced segments is also extremely restricted. The aforementioned treatment of OA *baka:* (e.g., the metathesis affecting the etymological plosives **bk*) is particularly indicative in this respect. Interestingly, underlying or historical dyadic obstruent clusters with [b] in first position do not seem to occur in CyA; observe, in this connection, the regular devoicing of historical **bd* in CyA /ptilt/ 'I changed' < **bdilt* < OA **badalt*. Significantly CyA here also retains the non-spirantized surface stop [p], yielding a minimal contrast with /ftilt/ 'I twisted'.

15.6. Synopsis and conclusion

It should be evident from this presentation that no strong case for postulating a systematic voicing contrast in underlying representations of CyA stops can be sustained on the basis of the data at hand. As has been noted, voicing of CyA stops occurs in fully or partially conditioning environments, i.e., after nasals, and, less predictably, in certain dyadic clusters which undergo voicing in certain morphophonemic contexts. In both cases, the potential functional role of the voicing feature in stops is anyway fairly negligible. The case of CyA *tt* : *dd* is also of marginal relevance to the issue of voicing, since neither sequence is in fact intrinsically and permanently voiced. The only other clear case of regular surface voicing affecting underlying CyA stops occurs in the clusters examined in the preceding section, where the cooccurrence of voicing and clustering makes an unambiguous appraisal of the functional role of voicing per se somewhat problematic.

I would like to suggest that the formal ambiguity obtaining vis-à-vis the functional role of the CyA voicing feature here is comparable to that of consonant length in Modern Hebrew. Observe, for instance, the following modern reflexes of Biblical Hebrew *ḥ-g-g* 'Fest' (Buhl 1954: 213; cf. Ar. *ḥaǧǧ* 'pilgrimage'), where etymological geminated **g* is simplified in items (a) and (b) but retained in (c), (d), and (e):

Modern Hebrew
(a) *ḥag*   'feast'
(b) *ḥag-ím*   'feasts'
(c) *laḥgóg*   'to celebrate'
(d) *ḥagigá*   'celebration'
(e) *ḥagigí*   'festive'

Though native Hebrew speakers undoubtedly perceive a clear semantic and derivational relationship between all these lexical items, functional loss of consonant length in Modern Hebrew has rendered the link between their surface and underlying form less transparent than it was for speakers of the ancient language.

In their reviews of Borg (1985), Hopkins (1990) and Singer (1991) argue for a "voicing" contrast in CyA, assuming too readily (despite indications to the contrary in Borg 1985: 12–16) that a stable correlation between phonetic and phonological voicing actually exists. In this they may have been misled by my use of the letters *p t k b d g*. Following traditional practice in phonological descriptions, I resorted to these symbols to characterize more than two different laryngeal states in phones and phonemes uttered in the labial, dental, and velar regions of the vocal tract, the "voiceless" set [p t k] being always assumed to represent the unmarked phonetic value within each allophonic split (voiceless : voiced; tense : lax; aspirated : non-aspirated). The adoption of these symbols for both phonetic and phonological representations has the drawback noted in Keating (1984: 287), e.g., that they

> are used for a variety of physical events. Strictly speaking, [b d g] are supposed to be reserved for stops with voicing during their closures, and [p t k] for voiceless unaspirated stops. The symbols defined in this way can be

used in Polish, French, and many other languages quite straightforwardly. In contrast, their use in English and other languages is more complicated: [b d g] occur mainly in medial position, sometimes in initial position; [p t k] occur after [s], and sometimes medially. But /b d g/ are used as broad-transcription symbols for both [b d g] and voiceless [b̥ d̥ g̊], which occur mainly in initial position. The latter set has been called voiceless lenis, or voiceless lax, or even 'voiced as in English'.

The reference to Indo-European plosive systems here is of more than tangential relevance to CyA. In his cursory survey of the role of aspiration in certain languages, Pétursson (1976: 169) remarks that

> À l'exception du néerlandais les langues germaniques ont la caractéristique commune de présenter dans leur système consonantique le phénomène phonétique appelé aspiration. ... Le grec est aussi un exemple de langue européenne non-germanique possédant le trait phonétique de l'aspiration....

Distinctive aspiration is not ordinarily associated with the Arabic vernaculars. The display in CyA of distinctive aspiration and of voiceless, lax, dental stops (i.e., [t:] ⇐ /dd/)—features which this vernacular imbibed through contact with CyG—yields a striking phonetic parallel with some of the aforementioned Indo-European stop systems, especially Greek; it also underscores the necessity for a phonological analysis of CyA stops that goes well beyond a mere conventional classification of stops into phonetically voiced and voiceless ones, since, as the preceding discussion showed, no such phonological correlation can be postulated for CyA stops, there being no clear instances of spontaneous (i.e., non-conditioned) voicing of individual stop segments in this vernacular.

As Abercrombie (1967: 148–49) noted, though not with reference to CyA, "There can ... be many intermediate points ... at which voicing sets in: from 'fully voiced' to 'voiceless fully aspirated' is a continuum." It would no doubt be very instructive to conduct an experimental study of CyA stop consonants in order to ensure clear and unassailable data on the exact function of voicing in this vernacular and on the extent of its correlation with other features (cf. Lisker and Abramson 1964, 1971; Chomsky & Halle 1968: 328ff.; Pétursson 1976; etc.). Such an investigation would almost certainly demonstrate the importance of laryngeal states other than vocal cord vibration to an analysis of the CyA stop series. In the absence of such a study I have resorted to a provisional phonological classification of CyA stops utilizing the tense : lax dichotomy familiar from traditional work on Indo-European languages, e.g., English.

15.7. Epilogue

All things considered, the special evolutionary path traversed by CyA, its continued interaction with Greek, and its present terminal state all suggest that it is probably unrealistic to approach the study of CyA phonology as if it were a completely integral and self-contained system in which, according to conventional wisdom, "tout se tient." A more plausible representational model of CyA phonology must take cognizance of its "parasitical" relationship with the sound system of Greek and allow for the possibility that the organization of surface phonology in CyA is sometimes achieved at the expense of overall paradigmatic transparency. The aforementioned parallel case of the formal opacity of consonant length in Modern Hebrew is particularly relevant here, since this circumstance is a byproduct of discontinuity in language transmission and language contact. Another case of this kind, involving ambiguity in the interpretation of surface phonetics in a variety of Arabic, was, for instance, noted by Heath's (1989) paper on the functional status of Moroccan affricates, in which the author concluded "that native speakers themselves are not entirely sure what is going on" (p. 133).

Thus, some systemically erratic traits in the voicing behavior of CyA stops noted in this chapter may ultimately also be symptomatic of this vernacular's advancing obsolescence. A special study of the impact exerted on CyA phonology by its current sociolinguistic situation in Cyprus should perhaps take within its purview relevant comparative data from another terminal language surviving in a Greek socio-cultural context, i.e., Arvanìtika (erstwhile Albanian) on mainland Greece (cf. Hamp 1989; Trudgill & Tzavaras 1977).

References

Abercrombie, David. 1967. *Elements of general phonetics*. Edinburgh: Edinburgh University Press; Chicago: Aldine.

Barth, Fredrik. 1969. "Introduction." In *Ethnic Groups and Boundaries*, ed. Fredrik Barth, pp. 11–38. Boston: Little, Brown.

Blanc, Haim. 1964. *Communal Dialects in Baghdad*. Cambridge: Harvard University Press.

Borg, Alexander. 1985. *Cypriot Arabic*. Stuttgart: Steiner.

Buhl, Frants. 1954 [1915]. *Wilhelm Gesenius' Hebräisches und Aramäisches Handwörterbuch über das alte Testament*, 17th ed. Leipzig: Vogel.

Cantineau, Jean, and Y. Helbaoui. 1953. *Manuel élémentaire d'arabe oriental*. Paris: Klincksieck.

Chomsky, Noam, and Morris Halle. 1968. *The Sound Pattern of English*. New York: Harper & Row.
Cohen, Marcel. 1912. *Le parler arabe des juifs d'Alger*. Paris: Champion.
El-Hajjé, Hassan. 1954. *Le parler arabe de Tripoli (Liban)*. Paris: Klincksieck.
Ferguson, Charles A. 1969. "The /g/ in Syrian Arabic: Filling a Gap in a Phonological Pattern." *Word* 25: 114–19.
Fischer, Wolfdietrich. 1961. "Die Sprache der arabischen Sprachinsel in Uzbekistan." *Der Islam* 36: 232–63.
Hagège, Claude. 1973. *Profil d'un parler arabe du Tchad*. Paris: Geuthner.
Hamp, Eric. 1962. "The Interconnection of Sound Production, Perception, and Phonemic Typology." In *Proceedings of the Fourth International Congress of Phonetic Sciences held at the University of Helsinki, 4–9 September 1961* (Janua Linguarum Series Maior 10), ed. Antti Sovijärvi and Pentti Aalto, pp. 639–42. The Hague: Mouton.
———. 1989. "On Signs of Health and Death." In *Investigating Obsolescence: Studies in Language Contraction and Death*, ed. Nancy C. Dorian, pp. 197–210.Cambridge: Cambridge University Press.
Heath, Jeffery. 1989. "Moroccan Affricates." In *Studia linguistica et orientalia memoriae Haim Blanc dedicata*, ed. Paul Wexler, Alexander Borg, and Sasson Somekh, pp. 133–35. Wiesbaden: Harrassowitz.
Hopkins, Simon. 1990. Review of Borg 1985. *Zeitschrift für arabische Linguistik* 22: 88–93.
Ingham, Bruce. 1994. "The Effect of Language Contact on the Arabic Dialect of Afghanistan." *Actas del congreso internacional sobre interferencias lingüísticas árabo-romances y paralelos extra-iberos celebradas en Madrid del 10 al 14 de diciembre de 1990*, ed. Jordi Aguadé, Federico Corriente, and Marina Marugán, pp. 105–17. Zaragoza: n.p.
Jacoby, David. 1979. "Citoyens, sujets et protégés de Venise et de Gênes en Chypre du XIIIe au XVe siècle." In *Recherches sur la Méditerranée orientale du XIIe au XVe siècle: Peuples, sociétés, économies* (Variorum Reprints 6), pp. 159–88. London.
Jastrow, Otto. 1973. *Daragözü: eine arabische Mundart der Kozluk-Sason Gruppe (Südostanatolien): Grammatik und Texte*, Nuremberg: Carl.
———. 1977. "Gedanken zum zypriotischen Arabisch." *Zeitschrift der deutschen morgenländischen Gesellschaft* 127: 258–86.
———. 1978. *Die mesopotamisch-arabischen Qəltu-Dialekte*, vol. 1. Wiesbaden: Harrassowitz.

Keating, Patricia A. 1984. "Phonetic and Phonological Representations of Stop Consonant Voicing." *Language* 60: 286–319.
Kieffer, Ch. M. 1980. "L'arabe et les arabophones de Bactriane (Afghanistan)." *Welt des Islams* 20: 178–96.
Levin, A. 1971. "The *imāla* in the Arabic Dialects." Ph.D. dissertation, Hebrew University, Jerusalem.
Lisker, Leigh, and Arthur S. Abramson. 1964. "A Cross-language Study of Voicing in Initial Stops: Acoustical Measurements." *Word* 20: 384–422.
———. 1971. "Distinctive Features and Laryngeal Control." *Language* 47: 767–85.
Lüdtke, Helmut. 1977. "Plurilinguismo e morfosintassi mista (comparazione del maltese con l'arabo cipriota)." *Bollettino dell'atlante linguistico mediterraneo* 18–19: 211–15.
Newton, Brian. 1964. "An Arabic-Greek Dialect." In *Papers in Memory of George C. Pappageotes*, ed. Robert Austerlitz (Supplement to *Word* 20/3), pp. 43–52.
———. 1972a. *Cypriot Greek: Its Phonology and Inflections* (Janua Linguarum Series Practica 121). The Hague: Mouton.
———. 1972b. *The Generative Interpretation of Dialect* (Cambridge Studies in Linguistics 8). Cambridge: Cambridge University Press.
Nöldeke, Theodor. 1904. Review of Stumme 1904. *Zeitschrift der deutschen morgenländischen Gesellschaft* 58: 903–20.
Pétursson, Magnús. 1976. "Aspiration et activité glottale: Examen expérimental à partir de consonnes islandaises." *Phonetica* 33: 169–98.
Röhricht, R. 1895. "Le pèlerinage du moine augustin Jacques de Vérone (1335)." *Revue de l'orient latin* 3: 178.
Roth, Arlette. 1975. "Le verbe dans le parler de Kormakiti (Chypre)." *Epetêris* (Nicosia) 7: 21–117.
Roth-Laly, Arlette. 1969. *Lexique des parlers arabes tchado-soudanais*. Paris: Centre national de la recherche scientifique.
Schwyzer, Eduard. 1938. *Griechische Grammatik*, vol. 1. Munich: Beck.
Selim, George Dimitri. 1967. "Some Contrasts between Classical Arabic and Egyptian Arabic." In *Linguistic Studies in Memory of Richard Slade Harrell*, ed. Don Graham Stuart, pp. 133–52. Washington, D.C.: Georgetown University Press.
Singer, Hans-Rudolf. 1991. Review of Borg 1985. *Orientalistische Literaturzeitung* 86: 408–9.

Sirat, A. S., and E. E. Knudsen. 1973. "Notes on the Arabic Dialect Spoken in the Balkh Region of Afghanistan." *Acta Orientalia* 35: 99–101.

Storrs, Sir Ronald, and Brian Justin O'Brian, eds. 1930. *The Handbook of Cyprus*, 9th issue. London: Christophers.

Stumme, Hans. 1904. *Maltesische Studien: Eine Sammlung prosäischer und poetischer Texte in maltesischer Sprache nebst Erläuterungen*. Leipzig: Hinrichs.

Trudgill, Peter, and G. A. Tzavaras. 1977. "Why Albanian-Greeks Are Not Albanians: Language Shift in Attica and Biotia." In *Language, Ethnicity and Intergroup Relations*, ed. Howard Giles, pp. 171–84. New York: Academic Press.

Tsiapera, Mária. 1969. *A Descriptive Analysis of Cypriot Maronite Arabic* (Janua Linguarum Series Practica 66). The Hague: Mouton.

Ullmann, Manfred. 1970. *Die Medizin im Islam*. Leiden: Brill.

Chapter 16
Maltese Phonology
Alexander Borg
Ben-Gurion University of the Negev

16.1. Introduction

The structural profile of contemporary Maltese represents the outcome of a diachronic process in which an erstwhile vernacular of spoken Arabic—brought to the Maltese Islands apparently in the late 9th century (A.D. 870 [?]; cf. Rossi 1936, Wettinger 1986, Barbato 1990)—evolved during most of the present millennium in virtually complete isolation from the mainstream Arabic vernaculars. Prolonged interaction with literary and dialectal varieties of Italian, the Mediterranean *Lingua Franca*—in the sense of Kahane and Tietze (1958)—and English, has acted as a strong catalyst of diachronic change accentuating the formal distinctiveness of Maltese (henceforth M) from native varieties of vernacular Arabic, particularly in the domains of lexicon, syntax, and phonology.

Though M is not infrequently referred to as an "Arabic dialect" in the linguistic literature, this designation would seem to be more appropriate as a genetic classification than as a synchronic one, since in its present form, M has structurally distanced itself far too profoundly from the norms of spoken Arabic to be regarded as anything other than a separate language. Two factors symptomatic of the highly alien character of the Maltese language community vis-à-vis the contemporary Arabic-speaking world deserve mention here:

(a) the Christian affiliation and European *Weltanschauung* of the Maltese, which renders them basically unreceptive to cultural and linguistic influences from the Arab countries. (Throughout its known history, the Maltese

AUTHOR'S NOTE: Abbreviations and symbols: /h/, in M words, stands for a phonemic segment that alternates freely between laryngeal, fricative, and velar points of articulation. The following abbreviations have been used: Ar., Arabic; Cal., Calabrian; Eng., English; It., Italian; Lat., Latin; M, Maltese; MLF, Mediterranean Lingua Franca; Mor., Moroccan; OA, Old Arabic; Sic., Sicilian; SM, Standard Maltese; Tk., Turkish; ⇐, derives synchronically from; ⇒, yields synchronically; { } enclose morphemic or allomorphic representations; | | enclose underlying representations. The letters of the M alphabet with notes relating to their most usual phonetic realizations are listed in § 16.8. I am indebted to Prof. A. Ambros (Vienna) for his comments on an earlier draft of this paper.

nation has stood distinctly outside the pale of such entities as 'urūba and umma.) The cultural and confessional aspects of the linguistic *Abstand* between M and Arabic are both strikingly reflected in the longstanding tradition of writing M by means of the Latin alphabet; cf. the use of the Hebrew alphabet in Judeo-Arabic.

(b) the absence of a literary Arabic tradition in Malta and the consequent non-existence of the so-called "diglossia" situation familiar from the Arab countries (cf. Ferguson 1959, but also El-Hassan 1977)—literary M being an independent local development deriving exclusively from colloquial M.

Thus whereas mainstream Arabic vernaculars form a symbiotic system with literary Arabic drawing on it both as a source of linguistic enrichment and as a cultural model, M lost its direct linguistic and cultural links with Arabic in the Middle Ages—presumably after the Norman invasion of 1090 and the subsequent expulsion of the Muslim community from the Maltese Islands in the 13th century (Wettinger 1986: 99)—and has since then looked to European languages (first Italian and later English) for cultural and lexical enrichment. Highly symptomatic of this profound and probably unbridgeable gap between M and the Arabic *Sprachraum* is the striking but rarely noted circumstance that notwithstanding its patently Arabic grammatical core, contemporary M is apparently unable, on both formal and cultural grounds, to draw on Arabic, e.g., as a source of lexical expansion.

A systematic attempt at assessing the extent of the formal drift of M from the Arabic dialect family and accounting for its apparent immunity against Arabic influences must take into account the aberrant evolutionary path that yielded the present M sound system. As in certain other residual varieties of dialectal Arabic spoken outside the Arab countries—e.g., in Cyprus (Borg 1985; Borg, this volume), and in Central Asia (Fischer 1961; Sirat and Knudsen 1973), all trace of velarization has been lost in the M consonant system, the OA emphatics having been fused with their plain counterparts. Far-reaching paradigmatic changes have also occurred among back consonants: reinterpretation of the OA velar and pharyngeal fricative pair ʕ and ɣ, chiefly as vocalic length; fusion of *OA x, ḥ*, and *h* into M /h/, loss of *hamza*, etc. M has furthermore integrated several foreign consonant segments, primarily through contact with Italian: /p/, /v/, /c/, /ʣ/, and /č/. As a result, the M sound system probably constitutes the most salient single factor accountable for the alien character and unintelligibility of the language to native speakers of Arabic. By the same token, the cumulative impact of these systemic departures from the phonological norms of spoken Arabic in M plausibly represents the most important single correlate of the linguistic and cultural distance of its speaker community from the Arabic-speaking world, and of the *rapprochement* of M to the Romance *Sprachbund*.

Some idea of the estrangement of M from the Arabic *Sprachraum* in the perception of native Arabic speakers can be gleaned, for instance, from explicit statements by Arabic language reformers concerning the "decadent" state of M. Thus in a statement reflecting his concern for the purity of literary Arabic, Al-Maghribi (1947 [1908]: 43–44) characterizes "the language of Malta" as "neither Arabic nor foreign" (cited in Stetkevich 1970: 62). In the same spirit, the Syrian Anis Sallum wrote in 1922: "Is there an educated person who wants his language to be like that of the people of Malta?" (cited in Chejne 1969: 154). In a less formal vein, the Egyptian novelist Ibrahim al-Mazini (in *Ṣunduːq al-dunyaː*, 26–31) attempts to convey to the reader the foreignness of M by mimicking certain phonological traits in the language commonly associated with nonnative Arabic speech (e.g., confusion of Arabic /ḥ/, /x/, and /h/).

The cultural distance of the Maltese nation from the Arabic-speaking world is clearly reciprocated in the self-perception of Maltese ethnic minorities abroad. Thus, whereas Maltese settlers in the West—England, Australia, and the U.S.—easily shift to the majority language, e.g., English (cf. Jeger 1963 cited in Dench 1975), M communities in North Africa and Egypt retained their ethno-religious distinctiveness (Nachtigal 1974 [1879]: 13–14; Vadala 1906, passim; Price 1954: 55f.) and their vernacular throughout their existence and did not simply shift to the local dialect of Arabic (cf. Saada 1986 on "Tunisian" Maltese, and Hull 1988 on "Egyptian" Maltese).

The phonology of M not only sets it apart from the mainstream Arabic vernaculars, but also constitutes the structural domain characterized by the greatest degree of internal dialectal differentiation, yielding a standard vernacular (henceforth SM)—spoken in the urban centers of the main island, Malta—and a number of nonstandard varieties traditionally associated with rural Malta and especially with the island of Gozo (for more detail, see Puech 1994: 16–22 and passim).

The consonantal inventory of M is virtually identical in all the dialects; fairly marked differences, however, obtain between SM and nonstandard M, as well as between the rural varieties themselves, in the domains of vocalic inventory and morphophonemics. Dialectal diversification in the rural vernaculars of M derives for the most part from differential historical treatment of the OA vowel system:

SM	Rabat (Gozo)	OA	
omm	*umm*	*umm*	'mother'
da:r	*do:r*	*da:r*	'house'
bɪ:b	*be:b*	*ba:b*	'door'

Thus, whereas SM has evolved a system of five vowels, all nonstandard varieties of M have four (Puech 1994: 17f.). In the realm of vowel morphophonemics, certain non-standard varieties of M display complex rules of vowel harmony (Puech 1978) and/or a set of vocalic alternations conditioned by syllabic, lexical, and pausal boundaries. Observe, for instance, the prejunctural diphthongization of OA *[i:] and *[u:] in the M dialect of Rabat (island of Gozo), where the secondary diphthong in the closed syllable alternates with the monophthong in the open syllable:

Rabat (Gozo)	SM	
zarbewn	*zarbu:n*	'shoes'
zarbu:na	*zarbu:na*	'a shoe'
treyd	*tri:d*	'you (sg.) want'
tri:da	*tri:da*	'you (sg.) want her'

Certain conservative speakers from this dialect area also display pausally conditioned diphthongization of these OA long high vowels (Borg 1976)—a feature that is unknown in SM but is, significantly, well attested in certain Eastern varieties of vernacular Arabic, such as the dialect of Šḥi:m (Lebanon; Fleisch 1974 [1962]: 203–20), and the North Palestinian dialect spoken by the Druze (Blanc 1953: 50).

The present sketch will focus primarily on the SM sound system as reflected in educated urban speech—e.g., among residents of Valletta, Sliema, etc.—and broadcast on the local radio and TV networks. Unless otherwise indicated, the immediate source of the SM linguistic corpus cited here is the present author's own idiolect, and M dialectal material comes from the author's fieldnotes.

16.2. The Consonants

16.2.1. The consonant paradigm

The SM sound system comprises the consonant segments in Table 16-1. Some consonants are restricted to a few but well integrated loanwords, e.g., /ž/ in /televížin/ 'television', /be:ž/ 'beige,' /ru:ž/ 'rouge', /dz/ in /gadzdzetta/ 'newspaper', /landzi:t/ 'bristle', /medzdza/ 'kind of basket', etc.

Table 16-1. Maltese Consonants

p	t				k	ʼ
b	d				g	
	f	s	š			h
	v	z	ž			
		c	č			
		dz	ǧ			
m	n					
	l					
	r					
w			y			

In addition to this consonantal paradigm, the M sound system has an "abstract phoneme" represented by the orthographical symbol għ (called [aːyn] in the M alphabet) and representing the reflex of the OA fricatives */ʕ/ and */ɣ/ (cf. § 16.2.4.12).

The schematic chart of M consonants displayed above characterizes the consonantal paradigm of SM. Certain nonstandard dialects show some minor differences; as noted in Puech (1994: 17), conservative speakers from the Gozitan villages of San Lawrenz, Għarb [aːrp], and Żebbuġ [zebbúːǧ] still retain residual traces of the voiced velar fricative [ɣ] continuing the same phoneme in Old Arabic. Archaic consonantal traits have also been retained by speakers on the island of Malta itself. Thus, in contrast with the glottal reflex of qāf in SM, conservative speakers from the towns of Cospicua and Senglea [séngleya] retain the uvular stop [q]—also noted for Valletta in the early years of the century in Stumme 1904 (passim). The dialect of Xewkija [šewkiyya] in Gozo, on the other hand, systematically fuses OA /q/ and /k/ into /k/ (for further detail, see Puech 1994: 31). Dialectal variation also extends to M reflexes of OA /r/; instead of the apical trill [r] that is the normal SM reflex of OA *r, some nonstandard dialects of M show the alveolar tap [ɾ] or the alveolar approximant [ɹ] (cf. Puech 1994: 17).

16.2.2. Phonological neutralization in consonants
16.2.2.1. Voicing
Voiceless stops in M are generally realized without a significant degree of aspiration when released, and voiced stops tend to be uttered with full

phonation outside automatically devoicing phonetic environments. Some speakers display optional secondary voicing of historically voiceless stops in resonant environment in certain Romance loans. The integral function played by the voicing opposition in the M obstruent series as a result of its integration of the new obstruents *p, v, č, g, c,* and *ž* (acquired both through internal change and via nativized loans) is also reflected to varying degrees in many mainstream Arabic vernaculars that have extended the paradigmatic range of the Old Arabic voicing contrast.

M obstruents are subject to a regressive voicing assimilation rule systematically converting all and every dyadic or triadic set of adjacent obstruent segments that are nonuniform in voicing into completely voiced or voiceless sequences. The voicing feature in Maltese is therefore non-distinctive in all but the last segment in a cluster. Automatic gain or loss of the voicing feature in obstruents has given rise to conditioned alternation between voiced and voiceless segments that can otherwise occur in positions of functional contrast, e.g., the voiced and voiceless bilabial stops /p/ and /b/:

[kítep]	'he wrote'	⇐ /kiteb/
[nígdbu]	'we write'	⇐ ḥiktbu/
/posta/	'mail'	< It. *posta*
/bosta/	'many'	< Ar. *baṣta*

The voicing opposition in M is also neutralized in prejunctural position (as in [kitep] 'he wrote'), where voicing contrasts are normally restricted to underlying representations. Word-final devoiced obstruents in M are phonetically indistinguishable from their underlying voiceless correlates, but will here be transcribed as phonologically voiced so as to distinguish them from historically voiced obstruents in which the voicing feature has been permanently lost: /art/ 'land' < Ar. *arḍ*, /niket/ 'sorrow' < Ar. *nakd*, etc. The present distribution of voicing in neutralizing environments is not accurately reflected by contemporary orthographical norms since the Maltese writing system tends to be etymological in this respect; thus it often indicates obstruent voicing in contexts where permanent neutralization has rendered it irretrievable to the contemporary speaker: <sibt> [sipt] 'Saturday' < Ar. *sabt*, <abt> [a:pt] 'armpit' < Ar. *ibṭ*, etc. The tendency towards hypercorrect voicing is also reflected in orthographical variants, such as <berghud/berghut> 'flea' < Ar. *baryu:θ*.

In effect, voicing neutralization in M has tended to obscure native speaker perceptions of the underlying and historical distribution of voicing in obstruents. This circumstance has occasioned re-etymologization of several M root morphemes, entailing, for instance, permanent gain or loss of the voicing feature in certain obstruents via back formation. Observe the following examples, where conditioned voicing of the M reflexes of OA *k and *ṣ in clusters has yielded permanent M /g/ and /z/: /gideb/ 'he lied' < Ar. *kaðab, /zebah/ ~ /zeba/ 'he painted' < Ar. *ṣabay. Permanent devoicing of historically voiced segments is also common: /tefa/ 'he threw' < Ar. *dafaʻ 'to push', /hafer/ 'he forgave' < Ar. *yafar, etc.

The propensity for this kind of back-formation in M has occasioned numerous instances of hypercorrect shifts, as in the case of /d/ in M /disa/ 'nine' (< Ar. tisʻa) back-formed from /tsata:š/ 'nineteen' popularly perceived as |dsata:š|.

16.2.3. Length

M has retained the OA length contrast in both vowels and consonants. Consonantal length is optimally retained intervocalically after stressed vowels:

ferah	'he rejoiced'
ferrah	'he made happy'
safar	'travel'
saffar	'he whistled'

Both in lineally inherited lexicon and in nativized loans, M displays a certain degree of interdependence between the length of a vowel and that of a following word-final consonant. Thus, in monosyllabic words, long M vowels inherited from OA occur optimally before single consonants:

ǧa:r	'neighbor'
ǧarr	'he dragged'
bɪ:l	'he urinated'
bill	'dip!'
vo:t (< It. *voto*)	'vote'
bott (< Sic. *botti*)	'tin can'

Rare contraventions of this canonic norm occur in the few cases were M has evolved secondary vowel length before a word-final CC sequence:

e:mm	'there' <	*hemm < Mor.Ar. *hamm* (Fischer 1959: 127 n. 2)
e:kk	'thus' <	*hekk	

M tends to neutralize consonantal length in prejunctural position:

[fomm-i]	'my mouth'
[fom]	'mouth'

Stressed phonetic -VC# word-final sequences in M derive uniquely from underlying /-VCC#/, since singly closed prejunctural syllables displaying short vowels are rarely if ever stressed. Thus, as in many Arabic dialects, foreign loans displaying stressed word-final -VC# in the lending language tend to undergo automatic gemination of their final consonant in M underlying representations: /klabb-iyɪːt/ 'club-s', /čekk-iyɪːt/ 'check-s', etc. This constraint on the syllabic structure of monosyllables in M occasionally yields free variation between the canonic forms CVCC and CV:C, e.g., in the loanword /ramm/ ~ /raːm/ 'copper' < Italian *rame*.

Many Arabic dialects tend to neutralize the length contrast in consonant clusters. Schabert (1976: 26) notwithstanding, however, many M speakers, including the present writer, often retain such contrasts, possibly under the influence of written norms:

nizlu	'they descended'
nizzlu	'they brought down'
čahdet	'she denied'
čahhdet	'she deprived'

Underlying and historical contrasts between long and ultra-long consonants are, however, always automatically neutralized:

šellel	'he basted'
šellet	'she basted' ⇐ |šelllet| ⇐ |šellel + et|
hazzez	'he scribbled'
hazzet	'she scribbled' ⇐ |hazzzet| ⇐ |hazzez + et|

16.2.4. Sound Classes

The present section illustrates the contrastive roles of M consonants and outlines pertinent phonetic and distributional features. Diachronic aspects of the M sound system are briefly touched upon whenever this can throw light on present distributional patterns or special morphophonemic processes.

16.2.4.1. Labials

The M labial series comprises the bilabial stops /p/ and /b/, the nasal bilabial /m/, and the labiodental fricatives /f/ and /v/:

SM		
	post	'place'
	bosta	'many'
	fost	'among'
	mošt	'comb'
	pošt (< Tk. *puşt*)	'scoundrel'

    rkoppa (< Ar. *rukba*)   'knee'
    kobba   'ball of wool'
    'offa   'wicker basket'
    komma   'sleeve'

The extent to which M has integrated the voiceless bilabial stop /p/ in its sound system is probably without a close parallel among the contemporary Arabic dialects, even those where the voiceless bilabial stop is a full denizen (e.g., Baghdadi Arabic, Blanc 1964: 18). M has, for instance, not only integrated foreign /p/ but has proliferated it in new lexical creations, especially in words of an onomatopoeic nature:

    SM   *čappas*   'he tainted'
          tappan   'he made dull (glass, mirror)'
          perper   'it fluttered in the wind (flag)'
          pačpač   'he chattered'
          pa'pa'   'he sounded the horn (of car)'
          pespes   'he whispered'

16.2.4.2. Labiodental fricatives

The labiodental fricative /v/ is understandably rare in lineally inherited words; note, however, its occurrence in the high-frequency SM term /iːva/ 'yes' < *aywa*, which yields a functional contrast with /f/ in /ǧiːfa/ 'fool'. A variant [iːwa] (generally perceived as nonstandard) also exists. The diachronic shift *w > v here presumably reflects the co-articulatory incompatibility of lip-spreading concomitant with [iː] and lip-rounding accompanying [w]. In fact, the sequence [iw] is altogether rare in M (cf. § 16.3.3).

The contrast between M /f/ and /v/ is well established by reason of numerous Italian loans displaying the voiced labiodental fricative in initial and medial positions:

    fiːni   'fine (pl.)'   < It. *fini*
    viːni   'veins'   < Sic. *vini*
    feːra   'he injured'   < It. *ferire*
    veːra   'true (f.)'   < It. *vera*
    naːfu   'we know'   < Ar. *naʻrafuː*
    traːvu   'beam'   < Sic. *travu*

In M the voiced labiodental fricative /v/ does not enjoy the distributional freedom of most other M consonants and, for instance, rarely occurs geminated outside certain morphological contexts, e.g., verbal inflection: /vvoːta, yivvoːta/ 'to vote'.

16.2.4.3. Dentals

M /t/ (< OA *t, θ,* and *ṭ*) and /d/ (< OA *d, ð, ḍ,* and *ð̣*) are usually realized as plain dental stops, whereas the segments /s/ (< OA *s* and *ṣ*), /z/, /n/, /l/, and /r/ all are articulated with a more retracted tongue position, i.e., against the alveolar ridge. The following word pairs illustrate functional contrasts within this sound class; it should, however, be borne in mind that M neutralizes the voicing opposition word-finally in obstruents:

t : d	*temm*	'he finished'	*demm*	'blood'
	'atel	'he killed'	*'adef*	'he rowed'
	wiret	'he inherited'	*bired*	'it (masc.) cooled'
s : z	*smɪːn*	'fat (pl.)'	*zmɪːn*	'time'
	nisel	'origin'	*nizel*	'he descended'
	biss	'only'	*wizz*	'geese'

16.2.4.4. Affricates

The M alveolar series also includes the voiced and voiceless affricates /c/ and /dz/ respectively:

c : z	*copp*	'lame (masc.)'	< Sic. *zoppu*
	dzoːna	'zone'	< It. *zona*
	pecca	'roll of cloth'	< Sic. *pezza*
	medzdza	'kind of basket'	< It. *mezza*
	pasticc	'cheesecake'	< Sic. *pastizzu*

Both segments tend to occur primarily in words of Italian provenance and usually retain their phonological length component in non-initial position. Observe, for instance, how the segment /c/ in fully integrated italianisms functions as a geminated radical when the root undergoes internal inflection: /bocca/ 'electric bulb' (pl. /bococ/) < It. *bozza* 'protuberance'. The voiceless affricate /c/ also shows up in M derivatives of Arabic *kuds* (pl. *akdaːs*) 'heap', which yields M /gocc/ (pl. /gcuːc/) 'heap', and the verbal forms /geccec, ygeccec/ 'to bundle together'.

16.2.4.5. Resonants

Aside from a few noteworthy cases of permutation and metathesis discussed in § 16.2.4.7 below, the OA resonants /l/, /m/, /n/, and /r/ have been largely retained without change in lineally inherited lexicon, where they contrast functionally in word-initial, medial, and final positions:

l : *m* : *n* : *r*:

laha'	'he reached'	*mela*	'he filled'	*dahal*	'he entered'
mahat	'he blew (nose)'	*rema*	'he threw away'	*šaham*	'grease'
naha'	'it brayed'	*fena*	'he weakened'	*tahan*	'he ground'
rahal	'village'	*mera*	'mirror'	*nahar*	'he snored'

The nasal continuants /n/ and /m/ do not contrast before stops but always agree with the latter in point of articulation:

yonfoh	[yoɱfoħ]	'he blows'
banda	[banda]	'side'
bank	[baŋk]	'bank'

The phonological neutralization of the labial/dental contrast in nasals before stop segments yields the nasal archiphoneme *N*; this abstract representation is borne out by the tendency of M speakers to extrapolate underlying /n/ from surface [ɱf] and [mp] clusters: M [ˈnɪːpen] 'bells', sg. [ˈampɪːna] < It. *campana*.

The M alveolar nasal /n/ also assimilates to stem-initial resonants in the imperfect paradigm of verbs: /mmuːr/ 'I go' ⇐ |nmuːr|, /rriːd/ 'I want' ⇐ |nriːd|, etc. In the dual or pseudo-dual ending {-eyn} the final /n/ is liable to alternate freely with zero, usually with concomitant secondary doubling of the preceding glide or, alternatively, lengthening of the steady state portion of the vowel nucleus: /tneyn ~ tneyy ~ tneːy/. The elision of /n/ here and in reflexes of Ar. **-ayn* is presumably conditioned by the synchronic morphological boundary between /y/ and /n/ in the pseudo-dual: /idey-h/ 'his hands', /saʼay-h/ 'his legs', etc. Note also, in this connection, the historical accretion of word-final /n/ in M /armayn/ 'too late' < It. *ormai*, and its proliferation as a secondary syllable coda after word-final long stressed vowels, where it presumably implements a strategy for integrating foreign words, e.g., by facilitating morphological inflection of nouns: /sufáːn/ (pl. /sufan+iyɪːt/) 'sofa' < It. *sofà*, /bluːn-a/ 'indigo' < Eng. *blue*, /skruːn/ (pl. /skreyyen/) 'propeller' < Eng. *screw*, /kafé/ 'coffeehouse' (pl. /kafen-iyɪːt/).

16.2.4.6. The Lateral Resonant

The lateral liquid /l/ in the inherited lexicon is generally invariable at the purely segmental level but is subject to grammatically conditioned alternation at morphemic level, e.g., as a definite article and as object marker. The definite article {(i)l-} generally assimilates to following coronal segments (*t, d, s, z, n, r*): /it-tiːn/ 'the figs', /iš-šemš/ 'the sun', /ir-raːs/ 'the head', /in-naːr/ 'the fire', /id-daːr/ 'the house', etc.; interestingly, the assimilation rule is asymmetrically implemented before the voiced and voiceless alveopalatal affricates /ǧ/ and /č/, respectively: *il-ǧisem* 'the body,' but *ič-čarruːta* 'the rag' (~ Ar. *šarṭuːṭa*). Non-assimilation of the lateral before /ǧ/ is the norm in Classical Arabic and certain Arabic colloquials.

In some Eastern Arabic dialects the definite article is subject to optional assimilation before [ǧ]: rural Palestinian [il- ~ iǧ-ǧaːr] (Bauer 1926: 5); this suggests that the voiced alveopalatal affricate is ambiguously categorized in the consonant systems of these vernaculars. Assimilation of /l-/ exclusively before the voiceless alveopalatal affricate in M may well hark back to a historical stage when this affricate was perceived by native M speakers as the cluster [tš]. (For further discussion of this point, see Comrie 1980.)

Like many mainstream Arabic dialects, M displays the optional assimilation of /l/ to a following /n/ exclusively at the morpheme boundary between a verb stem and the pronominal suffix {-naː} 'we, us': /kilna ~ kinna/ 'we ate', /hadilna ~ hadinna/ 'he took from us', etc. Another morphologically conditioned realization of /l/ occurs in the (direct and indirect) object marker {lil-}, which is prone to automatic gemination before an initial vowel: /lill-ommi/ 'to my mother' ⇐ |lil-ómmi| (but /lil-missɪːri/ 'to my father'), thus avoiding an open unstressed syllable.

16.2.4.7. Interaction between Lateral and Trill

In words of Italian origin there is an unsystematic though widespread synchronic trend (especially in certain very commonly used words) towards reshuffling of liquids such that the lateral occurs optimally in syllable-initial and the apical trill in syllable-final position. Historically, this has yielded permanent syllabic shifts such as the following:

SM		Italian
arblu	'mast'	< *albero*
porvli	'gunpowder'	< *polvere*
girgoːr	(name)	< *Gregorio*
perliːna	'sugar-coated almond'	< *pralina*
garigoːr	'spiral staircase'	< Sic. *caragolu*
gabiryoːla	'somersault'	< *capriola*
gamblu	'crayfish'	< Cal. *gambaru*
splenguːn	'brooch'	< Sic. *spinguluni*

Though rare in the Arabic lexical component, this type of syllabic restructuring may account for the root-final changes in the native words

M		Arabic
tamal	'dates'	tamar
fɪːtel	'lukewarm'	faːtir

presumably via back-formation from the feminine forms (tamla, fɪːtla) showing the resonant segment in syllable-initial position.

In M lexicon of Romance provenance the same distributional preference can also be observed in the historical diffusion of *secondary* liquids promoting closed syllabicity in unstressed positions, especially, though not exclusively, in the nautical lexicon: /skorfiːna/ 'nut (mech.)' < Sic. *scufina*, /arcnell/ (kind of fish) < M *arsnell ~ Sic. *asineddu*. Note also the proliferation of word-final /r/ from /l/, other resonants, or zero: /artaːl/ 'altar' < It. *altare*, /pinnuːr/ 'weathercock' < It. *pennone* 'flagpole', /ǧuvintuːr/ 'young men' < Sic. *guivintu*, etc.

Synchronically, this process is most noticeable in the speech of the uneducated, where the restructured forms implement the unmarked syllabic option: [pitlóryu] 'paraffin', [sturmént], 'musical instrument' [maskla] 'mask', vs. SM [pitrólyu] [strumént], [maskra], ultimately < It. *petrolio, strumento*, and *maschera*. The popular perception of secondary /r/ (< another resonant or zero) at syllable codas as a hallmark of uneducated M speech is sometimes consciously exploited in the dialogue sections of M literary works portraying life in rural Malta: *ipperparot* 'prepared' < It. *preparato*; *porpaganda* 'propaganda' (Mamo 1930–31: 24, 4). Certain nonstandard M speakers use the form /telefórn/ 'telephone', where insertion of the apical trill creates a secondary CC cluster regularizing word-final stress in this lexical item (for the M stress rule, see § 16.5 below).

In standard M speech, this process yields a certain amount of free variation between /l/ and /r/ at syllable codas: /ǧorf/ ~ /ǧolf/ 'giant' < (?) Ar. *ǧurf* 'cliff', /galbu/ ~ /garbu/ 'good manners' < It. *garbo*.

16.2.4.8. Alveopalatals
The M alveopalatal series comprises principally the voiceless fricatives /š/, and the voiced and voiceless affricates /ǧ/ and /č/, respectively. The following pairs illustrate the relevant contrasts:

s : š
sellef	'he lent'	šellef	'he blunted (blade)'
nesa	'he forgot'	meša	'he walked'
fluːs	'money'	truːš	'deaf (masc.)'

š : č : ǧ

šaham 'grease'	*čahad* 'he denied'	*ǧahan* 'Juha'
kašša 'box'	*kačča* 'hunt (n.)'	*gaǧǧa* 'cage'
baraš 'he scratched'	*'ar'ač* 'he scorched'	*taraǧ* 'steps'

Though initially M /č/ may well have been internally generated via historically bi-phonemic *tš or devoiced *ǧ in the inherited lexicon, the integration into M of a large number of Italian loans displaying the alveopalatal affricate in different positions had the effect of regularizing its distribution:

čavetta	'key'
kečča (< It. *cacciare*)	'he expelled'
'a'očč (< Sic. *cacocciula*)	'artichokes'

M nonetheless retains the formal distinction between the sequence /tš/ and /č/, since the former usually implies a morphological boundary between stop and fricative:

    ma-ra:t-š   'she did not see'

Thus, for instance, whereas for the purposes of stress assignment, a word-final /tš/ represents a consonant cluster and draws stress on a preceding short vowel, non-geminated /č/ does not:

ma-čarrtít-s	'she did not rip'
'ármeč	'he crunched'

The voiced alveopalatal affricate /ǧ/ has the optional allophone [ž] before stops, e.g., [ǧdi:d] ~ [ždi:d] 'new (masc.sg.)'. Loss of the occlusive onset probably represents a process of cluster simplification: [džd] > [žd]. It is presumably the synchronic alternation between [ǧ] and [ž] in this phonetic context that has had the effect of obscuring the historical phonemic boundary between reflexes of /ǧ/ and /š/: [ǧbi:n] ~ [žbi:n] 'chum, fellow', [ǧbayt] ~ [žbayt] 'I am sated', ultimately < Ar. **šbi:n* 'godfather' and **šabi't*, respectively.

16.2.4.9. *Velar Stops*

The opposition of the voiceless velar stop /k/ and of its voiced equivalent /g/ in M was generated internally within the Arabic-based lexicon via voicing assimilation, both progressive and regressive:

k : g

kerrah	'he made ugly'	(~ Ar. *kariha* 'he hated')
gerrem	'he gnawed (bone)'	(cf. M **nqarram* 'I gnaw' ~ Ar. *qarama* 'he gnawed')
tnikker	'he loitered'	
niggez	'he pricked'	(cf. M **nikkzu* ~ Ar. *nakaz*)

and has been reinforced by numerous Italian words displaying /g/ in most environments. The contrast between /k/ and /g/ is partially neutralized in contact with certain resonants, e.g., liquids: *sa:gru* ~ *sa:kru* 'holy' < Sic. *sacru*, *klassi* ~ *glassi* 'class' < It. *classe*, *kazi:n* ~ *gazi:n* 'club' (cf. *il-gazi:n*, ultimately from It. *casino*), etc.

16.2.4.10. M /g/ vs. /ǧ/

Occasional traces in M of a shift /ǧ/ > /g/ in the context of /z/ (e.g., /gzi:ra/ 'island' < Ar. *ǧazi:ra*)—a well known feature in certain Arabic dialects—suggest that phonologization of the *ǧ* : *g* contrast in Maltese was, at least in part, an inherited trait. Maltese appears to have itself expanded the lexical scope of this contrast, both via internal change (e.g., OA **q* and **k* > M *g*):

g : ǧ	M		Arabic
	garr	'he complained'	< *qarr*
	ǧarr	'he carried'	
	niggez	'he pricked'	< *nakaz*
	niǧǧes	'he fouled'	

and through subsequent heavy borrowing from Mediterranean languages and English: /ganč/ 'hook', /bagoll/ 'suitcase', /sso:gra/ 'he risked' (< MLF; cf. Ar. /so:gar/ 'he insured'), /gendu:s/ 'bull' (< Berber), /gara:š/ 'garage' (< Eng.), etc.

16.2.4.11. *The M fricative* /h/

As already noted, M has lost the distinctions between the OA voiceless phayngeal, velar, and laryngeal fricatives **ḥ*, **x*, and **h*, respectively. The unconditional merger of **ḥ* and **x* had probably already occurred in Medieval M; note, for instance, the use of the digraph *ch* for the reflex of both OA sounds in the late 15th century poem, *Peter Caxaro's Cantilena* (Wettinger 1968): <bachar> 'sea' < *baḥr*, <morchi> 'loose' < **marxī*. The contemporary orthography renders this consonant by <ħ>; in the present study, it is indicated by plain /h/.

Orthography	Phonemic representation		Arabic
ħajt	/hayt/	'wall'	< **ḥa:yiṭ*
ħajt	/hayt/	'thread'	< *xayṭ*
baħar	/bahar/	'sea'	< *baḥr*
daħal	/dahal/	'he entered'	< *daxal*
riħ	/rɪːh/	'wind'	< *ri:ḥ*
xiħ	/šɪːh/	'old man'	< *šayx*

Many M speakers tend to articulate /ħ/ as a pharyngeal fricative [ħ] and it is usually transcribed as such (ḥ) in descriptive work, e.g., Stumme (1904, passim), Schabert (1980: 287f.), and Puech (1994, passim), but other pronunciations, for instance as a voiceless velar fricative [x], or as a voiceless laryngeal fricative [h], also exist. These phonetic variants of /ħ/ do not appear to correlate with speakers' sociolectal backgrounds or with dialect boundaries. In the present author's usage, non-laryngeal pronunciations of /ħ/ are the norm in the context of gemination: [kaħħal] 'he plastered'.

Consonantal reflexes of the OA laryngeal fricative *h in M are phonetically identical with those of OA *ḥ and *x. The laryngeal fricative has nonetheless undergone a distinctive evolutionary process in M entailing large-scale elision and/or fusion with historically adjacent short vowels in certain contexts. This has yielded secondary vocalic length, as in

M		Arabic
e:dded	'he threatened'	haddad
e:na	'joy'	hana:

or morphophonemic alternation between M /h/ and zero:

Orthography	Phonetic realization	
iblah	[íblah]	'foolish (masc.)'
belha	[béla]	'foolish (fem.)'
ikrah	[íkrah]	'ugly (masc.)'
kerha	[kéra]	'ugly (fem.)'

The M orthography tends to be etymological with respect to OA /h/ and often shows <h> where its consonantal value has been entirely lost:

Orthography	Phonetic realization	
rahan	[ra:n]	'token'
huwa	[úwwa]	'he'
hija	[íyya]	'she'
bhejjem	[béyyem]	'animals' (< *bha:yim)

In a few residual cases, however, OA /h/ has yielded a phonemically stable consonant /h/: /naha', yinha'/ 'to bray', /nebbah, inebbah/ 'to enlighten'. Traditionally the M orthography also tended to retain the etymological distinction between the reflex of OA /ḥ/ and /x/—which it represents by <ħ>—and that of stable /h/, written <h>:

Orthography	Phonetic realization	
ħaffer	[ħáffer]	'he dug'
ħarab	[ħarab]	'he escaped'

However, the most recent dictionary of M, Aquilina (1987–90), follows the current trend in literary M and writes all instances of the stable radical /h/ as <h> irrespective of etymological source.

16.2.4.12. Maltese għajn

The term *għajn* refers to the digraph <għ> used in the M writing system for representing the reflexes of both OA /ˤ/ and /ɣ/. In his table of M consonants, Cohen (1970 [1966]: 127) designates this segment as a pharyngeal but later notes that the orthographical digraph 'au moins à La Valette et dans les villes, ne semble pas correspondre toujours à un trait acoustique audible' (p. 129).

In fact, the most common phonological reflex of these OA consonants in standard and non-standard varieties of M is vocalic length:

Orthography	Phonetic realization	OA
għamel	[aːmel]	ˤamal
għalaq	[aːlaʔ]	ɣalaq
sogħla	[soːla]	suˤla
ragħwa	[raːwa]	raɣwa

A few conservative rural communities (referred to in § 16.2.1) have nonetheless retained in a residual fashion the OA voiced velar fricative [ɣ]. In SM and most other varieties of M, consonantal reflexes of *għajn* are restricted to certain morphophonemic contexts, e.g., before the suffixed pronouns {-ha:} and {-hom} in verb inflection., where historical or underlying *għajn* is realized as /h/:

M			
	sema	'he heard'	< *samaˤ < OA samiˤ
	semahha	'he heard her'	< *samaˤha:

As can be inferred from the second syllable of M [séma], in positions where M neutralizes vowel length (e.g., prejuncturally), no surface reflex of these OA sounds occurs. Synchronic alternation of this kind is not restricted to M verbs but can also occur in nominal inflection; observe the morphophonemic alternation /h/ ~ /ø/ ~ /ɣ/ in the following nouns:

M		OA
[déma], [dmuːh]	'tear(s)'	damˤa, dumuːˤ
[ˈɪːh], [ˈiyaːn]	'bottom(s)'	qaːˤ, qiːˤaːn

Incidentally, orthographical *għ* in M does not always correlate synchronically with a specific phonological element in underlying phonology; thus it sometimes shows up as a purely otiose etymological residue in a number of M words (especially nouns) where its phonetic reflexes, primary or secondary, have been entirely lost: <nagħal> [na:l] 'horseshoe' < *na'al < OA na'l, xogħol [šo:l] 'work' < *šoγol < OA šuγl (both M words are monosyllabic). In some cases, orthographical għajn in M lacks an etymological basis altogether and is clearly the product of analogical change: laqħa [lá'a] 'meeting' (< Ar. liqa:'), jilqagħhom [yil'áħhom] 'he receives them', baqgħu [bá'aw] 'they remained', etc.

The resort to a digraph għ in the contemporary M orthography is an elegant practical solution for capturing the complex synchronic morphophonemics arising out of the phonetic reinterpretation of OA /'/ and /γ/ in the evolution of M. Thus basing himself principally on M verb morphophonemics, Brame (1972) concluded that setting up an abstract pharyngeal segment għajn in the M consonant paradigm facilitates the statement of formal regularities relating, for instance, to M word stress, distribution of stem vowels, etc., in this form class.

Phonological evidence in support of the synchronic reality of an abstract segment in M includes the noteworthy fact that for many M speakers secondary long vowels harking back to * '+ V (or vice versa) are phonologically marked and, unlike primary long vowels, are not subject to automatic reduction (in conformity with the length neutralization rule stated in § 16.3.2) when they undergo stress shift:

  á:mmar 'he dwelt' (< Ar. 'ammar)
  a:mmárt 'I dwelt'

It should, however, be noted that the generative interpretation of abstract għajn may ultimately prove more faithful to historical fact than to the synchrony of M. At all events, the notion that M speakers perceive an underlying 'pharyngeal segment' għajn finds little support in written usage, since the correct assignment of this digraph in written M remains a notorious source of error even among highly literate speakers. For an alternative analysis of M għajn, see Comrie (1986).

16.2.4.13. The glottal stop

Like many North African Arabic vernaculars, M no longer retains the automatic glottal catch preceding word-initial vowels: M /isem/ 'name', /omm/ 'mother' (not /'isem/, /'omm/), though occasional secondary vocalic length in this context may well hark back to OA hamza: /a:bt/ 'underarm' < 'ibṭ, /ewlı:mes/ 'the day before yesterday' < 'awwal 'ams.

M /'/ in standard speech represents a radical consonant usually continuing OA qāf, though certain nonstandard speakers (e.g., from Victoria and Xewkija, Gozo) fuse OA /q/ and /k/ into /k/. It is probably hypercorrect interference from these vernaculars that has yielded the SM variants /'a:'/, /ka:k/ 'round cakes' < Ar. *ka'k*, SM /serdu:'/, /serdu:k/ 'rooster' < Maghrebi Ar. *sardu:k*, etc.

The functional contrasts between SM /'/ and other backed consonants can be exemplified as follows:

': k	'attar	'it dripped'	kattar	'he increased'
	ba'ra	'cow'	sakra	'drunkenness'
	toro'	'streets'	torok	'Turks'
': h	'assar	'he shortened'	hassar	'he erased'
	ba'ar	'cows'	bahar	'sea'
	ba''	'bedbugs'	bahh	'nothing'

16.2.5. Phonaesthemes

Some M consonants, principally /č/, /c/, /p/, and /'/, sometimes assume a special expressive value, in the sense of Firth (1964: 184). The rich inventory of onomatopoeic lexical creations in M, particularly in the quadriliteral verb class, is of some interest in a phonological description since the spontaneous origin of such terms attests to the articulatory naturalness and phonological integration of these segments in the M sound system:

čarrat	'he ripped (cloth)' (cf. Ar. *šaraṭ*)
čekček	'he rattled'
čapčap	'he clapped'
čafčaf	'he splashed water'
'armeč	'he crunched (food)'
mečla'	'he ate noisily'
cekcek	'he tsked'
ci:ci	'poultry (nursery)'
pa'pa'	'he honked (the horn of a car)'
pačpač	'he chattered'
perper	'it fluttered in the wind (flag)'

M /č/ also has other expressive uses outside the standard lexicon and is particularly common in words pertaining to the register of abusive language. Here the voiceless alveolar affricate sometimes generates euphemistic variants of vulgar expressions or words inadmissible in polite usage: /ha'' alla ~ alleč/ 'by Jove', /il-madonna ~ il-madonneč/ 'by our Lady', etc. One of the most common terms of abuse in M is /ču:č/ (pl. /čwɪ:č/) 'jackass!' < It. *ciuco* 'donkey'.

16.2.6. Interference

Throughout Malta's colonial period under British rule (1800–1964), knowledge of English was the key to social preferment and professional advancement. Many Maltese are bilingual in M and English; the average M speaker's command of English can range from fairly rudimentary to virtually native competence. M speakers also habitually codeswitch very freely between the two languages so that a M utterance is as likely as not to display embedded English lexical components—sometimes with minimal formal integration of the loaned elements to the native M sound pattern. Thus the surface content of a M utterance is quite liable to include nonnative sound units such as [æ], [ə], [θ], and [ð], though several fully integrated English words that have been adapted to M phonology are normally pronounced in their merged form even by educated M speakers: /kitla/ 'kettle', /tayer/ 'tire', /praymos/ 'primus stove', /trakk/ 'truck', etc. M speakers who habitually speak English at home sometimes carry over certain English phonetic features into their M speech, e.g., the alveolar articulation of M /t/ and /d/.

M speakers are also very familiar with Italian, but though M has integrated to different degrees a very large number of Italian words, intake of new Italianisms into M appears to be minimal, and habitual codeswitching between M and Italian nonexistent.

16.3. The Vowels

16.3.1. Short Vowels

SM has the system of five short vowels shown in Table 16-2.

Table 16-2. Maltese Short Vowels

i			u
	e	o	
		a		

This contrasts with the situation obtaining in many rural M dialects which have a four-vowel system (Puech 1994: 26f.). The functional status of these short M vowels can be illustrated by means of the following word pairs:

i : e	nisa	'women'	nesa	'he forgot'
i : a	wisa	'breadth'	wasal	'he arrived'

i : o	ǧibna	'we brought'	ǧobna	'piece of cheese'
i : u	siwi	'value'	suwed	'black (pl.)'
e : a	mera	'mirror'	mara	'woman'
e : o	ǧenna	'heaven'	ǧonna	'gardens'
e : u	dewwa	'he healed'	duwwa	'medicine'
a : o	sakra	'drunkenness'	sokra	'lock'
a : u	dawwar	'he turned'	duwwa	'medicine'
o : u	lottu	'lotto'	luttu	'mourning'

As can be inferred from some of these pairs, vocalic contrasts involving /u/ are systemically weak in SM. Though /u/ is formally part of the M short vowel system—note its fairly widespread occurrence in unstressed syllables: /ǧuraːt/ 'grasshopper', /summıːn/ 'quails', /ǧurdıːn/ 'rat', etc.—it is virtually nonexistent in stressed syllables of lineally inherited lexicon, where it has undergone a systematic shift to /o/: /omm/ 'mother', /forn/ 'oven', etc. Many M words of Italian provenance have also undergone this shift: /šott/ 'dry' < *asciutto*, /ponn/ 'fist' < *pugno*, /dlonk/ 'frequently' < *di lungo,* etc. The low functional yield of the *u* : *o* contrast in SM misled Cohen (1970 [1966]: 140) into assigning the vowel [u] purely allophonic status in the SM sound system. However, there can be little doubt that the occurrence of stressed [u] in several well-integrated Italian terms of a learned nature and in certain recent loans from English justifies the assigning of full functional status to short stressed /u/:

luttu	'mourning'
lussu	'luxury'
pulptu	'pulpit'
bust	'bust'
multa	'fine (n.)'
ǧust	'fair'
futbol	'football'
šutt (< Eng. *shoot*)	'shot (football)'

The distributional restriction of native **u* to unstressed positions in SM has yielded a morphophonemic vowel alternation of /o/ ⇒ /u/ concomitant with synchronic stress shift (e.g., in morphological derivation and proclisis), as in the following words:

fost (< *fi wasṭ*)	'amid'	*fustáːni*	'middle (adj.)'
kóllu	'all of it (masc.)'	*kull-hádd*	'everybody'

This alternation between stressed /o/ and pre-stress /u/ is often carried over into the morphophonology of well-integrated Romance lexicon:

    gost (< Sic. *gustu*)   'delight'   *gustú:z*   'nice, handsome'
    yimpórta   'it matters'   *ma yimpurtá:š* 'it doesn't matter'
There are other restrictions on short vowel distribution in SM. A fairly strict constraint in native words disallows the short high vowels /i/ and /u/ in prejunctural singly closed syllables, where only their mid counterparts, /e/ and /o/, respectively, can occur: *ra:ǧel* 'man', *yɪ:kol* 'he eats'. Many lexical loans also conform to this stricture:

    la:pes (< It. *lapis*)   'pencil'
    so:der   'soda (for laundry)'
    beyken   'bacon'
    printes   'apprentice'
    pro:set/pro:sit (< It. *prosit* < Lat.)   'well done!'

Some, however, do not: /to:kis/ 'cinema'.

One consequence of the aforementioned general shift of stressed *u to /o/ is that the phonological rule affecting underlying or historical high vowels in stem-final VC sequences yields an unsymmetrical surface distribution for underlying /i/ and /u/; thus, whereas underlying /i/ in stem-final VC sequences shows up as such in surface structure in non-final position, /u/ does not:

    nízzel   'he brought down'
    nizzílom   'he brought them down'
    šórob   'he drank'
    šoróba (not *šorúba)   'he drank it'

16.3.2. Long Vowels

M has retained the OA distinction between long and short vowels in open stressed syllables, though the functional load and present distribution of the length contrast in M are, to an extent, both products of its special internal history:

    nizel 'he descended'   *ni:zel*   'descending (masc.)'
    ǧara 'it happened'   *ǧa:ra*   'her neighbor'
    omma 'her mother'   *o:mma* (< Ar. *ǧumma*)   'sadness'

Many speakers of SM automatically neutralize vowel length contrasts in unstressed positions:

    ferhá:n   'happy (sg.)'   *ferhani:n*   'happy (pl.)'
    barrá:ni 'foreign (masc.)'   *barraníyya* 'foreign (fem.)'

In view of the fact that short vowels in open syllables tend, as in many Arabic dialects, to be lost, most M final vowels in the native lexicon, except the

feminine ending {-a}, have an underlying length feature which is automatically lost in direct contact with word boundary, but is restored before consonantal suffixes:
 stí:dnu   'they invited'
 stidnú:h   'they invited him'
 ma stidnú:š   'they didn't invite'

The function of the vocalic length contrast is minimal in lineally inherited monosyllables since words of this canonic shape tend to display a certain metrical equivalence between VCC and V:C (cf., for instance, the M stress rule in § 16.5 below):
 ǧa:r 'neighbor' *ǧarr* 'he carried'
 ra:s 'head'   *rass* 'he tightened'

However, as already noted, the fusion of certain OA consonants with neighboring vowels in M has in some cases introduced new extra-long syllables of the type that are disallowed in many contemporary dialects: /e:dded/ 'he threatened' < OA *haddad*.

Vocalic length contrasts are also neutralized in monosyllables consisting of the canonic form CV:—a relatively rare type of monosyllable in M:
 ra(:)   'he saw'
 ǧɪ(:)   'he came'
 zu(:)   'get out of the way!' ⇐ |zu:l|
 hu(:)   'take! (sg.)'   ⇐ |hu:d| < Ar. *xud*

The etymologically long vowel in the underlying form |hu:d| represents the regular M reflex: /hu:du/ 'take! (pl.)' and /hu:dom/ 'take them!', OA *axaδ* and *akal* having been reconstructed as medially weak stems. The reflex of Ar. *la:* 'no!' is most often realized as *le(:)* or *le"*.

As in many Arabic dialects, primary vocalic length contrasts are also lost before a geminated consonant (mostly /ll/) in certain morphophonemic contexts:
 'a:l   'he said'
 'alli   'he said to me'
 zu:(l)   'Get out!'
 zulli   'Get out of my way!'
 kelli   'I had'   < *ki:n + li:*
 ikollu   'he will have'   < *iku:n + lu:*
 malli   'as soon as'   < *ma' illi*

Secondary vowel length in stressed syllables, however, tends to be retained before geminate consonants:

ǧa:nni   'he obliged me'   < *ǧa'al + ni
a:mmed   'he baptized'   < *'ammad

A striking feature of the SM long vowel system is its display of four degrees of aperture along the front of the vowel triangle as opposed to three along the back. It comprises the segments shown in Table 16-3.

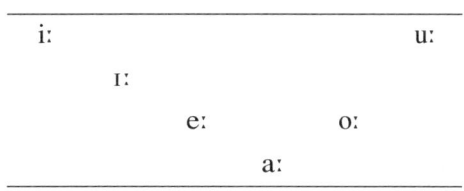

Table 16-3. Maltese Long Vowels

Functional contrasts between long vowels in SM can be illustrated by means of the following examples:

i: : ɪ:	zi:d	'increase!'	zɪ:d	'he increased'	
i: : e:	di:n	'this (f.)'	de:n	'intelligence'	< dihn
i: : a:	di:n	'this (f.)'	da:n	'this (masc.)'	
i: : o:	si:ba	'find her!'	so:ba	'repentance'	~ ṣ'b
i: : u:	li:ra	'pound'	lu:ra	'backwards'	< l + wara:
ɪ: : e:	wɪ:d	'valley'	we:da	'promise'	< *w'd
ɪ: : a:	sɪ:'	'leg'	sa:'	'he drove'	
ɪ: : o:	lɪ:ma	'which?'	lo:ba	'game'	< lu'ba
ɪ: : u:	sɪ:'	'leg'	su:'	'drive!'	
e: : a:	de:r	'he appeared'	da:r	'house'	
e: : o:	re:ba	'greed'	lo:ba	'game'	
e: : u:	de:r	'he appeared'	du:r	'turn round!'	
a: : o:	na:l	'horseshoe'	no:l	'freight'	< It. nolo
a: : u:	da:m	'he lingered'	du:m	'take your time!'	

Whereas the oppositions between the SM long vowels /i:/, /ɪ:/, and /u:/ continue historical contrasts between OA long vowels, the SM mid vowels /e:/ and /o:/ do not derive, as in most Arabic dialects, from /ay/ and /aw/, but usually represent the outcome of secondary developments, e.g., fusion of short *i and *u with adjacent velar, pharyngeal, and laryngeal fricatives:

SM	Meaning	Old Arabic	
šo:l	'work'	< šuɣl	
so:la	'cough'	< su'la	
de:n	'intelligence'	< *dihn	< ðihn

Phonological analyses of M that postulate an "abstract *għajn*" restrict the distribution of phonological length in vowels by implying that surface length in certain vowels can be interpreted as deriving from underlying biphonemic combinations of "*għ* + short vowel" (or vice versa).

The aforementioned asymmetrical patterning of long M vowels occasioned by the *ima:la*-shift presents a marked contrast with the situation obtaining among mainstream Arabic dialects showing a form of *ima:la šadi:da*, since these tend to fuse the resulting front vowel with the qualitatively closest available front vowel, i.e., with [e:] < *ay, or with *[i:].

The systemic asymmetry obtaining among the long vowels of SM naturally also extends to systemic relationships between long and short segments. Thus the morphophonemic lax correlate of destressed SM /ɪ:/ is traditionally /e/ rather than /i/:

bní:dem	'man'	bnedmí:n	'men'
í:ni (< ha:ni')	'glad'	enyí:n	'glad (pl.)'
mí:ra	'he contradicted'	merí:ni	'he contradicted me'
wí:hed	'one'	wehída	'alone (f.)'
kí:fer	'cruel'	kefrí:n	'cruel (pl.)'

Among SM speakers, however, this is a residual trait; thus outside specific morphophonemic or lexical contexts, the short vowel /i/ is by far the most common surface realization of a reduced /ɪ:/ in SM: /nɪ:zel/, pl. /nizli:n/ 'descending', /rɪ:'ed/, pl. /ri'di:n/ 'sleeping', etc. Lexicalization of the lax correlate of */ɪ:/ has occurred under stress in M /kell-/ 'to have' < *[kɪ:n + l-]: /kelli/ 'I had', where it is probably conditioned by the following cluster.

To nonnative ears the auditory difference between SM /i:/ and /ɪ:/ appears to be a very slight one. The phonetic quality of SM /i:/ closely approximates that of the vowel in Eng. *bead*, whereas the *ima:la* reflex is much closer to long Eng. [ɪ:] occurring before the voiced stops, e.g., *bid* [bɪ:d]. The functional contrast between SM /i:/ and /ɪ:/ carries a significant functional load supported by several minimal pairs of high frequency:

smi:n	'fat (masc.sg.)'	smɪ:n	'fat (pl.)'
sni:n	'years'	snɪ:n	'teeth'
ǧi:b	'bring!'	ǧɪ:b	'he brought'
'i:s	'measure!'	'ɪ:s	'he measured'

In SM the historical distinction between OA /i:/ and the *ima:la* reflex is neutralized before /'/ (< *q) and /h/ (< *ħ, *x, and *h) where only [ɪ:] occurs:

sɪ:'	'leg'	< sa:q
dɪ:'a	'narrowness'	< ḍi:qa

ǧɪːh	'honor'	< *ǧaːh*
fɪːh	'in him'	< *fiːh*

Many SM speakers (including the present writer) also neutralize this contrast in certain morphological contexts, e.g., in the first person plural inflectional suffix {-naː} before object suffixes {-k} and {-kom}:

ǧibna	'we brought'
ǧibnɪːk (~ -niːk)	'we brought you (sg.)'
ǧibnɪːkom (~ -niːkom)	'we brought you (pl.)'

16.3.3. Diphthongs

SM has the seven diphthongs shown in Table 16-4.

Table 16-4. Maltese Diphthongs

iw	ew	aw	ow
–	ey	ay	oy

The systemic asymmetry within the class of M diphthongs derives from the fact that SM /iː/ is usually realized as a monophthong rather than as a diphthongized [iy].

The diphthong /iw/ is highly marked in SM, no doubt on account of the already mentioned articulatory incompatibility of lip-spreading and lip-rounding entailed. This diphthong appears to be restricted to the term /liwya/ 'bend', and Aquilina (1987: 742) significantly notes the dialectal variant *lilwa* showing the shift of the problematic bilabial glide to the second syllable. Secondary /iw/ arising in morphological inflection tends to show up as surface [uː], e.g., in [uːsa] 'wider' ⇐ liwsaʻl < Ar. *awsaʻ*, the OA *afʻal* pattern generally yielding M *ifʻa/el*: /ikbar ~ akbar/ 'bigger (masc.)', /isbaħ/ 'more beautiful (masc.)', /ičken/ 'smaller (masc.)', /iswed/ 'black (masc.)', etc. The proliferation of new diphthongs in SM was principally a historical consequence of loss of emphasis:

newl	'loom'	< *nawl*
dawl	'light (n.)'	< *ḍawʼ*
seyf	'dagger'	< *sayf*
sayf	'summer'	< *ṣayf*

In SM, the first element in the diphthong /ew/ can be optionally rounded and backed in contact with the bilabial glide /w/, yielding free variants such as:

lewn ~ lown	'color'
bewl ~ bowl	'urine'

Note, for instance, the common SM realization of the English loanword 'bowl' as /bawl/ avoiding homophony with the M variant [bowl] 'urine'.

SM primary and secondary diphthongs continuing OA /aw/, /ay/, /iː/, and /uː/ after historical /ʕ/ tend to be synchronically marked in M (especially among conservative speakers) and are usually phonetically longer than other diphthongs: [aːyn] 'eye' < Ar. *ʿayn*, but /tayn/ 'mud' < Ar. *ṭiːn*. SM also has the diphthong /oy/, e.g., /voyt/ 'empty' < Sic. *voitu*, /boyy/ 'hey you!' < Eng. *boy*.

16.3.4. The Synchronic imaːla

The aforementioned *imaːla*-shift in M, a different variety of which was recorded for Mesopotamian Arabic in *Kitaːb* by Sibawayhi (died c. 800), presents the Arabist with what is possibly the most striking areal trait in this otherwise highly deviant offshoot of vernacular Arabic. The phonetic realizations of the *imaːla*-vowel in M vary considerably from one dialect to the next (cf. the folktexts in nonstandard M reproduced in Stumme 1904, and in Puech 1994). In SM *imaːla*-shift affects stressed long *[aː], usually, though not exclusively, in non-emphatic or non-back consonantal environments yielding, for instance, /ktɪːb/ 'book', /tiǧɪːǧa/ 'hen' < **ktaːb* and **da/iǧaːǧa*, as opposed to /saːr/ 'he became', /saːʔ/ 'he drove' < *ṣaːr* and *saːq*. In unstressed position, the M reflex of *[aː] retains the [low] feature: /ílma/ 'water' < **ilmáː*', /hobla/ 'pregnant' < *ḥublaː*, /mela/ 'therefore' (~ /immela/) < *'immaːlaː* (Dozy 1881, 1:36), /ébda/ 'none' < **'abdaː* < *'abadan* 'never', etc.

The mutual historical ordering obtaining between the stress-assignment rule and the *imaːla*-shift observable in Medieval Maltese has been integrated into the synchronic grammar of the language, where it has contributed a certain degree of formal complexity to the morphophonemics of verb inflection and suffixation.

In SM the synchronic *imaːla*-rule affects underlying long /aː/ chiefly: (i) in the stems of many finally weak verbs, (ii) in the subject and object pronominal suffix {-naː}, and (iii) in the 3rd person feminine suffix {-haː}. Observe, for instance, the derivations of surface forms from underlying |fela: + h| 'he scrutinized him' and |ráyna: + h| 'we saw him':

(1) The synchronic *imaːla*-rule in SM
    (a) Underlying form   *féla:* + h   'he scrutinized him'
        Stress shift   *feláːh*
        Imaːla-rule   *felíːh*
        Syncope   *flíːh*

(b) Underlying form   *ráyna: + h*   'we saw him'
    Stress shift   *rayná:h*
    Ima:la-rule   *rayní:h*

The circumstance that only synchronically stressed occurrences of SM /a:/ are affected by the *ima:la*-rule necessarily implies that grammatically complex strings displaying more than one instance of the low central vowel /a:/ (e.g., concomitant with two or three layers of person markers) cannot be simply derived via fronting the last /a:/ in the string, but require recurring application of the rule of stress assignment and of the *ima:la*-rule, in that order. A representative SM example of such a string is the verb phrase like <ma sraqnihilhiex> 'we did not steal it from her', which would seem to derive morphophonemically via cyclical application of the stress and *ima:la* rules to an underlying representation such as the following string: [ma [[[srá'na:]ha:]lha:]š] (cf. Brame 1974).

16.3.4.1. Morphophonemic ima:la in Romance Quadriliteral Plurals

The M synchronic *ima:la* shows up in another morphophonemic process: broken plural formation on the M scheme CCV:CVC (< Maghrebi Ar. *fa:lel*) for many quadriliteral roots which Maltese has derived from Italian singular forms.

Plural forms in this noun class select /a:/ or /ɪ:/ in accordance with a rule matching the advancement feature of the vowel in the plural with that of the stressed vowel in the singular. In other words, a stressed /i/ or /e/ in the singular form requires the *ima:la* vowel /ɪ:/ in the plural, whereas stressed non-front vowels (e.g., /á:/ or /ú:/) require /a:/:

Singular		Plural
ber[r]ítta	'cap'	*brí:ret*
furkétta	'fork'	*frí:ket*
čavétta	'key'	*čwí:vet*
kappéll	'hat'	*kpí:pel*
bastú:n	'walking stick'	*bsa:ten*
kaššú:n	'drawer'	*kša:šen*
pastá:s	'rude'	*psa:tas*
fardá:l	'apron'	*fra:dal*

As can be inferred from the last four examples, singular stems displaying the low stressed /á:/ require the low vowel /a/ in the final syllable of the plural, whereas singular stems displaying a non-low vowel (e.g., /i/ or /u:/) take /e/.

The morphophonemic rule assigning the *ima:la* vowel in quadriradical plurals of Romance singular nouns was presumably extrapolated by M speakers on the analogical basis of a perceived relationship between front and non-front vowels in certain frequently used quadriradicals pertaining to the inherited lexicon:

Singular		Plural
zarbuːna	'shoe'	*zraːben*
sikkiːna	'knife'	*skɪːken*
fartaːs	'a bald man'	*fraːtas*

16.4. Phonotactics

16.4.1. Consonant Clusters

Whereas consonant clusters in the native lexicon generally tend to enjoy stability both idiolectally and across the M speech community, those pertaining to the Romance lexicon are often susceptible to variation conditioned by stylistic and other factors, e.g., Low /stuːptu/ 'stupid', High /stuːpidu/ (< It. *stupido*).

The nature and distribution of initial clusters in the inherited lexicon of M are closely analogous to those obtaining in many Arabic dialects (Cantineau's *parlers non différentiels*) that generally elide all short vowels in unstressed open syllables: /klɪːb/ 'dogs', /trɪːʼ/ 'road', /traːb/ 'dust', /nifthu/ 'we open', /yiksru/ 'they break', etc. Many well-integrated Italian loans in M have also been adapted to these syllabic norms: /zguːr/ 'sure' < *sicuro*, /lvant/ 'east' < *levante*, /lment/ 'complaint' < *lamento*, /kampnaːr/ 'bell tower' < Sic. *campanaru*, but the effect of this acculturation process has not introduced radically novel clustering patterns in M.

In both native and borrowed lexicon, initial CC clusters beginning with a resonant require a prosthetic vowel after pause, [ilsíːn] 'tongue', [imwéyyed] 'tables', [ilvánt] 'east', [irvéll] 'disturbance', etc. The same goes for initial geminate clusters, which are particularly common in M denominal verbs of Italian origin: /irraːbya/ 'he became angry' ⇐ /raːbya/ 'anger', /ikkoːpya/ 'he copied' ⇐ /koːpya/ 'copy', /ipprɪːtka/ 'he preached' ⇐ /prɪːtka/ 'sermon', etc.

The occurrence of the definite article {(i)l-} before initial CC clusters does not necessarily trigger off an auxiliary vowel, but Italian clusters with initial sibilants do: /il-kbiːr/ 'the big one', /il-hrɪːf/ 'the lambs', but /l-iskoːla/, /l-ispaːg/ 'the string', /l-izball/ 'the mistake'. In relaxed speech, however, initial CC clusters with a resonant in first position often dispense with the secondary syllabic and show assimilation of the article: /ir-rmɪːd/ 'the ashes'. In certain words, the secondary prosthetic vowel has become lexicalized and appears exclusively after the article even though the initial CC cluster has been dissolved, e.g., via loss of historical *għajn*:

ma:š	'interest'	< **mʻa:š*	< *maʻa:š*	
ma:rfa	'spoon'	< **myarfa*	< **mayárfa*	< OA *mayrafa*
l-ima:š	'the interest'	< **l-imʻa:š*		
l-ima:rfa	'the spoon'	< **l-imyarfa*		

Free variation between /l/ and /r/ before a consonant in new syllables, as in /ilsi:r ~ irsi:r/ 'slave' < OA *yasi:r*, should probably be accounted for within the explanatory framework outlined in § 16.2.4.7 for optimal positions of liquids in the syllable. Preference for /r/ as syllable coda is also evident from historical shifts like M /irkant/ 'auction' < It. *incanto*.

The synchronic treatment of medial CCC clusters in the inherited lexicon conforms to patterns familar from other Arabic vernaculars, which generally show CVCC if medial C is a resonant: /yahílbu/ 'they milk', /yoʻórbu/ 'they approach', /yoʻómsu/ 'they hop', etc. The accent regularly falls on the secondary syllabic.

Where no medial resonants are involved in potential CCC clusters, M is strikingly tolerant to medial obstruent clusters and displays some highly marked phonetic sequences especially in onomatopoeic local creations: /ipačpču/ 'they chatter', /ipaʼpʼu/ 'they honk (car horn)', /ihašwšu/ 'they rustle (silk, paper)', /iʼasʼsu/ 'they cut out'.

Underlying word-final CC clusters with a final resonant are resolved in surface structure through anaptyctic vowels, as in many Arabic dialects: /iben/ 'son', but /ibni/ 'my son'. Word-final clusters in surface and underlying structure are rare in Italian loans, but note the synchronic elision of the final apical trill in M /surmast/ ⇐ |surmastr| 'schoolmaster', pl. /surmastr-iyɪ:t/.

16.4.2. *Vowels in Hiatus*

SM word phonology disallows the occurrence of vowels in immediate adjacency, i.e., without an intervening consonant. Thus, for instance, historical loss of intervocalic */ʻ/, */ɣ/, or */h/ invariably yields a secondary bilabial or palatal glide agreeing in advancement and lip-rounding with the preceding stressed vowel:

(2) Diachronic treatment of hiatus in SM

OA				Orthography	
šana:ʻa	> **šnɪ:ʻa*	> *šniya*		*xniegħa*	'rumor'
furu:ya	> **fru:ya*	> *fruwa*		*frugħa*	'emptiness'
*hubu:la	> **blu:ha*	> *bluwa*		*bluha*	'foolishness'

Closely analogous morphophonemic treatment of elidable /h/ intervocalically can be observed in the suffixation of the object pronouns {-h}, {-ha:}, and {-hom} to the stems of finally weak verbs. Note, for instance, the synchronic derivations of SM <ksieha> 'he covered it (fem.)', and SM <jixtruhom> 'they buy them', here presented in condensed fashion:

(3) Elimination of hiatus in verb stems with object pronouns
    (a) Underlying form   *késa:* + *ha:*   'he covered it (fem.)'
        Stress shift   *kesá:ha*
        Ima:la-rule   *kesí:ha*
        Syncope   *ksí:ha*
        Deletion of laryngeal   *ksíya*
    (b) Underlying form   *yíštru:* + *hom*   'they buy them'
        Stress shift   *yištrú:hom*
        Deletion of laryngeal   *yištrúwom*

As can be inferred from these two derivations, stressed stem-final high vowels undergo the following changes before the suffixed pronouns /-ha/ and /-hom/:

|-í:h-| ⇒ |-i:y-| ⇒ /-iy-/
|-ú:h-| ⇒ |-u:w-| ⇒ /-uw-/

which recapitulate the historical sound shift we observed word-internally in (2). Vocalic length reduction here can be plausibly attributed to the phonologically weak nature of the syllabic arrest provided by semivowels after long high vowels. It is not without interest in this connection that certain non-standard M dialects (e.g., that spoken in Nadur, Gozo) display secondary gemination of the post-stress bilabial glide with concomitant reduction of word-final |-u:| in verbs with pronominal suffixes: /triduwwim/ 'you want them' (Puech 1994: 87) < *tri:du:him*. Observe also the diachronic tendency in SM towards gemination of historical /y/ after a stressed long high vowel in reflexes of OA *fa'a:lil* and *fa'a:li:l* plurals:

M
kneyyes < *kne:yis* < *kana:yis*   'churches'
mweyyed < *mwe:yid* < *mawa:yid*   'tables'

On the other hand, stems which retain the low reflex of final /a:/ in the context of syntactic suffixes (e.g., /ra:/ 'he saw', /štara/ 'he bought', < *ṛa:* and *štaṛa:*) circumvent vocalic hiatus differently. M morphophonology here resorts to syllabic fusion, which is, as far as one can tell from the Arabic dialectal literature, unique to M. In its simplest form one can see it operating in the sequences <raha> 'he saw her' and <xtraha> 'he bought it (fem.)', both of which delete the intervocalic laryngeal and yield the monosyllables [ra(ː)] and [štra(ː)] respectively, with optional vowel length. A more extreme form of syllable fusion occurs in verb phrases with the object pronoun {-hom}, as in realizations of M <rahom> 'he saw them' [roːm] and <xtrahom> 'he bought them' [štroːm]:

(4) Elimination of vocalic hiatus via syllable fusion
- (a) Underlying form   *ráː+ hom*   'he saw them'
  Deletion of laryngeal   *ráːom*
  Syllabic fusion   *róːm*
- (b) Underlying form   *štáraː+hom*   'he bought them'
  Stress shift   *štráːhom*
  Deletion of laryngeal   *štráːom*
  Syllabic fusion   *štróːm*

These schematic presentations illustrate how M systematically eliminates hiatus present in the underlying form of verb phrases and generates surface structures that conform to the phonetic stricturess of M word phonology. There are, however, cases where unique solutions are not available for smoothing out potentially abrupt transitions in underlying structures. One such case occurs in finally weak verbs with a morphophonemically stable stem-final /aː/, i.e., one that is not affected by the synchronic *imaːla*-rule. When such stems display a double object: <xtrahomli> 'he bought them for me', <xtrahieli> 'he bought it for me', etc., word stress shifts to the direct object suffix yielding forms like [štra.ómli] and [štra.íːli]), etc., where the height and advancement discrepancies between the vowels flanking the syllable boundary render the hiatus highly marked. Many M speakers often simply retain the problematic hiatus. In relaxed speech, however, they often resort to different ways of smoothing the abrupt transition, e.g., by introducing the glide [y]: [štrayíːli]; or a geminated [ħ] on the analogy of stems displaying final abstract *għajn*: [štraħħómli] (cf. [refaħħómli] 'he carried them for me').

16.4.3. Roundness Assimilation

Unrounded short vowels in the inherited lexicon occur very freely in adjacent syllables:

tifel	'boy'	*siġar*	'trees'
wera'	'leaves'	*ħanek*	'gums'

By contrast, the distribution of the rounded mid back vowel /o/ (but not /u/) is subject to a rule of progressive roundness assimilation both intra- and intermorphemically:

to'ol	'weight'	*hodon*	'bosom'
borom	'cooking pots'	*torok*	'Turks'
šorob	'he drank'	*romol*	'he became a widower'

Across word boundary, the assimilation rule affects the allomorphy of the 2nd person suffix |-Vk|. There is a certain amount of dialectal variation in the phonemic realization of this suffix. In SM three allomorphs occur, i.e., {-ok} after stems with /o/, {-ak} after historically stem-final /ʕ/, and {-ek} elsewhere:

omm-ok	'your mother'	*tiy-ak*	'your'
oht-ok	'your sister'	*raːs-ek*	'your head'
hoǧr-ok	'your lap'	*sɪː-ek*	'your leg'
floːk-ok	'instead of you'	(< Ar. *fi + Sic. *locu*)	
post-ok	'your place'	(cf. Sic. *postu*)	

When {-Vk} is suffixed to verb stems, the "harmony rule" operates on underlying representations and copies the roundness feature of stem vowels that are subsequently elided at surface level:

Underlying form	*yɪːhod* + V*k*	'he takes you'
Roundness assimilation	*yɪːhodok*	
Syncope	*yɪːhdok*	

Further examples are: /yiǧbrok/ 'he picks you up' ⇐ |yiǧbor+Vk|, /yɪːklok/ 'he eats you up' ⇐ |yɪːkol+Vk|.

A less systematic, mostly optional, form of roundness assimilation (usually affecting /i/) also occurs in the Romance lexicon of M in the neighborhood of /u/ where it affects short unstressed vowels in the adjacency of /u/ bearing primary and secondary stress on: M /pùlicíyya ~ pùlucíyya/ 'police' < Sic. *pulizzia*, /kùritúːr ~ kùrutúːr/ 'corridor' < Sic. *currituri*, /pruzuntuːz/ 'rash' < Sic. *presuntusu*.

16.5. Stress

The assignment of word stress in native M words and in fully integrated loans is generally predictable by reference to their syllabic or morphemic composition. Like many Arabic dialects, M generally accentuates words without syntactical affixes on the VCC or V:C sequence closest to word boundary; in the absence of a VCC and V:C sequence, stress falls on penultimate syllables:

M	*háreǧ*	'he went out'
	wíːhed	'one (masc.)'

halli:l   'thief'
tuffí:ha   'apple'
gabillótt   'farmer'
purtiná:r   'janitor'

M shows very extensive historical loss of short vowels in unstressed open syllables; this factor has tended to restrict canonic forms in the native lexicon and in well-integrated foreign words to mono- or bi-syllabic shapes:

ktɪ:b   'book'   < kita:b
slɪ:m   'peace'   < sala:m
tra:b   'dust'   < tura:b
mizbla   'dump'   < mazbala
mahfra   'forgiveness'   < mayfira

Consequently most M words show stress on final or penultimate syllables. In synchronic terms, this means that when morphological inflection introduces additional syllables into underlying structure, morphophonemic adjustments occur in the surface form promoting closed syllabicity in unaccented positions and reducing the stem to one of the standard syllabic templates: ra'ad + u ⇒ /ra'du/ 'they slept'; dendel + u ⇒ /dendlu/ 'they hung', habbar + et ⇒ /habbret/ 'she announced', etc. M words of Italian provenance can vary considerably in length and syllabic structure, depending on the degree to which they have been formally adapted to native canonic shapes. Massive influx of Romance stems into M over a long period of time has introduced atypical canonic forms into the language, entailing greater variability in word length, an enhanced tolerance to open syllabicity, a freer and richer distribution of vowels often contravening inherited vocalic schemes (particularly in unstressed syllables), etc.

The differential treatment meted out to Italian lexical material in M (no doubt correlating with the diffusional path selected by the lexical item in question) can be exemplified in the following words which range from virtually "whole" Italian, like (a), to more fully "merged" Italian, like (c), which has been radically restructured to conform to the native class of Form II verbs (/kisser/ 'he broke', /nizzel/ 'he brought down', etc.):

(a) edukacyo:ni   'education'   < It. educazione
(b) peri:t   'architect'   < Sic. peritu
(c) pitter   'he painted'   ⇐ {p-t-r}   < It. pittore

Educated M speakers freely resort to Italian words of a learned nature which tend to contravene the canonic forms of M and show atypical stress patterns, e.g., Italian proparoxytones (sdrucciole), and words with final stress (parole tronche):

píllola ~ pínnola	'pill'	< It. *pillola*, Sic. *pinnula*
dé:boli ~ débboli	'weak'	< It. *debole*, Sic. *debbuli*
virtú	'virtue'	< It. *virtù*

Interestingly, in reflexes of certain recently borrowed Italian proparoxytones M speakers tend to hesitate between a native stress pattern and the Italian one: /fertí:li ~ fértili/ 'fertile' < It. [fértili]. However, most speakers of M have fully integrated the proparoxytonic accentual pattern via English loans like /šárabank/ 'bus', /télefown/, 'telephone'. As can be inferred from M /ferti:li/ here, M has phonologized the automatic phonetic length of Italian vowels in open syllables, and this often serves as the basis of stress assignment. That the integration in M of Italian words with open syllables at two removes from stress was a gradual process can be inferred from a lexical stratum showing secondary consonant gemination in this position:

annima:l	'animal'	< It. *animale*

The integration of these phonologically long canonic forms in M with concomitant retention of pretonic short vowels, can be said to have stabilized in M the category of phonetic "secondary stress" in isolated words.

Though stress assignment is highly predictable in M, even where morphological factors are involved, implementation of the stress rule can still be relatively complex since it invariably interacts with a number of phonological rules and constraints: short vowel elision, raising and fronting of /a:/, reduction of underlying length, etc. Brame (1974: 56), for instance, noted that the M stress assignment rule systematically discriminates between morphological and syntactic affixes on verb stems, as can be seen from the following surface forms of the M verb /hareğ/:

|háreğ + na|	'we went out'	⇒ *hriğna*
|háreğ + na|	'he took us out'	⇒ *hariğna*

where the open syllable is elided in the first example but not in the second. Interaction between the stress assignment rule and morphophonemic processes can be particularly complex in the case of phonological words deriving from syntactic strings, as already noted in the section on *ima:la* (§ 16.4.4).

16.6. Reduction of the *nisba*-ending {-íyy}

As in many mainstream Arabic vernaculars, the singular forms of the OA *nisba* {-íyy} yield the following reflexes in M: masc. *-i*, fem. *-iyya*, where the masculine form has undergone length neutralization concomitant with the diachronic shift of stress to the stem vowel:

masc.	fem.	
maːlti	*maltiyya*	'Maltese'
aːrbi	*arbiyya*	'Arab'
ramli	*ramliyya*	'sandy'

In the plural, the M form of the *nisba* for both genders has the invariant shape {-íːn} through haplology of the bisyllabic underlying and historical form *iyyiːn:

maltiːn	'Maltese people'
sʾalliːn	'Sicilians'
beltiːn	'people from Valletta'

16.7. A note on phoneme–grapheme correspondences in Maltese

The present M orthography, standardized in 1934, is the product of a long but intermittent literary tradition harking back at least to the end of the 15th century, when the earliest extant text in M was composed: *Peter Caxaro's Cantilena* (see Wettinger and Fsadni 1968). (The only other medieval texts discovered so far in the Maltese Islands are in a local form of Judeo-Arabic written in Hebrew characters; cf. Wettinger 1985).

However, it is only from the 18th century onwards that M has been written with any degree of continuity, though descriptive accounts of the language, necessarily entailing attempts at orthographic representation, were compiled before then: for instance, the recently discovered *Regole per la lingua maltese*, which is thought to date back to the late 17th century (cf. Cassola 1988: 63).

In view of the present lack of a modern systematic description of M in languages other than M itself, it may be useful to conclude this sketch of M phonology with some general indications as to how the letters of the M alphabet correlate with the sound system of the language, if only to enable the interested linguist to avail himself of printed texts in M.

The M orthography presents a number of pitfalls for those unfamiliar with the spoken language. Thus except for the digraph *ie*, which is generally realized long, M does not ordinarily mark vocalic length. The circumflex accent is sometimes used to avoid ambiguity: *qartas* 'to wrap in paper' as distinct from *qartâs* 'a paper funnel for wrapping groceries' (Aquilina 1990: 1134).

The distribution of diacritics differentiating between sounds represented by the same letter does not always follow generally accepted linguistic principles, e.g., restriction of a diacritic to the phonologically marked or statistically less frequent segment. Thus M oddly marks its native voiced alveolar fricative /z/ (< OA z) with a superscript dot <ż> to distinguish it from the alveolar affricate /c/ (< It. z) though the opposite procedure would have been more appropriate.

16.8. The Maltese alphabet

The letters of the M alphabet are here listed in the order usually adhered to in dictionaries; these are followed by their traditional names in square brackets, a phonetic description, and a few examples. (The digraph <ie> is not included as a separate symbol in the M alphabet.)

a, A [aː]—a low central vowel, long or short: *qam* 'he rose' [ʼaːm], *wasal* 'he arrived' [wásal]

b, B [beː]—a voiced bilabial stop: *bir* 'well' [biːr]; *aħbar* 'piece of news' [aħbáːr]; *bieb* 'door' [bıːp]

ċ, Ċ [čeː]—a voiceless alveolar affricate: *ċar* 'clear' [tšaːr]; *keċċa* 'he expelled' [kéttša]

d, D [deː]—a voiced dental stop: *dar* 'house' [daːr]; *beda* 'he began' [béda]

e, E [eː]—a mid front vowel, long or short: *erbgħa* 'four' [éːrba]; *deheb* 'gold' [deːp]; *dell* 'shadow' [del]

f, F [éffe]—a voiceless labiodental fricative: *fiehem* 'he explained' [fíyem]; *siefer* 'he traveled' [síːfer]; *ħlief* 'except' [ħlıːf]

ġ, Ġ [ğeː]—a voiced alveopalatal affricate: *ġar* 'neighbor' [ğaːr]; *riġel* 'foot' [ríğel]

g, G [gaː]—a voiced velar stop: *gżira* 'island* [gziːra]; *nigġeż* 'he pricked' [nígges]

għ, Għ [aːyn]—a digraph usually continuing OA [ʼ] and [ɣ] yielding mostly vocalic length in stressed positions: *għamel* 'he made' [aːmel], and [ħ] when closing word-final stressed syllables: *qiegħ* 'bottom' [ʼıːħ]

h, H [ákka]—a letter that continues etymologically the OA laryngeal fricative /h/; it is mostly realized as vocalic length: *hena* 'joy' [eːna]

ħ, Ħ [éħħe]—a voiceless fricative with a widely variable point of articulation including velar, laryngeal, but mostly pharyngeal realizations: *ħafer* [ħáfer] 'he forgave'; *baħar* 'sea' [báħar]; *riħ* 'wind' [rıːħ]

i, I [iː]—a high front vowel, long or short: *iben* 'son' [íben]; *irid* 'he wants' [iriːt] *j, J* [ye:]—a palatal glide: *jiena* 'I' [yí:na]; *sejjer* 'going (masc.sg.)' [séyyer]

k, K [ke:]—a voiceless velar stop: *kelb* 'dog' [kelp]; *beka* 'he wept' [béka]; *fenek* 'rabbit' [fének]

l, L [élle]—an alveolar lateral resonant: *lagħab* 'he played' [la:p]; *mielaħ* 'salty' [mí:laħ]; *dell* 'shadow' [del]

m, M [émme]—a bilabial nasal resonant: *mera* 'mirror' [méra]; *komma* 'sleeve' [kómma]; *tmiem* 'end' [tmɪ:m]

n, N [énne]—an alveolar nasal resonant: *neħħa* 'he took away' [néħħa]; *bnin* 'beneficial' [bni:n]

o, O [o:]—a mid back rounded vowel, long or short: *omm* 'mother' [ómm]; *għoli* 'high' [ó:li]

p, P [pe:]—a voiceless bilabial stop: *pastas* 'rude' [pastá:s]; *kappar* 'capers' [kappá:r]

q, Q ['a:]—a voiceless glottal stop: *qal* 'he said' ['a:l]; *qorti* 'law court' ['órti]; *triq* 'road' [trɪ:']

r, R [érre]—an apical trill: *raba'* 'fields' [rába]; *morr* 'bitter' [mor]

s, S [ésse]—a voiceless alveolar fricative: *seraq* 'he stole' [séra']; *kesa* 'he covered' [késa]; *biss* 'only' [bis]

t, T [te:]—a voiceless dental stop: *tar* 'he flew' [ta:r]; *kattar* 'he increased' [káttar]

u, U [u:]—a rounded high back vowel, long or short: *usa'* 'wider' [ú:sa]; *iżur* 'he visits' [izú:r]; *ġurat* 'grasshopper' [ǧurá:t]

v, V [ve:]—a voiced labiodental fricative: *venven* 'blow loudly (wind)' [vénven]; *iva* 'yes' [i:va]

w, W [wa:w] or [we:]—*wera* 'he showed' [wéra]; *sewwa* 'he repaired' [sewwa]; *raw* 'they saw' [ra:w]

x, X [éšše]—a voiced or voiceless alveopalatal fricative: *xorob* 'he drank' [šórop]; *televixin* 'television' [tèlevížin]

ż, Ż [za:]—a voiced alveolar fricative: *żar* 'he visited' [za:r]; *beża'* 'he feared' [béza]

z, Z [ca:]—a voiced or voiceless alveolar affricate: *gazzetta* 'newspaper' [gaddzétta]; *zekzek* 'he tsked' [cékcek]; *gezzez* 'he bundled together' [géttsets]

Bibliography

Al-Maghribi, 'Abd al-Qadir. 1947 [1908]. *Kitāb al ištiqāq wa al-taʻrīb*, 2nd ed. Cairo: n.p.
Aquilina, Joseph. 1987–90. *Maltese-English Dictionary*, 2 vols. Malta: Midsea Books.
Barbato, A. 1990. "Conquista e presenza arabo-islamica a Malta." *Annali dell'Istituto Universitario Orientale, Napoli* 50: 233–47.
Bauer, Leonhard. 1926 [1909]. *Das palästinische Arabisch*. Leipzig: Hinrichs.
Blanc, Haim. 1953. *Studies in North Palestinian Arabic*. Jerusalem: Israel Oriental Society.
———. 1964. *Communal dialects in Baghdad*. Cambridge, Mass.: Harvard University Press.
Borg, Alexander. 1976. "Reflexes of Pausal Forms in Maltese Rural Dialects?" *Israel Oriental Studies* 7: 211–25.
———. 1978. "A Historical and Comparative Phonology and Morphology of Maltese." Ph.D. dissertation, The Hebrew University, Jerusalem.
———. 1985. *Cypriot Arabic*. Stuttgart: Steiner.
———. 1994. "Observations on Some Evolutionary Parallels and Divergences in Cypriot Arabic and Maltese." *Actas del congreso internacional sobre interferencias lingüísticas árabo-romances y paralelos extra-iberos celebradas en Madrid del 10 al 14 de diciembre de 1990*, ed. Jordi Aguadé, Federico Corriente, and Marina Marugán, pp. 21–40. Zaragoza: n.p.
Brame, Michael. 1972. "On the Abstractness of Phonology: Maltese ʕ." In *Contributions to Generative Phonology*, ed. M. K. Brame, pp. 22–61. Austin: University of Texas Press.
———. 1974. "The Cycle in Phonology: Stress in Palestinian, Maltese, and Spanish." *Linguistic Inquiry* 5: 39–60.
Cassola, A. 1988. *Regole per la lingua Maltese*. Malta: Said International.
Chejne, A. G. 1969. *The Arabic Language*. Minneapolis: University of Minnesota Press.
Cohen, David. 1970 [1966]. "Le système phonologique du maltais." In *Études de linguistique sémitique et arabe*, pp. 126–49. The Hague: Mouton.
Comrie, Bernard. 1980. "The Sun Letters in Maltese: Between Morphophonemics and Phonetics." *Studies in the Linguistic Sciences* 10 (2): 25–37.

———. 1986. "The Maltese Pharyngeal." *Zeitschrift für Phonetik, Sprachwissenschaft und Kommunikationsforschung* 39: 12–18.
Dench, Geoffrey. 1975. *The Maltese in London*. London: Routledge and Kegan Paul.
Dozy, Reinhart. 1881. *Supplément aux dictionnaires arabes*. Leiden: Brill.
El-Hassan, S. A. 1977. "Educated Spoken Arabic in Egypt and the Levant: A Critical Review of Diglossia and Related Concepts." *Archivum Linguisticum* 9: 32–57.
Ferguson, Charles A. 1959. "Diglossia." *Word* 15: 325–40.
Firth, J. R. 1964. *The Tongues of Men* and *Speech* (Language and Language Learning 2). London: Oxford University Press. (Orig. publication 1937, 1930).
Fischer, Wolfdietrich. 1959. *Die demonstrativen Bildungen der neuarabischen Dialekte*. The Hague: Mouton.
———. 1961. "Die Sprache der arabischen Sprachinsel in Uzbekistan." *Der Islam* 36: 232–63.
———, and Otto Jastrow, eds. 1980. *Handbuch der arabischen Dialekte*. Wiesbaden: Harrassowitz.
Fleisch, Henri. 1974. *Études d'arabe dialectal*. Beirut: Dar al-Mashreq.
Hull, Geoffrey. 1988. "Vicende e caratteristiche del maltese parlato in Egitto." *Incontri Siculo–Maltesi: Atti del convegno su Malta–Sicilia, Contiguità linguistica e culturale (Malta, 4–6 aprile 1986)*. Malta: University of Malta.
Jeger, L. 1963. "London Maltese." *The Guardian*, Feb. 14.
Kahane, Henry, and A. Tietze. 1958. *Lingua Franca in the Levant*. Urbana: University of Illinois Press.
Mamo, J. 1930–31. *Ulied in-nanna Venut fl-Amerca* [Grandma Venut's children in America]. Malta: Author.
Nachtigal, Gustav. 1974 [1879]. *Sahara and Sudan*. London: Hurst.
Price, C. A. 1954. *Malta and the Maltese: A Study in Nineteenth Century Migration*. Melbourne: Georgia House.
Puech, Gilbert. 1978. "A Cross-Dialectal Study of Vowel Harmony in Maltese." *Chicago Linguistic Society* 14: 377–89.
———. 1994. *Ethnotextes Maltais*. Wiesbaden: Harrassowitz.
Rossi, E. 1936. "Malta." *Encyclopedia of Islam*, vol. 3, pp. 213–14.
Saada, Lucienne. 1986. "Maltais en Tunisie." *Gli interscambi culturali e socio-economici fra l'Africa settentrionale e l'Europa mediterranea: Atti del congresso internazionale di Amalfi, 5-8 dicembre 1983*. Naples: n.p.

Schabert, P. 1976. *Laut- und Formenlehre des Maltesischen anhand zweier Mundarten.* Erlangen: Palm & Enke.
———. 1980. "Text aus Malta." In Fischer and Jastrow 1980: 286–91.
Sirat, A., and E. E. Knudsen. 1973. "Notes on the Arabic Dialect Spoken in the Balkh Region of Afghanistan." *Acta Orientalia* 35: 99–101.
Stetkevich, Jaroslav. 1970. *The Modern Arabic Literary Language: Lexical and Stylistic Developments.* Chicago: University of Chicago Press.
Stumme, Hans. 1904. *Maltesische Studien: Eine Sammlung prosaïscher und poetischer Texte in maltesischer Sprache nebst Erläuterungen.* Leipzig: Hinrichs.
Vadala, G. 1906. *Malte et ses dépendances.* Malta: n.p.
Wettinger, Godfrey. 1985. *The Jews of Malta in the Late Middle Ages.* Malta: Midsea Books.
———. 1986. "The Arabs in Malta." In *Malta: Studies of its Heritage and History.* Malta: Mid-Med Bank.
———, and M. Fsadni. 1968. *Peter Caxaro's Cantilena.* Malta: n.p.
———. 1983. *L-Għanja ta' Pietru Caxaru* [Peter Caxaro's Cantilena], 2nd ed. Malta: n.p.

Chapter 17
Israeli Hebrew Phonology
Shmuel Bolozky
University of Massachusetts, Amherst

17.1. Introduction

Whether or not it is appropriate to talk of the "revival" (see Wexler 1990 and references to earlier discussions) of Hebrew as a verbal means of communication in Palestine (now Israel) about a century ago, the phonological inventory of Modern Hebrew as spoken in Israel today is significantly different from that of either Biblical Hebrew (henceforth BH; see Chapter 6) or Mishnaic Hebrew. Today's "Arabicized" Hebrew (see Blanc 1964 and elsewhere) maintains a few more phonemic distinctions than does Standard (or General) Israeli Hebrew (henceforth Modern Hebrew, MH)—notably the preservation of pharyngeals ʻ and ḥ, and for some groups the uvular stop q, the velarized denti-alveolar stop ṭ, and the glide w. It also tends to preserve a rolled denti-alveolar r, and here and there a velarized denti-alveolar ṣ. This chapter, however, focuses on MH phonology. The "compromise" between the Sephardi and Ashkenazi traditions of pronunciations of Hebrew that constitutes MH is a considerably simpler inventory of phonemes:

Table 17-1. Israeli Hebrew Consonants

Consonant	Bilabial	Labio-Dental	Denti-Alveolar	Palato-Alveolar	Palatal	Velar	Uvular	Glottal
Stop	p b		t d			k g		ʼ
Fricative		f v	s z	š (ž)			x	h
Affricate			c	(č) (ǰ)				
Nasal	m		n					
Liquid			l				r	
Glide					y			

The consonants in brackets occur only in borrowings. Comparison with BH suggests the following "mergers"/simplifications and other changes/correspondences:

(a) *t* and *ṭ* > *t*
(b) *k* and *q* > *k*
(c) ' and ʿ (and for some speakers *ḥ* as well) > ' or Ø (Optional realization as ' is most likely as onglide to a heavily stressed vowel.)
(d) *h* > Ø (Optional realization as *h* is most likely as onglide to a heavily stressed vowel.)
(e) *s* and *ś* > *s*
(f) *ḥ* and *x* as an allophone of /k/ > *x*
(g) *ṣ* > *c*
(h) denti-alveolar roll *r* > uvular *r*
(i) *w* and *v* as an allophone of /b/ > *v*
(j) MH no longer maintains gemination, except phonetically, across morpheme boundary: *yašán+nu* 'we slept', *avát+ti* 'I worked' (~*avádeti*).
(k) The stop–fricative alternation of BH is maintained only for *p*, *b*, and *k*, and even that part of the rule is rife with exceptions, making it very opaque. Moreover, segments that were historically geminate are not subject to spirantization, nor is historical /q/. *v* from BH *w* and *x* from BH *ḥ* add to further surface opacity. None of the fricatives concerned is an allophone of the corresponding stop.

Vowels: *i e a o u*
Changes from the BH Tiberian inventory:
(a) *e*, *ɛ*, and *ə* > *e* (phonetically *ɛ*)
(b) *a* and *ɔ* > *a*

It should be pointed out that the gap between the phonemic system of MH and earlier phases of the language cannot be regarded as evidence for MH having lost its Semitic character; phonological, phonetic, or syntactic deviations from what is conceived of as a language family norm quite commonly result from the inherent instability of these components of the grammar and should not be interpreted as evidence for severed relationship with the common source.

17.1.1. Characterizing the phonetic–phonological–morphological continuum

The following discussion will present some essential features of MH phonology in a phonetic–phonological–morphological continuum of processes, which can be motivated by a number of criteria. The primary criterion is universal **phonetic/phonological naturalness**, which declines from one end of the continuum to the other. Another is the degree of **automaticity** of a process from a **phonetic/phonological** point of view. An automatic phonetic process applies whenever its structural description is met. The majority of phonetic and phonological rules, however, are restricted in one way or another to particular categories (mostly morphological), to segments of the lexicon, to individual items, etc., and have lexically marked exceptions. It is also possible to view automaticity from a different angle: the degree to which a speaker is **aware** of the process having taken place. Normally, speakers are not conscious of the application of automatic phonetic rules, whereas the more morphologized a phonological process is, the more likely is the speaker to be aware of its existence—although there is still the question of whether s/he is aware of an actual process, or merely of the relationship between two related morphological patterns, one of which is our assumed process "output." A fourth criterion, which characterizes the continuum only partially, is the extent to which a process is **optional**, or more accurately **variable**, depending on various sociolinguistic factors (age, gender, education, socio-economic status, speech style or tempo, etc.). Owing to limitations of space, only a few illustrations will be provided for each of the categories below. For additional survey-type data, see Bolozky (1978).

17.2. Natural, automatic phonetic processes

17.2.1. 'Mechanical' secondary stress

In Modern Hebrew, as well as in Polish and in other languages, there exists almost-automatic alternation between stressed and unstressed syllables, where the main stress constitutes the base, and in most cases every other syllable before it receives secondary stress. Occasionally, **two** unstressed syllables are squeezed between two stressed ones. The existence of two consecutive unstressed syllables generally results from the non-realization of secondary stress when a penultimately stressed word is followed by a bi-syllabic word with final stress, as in *dóar avír* 'air mail', or when the secondary stress—or the lexical stress of grammatical words—would have "clashed" (see Bolozky 1982) with the main stress of adjacent words, as in *xàmišá mìxtavím* 'five letters' > *xamišá mixtavím, ù kará lànu séfer* 'he read us a book' > *ù kará lanu séfer*. The main stress of most grammatical words is essentially equal to that of regular secondary stress, and is thus subject to destressing in the same way. It is also more flexible than the primary stress of regular lexical items. Unlike the BH situation, where stress retraction (*nɔsog 'ɔhor*) occurred even in lexical items, as in Gen 1:5:

    vəlahóšex   qɔrɔ́   láylɔ
    and (to) the dark   he called night

                                > *vəlahóšex qɔ́rɔ láylɔ*

MH does allow adjacent main stresses across lexical items, as in *vèdarás kélev*:

    ù   naág   bemèirút mufrézet vèdarás   kélev
    he drove in speed excessive and ran over a dog

In grammatical words, on the other hand, clash of the main stress with another main stress results in reconfiguration of the stress pattern in a manner that avoids such clash:

    atà   bá 'are you coming?'
    you   come

                                  > *àta bá*

    ù   kará   lànu   abáyta 'he called us home'
    he called to us home

                                  > *ù kará lanù abáyta*

Under relatively rare conditions of very low contextual prominence (e.g. next to contrastive stress), the main stress of some lexical items is low, equivalent to that of secondary stress, and thus may undergo similar reconfiguration (see Kadmon 1983):

    ù   kará   pérek   xaméšesrè   lo   šéšesrè
    he read chapter fifteen   not sixteen

                                  > *ù kará perèk xaméšesrè lo šéšesrè*

    The opposition between stressed and unstressed syllables is a common phenomenon, and fixed repetition of this contrast in the form of rhythmic alternation is a natural phenomenon in the colloquial registers of a number of languages. Regular rhythmic alternation is frequently found in folk poetry, and is also characteristic of counting sequences or memorized numeral sequences. As shown in Bolozky and Haydar (1986), preference for the unsuffixed numeral set in colloquial Hebrew and for the suffixed one in the dialects of Arabic (e.g. Lebanese Arabic below) originates, at least in part, from

numeral paradigms in trochaic rhythm as chanted and acquired for the first time by children:
    MH: (a)xát—štáym šalóš arbá xaméš—šéš—šéva šmóne tésa éser
    Arab: wáḥed tnéyn—tléte 'árb'a xámse sítte sáb'a tméni tís'a 'ášra
Had the situation been reversed, the chanted sequences would not have flowed as naturally (a partial anapest in Hebrew, and staccato in Lebanese Arabic):
    exád šnáim šlošá arbaá xamišá šišá šivá šmoná tišá asará
    ... tlét 'árb' xáms sítt sáb' tmén tís' 'ášr
Alternating stress can also be observed in children's rhymes, e.g.
    mìmromím   pcacá   yorédet ...
    from the sky bomb   comes down
and in rhythmic counting by children for 'random selection' purposes, as in
    éven   nyár   umìsparáim ...
    rock   paper   and scissors
    én den díno sóf a lá katíno ... (random selection rhyme of un-
        clear origin, probably Mediterranean Lingua Franca)
as well as in rhythmic chants of groups at sports events and such (see Gil 1986):
    él—él—ìsraél   (sports chant to encourage Israeli team)
    àšofét   abáyta   'referee go home!'
    the referee home
Mechanical secondary stress assignment is a natural process, then, applying automatically whenever its structural description is met, and speakers are certainly unaware of its having taken place. It is also variable, at least in that it "cancels out" when clashing with an adjacent primary stress.

17.2.2. Voicing assimilation

MH voicing assimilation of obstruents is anticipatory/regressive, which is the unmarked direction for this kind of assimilation (**progressive** assimilation is unmarked when stems determine the realization of the suffix. Unless marked otherwise, the main stress always falls on the final vowel):

No Contact		Formal Alternant		Informal Variant
sagar	'he closed'	yisgor	'he will close'	yizgor
pagaš	'he met'	pgiša	'meeting'	bgiša
zaken	'old (m.sg.)'	zkenim	'old (m.pl.)'	skenim
dakar	'he stabbed'	yidkor	'he will stab'	yitkor

As shown in Bolozky (1978, 1985), there appear to be two types of exceptions: normally, *v* does not cause voicing assimilation, and *x* does not undergo it:

kvar	'already'	*exzir*	'returned (trans.)'
kviš	'road'	*yixboš*	'will conquer'
tikva	'hope'	*exdir*	'caused to penetrate'
tvia	'claim; drowning'		
itva	'outlined'		

It appears that *v* not causing voicing assimilation is due to substratum influence of Slavic languages such as Russian and Polish, where (owing to *v* originating from a historical glide *w*) the same phenomenon is observed (and furthermore, where at least intra-morphemically in Warsaw Polish, **progressive** assimilation occurs instead—which may also surface in the speech of some Polish-born Israelis). *x* does not readily undergo voicing assimilation apparently because speakers might be reluctant to assimilate *x* into something that sounds too much like an *r* that should not be there (Hebrew does not have a truly corresponding voiced fricative counterpart ɣ: r, the nearest voiced segment, does not have enough friction to qualify as an obstruent.) In (very) casual speech, however, these exceptions tend to be eliminated; the more casual the register and more rapid the tempo, the greater the likelihood of the process having no exceptions:

gvar	'already'	*eɣzir*	'returned (trans.)'
gviš	'road'	*yiɣboš*	'will conquer'
tigva	'hope'	*eɣdir*	'caused to penetrate'
dvia	'claim; drowning'		
idva	'outlined'		

We are dealing, then, with a natural phonetic process (uniformity of voicing clearly facilitates production), working in the unmarked (anticipatory/regressive) direction, which applies automatically whenever the structural description is met, and exceptions tend to be eliminated in fast/casual speech. It is normally not a conscious process; speakers will deny, for instance, that they ever pronounce *yisgor* as *yizgor*, etc. It is also variable, relative to the degree of casualness and tempo involved. The more casual the register and the faster the tempo, the more likely the assimilation.

17.3. Natural phonological processes with some restrictions

17.3.1. Avoidance of identical or homorganic consonant sequences

MH does not maintain the gemination of BH, but geminates may be formed across a morpheme boundary:

  dan 'he discussed'   *dánnu*   'we discussed'
  šavat 'he was on strike'   *šavátti*   'I was on strike'
  tamim 'naïve'   *hittamem*   'he feigned naïveté'

Within the stem, however, geminates are either broken with the minimal vowel *e* (the assumption that this *e* is epenthetic is based on pattern comparison):

    zalelan   'glutton'
    xatetan   'meddler'
 cf. *kamcan*   'miser'
    noxexut   'presence'
    holelut   'folly, hilarity'
 cf. *rokxut*   'pharmacology'

or the elision of a vowel separating between identical consonants is blocked (although reduction to *e* still takes place), as in

  xagag 'he celebrated' ~ *xagega* 'she celebrated'
 cf. *katav* 'he wrote' ~ *katva* 'she wrote'
  kucac 'it was cut' ~ *kucecu* 'they were cut'
 cf. *šupac* 'it was overhauled' ~ *šupcu* 'they were overhauled'
  itpalel 'he prayed' ~ *itpalela* 'she prayed'
 cf. *itlabeš* 'he got dressed' ~ *itlabša* 'she got dressed'

except for **very** casual/fast speech, in which elision may marginally occur, particularly when fricatives are involved (e.g. *em šàxexú* 'they forgot' > *èm šaxxú*). McCarthy (1986) regards the blocking of *e*-deletion in *xagega*, etc. as "antigemination": syncope rules are prohibited from creating clusters of identical consonants. This is an immediate corollary of his Obligatory Contour Principle (OCP), which prohibits adjacent identical elements at the melodic level (either consonantal or vocalic, in an autosegmental analysis). The OCP does not apply to the across-morpheme-boundary cases, since different morphemes are represented on different tiers.

The *šavátti* type above often undergoes *e*-insertion, which breaks the surface geminate or a homorganic *d+t* sequence (just as in English *prodded*, *wanted*—except that in English the process is obligatory):

  šavátti 'I was on strike' ~ *šaváteti*
  /avád+ti/ 'I worked' > *avátti* ~ *avádeti*

and needless to say, voicing assimilation and the splitting process will have to be mutually exclusive, to avoid *avátetí* (which can be achieved by Kiparsky's 1973 Elsewhere Condition, according to which the more specific rule applies before the more general one). Its not applying to *hittamem* suggests that the process is restricted to sequences involving an **inflectional** affix, and it is blocked in *dánnu* since **danenu* would have been interpreted as stemming from a geminate root *d.n.n* instead of the correct *d.w.n*.

The avoidance or splitting of identical or homorganic consonants is phonetically natural, but nevertheless restricted; speakers may or may not be aware of its having taken place.

17.3.2. The new imperative in colloquial Hebrew

In Bolozky (1979) it was argued that in colloquial Hebrew, commands are normally realized in future-tense form used imperatively. What appears to be partial colloquial resurrection of the normative formal imperative, as in *štok* 'shut up!', *lex* 'go!', etc., is in fact a future (BH imperfect) form whose prefix has been "chopped off":

Fut/Imp.	Reduction 1	Reduction 2	
tešev	*tšev ~ čev*	*šev*	'sit down! (m.sg.)'
telamed	*tlamed*	*lamed*	'teach!'
titlabeš		*tlabeš*	'get dressed!'
tizaer	*tzaer > dzaer*	*zaer*	'watch out!'

That this is **not** the normative imperative can be proven by the absence of the prefixal *h* required for the formal imperative in Hitpa'el and Nif'al (i.e. *hitlabeš* and *hiza(h)er*, respectively, would have been expected), as well as by the clearly-reduced new **suffixed** imperatives in Pa'al, which are distinct from their normative counterparts (illustrations are with the feminine suffix +*i*ˢ; the same applies to the plural suffix +*u*ˢ):

Normative	Fut/Imp.	Reduction 1	Reduction 2	
sigri	*tisgeri*	*tsgeri ~ cgeri ~ dzgeri*	*s/zgeri*	'close!'
pitxi	*tiftexi*		*ftexi*	'open!'

This is a natural phenomenon; many languages allow imperative use of their future forms (see Ultan 1978). Shortening increases the stress and urgency of the command: in BH, the shorter jussive form was used for negative imperatives (*'al tešt* 'do not drink!', full form *tište*) and for command or request in the third person (*yəhi 'or* 'let there be light!'). Although the first person "command," the cohortative, actually involves lengthening (*'ešmərà* 'I will observe, let me observe' vs. imperfect *'ešmor*), it does not involve the urgency of a shortened form, and the same can be said of other long-form imperatives (*qúma* 'arise' is less urgent than its variant *qum*). The process is also natural in that only deletion of the "minimal" vowels *e* and *i* is allowed; the *a* of Hif'il (*tasbir* 'explain!') is never affected. It is not automatic, though; it is essentially restricted to the future-used-imperatively, and only occasionally expands to non-imperative future forms. Speakers are at least somewhat aware of its having taken place, as can be shown from occasional orthographic evidence. For a recent, most detailed description of MH imperatives and their substitutes, see Henkin (to appear).

17.4. Morphologically constrained phonological processes that have no exceptions, but are not (or are no longer) phonetically motivated

17.4.1. Residues of Philippi's Law

Essentially, the general lowering of a stressed *i* or *e* in a closed syllable to *a* is now restricted to the verb system:

diber	'he spoke'	~ *dibárti*	'I spoke'
isbir	'he explained'	~ *isbárnu*	'we explained'
itlabeš	'he got dressed'	~ *itlabášta*	'you got dressed'

In the verb, however, it has no exceptions: *šévna* 'sit! (f.pl.)' etc. no longer exist in MH. It is not a variable rule, and speakers are aware of the alternation. For additional discussion, see Bolozky (1978).

17.4.2. Hitpa'el metathesis

In Hitpa'el, and in related derived nominalizations (e.g. *istalkut* 'going away', cf. *istalek* 'went away'), a coronal sibilant metathesizes with the prefixal *t*:

	Underlying	Surface	
(a)	/hit+labeš/	*itlabeš*	'got dressed'
(b)	/hit+saken/	*istaken*	'took risk'
	/hit+šameš/	*ištameš*	'used'
	/hit+zaken/	*izdaken*	'became old'
	/hit+camek/	*ictamek*	'shrank'

When voicing assimilation is involved (see § 17.2.2), the two processes should apply simultaneously, to block **istaken* for 'he became old' (see Bolozky 1978). Ordering voicing assimilation before metathesis would have also worked, but one would not wish to order a phonetic process before a morphologically restricted rule like this one.

Since this is an historical, established process, it might make more sense to ask not what the actual phonetic motivation for this rule is, but rather why it is not inverted or lost. One possible explanation is avoidance of single-unit affricate interpretation of a *t*-plus-sibilant, which would make the Hitpa'el prefix opaque, causing the forms concerned to look like infinitives or imperatives of Nif'al (e.g. /hit+saken/ > *hitsaken > *hicaken). It would also make the underlying root opaque. So the process can be explained on phonological–semantic grounds, and has no exceptions among Hitpa'el forms, but can hardly be motivated phonetically: even Hif'il forms with the same structural description, such as *hitsis* 'caused to ferment', *hitšiš* 'tired out (trans.)', do not undergo the rule, let alone other items (/t+šuv+a/ 'answer' > *tšuva*, not *štuva). It is strictly restricted to Hitpa'el. It is not a variable process; determining speakers' awareness of its application would require testing.

17.5. Other morphologically constrained phonological processes that are not (or are no longer) phonetically motivated

17.5.1. Pretonic and antepretonic a/e-deletion

In the verb, a non-high vowel is elided in a pretonic open syllable:

katav	'he wrote'	~ *katva*	'she wrote'
yikanes	'he will enter'	~ *yikansu*	'they will enter'
diber	'he spoke'	~ *dibru*	'they spoke'
sudar	'he/it was arranged'	~ *sudra*	'she/it was arranged'
itlabeš	'he got dressed'	~ *itlabšu*	'they got dressed'

Exception: the present/present participle of Pu'al (*mesudarim* 'are (m.) arranged', not *mesudrim). If a sequence of (any) three consonants or two identical ones (see above) would be formed in the process, they are broken/avoided by an intervening *e*:

tixtov	'you (m.) will write'	~ *tixtevi*	'you (f.sg.) id.'
nixtav	'it was written'	~ *nixtevu*	'they were written'
uxtav	'it was dictated'	~ *uxteva*	'she/it was dictated'

Two exceptions: the present/present participle of Nif'al (*nixnasim* 'enter (m.pl.)', not *nixnesim) and of Huf'al (*mustarim* 'are (m.) hidden', not *musterim).

This **could** have been a natural phonetic rule, since pretonic reduction and elision are (universally) expected. It is, however, restricted to the verb system, and even there one finds exceptions that are hard to account for. Reduction/elision does apply to one non-verbal pattern, as in:

M.Sg.	F.Sg.	M.Pl.	F.Pl.	
tipeš	tipša	tipšim	tipšot	'fool(ish)'
xiver	xivéret	xivrim	xivrot	'pale'

and to a few other items, like:

totax	'gun'	~ totxan	'gunner'
mišpat	'law'	~ mišpetan	'jurist'

but in most cases it is blocked because antepretonic *a*-deletion in non-verbal categories takes precedence:

M.Sg.	F.Sg.	M.Pl.	F.Pl.	
šamen	šmena	šmenim	šmenot	'fat'
šafan	šfana	šfanim	šfanot	'rabbit'
davar		dvarim		'thing'

Antepretonic *a*-deletion is **also** heavily morphologized, and is certainly less motivated phonetically. Historically, reduction of either pretonic or antepretonic vowels appears to have applied to any unstressed non-high vowel in an open syllable, regardless of distance from the main stress, that was not affected by pretonic lengthening or other tensing processes. Thus, since the second *a* in /davar+im/ was lengthened, and the second one in /šafann+im/ was closed by gemination, reduction could only apply to the first *a*. In MH, though, with no lengthening and no gemination, there is no particular phonetic reason for deleting a vowel **two** syllables before the stress, and the restriction to *a* to the exclusion of *e* (*terucim* 'excuses' > **trucim*, *pexamim* 'coals' > **pxamim*, etc.—see Bolozky and Schwarzwald 1990) makes it even less plausible as a phonetically motivated process. Another point: if complete deletion cannot take place, at least *a* is reduced to *e* (*yašar* 'straight' ~ *yešarim* (pl.), *ša(')ul* 'borrowed' ~ *šeulim* (pl.)). But reduction does not apply with *a* that was preceded by a now-lost low consonant:

ašir	'rich, m.sg.'	~ аširim	'rich, m.pl.', not *eširim
avud	'lost (m.sg.)'	~ avuda	'lost (f.sg.)'
arug	'killed (m.sg.)'	~ arugim	'killed (m.pl.)'

Historically, low consonants preferred a low vowel. Today, however, with no phonetic realization of such consonants, the blocking of reduction is hard to motivate. Furthermore, the loss of gemination in MH has also removed the motivation for blocking *a*-deletion in forms like:

Singular	Historical	Plural	Historical	
nagar	naggar	nagarim	naggarim	'carpenter'
patiš	pattiš	patišim	pattišim	'hammer'
šapud	šappud	šapudim	šappudim	'skewer'

Historically, deletion was blocked because its application would have created an impermissible three-consonant cluster, a geminate counting as two consonants. With MH degemination, *a*-deletion **should** have applied, had it been a phonetically motivated process.

Both deletion/reduction processes, then, have lost their phonetic motivation—*a*-deletion perhaps more so than *e*-deletion—and are morphologically restricted. They also are not variable in MH (*yoševim* for *yošvim* 'sit (m.pl.)', etc. may rarely be heard among former speakers of Judeo-Spanish—a very marginal phenomenon). Since these are not phonetic processes, it is hard to tell whether speakers actually derive one form from the other by deleting a vowel (e.g. *katav* 'he wrote' ~ /katav+a/ 'she wrote' > *katva*), or simply make the connection between two related patterns—e.g. CaCaC and a related CaCC+a feminine pattern. (Speakers are clearly aware of the relationships between patterns.)

17.5.2. Assignment of main stress

MH main stress is normally assigned to the final syllable, with a number of classes of exceptions that are sufficiently well defined for systematic treatment. One can first take care of these exceptions, and then let all the remaining forms, which constitute the majority, be assigned the unmarked final stress by the universal Elsewhere Condition.

In the verb system, the final vowel of the stem and main stress assignment appear to be mutually exclusive (see Bolozky 1978): a stem-final vowel that has not been affected by elision or reduction is assigned main stress. As noted above, pretonic deletion in the verb can hardly be regarded as a phonetically motivated process in MH. If so, one could let deletion or reduction of a non-high vowel at the end of the verb stem be triggered by a +V# or +VC# suffix irrespective of whether it is stressed or not, mark a few exceptions (*egena* 'she protected', *exela* 'she began'), and subsequently assign primary stress to all remaining final stem vowels (excluding derived ones resulting from reduction):

katávti	'I wrote'	*dibárta*	'you spoke'
káma	'she rose'	*hitlabášti*	'I got dressed'
kanínu	'we bought'	*isbíru*	'they explained'
macáti	'I found'	*egéna*	'she protected'
yakúmu	'they will rise'	*ekímu*	'they established'
nišbárti	'I broke'	*ipíla*	'she dropped (trans.)'
nimcénu	'we were found'		

Present/present participle forms will have to be excluded, to block *mazkíra 'remind (f.sg.); secretary', *mešubášim 'distorted (m.pl.), faulty', *mušlámim 'completed (m.pl., perfect)'—which is, perhaps, one of the arguments for considering the present participle as part of the non-verbal system.

As for the non-verbal system, there are a few sporadic exceptions, such as láma 'where', (')éfo 'where', (h)éna 'here', but in most cases penultimate stress applies to reasonably well defined groups. The main exception to final stress is the segolate class. Historically, this was hardly a problem, since stress assignment applied **before** the epenthesis of ε to break an unpermitted final cluster, when the surface penultimate vowel was still the final vowel:

/malk/ 'king' > málk > málɛk > mélɛk > mélɛx

Assuming an underlying /malk/ was based on the existence of alternants in which this stem surfaces, e.g. malka 'queen'. As pointed out in Bolozky (1978), however, in MH most segolates do **not** have CVCC alternants (if they do, they are confined to the literary register), e.g.

téred	'spinach'	xóken	'enema'
téfer	'seam'	šéten	'urine'
rótev	'sauce'	bóreg	'screw'
gézer	'carrot'	dófek	'pulse'
délek	'fuel'		

which suggests that segolate stress be assigned by surface sequences, i.e. to the penult in ...CeCeC# and ...CoCeC# nouns that are not directly derived from verbs (to exclude verbs, e.g. kotev 'write (m.sg.)', berex 'he blessed'— as well as verb-related agent nouns like šoter 'policeman'). If that final eC# sequence is an +etˁ suffix, verbs are penultimately stressed as well (i.e. not only miktéret 'pipe', but also kotévet 'write (f.sg.)').

When consequences of formerly low consonants are included, the list may also include ...Ca(x)aC#:

ráaš	'noise'	mikláxat	'shower'
náxal	'river'	šomáat	'hear'
mišmáat	'discipline'	šoláxat	'send (f.sg.)'

CeCeˁ (péle 'miracle', déše 'lawn'), CeCa(x)ˁ (téva 'nature', kérax 'ice'), Co(x)aCˁ (nóar 'youth', dóar 'mail', šóxad 'bribe'). Exceptions like nahar 'river', naxaš 'snake', šena 'sleep', koxav 'star', ge'e 'proud', kehe 'dark', which are a minority, will be marked as such.

Another group of words that is stressed penultimately involves a "furtive patax"—an a inserted before historical word-final h, ʕ, and ḥ when those were preceded by a vowel-other-than-a:

gavóa	'tall (m.sg.)'	historically *gavóah*
šoméa	'hear (m.sg.)'	historically *šoméaʿ*
potéax	'open (m.sg.)'	historically *potéaḥ*

If underlying low consonants are assumed, regular final stress applies before *a*-insertion:

/gavoh/ 'tall (m.sg.)' > *gavóh* > *gavóah* > *gavóa*

but since the low consonant is not ever realized, a more concrete approach would be preferable: stress a vowel-other-than-*a* that is immediately followed by word-final *a* that is not suffixal (to block **meví+a* for *mevia* 'bring (f.sg.)', **bí+a* for *bia* 'coming'. Exceptions, like *kia* from *kiha* 'he scolded', would be rare), or by *axʕ*.

Bolozky (1978) also discusses the influence of Yiddish stress, which in the colloquial shifts final stress to penultimate position in proper names,

yael > *yáel*
menaxem > *menáxem*
naftali > *naftáli*

occasionally creating "minimal pairs" of common and proper nouns,

rexovot	'streets'	vs. *rexóvot*	'Rehovot'
xaim	'life'	vs. *xáim*	'Chaim'

or of Hebrew and related Yiddishized versions:

taxlit	'aim, purpose'	vs. *táxles*	'business'
meci(')a	'finding, bargain'	vs. *mecíe*	'bargain (usu. ironic)'

as well as the colloquial tendency to shift stress to the first syllable when the word concerned is used in the context of games:

klafim	'cards'	vs. *kláfim*	'card game'
bulim	'stamps'	vs. *búlim*	'(collecting) stamps'
rišon	'first'	vs. *ríšon*	'first step in game'
xamiši	'fifth'	vs. *xámiši*	'fifth step in game'
monopol	'monopoly'	vs. *mónopol*	'Monopoly (game)'

This phenomenon seems to "spill over" to some common colloquial variants, where the alternative penultimate stress stays on the same syllable even after suffixation:

Singular		Plural		
Formal	Non-formal	Formal	Non-formal	
tiras	*tíras*	*tirasim*	*tírasim*	'corn'
pilpel	*pílpel*	*pilpelim*	*pílpelim*	'pepper'

In borrowed non-verbs, stress normally (but not always) maintains the position it holds in the language of origin, and stays in a steady relationship to specific suffixes (see Bolozky 1978). The addition of native suffixes does not affect the position of stress in borrowed words. Some familiar native words demonstrate similar behavior in all non-formal registers, not only when the basic stress is penultimate, as in *tíras* 'corn' above, but when it is final as well (see Bat-El 1989):

Singular	Plural		
Formal	Formal	Non-formal	
marak	*merakim*	*marákim*	'soup'
sabon	*sabonim*	*sabónim*	'nerd'

Note, however, that in its basic meaning, the plural of *sabon* 'soap', *sabonim*, has regular final stress.

It appears, then, that main word-stress can be reasonably well defined for a variety of penultimate (and some word-initial) environments, and once these are taken care of, final word stress applies elsewhere. As for speakers' awareness of it—one indication that they do is that they distinguish different meanings for minimal pairs that differ only in the location of their main stress.

17.5.3. Residues of historical low consonants

With the loss of low consonants or their mergers with other segments in MH, their role in the phonological component requires reevaluation. In the case of *ḥ*, for instance, the merger with *x* has indeed resulted in some degree of regularization, particularly in dispensing with the need for *a*-epenthesis to avoid a syllable-final *ḥ*:

  sixka   'she played' (rarely *sixaka*)
  maxku   'they erased' (rarely *maxaku*)
  saxkan   'actor' (*saxakan* only in very formal register)

but also in allowing variable regularization of the prefix, "returning" it to *i*, as in

  exzik   'he held'   ~ *ixzik* (cf. *isbir* 'he decided')
  exlit   'he decided'   ~ *ixlit*

and in variable choice of the stem-vowel in the future of Pa'al, with an option for using the regular *o* alongside the "guttural"-related *a* when *x* from *ḥ* is the **second** radical of the root:

  yivxar   'he will choose/elect'   ~ *yivxor*
  yivxan   'he will examine'   ~ *yivxon*

The "ex-guttural" impact is still strongly felt, however, in word-final position: choice of *a* rather than *o* in the future of Pa'al:

yišlax 'he will send' ~ **yišlóax*
yivrax 'he will flee' ~ **yivróax*
and insertion of *a* if the preceding vowel is not *a*:
/šalix/ 'messenger' > *šalíax*
/samex/ 'happy' > *saméax*
It is also maintained in the replacement of regular ...*éxetˤ* by ...*áxatˤ*:
šoláxat 'send (f.sg.)' (cf. *kotévet*)
mefatáxat 'develop (f.sg.)' (cf. *medabéret*)

Since in most cases *x* that corresponds to the historical allophone of *k* can also occur in the same environments (except for the *yivxar* group), *x* from *ḥ* still requires marking in some way to account for these consequences.

As shown in detail in Bolozky (1978), the ex-gutturals or their traces fulfill a role **even if not realized**: as occupiers of consonantal slots, to give speakers clues as to *miškal* (canonical morphological pattern) membership, as well as to account for deviation from regular *miškal* patterns, owing to processes which were historically natural, but are no longer transparent. There are essentially two ways of accounting for speakers' capability to relate deviant forms with formerly-low consonants to their regular *miškal*-base. One is to start from abstract representations based on regular *miškalim*, derive the forms concerned by means of morpho-phonological processes, then dispose of whatever is not realized phonetically. Assuming underlying low consonants would "motivate" the need to get rid of a low consonant at the syllable coda:

/macaʕ/ 'he found' > *maca*
/macaʕ+ti/ 'I found' > *macáti*
/gavah/ 'he was tall' > *gava* (MH only)
/šamaʕ/ 'he heard' > *šama* (MH only)

or to add a vowel, which would shift them to syllabic onset position:
/šo'el+im/ 'ask (m.pl.)' > *šo'l+im* > *šo'alim* > *šoalim*
(cf. /kotev+im/ 'write (m.pl.)' > *kotvim*)

and if a prefix is involved, it also echoes that vowel across it:
/ti+ʕbod/ 'you will work' > *taʕabod* > *taavod*
(cf. *ti+xtov* 'you will write')
/hi+ʔmin/ 'he believed' > *heʔemin* > *eemin*
(cf. *isbir* 'he explained')
/mi+ʕrav/ 'west' > *maʕarav* > *maarav*
(cf. *mi+zrax* 'east')

A low consonant is also not allowed with another consonant in the syllable onset:

(cf. /'ašir+im/ 'rich (m.pl.)' > 'širim > 'aširim > aširim
/zariz+im/ 'nimble (m.pl.)' > zrizim)
/hlix+a/ 'walking' > halixa > alixa
(cf. ktiv+a 'writing')
/ka'uv+im/ 'painful (m.pl.)' > k'uvim > ke'uvim > keuvim
(cf. /katuv+im/ 'written (m.sg.)' > ktuvim)
/t+'uf+a/ 'aviation' > te'ufa > teufa
(cf. t+rum+a 'contribution')

And a word-final low consonant other-than-a-glottal-stop can be used to account for the "furtive *patax*," i.e. the insertion of *a* when historical final *h*, *'*, and *ḥ* (see § 17.5.2) are preceded by a vowel-other-than-*a*:

/gavoh/ 'tall (m.sg.)' > gavóah > gavóa
/yode'/ 'know (m.sg.)' > yodéa' > yodéa

This is an abstract approach, and in most cases is problematic in that it assumes underlying **low** consonants for which there is no sufficient synchronic motivation. Speakers can be argued to refer to consonantal positions where the "gutturals" used to be, but not to actual "gutturals." A more realistic way of accounting for speakers' capability to assign forms with former "gutturals" to prototypical *miškalim* is to assume that they form recognition strategies based on regularities observed in surface configurations, and that although they extrapolate from them the existence of consonantal slots, these discovery procedures have nothing to do with the feature "low." Below are some initial formulations of possible slot-discovery procedures.

(i) Any syllable-initial vowel is an obvious indication of a lost "guttural" that used to function as its onset:

amar	'he said'	meir	'give light (m.sg.)'
oved	'he works'	yedia	'message'
šual	'fox'	eaxzut	'settlement'

Exception: *a* preceded by a stressed vowel-other-than-*a* and followed by a word-final *x* (e.g. *šalíax* 'messenger'), where this *a* is epenthetic (i.e. does not constitute part of the *miškal*).

(ii) When the syllable-initial and immediately preceding syllable-final vowels are identical, the ex-guttural may be signaled by a long vowel in casual speech:

ta+avod	'you (m.sg.) will work'		> ta:vod
e+evod	'I will work'		> e:vod
revi+i	'fourth'		> revi:
šiamum	'boredom'	> šiimum	> ši:mum

In **very** casual or fast speech, shortening (e.g. to *tavod, šimum*) is **also** possible, but is generally considered substandard; alternatively, it may be argued that a **trace** of length is **always** there, regardless of register. When the two adjacent vowels are identical and the first is prefixal, the second is epenthetic, while the first, which constitutes a component of the *miškal*, is underlyingly /i/ if it surfaces as *a* or *e* (*taavod, eevid*), and /u/ if it surfaces as *o* (*o+osak* 'he was employed').

(iii) A word-final vowel (*a* or *e*, but theoretically it could be any) that is preceded by a **stressed** vowel in the preceding syllable signals a **following** (syllable-final) low consonant that has been lost (*téva* 'nature', *pére* 'wild one, wildly').

(iv) When a word-final *a* that is **not** suffixal is immediately preceded by a stressed vowel-other-than-*a*, it signals a following (syllable-final) lost guttural, while the *a* itself is epenthetic (i.e. does not constitute part of the *miškal*):

yadúa   'known (m.sg.)'
gavóa   'tall (m.sg.)'   vs. *heví+a* 'she brought'
higía   'he arrived'   vs. *higí+a* 'she arrived'

So the historically low consonants are no longer low, and essentially function as occupiers of consonantal slots in order to account for *miškal* membership and deviations from *miškalim* that are fairly systematic but cannot be motivated independently on phonetic grounds. Normally, these deviations are not variable, with the notable exception of some processes related to *x* from historical *ḥ*. Speakers are probably aware of the existence of these "empty" slots.

17.5.4. Stop spirantization

As noted in § 17.1k, the post-vocalic spirantization of BH stops is restricted in MH to *p*, *b*, and *k*, and even that part of the rule is very opaque, owing to numerous exceptions and constant flux. Opacity is further increased by degemination, since degeminated segments continue to block spirantization as if they were still geminated, and so does *k* from historical *q*. *v* from BH *w* and *x* from BH *ḥ* add to further surface opacity. Residual spirantization has received considerable attention in the literature—see, for instance, Ben-Horin and Bolozky (1972), Barkai (1978), Bolozky (1980), Schwarzwald (1981)—most of which seems to suggest that it perhaps should no longer be regarded as a significant generalization. At best, one could point to tendencies for the rule to operate in a number of sub-environments, like word-finally (which is, essentially, the only environment in which the rule is rarely contradicted, and even **this** holds true only for the **native** lexicon):

kaf	'spoon'	~ *kapot*	'spoons'
dov	'bear'	~ *dubim*	'bears'
rax	'soft (m.sg.)'	~ *raka*	'soft (f.sg.)'

or after a prefix ending in a vowel:

katav	'he wrote'	~ *yi+xtov*	'he will write'
pitéax	'he developed'	~ *me+fatéax*	'develop (m.sg.)'
badak	'he examined'	~ *ni+vdak*	'he was examined'
		mi+xtav	'letter'
		ma+ftéax	'key'
		mi+vxan	'test'

or one could simply list stop–spirant alternations as associated with particular paradigms (within the verb and elsewhere), as in Schwarzwald (1981)—and then try to account for the numerous deviations by additional principles. In Ben-Horin and Bolozky (1972), for instance, it was pointed out that there is some correlation between the degree of opacity and its impact on either input or output of spirantization—and the degree and nature of deviation from expected norms. Thus, one would expect more violation of historical *k*~*x* alternations because of opacity in both input (historical *q*) and output (historical *ḥ*), with violations going both ways, whereas in the case of *b*-*v* increased opacity is only in the output (historical *w*), which consequently causes more output deviations (i.e. "overapplication" on the surface), and the same applies to *p*-*f*, owing to numerous borrowings with *f* in positions other than post-vocalic. But there are too many exceptions to this generalization—some of them due to even greater opacity since 1972. Barkai (1978) proposes that inapplication or overapplication be accounted for by avoidance of ambiguity—which again works only in some of the cases. It appears that the only way of accounting for the various numerous deviations is, as suggested in Bolozky (1980) and in Schwarzwald (1981), to attribute them to analogical leveling, directed towards already-existing opacity (which acts as a trigger, signaling that "it **can** be done"), or towards the unmarked form, or (less frequently) towards the realization that minimizes opacity. Furthermore, with some notable exceptions, the tendency for analogical leveling decreases with the decrease in derivational bond: it is stronger within inflections, but weakens with the increase in distance between an inflectional form and a related derivational one that is not automatically predictable (see Bolozky 1980). Below are a few illustrations, from Bolozky (1980).

At the end of the word (in native words) one always finds a spirant. Analogical leveling is not common; when occurring, however, the formal alternant is rarely used. Analogy is with the unmarked form with a spirant:

Formal		Alternant		Colloquial Var.
ratov/uv	'wet (m.sg.)'	retuba	(f.sg.)	retuva
metofef	'drummer'	tipuf	'drumming'	tifuf
musax	'garage'	musakim	(pl.)	musaxim

In the beginning of the stem (particularly in Pi'el), the *k~x* variation undergoes analogy in the direction of both stop and spirant—probably owing to the above-mentioned opacity with both output **and** input (*k* from BH *q* and *x* from BH *ḥ*); in *b~v* and *p~f* variations analogy is usually with the spirant—because of opacity with the output (*v* from BH *w*, and *f* because of opacity caused by numerous borrowed verbs with initial *f*—*fibrek* 'fabricated', *flirtet* 'flirted', *filéax* 'pilfered', *fisfes* 'missed', etc.). When the derivation is automatic, as in the case of derived nominalizations (gerunds), analogical leveling with the verb is almost as likely to occur as within a particular verb paradigm (inflected Past and Future forms below are in 3rd person masculine singular):

	Past	Future	Imperative	Gerund	
	kiven	yexaven	kaven	kivun	'aim'
coll.	xiven	yexaven	xaven	xivun	
or	kiven	yekaven	kaven	kivun	
	bikeš	yevakeš	bakeš	bikuš	'ask'
coll.	vikeš	yevakeš	vakeš	vikuš	
or	bikeš	*yebakeš	bakeš	bikuš	
	pitéax	yefatéax	patéax	pitúax	'develop'
coll.	fitéax	yefatéax	fatéax	fitúax	
or	pitéax	*yepatéax	patéax	pitúax	

Exception: in the case of quadriliterals, *b~v* pairs are subject to opacity (and consequently to analogy) with the stop only, owing to the tendency to keep reduplicated syllables identical:

	Past	Future	Imperative	Gerund	
	bilbel	yevalbel	balbel	bilbul	'confuse'
coll.	bilbel	yebalbel	balbel	bilbul	
	*vilvel	*yevalvel	*valvel	*vilvul	

Across *binyanim* (verb patterns), analogy is likely if the relationship is reasonably automatic, as in active–passive pairs:

Pa'al Past		Nif'al Past		Substandard Var.
katav	'write'	*nixtav*	'be written'	*niktav*
kavaš	'conquer'	*nixbaš*	'be conquered'	*nikbaš/nikvaš*

but not when the derivation is more specialized and less automatic, as in a causality relationship:

Pa'al Past		Hif'il Past		Potential Variant
katav	'write'	*hixtiv*	'dictate'	**hiktiv*
kašal	'fail (intrans.)'	*hixšil*	'fail (trans.)'	**hikšil*

In non-automatic derivation, analogical leveling is highly unlikely:

Pa'al Past		Derived Noun		Potential Analogy
katav	'wrote'	*mixtav*	'letter'	**miktav*
patax	'opened'	*mafteax*	'key'	**mapteax*
balat	'projected'	*tavlit*	'relief'	**tablit*

When the alternation affects the second radical of the root, analogical leveling with the stop is not that common: in Pa'al it only tends to occur in the imperative, probably because of the new imperative being derived from the future-used-imperatively (see § 17.3.2):

Formal Imperative		Future	Colloquial Imper.
šxav	'lie down!'	*tiškav*	*škav*
švor	'break!'	*tišbor*	*šbor*
šfox	'spill!'	*tišpox*	*špox*

with possible "spill-over" to the past stem in child language: *šabar* for *šavar* 'he broke', *šapax* for *šafax* 'he spilled' (but never **šakav* 'he lay down') and in the future of Nif'al in analogy with the past form:

Nif'al Past		Future	Colloquial
niškax	'be forgotten'	*yišaxax*	*yišakax*
nišbar	'be broken'	*yišaver*	*yišaber*
nišpax	'be spilled'	*yišafex*	*yišapex*

More commonly, however, analogical leveling in this position is with the fricative found in the base past-tense form of Pa'al:

Past		Future	Colloquial
raxav	'ride'	*yirkav*	*yirxav*
šavat	'strike'	*yišbot*	*yišvot*
tafar	'sew'	*yitpor*	*yitfor*

In the case of *p~f*, the colloquial variant with *f* almost totally replaces the one with the stop in some cases, and variants with *v* are more frequent than ones with *x*. Possible explanation: in this environment, *f* may only be derived from *p*, and occurrences in this position of *v* from historical *w* are rare, whereas *x* from historical *ḥ* is fairly frequent, i.e. inapplication of analogy prevents (potential) additional ambiguity. Clearly, however, the avoidance-of-ambiguity explanation can only account for **some** cases. As in stem-initial position, if the derivational relationship is not automatic, there is (normally) no analogy:

Pa'al Past		Derived Noun		Potential Analogy
zaxar	'remember'	*mazkir*	'secretary'	**mazxir*
šavar	'break'	*mašber*	'crisis'	**mašver*
šafax	'pour'	*mašpex*	'watering can'	**mašfex*

On the whole, then, it seems that analogy is affected by the frequency of "surface violations" to start with, owing to historical segment mergers, borrowings, etc.; that analogies with *f* and *v* are commoner because less potential ambiguity will result; and that the less inflectional and less automatic the derivation, the lower the likelihood of paradigmatic leveling. Spirantization is no longer a phonetically motivated process, and its application is severely restricted and certainly is not automatic. With the analogy factor, though, it has become fairly variable. Speakers are aware of the stop–fricative relationship.

17.6. Processes that use phonological information, but have always been morphological

17.6.1. Formation of segolate plurals

Segolate plural formation, as in

Singular	Plural	
mélex	*mlaxim*	'king'
kéves	*kvasim*	'sheep'
kélev	*klavim*	'dog'
bóker	*bkarim*	'morning'
séfer	*sfarim*	'book'
kótel	*ktalim*	'wall'

is often described as a phonological process, from the historical segolate base, as in

/malk+im/ 'king' > *malakim* (by *a*-insertion) > *mlakim* (by antepenultimate *a*-deletion) > *mlaxim*

As noted in § 17.5.1, the phonetic motivation for ante-pretonic *a*-deletion in MH is weak, and this ad hoc *a*-insertion cannot be motivated at all. Segolate plural formation, though defined in phonological terms, is a truly morphological rule, paralleling broken plural formation in Arabic. Speakers simply know that the plural of masculine segolates is CC*a*C+*im*. This is a large, prominent class, and its deviant plural pattern is reinforced by numerous members, i.e. is not likely to disappear or to be leveled.

The situation is different in segolate **feminine** nouns. Alongside commonly heard normative plurals like

Sing.	Plural	
giv(')a	gva(')ot	'hill'
dim(')a	dma(')ot	'tear'
yalda	yeladot	'girl'
ricpa	recafot	'floor'
simla	smalot	'dress*s*'
šimša	šmašot	'pane'

one also finds non-normative forms based on the singular:

Sing.	Normative Pl.	Colloquial	
darga	dragot	dargot	'rank'
kalba	klavot	kalbot	'bitch'
mišxa	mešaxot	mišxot	'ointment'
malka	mlaxot	malkot	'queen'

It appears that speakers are not aware of the "segolate origin" of these feminine nouns, which look no different from any other feminine noun with a stressed feminine suffix. They simply know that **some** nouns with +*aˤ* ending take the plural form CC*a*C+*ot*. It is also doubtful that speakers are aware of the non-segolate status of similar forms in which the initial #CV+ sequence is a prefix (usually ˤ*mi*+/ˤ*ma*+ or ˤ*ti*+/ˤ*ta*+), which accounts for their **not** being realized as CC*a*C+*ot*:

Sing.	Plural	
micva	micvot	'commandment'
mar'a	mar'ot	'mirror'
taxana	taxanot	'station'
tikva	tikvot	'hope'
tikra	tikrot	'ceiling'
misra	misrot	'position'

They simply add +*ot*ˤ to the base, just as they do in /kalba+ot/ 'bitches' > *kalbot*.

The formation of segolate plurals, then, has always been morphological, and has nothing to do with phonetic naturalness. Speakers are clearly aware of the relationships between the singular and plural patterns. If any variability is involved, it is restricted to some feminine plural segolates, which tend to be regularized in the colloquial register.

17.7. Conclusion

The phonetic–phonological–morphological continuum does not always work, but on the whole it provides a reasonably coherent picture of MH phonology, showing it to contain the whole gamut of processes and rules found in any other living language—even though it was "revived" as a living spoken medium after almost two millennia. They range from purely phonetic, automatic, variable processes, of which speakers are unaware; through phonological ones that are partially motivated phonetically and somewhat restricted morphologically; through rules that lost all phonetic motivation, have been morphologized, and have become quite opaque; to morphological rules that use phonological information but have always been morphological. With some notable exceptions, the continuum is also characterized by decreased variability and increased speaker awareness.

References

Barkai, Malachi. 1978. "Phonological Opacity vs. Semantic Transparency: Two Cases from Israeli Hebrew." *Lingua* 44: 363–78.

Bat-El, Outi. 1989. *Phonology and Word Structure in Modern Hebrew.* Ph.D. dissertation, University of California, Los Angeles.

Ben-Horin, Gad, & Shmuel Bolozky. 1972. "Hebrew *b*, *p*, *k*—Rule Opacity or Data Opacity?" *Hebrew Computational Linguistics* 5: 24–35.

Blanc, Haim. 1964. "Israeli Hebrew Texts." In *Studies in Egyptology and Linguistics in Honor of H. J. Polotsky*, ed. Haiím B. Rosén, pp. 132–52. Jerusalem: Israel Exploration Society.

Bolozky, Shmuel. 1978. "Some Aspects of Modern Hebrew Phonology." In *Modern Hebrew Structure*, ed. Ruth Aronson Berman, pp. 11–67. Tel Aviv: Universities Publishing Projects.

———. 1979. "On the New Imperative in Colloquial Hebrew." *Hebrew Annual Review* 3: 17–24.

———. 1980. "Paradigm Coherence: Evidence from Modern Hebrew." *Afroasiatic Linguistics* 7/4: 103–26.

———. 1982. "Remarks on Rhythmic Stress in Modern Hebrew." *Journal of Linguistics* 18: 275–89.

———. 1985. "The Domain of Casual Processes in Modern Hebrew." *Linguistic Analysis* 15: 19–27.

Bolozky, Shmuel, & Adnan F. Haydar. 1986. "Colloquial Gender Neutralization in the Numeral System of Modern Hebrew and Lebanese Arabic." *Al-'arabiyya* 19: 19–28.

Bolozky, Shmuel, & Ora R. Schwarzwald. 1990. "On Vowel Assimilation and Deletion in Modern Hebrew." *Hebrew Annual Review* 12: 23–48.

Gil, David. 1986. "A Prosodic Typology of Language." *Folia Linguistica* 20: 165–231.

Henkin, Roni. to appear. *The Imperative and Its Substitutes in Modern Colloquial Hebrew.* (*Mediterranean Language Review* supplementary series).

Kadmon, Nirit. 1983. "On Main Stress, Secondary Stress, Stress Changes, and Casual Speech Deletion in Modern Hebrew." Generals paper, University of Massachusetts/Amherst, ms.

Kiparsky, Paul. 1973. "'Elsewhere' in Phonology." In *A Festschrift for Morris Halle*, ed. Stephen R. Anderson and Paul Kiparsky, pp. 93–106. New York: Holt.

McCarthy, John J. 1986. "OCP Effects: Gemination and Antigemination." *Linguistic Inquiry* 17: 207–63.

Schwarzwald, Ora R. 1981. *Diqduq umeci'ut bapó'al ha'ivri*. Ramat Gan: Bar Ilan Press.

Ultan, Russell. 1978. "The Nature of Future Tenses." In *Universals of Human Language*, ed. Joseph Greenberg, Charles A. Ferguson, & Edith A. Moravcsik, vol. 3, *Word Structure*, pp. 83–123. Stanford: Stanford University Press.

Wexler, Paul. 1990. *The Schizoid Nature of Modern Hebrew: A Slavic Language in Search of a Semitic Past* (Mediterranean Language and Culture Monograph Series 4). Wiesbaden: Harrassowitz.

Chapter 18
Modern Aramaic Phonology
Robert D. Hoberman
State University of New York at Stony Brook

18.1. Introduction

Several entirely separate Aramaic languages are spoken today by a total of two or three hundred thousand people. The modern Aramaic languages fall into four distinct subfamilies, of which three are small both in the number of speakers and in the amount of dialectal diversity within the subfamily. These are: (1) the Ma'lūla group, spoken in three villages near Damascus; (2) the Ṭūrōyo group, including Ṭūrōyo proper, spoken in the Ṭūr 'Abdīn region of southeastern Turkey, and the language of the village of Mlaḥsô in east-central Turkey; (3) Mandaic, spoken in the city of Ahwaz, Iran, and perhaps also in Khorramshahr. These three subfamilies thus amount to four thoroughly distinct languages. (4) The fourth subfamily is modern Northeastern Aramaic. Spoken by the Christian and Jewish minorities of Kurdistan and Iranian Azerbaijan, that is, in northern Iraq and adjacent parts of Iran, Syria, and Turkey, it has far more speakers than all the other branches put together—possibly over two hundred thousand. It is impossible to say precisely how many distinct languages are in this subfamily, because of the vagueness of the distinction between language and dialect. Even so, it is realistic to say that modern Northeastern Aramaic comprises about six distinct languages, which are different in their grammatical structures and mutually comprehensible only with serious difficulty, if at all. Within modern Northeastern Aramaic the linguistic diversity, in terms of phonology, morphology, syntax, and vocabulary, is of the same order of magnitude as in all of colloquial Arabic. Together with the four languages of the other three subfamilies, the total number of modern Aramaic languages is thus about ten. In terms of time-depth of separation, the Ma'lūla group, representing western Aramaic, separated from all the others well over two thousand years ago. Modern Northeastern Aramaic and Ṭūrōyo bear significant similarities, and have been classed together by Jastrow (1990b) as two branches of a single subfamily, Central Neo-Aramaic.

This article will describe the phonologies of two very different Northeastern Aramaic languages, one in some detail and one mentioning just the highlights. For phonological information about the other modern Aramaic subfamilies, the reader can consult the following sources: on Maʻlūla: Arnold 1990; on Ṭūrōyo and Mlaḥsô: Jastrow 1985; on Mandaic: Macuch 1989 and the chapter by Malone in this volume.

18.2. Jewish dialects of northwestern Iraq

Within modern Northeastern Aramaic, the most conservative phonology is found in the Jewish dialects of northwestern Iraq, native to the towns of Zakho, Dohuk, Amadiya, Nerwa, Gzira, and others.[1] All the speakers of these dialects, aside from isolated individuals, are now in Israel. While these dialects differ among themselves in many details, they are all mutually comprehensible, their grammatical structures are the same in all fundamental respects, and their phonologies are likewise similar.[2] I take as representative of this group the dialects of the Jews of Zakho and Amadiya, abbreviated Z and Am. Previously published phonological studies of this group of dialects are Nakano 1969 and Hoberman 1989: 149–56.[3] The following description complements the one in Hoberman 1989, presenting some of the same ideas and information in different ways, but some topics are not duplicated.

Most speakers of these dialects also spoke fluent Kurdish, the language of the surrounding Muslim majority, and their Aramaic has many loanwords and structural influences from Kurdish (and via Kurdish also from Turkish and Arabic). They also knew a certain number of Hebrew terms even before migrating to Israel, but only a few individuals knew Arabic.

The description that follows is synchronic. However, for the interest of those who are familiar with historical Aramaic, some basic diachronic information is also given. For more detailed information on the history of modern Aramaic phonology see Sabar 1976: xxxiii–xli, Nöldeke 1868, and Maclean 1895.

1. In the Aramaic dialect being described the names of these towns are *zaːxo*, *dohŭk* or *dhoːk*, *ʕamĭdya*, *nerwa* or *neːrwa*, and *gziːra*. Amadiya in Modern Standard Arabic is *al-ʕamaːdiːya*.
2. These dialects differ significantly from (but are mutually intelligible with) the Christian dialects of the same region, which are therefore not covered by the following description. Christian dialects of the region are documented in Krotkoff 1982 and Sara 1974.
3. In addition to numerous published Zakho texts, I have obtained a great deal of the Zakho data and some important observations from two sources for which I am especially grateful: unpublished notes of the late H. J. Polotsky, used with his permission, and extensive conversations with Professor Yona Sabar of UCLA, a native speaker of Zakho Aramaic.

Modern Aramaic sounds and words are written here in italics in a broad phonetic transcription equivalent to the American descriptivist phonemic level, which corresponds biuniquely with the phonetics. (A more convenient, simplified way of representing the vowels is suggested in § 18.2.4.) The hyphen is used to assist the reader by showing a morpheme boundary, but it has no phonetic implication. The symbol = indicates the linkage of a word and a proclitic or enclitic (see § 18.2.5.1). Occasionally phonetic or morphophonemic representations are used (in square brackets [ ] or vertical lines | | respectively), though even then the transcription is mainly phonemic in the above sense and phonetic detail or morphophonemic abstraction is shown only for the particular details being illustrated. Many words are identical in the Zakho and Amadiya dialects and where this is so no dialect labels are used. Thus a label Z or Am. implies that the word is different or lacking (or sometimes merely unattested) in the other dialect. There is one extension to this policy: since nearly all words with *θ* in Amadiya have *s* in Zakho, a word written with *θ* and appearing without a dialect label exists in Amadiya as given, with *θ*, and in Zakho in identical form but with *s*; for example, *be:θa* implies Am. *be:θa* and Z *be:sa*. Stress in words of more than one syllable is most often on the penultimate syllable, and will not be indicated in that case but only when it is other than penult.

18.2.1. Consonants

18.2.1.1. Inventory, phonetics, and phonological processes

Table 18-1 shows the consonant phonemes of the Amadiya dialect, excluding the emphatics, which are discussed below. Zakho has the same inventory

Table 18-1. Amadiya Aramaic Consonants

Bilabial	Labio-dental	Dental	(Alveo)-palatal	Velar	Uvular	Pharyngeal	Glottal
p b		t d	č ǰ	k g	q	ʕ	ʔ
	f v	θ		x ɣ		ħ	
		s z	š ž				
m		n					
		l					
		r					
		w	y				h

except that it lacks θ, while the dialect of Dohuk has both θ and ð.

18.2.1.1.1. Phonetic specifications

All the symbols have their conventional values, and only a few details need to be mentioned specifically. The voiced pharyngeal ʕ is a stop, probably a glottal stop with simultaneous pharyngeal constriction, unlike some varieties of Arabic in which it is a frictionless continuant or a semivowel. The voiceless stops are slightly aspirated before a vowel. Before a velar stop *n* is velar and before a uvular it is uvular. The tap *r* and trill *rr* are often retroflex (but without the lip-rounding of some varieties of English). *w* is most often labiodental, less often bilabial. The fricative *v* occurs only in words borrowed from Kurdish; it is rare in Amadiya, since many words which contain *v* in Zakho have *w* in Amadiya, as Z *zvirre*, Am. *zwirre* 'he turned around'.

18.2.1.1.2. Emphatic coarticulation

The "emphatic" coarticulation is identical, both phonetically and phonologically, to the same phenomenon which is familiar in Arabic. The articulatory and auditory nature of emphasis is complex: its articulation is a complex of pharyngealization, velarization, and sometimes also laryngeal elevation, labialization, and increased tension. Studies of Arabic, as well as of a different variety of modern Aramaic (Odisho 1988: 114–19), have consistently shown the central component to be retraction of the tongue root producing constriction of the pharynx. Neighboring consonants and vowels assimilate in emphasis to an emphatic consonant. Hence there is normally more than one emphatic segment in a word, e.g. Am. *paːḷiṭ* 'that he go out', but emphasis does not always pervade a word; for Am. *m̩leːle* 'he filled', informants reject the pronunciation *m̩ḷeːḷe*. Emphasis also occurs in the absence of any emphatic consonant in the demonstratives Am. *ʔawaːha* (masculine) and *ʔayaːha* (feminine) 'that yonder'.

The presence or absence of emphasis is phonemic, as the following minimal and near-minimal pairs illustrate.

p	gupaːle 'crutches'		Am. guppalgaːya 'middle (adj.)'
			gimpaːleʔ 'he divides'
ḅ	baːš 'good'		Z baːžir 'city'
	Am. baːžir 'city'		baːθe 'he will come'
			baːte 'houses'
ṭ	Z tʔaːya 'to seek'		Z tʔaːra 'to wake up'
	ṣṭiːxa 'spread'		Z štiːqa 'quiet'
	Z ṣṭiːḥa 'lying down'		
	Z ṭreːle 'he drove (an animal)'		tre 'two'

Modern Aramaic Phonology 317

ḍ	qiṭla 'killing'	Z qitil 'murder'
ṣ	ʔo:ḍa, ʔo:ḍe 'room, rooms'	ʔo:da, ʔo:de 'slave, slaves'
ẓ	xa:ṣa 'back'	Z xa:sa (Am. xa:θa) 'sister, new'
	biṣla 'onion'	pisra 'meat'
	Z qa:ẓe 'that he arrange'	Z qa:ze 'ducks'
	Z qa:ẓax 'that we arrange'	Z qa:za 'duck'
	qaẓa:ne 'pot' Z sg., Am. pl.	
	Z qẓa:ya 'to spend time'	Z qza:la 'neck'
m̱	Z m̱a:ya, Am. m̱a:e 'water'	ma:yiθ 'that he die'
č̣	Z č̣me:la 'it was extinguished'	Z jmidla 'she froze'
	Z č̣o:ʔa 'smooth'	čo:l 'desert, wilderness'
	Z č̣eʔle 'he became smooth'	Z čehya 'tired (fem.sg.)'
	Z č̣ya:ʔa 'be smooth'	
	Z mač̣o:ʔe 'to smooth'	

m̱ and ḻ mḻe:le 'he filled' mle:le 'it sufficed'
gmaḻe 'he fills' Am. gma:le 'it is enough'
Z kma:le 'it is enough'

Z mʕamo:ṛe 'bother, boss around' Z maʔmo:re 'build'
Z ḻa:ma 'cheek'

ṛ   Z kṛe:le 'he rented' Z kre:le 'he was/became short'
Z kiṛya 'rented (adj., masc.sg.) Z kirya 'short (masc. sg.)
kiṛe 'rent, fee, payment' Am. giran 'expensive'
to:ṛa 'Torah' to:ra 'bull'
Am. gma:ṛix 'he smells' gma:reʔ 'it hurts'
Z qo:ṛi 'kettle' Z qo:ri 'my grave; they bury'
Am. ʔiṛxa 'guest' (Z ʔaṛxa) ʔirxe '(water-)mill'
Am. ʔuṛxa 'road' (Z ʔuṛxa) ʔurza 'male'
Am. ʔuṛwa 'big' ʔirba 'sheep, goats'

ṛ and p̣ Z ṛp̣e:le '(an animal) was sicced Z rpe:le 'was loose'
(released to attack)'
Z marp̣o:ye 'to sic (an animal)' Z marpo:ye to make loose'

p̣ and ḻ p̣aḻḻa 'burning coal' palge 'half, middle'
pḻi:ma 'crooked, twisted' pli:xa 'worked'
Z p̣aḻḻunka 'crippied'
Z ḻap̣p̣a 'paw'

p̣ and ẓ p̣o:ẓa Z 'face, countenance', po:xa 'wind'
Am. 'chin'
Z ẓap̣p̣a 'large turd'

p and č Z *ča:pa* 'slap'   Z *čippiksa* 'drop'
         Am. *čappa*, pl. *-e* 'handful'
         Am. *čappe* (Z *čappe*) 'left (side)'
ṛ and ẓ Z *gzirre* (or *gzịṛṛe*) 'he decreed'   Z *gzirre* 'he circumcised'
         Z *zaṛṛa* 'huge'   Z *zo:ra* Am. *zʔo:ra* 'small'
č and ṭ Z *čanṭa* 'suitcase'   Z *čanta* 'cloth shoulder bag'

Consonants occur geminated intervocalically: *libba* 'heart', *xiṭṭe* 'wheat', *sippa:θa* 'lips' (sg. *sipθa*), *ʔatta* 'now', *ʔizza* 'she-goat', *mxaθθo:θe* 'renew', *gᵾθθa*, pl. *gᵾθθa:θa* 'ball of yarn', Z *mijjo:ja* 'washed-out sliver of soap', Z *mažža* 'brain', *ʔaxxa* 'here', *šinne* 'years', *šimma*, pl. *šimma:he* 'name', *gilla:le* 'grasses, herbs', *hayya* 'quickly, early', *hawwa* 'good', Am. *ṣawwarči* 'photographer'; *saʕʕa* 'hour', Z *raḥḥat* 'calm, relaxed, at ease, healthy', Am. *šiḥḥa:ṭa* 'matchbox'. The glottals *ʔ* and *h* are not attested as geminates. At the beginning of a word a geminate consonant appears when a prefix is identical (either underlyingly or by assimilation) to the first consonant of the stem: *p-pa:yiš* |b+pa:yiš| 'he will become or remain' *b-ba:xe* 'he will cry', *m-ma:yiθ* |b+ma:yiθ| 'he will die', *q-qa:re* |k+qa:re| 'he studies'. Initial gemination is not always audible unless it is preceded by a vowel-final word.

Adjacent consonants assimilate regressively in voicing and emphasis, Am. |b+dabt+i| *bdapti* 'they will heal', |gxɨk+le| *kxɨkle*, |b+qa:re:| *pqa:re* 'he will read', |bɨxza:ya| *bɨyza:ya* 'seeing' (cf. *xa:ze* 'that he see'), *ṣḷo:θa* 'prayer', Z *mista* |mɨzzta| 'hair' (pl. *mizze*). In assimilation *ʔ* counts as voiced: *gʔa:riq* 'he runs'. In addition the future-tense prefix *b* becomes *m* before a following nasal: |b+na:pɨl| *mna:pɨl* 'he will fall', |b+ma:yiθ| *mma:yiθ* 'he will die'. The general present tense prefix *k-/g-* assimilates to an adjacent consonant in the usual manner illustrated above, but it also assimilates across an intervening vowel in verbs lacking an initial consonant, being voiceless in *ke:xɨl* 'he eats', *ke:θe* 'he comes', but voiced in *ge:mɨr* 'he says', Am. *ge:wɨd* Z *ge:wɨz* 'he does', *ge:zɨl* 'he goes'. (The future tense prefix does not alternate in this way, e.g. *ba:xɨl*.) The lexicalized nature of voicing in the *k-/g-* prefix is evident in Z *kma:le* 'it suffices' (in contrast to the usual case, where the prefix is voiced before nasals: *gma:le* 'he fills', *gma:yiθ* 'he dies', and Am. *gma:le* 'it suffices').

Like other consonants, *ʔ* can appear in any position within a syllable or word: *ʔza:la* 'to spin (thread)', *qaṭʔa* 'that she cut', *tarʔa* 'door', *paʔla* 'laborer', *qteʔle* 'he cut', *daʔra* 'that she return', *ša:meʔ* 'that he hear', *qa:teʔ* 'that he cut'. Initially before a vowel there is no opposition between *ʔ* and zero, and *ʔ* is usually pronounced; thus *ʔa:zɨl* ([ʔa:zɨl] or [a:zɨl]) is ambiguous between |ʔa:zɨl| 'that he spin' (from the root *ʔzl*, historical *ʕzl*), and |a:zɨl| 'that he go' (from the root zl or ∅zl, historical *ʔzl); the difference is apparent in other forms: bʔa:zil 'he will spin', ba:zil 'he will go', ʔzilla 'she spun', zilla 'she went'. Nonetheless ʔ may elide optionally, especially in a syllable coda, as in ša:meʔ, qṭeʔle, for which ša:me, qṭe:le are also heard.

18.2.1.2. Historical excursus

More than two thousand years ago Aramaic underwent a sound change known as spirantization, in which *p b t d k g* changed into the corresponding fricatives when postvocalic and not geminate. These fricatives were at first allophones, but the loss of many short vowels and of some instances of gemination caused them to be phonemic and spirantization to be a morphophonemic rule. In modern Aramaic the rule is dead, all the words with a given root having either the stop or the fricative, for instance, from historical *lbš: lwa:ša 'wearing, putting on (clothing)', la:wiš 'that he wear', malwo:še 'dressing'. There are only a few relic alternations, which are listed below. Hand in hand with the loss of alternation, subsequent sound changes affected three of the fricative variants, so that they are less similar to the corresponding stops than they were at first. Spirantized *b, which was at first undoubtedly a bilabial fricative, has merged with historical *w as w, as in *kātebā which became kaθwa 'that she write', or *dābeq which is now da:wiq 'that he hold'; it frequently formed diphthongs, most of which are reduced to long vowels, as in do:qa ldawq-al 'that she hold', ytu:la lyti:w+l+al 'she sat down', Z mʉt(t)o:ta Am. mʉttawta 'placed, seated (fem.sg.)'. Spirantized *g has merged with the reflexes of *ʕ and *ʔ as ʔ, such as peʔla 'radish'. Spirantized *p has merged back with the stop as p, as in na:piq 'that he go out', la:yip 'that he learn'. However, it remained as w (more precisely, it is reflected in coalesced diphthongs o: or u:) in three words: mno:š- 'by oneself' from *b+napš-; ṭlo:xe 'lentils', cf. Syriac *ṭlāp̄ē; ru:ša 'shoulder', cf. Syriac rap̄šā 'shovel'.[4] The fricative variant of *k remains as x: xille 'he ate'.

The interdentals θ ð exist as such in the dialect of the Jews of Dohuk, one of the same group of dialects with Zakho and Amadiya, as well as in many Christian dialects. In Zakho these have become sibilants s z. In Amadiya *θ remained, while *ð became a stop, d. Speakers from Nerwa took the

---

4. On the etymology of ru:ša, a loanword from Akkadian, including the semantic connection of 'shovel' and 'shoulder', see Krotkoff 1985: 126–27. The change of f to w also applied in a couple of loanwords, Am. táwsir 'translation of a religious text' (from Arabic tafsi:r), Am. tawtíš 'inspection' (from Arabic tafti:š).

Amadiya pattern one step further, shifting the θ to s.[5] The correspondences, to which there are only very rare exceptions, are thus as follows:

	'house'	'hand'
Dohuk	beːθa	ʔiːða
Zakho	beːsa	ʔiːza
Amadiya	beːθa	ʔiːda
Nerwa	beːsa	ʔiːda

Older Aramaic ħ and ʕ shifted to x and ʔ respectively, merging with the reflexes of spirantized *k and *ʔ. Pharyngeal ħ and ʕ are pronounced, however, in numerous words of Arabic origin, some of them otherwise completely Aramaicised, such as maħkoːye 'speaking'. It would be incorrect to say that ħ and ʕ were first lost and then restored as borrowed phonemes; in reality there was never a stage of the language that lacked ħ and ʕ. This is true because they survive in a few native Aramaic words, especially in the environment of emphatics and q: raħuːqa 'far' and the verb rħaːqa 'be far', ṛumħa 'spear', ʕuṭma 'hip', ʕapṣa 'gall nut', mʕaṛoːṭe 'farting', ʕamuːqa 'deep'. They are also pronounced in numerous borrowings from Hebrew, and such borrowing must have been taking place continuously since ancient times. In any case, ħ and ʕ are plentiful and fully integrated in the modern language.

18.2.1.3. Relics of spirantization

Frozen relics of the formerly productive (originally allophonic) process of spirantization remain in a few lexicalized alternations.

b ~ w: zaːwin 'that he buy', mzaːbin 'that he sell'; kalba 'dog', pl. kalwe; ʔirba 'sheep', pl. ʔirwe; xšaːwa 'to think', xižboːna 'thought'; and perhaps b 'in', xa-w-ʔiṣra 'ten times as much'.

g ~ ʔ or ʕ: palge 'half', mpaloːʔe 'to split'; gaːw- 'in', l-ʕoːya 'inside' (cf. l-warya 'outside' from *l-bar).

t ~ Am. θ, Z s: beːθa, 'house', pl. baːte. There are two partially rule-governed patterns of alternation. (1) The two variant forms of the feminine ending -ta ~ -θa (Z -sa) are selected partly on a lexical basis,[6] but in deverbal nouns and adjectives they are governed by a simple rule: the suffix is -ta after conso-

---

5. An identical assymetry between the reflexes of *θ and *ð is found in the dialect of the Jews of Azerbaijan (Garbell 1965), in which *ð became d but *θ became l, remaining a continuant (thus ida 'hand', bela 'house'), and also in the Ashkenazic pronunciation of Hebrew, with s for *θ but d for ð... yod 'hand', bayis 'house'. Jewish dialects of southeastern Kurdistan have l for both. The Christian Urmi dialect and Iraqi Koine have stops: beːtʰa, iːda.

6. Sara 1993 analyzes the complex patterning of these two variants in a closely related dialect.

nant-final stems (e.g. Am. *ptixta* 'open') and after the vowels *o:* and *u:* derived from coalescence of a vowel with a final *w* from historical spirantized *b*: Am. *kθu:ta* (historical *kθībtā) 'written', but it is -*θa* after vowel-final stems derived from final-*y* roots: *gli:θa* 'revealed, exposed'. (2) A second fairly regular process changes stem-final *θ* (and its reflex *s* in Zakho) to *t* before a suffix beginning with *l*. This happens in preterite forms of the verb *mya:θa* 'die', such as *mitle* |miθ+le| 'he died'; in Zakho the intervening suffix -*wa:*- 'past' prevents this, so *miswa:le* 'he had died', but in Amadiya the *t* is characteristic of the preterite stem even with -*wa:*-, thus Am. *mitwa:lu* 'they had died'. Similarly Am. *ʔi:θ* Z *ʔi:s* 'there is', *ʔitle*, Z *ʔiswa:le* 'he had', for which Amadiya has both *ʔiθwa:le* and *ʔitwa:le*.

18.2.2. Syllable types

The basic syllable types, which may appear in any part of a word, are: CV, CV:, and CVC.[7] At the beginning of a word an extra consonantal position may be added to any of these, allowing for an unlimited variety of initial consonant clusters.[8] These are so common and varied primarily because the most common verb template is of the form CCV:C. At the end of a word an extra consonantal position may also be added, although this is relatively rare, yielding two additional syllable types: CV:C and CVCC. Of these two, CVCC is the rarer, occuring in about 1% of the vocabulary, all in words borrowed from Arabic and Kurdish, including Am. *dawramand* 'wealthy man',

---

7. In Amadiya, where intervocalic *ʔ* and *y* before front vowels tend to elide, there are a number of sequences of vowels and thus of medial syllables beginning with a vowel: *ki:e* 'he knows', *ki:in* 'I (masc.) know', *ki:a* 'she knows' (for *ki:ʔe* etc.), Am. *ma:e* 'water' (for *ma:ye*), and in general all sequences of *a:ye* or *a:yi*, as in many verbs like *pa:yiš* 'become, remain', may be pronounced [a:e], [a:i], also *ʔamo:(y)i* 'my paternal uncle' for *ʔamo:y-i*, cf. *ʔamo:yʉx* 'your paternal uncle'.

The rare tense vowels in closed medial and closed unstressed final syllables are phonetically rather short, as in Z *brindar* 'wounded' (cf. *bri:n* 'wound'), Am. *zilga* 'a match (for lighting)', *nerwa* (name of a town), *gmenxa* 'she looks' (cf. *gme:nix* 'he looks'), Am. *jemke* 'twins', *bemke* 'pine nuts', Am. *ʔitwa* (in free variation with *ʔitwa* 'there was', *bista:na* 'garden', Am. *fista:na* (but Z *fista:na*) 'woman's dress', Am. *qʉrduθkí* 'in Kurdish', *siruθkí* 'in Christian Aramaic' (cf. *qʉrduθ* 'the Kurds, Kurdish language', *siruθ* 'Syriac Christendom'), *taxmin* 'thought', *hakim* 'physician'. It is difficult to determine whether there is a contrast of vowel length between words like *ne(:)rwa* or *be(:)mke* and words like Am. *herge* 'clothing', Am. *meθya* 'that she bring', since there are few words of either class and the nature of the following consonants, whether sonorants or stops, seems to play a role.

8. Detailed listings of consonant clusters in other dialects are given in Sara 1974: 41–47 and Odisho 1988: 64–78.

Am. *dirist* 'straight', Z *xụṛṭ* 'violent', *ṛast* 'right', *bass* 'only', Z *mịjǰ* 'fog', Z *sirr* 'deep cold'. Final syllables of the form CV:C exist only when stressed, and occur productively in the imperative singular and (in Amadiya only) the bare preterite of first conjugation verbs and in certain inflectional suffixes. Examples: *bri:n* 'wound', *ba:š* 'good', *čo:l* 'wilderness, desert', *ye:r* 'other', *hi:l* 'until', *he:š* 'yet, still', *ʔi:θ* 'there is', Am. *li:t* Z *le:s* 'there is not', *ḥa:l* 'situation', *jwa:n* 'young', *jwi:n* 'side, party'; for verbs see the following section.

18.2.3. *Canonical shape and minimal length of words*

Native Aramaic nouns and adjectives are at least of the structure CVCCV or CV:CV, and there may be additional preceding material: Am. *šimša* 'sun', Am. *garma* 'bone', Am. *ʔụtma* 'thigh', Am. *gụpta* 'cheese', Am. *ke:pa* 'stone', Am. *go:ra* 'man', Am. *ga:re* 'roof', Am. *ʔirxe* 'mill', *ʔiro:ta* 'Friday', *ʔili:θa* 'fat tail of sheep', Am. *raki:xa* 'soft', Am. *ʕaṛmo:ta* 'pomegranate', Am. *qinya:na* 'large domestic animal', Am. *gụppalga:ya* 'middle (adj.)'. Loanwords may be shorter, and may end in a consonant: *giran* 'expensive', *čo:l* 'wilderness', Am. *gaha* 'knuckle', *kịṛe* 'fee, payment'.

The syllabic shape of verbs is strictly governed by the canonical forms of the system of discontinuous (nonconcatenative) morphology in the usual Semitic mold, in which the shortest regular verb forms, first conjugation imperatives, have the shape (C)CV:(C): *šqo:l* 'take', *xo:l* 'eat', *χzi:* 'see'. A few irregular imperatives are shorter: *hal* 'give', *mar* 'say', *θa* 'come'.

Adverbs, prepositions, exclamations, and other closed-class items are frequently very short: *biš* 'more', *ču* or *čụ* 'no', *ʔe(:)* 'this', *xu* (exclamation of surprise), *dị* (exclamation of offering, giving: 'here!'), *ba* (exclamation: 'but, so'), *b* 'with, at, by', *d* 'that, of', *w* or *u* 'and'.

18.2.4. *Vowels*
18.2.4.1. *General properties*

There are seven distinct vowel qualities, *i ị e a o ụ u*, and a feature of vowel length, V:. These are organized into a system of five long and three short vowel phonemes: *i: e: a: o: u: i a ụ*; there are in addition a few mostly rule-governed occurrences of short *i, e, u,* and *o. ị* and *ụ* are always short, while the others—the five peripheral vowel qualities—occur phonetically both long and short. However, the only vowel quality for which there is a secure phonemic opposition of long and short quantity is *a*. For the other four peripheral vowels, *i e o u,* the long and short variants are in complementary distribution; they are short in closed non-final syllables and in unstressed final syllables whether open or closed, and long otherwise; details will be specified below.[9] In the position of maximal inventory of vowel oppositions, open non-final syllables, there are thus eight phonemic vowels, five long and three short: *i: e: a: o: u: i a ʉ*. In the position with the smallest inventory, non-final syllables closed by an obstruent (other than glottal), there are three vowels, all short: *i a ʉ* (plus short *i* and *u* in a handful of items each). In final open unstressed syllables, there are five vowels: *i e a o u*. For details of these inventories, see Hoberman 1989: 153–54.

The transcription used here could be simplified without loss of information in the following way. Instead of *i* and *ʉ* write *i* and *u*, and write [i] and [u] always with the sign of length, even when they are short but tense: *i:* and *u:*. This causes no confusion because [i] and [i:], [u] and [u:] are in complementary distribution, as mentioned above. Thus the words *zilla* 'she went', Am. *zilga* 'match', *bista:na* 'orchard', *ħakim* 'physician', *ʔʉrza* 'male', *siruθ* 'Syriac Christendom', *si:* 'go (imperative)', *di* (an interjection associated with offering) would be written as *zilla, zi:lga, bi:sta:na, ħaki:m, ʔurza, siru:θ, si:, di*. The sign of length can be omitted in unstressed final vowels, where all vowels are short except in certain intonation contours (discussed below) and *i* and *ʉ* do not occur: *kxa:ze* 'they see', *kθu:li* 'I wrote'. Although for the purpose of this article I chose to use a more phonetically revealing system, the simpler system just described is phonemically adequate and would be suitable for such purposes as the publication of texts, lexicons, and grammatical analysis.[10]

18.2.4.2. Vowel quality

The vowels *i* and *ʉ* are more central and distinctly lower than *i* and *u, i* varying from [ɪ] to [ə] and *ʉ* from [ʊ] to [ɵ].[11] Thus *i* and *ʉ* differ mainly in terms of rounding, rather than in the front–back dimension, while the contrast between *i* and *i(:)*, and similarly between *ʉ* and *u(:)*, is more in respect to quality than it is in quantity. The phonemic opposition between *i* and *ʉ* is

---

9. There is a marginal phonemic opposition of quantity in the cases of *i* and *e*. In *xamší=ba:te* 'fifty houses' the stressed *i* is short but tense, as opposed to long *i:* in *si:* 'go (imperative)' and to lax *i* in *dí* (an interjection associated with offering). In *méθi:li* 'bring me (imperative)' the *e* is usually short, as opposed to long *e:* in *me:θi* 'bring (imperative)'. Short *e* and *o* are discussed in more detail below.

10. This system was used in Avinery 1988, following unpublished work by H. J. Polotsky. A different sort of simplification, taking advantage of the low functional load of vowel quantity to reduce the number of symbols, was used in Hoberman 1989, following Nakano 1969.

11. Because of this central quality some authors have written *ʉ* as *ü*.

demonstrated by such pairs as *ʔirba* 'sheep, goats' vs. *ʔurza* 'male', Am. *ʔurwa* 'big', Am. *witwa* 'you (masc.sg.) were' vs. Am. *wutwa* 'you (pl.) were', *šargume* 'turnips' vs. *ṭlimme* 'thin, flat breads', *gilla* 'herb, grass' vs. *julle* 'clothing', Am. *ʔirxa* 'guest' vs. *ʔurxa* 'road, way'. However, in some environments the opposition is neutralized, adjacent labial and emphatic consonants tending to produce a sound that is more like *u*, as in *ṣruxlu* for |ṣri:x+lu| 'they shouted', and there is sometimes free variation, as between *ʔidyo* and *ʔudyo* 'today', *pumma* and *pimma* 'mouth', *či=mindi* and *ču=mindi* 'nothing'.

Some speakers pronounce *o:* as distinctly fronted, sometimes almost to the point of IPA [ø], as in [pø:ši:ya] 'turban', Z [pø:xa] 'wind'. This fronting is prevented by a neighboring emphatic, [po:ẓa] Am. 'chin', Z 'face and upper body', but not by *q*: [šø:qi:] 'that they leave', Am. [pø:qa] 'nostril'. *u:* is not similarly fronted: [gø:ra] 'man', [gu:re] 'men'.

Long *a:* and short *a* are low central vowels in most environments, low back in the neighborhood of emphatics. Some Zakho speakers front short *a* [æ] before an *r* in the same syllable, provided it is not preceded by an emphatic: [kærma] 'orchard, vineyard', [qærsa] 'cold', but [ṭarpa] 'leaf'. In Amadiya final *a* is strikingly rounded and raised to [ɔ] regardless of the preceding consonant. In Amadiya too *a:* is rounded and raised to [ɔ:], almost [o], next to an emphatic labial consonant, as in [bɔ:š] 'good' (but Zakho [ba:š]), Am. [bɔ:žir] 'city' (Z [ba:žir]), Am. [gmɔ:le] 'he fills', Am. [mɔ:li] 'my property', but no rounding in Am. [gma:le] 'it is enough, stop!', [ba:be] 'his father', [ṭa:le] 'to him', Am. [gma:ṛɨx] 'he smells'.

Short *e* and *o* are only marginally phonemic, as nearly all of their occurrences are predictable by three simple and superficial rules:

1. All word-final unstressed vowels are short, though tense and peripheral, including *e* and *o* as in Am. *de:re* 'monastery', Am. *ka:lo* 'bride', Am. *ʕe:qo* 'trouble', *kxa:ze* 'he sees'.
2. Before *ʔ* or *h* we find *e* and *o* instead of *i* and *u* respectively. This rule is quite regular in verb conjugation and in deverbal nouns and adjectives, so that corresponding to *ptixle* 'he opened' we have *šmeʔle* 'he heard'.[12] Similarly *e* and *o* appear before *h* or *ʔ* in other nouns and adjectives: *behna* 'breath, moment', *dehwa* 'gold', *sehra:ne* 'communal festive picnic', *beʔta*

---

12. It apparently does not apply in preterite and perfect forms of second-conjugation verbs with a first root consonant *ʔ*: Z *muʔimra* 'built', Am. *muʔwiṛe* 'he caused to enter', *muʔu:ra:le* 'he caused her to enter'.

'egg', be?e 'eggs', Am. šmo?ta 'fame', zdo?θa 'fear', Z čo?ta 'smooth (fem.sg.)'.[13]

3. Short e and o appear in a few morphemes, especially in Zakho, as a free variant of the more frequent i and ʉ. All of these alternate morphologically with eː and oː respectively. These items are the following:

- the suffix -et ~ -it 'second person masculine singular' in ʔaːhet ~ ʔaːhit 'you (masc.sg.), wet ~ wit 'you are', which has morphologically conditioned or free alternates -eːtin (verbal agreement marker) and plural -eːtuːn;
- the second person masculine singular possessive suffix Z -ox, sometimes -oːx (Am. -ʉx), plural -oːxuːn;
- the extended diminutive suffix -ʉn-ka ~ -on-ka ~ -in-ka ~ -oːn-ka, e.g. Z ǰwanqonkat 'lads', the first part of which appears alone in historical diminutives such as broːna 'son';
- the enclitic form of xeːta 'other', which may be pronounced xeːt, xet, or xit.

Aside from these rule-governed instances of e, there are a few items showing that it is a phoneme marginally distinct from other vowels. They are mɨθya 'brought (participle, masc.sg.)' versus Am. meθya (Z masya) 'that she bring' (cf. meːθe 'that he bring'); Am. begwiːne (also Am. bʉgwiːne) but not *bigwiːne 'eyebrows' versus bigwaːra 'marrying';[14] Am. ʔeyya 'this (masc. and fem.)' vs. hayya 'quickly'. It is clear from all this that the phonemic status of e is more secure than that of o.

18.2.4.2.1. DIPHTHONGS

The older Aramaic diphthongs ay and aw generally coalesced to eː and oː respectively in these dialects. However, they exist in a small number of words, many of them borrowed, with considerable dialectal variation: Am. kawdɨnta 'mule' (Z koːzinta), Am. ʔawraːza (Z ʔavraːza) 'hill', Z gawda 'trunk (of body)', Am. mʉttawta (Z mit(t)oːta) 'having been seated, placed', Z xaw?isra

---

13. In Amadiya some words show free variation: Am. dehna and dihna 'oil rendered from meat', šeʔde and šiʔde 'almonds' (in Zakho only dehna, šeʔze), but not all do: Am. šʉʔla 'work; thing, matter' does not have the alternate *šoʔla (cf. Z šuːla). Before pharyngeals and liquids the vowel sometimes sounds more like e than like i, as in moːṣel 'Mosul', mfoːṣel 'cut', Am. baːžer 'city', Am. moːdeʕlu 'they lost', Am. piːramer 'old man', but they are in free variation with i. Both Am. herge and hirge 'clothing' are heard (but in Zakho only hirge 'ragged, poor clothing').

14. begwiːne was etymologically a compound, *beː(θ) + gwiːne, cf. classical Syriac gḇīnē 'eyebrows'.

'ten times as much', Am. *tawsir* (Z *tafsir*) 'translation of a religous text', Am. *tawtĭš* 'search, examination', Z *ʔaw* 'that (masc.), *ʔay* 'that (fem.)', *fayda* 'benefit, use', *mayle* (or *ma=yle*) 'what=is'. Several forms of the verb Am. *msahoːwe* contain the diphthong *ew*: *gimsaːhew* 'he gets frightened', *msoːhewli* 'I got frightened' (in Zakho the verb is not used and the related noun Z *sahve* 'fear' and adjective *sahvaːna* 'awesome' have *v*).

18.2.4.3. Vowel quantity

Long *iː eː aː oː uː* are longest in open syllables and when stressed, shorter in closed syllables and when unstressed. Unstressed at the end of a word, such as the *i* of *kšaqli* 'they take', vowels are normally short, though tense. This is true whether the word is in the middle of a phrase or at the end of a sentence, but at the end of a phrase or clause which does not end a sentence, i.e. in a situation which would call for a comma in English orthography, such vowels are long.

Vowel quantity is phonemic, and it is not too hard to find minimal or near-minimal pairs to prove it: *bale* 'but' vs. *baːle* 'his attention'; Z *bala* 'trouble' vs. *baːla* 'attention'; *maːne* 'that he/they count', *mani* 'who'; *gibe* 'he wants' vs. *geːbe* 'his direction'; Am. *šargume* 'turnips' vs. Am. *guːma* 'hole, pit' vs. *koːma* 'black'; *meːθi* 'bring (imperative singular)' vs. *méθiːli* 'bring me'. However there are strong statistical correlations between vowel length and syllable type: open syllables tend to have long vowels, and closed syllables tend to have short vowels. Thus the functional load of vowel quantity in modern Aramaic is rather low. If we define UNMARKED QUANTITY as long in open syllables and short in closed syllables, then only about 8% of all syllables in a running text have vowels of marked quantity.[15] To see the significance of this we can compare it with another Semitic language which likewise has an opposition of vowel quantity and which moreover belongs to the same *Sprachbund* as the Aramaic dialects being described: the Arabic spoken by the Jews of Aqra and Arbil (Jastrow 1990a). In this Arabic dialect, marked syllables make up about 40% of the total: five times the proportion in the Aramaic of Zakho and Amadiya.[16] We can go further by

---

15. For this purpose final unstressed vowels (as in *baxta* 'woman' or *šaqli* 'that they take') are counted as long. Although their phonetic length is variable, as described above, they are tense, not lax. Moreover they are long when any suffix is added: *šaqliːle* 'that they take him'.
16. The distinctiveness of modern Aramaic vis-à-vis languages of the world lies in the unusually high frequency of long vowels in Aramaic. Thus the text frequency of all long vowels in a Zakho or Amadiya Aramaic text is about 64% of all vowels (or 29% if we exclude final unstressed tense vowels such as that in *šaqli*). Compare this with 45% (or 31%)

looking at specific types of syllables. Of marked syllables, the most prevalent type is an open syllable with a short vowel. These amount to about 5% of all syllables. Of marked syllables in which the vowel is long, the majority (2% of all syllables) are stressed monosyllabic words, such as *čo:l* 'wilderness', *dmo:x* 'go to sleep (imperative)'.

The preponderance of what I have called unmarked syllables—closed syllables with short vowels and open syllables with long vowels—is supported by numerous and productive alternations of the type *kša:qil* 'he takes', *kšaql-a* 'she takes'. The proper analysis of such alternations is not certain, however, because there are many other types of alternations between long and short vowels and there are a fair number of deviations from this pattern of alternation. Long and short vowels alternate in the following kinds of situation. Note that in most of these alternations *i* is the short counterpart of both *i:* and *e:*, and *u* is the short counterpart of both *u:* and *o:*.

1. Open versus closed syllable with syncope or epenthesis of *i*, V:C*i*C (or V:C*i*C-C) ~ VCC-V. This pattern is extremely common, being totally productive in verb inflection. Examples: Am. *kpa:tix* 'he opens', *kpa:tixlu* 'he opens them', *kpatxa* 'she opens', *kpatxa:lu* 'she opens them', *kpatxin* 'I open', *kpatxe:tu:n* 'you (pl.) bring'; Am. *mo:rimle* 'he lifted, raised', *murmi:le* 'he raised them', *ke:xil* 'he eats', *kixli* 'they eat', *kixle:tu:n* 'you (pl.) eat', *gme:θe* 'he brings', *gme:θax* 'we bring', Am. *gmeθya* Z *gmasya* 'she brings'.

COUNTERINSTANCES: Several borrowed nouns and adjectives of the same shape do not lose the *i* or shorten the vowel when a suffix is added: *ʕa:qil* 'mind', *ʕa:qile* 'his mind', *ʕa:qilo:xun* 'your (pl.) mind' (all with the usual penultimate stress). Several native Aramaic prepositions exhibit similar syncope or epenthesis of *i* but the vowel is always short: *baθir* 'after', *baθri* 'after me', and the construct states of many nouns of the shape CVCCV, where the third consonant is *n*, *l*, or *r*, are similar: *pisir* 'meat of' (from *pisra* 'meat'); *ṣadir* 'chest of' (from *ṣadra* 'chest').[17]

2. Open versus closed syllables, with vowel-initial or consonant-initial suffixes respectively, V:C-V, VC-C. This pattern too is common and productive in several noun and adjective forms, including participles and verbal

in the Arabic of Aqra and Arbil, or with 33% (or 14%) in Cairo Arabic. Greenberg 1966: 18–20) examined seven languages with an opposition of vowel quantity and found that long vowels were from 8 to 25 percent of all vowels in a text.

17. It would be easy to distinguish these three types (*ša:qil/šaqla*, *ʕa:qil/ʕa:qile*, *baθir/baθri*), and non-alternating words like *rast*, *raste* 'left' too, by means of distinct abstract underlying shapes and diacritic rule features, but the correct approach is not obvious and this is not the place to work out all the details.

nouns. Examples: *pti:xa:le* 'he opened her/it', *ptixle* 'he opened'; *pti:xa* 'taken (masc.sg.)', *pti:xe* 'taken (pl.)', *ptixta* 'taken (fem.sg.)'; *smo:qa*, *smɨqta* 'red (masc., fem.)', *rɨqta* '(an act of) spitting', *ro:qe* 'saliva', pl. *rɨqya:θa*; Am. *ši:da:na*, *ši:danta*, Z *šiza:na*, *šizanta* 'crazy (masc., fem.)', *ħako:ma* 'king', *ħakɨmta* 'queen', *raħu:qa*, *raħɨqta* 'far (masc., fem.)'.

3. Second-conjugation verbs with single middle consonants (historical *afʕel*) and those with two middle consonants (historical *paʕel*) differ in the vowels of the jussive, preterite, and imperative stems. The one-consonant shape is C(C)V:CVC, as in *ma:lip* 'teach', *mša:dir* 'send', *na:bɨl* 'take'; the two-consonant shape is (C(C)VCCVC, as in *manxip* 'shame', *mašmiš* 'fondle', *mparčik* 'pluck (a fowl)', *mxallil* 'wash'. These differences correlate exactly with the open or closed nature of the first syllable:

'teach'   'shame'
gma:lip   *gmanxip*   'he teaches, shames'
mo:liple *mɨnxiple*   'he taught, shamed'

4. Long vowel when stressed, short when unstressed (both in open syllables). This pattern is productive in certain categories of second conjugation verbs, such as Am. *mšo:dir* 'sent (preterite)', *mšɨdarta* 'sent (stative participle, fem.sg.)'. It also applies to *a:* in a number of nouns, both native and borrowed, such as Am. *ʔa:xa* (Z *ʔaxo:na*) 'brother', pl. *ʔaxawa:θa*; *ja:sus* 'spy', pl. *jasu:se* 'spies'; *za:xo* 'Zakho', *za(:)xo:na:ya* 'of Zakho (adj.)', Z *su:ris* (Am. *siruθ*) 'Syriac Christendom', *sɨra:ye* '(Aramaic-speaking) Christians'. In nominals (nouns, adjectives, and infinitives) only *a:* alternates in this manner, other vowels remaining constant whether stressed or unstressed: *ʔi:la:na* 'tree', *ʔi:za:la* 'going', *po:ši:ya* 'turban', Am. *be:da:θa* 'long decorative sleeve cuffs'.

COUNTERINSTANCES: There are words which retain a long vowel even when not stressed, such as *ba:ba* 'father', pl. *ba:bawa:θa*. Here the first *a:* is phonetically shorter than the second, stressed one, but yet not as short as the fully short first vowel in *ʔaxawa:θa* 'brothers'. This retention of vowel length in unstressed position is productive in verb forms containing one or more of the unstressable suffixes (discussed in § 18.2.5), thus Am. *kpa:tix* 'he opens', *kpa:tixle* 'he opens it', *kpa:tíxwa:le* 'he used to open it'; Am. *mo:qid* '(they) burnt him, he was burnt', *mo:qidle* 'he burnt'. These cases can be analyzed as involving cyclic stress assignment and vowel lengthening (Hoberman 1989: 116–18).

5. The short vowel of a final closed syllable corresponds to a long vowel when the stem has a vowel-initial suffix, VC# ~ V:C-V. This happens in both stems and suffixes. Examples: Am. *ba:žir* 'city', pl. *ba:že:re*; *ja:sus* 'spy', pl.

ǰasu:se; Z ḥe:wan 'animal', pl. ḥe:wa:ne (Am. ḥaywan, ḥaywa:ne); kɨmmaṛ Am. 'high-ranking Christian cleric, priest', Z 'habitually angry person', pl. kɨmma:ṛe; Am. qa:ẓan 'cooking pot', pl. qa:ẓa:ne; gma:lɨš 'he dresses (transitive)', gmálu:ša 'she dresses' (on the shortening of the a see paragraph 7 below); kpalxɨt 'you (masc.sg.) work', kpalxe:tun 'you (pl.) work', Am. plɨxlɨx Z plɨxlox 'you (masc.sg.) worked', plíxlo:xun 'you (pl.) worked'. A similar case is ʔi:la:na 'tree', ʔi:lán 'tree of' (construct state). In the subject-agreement suffixes of verbs, first and second person singular, there are pairs with no difference of meaning, of the following types, illustrated by forms for 'I/you work': kpalxɨn / kpalxe:na (1.masc.), kpalxan / kpalxa:na (1.fem.), kpalxɨt / kpalxe:tin (2.masc.), kpalxat / kpalxa:tin (2.fem.). There are nouns and adjectives, especially but not only of the pattern |CaCi:C|, such as ḥakim 'physician', pl. ḥaki:me, sarbor 'anecdote, incident', pl. sarbo:re, in which the final stem vowel, when suffixless, is unstressed and short, but not centralized; similarly a suffix forming abstract nouns has the two forms -uθ and -u:θa (the distribution is lexical), as in xli:muθ 'thickness', Am. siruθ 'Syriac Christendom', (also siruθkí 'in Christian Aramaic'), versus ḥawu:θa 'good(ness), benefit'.

6. Monosyllabic words of the form C(C)V:C shorten the vowel when a consonant-initial suffix is added. This occurs in first-conjugation imperatives and (in Amadiya but not Zakho) preterites, and in forms of the existential predicator ʔi:θ. Examples: pto:x 'open (imperative)', ptɨxle 'open (imperative) it'; Am. pti:x '(they) opened it, it was opened (preterite)', ptixle 'he opened'; ʔi:θ 'there is/are', ʔitle 'he has', ʔiθwa 'there was/were', Z le:s Am. li:θ ' there is/are not', Z laswa Am. liθwa 'there was/were not', Z latle Am. litle 'he doesn't have'.[18] All of these monosyllables have alternative forms, with no discernable difference of meaning, with an added -in: pto:xɨn, pti:xɨn, ʔi:θin, le:sin / li:tin, which has the effect (we might even say purpose) of eliminating the occurrence of a marked closed syllable with a long vowel, creating an unmarked open syllable. In Zakho this -in is obligatory with unsuffixed monosyllabic preterites.[19]

7. In a stressed antepenultimate syllable the vowel is often short. Examples: ptɨ́xu:le 'open (pl.) it' (cf. pto:xun 'open (pl.)'), ptɨxle 'open (sg.) it';

---

18. In Amadiya all the forms of the existential predicator with θ can also be pronounced with t.

19. This -in is similar in its apparent meaninglessness to the -in that attaches optionally to the first and second person subject markers mentioned just above, where it does not have the same effect of opening a long-voweled syllable. An apparent difference in function between forms with and without -in is discussed in Sabar 1976: 40 n. 34.

kpatxítu:le 'you (pl.) open it' (cf. *kpatxe:tun* 'you (pl.) open'); *gmáhi:bin* 'I like' (cf. *gma:hib* 'he likes'); *méθi:le* 'bring him (imperative)' (cf. *me:θi* 'bring (imperative)').

COUNTERINSTANCES: *mšá:dirre* 'send (imperative) him' and all such imperatives of second-conjugation verbs with a single middle consonant.

8. As mentioned above, final unstressed vowels are normally short. If suffixes are added, in most cases these vowels are lengthened (or it may be said that they are underlying long and shorten in final position): *kšaqli* 'they take', *kšaqli:lu* 'they take them'.

9. In a clitic pair, if the first element ends in a stressed vowel it is usually short: *go:rá=go:ra* '(man=man) = each man'; *la=θe:le* '(not=he.came) = he did not come'; *la=ba:š* 'no=good'; *xamšá=ba:te* 'five=houses'; *čɨ=na:ša* 'no=person'. In Amadiya the first consonant of the second element of the clitic pair is sometimes geminated after the short stressed vowel (thereby creating an unmarked syllable type): Am. *čɨ=gga* 'never', Am. *čɨ=xxa* 'no=one', Am. *gɨ=ttu:ra* 'in mountain'. This has been lexicalized in the adjective Am. *guppalga:ya* 'middle', from *gu* 'in' + *palg-* ' half' + *-a:ya* (adjectivalizing suffix).

Several typical situations in which marked syllables are found have been mentioned up to this point. In addition to those already mentioned, short vowels in open stressed syllables occur in many loanwords, such as *šargɨme* 'turnips', include those with the feminine suffix *-ita* (stress on the penult as usual; from Arabic *-at* via Kurdish or Turkish), such as *xilmita* 'work', *qu:wi-ta* 'strength', and also in a few native words such as *gibe* 'he wants', *mare* 'possessor of, one with', *mani* 'who'.

18.2.5. Stress and clitic units

Stress in words of more than one syllable falls most often on the penultimate syllable. Throughout this chapter stress is indicated only when it is other than penultimate. In this section, however, stress is indicated in all cases.

Stress is phonemic, as the following minimal pairs demonstrate: *bále* 'but' versus Z *balé(:)* 'certainly', *má:liple* 'teach him (imperative singular)' versus *ma:líple* 'that he teach him' (and similarly with all verbs of the second conjugation). However, stress shifts fairly readily for emphasis, either a vague semantic emphasis or to emphasize the length or shortness of a vowel for the benefit of the inquiring linguist (stressed long vowels are longer and short vowels more clearly short than unstressed).

In words other than verbs, stress is uniformly penultimate. This is true even in loanwords where the stress in the source language is in another position (except for the most unassimilated, conscious borrowings), such as the following words from Arabic: Am. ħákim 'physician', Am. ħáywan 'animal', Am. májbuṛ 'compelled' (but with an enclitic copula majbú:ṛ=i:win 'I am compelled'), Am. samáwi 'sky blue', quwwíta 'strength'; and from Hebrew: ba:ruxxábba 'welcome'. There are a small number of lexical exceptions, almost all of them adverbs: Am. derħál 'thereupon', Am. hammán 'slightly, hardly', Am. dúrtidyom 'on the next day' (Z dịrtyom), Am. š-xáflati 'suddenly', Am. ṭamá(:) 'why', Am. siruθkí 'in Syriac (Christian Aramaic)', Am. qụrduθkí 'in Kurdish', Am. bínafši 'purple', l-báxxati 'on my conscience, mercy', Am. tawtíš (Z táftiš) 'search, examination', Am. ʔárbu:šụb (Z ʔarbó:šib) 'Wednesday'.

In verbs stress is governed by morphological rules, though even here the penultimate pattern is still evident as the default. In general, a verb form has the following morphological makeup:[20]

(TENSE.ASPECT)–STEM–(GNP)–(wa:)–(l-GNP)–(l-GNP)

The following rules specify the place of stress in verbs:

1. Imperative forms (which have no prefix) have initial stress: Am. šqúl-u:-l-i 'take (plural) me', Am. má:lip-l-e 'teach (sg.) him', Z máʔu:r-u:-l-e 'bring (pl.) him in', Z máyze:-l-e:-l-i 'show him to me'.

2. Otherwise stress is as close to the penult as permitted by the following restrictions:

    (a) In certain second-conjugation verbs a penultimate vowel i: or u: is a non-syllabic semivowel at a more abstract level of analysis; this syllable does not count in stress placement, and the words consequently have antepenultimate stress: Am. g-málu:š-a |g-malwš-a| 'she dresses' (derived from lwa:ša 'to wear'), g-máħi:b-in 'I like' |g-maħyb-in|. When further suffixes are added the stress shifts: g-malu:š-á:-l-e 'she dresses him', g-maħi:b-ín-n-u (|-in-l-u|) 'I like them'.

    (b) Stress does not fall on suffixes of either of two classes: the past tense marker -wa:- and the set of GNP markers which are preceded by -l- (though stress can freely fall on suffixes of the other GNP set). If the word contains one or more such suffixes amounting to two or more syllables, stress will be earlier than

---

20. "GNP" stands for a suffix marking the gender, number, and person of the subject, direct object, or indirect object of the verb; there are two different sets, one of which is always preceded by the element l. The suffix wa: is a past tense marker. Various combinations of prefixes and suffixes are permitted in various tense/aspect categories, but their order is always the same.

penultimate: *šqíl-wa:-l-ʉx* 'you had taken' *šqíl-l-o:xu:n* 'you (pl.) took'. Occasionally in continuous speech (though not in citation) this prohibition is violated.

(c) The second syllable of the second person plural suffix *-e:tu:n ~ -itu:-* is never stressed: *k-šaql-é:tu:n-wa* 'you (pl.) would take', *k-šaql-ítu:-l-e* 'you (pl.) take him'.

(d) Otherwise stress is penultimate: Am. *k-pá:tix* 'he opens', *k-patx-é:tun* 'you (pl.) open', *gi-mšádr-ax* ' we send', *gi-mšadr-é:tun* 'you send', *qam(m)šadr-áx-l-u* 'we sent them', *k-pa:tíx-wa* 'he would open', *k-patx-í:-wa* 'they would open'.

18.2.5.1. Clitic groups and stress shift

In certain kinds of two-word collocations the normal stress on the second word is reduced or eliminated, the main stress being on the first word.[21] This is indicated by the symbol = between the two words. Such cliticization occurs in phrases of the the following types:

1. The present positive copula is normally enclitic to the noun, adjective, etc. that precede it, as in *dawrámand=i:le* 'he is a rich man'. In Amadiya words that end in *-a* (i.e. most nouns) have that vowel coalesce with the vowel of the copula, as in *kaθá:wa* 'scribe' with *i:le* 'he is', pronounced [kaθáwe:le] 'he is a scribe' (Z [kasá:wale]). In such cases there is no fully satisfactory place to write the = boundary, because to write *kaθa:we=le* incorrectly implies that the noun is the plural *kaθá:we* (cf. *kaθa:we=lu* 'they are scribes'). I opt for *kaθa:we=le* nonetheless, because it correctly indicates the pronunciation, including the stress; *kaθá:w=e:le* would be more misleading, because it would suggest that the location of the stress is irregular. After vowels other than *a* the *i:* is absent: *ká:lo=la* 'she is a bride'.

2. Verbs preceded by the negative marker *la*, such as *lá=kšaqlìn-wa:lu* 'I would not take them', or by the negative copula, *le:we=gwi:ra* [lé:wegwì:ra] 'he is not married', and generic nouns with the negative marker *ču ~ čʉ*, such as *čʉ́=mindi* 'nothing' or with *kʉll-* or *kʉd* 'all': Am. *kʉ́lle=mìndi* 'everything'.

---

21. Such a collocation is termed a "secondary stress unit" by Krotkoff (1982: 16–17) and a "Betonungseinheit" or "Akzentkompositum" by Jastrow (1985: 29–32, 1988: 20–21).

3. Participles or infinitives followed (in Amadiya but not Zakho) by the object marker =ll- (a reduced form of the preposition ʔill-) plus GNP suffixes: bi-γzá:ya=llʉx 'seeing you'.
4. Numerals with following enumerated noun: xamší=bà:te 'fifty=houses'. The stress in the numeral generally shifts to the final syllable.
5. Reduplications: he:dí=hè:di 'slowly', go:rá=go:ra '(man= man) = each man', ṭu:ré=ṭu:re 'full of mountains, along the mountains', xabrá=p=xabra 'word by word', kò:la:ná=b= ko:là:na 'street by street'. In these, too, stress shifts to the end of the first member.

18.3. The Christian dialect of Urmi and Koine

The Aramaic dialects described above are phonologically the most conservative of modern Northeastern Aramaic. To illustrate the degree of variation found in this subfamily I will take the dialect of the Christians of Urmi, Iran, and its offshoot, the Modern Aramaic Koine of the Assyrians in Iraq. This is probably the most widely spoken Aramaic language today. The phonology of these varieties has been described before (Marogulov 1935/1976, Polotsky 1961, Hetzron 1969, and especially Odisho 1988), so I will merely mention four important innovations.

18.3.1. The distribution of emphasis
In these varieties of Aramaic a word is either emphatic or plain as a whole. Thus emphasis affects all the sounds of the word .muddírtela 'she has given back' (it is indicated here by the dot before the word), which thus contrasts as a whole with muddírtela 'she has dared' (Hetzron 1969: 113). There are only very limited exceptions, such as i.ša:rat 'sign, signal', in which i is plain but .ša:rat is emphatic. The entire phenomenon, sometimes called "synharmonism," has been very well described in both its synchronic and its diachronic aspects by Jušmanov (1938), and its articulatory and acoustic phonetics are treated in detail in Odisho 1988: 114–19.[22]

18.3.2. Aspiration
The voiceless stops and affricates p t č c (also the rare k, but not q) are distinctively aspirated or unaspirated, with minimal pairs like .pa:rı 'odd

---

22. The same phenomenon exists in the Jewish dialect of Urmi and the surrounding area. The phonology of emphasis in this dialect has been analyzed in detail in Hoberman 1988.

numbers' vs. .pʰaːrɪ 'lambs'. This is the case in both emphatic and plain words. There is thus a six-way opposition for stops and affricates, illustrated by dyaːla 'giving birth', tyaraːya 'a member of the Tiari tribe', tʰyaːwa 'sitting', .dyaːra 'returning', .tyaːpʰa 'bending', .tʰlaːma 'punishing'.

18.3.3. Fronting of uvulars and velars
In the Urmi dialect k, g, and q have shifted forward, the velars to palatal c ɟ (remaining distinct from the affricates č ǰ) and the uvular to k. In the Iraqi Koine q remains uvular while the velars are shifted to the palatal position, with the result that velar k and g exist only in a handful of baby-talk words and recent loanwords (Odisho 1988: 46).

18.3.4. Vowel quantity
The functional load of vowel quantity has been much reduced. Vowel length is almost entirely determined by syllable type and stress, although there are a few syllable types in which both long vowels and short ɪ can appear.

References

Arnold, Werner. 1990. *Das Neuwestaramäische*, vol. 5: *Grammatik* (Semitica Viva 4). Wiesbaden: Harrassowitz.

Avinery, Iddo. 1988. *Ha-niv ha-Arami shel Yehudey Za'kho* (The Aramaic dialect of the Jews of Zakho). Jerusalem: Israel Academy of Sciences and Humanities.

Garbell, Irene. 1965. *The Jewish Neo-Aramaic Dialect of Persian Azerbaijan* (Janua Linguarum Series Practica 3). The Hague: Mouton.

Greenberg, Joseph H. 1966. *Language universals with special reference to feature hierarchies* (Janua Linguarum Series Minor 59). The Hague: Mouton.

Hetzron, Robert. 1969. "The morphology of the verb in Modern Syriac (Christian colloquial of Urmi)." *Journal of the American Oriental Society* 89: 112–27.

Hoberman, Robert D. 1988. "Emphasis harmony in a modern Aramaic dialect." *Language* 64: 1–26.

———. 1989. *The syntax and semantics of verb morphology in modern Aramaic: A Jewish dialect of Iraqi Kurdistan* (American Oriental Series 69). New Haven.: American Oriental Society.

Jastrow, Otto. 1985. *Laut- und Formenlehre des neuaramäischen Dialekts von Mīdin im Ṭūr ʿAbdīn*, 3rd ed. Wiesbaden: Harrassowitz.

———. 1988. *Der neuaramäische Dialekt von Hertevin (Provinz Siirt)*. Wiesbaden: Harrassowitz.

———. 1990a. *Der arabische Dialekt der Juden von 'Aqra und Arbīl*. Wiesbaden: Harrassowitz.

———. 1990b. "Personal and demonstrative pronouns in Central Neo-Aramaic." In *Studies in Neo-Aramaic*, ed. Wolfhart Heinrichs (Harvard Semitic Series), pp. 89–103. Atlanta: Scholars Press.

Jušmanov, N. V. 1938. "Singarmonizm urmĭskogo narečija." *Pamjati akademika N. Ja. Marra*, pp. 295–314. Moscow & Leningrad: Akademija Nauk SSSR, Institut Jazyka i Myšlenija.

Krotkoff, Georg. 1982. *A Neo-Aramaic dialect of Kurdistan* (American Oriental Series 64). New Haven: American Oriental Society.

———. 1985. "Studies in Neo-Aramaic lexicology." In *Biblical and related studies presented to Samuel Iwry*, ed. Ann Kort and Scott Morschauser, pp. 123–34. Winona Lake, Ind.: Eisenbrauns.

Maclean, Arthur John. 1895. *Grammar of the dialects of vernacular Syriac*. Cambridge: Cambridge University Press. Repr. Amsterdam: Philo, 1971.

Macuch, Rudolf. 1989. *Neumandäische Chrestomathie mit grammatischer Skizze, kommentierter Übersetzung und Glossar*. Wiesbaden: Harrassowitz.

Marogulov, Q. I. 1935/1976. *Grammaire néo-syriaque pour écoles d'adultes (dialecte d'Urmia)*, trans. Olga Kapeliuk (Comptes Rendus du Groupe Linguistique d'Études Chamito-Sémitiques, Suppl. 5). Paris: Geuthner.

Nakano, Akio. 1969. "Preliminary reports on the Zaxo dialect of Neo-Aramaic: Phonology." *J. of Asian and African Studies* (Tokyo) 2: 126–42.

Nöldeke, Theodor. 1868. *Grammatik der neusyrischen Sprache*. Leipzig: Weigel. Repr. Hildesheim: Olms, 1974.

Odisho, Edward Y. 1988. *The sound system of modern Assyrian (Neo-Aramaic)* (Semitica Viva 2). Wiesbaden: Harrassowitz.

Polotsky, H. J. 1961. "Studies in modern Syriac." *Journal of Semitic Studies* 6: 1–32.

Sabar, Yona. 1976. *Pəšaṭ Wayəhî Bəšallaḥ: A Neo-Aramaic midrash on Beshallaḥ (Exodus)*. Wiesbaden: Harrassowitz.

Sara, Solomon I. 1974. *A Description of Modern Chaldean* (Janua Linguarum Series Practica 213). The Hague: Mouton.

———. 1993. "Marked gender in Modern Chaldean [ta/θa] suffix." In *Semitica: Serta philologica Constantino Tsereteli dicata*, ed. R. Contini et al., pp. 299–308. Turin: Zamorani.

Chapitre 19
La phonologie des langues sudarabiques modernes
Antoine Lonnet et Marie-Claude Simeone-Senelle
C.N.R.S. et Université de Paris 3 - Sorbonne Nouvelle

19.1. Présentation

Au sud de la Péninsule arabique, à l'ouest du Sultanat d'Oman, à l'est de la République du Yémen et dans les îles yéménites du golfe d'Aden, vivent quelque deux cent mille Arabes dont la langue maternelle n'est pas l'arabe mais une des langues sémitiques que la tradition scientifique européenne a nommé *sudarabique moderne* (désormais: SAM).[1]

Cette appellation pourrait malencontreusement laisser entendre qu'il s'agit de dialectes arabes; or il n'en est rien. L'intercompréhension n'est pas possible entre le sudarabique et l'arabe même si l'un et l'autre appartiennent, avec le *sudarabique ancien* (épigraphique) et les langues sémitiques d'Ethiopie, à la branche méridionale du sémitique de l'ouest. Le groupe SAM est subdivisé en six langues: mehri, harsusi, bathari, hobyot, jibbali et soqotri (phonétiquement, [mɛhri], [ḥarsūsi], [baṭhari], [həwbyūt], [ǧibbāli] et [soqoṭri]).

19.1.1. *Localisation (se reporter à la carte)*
Les langues SAM sont parlées aujourd'hui dans deux pays.
   a) Au Yémen:
      - le mehri est parlé dans le gouvernorat le plus oriental, celui du Mahra;
      - le hobyot est parlé sur une aire réduite, à l'extrême est du Mahra, à la frontière du Sultanat d'Oman;
      - le soqotri est parlé dans l'île de Soqotra et les petites îles voisines de 'Abd-al-Kūrī et Samha (l'îlot de Darsa n'est pas habité).

---

1. La recherche de terrain menée par la Mission Française d'Enquête Linguistique au Sud-Yémen (MFELSY), aujourd'hui Mission Française d'Enquête sur les Langues du Yémen, fondée en 1982 par les auteurs, est soutenue par le Ministère des Affaires Etrangères (Direction de la coopération Scientifique et Technique), l'Université d'Aden, le C.N.R.S. et l'Université de Paris 3 - Sorbonne Nouvelle. Cet article est adapté des chapitres correspondants de notre ouvrage à paraître *Les langues du pays de l'encens: le sudarabique moderne*.

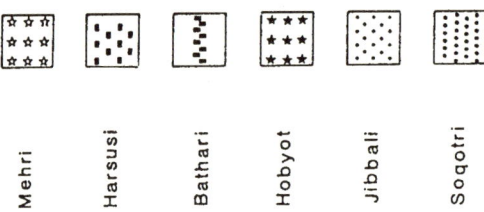

Mehri Harsusi Bathari Hobyot Jibbali Soqotri

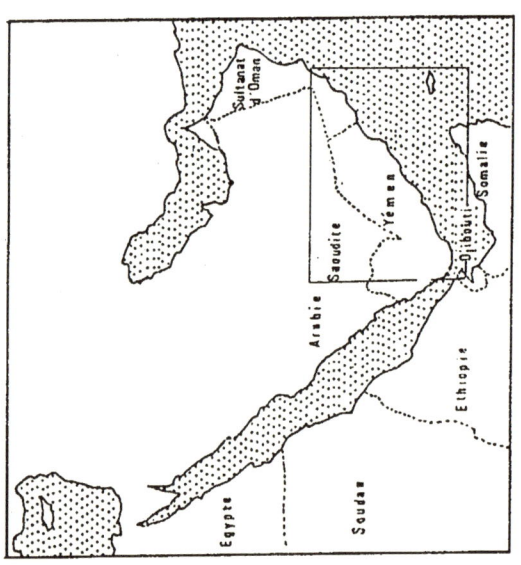

Map 2. Les langues sudarabiques modernes

La phonologie des langues sudarabiques modernes

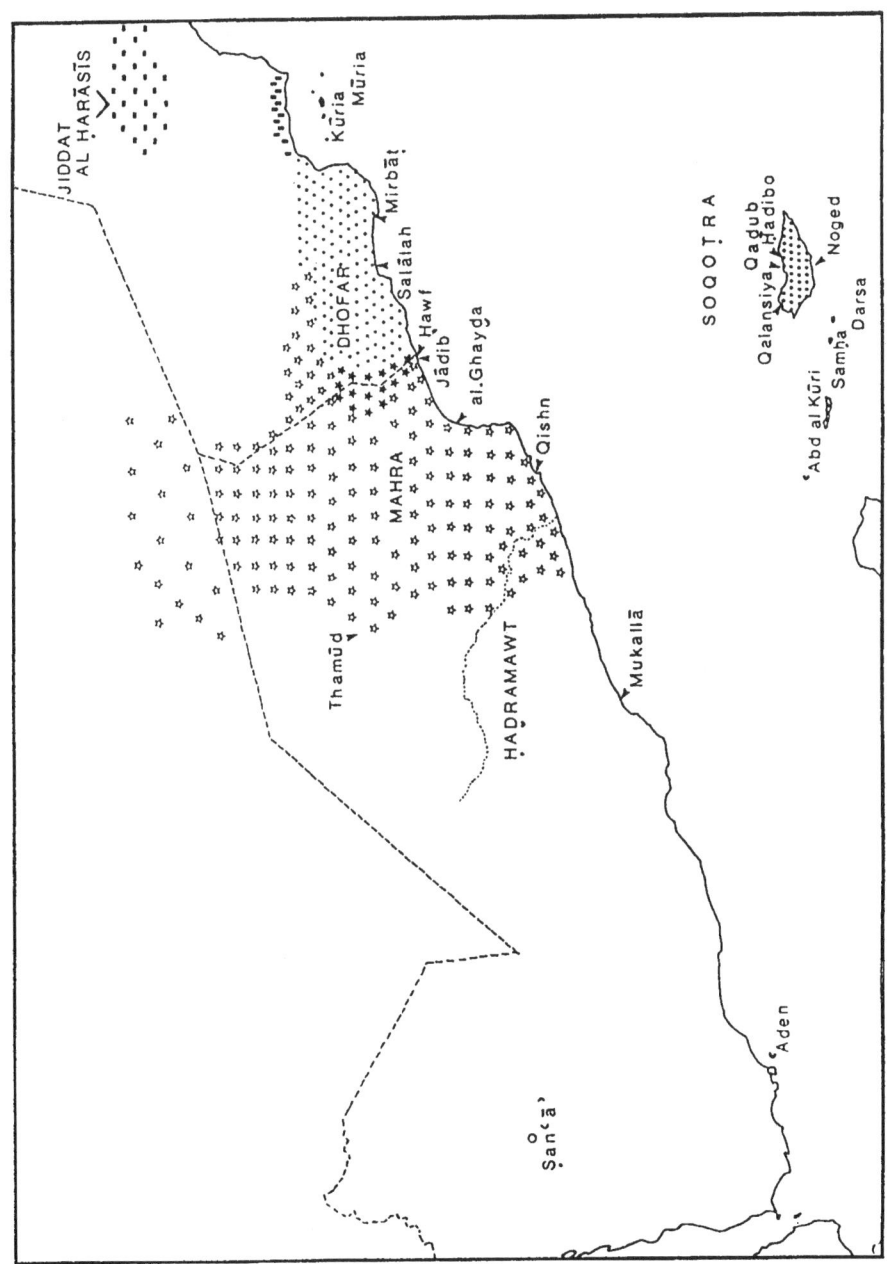

b) Dans le Sultanat d'Oman:
- le mehri est parlé à l'ouest, dans les montagnes du Dhofar;
- le jibbali est parlé dans la même région jusque dans les villes côtières et dans les îles Kuria Muria;
- le hobyot est parlé dans la montagne près de la frontière du Yémen;
- le harsusi est parlé dans la zone nommée Jiddat al-Ḥarāsīs;
- le bathari est parlé sur la côte, face aux îles Kuria Muria.

c) Il faut ajouter que nombre d'émigrés dans les pays du Golfe et en Afrique de l'est constituent des communautés qui ont conservé leur langue.

19.1.2. Situation linguistique
19.1.2.1. Les langues sudarabiques et l'arabe

La langue sudarabique est la langue première des communautés sudarabophones. Les locuteurs l'utilisent dans la vie domestique et dans toutes les relations sociales, et parfois même administratives, internes à la communauté.

Dans les régions limitrophes entre les langues sudarabiques, et dans les régions où plusieurs coexistent, la règle est le plurilinguisme: il n'est pas rare de rencontrer des personnes parlant trois langues sudarabiques en plus de l'arabe.

Dans le Mahra, au Yémen, plusieurs langues exercent une pression à des degrés divers: à l'ouest, le Hadramout est une aire de langue arabe et, à l'est, au Dhofar (Sultanat d'Oman), coexistent le jibbali, le mehri et l'arabe (sans compter le hobyot de la région frontalière).

L'arabe, langue officielle, est la langue seconde apprise à l'école et utilisée dans la majorité des activités de la vie de citoyen. Les progrès de la scolarisation et le développement des moyens de communication font que la quasi-totalité des sudarabophones de moins de quarante ans comprennent et parlent l'arabe. Seuls certains adultes âgés (surtout des femmes) des régions reculées connaissent encore très mal l'arabe. Il faut préciser que l'intercompréhension est exclue entre le soqotri et les langues SAM "continentales". Parmi celles-ci, le jibbali est difficilement compréhensible aux locuteurs des autres langues, c'est-à-dire du mehri et des trois langues qui en sont très proches. Dans de telles conditions, l'arabe, langue nationale, est amené à servir de langue de relation.

19.1.2.2. Ecriture
Aucune de ces langues n'a de tradition d'écriture; quelques expériences montrent que l'alphabet arabe permet d'écrire le mehri moyennant un aménage-

ment très simple. Plus difficile est l'adaptation au jibbali; le soqotri noté en lettres arabes nécessite une *scriptio plena* très lourde: les (nombreuses) voyelles doivent être notées.

19.1.2.3. Dialectes
Les langues sudarabiques ont une riche dialectologie, dont un aperçu peut transparaître dans les exemples qui illustrent le présent article, volontairement et explicitement choisis dans la plus grande variété dialectale.

Pour se limiter au plan phonétique, nos enquêtes sur le terrain yéménite ont permis de dégager pour le mehri des critères de classement: coalescence dentales-interdentales, vocalisation de la fricative laryngale /'/, timbres des voyelles et des diphtongues, glottalisation ou laryngalisation des emphatiques.

Dans les dialectes soqotri: coalescence des fricatives vélaires et pharyngales, durée des voyelles, voix murmurée, labialisation des voyelles postérieures, degré de palatalisation des vélaires, sonorisation des emphatiques, réalisation fricative de /l/.

En hobyot, il semble que malgré le très petit nombre de locuteurs, des différences dialectales assez importantes apparaissent.

Pour le jibbali, Johnstone (*JL*) distingue le dialecte de l'est et celui du centre, ne faisant qu'évoquer celui de l'ouest et celui des îles Kuria Muria.

19.1.3. Découverte des langues sudarabiques modernes
Au dixième siècle de notre ère al-Hamdani indique dans sa *Description de l'Arabie*:[2] "les Mahra ont un parler barbare, on dirait des étrangers". Le terme Mahra désigne évidemment pour lui toutes les populations de langue SAM.

Les savants arabes n'ignoraient donc pas l'existence des langues sudarabiques vivantes de leur époque mais la science linguistique arabe, pour des raisons historiques et culturelles, ne s'est pas intéressée à d'autres langues que l'arabe. On peut donc véritablement parler de découverte lorsqu'au dix-neuvième siècle la science occidentale constata que ces langues étaient toujours parlées.

Cette découverte s'est faite, souvent au gré du hasard ou de l'aventure, en plusieurs épisodes dont le plus fructueux reste l'Expédition Sudarabique de 1898.

---

2. Hamdani 1884: 134 (éd. Müller), ou Hamdani 1983: 248 (éd. al-Akwaʿ).

Les premières informations linguistiques sur les langues SAM apparaissent au dix-neuvième siècle. J. R. Wellsted publie une liste de mots soqotri et mehri (1835 et 1840). F. Fresnel donne une brève description du jibbali, sous le nom de "*ehhkili*" (1838). Puis le corpus sudarabique s'enrichit des contributions de quelques voyageurs, navigateurs, explorateurs, missionnaires, savants, répertoriées par Leslau (1946), et, en 1898, l'Académie Impériale des Sciences de Vienne organise une expédition scientifique de grande envergure sous la direction conjointe de C. de Landberg et de D. H. Müller. Moins de trois ans après le retour de l'Expédition, l'ethnographe autrichien W. Hein est envoyé par l'Académie dans le Mahra pour compléter les études sudarabiques.

Ces voyages et ces collaborations ont permis de constituer une véritable bibliothèque sur les langues SAM. Les prestigieux volumes édités entre 1900 et 1909 par l'Académie dans la collection *Südarabische Expedition*, les comptes rendus de séances de l'Académie, les communications, les articles de revues scientifiques, sont les fondements des études sudarabiques: plus d'un millier de pages constituant aussi les premières archives de ces populations sudarabiques et une image de leurs sociétés il y a un siècle.

Les langues traitées étaient donc les mêmes que celles qui avaient été découvertes à partir de 1834: soqotri, mehri, jibbali (nommé *šḫauri*).

M. Bittner, dès 1908, sut tirer de ces matériaux des études comparatives et descriptives dont une grande partie reste encore valide aujourd'hui, et, jusqu'à très récemment, c'est toujours l'Expédition sudarabique qui a alimenté les travaux en linguistique SAM, parmi lesquels les deux ouvrages fondamentaux: *Lexique soqoṭri* de W. Leslau (1938) et *Syntax der Mehri-Sprache* d'E. Wagner (1953).

Les autres langues sont découvertes au vingtième siècle: B. Thomas révèle en 1929 le harsusi et le bathari, deux dialectes mehri ayant connu une évolution particulière. Il en publie un corpus en 1937, avec du mehri et du jibbali (sous le nom de *shahari*).

L'existence du hobyot au Dhofar est évoquée par T. M. Johnstone en 1981; le premier article présentant le hobyot parlé au Yémen est publié par la MFELSY en 1985.

La fin du vingtième siècle est marquée par les importants travaux, en particulier les dictionnaires harsusi, jibbali et mehri (du Dhofar), de T. M. Johnstone, les travaux d'ethnolinguistique soqotri de V. V. Naumkin et V. Ja. Porxomovskij et dernièrement les travaux linguistiques d'A. Lonnet et

M.-Cl. Simeone-Senelle (MFELSY). D'autres chercheurs ont abordé le SAM: Ch. Matthews, A. Nakano et M. Morris.

19.1.4. Dénominations des langues
19.1.4.1. Le groupe sudarabique moderne
Ce groupe de langues aujourd'hui appelé le plus couramment *sudarabique moderne* ou *néo-sudarabique* (Neusüdarabisch, Modern South Arabian) a parfois reçu d'autres noms qu'il est utile de signaler: Contemporary South Arabian, (néo-)himyarite, mehritique, sudarabe, Modern South Arabic, et même arabe méridional (!).

19.1.4.2. Le jibbali
C'est le nom le plus récent et désormais le plus général pour cette langue; il succède à *šḫauri* qui, choisi à tort par D. H. Müller en 1907, a servi pendant plus d'un demi-siècle à la désigner chez les orientalistes. Or les véritables noms de la langue étaient déjà connus à cette époque: *śḫari, qarāwi, eḥkili*.

Il faut attendre 1969–70 et les articles de Ch. Matthews puis T. M. Johnstone pour avoir quelques éclaircissements sur ces noms.

Ğibbāli (*jabbālīyah* pour Matthews) et *šaḥri* sont deux traductions dans le dialecte arabe local de *śḥeri* 'montagnard, paysan', dérivé de *śḥer* (arabe local *šiḥr*) 'montagne, campagne'. Le mot 'jibbali' a l'avantage d'être dépourvu de la connotation péjorative de *śḥeri* qui s'applique à un homme sans statut tribal, un serf. On retient donc, avec T. M. Johnstone, le terme qui ne signifie que 'langue de la montagne'.

La langue est aussi parlée par la tribu dominante dont le nom arabe est *qarā* (singulier *qarāwi*) et le nom jibbali *əḥklo* (singulier *əḥkli*).

En définitive les diverses appellations de la langue, sans préjuger de la diversité dialectale qui apparaît dans les diverses publications, sont les suivantes:

ğibbāli, ğabbāliyah, ğəblét; śḥeri, śheri, śiḥri, śḥerēt, šaḥri, šiḥri, shahari; əḥkli, eḥkili, ḥakili; qarāwi, grawi, qarauwi, grauwi; sans compter une appellation géographique plus vague, *ḍofāri*.

Quant à *šḫauri* (*shkhawri, šxawri*), c'est ainsi que l'informateur de D. H. Müller nomma un jour cette langue, expliquant que le mot signifie 'pauvre, faible', par opposition à 'tribal'. Ce mot n'est pas usité, mais on peut penser (Leslau 1938: 211) à la racine sudarabique <šxr>: mehri 'vieillard', jibbali 'vieillard, faible, pauvre', soqotri 'pauvre, faible, homme, individu'; le statut non tribal est dit 'faible', arabe *ḍa'īf*.

19.1.4.3. *Les autres langues*

- Pour le *mehri*, [mɛhri], signalons que le nom mehri de cette langue est, en fonction de la morphologie du dialecte, *məhrīyət* à l'ouest du Mahra, *məhriyōt* à l'est, et *məhráyyət* au Dhofar.
- Le *soqotri*, [soqoṭri], est désigné en soqotri par une périphrase: "la langue de Soqotra [sʌḳʌṭri]".
- Le *harsusi*, [ḥarsūsi], est désigné dans la langue par *ḥərsīyət*.
- Pour le *bathari*, [baṭḥari], on trouve chez B. Thomas *botahari*, *bautahari*.

Tous ces noms de langues ont été empruntés à l'arabe dialectal de la région (remarquons qu'ils sont au masculin en arabe et au féminin en sudarabique).

- Pour le *hobyot*, nous avons conservé le nom sudarabique ([həwbyūt]), que l'on pourrait arabiser en "*hobi*".

19.1.5. *Parenté sémitique*

Il existe plusieurs théories sur la place exacte du sudarabique. Celles qui le rapprochent particulièrement de l'araméen ou de l'akkadien le font sur des bases désormais considérées comme inexactes. Tout confirme au contraire la proximité, dans un groupe sud-sémitique, avec le sudarabique ancien, les langues sémitiques d'Ethiopie (guèze, amharique ...) et l'arabe. Voir D. Cohen 1988.

Il est désormais acquis que l'existence de consonnes glottalisées et celle de fricatives latérales sont deux traits du sémitique commun. Le premier ne s'est conservé que dans les langues éthiopiennes et sudarabiques (modernes et peut-être anciennes). Le second ne s'est conservé que dans les langues sudarabiques (modernes et peut-être anciennes).

On trouvera ci-dessous les correspondances phonétiques, illustrées d'exemples, qui mettent en évidence cette parenté.

Aussi loin dans le temps que remontent nos connaissances des populations arabes, nous trouvons la division: Arabes du Nord et Arabes du Sud; les premiers parlaient des *langues nordarabiques*, desquelles a émergé l'arabe, les autres ont inscrit dans la pierre les langues que l'on regroupe aujourd'hui sous le nom de *sudarabique ancien* ou *épigraphique*. A. F. L. Beeston (1984) propose *Sayhadic languages* pour cette famille de langues dont les premières inscriptions apparurent toutes autour du prolongement occidental du grand désert *al-rubʿ al-xālī*. En effet, cette bande de sable, aujourd'hui *ramlat al-sabʿatayn*, était nommée *ṣayhad* au moyen-âge. La parenté des langues sudarabiques modernes avec celles de ces inscriptions datant des royaumes antiques du Yémen (Saba', Ma'īn, Qatabān, Ḥaḍramūt ...) est très probable, mais les recherches récentes montrent qu'il est exclu de voir dans les langues dites modernes le simple résultat de l'évolution de langues anciennes attestées. Elles proviennent assurément de langues parlées dans la région à l'époque des inscriptions, dont il n'a pas été trouvé de traces écrites.

Les dernières inscriptions sudarabiques précèdent de quelques années les premières observations linguistiques des savants arabes. Les données que l'on peut tirer de ces auteurs ne concernent qu'exceptionnellement—et sur des points mineurs—le sudarabique; ils accordent leur attention au *himyarite*, terme qui désignait des dialectes arabes très singuliers. Ces dialectes ont sans doute coexisté avec le sudarabique et laissé des traces dans des dialectes arabes yéménites jusqu'à nos jours.

19.2. Phonétique et phonologie

Le SAM considéré dans son ensemble présente des traits originaux au sein de la famille sémitique. Nous exposons brièvement d'une part ce qui constitue cette originalité et d'autre part ce qui caractérise chacune des langues à l'intérieur de la famille SAM. Pour une comparaison sémitique générale, voire chamito-sémitique, nous renvoyons à D. Cohen (1988, en particulier 33–35 et 11–14).

Une présentation des traits communs de la phonétique et de la phonologie des langues SAM se fait sur la base de la comparaison avec l'arabe et plus généralement avec les langues sud-(ouest-)sémitiques. C'est pourquoi, nous commencerons par donner un tableau général des correspondances consonantiques dans les langues sud-sémitiques, pour proposer ensuite le tableau du système des consonnes du SAM, avec les précisions nécessaires sur certaines articulations caractéristiques.

19.2.1. Consonnes
19.2.1.1. Correspondances
En ce qui concerne les consonnes, la comparaison entre les mots des différentes langues sémitiques met en évidence des correspondances très régulières.

Le cas trivial est celui des phonèmes qui apparaissent inchangés dans les mots homologues des diverses langues.

Ainsi reconstitue-t-on facilement le mot *ba'l, 'maître', dans la langue antique qui est à l'origine des langues sémitiques, à partir de la série des mots suivants signifiant 'maître':
   akkadien *bēlu*, ougaritique et phénicien *b'l*,[3] hébreu *ba'al*, araméen *ba'ᵃlā*, arabe *ba'l*, guèze *bā'l*, tigrigna *ba'al*, tigré *bä'l*, amharique *bal*, sabéen *b'l*, mehri *bɛ'l*, *bēl*, *bāl*, harsusi *bāl*, bathari *ba'l*, hobyot et jibbali *bá'al*, soqotri *ba'l*.

Tableau 19-1. Correspondances consonantiques en sémitique méridional

sémitique reconstruit	mehri	jibbali	soqotri	sudarabique épigraphique	éthiopien classique	arabe
interdentales						
*θ	θ	θ	t	θ	s	θ
*ð	ð	ð	d	ð	z	ð
*θ̣	θ̣, ð̣	θ̣	ṭ	θ̣	ṣ	ð̣
latérales						
*ś	ś	ś	ś	s²	š	š
*ṣ́	ṣ́	ṣ́	ṣ́	ḍ	ḍ	ḍ
sifflantes						
*s	s	s	s	s³	s	s
chuintantes						
*š	h	š	š/y/h	s¹	s	s
occlusives vélaires						
*ḳ	ḳ	ḳ	ḳ	ḳ	ḳ	q
fricatives post-vélaires						
*ɣ	ɣ	ɣ	ɣ	ɣ	ʻ	ɣ

En outre, *se présentent identiques* dans toutes ces langues les consonnes:
   labiales   *f, *b, *m   fric. post-vélaire *x
   dentales   *t, *d, *ṭ, *n, *l, *r   pharyngales   *ḥ, *ʻ
   sifflantes *z, *ṣ   laryngales   *ʼ, *h
   occl. vélaires *k, *g   semi-consonnes *w, *y

---

3. Sans voyelles car les écritures ougaritique, phénicienne et sabéenne (sudarabique ancienne) ne notent que les consonnes.

La comparaison et la reconstruction sont aussi possibles entre des mots présentant des différences importantes mais montrant des correspondances régulières.

Ainsi reconnaît-on la correspondance entre ḍ, ṣ, ṭ, ḏ, ṣ́, ʿ, résultats divers de l'évolution du même phonème sémitique *ṣ́, dans les mots suivants:

'ennemi': akkadien ṣerru, araméen ʿār;
'être hostile': hébreu ṣārar, guèze 'aḏrara, sabéen ḏrr;
'faire souffrir': ougaritique ṣrr, arabe ḏarra, M et Ḥ ṣ́ər(r), J ṣ́err;
'frapper': S ṣ́er;

comme étant celle qu'on voit aussi dans de très nombreuses séries, dont:

akkadien raxāṣu, ougaritique rḫṣ, hébreu rāḥaṣ, araméen rḥʿ, arabe raḥaḍ, guèze raḥaḍa, sabéen rḥḍ, M et Ḥ rəḥāṣ́, J raḥáṣ́, S ráḥaṣ́, etc… pour 'laver'.

Dans les correspondances du tableau 19-1, nous ne faisons figurer que le sudarabique et les autres langues sémitiques méridionales.

REMARQUES sur le tableau 19-1:

Le mehri, le jibbali, le soqotri et l'arabe présentés ici sont plutôt les proto-langues que tel ou tel dialecte. Ainsi, le harsusi, le bathari et le hobyot occupent-ils implicitement dans ce tableau la même colonne que celle du mehri. Pour l'éthiopien, on considère ici le système archaïque dont témoigne l'écriture du guèze et non la prononciation traditionnelle.

Le phonème occlusif post-palatal (g) ou palatal sonore (A.P.I. ɟ) ou encore chuintant prépalatal sonore (A.P.I. ʒ, ici ž) des diverses langues, est uniformément noté g dans ce tableau.

On constate une concordance des consonnes presque totale, les seules discordances étant les suivantes:

- la sifflante *š s'est confondue avec s en arabe et en éthiopien. Il lui correspond h presque toujours en mehri et h, y̤ ou š en soqotri; le symbole y̤ représente le phonème palatal murmuré, souvent interprété comme la séquence y+h ou h+y, alors qu'il s'agit de l'articulation de y avec une vibration particulière ("murmure") des cordes vocales. Dans certains cas c'est un y simple qui est le résultat de l'évolution: MQn yittīt 'six', ML yəfə́wwəl 'ventres', pluriel de hōfəl (en MQn ce pluriel est fūl: š > y̤ > h > ∅).

- Les interdentales ont été confondues en soqotri (et dans certains dialectes mehri) avec les occlusives dentales: ð > d, θ > t, θ̣ > ṭ; mais en éthiopien c'est avec les sifflantes qu'a eu lieu la confusion.

- Les fricatives vélaires *x* et *ɣ* ne sont pas absentes du soqotri, contrairement à ce qui est généralement affirmé; ce n'est que dans certains dialectes qu'elles se sont confondues avec les pharyngales (ce qui s'est aussi produit en éthiopien, mais seulement pour *ɣ* > ʻ);
- de même la pharyngale ʻ ne manque que dans certains dialectes mehri.

Le tableau des correspondances met aussi en évidence la remarquable unité des langues SAM; il en ressort immédiatement l'identité des consonnes du sudarabique moderne commun, c'est-à-dire du *proto*-SAM à partir duquel ont évolué les diverses langues.

Le trait le plus saillant de ces langues est la présence de trois sifflantes /s/ /š/ /ś/: seul le sudarabique a conservé la distinction entre ces trois phonèmes du sémitique commun. Le sudarabique épigraphique distinguait dans l'écriture trois lettres, ḥ, ≥, ẋ, correspondant à trois phonèmes distincts, /s¹/, /s²/, /s³/, dont le détail de l'articulation nous échappe encore (Beeston 1984: 8–10).

19.2.1.2. *Fricatives latérales*

En SAM le phonème /ś/ et son homologue emphatique /ṣ́/ (d'ordinaire notée *ź* par commodité et tradition) ont une articulation alvéolaire fricative latérale[4] (A.P.I. ɬ) que l'on peut sommairement décrire ainsi: la langue est dans la position de l'articulation de [t], partout en contact avec les alvéoles à l'exception d'un étroit passage latéral (en général à droite) par où l'air s'échappe avec un bruit de friction amplifié au contact de la paroi intérieure de la joue et du coin de la bouche très légèrement rétracté. Notons que son homologue arabe, *ḍ*, connaît et a connu diverses réalisations, la plus anciennement décrite (Sibawayhi, 8ème siècle, 1889: 453) étant une latérale.

19.2.1.3. *Emphase*

L'autre trait remarquable est l'articulation des phonèmes emphatiques: les trois séries, sourde, sonore, emphatique, du sémitique (et même du chamito-sémitique) se retrouvent en SAM avec la configuration normale; mais au lieu de la pharyngalisation de l'arabe, que l'on prend à tort comme référence en général, c'est une glottalisation qui est ici la marque de l'emphase. La réalisation dominante est celle d'une glottalisée éjective: la pression de l'air dans la cavité buccale provient non du soufflet des poumons mais du piston constitué par le larynx hermétiquement clos se déplaçant vers le haut. Ce type

---

4. Articulation proche du *ll* du gallois ou du *tl* de certaines langues amérindiennes.

articulatoire, courant dans les langues du monde, ne se trouve aujourd'hui en sémitique qu'en éthiopien[5] et en SAM (et dans quelques rares dialectes arabes marginaux). Ajoutons que dans le dialecte mehri de Qishn (Lonnet et Simeone-Senelle 1983), l'occlusion laryngale est relâchée provoquant une laryngalisation (*creaky voice*) qu'il est difficile de prime abord de distinguer du voisement ordinaire. Certains dialectes soqotri connaissent aussi un affaiblissement de l'emphase.

19.2.1.4. *Système phonologique*

Le système consonantique du SAM commun se présente donc ainsi:

Tableau 19-2. Système consonantique du sudarabique moderne commun

	sourde	sonore	glottalisée	nasale	vibrante	semi-voyelle
labiales	f	b		m		
interdentales	θ	ð	θ̣			
dento-alvéolaires	t	d	ṭ	n	r	
latérales	ś	l	ṣ́			
sifflantes	s	z	ṣ			
chuintante(s)	š		(ṣ̌)			
palatale						y
vélaires (occlusives)	k	g	ḳ			labio-vélaire w
post-vélaires (fricatives)	x	ɣ				
pharyngales	ḥ	ʿ				
laryngales	h	ʾ				

On reconnaît là le système sémitique commun, *augmenté d'un seul phonème*, la chuintante glottalisée ṣ̌.

---

5. Nous entendons par *éthiopien* la famille des langues sémitiques d'Ethiopie ("éthiosémitique" de certains auteurs).

19.2.1.5. *Le phonème chuintant glottalisé*

Il a été placé entre parenthèses pour signifier que son appartenance au SAM commun n'est pas certaine. Toutes les langues contemporaines présentent le ṣ̌, mais on ne trouve guère de mots en ṣ̌ homologues dans toutes les langues.

SQa *ša'ṣa'* 'boire une petite gorgée (dans la main)' n'a pas d'homologue en M, J, Ḥ.

ML, Ḥ *ṣ̌ərōm* 'gifler' n'a pas d'homologue en J, S.

J *ḳóṣ̌ól*, ML Ḥ *ḳəṣ̌áwl* 'briser' n'a pas d'homologue en S. (Pour š̃, voir §§ 19.2.1.6. et 19.3.2.1.4.)

L'articulation ṣ̌ se rencontre dans trois sortes de mots.

a) Ceux où elle provient de la palatalisation de *ḳ*[6] (parallèle à celle de *k*, voir ci-dessous), c'est le cas le plus fréquent:

SHr *šédhər* 'marmite' (MQn *ḳādər* - Ḥ *ḳédər*) - SHr *méṣ̌əher/məṣ̌éri/máḳəhɔr* 'étable' - J *minṣ̌érɔ́t* 'majeur' (doigt) (MQn et H *mənḳīrṓt*); *miṣ̌ɔ́rfɔ́t/moḳóruf, moṣ̌óruf* - MQn *ṣ̌ʌbṣ̌āb* 'porcelaines' (cauris) (arabe *qibqib*).

b) Ceux où elle résulte d'une évolution particulière de *ṣ*. Ainsi le mot 'doigt' comporte-t-il un ṣ̌ dans:

MQn *haṣ̌bá/haṣ̌óba*; MQnB *ṣ̌əbá'/ṣ̌óba*; MJb *hīṣ̌əbá', īṣ̌əbá'/īṣ̌óba*; ML *ṣ̌əbá'/ṣ̌ába'* - H *hīṣ̌əbá'/hīṣ̌óba*; H(ML) *eṣ̌əbá'* - B(ML) *haṣ̌bá'* - Ḥ *haṣ̌bá'/həṣ̌ába'* - JE(ḤL) *'eṣ̌bá'*.

Mais dans d'autres dialectes c'est la forme sémitique en *ṣ* qui apparaît:

J *'iṣbá'/eṣē'* - H *'īṣəba'/'ʌ̄ṣābʌ'*,

comme en soqotri:

SQb *'ə́ṣba'/'əṣā́bə'*.

D'autre part le mot mehri ML *yə̄ṣ̌*, JE(ML) *yéṣ̌*, 'avaler à grandes lampées', est peut-être à rapprocher de l'arabe *yaṣṣa* 's'étouffer en avalant'.

c) Ceux où elle résulte d'une évolution particulière de *ṣ́(ẓ́)*. Ainsi:

ML *ṣ̌əfdḗt*, Ḥ *ṣ̌əfdáyt* 'grenouille' (arabe *ḍufda'ᵗ*: racine *ẓ́fd'*).

Enfin, quelques cas ne peuvent s'expliquer par *ḳ*, *ṣ* ou *ṣ́(ẓ́)*, tels que:

'coude' MQn *ṣ̌affī* - H *ṣ̌ífē* - B(ML) *ṣ̌əffáyh* - Ḥ *ṣ̌əffɔ́y* - J(ML) *ṣ̌éféf* (racine non attestée en soqotri); 'gros bâton' H *təḳəṣ̌ɔ́'* (mais J *təḳṣ̌ɔ́'* - ML *təḳṣ̌ɛ̄*); 'arc' ML *mənṣ̌əbēt* - Ḥ *nəṣ̌íbət* (mais J *mənṭɔ̄t*).

---

6. La palatalisation de *ḳ* en jibbali du centre (celui de JL) aboutit à ṣ̌, parallèle à š̃ qui résulte de *k*.

19.2.1.6. *Palatalisation de k et g*
La palatalisation de *k* (et de *ḳ*) est un phénomène très marqué dans les langues SAM. Il affectait déjà (dans une faible mesure) le proto-SAM puisqu'un mot sémitique en *k* est attesté avec *š* dans tout le SAM:
  'foie': M*Qn*, ML et B*(ML) šəbdīt* - Ḥ *šəbdēt* - J *šəbdét* - S *šə́bdeh*
  - H *šebdét*.
En jibbali du centre le son palatalisé est *s̃* (décrit dans JL et Johnstone 1984) qui se distingue donc de *š* au point que dans ce dialecte il constitue un phonème indépendant. Une paire minimale importante est celle qui oppose -*s̃* (pronom suffixe 2fs) à -*š* (pr. suff. 3ms). Notons aussi *ys̃érɔ́k* 'il fait' :: *yśérɔ́k* 'il grimpe'. (Pour *s̃*, voir aussi § 19.3.2.1.4.)
  Synchroniquement les alternances *k/š(s̃)* sont très nombreuses dans toutes les langues mais particulièrement productives en jibbali. En soqotri on trouve aussi des degrés de palatalisation différents: *c* (occlusive palatale) et *ç* (éjective) dans certains dialectes:
  S*Qb ycṓtəb* 'il écrit' (*ktb*); *dça'r* 'de la maison' (< *di-ḳa'r*).
On observe aussi une palatalisation de *g* en soqotri et en jibbali:
  SH*r tenḗžəh* sorte de pamplemousse, S*Qa ɣážəh* 'femme';
  J *ɣég/ɣṓži/ɣég*, dim. *ɣížég* 'homme' - *ɣažét* 'grande fille' (cf. S*Qa* ci-dessus). (Pour *ž*, voir aussi § 19.3.2.1.4.)

19.2.2. *Voyelles*
19.2.2.1. *Timbres*
Pour ce qui est des voyelles, la seule caractéristique générale est, par rapport au sémitique commun, un élargissement de la gamme des timbres: y figurent toujours les voyelles *a, i, u, o, e, ɛ, ə*. Ces timbres s'organisent dans des systèmes assez variés, présentant ou non une opposition brève/longue, une nasalisation, etc. Ils seront précisés plus loin lors de la présentation de chaque langue. Il n'est pas possible encore de proposer un système de voyelles pour le proto-SAM, qui serait intermédiaire entre le système sémitique (*a u i - ā ū ī*) et les systèmes actuels; il faut en particulier déterminer si les voyelles *o* et *e* étaient ou non en place avant la séparation des langues.

19.2.2.2. *Correspondances*
Dans les langues SAM, lorsque les lexèmes se correspondent, et dérivent donc a priori du même mot sud-sémitique, il arrive, dans un nombre de cas limité seulement, que les timbres des voyelles soient voisins ou identiques:
  'genou' *bark* en M, B, S, H, et *bɛrk* en H, J. (< **bark*);

'chèvres' MQn hēráwn, Ḥ ḥəwərūn, H ḥeywurṓn, B(ML) 'ā́ərān, J 'ɛrún, S 'ɔ́rəhɔn (< *'arṓn < *'arān).

Le plus souvent, les voyelles sont différentes, résultant de règles historiques d'évolution qui produisent des correspondances régulières:
    ML həfhṓś H 'ɛfhóś J efhéś 'cuire à l'eau' (< *√hafhaś);
    ML həɣlṓṭ H aɣlṓṭ J aɣlɛ́t 'se tromper' (< *√haɣlaṭ).

On aperçoit à travers trois des quatre exemples précédents une évolution phonétique changeant *a* en *o* dans certaines conditions, variant selon les langues; dans le sémitique méridional, seul le SAM est dans ce cas.

Malgré l'impression de régularité que peuvent donner les exemples précédents, on constate que les voyelles s'organisent dans des systèmes phonologiques structurellement très différents; il en résulte des correspondances très complexes encore obscurcies par une harmonisation vocalique partielle dans certaines langues et des discordances morphologiques entre les langues portant précisément sur les voyelles, la structure syllabique et l'accent.

    'tendon d'Achille, talon' *ML* mədrɛ́m *J* mədrúm *SQb* médrəhem;
    'sourcil' *MQn* gəfṓn *J* gɛfn *SHo* gḗfən;
    'rein' *ML* kəlyī́t *J* kuLɛ́t *SQb* kəlɔ́yət. (Pour *L*, voir § 19.3.2.1.3.)

On ne s'étonnera donc pas de ne pas trouver ici de tableau de correspondances vocaliques pour le SAM. Il est cependant possible de donner des séries de correspondances entre les schèmes vocaliques des formes nominales et verbales qui constituent la base du lexique.

a) noms
    sud sém. *CaCaC   M CəCēC
                                            J C(ə)CɛC, CéCɛ́C
    sud sém. *CaCC   M CaCC, CōCəC, CēCəC
                                            J CɛC(ə)C, CɔCC, CəCC

b) suffixe nominal de féminin
    sud sém. *-at   M -ṓt, -ḗt, -ət, -t
                                            J -ɔ́t, -ɛ́t, -ət, -t
                                           S -ɔh, -ɛh, -əh, …

c) verbes
    sud sém. *CaCaCa/yaCCuCu/yaCCuC   M CəCū́C/yəCū́CəC/l-əCCḗC
                                           J C(ə)Cɔ́C/yCɔ́CəC/yɔ́CCəC
                                           S Cɔ́CəC,
                                                 CCɔC/yCɔ́CəC/l-iCCɛ́C
    sud sém. *CaCiCa/yaCCaCu/yaCCaC   M CĩCəC/yəCCɔ́C/l-əCCṓC
                                           J CéCəC/yCéCɔ́C/yəCCɔ́C
                                           S CéCəC/yCéCəC/l-iCCɔ́C, &c.

19.2.2.3. Rôle des voyelles dans la morphologie

a) Dans les verbes, les voyelles participent aux schèmes de la dérivation verbale, à l'opposition de genre, de nombre, de personne et de diathèse, selon le fonctionnement régulier des langues sémitiques. Mais une particularité est l'existence de certaines alternances vocaliques pour les oppositions de genre et de nombre.

- genre (masculin\féminin)
    'tu écris' MQn *təkūtəb\təkītəb*; J *tkɔ́təb\tkítəb*; SQa *tkṓtəb\tkḗtəb*
    'que tu écrives' J *tɔ́ktəb\tíktib*.
- nombre (singulier/pluriel)
    ML *kətūb* 'il a écrit'/*kətawb* 'ils ont écrit'.
    J *yféðɔ́r* 'il tremble de peur'/*yféðér* 'ils tremblent de peur'.
    SQa *ykṓtəb* 'il écrit'/*ykḗtəb* 'ils écrivent'; *ktöb* 'il a écrit'/*kteb* 'ils ont écrit'.

b) Dans les noms, de même, on remarque le rôle particulier de l'alternance vocalique pour les oppositions de genre (S et J seulement) et de nombre essentiellement dans les quadrilitères:

- genre (masculin\féminin)
    SQa *ṭáḥrər\ṭáḥrer* 'chèvre sauvage', *śíbœb\śíbib* 'vieux', *xálxal\xálxel* 'grisonnant' (poil); S(JL) *šə́źrhar\šə́źrhir* 'jaune', *kérkam\kérkim* 'jaune'.
    J *šḥamúm\šḥamím* 'brun de peau', *ṣaḥbɔ́b\ṣaḥbéb* 'brun clair', *šə́źrɔ́r\šə́źrér* jaune, *ṣɔfrɔ́r\ṣəfrér* 'jaune', *xɔzgɔ́g\xazgég* 'fin' (tissu).
- nombre (singulier/pluriel):
    Ḥ *'ardīb/'ardōb* 'nuque' - MQn *bərṣén/bərṣṓn* 'articulation de la hanche' - J *məṣḥérér/məṣḥérɔ́r* 'os du tibia' - SQb *náḥrər/náḥrur* 'nez'.

19.2.2.4. Variation morpho-phonologique

Des phénomènes de variation affectent les noms et les verbes: quand ils sont construits avec un pronom suffixe personnel, on observe des modifications de timbre vocalique, de durée, d'accent, de structure syllabique.

MQn *'abšóš* & *'abšéšiä* 'les lèvres' & 'mes lèvres'; MQnB *kʌšawl* & *kʌšaleh* 'il a brisé' & 'il l'a brisé'; *ḥɔ́rəm* & *hárᵊmi* 'chemin' & 'mon chemin';

Ḥ *əlbədtō* & *əlbədtáyhəm* 'elles deux ont frappé' & 'elles deux les ont frappés'; *bəxáṣ̌* & *bəxṣéni* 'cela a fait mal' & 'cela m'a fait mal'; *yəmṓt* & *yémtəh* 'il a maltraité' & 'il l'a maltraité'; *yərṓb* & *yərbéni* 'il a reconnu' & 'il m'a reconnu'; B *nōkaʿ* & *nekeʿēn* 'il est venu' & 'il est venu à nous'; B(ML) *ḥāṭər* & *ḥóṭri* 'chevreau' & 'mon chevreau'; J *šúyəl* & *šɔ́yɔ́lš* & *šúylən* & *šuɣlək* 'travail' & 'son travail' & 'notre travail' & 'ton travail'; *yéxtər* & *yəxtérsən* 'qu'il retire du feu' & 'qu'il les retire du feu'; *ɔ́ḳɔ́l* & *ʾéḳíləš* 'il a fait coucher' & 'il l'a fait coucher'; *effɔ́śəl* & *effīšílɔ́hum* 'il embarrassa' & 'il les embarrassa'.

19.2.3. Syllabe - accent
19.2.3.1. Mehri et langues voisines

On se bornera ici à indiquer que le système le plus simple, et sans doute celui qui a le moins évolué, est celui du mehri.

En règle générale, la *syllabe* est de type CV(C) ou CV̄, à l'initiale (C)CV(C) ou (C)CV̄, à la finale CV(C(C)) ou CV̄(C).

L'*accent* tombe sur la (dernière) syllabe longue {CVC(C), CV̄(C)} ou, si toutes les syllabes sont brèves {CV}, sur la première (CVC en fin de mot compte pour brève).

ML *məlū́k* 'posséder'; *kāláyn* 'le soir'; *rīḳṓḳ* 'fins'; *bə́hi* 'par eux deux'; *yəhánsəməm* 'ils respirent'; *təhənáwdəxən* 'elles fumigent'; *mənḳərbəṭáwtən* 'tordues de douleur'.

Il y a quelques exceptions: ML *fənwə́hi* (?< *fənwī́hi*) 'devant eux deux', et le suffixe *-ən* de certaines conjugaisons est hors unité accentuable: ML *yarkəbáyən* (*yarkəbē+ən*) 'eux deux mettent sur le feu (une marmite)'; les voyelles non phonologiques ne comptent pas: ML *ənxálihəm* (= /nxalihəm/) 'sous eux'; *θə́bərkəm* (< *θə́brəkəm*) 'vous êtes cassés'. Le ʿ 'compte comme une consonne, même lorsqu'il a disparu laissant pour trace une influence sur la voyelle (ouverture, allongement): *yənákam* (< *yənákʿəm*) 'ils viennent'. Il en est de même pour ʾ.

Au contact de deux mots, une voyelle de disjonction se présente pour rétablir la structure syllabique menacée par le contact des consonnes:

MQ*n ḥamš-ə-ttī́yəs* 'je veux que tu la manges' [-*š*, -*s*: pr. suff. 2fs, 3fs].

Cependant certains groupes consonantiques sont admis:

MQ*n ḥamk ttah* 'je veux que tu le manges' [-*k*, -*h*: pr. suff. 2ms, 3ms].

La phonologie des langues sudarabiques modernes   355

De plus, de tels groupements admissibles se produisent dans les mots, par chute d'un ə:

> M *Qn dekkk* 'ton coq' (*dekk-k*) - M *QnB ftkkōt* (*f* syllabique) 'elle s'est détachée, libérée'.

Le harsusi et le bathari gardent l'accentuation du mehri malgré l'abrégement de certaines voyelles:

> Ḥ *šəlŕbəd* (< *šəlēbəd) 'il a essayé de tirer (au fusil)'; *təxŕm* (< *təxaym) 'tu veux'; *ḳäbəlét* (< *ḳäbəlēt) 'sud'.

Le harsusi admet la syllabe CV̄C en position non finale: *yeḵerōbhem* 'il s'approche d'eux'; de même que le bathari: *a'ayāntha* 'ses (m.) yeux'.

Les langues autres que le mehri occidental ont, en plus, la possibilité d'avoir une voyelle à l'initiale de mot:

> J *efḳáḥ* 'briser en deux'; *énúf* 'lui-même' - ML *amōdəḥ* 'flatter';
> *ayáyg* 'l'homme' - Ḥ *aḵṣōm* 'rafraîchir'; *ayāh* 'son frère' - B *exuft* 'la plante du pied'.

Il s'agit en général d'un préfixe de dérivation verbale ou d'un article défini.

19.2.3.2. Le système jibbali (jibbali du centre)

Il a connu une évolution particulière. Le contraste V̄ :: V̆ est perdu et l'accent n'est pas de culmination: un mot peut avoir plusieurs syllabes également proéminentes: *ənkɔ́zbɔ́zɔ́t* 'elle a soupiré'.

Lorsque le mot mehri apparenté existe, avec un schème analogue, la comparaison montre que, lorsque le mot jibbali n'a qu'un accent, celui-ci est situé sur la syllabe homologue de la syllabe accentuée du mot mehri.

> ML\J: *nídəm\nídəm* 'se repentir'; *həndū́m\endím* 'aider'\'faire repentir'; *náddəm\nútdəm* 'regretter'; *šəndū́m\šəndím* 'revendiquer'; *nədmít\nədmét* 'regret'.

Mais on peut pousser la comparaison plus loin: dans une série de mots de même schème, le nombre d'accents varie selon l'environnement consonantique; la dernière syllabe accentuée correspond alors régulièrement à celle qui porte l'accent en mehri.

> ML\J: *həsū́f\hsɔf* 'il a humilié'; *həgū́s\hɔ́gɔ́s* 'il a pensé' (< *CaCaCa); *kəfɛ́n\kfɛn* 'linceul'; *yəlɛ́ṭ\yálɛ́ṭ* 'faute' (< *CaCaC).

On peut en conclure que le proto-jibbali avait la même accentuation que le mehri et que l'énergie accentuelle a eu tendance à se répartir vers le début du mot.

De ce point de vue, le jibbali de l'est est conservateur:

ML kəláwkəl, JE kəlébkəl, J kélébkəl 'rafales de vent'
(< *kalākil); ML məkhayrīr, JE məṣhayrér, J məṣḥérér 'tibia'.

Une exception importante à la correspondance formelle entre le mehri et le jibbali est celle du subjonctif des verbes simples de type transitif (< sémitique *faʻala, par opposition à *faʻila):

ML kətūb/ykūtəb/yəktéb, J ktɔb/ykɔ́təb/yɔ́ktəb 'écrire'.

Mais divers indices, dont la 1ère personne du pluriel nəktéb et l'impératif J ktɛb conforme au M ktēb, permettent de supposer que le subjonctif en J ait eu secondairement une transformation accentuelle particulière.

19.2.3.3. *Le système soqotri*

Le soqotri a poussé cette tendance plus loin: la syllabe initialement accentuée a perdu son accent qui est remonté vers le début du mot, en même temps que l'opposition de durée était abolie. Comparer:

'morceaux de bois' M θayrū́b, J ðɔ́rɔ́b, SQa ṭáyrəb;
'cinq' (+ nom masculin) MQn xmoh, H xəmmóh J xōš, SQa xɔ́mʌy;
'écorce d'arbre' MQn ḳalīfɔ́t, J ḳiLifɔ́t, SQa ḳályēfəh;
'enfant' H mɛbəré' J əmbéré' SQa mɔ́brəhɛ';
'feuille' MQnB ṣyāfɔ́t, J źyiLfɔ́t, H ṣyɛlfɔ́t, SQa ṣɔ́yləfəh;
'il vole (oiseau)' MQn yifərū́r, J yəfrér, SQa yífrör.

Dans le cas où une voyelle longue perd son accent et sa durée, il s'est développé un dédoublement de cette voyelle au moyen de h: J ḳaṭmim, S ḳáṭməhim 'beurre'. C'est ce qu'on appelle le 'h parasite', voir § 19.3.3.1.2.

19.2.4. *Gémination consonantique*[7]

19.2.4.1. *Existence de la gémination*

En comparant à l'arabe, on constate l'absence de la gémination comme morphème de dérivation verbale. Pour opposer 'mettre en garde' :: 'prendre garde', par exemple, l'arabe utilise une gémination à valeur morphologique: arabe ḥaðira :: ḥaððara. Le SAM ne présente, dans les formes équivalentes, que des consonnes simples:

M ḥəðūr :: ḥōðər - J ḥɔ́ðɔ́r :: oḥóður - S ḥə́dɔr :: ḥódər.

Et ceci même dans des emprunts à l'arabe: mu/aʻallim 'professeur' est devenu J m'alm et MQn mɔ́ləm.

Il en a été tiré, à tort, la généralisation selon laquelle *il n'y aurait pas de gémination* en SAM. Or il suffit, pour prouver le contraire, de présenter les

---

7. Voir, pour le jibbali, Johnstone 1980.

La phonologie des langues sudarabiques modernes 357

quelques faits suivants qui concernent les langues autres que le soqotri (voir REMARQUE le concernant).

La gémination est attestée partout mais de façon variable selon les langues et les dialectes; ainsi pour le mot 'coude':

MQ*n* šaffī/šəffyū́tən; MM*f* šəfī/šəfṓwyət; ML šəffáy/šəfṓf, šə-fáwwət, šəfū́tən - B šəffáyh - Ḥ šəffəy/šəffā́yət - H šī́fḗ/šəfiy-ṓtə, šəffṓtə' - J šéféf/šáffətə.

Comparer aussi: MQ*n* xaff mais ML xaf 'pied'.

19.2.4.2. Types et variation

Il existe en SAM deux causes de gémination phonétique.

a) Soit la présence d'une racine de type $C_2 = C_3$ ou $C_3 = C_4$ (*gémination d'origine radicale*):

MQ*n* śəllū́t 'elle a pris'; ML ḳətəbbū́t 'poupée en bois'; ḳətəf-fáwtən 'petites plumes' - J dəkkét 'banc'; xazəggún, 'très fins' (vêtements) - B dəśśít 'pierre taillée' - Ḥ heddōt 'berceau'; γemellḗt 'nuages amoncelés' - H γəllɔ́t 'brouillard';

on a même $C_4 = C_5$ dans MQ*n* śxūllū́t 'elle s'est assise' (śxwll).

b) Soit le contact (et l'assimilation) de la consonne du morphème infixé -t- avec une consonne radicale homorganique ou quasi-homorganique (*gémination d'origine morphologique*):

MQ*n* 'ássʌd ('-t-ṣd) 'être inquiet'; fʌṭṭáwn (f-t-ṭn) 'essayer de se souvenir'; kássər (k-t-sr) 'être humilié'; ML ḳáṣ́ṣ́əl 'être cassé' (ḳ-t-šl); ḳáśśər (ḳ-t-śr) 'être dépouillé'; xázzəl 'plaisanter' (x-t-zl); xáššəl 'être percé' (x-t-šl).

Dans le dialecte de ML, t s'assimile avec: d, ṭ; š, ṣ̌; ś, ź; z, s, ṣ; θ, ð, θ̣.

Le traitement des formes comportant une gémination (de l'une et l'autre origine) est très original en SAM. Il suffit d'observer le paradigme de verbes tels que:

J terr/yətrér/yɔ́ttər 'tirer' - MQ*n* haḵráwr/yhaḵráwr, f. haḵʌrráwt/lháḵḵar, participe actif məháḵḵar 'partir' - ML ráttəṣəm/yərtəṣáyṣ/yərtə́ṣṣəm (pluriel) 'être en foule',

pour constater que, dans la variation morphologique, la gémination consonantique ne suit pas toujours la même consonne; selon les langues et les dialectes, les situations sont variables et complexes; nous ne donnerons ci-dessous qu'un aperçu de ce transfert de gémination.

REMARQUES

- Même sans transfert de gémination, la différence avec l'arabe est remarquable: si à l'accompli arabe, par exemple, *tamma* 'être terminé' correspond le mehri (MQn) *təmm*, à l'inaccompli *yatimmu* correspond MQn *yitəmū́m* (et le subjonctif *lətmḗm*) sans gémination.

- La réorganisation syllabique en présence d'un suffixe peut faire apparaître une gémination phonétique: J *ɛhdéd* 'il a menacé', *ɛhəddə́š* 'il l'a menacé'.

19.2.4.3. Transfert de gémination
19.2.4.3.1. Verbe et participe

La gémination porte, au gré de la morphologie, selon les formes dérivées, les personnes …, sur la deuxième *ou la première* consonne radicale (troisième ou deuxième pour les quadrilitères), ou non-radicale dans le cas du -*t*- infixé:

J *kerr/yəkrér/yɔ́kkur* 'sauter' - MQn *šḥʌźáwź/yšḥʌźáwź/lšáḥḥaź* 'suivre à la trace' - J *axlél* 'laisser passer la pluie' (toit), participe actif *míxxəl*; *aḥaðnín/yḥaðnín/yḥáððən* 'regarder fixement'.

Avec -*t*-:

Ḥ <śll> *śáttəl/yəśtəlól/yəśtól* 'transhumer' - MQnB <fkk> *féttᵃk* 'se détacher' (f. *ftkkōt*).

REMARQUES

- Le transfert d'une gémination d'origine morphologique provoque une gémination sur les racines non géminées. Ainsi, MQn *ḳʌṣṣáwr* (< ḳ-t-ṣr) 'rétrécir (au lavage)' a pour féminin *ḳʌṣarrū́t* dans lequel l'infixation de -*t*- n'est plus apparente, l'apparence étant celle de *ḳṣrr*.

- Une autre conséquence du transfert de gémination s'observe dans certaines homonymies telles que J *kɔ́ttəb* 's'écrire les uns aux autres' <k-t-tb> et *kɔ́ttəb* 'être réticent' <k-t-bb> (transfert).

19.2.4.3.2. Nom

Il existe des noms comportant une consonne géminée; leur pluriel présente dans certains cas un transfert de gémination.

a) Gémination d'origine radicale:

ML *ḳəwwḗt* 'force'; MQn *sənnɔ́rt/sənɔ́rər* 'chatte' - Ḥ *ḳəṭṭəbṓt/ḳəṭəbā́b* 'poupée' (taillée dans le bois ou l'os).

b) Gémination d'origine morphologique (schème sémitique *CaCCāC):

MQn *bəḥḥṓr* 'marin'.

c) Par ailleurs, certains noms déverbaux à préfixe comportent, par transfert, une gémination différente de celle de la racine:

J *middḗk* 'percuteur de fusil' (*dkk*), *múxxud* 'épingle à cheveux' (*xdd*).

d) La gémination apparaît aussi dans une série de pluriels:
   ML ḳāṣər/ḳəṣáwwər 'pièce au premier étage'; kōbən/kəbúwwən
   'bouse sèche' - Ḥ ḳəḥōr/ḳəwáḥḥər 'chamelle suitée'.
e) En outre, il existe, en mehri, hobyot et harsusi, quelques occurrences de gémination difficilement explicables:
   ML ḥənnūk, Ḥ ḥénnek 'palais et gencive' (J ḥónúk, MQn ḥank).
   Ḥ θəmméni 'huit' (MQn təmōni, J θōni).

19.2.4.4. Remarques concernant la gémination en jibbali
Le jibbali présente aussi une gémination de la première consonne du mot lorsque lui est préposée une voyelle, ce qui se produit dans trois circonstances pour les verbes et une pour les noms, à condition que cette première consonne soit dans la liste suivante: C_1 = ś, š, s̃, f, t, k, y (dans les verbes, occasionnellement d, θ, ð, g, z, γ, x, ḥ, h, et exceptionnellement ḍ, z̃).
a) Les verbes intensifs-conatifs (correspondant aux formes II et III de l'arabe) sont de type eCóCeC, les causatifs (forme IV de l'arabe) sont de type (a)CCeC, et les quadrilitères de type (e)CɛCCéC. Tous développent, tantôt à l'accompli, tantôt à l'inaccompli, une gémination de C_1:
- eCCóCeC:
   eśśóḳər/iśśóḳərən/iśśóḳər 'plisser des yeux au soleil';
   eθθúḳul/íθθúḳələn/yθɔ́ḳəl 'charger'; axlé/íxxɔ́lɛ/yáxlɛ 'consacrer';
- (a)CCéC:
   etlék/ittélɔ́k/yétlək 'marcher derrière une bête attachée par la patte';
   eklé/ikkɔ́lɛ/yékle 'amener à la maison' (mariée, ses animaux);
   aḥrér/íḥḥrér/yéḥḥər 'parquer les chevreaux'.
   Remarquer que pour ce dernier verbe la gémination ḥḥ est, à l'indicatif, due à la voyelle préfixée, et, au subjonctif, au transfert de rr.
- (e)CCɛCCéC:
   ettɛrtér 'mener rudement'.
b) Les noms déterminés par l'article (constitué par une voyelle):
   ɔ-xxɔ́bz 'le pain'; a-xxaf 'la sole du chameau', mais ɔ-(x)xɔ́fét 'la fenêtre'; ɔ-(x)xɔ́rf 'les pluies de la mousson'; e-ffá'm 'le pied', mais e-fénús 'la lampe'; e-kkɔ́b 'le chien', mais e-(k)kēr 'le cheikh'; e-tté 'la viande'; i-yyúm 'le jour', 'le soleil'; e-ssáḥart 'la sorcière'; ɛ-śśá'b 'la vallée, le cours d'eau'; ɛ-šš ɔ́ 'le dos', mais e-(š)šúm 'le nom'; e-s̃s̃írs̃ 'le ventre'.

Un phénomène de *gémination compensatoire* apparaît lorsque, pour des raisons de contexte la première consonne radicale est élidée (c'est le cas de *b* à l'intervocalique), la deuxième radicale est alors géminée:

J *ebhím/íɔ̄hhúm* (< * *íbɔhúm*) 'ne pas se décider'; *ebšél/yēššɔ́l* 'cuisiner'.

Dans le cas où C₂ est une consonne qui s'élide, c'est C₁ qui est géminée:

J *eźbéṭ/íźźiɔ̄ṭ* 'donner du lait'.

19.2.4.5. Remarques concernant la gémination en soqotri

D'une façon générale, la gémination est quasi absente en soqotri; elle est en général réduite: SQa *'ɔṣ*, f. *'ɔ́ṣɔh/yɔ́ṣɔṣ/l-iṣáṣ* 'avoir peur'; et S *śfɛh* à côté de MQn *śəffít* 'cheveu'.

- Gémination d'origine radicale (dans les noms exclusivement):
    SQaB *'ərébbəh*, SQb *'ərbéboh* 'cuisse'; S *ḵɔ́ṣṣəh* 'cheveux coupés'.
- Gémination d'origine morphologique:
    S *ḥódder* (< ḥ-t-dr) 'prendre garde'; *lɔ́ttəm* 's'envelopper le visage'; *házzaḵ* 'plaisanter'.
- Gémination d'origine phonétique. La voix murmurée (cf. supra) provoque un allongement consonantique qui peut parfois aller jusqu'à une gémination:
    SQa *léšʰɛn*, SQaB *léššʰɛn* 'langue'.

Pour le mot SQa *mɛ́šhɛ'*, S(ML) *mɛ́ssɛ* 'pluie', on peut aussi penser au résultat de l'assimilation de *l*, la racine étant <lsw> (MJb *məlsé'*).

Notons enfin que l'apparition de la gémination est parfois limitée à certains dialectes.

19.3. Particularités des langues

Nous présenterons ici les trois langues les mieux connues, le mehri, le jibbali et le soqotri. Les autres seront évoquées incidemment, le harsusi et le bathari étant phonétiquement très voisins du mehri, le hobyot étant, selon ses dialectes, proche du mehri de Jadib ou du jibbali.

19.3.1. Mehri

Le mehri est la langue qui a le moins divergé du proto-SAM, la langue parlée avant la séparation en plusieurs langues: elle n'a connu ni les transformations phonologiques du soqotri et du jibbali, ni les développements morphologiques et syntaxiques du soqotri.

19.3.1.1. Consonnes[8] (voir Lonnet et Simeone-Senelle 1983)
19.3.1.1.1. SYSTÈME COMPLET
Le système consonantique est le système complet du sudarabique, c'est-à-dire celui du sémitique, comme le montre le tableau comparatif (tableau 19-1); une seule exception, mais très caractéristique du mehri (et, dans une moindre mesure, du soqotri), est l'évolution de *š en h.

MQn hemm 'nom' (J šum, S šem);
MQn ḥroh 'tête' (J rɛš, SHr rī´/ríhi/ə́rəš);
MQn bəhḗl 'être cuit' (J bésəl, S béhɛl);

dans un cas le h passe même à ḥ: mźrāḥ 'dent' (arabe ḍirs) où š > h > ḥ.

Il reste quelques š non passés à h, tels que:

ML šəṭáwf, J šṓṭə́f 'blesser légèrement'; ML ləšēn, J ɛlšén, SHo líšin 'langue'.

19.3.1.1.2. INTERDENTALES
Dans quelques dialectes, essentiellement citadins, s'est produite la coalescence des dentales et interdentales. C'est le cas bien connu du parler de Qishn où 'sein', 'cuisse', 'sur' se disent tṓdi, fxād, ṭār, mais ailleurs θṓdi, fxāð, θār.

19.3.1.1.3. FAIBLESSE DE ʿ
La fricative pharyngale sonore (le ʿayn de l'arabe) manque partiellement, parfois presque totalement, dans certains dialectes, en particulier à Qishn, Ṣaqr, et dans le dialecte du Dhofar, décrit dans ML.

MQn\MJb: ʿāḵā́b\ʾaḵā́b 'oiseaux'; tərā̀\tərʿá 'elle garde le troupeau', šīrḗ\šīrɛ̄ʿ 'nombril'.

Il arrive que la même racine se manifeste chez le même locuteur avec et sans ʿayn: lāθī́t/lī´áθtən 'scinque', sorte de lézard.

19.3.1.1.4. RÉTROFLEXES
Apparemment plus fréquentes à l'ouest qu'à l'est sont les réalisations rétroflexes des groupes r + dentale.

MQn mərdəbṍn [ʈḍ] sorte de jarre; MMf réźəm/hārźōm [ʈṣ̌] 'dessus du pied', ḵornḗt [ʈɳ]/ḵarā́n 'utérus'.

Notons que la durée de la voyelle qui précède le [ʈ] est allongée, et que ce [ʈ] rétroflexe peut avoir des réalisations faibles, jusqu'à disparaître, ce qui rappelle la situation de certains dialectes de l'anglais.

---

8. Nous avons, en notant systématiquement g, neutralisé les diverses réalisations dialectales : ce g représente [ɟ] de MQn, le g de ML, etc.

19.3.1.1.5. Vélarisation de *l*
Inversement, on observe, à l'est et pas à l'ouest, la vélarisation de *l*. Le contexte est celui d'une fermeture de syllabe non finale:
ML həwbūs (MQn həlbūs) 'habiller qqn'; kəwθēt (MQn kəltēt) 'histoire, conte'.
Et ceci même quand la voyelle qui précède est une voyelle épenthétique:
ML əwbōn (MQn ləbōn) 'blanc'.
Dans le cas où la syllabe est accentuée, on peut avoir chute de *l* et allongement de la voyelle: ML sḗmək 'je suis sauf' (< sə́lmək).
Cependant, la vélarisation ne se produit pas quand *l* est suivi d'une pharyngale ou d'une laryngale.

19.3.1.1.6. Développement de '
Le ḥ et le h initiaux, non étymologiques, sont souvent le développement d'une occlusive glottale ['].
'père' ('b) MQn Ḥ ḥayb; H ḥɛb; J 'iy (b > ∅);
'mère' ('m) MQn hāmē; Ḥ ḥām; H hāmɛ́; J 'ɛm;
'chemin' ('rm) MQn ḥawröm; Ḥ wōrəm; H hɔ̄́rəm; J 'ɔrm;
'femmes' ('nθ) MJb ḥaynēθ; Ḥ ḥáynɛθ; Ḥ ḥānīθ; J 'inɛ́θ;
et peut-être parfois la trace d'un article qui ne subsiste fonctionnellement qu'en mehri du Dhofar:
'tête' (rš < r'š et h < š) MQn ḥroh; Ḥ ḥérih; H ḥarɛ́h; J réš.

19.3.1.1.7. Glottalisation à la pause
Dans certains dialectes, on observe une fermeture de la glotte après la dernière voyelle lorsqu'elle est longue et suivie d'une consonne. Il en résulte une articulation éjective de cette consonne:
MJb dəmḗy > [dəmēx'] 'cerveau', MQnB bīr > [bīr'] 'puits'.
Lorsqu'il s'agit d'une nasale, elle se réduit à un souffle nasal (sourd), la nasalité pouvant affecter la voyelle.

19.3.1.2. *Voyelles*
Le système vocalique comprend deux ou trois voyelles brèves (selon les dialectes) a, ə/ʌ, (ɛ), six voyelles longues: ā, ɛ̄, ē, ī, ō/ɔ̄, ū et deux diphtongues ay, aw. Du point de vue diachronique un certain nombre de régularités apparaissent. En comparant le verbe de base kətūb/yəkū́təb/yəktḗb 'écrire' qui comporte des consonnes 'neutres' aux verbes nəhāg/yənū́həg/yənhā́g 'danser, jouer', nəḳáwr/yənū́ḳər/yənḳā́r 'vider un chargeur', on constate l'influence des consonnes telles que pharyngales et vélaires (ḥ, x, ɣ) d'une part, et des emphatiques (glottalisées) d'autre part. Les mêmes phénomènes se produi-

sent dans les noms: comparer ḵəffḗt 'panier' et ḵəṣṣā́t 'frange', ḥərū́ź 'acacia' et ḵəźáwb 'fauve' (non identifié).

Nous donnons ici quelques exemples de paires minimales pour des voyelles de faible contraste (MQn):
    hətt 'six' :: hɛtt 'donne!'
    kəbkēb 'entrée' :: kəbkīb 'étoile'
    tawmər 'elle dit' :: tōmər 'dattes'
    fām 'jambe' :: fawm 'jambes'
    ktūb 'il a écrit' :: ktōb 'livre'
    ɣáydəl 'il a porté' :: ɣādəl 'porter'
    tʌébyən 'tu (m.) remplis' :: tʌébyən 'tu (f.) remplis'.

19.3.1.3. Diphtongues

Nous renvoyons aux exemples de mehri, de hobyot et de harsusi du présent article: l'abondance des diphtongues *aw* et *ay* y est manifeste par rapport à leur rareté en jibbali et en soqotri. Elles sont équivalentes à une voyelle longue et majoritairement conditionnées par la présence d'une pharyngale, d'une vélaire ou d'une emphatique; mais certaines diphtongues ne peuvent s'expliquer par ce conditionnement.

19.3.2. Jibbali

Le jibbali se caractérise, phonétiquement, par la transformation de son accentuation (voir § 19.2.3.2), par la vocalisation des bilabiales *b* et *m*, l'occlusion de la bilabiale *w* ou son amuïssement, la réalisation fricative de *l*, la perte de l'opposition de quantité vocalique du proto-SAM, compensée par l'abondance des timbres vocaliques. Ces phénomènes empêchent l'identification directe de la racine. Ainsi, la plante *iźyet* est-elle *wəblīt* en mehri (même racine *wbl*).

En outre, le jibbali du centre, non celui de l'est, présente des sifflantes particulières (à côté de *š, ś, s*) fortement labialisées: *s̃, s̰̃* et *z̃*.

Les exemples ci-dessous sont uniquement pris en jibbali du centre, celui de *JL*, sauf indication contraire, *JE*, pour le jibbali de l'est.

19.3.2.1. Consonnes

19.3.2.1.1. Vocalisation de *b* et *m*

b et *m*, en position intervocalique se vocalisent, produisant les seules voyelles longues de la langue (nasalisées dans le cas de *m*):

ɛrḥī́t, f. de ɛrḥím 'beau' (MQn rḥaym, rḥáymət);
yṓri (ML yəbṓri) 'djinns'; ḫēr (ML ḫáybər) 'se refroidir';
ou produisant des hiatus: JE yiér (MQn yəbēr) 'dauphin'; JL giél (MQn gəbḗl) 'montagne'. Dans ce dernier cas le pluriel a été formé sur le singulier réduit: géĺətə (mais MQn gəbəlī́n).

Il arrive qu'un mot, dont la racine contient deux b, soit réalisé avec un ou zéro b, selon les contextes: *sabab > *səbɛb > siēb 'cause', et avec suffixe -Vk: essiēk.

19.3.2.1.2. Évolution de w

Le w radical passe à b ou à une voyelle, selon les contextes, et n'est normalement jamais réalisé w:

šəbḥéd 'être livré à soi-même' (wḥd), egbéz 'rendre licite' (gwz);
ék̲t 'temps' (wk̲t), éléd (wld) 'enfants'.

La voyelle peut être longue: əštṓḫ (šwḫ) 'pleurer amèrement'.

19.3.2.1.3. L: l fricatif

Dans des contextes palatalisants, l peut avoir une variante fricative: L (notée ź dans JL). Elle est sonore et ne peut être confondue avec la sourde ś ni avec l'éjective ź (notée ẓ́ dans JL): gíLɔ́l (ML gīlɔ́l) 'nourriture cuite'.

19.3.2.1.4. Sifflantes labialisées š̃, ṣ̃ et z̃

Ces articulations sont "réalisées avec approximativement la même position de la langue que pour š, mais il n'y a pas de contact entre le haut de la langue et les alvéoles. L'air est expulsé au-dessus de la langue et les lèvres sont simultanément arrondies en une moue" (JL: xiv).

- š̃ (voir § 19.2.1.6) a pris une indépendance phonématique par rapport à š. Rappelons la paire minimale fondamentale des pronoms suffixes -š 3ms :: -š̃ 2fs (confondus en JE); et ajoutons šəbdún 'courageux' :: š̃əbdún 'à plat ventre'. C'est souvent une simple variante palatalisée de k: š̃irś/ekrέš̃ 'ventre'.

Mais elle peut s'opposer à k: eš̃ḥéf 'perdre' :: ekḥéf 'faire affronter'.

- ṣ̃ est son homologue emphatique (voir § 19.2.1.5). Elle s'oppose à ḳ:
ṣ̃eff 'coudre grossièrement' :: ḳeff 'se détourner'.

Mais elle en est le plus souvent une variante:
fɔk̲ḫ/fúṣ̃ḥi 'une/deux moitié(s)'.

- z̃ (voir § 19.2.1.6) est une simple variante palatalisée de g: z̃énúzt/généz 'cadavre'.

19.3.2.2. Voyelles

L'opposition de quantité originelle a disparu et les timbres sont nombreux: a, ɛ, e, i, ə, u, o, ɔ.

De nouvelles voyelles longues sont produites par l'intégration de *b*, *w* et *m* (voir § 19.3.2.1.1–2). Dans ce dernier cas, il y a en outre nasalisation. L'article défini s'amalgame à une voyelle initiale (précédée de ') et l'allonge. Nous présentons ici quelques paires minimales particulièrement révélatrices.

ra yáź 'devenir doux' :: *rə yáź* 'doux'
réš 'tête' :: *réš* 'têtes'
ɛrdé 'rejeter' :: *erdé* 'abandonner'
ḥálɔ́l 'licéité' :: *ḥálúl* 'laxatif'
ɔz 'chèvre' :: *ɔ̄z* 'la chèvre'
'a yá 'frère' :: *'ā yá* 'le frère'
'irɔ́z 'riz' :: *'īrɔ́z* 'le riz'
lun 'sorte' :: *lūn* 'blanc'
essólm 'il sauva' :: *əssólm* 'que je sauve'
éléd 'enfants' :: *íléd* 'qu'il ait des enfants', ...

Quant à *a* et *ɛ* ils sont en distribution complémentaire: *a* est toujours en contexte vélaire ou pharyngal; de même *u*, *o* et *ɔ* sont vraisemblablement les variantes de deux phonèmes, bien que les notations de Johnstone laissent subsister un doute: comparer *ub* 'coeur', *ób* 'non', *ɔb* 'porte', *ɔ̄b* 'la porte'.

La disparition de *w* a entraîné la perte des diphtongues V*w*. Il y a quelques rares diphtongues V*y*: *'iy* 'père'. Plus fréquent est le hiatus: *yšīūn* 'il croit' (*'mn*); *modōi* 'étables' (*dwm*); *idīə́s* (*dyb*) 'il l'a punie'.

19.3.3. Soqotri

Le relatif isolement géographique du soqotri a permis des évolutions linguistiques particulières qui en font une langue très originale dans le groupe sudarabique et dans la famille sémitique. Dans la brève présentation qui suit, on trouvera ces traits originaux et d'autres caractéristiques résultant d'évolutions plus répandues dans les langues sémitiques.

19.3.3.1. Consonnes

19.3.3.1.1. Coalescence de phonèmes

a) Dans tous les dialectes connus, les interdentales θ, ð, θ̣ se sont confondues avec les occlusives dentales *t*, *d*, *ṭ*. Ainsi 'sang' (racine sudarabique *ðrw/y*): *dərʰ*, *dōr*, *dōṛ*,... selon les dialectes soqotri, mais *ðor* en jibbali. De même S *ṭarb* 'morceau de bois', *trih* 'deux', M Ḥ B H J mêmes mots, mais avec θ̣ et θ.

b) Inversement, nous sommes désormais en mesure d'affirmer que ce n'est que dans certains dialectes que les fricatives vélaires ɣ et x se sont confondues avec les pharyngales ʽ et ḥ:

SQa tóɣəd, SHo, Qb tə́ʽöd 'tu vas'; SQa xɔ̃mʌy̰, Qb ḥóymʌh 'cinq'.

19.3.3.1.2. Le h parasite

Son caractère "parasite" apparaît quand on compare certains mots soqotri à leurs homologues d'autres langues sudarabiques ou d'autres langues sémitiques. Le h intercalé perturbe la correspondance entre les consonnes des racines. Ainsi, le mot 'oreille' (racine ðn) se présente-t-il sous les formes: akkadien uzn, ougaritique ʼudn, hébreu ʼozen, araméen ʼudnā, arabe ʼuðn, éthiopien ʼəzn, mehri ḥayðēn, jibbali ʼiðɛ́n, harsusi ḥəyðən, hobyot ḥáyðən, et soqotri ʼídehɛn. De même: S dɔ́ḳəhɔn (ðḳn) 'menton', 'barbe'; ʼíhɔ́ntən (ʽyn) 'yeux'; ʼírhɛz (ʽrz) 'riz', etc.

Ce h n'a aucune valeur morphologique, il est le résultat d'une évolution phonétique des voyelles longues dont une reconstitution est proposée par Leslau (LS: 22). Voir aussi Bittner (1913: 5 n.), Prætorius (1908: 708–13) et Rhodokanakis (1915: 12–56).

19.3.3.1.3. Voix murmurée

Parallèlement au "h parasite", phonème de plein statut, existe une "voix murmurée", apparemment réalisée par une ouverture partielle des cordes vocales (en vibration ou non selon le contexte). Ce type phonatoire se propage sur un, deux phonèmes, rarement plus. Nous le notons par un ʰ, placé arbitrairement après une consonne murmurée, alors que la voyelle suivante et/ou la voyelle précédente peuvent être aussi murmurées:

SQa ḳårʰ 'gorge', léšʰən 'langue', tʰáʽɛləh 'ver'.

C'est peut-être un développement de ce murmure qui a permis l'émergence du h "parasite". Dans gémʰɛl/gemíli/gémʌhɔL 'chameau', le singulier comporte un murmure, le pluriel un h parasite, l'un et l'autre absents du duel.

Inversement, le -h du féminin singulier nominal et verbal (accompli 3ème personne) est parfois réduit à un murmure de la voyelle précédente ou même à zéro.

Ce murmure provoque sur /l/ l'apparition d'une variante légèrement fricative (ici notée L). Dans un dialecte (Qalansiya) la friction est telle que la réalisation de ce phonème converge avec celle de /ź/ (souvent déglottalisée en soqotri). Ainsi pour le mot 'côte', nous avons relevé: źalʽ, źɔ́ləʽ, ... et, à Qalansiya, źáźəʽ.

La phonologie des langues sudarabiques modernes   367

19.3.3.1.4. Articulation de /ˤ/
Elle n'est fricative pharyngale sonore qu'entre deux voyelles. Ailleurs elle est, dans certains dialectes occidentaux, occlusive ou plutôt affriquée: occlusive pharyngale à détente fricative pharyngale. Cette occlusion est, à la première écoute, difficilement discernable d'une occlusion glottale. Quant à la friction, elle est normalement sonore mais en fin de mot elle est dévoisée comme toute consonne. Il s'ensuit la perception de [ˤḥ#] (dans les autres dialectes il y a généralement un simple [ḥ#]).

19.3.3.1.5. Palatalisation (voir § 19.2.1.6)
La palatalisation contextuelle de /k/ connaît des degrés divers selon les dialectes. Elle peut aboutir à [c] qui ne semble pas avoir un statut de phonème dans les dialectes que nous avons observés; quant à /g/ ([ɟ], [g]) sa réalisation avancée [ž] (A.P.I. [ʒ]) a, au moins dans un dialecte, un statut phonologique à faible rendement d'opposition. Nous n'avons relevé qu'une paire minimale: SQaB *máḥže* 'lobe de l'oreille' :: *máḫge* 'enclos'.

19.3.3.1.6. Affaiblissement de l'emphase
Plusieurs dialectes ont une articulation faiblement éjective pour les occlusives (*ṭ*, *ḳ*) et quasi-sonore pour les fricatives (*ź*, *ṣ*, *ṣ̌*). Lorsque *ḳ* se palatalise (voir § 19.2.1.5), l'affrication quasi-sonore fait converger la consonne avec *g*: SQa *gə́rbʌḳ/gərbḗgi/gərébič* ou *gərḗbeg* 'chat'. On trouve même, dans certains dialectes, la convergence *ḳ-ž*: 'abreuver' *héžə*, dont le réfléchi est *téḳi* 'boire' (racine *šḳy*).

19.3.3.2. *Voyelles*

L'opposition de longueur n'apparaît qu'exceptionnellement dans les dialectes connus et avec un rendement infime. Un résidu des voyelles longues sémitiques et proto-sudarabiques est sans doute le *h* parasite (cf. ci-dessus).

Le système vocalique est riche en timbres dans tous les dialectes; certains comportent moins de voyelles labialisées que les autres, mais l'inventaire phonématique est conservé, [ɔ] et [o] étant remplacés par des réalisations [ɤ] et [ɯ] qui restent en opposition avec les voyelles antérieures.

Ainsi SQa présente, pour l'inaccompli de *sed* 'mettre à chauffer sur le feu', les formes suivantes (sans préfixe, cf. Johnstone 1968): 2ms [sɤd], 2fs [sɪd], 2mpl [səd] qui, dans d'autres dialectes sont respectivement [sɔd], [sid], [səd].

Signalons que le timbre *u* n'apparaît pratiquement que dans le passif inaccompli (sans marque personnelle) des verbes: SQa *túḳɔṭ* 'il se fait réveiller' (actif: *itā́ḳəṭ* 'il réveille'). On remarque que, dans l'ensemble, contrairement au mehri, les timbres moyens dominent largement les timbres extrêmes.

Bibliographie[9]

Abréviations
>BSOAS: *Bulletin of the School of Oriental and African Studies*
>JSS: *Journal of Semitic Studies*
>KAWW: Kaiserliche Akademie der Wissenschaften in Wien
>MAS-GELLAS: *Matériaux Arabes et Sudarabiques*. Paris: Univ. Paris-3, Groupe d'Etudes de Linguistique et de Littératures Arabes et Sudarabiques
>SAE: Südarabische Expedition
>SBKAWW: *Sitzungsberichte der KAWW*, phil.-hist. Klasse
>ZAL: *Zeitschrift für arabische Linguistik*
>ZDMG: *Zeitschrift der deutschen morgenländischen Gesellschaft*

Beeston, A. F. L. 1984. *Sabaic Grammar*. Manchester: University of Manchester (*JSS* Monograph 6).

Bittner, Maximilian. 1909–15. "Studien zur Laut- und Formenlehre der Mehri-Sprache in Südarabien, 1–5." *SBKAWW* 162/5, 168/2, 172/5, 174/4, 176/1, 2, 178/3.

———. 1913–18. "Vorstudien zur Grammatik und zum Wörterbuche der Soqotri-Sprache, 1–3." *SBKAWW*, 173/4, 186/4, 5.

———. 1916–17. "Studien zur Šḫauri-Sprache in den Bergen von Ḍofâr am Persischen Meerbusen, 1–4." *SBKAWW* 179/2, 4, 5, 183/5.

Cohen, David (éd. par). 1988. *Les langues chamito-sémitiques*. Paris: C.N.R.S. (Les langues dans le monde ancien et moderne, éd. par J. Perrot, 3).

Fresnel, Fulgence: voir Lonnet 1991.

al-Hamdani (10ème siècle). 1884–91. *Al Hamdānī's Geographie der arabischen Halbinsel [Ṣifat Jazīrat al-'Arab]*. Ed. par D. H. Müller. Leyden: Brill.

———. 1983. *Ṣifat Jazīrat al-'Arab*. Ed. par M. b. 'A. al-Akwa'. Ṣan'ā': Markaz al-dirāsāt w-al-buḥūṯ al-yamanī.

Hein, Wilhelm. 1909. *Mehri- und Ḥaḍrami-Texte gesammelt im Jahre 1902 in Gischin von Dr. —*, bearbeitet und herausgegeben von Dav. Heinr. Müller. Vienne: Alfred Hölder (KAWW, SAE, 9).

---

9. Nous donnons ici une bibliographie sommaire. Pour approfondir, on se référera à Leslau (1946) et Robin (1977).

Jahn, Alfred. 1902. *Die Mehri-Sprache in Südarabien. Texte und Wörterbuch.* Vienne: Alfred Hölder (KAWW, SAE, 3).

———. 1905. "Grammatik der Mehri-Sprache in Südarabien." *SBKAWW* 150/6.

Johnstone, T. M. 1968. "The Non-occurrence of a *t-* Prefix in Certain Socotri Verbal Forms." *BSOAS* 31: 515–25.

———. 1970. "A Definite Article in the Modern South Arabian Languages." *BSOAS* 33: 295–307.

———. 1975a. "The Modern South Arabian Languages." *Afro-Asiatic Linguistics* 1/5: 93–121.

———. 1975b. "Contrasting Articulations in the Modern South Arabian Languages." *Hamito-Semitica*. Ed. par J. et Th. Bynon, 155–59. La Haye: Mouton (Janua Linguarum Series Practica, 200).

———. 1977. *Ḥarsūsi Lexicon and English-Ḥarsūsi Word-List*. Londres: Oxford University Press (= *ḤL*).

———. 1980. "Gemination in the Jibbali Language of Dhofar." *ZAL* 4: 61–71.

———. 1981. *Jibbāli Lexicon*. Londres: Oxford University Press (= *JL*).

———. 1984. "New Sibilant Phonemes in the Modern South Arabian Languages of Dhofar." *Current Progress in Afro-Asiatic Linguistics: Papers of the Third International Hamito-Semitic Congress.* Ed. par J. Bynon, 389–90. Amsterdam-Philadelphie: Benjamins (Current Issues in Linguistic Theory, 28).

———. 1986. "Mahrī." *Encyclopédie de l'Islam*, nouv. éd., 6: 82–83.

———. 1987. *Mehri Lexicon and English-Mehri Word-list* (= *ML*), avec: *Index of the English Definitions in the Jibbāli Lexicon*, compiled by G. Rex Smith. Londres: SOAS.

Leslau, Wolf. 1938. *Lexique Soqoṭri (Sudarabique Moderne) avec comparaisons et explications étymologiques*. Paris: Klincksieck (Coll. ling. pub. par la Soc. de Ling. de Paris, 41). (= *LS*)

———. 1946. "Modern South Arabic Languages. A Bibliography." *Bulletin of the New York Public Library* 50/8 (August): 607–33.

Lonnet, Antoine. 1985. "The Modern South Arabian Languages in the P.D.R. of Yemen." *Proceedings of the Seminar for Arabian Studies* 15: 49–55.

———. 1991. "La découverte du sudarabique moderne: le eḥkili de Fresnel (1838)." *MAS-GELLAS* n.s. 3: 15–89.

Lonnet, Antoine et M.-C. Simeone-Senelle. 1983. "Observations phonétiques et phonologiques sur les consonnes d'un dialecte mehri." *MAS-GELLAS* 1: 187–218.

Matthews, Charles. 1967–70. "On the Border of the Sands." *Univ. of South Florida Language Quarterly* 6/1–2: 39–47, 6/3–4: 7–12, 7/1–2: 41–48, 7/3–4: 43–48, 8/1–2: 43–47, 8/3–4: 11–19.

Morris, Miranda. 1983. "Some Preliminary Remarks on a Collection of Poems and Songs of the Baṭāḥirah." *Journal of Oman Studies* 6: 129–44.

Müller, David Heinrich. 1902. *Die Mehri- und Soqoṭri-Sprache. I. Texte.* Vienne: Alfred Hölder (KAWW, SAE, 4).

———. 1905. *Die Mehri- und Soqoṭri-Sprache. II. Soqoṭri-Texte.* Vienne: Alfred Hölder (KAWW, SAE, 6).

———. 1907. *Die Mehri- und Soqoṭri-Sprache. III. Šḫauri-Texte.* Vienne: Alfred Hölder (KAWW, SAE, 7).

Naumkin, Vitalij V. et V. Ja. Porxomovskij. 1981. *Očerki po etnolingvistike Sokotry* [Essais d'ethnolinguistique de Soqotra]. Moscou: Nauka.

Prætorius, Franz. 1908. "Zur Frage über das parasitische *h* des Minäischen." *ZDMG* 62: 708–13.

Rhodokanakis, Nikolaus. 1915. "Der Zweigipflige Akzent im Minäo-Sabäischen (Studien zur Lexicographie und Grammatik des Altsüdarabischen, I)." *SBKAWW*, 178/4: 12–56.

Robin, Christian (éd. par). 1992. *L'Arabie antique de Karib'îl à Mahomet. Nouvelles données sur l'histoire des Arabes grâce aux inscriptions.* Aix-en-Provence: Edisud (*Revue du monde musulman et de la Méditerranée* 61, 1991–93).

[Robin, Christian]. 1977. "Langues et dialectes modernes de l'Arabie du sud." *Bibliographie générale systématique, Corpus des inscriptions et des antiquités sud-arabes*, chap. 18, 89–99. Louvain.

Sibawayhi (8ème siècle). 1881–89. *Le livre de —, Traité de grammaire arabe.* Paris. Ed. par H. Derenbourg. Repr. Hildesheim - New York: Olms, 1970.

Simeone-Senelle, Marie-Claude. 1991a. "Récents développements des recherches sur les langues sudarabiques modernes." *Proceedings of the International Hamito-Semitic Congress, 1987*, Ed. par Hans G. Mukarovsky, vol. 2, 321–37 Vienne (Beiträge zur Afrikanistik, 41).

———. 1991b. "Notes sur le premier vocabulaire soqotri: le Mémoire de Wellsted (1835). Première partie." *MAS-GELLAS* n.s. 3: 91–135.

———. 1992. "Notes sur le premier vocabulaire soqotri: le Mémoire de Wellsted (1835). Deuxième partie." *MAS-GELLAS* n.s. 4: 13–82.

Simeone-Senelle, Marie-Claude et A. Lonnet. 1986. "Lexique des noms des parties du corps dans les langues sudarabiques modernes. Première partie: la tête." *MAS-GELLAS* 3: 259–304.

———. 1988–89. "Lexique des noms des parties du corps dans les langues sudarabiques modernes. Deuxième partie: les membres." *MAS-GELLAS* n.s. 2: 191–252.

———. 1991. "Lexique Soqotri: les noms des parties du corps." *Semitic Studies in Honor of Wolf Leslau on the Occasion of His Eighty-fifth Birthday, November 14th, 1991.* Ed. par Alan S. Kaye, vol. 2, 1443–87. Wiesbaden: Harrassowitz.

———. 1992. "Compléments à *Lexique Soqotri: les noms des parties du corps.*" *MAS-GELLAS* n.s. 4: 85–108.

Thomas, Bertram. 1929. "Among some Unknown Tribes of South Arabia." *Journal of the Royal Anthropological Institute of Great Britain and Ireland* 59: 97–111.

———. 1937. "Four Strange Tongues from South Arabia: the Hadara Group." *Proceedings of the British Academy* 23: 231–331.

Wagner, Ewald. 1953. *Syntax der Mehri-Sprache unter Berücksichtigung auch der anderen neusüdarabischen Sprachen.* Berlin: Akademie Verlag (Deutsche Akademie der Wissenschaften zu Berlin, Institut für Orientforschung, Veröffentlichung 13).

Wellsted, James R.: voir Simeone-Senelle 1991b, 1992.

Abréviations et Conventions de lecture

Langues

a) Les exemples sont tirés des corpus relevés par nous sur le terrain, sauf:

B: bathari relevé par M. Morris, sauf, si précisé *(ML)*, par Johnstone.
H(ML): hobyot du Dhofar relevé par Johnstone dans le *Mehri Lexicon*.
Ḥ: harsusi, dans le *Ḥarsūsi Lexicon* (Johnstone 1977).
J: jibbali du centre, dans le *Jibbāli Lexicon* (Johnstone 1981).
JE: jibbali de l'est relevé par Johnstone.
LS: soqotri (Müller), compilé dans *Lexique Soqotri* (Leslau 1938).
ML: mehri du Dhofar, dans le *Mehri Lexicon* (Johnstone 1987).

b) Nos propres données sont introduites par l'abréviation du nom de la langue suivi du lieu d'enquête (voir la carte):

MQn: mehri de Qishn.
MQnB: dialecte bédouin de la région de Qishn.
MMf: mehri de Muḥayfif (région d'al-Ghayḍah).
MJb: mehri de Jādib.
S: soqotri.
SHo: soqotri de Ḥadibo.
SHr: soqotri de la montagne Ḥagher (dialecte bédouin).
SQa: soqotri de Qalansiya.
SQaB: soqotri des bédouins de la région de Qalansiya.
SQb: soqotri de Qadhub.
H: hobyot de la région de Ḥawf.

Autres abréviations

SAM sudarabique moderne; sém. sémitique; pr. pronom; suff. suffixe; m. masculin; f. féminin; 2ms = 2ème pers. masculin singulier, etc…

Autres conventions de lecture

    La morphologie des noms est présentée ainsi:
        singulier/duel/pluriel ou: singulier/pluriel;
  et celle des verbes:
        accompli/inaccompli indicatif/inaccompli subjonctif (à la 3ème personne du masculin singulier).

Chapter 20
Chaha (Gurage) Phonology
Wolf Leslau
University of California, Los Angeles

Chaha is a Gurage (Guragué) dialect.[1] It belongs to the branch of the Semitic language family of which the others members are Geʻez (at present the language of the liturgy), Tigre, and Tigrinya in the north; Amharic, Argobba, Harari, Gafat, and Gurage in the south.

Gurage has at least twelve dialects, some of them having variants. There are three distinct groups of this cluster: West Gurage, which includes Chaha, Endegeň, Inōr (or Ennemor), Eža, and Gyeto; East Gurage, which includes Selṭi, Wolane, Ulbarag (or Urbarag), and Zway; North Gurage, with Soddo as its only representative; and Muher, Masqan, and Gogot, the positions of which still remain to be investigated.

Note that Chaha is called *čäha* by the speakers, and *čäha* or *čəha* by the Amharas.

East Gurage is linguistically related to Harari, and Soddo (or Kəstanəňňa) is related to Gafat (Leslau 1950b). As for West Gurage, even though it has South Ethiopian features and a few notable North Ethiopian features, it still has no particularly close connection with any specific South Ethiopian language. For the position of Muher, Masqan, and Gogot, see above.

Hetzron (1972, 1977) suggested another classification, but see Leslau 1969; 1979, 1: xi–xii.

The region of Gurage is situated southwest of Addis Ababa, the capital of Ethiopia, at a distance of about 120 miles. It is bordered on the north by the river Awash, on the east by Lake Zway, and on the south and west by the river Omo.[2]

---

1. ABBREVIATIONS: Amh., Amharic; Ar., Arabic; C, consonant; C., Chaha; E., Eža; Ed., Endegeň; En., Ennemor; G., Geʻez; Go., Gogot; Gt., Gyeto; Had., Hadiya; Har., Harari; Hebr., Hebrew; Kam., Kambata; M., Muher; Ms., Masqan; Qab., Qabenna; Sid., Sidamo; So., Soddo; Te., Tigre; Tňa., Tigriňa; V, vowel; W., Wolane; Z., Zway. A lexeme *not* preceded by C. refers to Chaha.

2. For more details, see Leslau 1979, 1: ixff. For a description of the Western part of Gurage, see Shack 1966.

Most normally, the point of departure is a Chaha feature in relation to the feature of the other Gurage dialects. Occasionally a phonetic feature is mentioned in the various Gurage dialects with the exclusion of Chaha.

20.1. Labials and labialization

The labials are: *b m f w*, allophone *p*; rounded *b^w m^w f^w*, allophone *p^w*.

20.1.1. *b*

b corresponds to Semitic and Ethiopic *b*. Example: C. *bäna* (for *l* : *n*, see § 20.7.1.2) 'eat', Ar. *bali'a*, G. *bäl'a*, Amh. *bälla*.

Minimal pairs *b*:*b^w* in *bər* 'silver' : *b^wər* 'main'; *bärä* 'leaf of the *äsät*-plant that is torn' : *b^wärä* 'cow that has a white spot on the forehead'; *bəṭər* 'kind of bush' : *b^wəṭər* 'eighth of a loaf of bread'.

In intervocalic or final position *b* may become *w*. Examples: C. *äwawt* 'roundworm' (Go. *äbabut*); C. *äwä* 'dew' (G. *həbo*); C. *səwä* 'animal fat' (from *säbba* 'be fat'); C. *šəwät* 'gray hair' (from *šəbät*); C. *nəzəw* 'flexible' (from **nəzəb, ləzəb*).

b became *y* in C. *əngäyä* 'kind of berry' (Gt. *əng'aba*).

-*äb*V- became *o* in C. *wəg'o* 'violent rain with wind' (Go. *wäg'äbä*); C. *aso* 'salt' (S. *asäbo*).

-*əbə*-, -*əb* became *u* in *sur* 'broken' (from *səbər, səwer*); *ṭu* 'breast' (from *ṭəb, ṭəw*).

Alternation between C. *b* and Gurage *m* occurs in C. *qaribo* 'kind of beer' and M. *qarimo*.

Alternation between C. *b* and *f* occurs in C. *bəṭərq bärä*[3] 'feel excitement' and M. *fəṭərq beä*; C. *anqəbäqäbä* and *anqəfäqäfä* 'cut down branches'.

The labial *b* is occasionally inserted after *m*: C. *ambər* 'cabbage' (W. *aməl*); C. *qambisa* and *qämis* 'shirt' (*qämis* borrowed from Arabic).

For devoicing of originally geminated *b*, *b^w* becoming *p*, *p^w*, see § 20.10.1; § 20.10.2.

20.1.2. *b^w*

b^w of the various Gurage dialects may become *w* in Chaha: thus, C. *wäz* 'slave' (En. *b^wäz*); C. *wəyä* 'go down to a lower place' (Ms. *b^wəyä*); *däwä* 'relatives' (E. *däb^wä*).

---

3. The final -*m* of the Chaha perfect (*barä-m*) will be omitted.

Intervocalic: C. *a-wäka* 'make dough' (from *a-bʷäka*); *yä-wänet* 'of the husband's sister' (for *yä-bʷänet*); *yä-wəya* 'of the *bʷəya*-liquid'.

bʷ instead of *w* by pseudo-correction (see § 20.17) in *bʷər* 'main' instead of *wər*.

Note C. *bʷə*- as against *bu* of the other Gurage dialects: C. *bʷəko* 'dough', E. *buko*.

20.1.3. f

f corresponds to *f* of Semitic and Ethiopic: C. *fäta* 'untie, loosen', Ar. *fataḥa* 'open', G. *fätḥa*.

Minimal pairs *f* : *fʷ* in C. *āf* 'mouth' : *āfʷ* 'bird'; *fäkärä* 'multiply' : *fʷäkärä* 'boast'.

f occasionally nasalizes the preceding *a*: thus, *āfraxʷa* 'pregnant cattle'; *āfwat* 'odor'; *zāfʷa* 'afterbirth of cattle'.

For the alternation *f* : *b*, see § 20.1.1.

Note that Chaha *fʷä* becomes *fo*, and C. *fʷə* becomes *fu* in the other Gurage dialects. Thus, C. *fʷägägä anṭä* 'cut off something very close', but Gt. *fogägä anṭä*; C. *fʷəgəg* 'last day of the full moon', but E. En. *fugəg*.

20.1.4. m

m corresponds to *m* of Semitic and Ethiopic: *mänṭä* 'strip off', Ar. *malaṭa* 'shave', G. *mäläṭä* 'strip off'. (for *l* : *n*, see § 20.7.1.2).

Minimal pairs of *m* : *mʷ* in C. *mar* 'beeswax' : *mʷar* 'share'; *mena* 'action' : *mʷena* 'maternal uncle'; *əmər* 'stone' : *əmʷər* 'strength'.

m in dialects other than Chaha may become *w*: thus, *w* of Ed. *əwān* 'louse' goes back to *m* of M. *qəmal*, C. *qəmar* (for *l* : *r*, see § 20.7.3); Ed. *žəwān* 'red core of the trunk', but C. *žəmar*, Ed. *qəwāččä* 'be bashful', but C. *qəmäčä*.

Final *-äm* of Ethiopic is reduced to *-o* in Chaha: e.g., G. *mäskäräm*, name of the 1st month, > C. *mäsxäro*.

Final *-m* is lost in *axu* 'you' (pl.) for *axum*.

Note that Chaha *mʷä* becomes *mo* and *mʷə* becomes *mu* in the other Gurage dialects. Thus, C. *mʷänä* 'bladder', but Ed. *monä*; C. *mʷəst* 'ill-mannered', but En. *must*.

20.1.5. w

w corresponds to *w* of Semitic and Ethiopic: e.g., C. *wäṭäqä* 'fall', Ar. *wadaqa* 'fall in drops' (for *ṭ* from *d*, see § 20.14.1.5), Amh. *wäddäqä* 'fall'.

20.1.5.1. w from consonants

w < *b*: thus, C. *äwa* 'dew' (G. *həbo*); C. *äwawt* 'roundworm' (Go.*äbabut*).

w < *bʷ*: C. *wäz* 'slave' (En. *bʷäz*); C. *wəyä* 'go down to a lower place' (Ms. *bʷəyä*); C. *däwä* 'relatives' (E. *däbʷä*).

w < *mʷ*: thus, C. *wämaka* 'proverb' (En. *mʷamʷaka*); C. *wətətənyät* 'upper part of the rolled-up leaf of the *äsät*-plant' (Gt. *mutətənyät* < *mʷətətənyät*). For *w* < *m* by dissimilation, see § 20.15.3.

w < *kʷ* in C. *näwšašä* 'the young of a goat' (Ed. *nokšašä* from *näkʷšašä*), and probably C. *wašwašinyät* and *kʷaškʷašiyä* 'kind of bush'.

w < *gʷ* in C. *wərawər* 'throat' and *gʷärärä*.

w < *h* in C. *wəsača* 'day when the *äsät*-plant is scraped', from Kambata *hasačča*.

20.1.5.2. Contractions involving w

wä > *o*: C. *wägät* and *ogät* 'public discussion'.

-*äw* > *o*: C. *ṭona* 'strength' (Gt. *ṭäwna*).

aw > *o*: C. *od* 'threshing field' (En. *awd*); C. *ozat* 'flour boiled in water' (Gt. *awzat*).

-*äwä* > *o*: C. *boxe* 'well', from *bäwäxe*; *bogäret* 'well', from *bäwägäret*; *yorčä* 'of the front leg' from *yäwärčä*.

-*äwə* > *o*: C. *yok'äränä* 'one who participates in the monthly gathering', from *yäwək'äränä*; *yosa* 'of the bread made of the *äsät*-plant', from *yäwəsa*.

awä > *a*, *ọ*: e.g., C. *aṭa*, *ọṭa* 'bring out', from *awäṭa*; *andä*, *ọndä* 'lower' (from *awändä*, M. *awärrädä*).

20.2. Labialization

While the labiovelars and the rounded labials are phonemes in Gurage and in the other Ethiopian languages outside of Tigre and Harari, they are also phonetically conditioned.

In the impersonal of Gurage of the type 'one says' a labializable consonant is labialized. The labializable consonants are the labials *b* > *bʷ*, *f* > *fʷ*, *m* > *mʷ*, *p* > *pʷ*, and the velars *g* > *gʷ*, *k* > *kʷ*, *x* > *xʷ*, *q* > *qʷ* (see Leslau 1967). Thus, *bʷänem* (from *bäna-m* 'eat'); *čäfʷärim* (from *čäfärä-m* 'put into the mouth'); *mʷänem* (from *mäna-m* 'fill'); *säpʷärim* (from *säpärä-m* 'break'); *šägʷärim* (from *šägärä-m* 'change'); *məsäkʷärim* (from *məsäkärä-m* 'bear witness'); *xʷarim* (from *xarä-m* 'know'); *qʷäṭärim* (from *qäṭärä-m* 'kill').

20.3. Velars

The velars are: *g*, *k*, *q*; spirant *x*; palatalized *g'*, *k'*, *x'*, *q'*; labiovelars *gʷ*, *kʷ*, *xʷ*, *qʷ*.

20.3.1. Velar g

g corresponds to Arabic ǧ (*g*), Ethiopic *g*: e.g., C. *gamera* 'camel', Ar. *ǧamal*, G. *gämäl*.

In Arabic loanwords, C. *g* corresponds to Ar. ǧ (*g*), ġ: e.g., C. *ləgʷam* 'bridle', Ar. *luǧām*; C. *gaz* 'battle', Ar. *ġazʷ*.

Minimal pairs *g* : *g'* in *gärä* 'buttocks' : *g'ärä* 'leaf of the *äsät*-plant that is not torn'; *gätärä* 'put to sleep' : *g'ätärä* 'be lenient toward someone'.

Minimal pairs *g* : *gʷ* in *gaz* 'raid' : *gʷaz* 'caravan'; *gəbər* 'utensil' : *gʷəbər* 'hunchbacked'; *gär* 'mild' : *gʷär* 'harvest'.

For the originally geminated *g*, *g'*, *gʷ* becoming *k*, *k'*, *kʷ*, see § 20.10.4; § 20.10.5; § 20.10.6.

For *g* becoming palatalized *g'*, see § 20.9.

For labialization of *g* into *gʷ*, see § 20.2.

C. *gʷ* alternates with *w* in *gʷäräro* 'throat' and *wərawər*.

C. *gu*- (from *gʷə*-) may become *w* in the other Gurage dialects: thus, C. *gudella* (from *gʷədella*) 'strap around the tail of the horse' as against M. So. *wəddəlla*.

C. *gʷä* may become *go* in the other dialects: thus, C. *gʷäǧä* 'well, pit', Ed. *goǧä*.

20.3.2. k

k corresponds to *k* of Semitic and Ethiopic: C. *käfana* 'shroud', Ar. *kafana* 'envelop in a shroud', Te. *käfna*.

Minimal pairs of *k* : *k'* in C. *wäka* 'beam' : *wäk'a* 'loan of a cow'.

Minimal pairs in *k* : *kʷ* in C. *täkäsä* 'set on fire' : *täkʷäsä* 'shoot'; *käšä barä*- 'have dysentery' : *(a)kʷäšä* 'remove the layers of the trunk of the *äsät*-plant'.

k is in alternation with *q* of the other Gurage dialects: C. *korbeša* 'the young of a goat', Ed. *qorbešša*; C. *äkäsä* 'be delayed', So. *iqqäsä*; C. *kʷätä* 'loft', En. *qʷätä*; C. *kärä* 'day', M. *qänä* (for *n* : *r*, see § 20.7.3.1).

Original *k*, *kʷ* has a tendency of becoming a spirant *x*, *xʷ*. There are nearly as many nouns and verbs with *k* as there are with *x*.

Initial position: C. *xarä* 'know', root *khl*; C. *xənnä* 'cubit', So. *kərrä*; C. *xabä* 'do something again', G. *käʿabä*; C. *xäpt* 'liver' (§ 20.14.1.3), G. *käbəd*; C. *xʷä* 'spill', G. *käʿawä*; C. *xʷäxʷäb* 'star', G. *kokäb*.

In medial position: C. *äxər* 'cereal', root *äkəl*; *bäxər* 'first-born', root *bäkər*; *naxä* 'send', Amh. *lakä* (for *l* : *n*, see § 20.7.1.2); *tä-xätärä* 'put on a dress', root *kdn* 'cover'; *fänäxä* 'be patient', So. *färräkä*.

In final position: C. *sox* 'thorn', So. *äsok*.

Before or after a consonant: C. *mäsxäro*, name of the first month, Amh. *mäskäräm*; *šäxra* 'clay', So. *šäkla*.

In the verbal class C*ky*, *k* may become palatalized into *k'*: thus, C. *bäk'ä* 'cry', root *bky*; C. *säk'ä* 'flee', root *sky*.

k may become palatalized into *č*: thus, C. *wärčä* 'front of leg' (also Amh. *wärč*), from *wärk-e*; C. *čəff*, interjection used to chase away a cat, Amh. *kəff*.

For *k* becoming labialized *k*ʷ, see § 20.2.

C. *k*ʷä may become *ko* in the other Gurage dialects: thus, C. *k*ʷ*äfita* 'plaited turban worn by Muslims', E. *kofita*.

20.3.3. *x*

x most often comes from *k* (see § 20.3.2).

It also corresponds to *h* in Cushitic loanwords (as in C. *xäbər* 'uncultivated pasture land', from Qab. *haburra*), and to *h*, *ḥ*, and *ḫ* in Arabic loanwords (as in C. *xawa* 'empty', Ar. *hawā*'; *saxən* 'plate', Ar. *ṣaḥn*; *xädämä* 'render service', Ar. *ḫadama*; *xamis* 'Thursday', Ar. *ḫamīs*).

Minimal pairs *x* : *x'* in C. *tä-xätärä* 'put on a dress' : *tä-x'ätärä* 'follow'; *mäxäna* 'six-month period of growing' : *mäx'äna* 'bull in his prime'.

Minimal pairs *x* : *x*ʷ in C. *xəm* 'that' : *x*ʷ*əm* 'thousand'.

For *x* labialized into *x*ʷ, see § 20.2.

For *x* palatalized into *x'*, see § 20.9.1.

In the verbal class C*ky*, the final *k'* may become *x'* in some nominal forms: e.g., C. *bix'ä* 'mourning', from *bäk'ä*.

C. *x*ʷä may become *xo* and C. *x*ʷə may become *xu* in the other Gurage dialects: thus, C. *x*ʷ*ärinä* 'dress made of hare's skin', Gt. *xorinä*; C. *x*ʷ*əm* 'thousand', Gt. *xum*.

20.3.4. *q*

q corresponds to *q* of Semitic and Ethiopic: e.g., C. *qomä* 'stand', Ar. *qāma*, G. *qomä*.

Minimal pairs *q* : *q*ʷ in C. *qänärä* 'be light': *q*ʷ*änärä* 'finish the top of the roof'; *qəyä* 'stone delimiting the boundary': *q*ʷ*əyä* 'ball made of cloth or fiber'.

Minimal pairs of *q* : *q'* in C. *qäpärä* 'help' : *q'äpärä* 'plant'; C. *qäṭärä* 'kill' : *q'äṭärä* 'join by attaching'; C. *bäqärä* 'germinate' : *bäq'ärä* 'brew beer'.

C. *q* alternates with *k* of the other Gurage dialects: thus, C. *qəṭär* 'leaf', En. *kä'är*; C. *qanča* 'fiber of the *äsät*-plant', Ed. *ke'ä*; C. *wäqt* 'time' (from Arabic), W. *wäkt*.

For *q* becoming a labialized *qʷ*, see § 20.2.

For *q* becoming palatalized *q'*, see § 20.9.1.

For Ethiopic *q* alternating with *k* of Chaha, see § 20.3.2.

q' of Chaha may become *č* in the other dialects: e.g., C. *aq'ä* 'crunch', but So. *ač̣č̣ä*; C. *q'äṭä* 'be weak', but W. *č̣eṭä*.

C. *qʷä*- as against *qo*-, and C. *qʷə*- as against *qu*- in the other Gurage dialects: thus, C. *qʷämärä* 'become strong', En. *qomärä*; C. *qʷərər* 'light', En. Ed. *qurər*.

C. *qə*- (probably from *qʷə*-) as against *w* in the other dialects; thus, C. *qənčuwät* 'woman who has power of stopping rain', Gt. *wīnčuwät*.

20.4. Dentals

The dentals are: *d*, *t*, *ṭ*.

20.4.1. d

d corresponds to *d* of Ethiopic. Examples: *däfärä* 'dare' (Amh. *däffärä*).

In Arabic loanwords *d* corresponds to *d*, *ḍ*. Examples: C. *xädämä* 'support one's parents', from Ar. *ḫadama* 'serve'; *qabd* 'object taken as a guarantee', from Ar. *qabḍ*.

Minimal pairs of *d* : *ǧ* in C. *däpärä* 'add, join': *ǧäpärä* 'accomplish'.

By assimilation to a glottalized, *d* has become *ṭ*: thus, C. *wäṭäqä* 'fall' (Amh. *wäddäqä*); see § 20.14.1.5.

By assimilation to a voiceless *p*, *d* became *t* in C. *xäpt* 'liver', from *käbd* (see § 20.14.1.3).

For *ṭ-g* of the various Gurage dialects becoming *d-g* in Chaha, as in *dəgär* 'hair' (but Z. *ṭəgär*), *däg'ä* 'honeyed water' (but W. *ṭəgay*), and for *ṭ-d* becoming *d-d*, as in C. *mədad* 'griddle' (but in So. *məṭad*), see § 20.14.1.5.

For an originally geminated *d* becoming a devoiced *t*, see § 20.10.3.

20.4.2. t

t corresponds to *t* of Semitic and Ethiopic: C. *täfa* 'spit', Ar. *taffa*, Amh. *täffa*.

In Arabic loanwords Chaha *t* corresponds to *t*, *ṭ*: e.g., C. *tarik* 'story' (Ar. *ta'rīḫ*); C. *tumma* 'garlic' (Ar. *ṭūm*).

Minimal pairs of *t* : *č* in C. *tərätärä* 'unroll thread used for weaving' : *čəräčärä* 'practice small trade'.

Original *t* of Chaha alternates with *ṭ* of the other Gurage dialects: thus, *tata* 'twist two or more threads', Go. So. *ṭaṭṭa*.

Original *ṭ* of Ethiopic alternates with *t* of Chaha: C. *atebät* 'finger' (Ms. *aṭebäṭ*; Amh. *ṭat*); see also § 20.11.2.

By assimilation to a palatal, *t* may become *č*: e.g, C. *gučəča* 'earring' (En. *gutəča*).

For the palatalization of *t* see § 20.9.1.

20.4.3. *ṭ*

ṭ corresponds to 1) Ar. *ṭ*, G. Te. Tna. *ṣ*, South Ethiopic *ṭ*: e.g., C. *ṭäma* 'be thirsty', Ar. *ṭami'a*, G. Te. *ṣäm'a*, Amh. *ṭämma*.

2) Ar. *ḍ*, G. *ḍ*, Te. Tna. *ṣ*, South Ethiopic *ṭ*: e.g., C. *ṭämädä* 'yoke', Ar. *ḍamada*, G. *ḍämädä*, Te. *ṣämda*; Amh. *ṭämmädä*.

3) Ar. *ṭ*, North and South Ethiopic *ṭ*: C. *ṭäpʷä* 'suck', Ar. *ṭiby* 'teat', G. *ṭäbäwä* 'suck', Am. *ṭäbba*.

Minimal pairs of *ṭ* : *č̣* in *ṭəra* 'grudge' : *č̣əra* 'fly whisk'.

The glottalized *ṭ* of Chaha alternates with the original *t* of the other languages: thus, C. *dəsṭ* 'kind of pot' (So. *dəst*); *šäfäṭä* 'become a rebel' (Ed. *šäffätä*).

For the glottalized *ṭ* of C. *aräqəṭ* 'leech' in relation to *aläqət* of the other Ethiopian languages, and of C. *wäṭäqä* 'fall' in relation to *wdq* of the other languages, see § 20.14.1.5.

For the palatalization of *ṭ* to *č̣*, see § 20.9.1.

20.5. Sibilants

The sibilants are: *z*, *s*, (*ṣ*).

20.5.1. *z*

z corresponds to *z* of Semitic: e.g., C. *zäbär* 'time', Ar. *zamān*, G. *zämän*.

It also corresponds to Ar. *ḏ*, Hebr. *z*, Ethiopic *z*: e.g., C. *zəmb* 'fly', Ar. *ḏubāb*, Hebr. *zəḇūḇ*, Amh. *zəmb*.

In Arabic loanwords *z* corresponds to Ar. *z*, *ḏ*, *ẓ*: e.g., C. *ǧeza* 'gratitude', Ar. *ǧazā*; C. *kəzəb* 'lie', Ar. *kiḏb*; C. *zəxur* 'midday', Ar. *ẓuhr*.

Minimal pairs *z* : *ž* in *zänärä* 'jump' : *žänärä* 'block the view with a curtain'.

For the palatalization of *z* into *ž*, see § 20.9.1.

An originally geminated *z* has become a devoiced *s*: e.g., C. *bäsa* 'abound', E. *bäzza*; *zasa* 'act mad' as against E. *zazza* (see § 20.10.8).

The voiced *z* remained *z* in the verbs with identical second and third radicals: thus, C. *fäzäzä* 'be better', E. *fäzzäzä*.

It also remained *z* in Amharic loanwords: e.g., C. *tä-razäzä* 'make the last will' from Amh. *tä-nazzäzä*.

For the palatalization of *z* to *ž*, see § 20.9.1.

20.5.2. s

s corresponds to 1) Ar. *ṭ*, Hebr. *š*, G. *ś*, other Ethiopian languages *s*: e.g., C. *sost* 'three', Ar. *ṭalāṭ*, Hebr. *šāloš*, G. *śäläs*, Amh. *sost*.

2) Ar. *ṭ*, Hebr. *š*, Ethiopic *s*: e.g., C. *samt* 'eight', Ar. *ṭamān*, Hebr. *šəmonɛ*, Amh. *səmmənt*.

3) Ar. *s*, Hebr. *š*, Ethiopic *s*: e.g., C. *sämma* 'hear', Ar. *samiʾa*, Hebr. *šåmaʿ*, G. *säm'a*.

4) Ar. *š*, G. *ś*, other Ethiopian languages *s*: e.g., C. *säpa* 'be fatter than expected', Ar. *šabḥ* 'large', G. *śäbḥa* 'be fat', Amh. *säbba*.

In Arabic loanwords C. *s* corresponds to Ar. *s*, *ṣ*: e.g., C. *säbäb* 'cause', Ar. *sabab*; C. *asər* 'time of day about 4 o'clock in the afternoon', Ar. *ʿaṣr*.

Minimal pairs *s* : *š* in C. *sägärä* 'amble' : *šägärä* 'change'.

For *s* going back to a geminated *z*, see § 20.10.8.

For *s* palatalized into *š*, see § 20.9.1.

20.5.3. ṣ

ṣ is preserved in loanwords from Geʿez through Amharic: e.g., *ṣälot* 'prayer', Amh. *ṣälot* (from Geʿez).

Geʿez *ṣ* has become *ṭ* in Chaha.

20.6. Laryngeal h

h, the only laryngeal in Chaha, exists in a few Amharic loanwords: *haymanot* 'belief', *har* 'silk'.

20.7. Liquids

The liquids are: *l*, *n*, *r*.

20.7.1. *l*

There are a few lexemes in Chaha that have a simple or a geminated *l*. Nearly all the verbs and nouns that have retained *l* are loanwords from Amharic, Arabic, or Cushitic.

In initial position: *ləbəč̣ barä* 'become lukewarm' (probably from Cushitic); *lul* 'pearl' (from Ar. *lu'lu'*); *lämča* 'twin' (from Oromo).

Medial position: *agälgəl* 'basket' (from Amharic); *bučəlla* 'puppy' (from Oromo through Amharic); *atäla* and *atära* 'lees of beer' (from Amharic); *ella* 'covet' (from Cushitic).

Post-consonant position: *abläšä* (also *abräšä*) 'spoil' (from Amharic).

20.7.1.1. Loss of original medial *l*

Original medial *l* is occasionally lost through palatalization or through weakening of *l*. Examples: C. *gef* 'tall' (root *glf*); *beṭ* 'clever' (root *blṭ*); *eb* 'milk' (from *alib*); *gaba* 'trodden straw' (Go. *gäläba*).

Normally, original *l* became *n* or *r* (see below).

20.7.1.2. *l* > *n*

The original liquid *l* has become *n* in initial position and in medial position when originally geminated.

Initial position: *naba* 'waist' (M. *laba*); *näma* 'flourish' (Amh. *lämma*).

Medial position: *mʷāšəna* 'kind of millet' (Amh. *mašəlla*); *bäna* 'eat' (Amh. *bälla*); *säna* 'arrive' (M. *sälla*); *anäbä* 'to milk' (Amh. *alläbä*).

20.7.1.3. *l* > *r*

The liquid *l* becomes *r* in non-initial position when originally not geminated.

In intervocalic position: C. *ənqura* 'egg' (Ed. *ənqulä*); *gamera* 'camel' (Amh. *gəmäl*); C. *qäpärä* 'decrease' (S. *qäbälä*).

Pre-consonant position: *darka* 'dewlap' (M. *daləgga*); *wärd* 'child' (root *wld*).

Post-consonant position: *amre*, name of the eleventh month (Amh. *hamle*); *a-mrana* 'be slippery' (M. *a-mlalla*); *a-č̣ranämä* 'be dark' (M.*a-č̣lallämä*).

Final, post-vocalic position: *bar* 'holiday' (Amh. *bal*); *ambər* 'cabbage' (S. *aməl*; for inserted *b*, see § 20.12.3).

20.7.1.4. *l* > *y*

When preceded by a palatalizing vowel, *l* is palatalized into *y*: thus, *gədiya* 'sleep' (n.), from *gätärä*, root *gdl*; *dəbiya* 'addition', from **dbl*.

20.7.2. n

n remains *n* in initial position: *näpärä* 'it was'; *nəb* 'bee'.

n remains *n* in intervocalic position when originally geminated: C. *anäsä* 'be little' (Amh. *annäsä*); *āfuna* 'nose' (E. *āfunna*).

A non-geminated *n* in intervocalic position remains *n* in Amharic and Cushitic loanwords: *fənäda* 'explode' (Amh. *fänädda*); *dina* 'enemy' (Oromo *dina*); *eyana* 'luck' (Kam. Had. *ayana*).

It remains *n* in medial, pre-consonant position: *andər* 'small drum'; *čanqʷa* 'not yet ripe'.

It likewise remains *n* in loanwords in final post-vocalic position: *saxən* 'dish' (from Ar. *ṣaḥn*).

A non-geminated *n* in intervocalic position becomes *r*: e.g., *amärä* 'believe' (Amh. *ammänä*); *qʼärä* 'bladder' (M. *qʼäna*); *arat* 'top of head' (M. *anat*).

In final postvocalic position *n* becomes *r*: e.g., *ənzər* 'ear' (M. *ənzən*, W. *əzən*); *gunär* 'head' (M. *gunnän*).

In verbs ending in *ñ* in the various Gurage dialects (often going back to a verb ending in *y*) Chaha has *n*: thus, *tänä* 'swear', but En. Gt. *täñä*, Ed. *täññä* (root *try*); C. *qʷänä* 'roast grain or coffee', but En. *qʷäñä*, Ed. *qʷäññä*; C. *a-fʷänä* 'take a rest', but En. Gt. *a-fʷäñä*, S. *a-fōye*; C. *tä-kranä* 'rent', but En.Gt. *tä-krañä*, Ed. *tä-krayyä*, Amh. *tä-kärayyä*.

The nasal *n* may be absorbed in the nasalized vowel: *āxʷärä-n* 'immature' (for *an-xʷärä-n*, lit. 'it is not for him'); *āfuna* 'nose' (root *'nf*).

20.7.3. r

An original non-geminated *r* remains *r*.

In medial position: *däfärä* 'dare' (Amh. *däffärä*); *atärä* 'spend the night' (Amh. *addärä*; for *t:d*, see § 20.10.3).

In pre-consonant and post-consonant position: *bärča* 'misfortune'; *boträka* 'crack in the ground after the rainy season'.

In final position: *ägər* 'foot'.

20.7.3.1. r > n

The liquid *r* becomes *n* in initial position and in non-initial position when originally geminated.

Initial position: *notä* 'run' (Amh. *rotä*); *nesa* 'corpse' (Amh. *resa*).

Medial position, originally geminated: *ṭänäqä* 'be dry' (Amh. *därräqä*); *bändä* (for *bänädä*) 'be cold' (Amh. *bärrädä*); *bəna* 'clear weather after rain' (Ms. *bərra*).

In loanwords *r* either remains *r* or it becomes *n*: *rux* 'spirit' (but also *lux*, from Ar. *rūḫ*), *qāna* 'read the Koran' (from Ar. *qara'a*).

20.7.3.2. *r > y*
Palatalization of *r* into *y* occurs in the verb and in the noun. Examples: C. *qəyä* 'wait' (W. *qerä*, Har. *qēraḫa*); *səyä* 'buy' (Go. *sərä*); *tä-wyanä* and *tä-wranä* 'be confused in making a decision'; *a-šränä* and *a-šräyä* 'distinguish'; *wanṭiyä* 'bamboo filter' (from *näṭärä*); *ang"äya* 'not yet ripe (coffee, fruit)', Ms. *ang"ar*.

The liquid is also lost through palatalization in the imperfect 2nd feminine singular: *təgäfi* from *gäfärä* 'release'; *təbädi* from *bätärä* 'advance'.

There are occurrences where *r* is lost in medial position: *qem* 'gleanings' (W. *qärma*); *čəyä* 'melted butter that runs down from the face of a woman's hair' (M. *čərəyä*).

20.7.3.3. Other *r* processes
By pseudo-correction (see § 20.17) *r* has become *l*: *sulle* 'kind of breeches' (Amh. *surre*); *fällämä* 'sign' (Amh. *färrämä*).

For the insertion of *r*, see § 20.12.2.

20.8. Palatals and palatalization

The palatals are : dentals and sibilants *ǧ č č̣ ž š ñ*; velars *g' k' x' q'*; and *y*. Note that palatal velars occur in West Gurage and in Muher, less in Masqan and Gogot. The number of the palatal velars in So., W., and Selti is small.

For originally geminated *ǧ* becoming *č*, for *ž* becoming *š*, and for *g'* becoming *k'*, see § 20.10.

20.8.1. Minimal pairs
d : *ǧ* in *däpärä* 'add, join' : *ǧäpärä* 'accomplish'.

t : *č* in *tərätärä* 'unroll thread used for weaving' : *čəräčärä* 'practice small trade'.

ṭ : *č̣* in *ṭəra* 'grudge: *č̣əra* 'fly whisk'.

s : *š* in *sägärä* 'amble' : *šägärä* 'change'.

z : *ž* in *zänärä* 'jump' : *žänärä* 'block the view with a curtain'.

g : *g'* in *gära* 'buttocks' : *g'ära* 'leaf of the *äsät*-plant that is torn'; *gätärä* 'put to sleep' : *g'ätärä* 'be lenient toward someone'.

k : *k'* in *wäka* 'beam' : *wäk'a* 'loan of a cow'.

x : x' in tä-xätärä 'put on a dress' : tä-x'ätärä 'follow'; mäxäna 'the six-month period of growing and harvesting' : mäx'äna 'bull in his prime'.

q : q' in qäpärä 'plant' : q'äpärä 'help'; qätärä 'kill' : q'ätärä 'join by attaching'.

20.8.2. Alternation of palatals

č : š, š : č in C. čəmbəra 'chickpea' : M. šəmbura; gʷäčä 'appointment' from Sid. gēšša; C. wərš, interjection used to chase away a calf, Ed. wərč.

ž : ǧ in C. qʷäžä 'defecate ': Z. qūǧi.

20.9. Palatalization

It was seen above (§ 20.8) that the palatals are phonemes. They are also, however, phonetically conditioned. As a rule, a palatal consonant is brought about by the presence of a final -i, -e, and of a semivowel y. The final -i occurs in the imperfect, jussive, and imperative of the 2nd feminine singular, in the participle, and in the impersonal. The palatalizable consonants are the dentals d, t, ṭ, the sibilants z, s, and the velars g, k, x, and q.

20.9.1. Examples

d > ǧ: tərämǧ 'you (fem.) love' (from nämädä); participle zamaǧ 'runaway horse' (from zämädä); impersonal agʷäǧim 'one binds' (from agädä).

t > č: təkäfči 'you (fem.) open' (from käfätä); äčoči 'which one plowed' (from čotä).

ṭ > č̣: təṭäbč̣i 'you (fem.) seize' (from ṭäbäṭä); yarč̣i 'which one slaughters' (from anṭä).

z > ž: tačänž 'you (fem.) crouch down' (from a-čänäzä); impersonal tä-g'ag'äžim 'one is haughty' (from tä-g'ag'äzä).

s > š: təqämš 'you (fem.) taste' (from qämäsä); impersonal näkʷäšim 'one bit' (from näkäsä).

k > k': təsäk'ək 'you (fem.) drive a peg into the ground' (from säkäkä); note the palatalized first k' by assimilation.

x > x': təfärx' 'you (fem.) are patient' (from fänäxä).

q > q': təṭärq' 'you (fem.) draw water from a container' (from ṭänäqä). Nominal pattern: wəṭaq'ä 'act of falling down' (from wäṭäqä).

20.9.2. Verbs with 3rd radical y/w

In the verbs in which the 2nd radical is palatalizable and the 3rd radical is y, w, the 2nd radical becomes palatalized and y, w is absorbed in the palatalization. Examples: *ačä* 'close' (G. *'aṣäwä*), *a-räšä* 'build' (G. *räsäyä* 'place'), *ažä* 'see' (root *ḥzy*), *bäk'ä* 'cry' (G. *bäkäyä*), *aq'ä* 'crunch' (root *ḥqy*).

The same feature occurs in the other Gurage dialects: *d* > *ǧ* as in E. *aǧǧä* 'sweep' (G. *'adäwä*); *t* > *č* as in S. *säče* 'drink' (G. *sätäyä*); *k* > *č* as in S. *bäče* 'cry' (G. *bäkäyä*).

For the palatalization of the liquids, see § 20.7.1.4, § 20.7.3.2.

20.10. Devoicing

The voiced *b*, *bʷ*, *d*, *g*, *g'*, *gʷ*, *ǧ*, *z*, *ž* if originally geminated have normally become devoiced. Thus, *bb* > *p*, *bbʷ* > *pʷ*, *dd* > *t*, *gg* > *k*, *gg'* > *k'*, *ggʷ* > *kʷ*, *ǧ* > *č*, *z* > *s*, *žž* > *č*.

20.10.1. *b*

Originally geminated voiced *b* has become devoiced *p*. Verbs: *däpärä* 'add', E. *däbbärä*; *šäpätä* 'choose, prefer', E. *šäbbätä*; *gäpa* 'enter', E. *gäbba*.

Nouns: *ǧipä* 'mat made of fiber', E. *ǧibbä*; *dəpeya* 'stick for hitting a ball', E. *dəbbe*.

In final, postvocalic position: *top*, interjection used to chase away a horse, E. *tobb*; *žäp* 'lion', E. *žäbb*.

Note also the devoicing of *b* in *xäpt* 'liver', from *käb(ə)d*, by assimilation to the final *t* (see also § 20.14.1.3).

The originally geminated *b* remains *b* in Amharic loanwords: e.g., *a-näbäbä* 'read' from Amh. *a-näbbäbä*; *g'äbärä* 'pay taxes' from Amh. *gäbbärä*, and others.

20.10.2. *bʷ*

Originally geminated voiced *bʷ* has become devoiced *pʷ* in Chaha *kapʷat* 'mattress made of unsplit rope and fiber' as against E. *kabbʷat*.

20.10.3. *d*

Originally geminated voiced *d* has become devoiced *t* in Chaha. Verbs: *gätärä* 'put to sleep, E. *gäddärä*; *bätärä* 'advance', E. *bäddärä*.

Nouns: *agdata* 'partition in the house', E. *agdadda*; *data* 'chest', E. *dadda*.

In verbs with identical second and third radicals the original *d* remains *d* in order to avoid the succession *t-d*: thus, *sädädä* 'send' (however En. Gt. have *sätädä*, Ed. *sättädä*); *gädädä* 'tear' (but En. Gt. *gätädä*, Ed. *gättädä*).

It so happens that in verbs with final *r*, Chaha has preserved the voiced *d*: thus, *xädärä* 'thatch a house' (but En. Gt. *xätärä*); *nädärä* 'bore a hole' (but Ed. Gt. *nätärä*).

Chaha has also kept the original *d* in Amharic loanwords: *näda* 'help' (Amh. *rädda*; for *r* : *n*, see § 20.7.3.1); *tä-ṭadäfä* 'hurry' (Amh. *tä-ṭaddäfä*).

There are also doublets: *adärä* and *atärä* 'spend the night'; *adägä* and *atägä* 'throw away'.

20.10.4. g
Originally geminated voiced *g* has become devoiced *k*. Verbs: *ğäkämä* 'hit with the fist or elbow', E. *ğäggämä*; *mäkärä* 'suppurate', E. *mäggärä*; *näka* 'coagulate', E. *nägga*, Amh. *rägga*.

Nouns: *däk* 'calf of a certain age', E. *dägg*; *gäkäbät* 'chest of animal', E. *gäggäbät*.

The presence of another voiced in the root prevented the devoicing of *g* into *k*: thus, *zägädä* 'remember', but En. Gt. *zäkädä*; *agädä* 'bind', but En. Gt. *akädä*.

The voiced *g* is also preserved in Amharic loanwords: *agäzä* 'help', Amh. *aggäzä*; *sägädä* 'worship', Amh. *säggädä*; *nägäsä* 'reign', Amh. *näggäsä*.

20.10.5. g'
Originally geminated voiced *g'* has become devoiced *k'*. Verbs: *g'äk'ätä* 'accompany', E. *g'ägg'ätä*; *g'äk'ärä* 'straighten out', E. *g'ägg'ärä*.

Nouns: *wək'är* 'evening gathering', E. *wəgg'är*; *muk'ik'a* 'grass growing in the *äsät* plantation in the rainy season', E. *mug'igg'a*.

20.10.6. gʷ
Originally geminated voiced *gʷ* has become devoiced into *kʷ*. Examples: *ğäkʷärä* 'become flexible having been put on the fire', E. *ğäggʷärä*; *gʷäkʷä* 'main root of the *äsät*-plant', M. *goggʷä*; *gʷäräkʷärä*, expression of thanks to God having eaten something for the first time, E. *gʷäräggʷärä*.

20.10.7. ǧ
Originally geminated voiced *ǧ* has become devoiced *č*. Examples: *gačä* 'rope an animal to kill it', E. *gaǧǧä*; *məǧača* 'fireplace', E. *məǧaǧǧa*.

20.10.8. z, ž
Originally geminated voiced *z* becomes *s*, and geminated *ž* becomes *š*. Examples: *bäsa* 'abound', E. *bäzza*; *zasa* 'act mad', W. *zazza*; *zəmäsämä* 'be

wet', E. zəmäzzämä; zəsər 'span', E. zəzzər.

The voiced z has remained z in verbs with identical second and third radicals: thus, fäzäzä 'be better', E. fäzzäzä; bazäzä- 'be in low spirits', E. bazzäzä-.

It has also remained z in Amharic loanwords: tä-razäzä 'make the last will', from Amh. tä-nazzäzä (for n : r, see § 20.7.2); näzäbä 'be flexible', from Amh. läzzäbä (for l : n, see § 20.7.1.2).

Examples for *žž becoming š: žäšä 'be cold', E. žäžžä; gašä 'raid', E. gažžä; ašä 'see', E. ažžä; bräšä 'bolt and run away', E. bəräžžä.

20.11. Glottalized and non-glottalized

There are several examples of alternation between q:k, ṭ:t, and č̣:č regardless of whether the original consonant is the glottalized (q, ṭ, č̣) or the non-glottalized (k, t, č). While in some examples the alternation of glottalized versus non-glottalized could be explained through assimilation as may be the case of aṭebät 'finger' (M. Ms. Go) as against atebät (C. E), that is, ṭ-t becoming t-t, this is not the case of the other examples. For a possible Cushitic influence, see Leslau 1952.

20.11.1. k : q

Original k in alternation with q: C. äkäsä 'be delayed', So. iqqäsä; C. korbeša 'the young of a goat', Ed. qorbeššä.

Original q in alternation with k: E. qurä 'crow', C. kurä; C. qanča 'fiber of the äsät-plant', Ed. ke'ä (for the alternation of glottalized with the glottal stop, see Leslau 1992: 82–84).

20.11.2. t : ṭ

Original t alternates with ṭ: thus, C. šäfätä 'become a rebel', but Ed. šäffätä; M. aläqət 'leech', but C. aräqeṭ 'leech' (possibly through assimilation of glottalization, namely q-t becoming q-ṭ); C. atebät 'finger', but So. aṭabät.

20.11.3. č : č̣

In C. čäfa 'marshland', but En. č̣äfa; C. č̣əra 'liquid mud', but En. čära; C. č̣əyä 'hump of a cow', but En. čəyä; C. a-x'ač̣ä 'encourage', but Ed. a-xečcä.

20.12. Insertion of a non-etymological *n, r, b*

Insertion of these consonants occurs mostly in roots with a velar *g, k, q*. The majority of occurrences with inserted *n, r* occurs in East Gurage.

20.12.1. *n*

Examples of Chaha roots with inserted *n*: *grangər* 'the young of an animal' (Amh. So. *gəlgəl*); *atankərt* 'eucalyptus' (So. Amh. *atakəlt*); *mänkina* 'car' (Amh. *mäkina*); *xendä* 'tread' (G. *kedä*); *ənk'ak'ä* 'scab' (C. *akäkä* 'scratch when it itches'); *ənzər* 'ear' (W. *əzən*); *genzo* 'ax' (Ms. *gezo*); *gʷänčä* 'hyena' (E. *gʷäčä*); *sončä* 'part of the tapeworm that emerges after medication' (E. *sočä*); *wägänǧa* 'bamboo spatula' (M. *wälgäǧa*>*wägäǧa*); C. *wanq'äba* 'wooden plate for measuring coffee', E. M. *waq'äma*.

There are occurrences of the prefix *ən-*: *ənqura* 'egg' (Amh. *qura* 'testicle'); *ənqurquna* 'excrement of a sheep or goat' (So. *qʷäräqʷärya*); *ənbərbäya* 'butterfly' (Amh. *birabiro*).

20.12.2. *r*

ənqərča 'a kick' (from *näqäṭä* 'kick'). Insertion of *n* and *r* occurs in *ənqurfit* 'obstacle' (G. *'əqf-ät*).

20.12.3. *b*

The labial *b* after *m* is inserted only in *ambər* 'cabbage' (W. *aməl*); *qambisa* and *qämis* 'shirt' (*qämis* is borrowed from Arabic).

20.13. Gemination

Chaha is a non-geminating dialect. Thus, the perfect has a non-geminated consonant (e.g., *näkäsä*) as against the other South Ethiopian languages in which the 2nd radical is geminated (e.g., *näkkäsä*). From a diachronic point of view, however, there are indications of an early stage of gemination. Indeed, whenever an originally voiced consonant is expected to be geminated it became voiceless. This is the case of *b, bʷ, d, g, g', gʷ, ǧ, z, ž* having become voiceless *p, pʷ, t, k, k', kʷ, č, s, š* (see § 20.10).

Occasionally one encounters occurrences with a geminated radical, as in *ella* 'covet', *at-ənnä* 'put to sleep', *tobbätä* 'become Muslim', *əmmat* 'an only one', *əkkəm* 'in vain', *ənnəm* 'all', *attəm* 'any'. Some of these lexemes are loanwords.

Note also that gemination resulting from assimilation occurs in morpheme boundaries: e.g., *fəqunnät* 'fatness', from *fəqur-nät*; *bučənnät* 'difference', from *bučər-nät*; *fʷänniyä* 'upward', from *fʷär-niyä*; *yəxʷəllä* 'it is possible for him', from *yəxʷər-lä*; *bibənna* 'when he says to her', from *bibərna*; *säpännä* 'we broke', for *säpär-nä*.

Gemination also occurs when two homologous phonemes meet: *nəqqar* 'much' for *nəq qar*.

20.14. Assimilation

The consonants that are most susceptible to assimilation are the liquids, the labials, and the dentals. The glottalized consonants in the environment of non-glottalized consonats are either assimilatory or assimilated consonants.

In the partial assimilation voicing and unvoicing play a considerable role.

20.14.1. Partial assimilation
20.14.1.1. Assimilation of the dental n in a contiguous position
The dental *n* is assimilated and becomes a labial *m* when in contact with the labials *b*, *f*. In this combination *nb* > *mb*, and *nf* > *mf*.

nb > *mb*. Examples: Amh. *ənba* 'tear' > C. *əmba*; Amh. *gənb* (also *gəmb*) 'stone wall' > C. *gəmb*; Z. *gänbälä* 'black' > C. *gämbänä*.

nf > *mf*. Examples: C. *ənfačä* and *əmfačä* 'nasal mucus'; **ənfas* 'air, wind' > C. *əmfas*.

20.14.1.2. Assimilation of the labial m in a contiguous position
The labial *m* is assimilated and becomes dental *n* in contact with the dentals *d*, *t*, *ṭ*, the sibilant *z*, the palatals *š*, *č*, and the velar *q*. Thus, *md* > *nd*, *mt* > *nt*, *mṭ* > *nṭ*, *mz* > *nz*, *mš* > *nš*, *mč* > *nč*, *mq* > *nq*.

md > *nd*. Examples: E. *dumd* 'joined' > C. *dund*; E. *ṭəmd* 'pair of oxen' > C. *ṭənd*; E. *nəmʷd* 'expensive' > C. *nund*.

mt > *nt*. There are no examples of Chaha *mt* > *nt*, but this partial assimilation occurs in the other West Gurage dialects in relation to Chaha. Thus, C. *xumtət* 'stiff, horny' > Ed. *huntut*; C. *qʷämät* 'gourd' > Gt. *qōnt*.

mṭ > *nṭ*. E. *amṭ* 'kind of grass' > C. *anṭ*; En. *samṭ* 'branch without leaves' > C. *sonṭ*; Gt. *amṭərəyä* 'dough that has a sour taste' > C. *onṭərəyä*.

mč > *nč*. Example: En. *lumča* 'kind of bush' > C. *nunčä* (for *l* : *n*, see § 20.7.1.2).

mz > *nz*. Example: En. *gamziyä* 'three fireplace stones on which the cooking pot rests' > C. *gʷänziyä*.

mš > *nš*. This assimilation is attested in dialects other than Chaha. Thus, Z. *qolomšoši* 'basket used for grain', W. *qʷälänše*.

mq > *nq*. Example: Ed. *šəmqəq* 'knot made in a belt' > C. *šənqəq*.

20.14.1.3. Assimilation of voiceless-voiced > voiceless-voiceless
*xäbd 'liver' > *xäpd > xäpt.

20.14.1.4. Non-contiguous regressive assimilation of palatalization
A non-palatal followed by a palatal in a non-contiguous position becomes palatal. Examples: En. *gutəča* 'earring' > C. *gučəča*; En. *futfuča* 'bread crumbs' > C. *fučfučä*.

In the dialects other than Chaha: S. *liṭačča* 'bark of tree' > W. *ləččače*; E. *dənǧər* 'fat', M. *ǧänǧən*; S. *mədaǧǧa* 'fireplace', E. *məǧaǧǧa*.

20.14.1.5. Assimilation of lexemes in which a glottalized is involved
ṭ-g>d-g (glottal-voiced > non-glottal voiced) in Z. *ṭəgär* 'hair' > C. *dəgär*; W. *ṭəgay* 'honeyed water' > C. *däg'ä*.

q-d > *g-d* in G. *ʾaqädä* 'tie' > C. *agädä*.

q-t > *q-ṭ* in M. *aläqət* 'leech' > C. *aräqəṭ* (for *l* : *r*, see § 20.7.1.3).

ṭ-d > *d-d* in So. *məṭad* 'griddle' > C. *mədad*.

d-q > *ṭ-q* in S. *wädäqä* 'fall' > C. *wäṭäqä*; Ed. *däqäqä* 'be ground finely' > C. *ṭäqäqä*.

20.14.2. Total assimilation
Total assimilation occurs only when the two consonants are in contact. It is mostly regressive. The consonants that are frequently assimilated are the liquids *r*, *n*, but also other consonants.

20.14.2.1. r
r is assimilated to various consonants, mostly in dialects other than Chaha. Examples: C. *wärčä* 'front leg of cattle', Ed. *wäččä*; C. *qärčat* 'basket made of bamboo', En. Ed. *qäčät*; C. *gurda* 'strong oath that should not be broken', M. *gudda*.

rn > *nn* in morpheme boundaries: Gt. *fuqur-nät* 'fatness', C. *fəqunnät*; *bučər-nät* 'difference', C. *bučənnät*; *fʷär-niyä 'upward', C. *fʷänniyä*.

20.14.2.2. n
n is assimilated to various consonants, mostly in dialects other than Chaha. Note that gemination that should have resulted from the process of

assimilation does not always occur. Examples: E. *kənčəf* 'chin', Ed. *kučəf*; C. *känfär* 'lip', Ed. *käfär*; C. *wänfit* 'sieve', Z. *wäfit*; C. *tənkiyä* 'kind of jar', Ed. *təkkiyä*; C. *manṭa* 'liquid of the intestine', Ed. *maṭä*.

20.14.2.3. Liquids and labials
In dialects other than Chaha: *angät lä-där 'upward slope', Z. *angällädär*; E. *atšaqətyä* 'kind of *äsät*-plant', En. *ašaqət*; C. *fərfər* 'kind of worm', Ed. *fəffər*; M. *əmbuq balä* 'take a mouthful of liquid', So. *əbbuq balä* (unless M. *əmbuq* is for *ənbuq*, with inserted *n*, for which see § 20.12); Gt. *amṭarəyä* 'dough that has a sour taste', M. *oṭarəyä*; C. *käbsasa* 'fiber of the *äsät*-plant', En. *kasasa*.

20.15. Dissimilation
Dissimilation can be contiguous and non-contiguous, progressive and regressive. Dissimilation may also result in deglottalization and in voicing of one of the consonants.

20.15.1. Progressive, non-contiguous
ṭ-q > *d-q* in Amh. *saqä* 'laugh', Gaf. *ṣaqä* > *ṭaqä, C. *daqä*.

In dialects other than Chaha: M. *ṭärraqqa* 'moon', So. *därraqqa*; M. *aṭq* 'joint of bamboo', En. *andəq* (for inserted *n*, see § 20.12).

Dissimilation of voice resulting in voiced-voiced > voiced-voiceless. Examples: C. *tä-g'ag'äzä* 'be proud', but E. *tä-g'agg'äsä*.

Voiceless-voiceless > voiceless-voiced in M. *näqq'äsä* 'limp', but E. *näqq'äzä*; E. *a-čeqä* 'make sure' > *a-čekä > *a-čegä*.

In verbs with medial *b* for which one would expect *p* in Chaha (see § 20.10.1), the voiced *b* is retained when preceded by a voiceless emphatic. Thus, C. *ṭäbäqä* 'be tight' instead of the expected *ṭäpäqä*; C. *ṭäbäsä* 'roast' instead of the expected *ṭäpäsä*.

20.15.2. Progressive contiguous
Dissimilation of voice resulting in voiced-voiced > voiced-voiceless in C. *dəmʷd* 'meeting place of two rivers', but En. *dəmʷt*; C. *gungərəyä* 'kind of knife', but Gt. *gunčərəyä*.

20.15.3. Progressive dissimilation
Progressive dissimilation of two homorganic sounds either in Chaha in relation to the other Gurage dialects or in the various dialects outside of Chaha.

f-f > *b̲-f* as in E. *kəfäkkäfä* 'thatch the roof with the tip of grass pointing up', but En. *kəb̲äkäfä* (note Ed. *kəwäkkäfä*); C. *k'əfäk'äfä* 'spray water', but En. *k'əb̲äk'äfä*.

q-q > *b̲ (w)-q*: C. *č̣əqäč̣äqä* 'annoy by talking', Gt. *č̣əb̲äč̣äqä*, Ed. *č̣əwäč̣č̣äqä*.

g-g > *b̲-g* as in Amh. *dägäddägä* 'level off the floor of the house', En. *dəb̲ätägä*.

x-x > *b̲-x*: C. *səxäsäxä* 'shell corn by grinding slightly with a pestle', En. *səb̲äsäxä*.

In the instrumental that is formed with the prefix *m*, the labial *m* became *w* in roots containing a labial. Thus, *wäfč̣ä* 'grinding stone', *wäfteya* 'spindle' (root *ftl*), *wägäpäča* 'horse-racing field' (root *g'äpätä* 'gallop, race').

Note the same feature in some nouns without a labial: *wädrägya* 'hammer' (root *dng* 'hit' going back to *drg*); *wanṭiyä* 'filter' (root *nṭr*).

20.15.4. Dissimilation of gemination

A geminated consonant may be dissimilated through the liquid *r*, occasionally through *n*. Examples: Ms. *mäddäd* 'sickle', but C. *märdäd*; E. *gədd* 'misery', but C. *gərd*; E. *k"ädda* 'water bottle', C. *k"ärda*; *šəšəra* 'liquid that exudes from the *äsät*-plant', also *šəršəra* (undoubtedly from *šəššəra*).

In dialects other than Chaha: W. *iddä* 'carding bow', En. *irda*.

20.16. Metathesis

Metathesis can be contiguous and non-contiguous. There are not enough examples in the same dialect, and, for that matter, not enough examples by comparing various dialects to warrant a definite statement on the phonetic conditions in which metathesis occurs.

20.16.1. Contiguous metathesis

The examples that follow are taken from Chaha as well as from the other Gurage dialects. Only a selection is given from the dialects other than Chaha.

Velar as 1st consonant: C. E. *əgzer* 'God', but Ms. Go. *əzger*; C. *əndäxreč̣ä* 'kidney', but Ms. *əndärheč̣č̣ä*; C. *azgart* 'cloth belt', M. *azgaləd*, but Ms. *azlagəd*.

Liquid as 1st consonant: En. *bərč̣əqo* 'drinking glass', but C. *bəč̣ərqo*; C. *arwa* 'soul', but W. *awrä*.

Dental as 1st consonant: C. *gʷädrät* 'mound around the fireplace', but M. *gʷärdät*; C. *aṭmet* 'solidified juice of the white part of the *äsät*-plant', but En. *amīʾid* (for ʾ for *ṭ*, see Leslau 1992: 84).

20.16.2. Non-contiguous metathesis

Velar as 1st consonant: So. *käsäl* 'charcoal', C. *käsär* (for *l*: *r*, see § 20.7.1.3), but Z. *sähal*.

Labial as 1st consonant: C. *käbäro* 'drum', but Ms. *käräbo*; C. *wäfänča* 'doorway', but Ed. *wänäfč-ar* 'section of the house from the entrance to the pillar'.

Liquid as 1st consonant: W. *gälämä* 'sew leather on the cover of the basket', but C. *gämärä* (for *l*:*r*, see § 20.7.1.3); Ms. *borkätta* 'crack of the ground after the rainy season', but C. *boträka*.

Sibilant as 1st consonant: C. *kəzəb* (from Arabic) 'lie', but Ed. *kəbz*.

Palatal as 1st consonant: *fišara* 'sediment of water', but Go. *fəršа*.

20.17. Pseudo-corrections

There are a few occurrences of pseudo-corrections in the various dialects.

Since *b* may become *w* (see § 20.1.1) there are examples of *w* becoming *b*: thus, E. *kaba* 'light, useless', C. *kaba*, the correct form being C. *xawa*, from Ar. *ḫawā* 'empty'; C. *bʷər* 'main' instead of *wər*.

The labial *m* may become *w* (see § 20.1.4). An example of *w* becoming *m* by pseudo-correction is M. Go. *tamuyä* 'orphan', to be identified with C. E. *tawəyä*.

For *qʼ* becoming *č* (see § 20.3.4), one also finds examples of *č* becoming *qʼ*, as in C. *wanqʼäbä* 'wooden plate for measuring coffee' going back to Ed. *wačäba*, from Kamb. *wačäba*; C. *qʼäf barä* 'be near to overflowing' to be compared with Ed. *čəff barä*, Amh. *čäfäff alä*; C. *mäqʼ*, interjection used to chase away a horse, but Ed. M. Amh. *mäčč*.

The original *l* may become *r* in Chaha (see § 20.7.1.3). Occurrences of pseudo-corrections of *r* becoming *l* are: C. *fällämä* 'sign' from an original *färrämä*; C. *lux* 'spirit', from Ar. *rūḥ*.

20.18. Vowels

The vowels that occur in all the dialects are seen in Table 20-1.

Table 20-1. Chaha Vowels

	front	central	back
high	i	ə	u
mid	e	ä	o
low		a	

20.18.1. Additional vowels
Chaha has additional vowels: *ạ̈* (open *ä*), *ọ* (open *o*); nasalized allophones *ã*, *õ*; allophone *å* of *ä*, and allophone *ŭ* of *ə* when preceded by a labial.

Minimal pairs *ä* : *ạ̈* in *bätärä* 'be first' : *bạ̈tärä* 'distinguish, separate'; *wärät* 'special share of a slaughtered cow' : *wärạ̈t* 'sleep'.

20.18.2. *ä*
Initial *ä* alternates with *ə* of Amharic: e.g., C. *äbäṭ* 'furuncle', Amh. *əbäṭ*; *äčä* 'wood', Amh. *ənčät*; C. *äxər* 'cereal', Amh. *əhəl*.

ä is a variant of *e* within Chaha and of *e*, *ə*, *i* of the other dialects. Examples: *wärät* and *wäret* 'sleep'; *ärä* and *äre* 'cows'; *etäniyä* and *eteniyä* 'in which direction?'; C. *särạ̈fər* and E. *särefər* 'kind of breeches'; C. *dạ̈yä* 'palm', but E. *dəyä*, W. *diyä*.

ạ̈ is also contracted from -*ay*, as in C. *ozạ̈* 'evil eye', but En. Gt. *ozay*; C. *sənạ̈* 'wheat', but Gt. *sənay*.

ạ̈ also results from a combination *a-e*: thus, *yagdatạ̈* 'section of the house near the partition' from *yä-agdata-e*.

20.18.3. *o*
Minimal pairs of *o* : *ọ* in *odä* 'tell': *ọdä-* 'be necessary'.

o may result from the reduction of final -*äm*: thus, C. *mäsxäro*, name of the 1st month, Amh. Z. *mäskäräm*.

Initial *wä*, *aw*, *äw* may become *o*. Examples: C. *wägät* and *ogät* 'assembly'; C. *od* 'threshing field' as against En. Gt. *awd*; C. *ṭona* 'strength', Gt. *ṭäwna*.

o also results from the reduction of *aw-*, *awä-*: e.g., C. *ọtät* 'one who leads the singing', En. Gt. *awṭayt*; C. *ọndä* 'lower', from *awändä*.

20.18.4. *e*
e also results from contraction of *ay*: e.g., C. *en* 'eye', Gt. *ayn*; *čet* 'sun', Gt. *čayt*; C. *eb* 'milk', S. W. *ayb*; C. *xäde* 'roof thatcher', E. *xäday*.

20.18.5. i

i also results from contraction of *-əyə, -äyə, -äəy*: e.g., *tiqäms* 'while he tastes' from *təyəqäms*; *tina* 'with us', from *tä-yəna*; *tiya* 'with me', from *ta-əya*.

20.18.6. ə

ə alternates with *i* of the other dialects: C. *təbre* 'animosity between two people', Ed. *tibre*.

20.18.7. u

u may go back to *əb* (passing through *əḇ, əw*): e.g., C. *ṭu* 'breast', Ms. *ṭəb*, E. Ed. *ṭəw*; C. *sur* 'broken', Go. So. *səbur*, C. also *səwər*.

20.18.8. Long vowels

Occasional long vowels occur in onomatopoetic expressions, such as *bā̰ barä, mā̰ barä* 'bleat'; also in *ō* 'yes', *yō* 'here I am'.

20.19. Vocalic initial

Vocalic initial goes back to Semitic and Ethiopic ' ' *h ḥ ḫ*. Examples: *äxər* 'cereal' (G. *əkəl*); *āf*ʷ 'bird' (G. Te. *'of*); *äčä* 'tree' (G. *'əḍ*); *anä* 'there is' (G. *hallo*); *akäkä* 'scratch' (G. *ḥakäkä*); *adägä* 'throw away' (G. *ḥadägä*); *amə̄st* 'five' (root *ḫms*).

In Arabic loanwords: *axera* 'future life' (from Ar. *'āḫira*); *əmar* 'donkey' (from Ar. *ḥimār*); *amd* 'thanks' (from Ar. *ḥamd*).

In Cushitic loanwords: *äčba* 'central pillar of the house' (from Kam. *utubu*); *āfraxʷa* 'pregnant' (from Had. *hafʷrakko*).

The initial vowel may be preceded by *y*. Thus, *yäčba* and *äčba* 'central pillar of the house'; *yärbat* and *ärbat* 'evening meal'; *yəra* 'wet', but Ms. *ira*; *yədar*, name of the third month, but Ms. W. *ədar*; *yəna* 'we', but En. Gt. *ina*.

20.20. Prothetic ä, ə

Prothetic *ä*, also *ə*, occurs before *r*, and occasionally before *s*. Examples: *äram* 'cow', *äräqʷe* 'far', *ärč* 'boy', *äro* 'Wednesday' (Amh. *rob*); *ərkus* 'impure'.

Before *s*: *äsər* 'root', *əset* 'young grain'.

20.21. Meeting of vowels

Chaha avoids the coming together of two vowels. If, for morphological reasons, two vowels should come together, the following may occur: elision of one of the vowels, or introduction of a glide semivowel *y* if the preceding vowel is *u*.

20.21.1. Elision

a-e > *ą̈*: *yä-agdata-e* > *yagdatą̈* 'of the section of the house near the partition'
ä-ä > *ä*: *yä-äčba* > *yäčba* 'of the pillar'
ä-a > *a*: *yä-adot* > *yadot* 'of the mother'
ä-e > *e*: *yä-eb* > *yeb* 'of the milk'
ä-ə > *ə*: *yä-əmfas* > *yəmfas* 'of the wind'

20.21.2. Insertion of a semivowel

i-u > *i^yu*: *wami-u* > *wami^yu* 'it is (necessary) to do'
e-y > *e^yu*: *f^wäre-u* > *f^wäre^yu* 'it is above'
ä-u > *ä^yu*: *wäsä-u* > *wäsä^yu* 'it is necessary to buy'.

20.22. Syllabic structure

A word may begin with any vowel except with *i*: thus, *ab* 'father', *äčä* 'tree', *ą̈šam*, form of greeting to welcome someone returning from a trip, *ebar* 'without', *əfəf barä* 'blow', *odä* 'tell', *ǫna* 'empty', *ux barä* 'sigh'.

A word may end with any vowel except with *u*:[4] thus, *angača* 'cat', *ənkurkuyä* 'lumpy', *asą̈* 'coward', *ete* 'where?', *xə* 'that', *atawari* 'one who spies out', *angädo* 'cattle pen outside the house', *čuču* 'chick'.

Needless to say, some of the vowels either at beginning of the word or at the end of the word are rare.

For the reduction of syllables, see the individual vowels mentioned above.

20.23. Consonant cluster

Chaha has an initial consonant cluster only if the 2nd radical is *r*, the 1st radical being either the labial *b*, *f*, the velar *g*, *k*, rarely *d*. Examples: *bre* 'insect that eats human skin or cereal', *brät* 'iron, rifle'; *fräta* 'sprinkle water', *fräntä* 'break bread into pieces'; *grängər* 'the young of an animal', *greğät* 'young women of the same clan'; *krəstiyan* 'Christian', *kräta* 'lift up a heavy object'.

---

[4]. It is quite possible that initial *i* and final *u* occur in the language, but I did not record lexemes with these vowels in Leslau 1969.

Bibliography

Cohen, Marcel. 1931. *Etudes d'éthiopien méridional*. Paris: Geuthner. [Pp. 104–33 deals with the phonology of various Gurage dialects.]

Hetzron, Robert. 1972. *Ethiopian Semitic: Studies in Classification* (Journal of Semitic Studies Monograph 2). Manchester: The University Press.

———. 1977. *The Gunnän-Gurage Languages* (Istituto Orientale di Napoli. Ricerche 12).

Leslau, Wolf. 1948. "Le problème de la gémination du verbe tchaha (gouragué)." *Word* 4: 42–47.

———. 1950a. *Ethiopic documents: Gurage* (Viking Fund Publications in Anthropology 14). New York: The Viking Fund.

———. 1950b. "La position du gafat parmi les langues sémitiques de l'Ethiopie." *Comptes rendus du groupe linguistique d'études chamito-sémitiques* 5: 47–48.

———. 1952. "The Influence of Sidamo on the Ethiopian Languages of Gurage." *Language* 28: 63–81.

———. 1967. "The Impersonal in Chaha." In *To Honor Roman Jakobson* (Janua Linguarum Series Maior 32), vol. 2, pp. 1150–62. The Hague: Mouton.

———. 1969. "Toward a Classification of the Gurage Dialects." *Journal of Semitic Studies* 14: 96–109.

———. 1979. *Etymological Dictionary of Gurage (Ethiopic)*, vol. 3: *Etymological Section*, pp. xv–xcii. Wiesbaden: Harrassowitz. [See also 1992.]

———. 1983. *Ethiopians Speak: Studies in Cultural Background*, part 5: *Chaha-Ennemor* (Aethiopistische Forschungen 16).

———. 1992. *Gurage Studies: Collected Writings*. Wiesbaden: Harrassowitz. [Pp. 1–113, reproduction of 1979; pp. 117–20, reproduction of 1950a; pp. 138–40, reproduction of 1983: 8–10; pp. 430–42, reproduction of 1967.

Polotsky, Hans Jakob. 1938. "Etudes de grammaire gouragué." *Bulletin de la société de linguistique de Paris* 38: 137–75.

———. 1951. Notes on Gurage Grammar (Oriental Notes and Studies 2). Jerusalem: Israel Oriental Society.

———. 1971. *Collected Papers*. Jerusalem: Magnes Press. [Pp. 477–515, reproduction of 1938; pp. 521–73, reproduction of 1951.]

Shack, W. A. 1966. *The Gurage: A People of the Ensete Culture*. London: Oxford University Press.

Chapter 21
Amharic Phonology
Wolf Leslau
University of California, Los Angeles

Amharic is the national language of Ethiopia. It belongs to the branch of the Semitic language family of which the other languages are Ge'ez (at present the language of the liturgy), Tigre and Tigrinya in the north (closely related to Ge'ez). The languages of the center and of the south are Amharic, Argobba (closely related to Amharic), Harari (or Adare, spoken only in the city of Harar), Gurage (a cluster of at least twelve dialects), and Gafat (for which the present writer found only four speakers in 1946).

In relation to the Ge'ez phonological system the Amharic phonology is characterized by the loss of the laryngeals and of the velar ḫ (for the glottal stop and h, see § 21.1.3.1, § 21.1.3.2), and by the palatalization of the dentals, of the sibilants and of *l, n*.[1]

21.1. The sounds

21.1.1. Phoneme inventory
There are 30 consonants and 7 vowels in Amharic. For the consonants, see Table 21-1.

For the other rounded consonants, see § 21.3.

The sounds *s, š, z, ž, ṣ* are also called "sibilants."

21.1.2. Pronunciation of the Amharic consonants
21.1.2.1. Comparison with English
Some Amharic sounds are the same, or nearly the same, as the English sounds, whereas others have no counterpart in English.

The sounds that are approximately the same as in English are: *b, p, m, f, w, s* (as in 'sun'), *z, y, g* (as in 'go'), *k*, and *h*.

In addition to these, however, some sounds that are the same or nearly the same as English sounds are rendered in the phonetic script by special symbols. These are:

---

1. ABBREVIATIONS: Amh., Amharic; Ar., Arabic; C, consonant; G., Ge'ez; V, vowel.

Table 21-1. Amharic Consonants

		Labials	Dentals	Palatals	Velars	Laryngeals
Stops	voiceless	p	t	č	k	(ʔ)
	voiced	b	d	ǧ	g	
	glottalized	p̣	ṭ	č̣	q	
	rounded				kʷ, gʷ, qʷ	
Spirants	voiceless	f	s	š		h
	voiced		z	ž		
	glottalized		ṣ			
	rounded					hʷ
Nasals	voiced	m	n	ň		
Liquids	voiced		l, r			
Semivowels		w		y		

č ቸ   corresponding to *ch* in 'church'
š ሸ   corresponding to *sh* in 'shoe'
ǧ ጀ   corresponding to *j* in 'joke'
ž ዠ   corresponding to *s* in 'pleasure'
ň ኘ   corresponding to *ni* in 'onion'

The Amharic sounds that are found in English but are pronounced somewhat differently are *d* and *t*. In Amharic they are of the dental type, that is, the tip of the tongue touches the upper part of the teeth, whereas in English they are of the alveolar type, that is, the tip of the tongue touches the alveolar ridge above the teeth.

The Amharic *l* is of the "light" type as in French, German, or Spanish. That is, the tip of the tongue touches the alveolar ridge and the middle of the tongue is closer to the roof of the mouth than it is for the English *l*. The Amharic *l* is more like the English *l* at the beginning of the word (as in 'light') rather than the English *l* that in other positions is of the "dark" type, that is, the back of the tongue is depressed.

The Amharic *r* is a flap as in Spanish or in Italian,[2] the tip of the tongue striking the gum ridge behind the upper teeth.

The glottal stop *ʔ* corresponds to the pronunciation of English 'uh-uh' used as a negation or 'oh-oh', as an expression of surprise or warning.

---

2. The geminated *r* is a trill.

21.1.2.2. Consonants without English parallels

The sounds that are characteristic of Amharic and are not found in English are ጠ *ṭ*, ጭ *č̣*, ጰ *p̣*, ቅ *q*, and ጸ *ṣ*.[3] These sounds are called "glottalized" or "ejectives." These glottalized sounds have their counterpart in nonglottalized sounds as follows:

    glottalized *ṭ* — nonglottalized *t*
    glottalized *q*[4] — nonglottalized *k*
    glottalized *p̣* — nonglottalized *p*
    glottalized *č̣* — nonglottalized *č*
    glottalized *ṣ* — nonglottalized *s*

The difference between glottalized and nonglottalized consonants is best described as follows:

1. Nonglottalized consonants are aspirated as in English, whereas glottalized consonants are not.

2. Nonglottalized consonants are pronounced as described above, whereas in pronouncing glottalized consonants the stream of air coming from the lungs is shut off by closure of the glottis. The air above it is then forced out through a stricture somewhere along the vocal organ. The stricture is at the lips for ጰ *p̣*, at the teeth for ጠ *ṭ*, ጸ *ṣ*, at the palate for ጭ *č̣*, and at the velum for ቅ *q*.

21.1.3. Observations on the consonants

21.1.3.1. ʔ

አ *ʔ* may be pronounced in initial pre-vocalic position, and in medial position between vowels, as is *antä* or *ʔantä* 'you', *säʔat* and *säat* 'hour', *bəʔər* and *bəər* 'pen'. It is also pronounced in the position VʔC, as in *məʔrab* 'west', *maʔzän* 'angle'.

For *ʔ* pronounced regionally instead of *q*, see § 21.1.3.5.

21.1.3.2. h

ሀ *h* (going back to *h*, *ḥ*, *ḫ*) occurs in words borrowed from Geʻez: e.g., *haymanot* 'belief', *hayl* 'power', *həgg* 'law'.

It occurs in free variation with *zero*: thus, *hagär* and *agär* 'country', *hassab* and *assab* 'thought', *hamus* and *amus* 'Thursday'.

---

3. These sounds are also transcribed as *t'*, *č'*, *p'*, *k'*, and *s'*.
4. The transcription with *ḳ* would be more consistent, but because *q* is available in the Latin alphabet, it has been used for the glottalized *k*.

An original laryngeal is *zero* in the verb, but it appears in the noun. Thus, *azzänä* 'be sad', but *hazän* 'sadness'; *allämä* 'to dream', but *həlm* 'dream'; *ammämä* 'be sick', but *həmäm* 'disease'; *annäṭä* 'build', but *hənṣa* 'building'.

In initial position it may be derived from *k*. Examples: *honä* 'be' (G. *konä*), *hod* 'stomach' (G. *käbd*), *hedä* 'go' (G. *kedä* 'tread'), *hulätt* 'two' (G. *kəlʔe*), *hullu* 'all' (G. *kʷəllu*).

21.1.3.3. d ~ r

Medial *d* in contact with a following consonant may occasionally be pronounced like *r*: thus, *qädmo* 'before' pronounced *qärmo*; *hedku* 'I went' pronounced *herku*; *gud näw* 'it is extraordinary' pronounced *gur näw*.

Variants of *d* and *r* occur in writing: *gədgədda* and *gərgədda* (by dissimilation) 'wooden wall'; *gudgʷad* and *gurgʷad* (by dissimilation) 'pit, hole'.

An original *rn* of Geʻez (passing though *nr*) may become *nd* in Amharic. Thus, *qärn* 'horn' > **qänr* > Amharic *qänd*; *śərnay* 'wheat' > **śənray* > Amh. *sənde*; *qərnəb* 'eyebrow' > **qənrəb* > Amh. *qəndəb*; *kʷərnaʕ* 'cubit' > **kʷənraʕ* > *kənd*.

21.1.3.4. ṣ

The glottalized አ *ṣ* normally became ጠ *ṭ*, though it is still preserved in the region of Gojjam and Gondar; in the dialect of Wollo only ጠ *ṭ* is used.[5] Whenever palatalization occurs (see § 21.5), *ṣ* is palatalized into *č̣* as is the case of *ṭ* (see § 21.5.1).

ṣ is preserved in expressions dealing with religion and culture. Thus, *ṣomä* (also *ṭomä*) 'fast', *ṣadəq* 'just', *mäṣhaf* 'book', *ṣähay* 'sun', *ṣəgge* 'flour', and others. In the rural areas these words are pronounced with *ṭ*: thus, *ṭähay*, *ṭay* 'sun', *mäṭaf* 'book', *ṭadq-an* 'righteous, pious' (pl.), *ṭəgge* 'flower', and so on.

21.1.3.5. q

The glottal *q* has a regional variant of a glottal stop: thus, *bäʔlo* 'mule' for *bäqlo*; *baʔela* 'bean' for *baqela*; *mäʔäs* 'scissors' for *mäqäs*; *təlləʔ* 'big' for *təlləq*. There are also spelling variants with አ used for ቀ: thus, ኡርዝ *urz* 'uncircumcised' for ቁርዝ *qurz*; አርፋፋ *(ʔ)arfaffa* 'tall, clumsy and ungainly' for ቀርፋፋ *qärfaffa*; ቡአ *buʔa* 'hernia' for ቡቃ *buqa*.

---

5. By hypercorrectness some words are written with አ ፡ ዐ instead of ጠ: e.g., ጸብ 'quarrel' instead of ጠብ; ዐባይ instead of ጠባይ.

21.1.3.6. č̣

Medial č̣ in contact with a following consonant may be pronounced like a glottal stop or y: e.g., *afʷač̣tʷall* pronounced *afʷaʔtʷall* or *afʷaytʷall* 'he has whistled'; *tägač̣tʷall* also pronounced *tägaytʷall* 'it collided'; *näč̣č̣ šənkurt*, also pronounced *näʔ šənkurt* 'garlic'.

21.1.3.7. p

p appears in Greek loanwords borrowed through Ge'ez: *pappas* 'bishop', *ṭäräppeza* (also pronounced *ṭäräbbeza*) 'table'. For *ityoppəya* 'Ethiopia' pronounced *ṭobbəya*, see § 21.10.3.

p appears in modern loanwords: *polis* 'police', *posta* 'mail', *parlamänt* 'parliament', *polätika* 'politics'. In the rural areas this letter is pronounced *b* (occasionally *f*): thus, *bosta, bolätika, bolis* (also *folis*).

v appears in modern loanwords: e.g., *viza* 'visa', *vino* (also *bino*) 'wine'.

21.2. Phonemic status of consonants

21.2.1. Minimal pairs

All consonants except *ʔ* are phonemes, that is, the unit of a sound when contrasted with another unit within the same environment brings about another meaning. Only minimal pairs of glottalized versus nonglottalized, of labiovelars versus plain velars, and of palatals versus nonpalatals are given below.

21.2.1.1. Glottalized versus nonglottalized

t-ṭ: *tälla* 'become wormy': *ṭälla* 'hate'; *mätta* 'hit': *mäṭṭa* 'come'
s-ṣ: *sällälä* 'become paralyzed': *ṣällälä* 'become clear'
č-č̣: *mäči* 'one who hits': *mäč̣i* 'one who comes'
k:q: *kämmämä* 'trim': *qämmämä* 'season, spice'

21.2.1.2. Labiovelars versus plain velars

g-gʷ: *gäddälä* 'kill': *gʷäddälä* 'be incomplete, miss'
k-kʷ: *kässäsä* 'accuse': *kʷässäsä* 'become meager'
q-qʷ: *qäṭṭärä* 'hire': *qʷäṭṭärä* 'count'

21.2.1.3. Palatals versus nonpalatals

t-č: *tärättärä* 'unravel': *čäräččärä* 'sell at retail'
ṭ-č̣: *ṭarä* 'try very hard': *č̣arä* 'scrape'
s-š: *sällälä* 'spy': *šällälä* 'sing a war song'

21.2.1.4. ž ~ ǧ

Minimal pairs of z-ž and of d-ǧ are more difficult to establish, as ž and ǧ normally alternate. As a result, a verb such as ǧämmärä 'begin' might be considered a member of the minimal pair of zämmärä 'sing' or dämmärä 'sum up'.

21.3. Rounding

21.3.1. General

Nearly all the consonants may be pronounced with a slight rounding of the lips, which is expressed by the phonetic symbol of a raised ʷ, as in m^w, $š^w$, k^w, q^w, f^w, and so on. Only the velars, however, that is, g, k, q, and h (representing ḫʷ),[6] have a complete set of graphic symbols for rounding, as, for instance, ቈ q^wä, ቍ q^wi, ቋ q^wa, ቌ q^we, ቊ q^wə; whereas the other consonants have a set only for the vowel a, as in ቧ b^wa, ሏ l^wa, ሷ s^wa. For the labiovelars as phonemes, see § 21.2.1.2.

21.3.2. Loss of labialization in velars

A labiovelar in any position followed by ä may become a plain velar followed by the labial round vowel o. Thus, q^wäṭṭärä or qoṭṭärä 'count'; g^wärräfä or gorräfä 'flood, overflow'; k^wännänä or konnänä 'condemn'. As 2nd or 3rd radical: däqq^{w}äsä or däqqosä 'grind to a fine powder'; dägg^{w}äsä or däggosä 'make designs on a book cover with a metal tool'; mäk^{w}ännən or mäkonnən 'governor, noble'.

A labiovelar in any position followed by ə usually becomes a plain velar followed by the labial rounded vowel u. Thus q^wərs or qurs 'breakfast'; g^wədday or gudday 'affair'; k^wəllab or kullab 'hook of iron'.

21.3.3. Loss of labialization in other consonants

As stated above, the consonants other than the velars may also be pronounced rounded, the rounding being expressed in writing only when the consonants are followed by the vowel a, as in ቧ b^wa. It so happens that the labials b, m, f, the dental d, and the palatal š may be followed by the vowel o in the verb or in the noun: thus, molla (and mälla) 'be full', monnänä 'become simple, foolish', bonnänä 'rise (dust)', foqäffoqä 'be fat', šolläkä 'slip out', domäddomä 'be dull', and others. Although the round labial vowel o following a labial may be owing to the preceding labial by assimilation, the vowel o preceded by d, š cannot be explained by assimilation to the preced-

---

6. h^{w}a is written only ኋ, originally ḫ^{w}a, pronounced h^{w}a.

ing consonant. Neither in writing nor in pronunciation is there any indication that the above-mentioned consonants may be variants for original rounded consonants, that is, $b^w\ddot{a}$, $m^w\ddot{a}$, $\check{s}^w\ddot{a}$, $d^w\ddot{a}$, and so on, but the imperfect or jussive of the above-mentioned verbs is a clear indication that these consonants were rounded. Indeed, the jussive of these verbs is pronounced rounded: thus, *yəm"la*, *yəb"nän*, *yəš"läk*. The imperfect of the quadriradicals is likewise pronounced *yəboräbb"ərall* or *yəboräbburall*, *yədomädd"əmall* or *yədomäddumall*.[7]

As Amharic has no way to express in writing the rounded consonant + *ə* for consonants other that the labiovelars, it uses the spelling of the plain consonant + *u*: thus, *yəmula*, *yədomdum*, *yəšuläk*, *yəboräbburall*, *yədomäddumall*, and so on.

21.3.4. Loss of rounding

At times a labiovelar or any rounded consonant may lose its rounding; it is transferred to the preceding consonant which is then followed by the round vowel *o* or *u*, depending on the vowel of the labiovelar or on the vowel of the consonant preceding the labiovelar.

Examples for *o* transferred to the preceding consonant: *bäqq"ält*, *bäqqolt* > *boqqält* 'sprout'; *nägg"ädä* > *noggädä* 'thunder'; *faggorä* > *foggärä* 'paw the ground'; *mänäk"se* > *mänokse* 'monk'; *mäg"zit* > *mogzit* 'nursemaid'.

Examples for *u* transferred to the preceding consonant: *ləg"am* > *lugam* 'bridle'; original *yəš"läk* written *yəšuläk* is also written and pronounced *yušläk*.

The rounding may also be transferred to the following consonant: thus, *ak"səm* 'Axum' became *aksum*.

21.4. Gemination

21.4.1. General

All the consonants except *ʔ* and *h* may occur in either a geminated or a nongeminated form. Gemination is most conveniently described as lengthening of the consonant.

Gemination permeates every aspect of the morphology; hardly a sentence lacks a geminated consonant. There may be as many as five geminated consonants in one word: *lämmənnəttämammänəbbät* 'to the one in whom we have confidence'.

---

7. Note that in the West Gurage cluster all the labials and velars may be rounded.

Words with two, three, or four geminated consonants are frequently seen in the language: *wättaddär* 'soldier', *ṭäffabbäññ* 'it disappeared to my detriment', *bämmättädärsubbät* 'in that you will arrive at it'.

21.4.2. Position
Gemination occurs only in medial or final position.

Examples for medial position: *läbbäsä* 'wear (a garment)', *allä* 'there is', *yəmmättall* 'he is hit'.

For final position, note the contrast between the nongeminated and the geminated consonants in *ləǧ* 'child' as against *əǧǧ* 'hand'; *bäg* 'sheep' as against *dägg* 'kind'; *ǧəb* 'hyena' as against *ləbb* 'heart'.

21.4.3. Final
The gemination of a final consonant which at times may hardly be audible becomes evident when the consonant is followed by a vowel: thus *wändəm(m)* 'brother', but *wändəmme* 'my brother'. The gemination of the final *l* in the compound imperfect as in *yənägrall* is more audible when followed by a vowel as in *yənägrallu*.

21.4.4. Phonemic status
Gemination is phonemic in Amharic. The following minimal pairs illustrate this feature: *gäna* 'still' : *gänna* 'Christmas'; *alä* 'he said' : *allä* 'there is'; *šəfta* 'outlaw' : *šəffəta* 'rash'; *fəraš* 'mattress' : *fərräš* 'remains, ruin'; *yəmätall* 'he hits' : *yəmmättall* 'he is hit'.

21.4.5. Assimilation
Gemination also results from the assimilation of one consonant to another: thus, *yəssäbbär* 'it is broken', from *yətsäbbär; *əssu* 'he' and *ərsu*; *arrässamm* 'he didn't forget', from *alrässamm*.

21.4.6. Lexical and morphological
Gemination is either a lexical or a morphological feature. Gemination as a lexical feature cannot be predicted. Thus, for instance, ዋና may be read *wanna* meaning 'main, principal' or *wana* meaning 'swimming'.

As a morphological feature gemination is more predictable in the verb than in the noun. Thus, the 2nd radical of a triradical verb or the 3rd radical of a quadriradical verb is always geminated in the perfect (*säbbärä*, *mäsäkkärä*). Likewise, the gemination or the nongemination of the 2nd radical in the imperfect is predictable when the type of the verb is known. Indeed, in type A the 2nd radical is not geminated (*yəsäbr*), whereas in a type-B verb the 2nd radical is geminated (*yəfälləg*).

The situation with the noun is less clear. In a primary noun there is no way of knowing whether any one of the radicals is geminated or not. Thus, ሠረሪት could be read *šärärit*, *šärrärit*, *šärärrit*, or even *šärrärrit*.

In some patterns of the derived nouns the gemination of a radical is predictable, whereas in other patterns this is not. Thus, whereas in the pattern ቀተተል the 3rd letter is geminated regardless of whether the noun derives from a type-A or a type-B verb, as in *nəgəggər* 'speech' (type A), *ləwəwwəṭ* 'exchange' (type B)—in the pattern ቀታል *qät(t)äl* of type A, *sänäf* 'lazy' has no gemination, but *addäg* (likewise of type A) 'one who has grown' has gemination.

For the dissimilation of gemination, see § 21.10.2.

21.5. Palatalization

21.5.1. General

As noted above (§ 21.2.1.3), the palatals are phonemic. The process of palatalization is also a phonetic feature. Indeed, the dentals *d*, *t*, *ṭ*, *l*, and *n*, and the sibilants *s*, *z*, and *ṣ* are palatalized when followed by the vowel -*i*, -*e*, or -*iya*. The resulting sounds are: *di* > *ǧ*, *ti* > *č*, *ṭi* (*ṣi*) > *č̣*, *li* > *y*, *ni* > *ň*, *si* > *š*, *zi* > *ž*.

Palatalization occurs in verbs and in verbals, that is, the active participle and the instrumental, nouns that are derived from the verb.

21.5.2. In verbs

The forms that end in -*i* are the imperfect, jussive, and imperative, the singular 2nd person feminine, and the active participle; the form that ends in -*e* is the gerund, 1st person singular; and the form that ends in -*iy(a)* is the verbal noun.

The vowel *i* following the above-mentioned consonants may either be kept with the palatal or, more usually, be absorbed. Thus,

   wəsäǧ or *wəsäǧi* 'take!' from *wässädä*
   kəfäč or *kəfäči* 'open!' from *käffätä*
   bəläč̣ or *bəläč̣i* 'exceed!' from *bälläṭä*
   kəfäy or *kəfäyi* 'pay!' from *käffälä*
   lämməň(ň) or *lämməňňi* 'beg!' from *lämmänä*
   mälläš or *mälläši* 'return!' from *mälläsä*
   märräž or *märräži* 'poison!' from *märräzä*

In the active participle the final *-i* is normally absorbed in the palatal: *araš* (from *arräsä*) 'he who plows'. In some isolated participles, however, the final dental or sibilant is not palatalized. The participles *därasi* 'author, writer' and perhaps *anaṭi* 'carpenter' may be borrowed from Geʿez, but the same is not true of *adli* 'one who is partial' (from *a-dälla*).

21.5.3. In the gerund
The expected vowel *e* in the gerund, 1st singular, may be pronounced and written *ä* after the palatals: thus, *mälləšše* or *mälləššä* 'I having returned'; *käfəčče* or *käfəččä* 'I having opened' (see § 21.21.2).

21.5.4. In the instrumental
The instrumental is *mälqäm-iya* or *mälqäm-ya*. The sequence *-iya* or *-ya* causes palatalization of the sibilants and dentals and is absorbed in the palatal. Examples: *mäkfäča* 'key' from **mäkfätiya*; *maräša* 'plow' from **maräsiya*. In a verb ending in *l*, *-liya* becomes *-ya*; thus, *mänqäya* 'instrument for pulling out', from *mänqäliya*.

21.5.5. In nouns
The final vowel *e* in a noun does not cause palatalization of a dental or a sibilant: thus, *bet-e* 'my house'. Some nominal patterns, however, bring about palatalization, such as the patterns *qättil, qəttali, qərtali, qətləya, qətləyya*, and the pattern ending in *-yyo*.

Examples for *qättil*: *aččir* 'short' (from *aṭṭärä*), *räžžim, räǧǧim* 'long' (from *räzzämä*), *qäččin* 'thin' (from *qäṭṭänä*), but without palatalization in *addis* 'new', *qällil* 'light'.

Examples for *qəttali, qərəttali*: *məllaš* 'answer' (from *mälläsä*), *fərraš* 'ruin' (from *färräsä*), *gʷədday,* 'incomplete, wanting' (from *gʷäddälä*), *gəžži* or *gəžž* 'purchase' (from *gäzza*), *kətəkkač* 'chopped up' (from *kätäkkätä*).

Examples for *qətləya, qətləyya*: *mərča* 'choice' (from *märräṭä*), *wərǧa* 'miscarriage' (from *wärrädä*), *ərša* 'field' (from *arräsä*), *ərməǧǧa* 'step, pace' (from *tärammädä*), *gədəyya* 'killing' (from *gäddälä*).

Examples for nouns ending in *-yyo*: *mälašo* 'salt given to cattle to lick' (from *lasä*), *mäqqačo* 'fine' (from *qäṭṭa* 'punish').

21.5.6. In other parts of speech
Palatalization also occurs in other parts of speech. Thus, *anči* 'you' (fem.) from *anti*; *mäčä* 'when?', from **matay*.

21.5.7. Regional palatalization

Outside the special nominal patterns there are also regional (Gojjam, Gondar, Wollo) occurrences of palatalization of consonants followed by the vowel *i, e,* or *ə*. Thus,

k>č: *kidan* 'pact'>*čidan*; *ənki* 'take!'>*ənči*
q>č̣: *qes* 'priest'>*č̣es*; *duqet* 'flour'>*duč̣ät*
g>ǧ: *gize* 'time'>*ǧəze* (Gojjam); *aroge* 'old'>*aroǧe*
d>ǧ: *dəngula* 'stallion'>*ǧəngula*
ṭ>č̣: *əṭege* 'head of the Ethiopian monks'>*əč̣ege*

21.5.8. Depalatalization

By an inverse process *ǧ* may become *g* in various regions: *əǧǧeta* and *eggeta* 'sleeve'; *ǧärba* and *gerba* 'back'; *ǧoro* and *gero* 'ear'.

21.6. Weakening of consonants

21.6.1. ǧ ~ y

The palatal *ǧ* may occasionally become *y*. Examples: *dawǧa* and *dawya* 'mat woven of reeds', *täzägagtäwall* and *täzägaytäwall* 'they are ready'.

By an inverse process *y* may become *ǧ*: thus, *əyubbəññ* and *əǧubbəññ*, formula for making someone one's attorney; *moyale* and *moǧale* 'a small flea'.

21.6.2. w ~ y

The labial *w* may become *y*. Examples: *särawit* and *särayət* 'army', *dawit* and *dayət* 'Psalter', *mästawät* and *mästayät* 'mirror'.

The labial *b* passing through the spirantized *ḇ* may become *y*: thus, *ṭäbib* and *ṭäyəb* 'smith', *zäbib* and *zäyəb* 'raisin'.

21.7. Spirantization

21.7.1. b ~ ḇ

A nongeminated intervocalic *b* is spirantized and pronounced *ḇ*: thus, *səbär* 'break!'. The city of *addis abäba* is pronounced *addis aḇäḇa* and, by haplology, *addisaḇa*.

The alternate forms of *wäbo* and *wäwo* 'rear guard' (perhaps by assimilation), of *səlbabot* and *səlbawät* 'film on the surface of hot milk' (perhaps by dissimilation of *b-b > b-w*; see § 21.10.1.1), and of *abʷara* and *awwara* 'dust' are also examples of spirantization.

Historically Amh. *säw* 'man, person' goes back to Ge'ez *säbəʔ*, and *ṭwat* 'morning' goes back to Ge'ez *ṣəbḥat*.

An inverse process of *w* becoming *b* occurs in *abol* 'first infusion of coffee' from Arabic *ʔawwal* 'first'.

21.7.2. k ~ h

A nongeminated intervocalic *k* may likewise regionally become a spirantized *h*. This is the case of *nəka* 'touch!' becoming *nəha*; *yənäkall* 'he touches' becoming *yənähall*; *käbbädä* 'be heavy', but *yähäbbädä* 'that which is heavy' in the dialect of Mänz. For the alternation of *k:h*, see § 21.8.2.1.

21.8. Sporadic alternation

This feature refers to the unpredictable substitution of one phoneme for another. It occurs with labials, velars, liquids, and palatals versus nonpalatals. Although some occurrences of sporadic alternation might be explained through regional or colloquial usage, in other occurrences assimilation might have played a role. Sporadic alternation also occurs in loanwords.

21.8.1. Alternation of labials
21.8.1.1. m-b, b-m

m instead of *b*: *məntä* 'for the sake of' instead of **bəntä* (from Ge'ez *bäʔəntä*).

Arabic loanwords: *qalib* and *qalim* 'mold' (Ar. *qālib*); *ṭäbänǧa* and *ṭämänǧa* 'rifle' (Ar. *ṭabanǧa*, of Turkish origin).

m instead of *f*: *əffuññit* and *əmmuññit* 'viper'.

b instead of *m*: *mahtäb*, *matäb* 'seal' instead of *mahtäm*; *zäbän* 'time' instead of *zämän*.

Arabic loanwords: *bilqaṭ* 'perfume bottle' (Ar. *milqaṭ*); *əlləmat* and *əlləbat* 'bookmark' (Ar. *ʕilāma*).

b instead of *f*: *näfs* and *näbs* 'soul'; *bulad* 'flint, steel', from Arabic *fūlāð*.

f instead of *b*: *kʷäräbta* and *kʷäräfta* 'hill'.

In loanwords: *p* instead of *b*: *lamba* and *lampa* 'lamp' (from Arabic *lamba* or perhaps from Italian *lampa*).

b instead of *p*: *pakko* and *bakko* 'pack (of cigarettes)' from Italian *pacco*; *polätika* and *bolätika* 'politics'.

b instead of *p*: *zopi* and *zobi* 'ebony'.

f instead of *p*: *polis*, *bolis*, and *folis* 'police'.

21.8.2. Alternation of velars
21.8.2.1. k-h, h-k

Amharic *h* goes back to *h*, *ḥ*, and *ḫ*. In fact, these letters are used in the orthography, but they are pronounced as *h* (see § 21.1.3.2). Examples: *haket* 'indolence' (Geʿez *hakäyä* 'be indolent'); *həyaw* 'immortal' (G. *ḥəyaw*); *həllina* 'conscience' (G. *ḫəllina*).

The verbal suffixes of the perfect *-hu* (1st person), *-h* (2nd person) go back to *-ku*, *-k*, as in *näggärhu*, *näggärh*ʷ 'I said', from *näggärku*; *näggärh* 'you said', from *näggärk*. See also § 21.8.2.1.1.

21.8.2.1.1. h < k

Some lexemes with Amharic *h* go back to *k*. Examples: *hullu* 'all' (G. *k*ʷ*əllu*); *hulätt* 'two' (G. *kəlʔe*); *h*ʷ*ala* 'after' (G. *käwäla* 'behind, back'); *honä* 'be' (G. *konä*); *hod* 'stomach' (G. *käbd*); *hedä* 'go' (G. *kedä* 'tread'). See also § 21.8.2.1.

21.8.2.1.2. k ~ h

In Amharic itself there are several lexemes with an etymological *k* which have variants with *h*. Thus: *k*ʷ*ämäṭṭäṭä* 'be sour, acid' and *homäṭṭäṭä*; *kudade* 'Lent' and *hudade*; *məknəyat* 'cause, reason' and *məhnəyat*; *säkona* 'sole of the foot' and *sähona*; *əšok* 'thorn' and *əšoh*.

It also happens that a false reconstruction of an original *h* becomes *k*, as in *homär* (from Ar. *ḥumar*) and *komär* 'tamarind'; *kamsa* 'fifty' for the existing *hamsa*.

21.8.2.2. k-q

karra and *qarra* 'steel knife'; *əmb*ʷ*aka* and *əmb*ʷ*aqa* 'coward'.

21.8.2.3. g-k, k-g

*g*ʷ*ärrätä* and *k*ʷ*ärrätä* 'make a pile of stones'; *gäwgawwa* and *käwkawwa* (also *qäwqawwa*) 'who wanders about aimlessly'; *kufeta* 'skullcap' (from Arabic *kūfiya*) and *gufta* 'scarf'.

21.8.3. Alternation of liquids
21.8.3.1. l ~ n

l instead of *n*: *mänäk*ʷ*se* and *mäläk*ʷ*se* 'monk'; *ǧanmeda* and *ǧalmeda* 'racecourse in Addis Ababa'; *zäläb* 'tail', from Arabic *ḏanab*.

n instead of *l*: *qəmal ǧər* and *qəman ǧər* 'licelike body parasite'; *läqämt* and *näqämt*, city in the Wollega region.

21.8.3.2. n ~ m

n instead of *m*: *šämqäqqo* and *šänqäqqo* 'snare for trapping animals'.
m instead of *n*: *konso* and *komso* 'a kind of handmade cotton blanket'.
From Turkish-Arabic: *barneṭa* and *barmeṭa* 'European-style hat'.

21.8.3.3. r ~ l

r instead of *l*: *gələmbiṭ* and *gərəmbiṭ* 'opposite, contrary' (from *gäläbbäṭä* 'turn upside down').
Note that in some occurrences assimilation or dissimilation may have brought about the alternance of the liquids.

21.8.4. Alternation of sibilants
21.8.4.1. s-š

säkʷäna and *šäkʷäna* 'hoof, foot'; *sənṭər* and *šənṭər* 'splinter'; *mist* and *mišt* 'wife'; *wägessa* and *wägešša* 'traditional medical practitioner'.
From Arabic: *sämbuq* and *šämbuq* 'small sailing vessel with sail'; *särṭan* and *šärṭan* 'crab'; *qərṭas* and *qərṭaš* 'piece of paper'.

21.8.4.2. z-ž-(ǧ)

(*a*)*mänäzzähä* and (*a*)*mänäžžähä* 'chew'; *mize* and *mənǧe* 'best man' (for inserted *n*, see § 21.12); *zəgra* and *žəgra* 'guinea hen'.

21.8.5. Alternation of palatals

21.8.5.1. š ~ č ~ ǧ

š:č: *šəfal* and *čəfal* 'eyebrow'; *čəgəñ* and *šəgəñ* 'seedling, plant shoot'; *čəggər* and *šəggər* 'trouble, difficulty'; (*a*)*ššännäfä* and (*a*)*čännäfä* 'overcome'.
š:ǧ: *šəgəl* and *ǧəgəl* 'gonorrhea'.

21.8.5.2. ž ~ ǧ

ž is in free variation with *ǧ* in any position. Initial: *žəgra* and *ǧəgra* 'guinea hen'; *žämmärä* and *ǧämmärä* 'begin'; *žoro* and *ǧoro* 'ear'.
Medial: *bäžäd* and *bäǧäd* 'abdomen'; *anžät* and *anǧät* 'bowels'.
Final: *goǧǧo* and *gožžo* 'small hut'; *gʷämäǧǧä* and *gʷämäžžä* 'desire eagerly'.

21.9. Assimilation

21.9.1. Total regressive assimilation
21.9.1.1. Consonants
Total assimilation occurs when two consonants are in contact. It affects the dentals *d, t, ṭ*; the liquids *l, r*; the sibilants *s, z*; and the velars *g, q*.

21.9.1.2. Morpheme *t*
The morpheme *t* of the imperfect, jussive, and of the verbal noun of the *tä*-stem is assimilated to any consonant with which it is in contact: thus, from *täkäffätä* 'be opened': imperfect *yəkkäffät* for *yətkäffät*, jussive *yəkkäfät* for *yətkäfät*, verbal noun *mäkkäfät* for *mätkäfät*, instrumental *mäkkäfäča* for *mätkäfäča*.

The derived stem *annaggärä* likewise derives from *atnaggärä.

The liquid *l* may be assimilated to an initial *r* of the verb: thus, *arräddamm* 'he didn't help' (for *alräddamm*), but also *alräddamm*.

The liquid *r* is assimilated to *s* in *əssu* 'he', *əssʷa* 'she', but also *ərsu, ərsʷa*.

21.9.1.3. Dentals
The glottalized *ṭ* is assimilated to the following *t* in the gerund: thus, *mätto* 'he coming' for *mäṭto*; *wätta* 'she going out' for *wäṭta* (but also *mäṭto, wäṭta*; see § 21.9.2).

The dental *d* becomes assimilated to the following *t* in the gerund: thus, *nädto* 'he driving', pronounced *nätto*; *kädto* 'he betraying', pronounced *kätto*; *ṣädto* 'it being clean', pronounced *ṣätto*.

The dental *d* is assimilated to the following *ǧ*: thus, *təwädǧ* 'you (fem.) love' (from *wäddädä*) becomes *təwäǧǧ* or *təwäǧǧi*.

21.9.1.4. Sibilants
The final *s* of the morpheme *as-* becomes assimilated to the initial *z, š*, or *ṣ* of the verb: thus, *azzämmätä*, for *aszämmätä* 'have someone go on campaign'; *aššällämä*, for *asšällämä* 'have someone decorated'; *aṣṣäyyäfä*, for *asṣäyyäfä* 'fill with disgust'.

In other occurrences, too, the succession *sš* becomes *šš*, *zž* becomes *žž*, and *zš* becomes *šš*: thus, *təkäšš* or *təkäšši*, from *təkäss* 'you (fem.) accuse' (from *kässäsä*); *tažž* or *tažži* 'you (fem.) command' (from *azzäzä*).

21.9.1.5. Lexical items
In the frequently used verbs *gäddälä* 'kill', *gʷäddälä* 'be missing', *d* is assimi-

lated to the following *l*: thus, *gällo* 'he killing', for *gädlo*; *yəgällall* 'he kills', for *yəgädlall*; *gʷällo* 'it missing', for *gʷädlo*; *yəgʷällall*, for *yəgʷädlall*.

Likewise the frequently used *dägmo* 'again, furthermore' is pronounced *dämmo*.

For the frequently used *adärrägä*, see § 21.14.

21.9.1.6. *Velars*
The velars *q, g* become assimilated to the suffix pronoun -*k* of the 1st and 2nd singular: thus, *särräkk* 'you stole', for *särräqk*; *fälläkk* 'you wished', for *fällägk*; *alṭäyyäkkumm* 'I didn't ask', for *alṭäyyäqkumm*.

21.9.1.7. *Miscellaneous*
Isolated occurrences of assimilation: *ṭunča* becoming *ṭučča* 'shoulder blade'; *mənčät* becoming *məččät* 'jar, pot'; *səlsa* and *səssa* 'sixty'; *əndet näw?* 'how is he?' becoming *əndennäw*.

21.9.2. Total progressive assimilation
Total progressive assimilation occurs in contact of *t* of the gerund with the final *ṭ* of the verb: thus *mäṭṭo*, for *mäṭto* 'he coming'; *wäṭṭa*, for *wäṭta* 'she going out' (but also *mätto, wätta*, for which see § 21.9.1.3).

21.9.3. Partial assimilation
21.9.3.1. *Contiguous assimilation*
nb may become *mb*. Thus, *šənbəra* and *šəmbəra* 'chick-pea'; *anbässa* and *ambässa* 'lion'; *ənbərt* and *əmbərt* 'navel'; *wänbär* and *wämbär* 'chair'.

Likewise *nf* may become *mf*: *qərənfud* and *qərəmfud* 'clove'; *gänfo* and *gämfo* 'porridge'.

21.9.3.2. *Assimilation of voicing*
Voiced-voiceless > voiceless-voiceless in *täzkar* and *täskar* 'memorial service held on the 40th day after death'; *gugs* and *guks* 'kind of polo'; *magsäñño* and *maksäñño* 'Tuesday'.

21.9.3.3. *Isolated occurrences of partial assimilation*
mṭ may become *nṭ* (the labial *m* becoming the dental labial *n* in contact with the dental *ṭ*) in *amṭa* and *anṭa* 'bring!'.

md may become *nd*: e.g., *təmd* and *tənd* 'pair, couple'.

ṭm became *ṭn* in *aṭənt* 'bone', from *ʕṣm, ʕṭm*.

ln > nn in *təlantənna* and *tənantənna* 'yesterday'.

21.9.3.4. Noncontiguous assimilation of voicing
gutəčča and kutəčča 'earrings'; səgaǧǧa (from Arabic saǧǧāda) and zəgaǧǧa 'prayer rug' (also səǧaǧǧa); tämäräkkʷäzä and tämäräggʷäzä 'lean upon'.

Of labials m-b > m-m: mabär and mamär 'association'.

Of liquids l, n: kuntal and kuntan 'quintal' (n-l > n-n; the original form is qinṭar, from Arabic qinṭār).

Of glottalization: k-ṭ > q-ṭ: kärāṭit (from Arabic ḫarīṭa) and qäräṭit 'pouch' (from Ar. ḫarīṭa).

q-ṭ > q-q in qärṭäm > qärqäm 'kind of plant resembling cress'; qənṭəš > qənqəš 'kind of sorghum'.

Of palatals: sanǧa and šanǧa 'bayonet'; säläččä- and šäläččä- 'be bored'.

21.10. Dissimilation

21.10.1. Contiguous dissimilation of voicing
žg > šg in mäžgär and mäšgär 'tick'; qṭ > gṭ in aqṭaččä and agṭaččä 'direction toward something'.

21.10.1.1. Noncontiguous dissimilation
The labial m of a noun expressing an instrument becomes w if there is a labial b, m, or f in the noun: thus, wämbär 'chair' (from *mänbär), waggəmt 'cup used for drawing blood' (from aggämä 'draw blood by cupping'), wäṭmäd 'snare, trap', wäqlämt and mäqlämt 'small knife', wäsfe 'awl', wänaf 'bellows', wänṭäft 'strainer', wänfit 'sieve', wäfčo 'grindstone', wäsfänṭər 'springy stick which is made into a snare' (from fänäṭṭärä 'spring out').

m-m may become m-b, as in mahtäb, matäb 'seal' instead of mahtäm; mäharäm, mäharäb 'handkerchief', from Arabic maḫrama.

Of two labials: fälässäfä and fälässämä 'philosophize, discover, invent'; anboləp and anboləkk 'envelope'.

n-n > l-n, or n-l: nišan 'medal' (from Arabic nišān) became lišan; ganen 'demon' became ganel.

21.10.1.2. Of voicing
gubbəta and qubbəta 'hill, hillock'; sənag and sənaq 'palate'.

Of glottalization (a voiceless glottalized becomes voiceless nonglottalized): qärqäha and qärkäha 'bamboo'; qawṭ and qawt 'kind of tree used for plow beams'.

Of glottalization and voicing (a voiceless glottalized becomes voiced nonglottalized): *qənṭar* and *gənṭar* 'quintal'; *ṭäräppeza* and *ṭäräbbeza* 'table'; *wäqqäṭä* and *wäggäṭä* 'pound'.

21.10.2. Dissimilation of gemination
The intensive action of type A of the composite verbs is expressed by *kəffətt adärrägä* 'open completely and suddenly', with gemination of the 2nd radical. In the verbs with identical second and third radical ("1.2.2"), however, the form is *wədədd alä*, with a nongeminated 2nd radical. The identity of the last two radicals brings about the dissimilation of gemination and, as a result, the 2nd radical is not geminated. The situation is the same in type-B verbs in which the attenuative action is expressed by the gemination of the 2nd radical: thus, *läzzäbb alä* 'be somewhat soft'. In 1.2.2 verbs, again by the dissimilation of gemination, the 2nd radical is simple: thus, *läṭäṭṭ alä* 'stretch somewhat'.

21.10.3. Reciprocal assimilation and dissimilation
qərṭas 'piece of paper' > **kərṭas* (by dissimilation) > *kərtas* (by assimilation); *ṭənčäl* 'hare, rabbit' > **čənčäl* (by assimilation) > *čəntäl* (by dissimilation); *ityoppəya* > **iṭyoppəya* (by assimilation) > *ṭobbəya* (by dissimilation); *čäqäččäqä*, and *čäkäččäkä* 'pester'.

21.11. Metathesis

21.11.1. Liquids and sibilants
Because of the relatively small number of occurrences with metathesis it is difficult to explain the reason for this feature. In the majority of occurrences the liquids *l, n, r* are involved.

With *r*: *səfra, sərfa* 'place'; *mäträbiya, märṭäbiya* 'axe'; *käbäro, käräbo* 'drum'; *bärtä qaqan, bäträ qaqan* 'iron bar'; *qərfəndo, qəfrindo* 'kind of plant'; *gärräzä, gäzzärä* 'circumcize'.

From Arabic: *märbuṭ, mäbruṭ* 'kind of rifle'; *mänäṭṭär, märäṭṭän* 'telescope'; *kəbrit, kərbit* 'matches'.

With *n*: *qəbanug, qənabug* 'oil from the *nug*-seed'; *qənṭəš, ṭənqəš* 'kind of sorghum'; *šännäṭä, näššäṭä* 'arouse great enthusiasm'.

With *l*: *sälen, sänel* 'palm mat'; *bäläṭṭägä, bäṭällägä* 'become rich'.

With the sibilants *s* and *z*: *maksäñño, maskäñño* 'Tuesday'; *betäksiyan, betäskiyan* 'church'; *sämmäṭä, säṭṭämä* 'get drowned, sink'.

With *z*: *əgzer, əzger* 'God' (but also with *r* in the root); *hullägize, hulläzge* 'always' (but also with *l* in the root).

21.11.2. Metathesis in Amharic roots in relation to Ge'ez roots

Amh. läwwäṭä 'change', Ge'ez wälāṭä; Amharic annäsä 'be little', Ge'ez nəʔəsä; Amharic təlant 'yesterday', from təlam-t, Ge'ez təmal-əm; Amharic awre 'wild animal', Ge'ez arwe.

21.12. Insertion of n, r

21.12.1. With quadriradicals

The dental-nasal n is occasionally intercalated between two radicals. This process of nasalization occurs most frequently when the root contains a velar g, q, or k.

With a velar in quadriradicals: gärägäre and gärängäre 'resinous bush'; gərgərit and gərəngərit 'tying the hands behind the back'; gədgədi and gədəngədi 'kind of hawk'; därägot and därängot 'a morsel of bread'; balägara and balängara 'opponent'. In the preceding examples n is placed before the velar.

Placed after the velar in duqduq and duqənduq 'dung worm'.

With other consonants: dəbəlbəl 'round', and dənbəlbəl 'sphere, ball'; ǧəlaǧəl and ǧəlanǧəl 'imbecile'; gələnbiṭ 'contrary, opposite', from gäläbbäṭä 'turn upside down'.

21.12.2. With biradicals and triradicals

Involving a velar: qug and qung 'snapper of a whip'; roqe and ronqe 'marsh'.

With other consonants: däf and dänf 'threshold'; mize and minǧe 'best man'; əntəff alä 'spit' (cf. əttəff alä, täffa 'spit'); qəfəd and qəfənd 'pus in the eye owing to inflammation'; wänčəf 'sling' from wäččäfä 'hurl with a sling' (cf. Ge'ez moḍäf 'sling', from * mäwḍəf, without n); qäbäṭ and qänbäṭ 'bud'; gäzzärä 'circumcise' and gänäzzärä 'cut'.

In nouns with a final -t: mağrat and manžərat 'nape of the neck'; säräbät and säränbät 'kind of bread made of chickpea flour'; məzəllat and mənzəllat 'great-great-grandparents'.

21.12.3. Lexical item

Amharic wänd 'male' is derived from * wäld becoming * wädd by assimilation (cf.Tigrinya wäddi) > wänd, with inserted n.

21.12.4. Miscellaneous

A few roots with a velar and an inserted n in relation to Ge'ez or to the other Semitic languages: anäqqäfä 'stumble', G. (ʔa)ʕqäfä; anäkkäsä 'limp',

Ar. ḥakasa; däqqä mäzmur and dänqä mäzmur 'student, disciple' (G. däqq); däqäl and dänqäl 'mast of a ship'.

With a consonant other than a velar: anäṭṭäsä 'sneeze', Geʿez ʿaṭäsä; ənčät 'wood', G. ʿəḍ; wänz 'river' (G. wəḥzä 'flow'); and 'one' from *ad (Geʿez ʔaḥadu).

21.12.5. r
A few nouns have an inserted r: qurqumba and qurqurəmba 'bottle-shaped container'; qumbus and qərənbus 'dung maggot'.

21.13. Abbreviations and haplology

21.13.1. Abbreviations
Frequently used nouns are abbreviated: əgzer (also əzger) for əgziabəher 'God'; betäksiyan and betäskiyan for betä krəstiyan 'church'; šaqa, or yäšaqa for šaläqa 'captain'; blatta for blattengeta, honorific title; däǧǧačč for däǧǧazmačč, honorific title; əče for əčege 'head of the Ethiopian monks'.

wätte emphasizes the attributes of the wättaddär 'soldier'; däbte emphasizes the attributes of the däbtära 'unordained member of the clergy'; šəme is used by children to make fun of the šəmagəlle 'old man'; šärme is used to make fun of the šärmuṭa 'prostitute'.

21.13.2. Haplology
addis aba for addis abäba 'Addis Ababa'; yäneta, yänta for yäne geta 'my master', term used by traditional church students in addressing teachers; əmmete, əmmäyte, for əmmä bete 'madam', lit. 'mother of the house'; filäfit and fit läfit 'directly in front of'; təlammata for təlant mata 'last night'.

21.14. Loss of consonants
The frequently used verb adärrägä 'do, make' loses the dental d without leaving a trace in the verb: thus, perfect arägä (note the nongemination of the r), imperfect yarägall for yadärgall, imperative arg for adrəg, gerund argo for adrəgo, and so on.

The d is likewise lost in qəmayat for qədmayat 'great-grandfather'.
The nasal-dental n is lost in mədəǧǧa 'fireplace', from näddädä 'burn'.
In the frequently used verb awwäqä 'know', the consonant w may be omitted: thus, yaqall for yawqall 'he knows', ayaqəmm 'he doesn't know' for

ayawqəmm, yämmiyaq 'he who knows' for *yämmiyawq, yämmayaq* 'he who doesn't know' for *yämmayawq*.

The consonant *y* is lost in *adollämm, adällämm* for *aydollämm, aydällämm* 'he is not'.

21.15. Vowels

21.15.1. Inventory
There are seven vowels in Amharic. The traditional order is: *ä, u, i, a, e, ə, o*. Table 21-2 illustrates the position of the vowels.

Table 21-2. Amharic Vowels

	front	central	back
high	i	ə	u
mid	e	ä	o
low		a	

There is no precise correspondence in the pronunciation of Amharic and English vowels.

21.15.1.1. *i*
The vowel *i* is pronounced somewhat like the 'ee' in 'feet' but without the /y/ glide of English: *fit* 'face', *anči* 'you' (fem.).

In a final palatal the expected *i* may be omitted in certain forms in writing and in pronunciation: thus, *kəfäči* and *kəfäč* 'open!' (fem.); *ləbäši* and *ləbäš* 'get dressed!' (fem.).

21.15.1.2. *e*
The pronunciation of the vowel *e* is approximately like that of the vowel 'a' in 'state' but without the /y/ glide of English: *bet* 'house', *nuzaze* 'will'. Note that in regions outside Addis Ababa all the consonants have slightly palatalized allophones when preceding the vowel *e*: thus, *bʸetʸe* 'my house'.[8] See also the vowel *o*, § 21.15.1.5.

---

8. This statement is in contradiction with some grammars which state that the vowel *e* is diphthongized as ʸ*e*. In fact, even in regions where ቤቲ is pronounced *bʸete*, the vowel is never diphthongized after a palatal (thus, ደረሰ *därässe*, not *därəššʸe*) or initially, as in እሊ *eli* 'tortoise'.

In palatals and with *y* the expected *e* may be written and pronounced *ä*; thus, *käfäčče* and *käfäččä* 'I opening'; *ǧela* and *ǧälä* 'be foolish'; *səraye* and *särayä* 'my job'.

21.15.1.3. ä
The vowel *ä* is pronounced like the sound one makes while hesitating in speaking; it is represented in writing by 'uh': *nägä* 'tomorrow', *gäräd* 'servant'. It is a mid-low central vowel, halfway between [ə] and [a].
No word in Amharic begins with *ä* except *ärä* 'then, so then, really?'

21.15.1.4. a
The vowel *a* is pronounced like the vowel *a* in 'father': *addärä* 'spend the night', *na* 'come!'.

21.15.1.5. o
The vowel *o* is pronounced approximately like the English 'a' in 'also': *roṭä* 'run', *of* 'bird. Note that in some regions outside Addis Ababa all consonants in contact with *o* are pronounced with rounded lips, resulting in a slight *w* off-glide: thus, *män^wor* 'existence, presence', *m^wotä* 'die', *s^wost* 'three'. See also § 21.15.1.2.

21.15.1.6. u
The vowel *u* is pronounced approximately like the English 'o' in 'who' but without diphthongization: *hullu* 'all', *ṭut* 'breast'.

21.15.1.7. ə
The vowel *ə* is pronounced approximately like the English 'e' in 'roses': *əssu* 'he', *sənt* 'how much?'
The vowel *ə* is phonemic: thus, አልቆ, the gerund of *alläqä* 'come to an end', is pronounced *alqo*, but አለቆ, the gerund of *a-laqä* 'make more, increase', is pronounced *aləqo* (likewise አርሶ, the gerund of *arräsä* 'plow', is pronounced *arso*, but አረሶ, the gerund of *a-rasä* 'wet, drench', is pronounced *arəso*); ይስማቸው is pronounced *yəsmaččäw* 'may he listen to them', but *yəsəmaččäw näbbär* 'he used to kiss them'; ጦምህ 'you fasted' is pronounced *ṭomh* or *ṭoməh*, but ጦምህ 'your fast' is pronounced only *ṭoməh*.

21.15.1.8. Final ə
No Amharic word ends in the vowel *ə* except the interrogative particle -ን -*nə*, which is pronounced with a rising intonation, and the interjection ሁ

əhə used by a listener to encourage the speaker to continue talking. Likewise in poetry, for reasons of prosody, if the final word of a line ends in a consonant, a vowel ə may be added.

For a prothetic ə, see § 21.18.

21.16. Vocalic length

The Amharic vowels are short. Vocalic length occurs only occasionally. Thus, the combination of a final -a with the enclitic -a may results in ā: e.g., käbbädä yännatun mot tärāddā (from tärädda-a) 'so, finally Käbbädä learned of his mother's death'.

The vowel is likewise long in näyī, the equivalent of näw əngi 'so it is!'; in a form such as sämmū wäy 'you, there! do you hear me!'; and in āy 'no', as in məsahən bällah? āy 'have you had lunch?' (lit. 'have you eaten your lunch?'). 'No'.

A long vowel is also connected with a special tone in the occurrences of a verbal noun at the end of the sentence. Examples: zənam limäta näw, mən yəššalall? tolo tolo mähēd 'it is starting to rain. What is best (to do)? Walk fast'; səfra lämagñat bägize männäsāt 'to get a seat one should start out early'; ṣähafiwa səra fätta səttəččawwät aläqawa kätäf malāt (with long ā̊) 'when the secretary was idly playing about, the boss suddenly showed up'.

21.17. Allophonic vowels

21.17.1. å

The vowel ä has a phonetic variant å (that is, a sound tending toward o) when preceded by a w or by a labialized consonant ending in ä, such as qʷä: thus, wåndəmm 'brother', wåmbär 'chair', täwållädä 'he was born', qʷårräṭä as against läbbäsä.

This feature is also expressed in the orthography. Indeed, one finds numerous words spelled with the vowel o after w. Examples: wäba and woba 'malaria mosquito', wäf and wof 'bird', wämo and womo 'Omo River', wädoma and wodoma 'plant that causes a goiterlike swelling in the necks of sheep'.

21.17.2. ə > ŭ

Likewise, the vowel ə has a variant ŭ (that is, a sound tending toward u) when preceded by a w: e.g., wŭsäd 'take!' as against ləbäs. The final ə of a labiovelar (such as qʷə) also has a variant ŭ: e.g., qʷŭräṭ 'cut!' as against ləbäs.

Some words are written either with the vowel ə or with the vowel u: thus, wəma and wuma 'symbol', wəha and wuha 'water'.

21.18. Prothetic ə and loss of initial ə

21.18.1. Prothetic ə before r
A prothetic ə often occurs before initial r, rarely before the sibilants s, š, z, and occasionally before other consonants.

The prothetic ə precedes r mostly if the initial r has the vowel ə. Examples: rəsas, ərsas 'lead, pencil', rəguz, ərguz 'pregnant', rəgo, ərgo 'coagulated milk'.

It also occurs with r having a vowel other than ə: thus, rab, ərab 'hunger', ras, əras 'head', rat, ərat 'dinner'.

A prothetic ə without an alternate form occurs in ərsu 'he', ərsʷa 'she', ərsaččäw 'they'.

21.18.2. Before other consonants
Examples for s: sar, əsar 'grass', set, əset 'woman'.

Examples for š: šəkokko, əškokko 'rock hyrax', šät, əšät 'almost mature grain', šok, əšok 'thorn'.

Before other consonants such as ṭ, l, and m. Examples for ṭ: ṭub, əṭub 'brick', ṭiy, əṭi 'gland'.

Example for l: əlqəmoš 'game consisting of catching stones tossed up in the air' (from läqqämä 'collect').

Examples for m: mäbällät, əmäbällät 'elderly widow', märr, əmmärr, exclamation to urge one's mount to jump over an obstacle.

21.18.3. Loss of initial ə
Loss of original ə (going back to ʔ, ʕ) occurs in ṭat 'finger' for əṭat (going back to Geʻez ʔaṣbāʕət, Semitic root ṣbʕ); sat 'fire' for əsat; zab 'reins' for əzab; rat 'dinner' for ərat; məs for əms 'vagina'; wənät for əwnät 'truth'; qubat 'concubine' for əqubat.

21.19. Meeting of vowels
As a rule, Amharic avoids the coming together of two vowels in pronunciation as well as in writing. If, for morphological reasons, two vowels should come together, the following may occur:

Amharic Phonology 423

1. Elision of one of the vowels.
2. Introduction of a glide semivowel *w* or *y* between the two vowels.

21.19.1. Elision
Elision of one of the vowels occurs: (1) if the two vowels are the same; (2) if the 1st vowel is a central vowel and the 2nd vowel is other than a back vowel.

21.19.1.1. Same vowels
a-a > a: **sämma-aččäw* 'he heard them' > *sämmaččäw*; *asa aṭmağ* 'fisherman' > *asaṭmağ*.
ə-ə > ə: **lə-əsäbər* 'so that I break' > *ləsäbər*.
o-o > o: either elision of one *o* (**bäqlo-očč* 'mules'>*bäqločč*) or a semivowel *ʷ* is produced (*bäqloʷočč*).

21.19.1.2. Different vowels
If the 1st vowel is a central vowel *ä*, *a*, or *ə*, and the 2nd vowel is a vowel other than a back vowel *o* or *u*, one of the vowels is elided. Thus,
ä-ə > ä: **yä-əğğ* 'of the hand' > *yäğğ*
ä-a > a: **yä-amarəñña* 'of Amharic' > *yamarəñña*
a-ə > a: *amsa əgər* 'centipede' > *amsagər*
a-ä > ä: *ṭena-äñña* 'healthy' > *ṭenäñña*
ə-a > a: **sə-alf* 'while I pass' > *salf*; **yə-awqall* 'he knows' > *yawqall*; **ə-alläbbät* becomes *alläbbät* 'that which is in it'.
    A form such as *šaläqa* 'major' arose from an original *ši-aläqa* becoming **šə-aläqa > šaläqa*.

21.19.1.3. With plural marker
In a plural noun, any final vowel of a singular noun may be elided when the plural marker *-očč* is added to it. Thus, **tämari-očč* 'students'>*tämaročč*; **wəšša-očč* 'dogs'>*wəššočč*. Note, however, that the vowel may be kept and a semivowel is then produced: thus, *tämariʷočč*, *tämariʸočč* (see below).

21.19.2. Insertion of a semivowel w, y
A semivowel *w* or *y* is inserted under the following conditions:
    1. If the 1st vowel is a back vowel *u* or *o*, the semivowel *w* is inserted.
    2. If the 1st vowel is a front vowel *i* or *e* and the 2nd vowel is the central vowel *a*, the semivowel *w* is inserted.

3. If the 1st vowel is a front vowel *i* or *e* and the 2nd vowel is the back vowel *o*, a semivowel *w* or *y* is inserted.

4. If the 1st vowel is a central vowel and the 2nd vowel is the back vowel *o*, a semivowel *w* is inserted.

Only a few occurrences will be given.

o-a > *o^wa*, *-wa* (without *o*): *bäqlo-aččən > *bäqlo^waččən* or *bäql^waččən*

u-a > *u^wa* or *wa* (without *u*): *näggäru-aččäw 'they told them' > *näggäru^waččäw* or *näggär^waččäw*

i-o > *i^yo*, *i^wo*: *tämari-očč 'students' > *tämari^yočč*, *tämari^wočč*

e-o > *e^yo*, *e^wo*: *bäre-očč 'oxen' > *bäre^yočč*, *bäre^wočč*

a-o > *a^wo*: *geta-očč 'masters' > *geta^wočč* (but also *getočč*)

21.20. Contraction of syllables

21.20.1. General

The succession -*Cäyä*- becomes *Ce*: thus, *wädet* 'where to?' from *wädä-yät*; *əndet* 'how?' from *əndä-yät*.

Cäyə- becomes *Ci*: e.g., *əndih* 'such' from *əndä-yəh*, lit. 'like this'; *əndičč* 'like this' (fem.) from *əndä-yəčč* (*yəhəčč*).

The syllable *Cäy*- may be contracted in pronunciation and in spelling into *Ce*-: e.g., *säyf* and *sef* 'sword'; *wäyzäro* and *wezäro* 'madam, lady'.

Cyä becomes *Ce*: e.g., *gəddelläš* and *gəddyälläš* 'carefree, unworried'.

Cyə becomes *Ci*: e.g., *asizo* 'he having someone seized' from *asyəzo*; (in proper names) *bärrihun* (from *bärr yəhun*) 'may he be the defense'.

Cəyə becomes *Ci*: e.g., *sisäbər* 'when he breaks' from *səyəsäbər*; *binägru* 'if they tell' from *bəyənägru*.

Cäw becomes *Co*: e.g., *läwz* and *loz* 'almond'; *mäbräd* 'file' (from Arabic) > *mäwräd > *moräd*.

Cäwä may become *Co*: e.g., *dämäwäz* and *dämoz* 'salary' (lit. 'blood and sweat'); *zäwätər* and *zotər* 'always'.

Cwä may become *Co*: e.g., *təlwät* and *təlot* 'dowry'; *ləbb wälläd* and *ləbbolläd* 'fiction'; *aswässädä* and *asossädä* 'have someone take'.

Cəw may become *Cu*: thus, *muläd* 'place of origin' (from *məwlad*); *həwkät* and *hukät* 'disturbance'.

21.20.2. Final V*ya* > *a*

bäzziya and *bäzza* 'there'; *läzziya* and *läzza* 'for that'; *mankiya* and *manka* 'spoon'; *ṭariya* and *ṭara* 'roof'; *maldäya* and *malda* 'brass arm bracelet'; *waləya* and *wala* 'Walia ibex'; *frəmbiya* 'cow's chest' and *frəmba*.

21.21. Alternation of vowels

21.21.1. Alternation i-ə
These two vowels are occasionally in free variation, particularly with the palatal š and occasionally with other palatals: thus, šəro and širo 'stew made from the flour of parched beans'; ǧər and ǧir 'a small military following a noblemen'; männəta and männita 'sleep, slumber'.

The forms of the perfect 2nd fem. singular ending in -š, or 3rd fem. singular ending in -äčč, are combined with the object suffix pronouns through the vowel i or ə: thus, and säddäbšəññ and säddäbšiññ 'you (fem.) insulted me'; säddäbäččəññ 'she insulted me' and säddäbäččiññ.

With other consonants: dəda and dida 'dumb, mute'; məst, məšt and mist 'wife'; məyazəya and miyazəya 'May'.

The instrumental is also written and pronounced mängäriya and mängärəya.

21.21.2. Alternation e-ä
In the gerund1st person singular, the regular final vowel -e (as in nägərre) alternates with ä in verbs ending in a palatal or in y. Thus, käfəčče and käfəččä 'I opening'; läbəšše and läbəššä 'I getting dressed'; bəyye and bəyyä 'I saying'.

21.21.3. Initial e, i, ə, o, u
Some nouns with an initial vowel e, i, or ə have variants with initial y + vowel. Examples: eli 'tortoise' and yäli; ečč, expression of disgust, and yäčč; itot 'nun' and yətot; imənt 'a nobody' and yəmənt.

In Arabic loanwords: yəmama 'turban', from Ar. ʕimāma; yəmam (also imam) 'leader of the Friday service', from Ar. ʔimām; yəmana 'money left in trust', from Ar. ʔimāna; yəlama 'target', and ilama, from Ar. ʕilāma.

A few nouns with initial o or u have variants with w: ona 'bare place without any people', and wäna; of 'bird', and wäf, wof; uqabe 'guardian spirit', and wəqabe.

21.22. Vowel harmony

21.22.1. Central vowels become rounded
When a rounded vowel u or o occurs in the root, the tendency is to harmonize the vowels ə and ä with the rounded vowels. Thus, the sequence ə-u may

become *u-u*: *qəmburs* and *qumburs* 'fat white grub'; *buruk* 'blessed' instead of *bəruk*; *səlluse* and *sulluse* 'ornamental collar for mules'.

ə-o may become *u-o*: *məšo* and *mušo* 'dirge'; *šəro* and *šuro* 'flour of roasted peas, sauce made from such flour'.

u-ə may become *u-u*: *šullə̣da* and *šulluda* 'flesh of the thigh'; *šurrəbba* and *šurrubba* 'braided hairdo'.

ä-o may become *u-o* or *o-o*: *mägogo* and *mugogo* (also *məgogo*) 'griddle'; *tälo* and *tolo* 'soon'.

o-ä may become *o-o*: *wärräta* (pronounced *worräta*) and *worrota* 'benefit, favor'.

21.22.2. Rounded vowels become centralized

Note that, because for some of the above-mentioned examples the origin is unknown, it is quite possible that the rounded vowel *u* or *o* was the original one and it became dissimilated into *ə* owing to the preceding or following *u*: thus, an original *šulluda* may have become *šulləda*.

21.23. Syllabic structure

To illustrate the syllabic structure, the symbol C is used for a consonant, C̄ for a geminated consonant, and V for a vowel.

The following syllables occur in Amharic:

V:	*u*, exclamation of surprise
VC:	*af* 'mouth'
VC̄:	*əǧǧ* 'hand'
VCC:	*ərf* 'plow beam and handle of the plow'
CV:	*na* 'come!'
CVC:	*mot* 'death'
CVC̄:	*ləkk* 'correct, size'
CVCC:	*səlt* 'method'

These syllables may constitute words by themselves as in the examples cited above, or they may be part of multisyllable words.

An Amharic word may begin with any consonant, although initial *ň* is very rare. As for *p* and *p̣*, they are rare and are usually of foreign origin.

An Amharic word may begin with any vowel except *ä*. The only exception to this rule is the word *ärä* 'oh, really!'.

An Amharic word may end in any vowel. A final *ə* occurs only in the interrogative particle *nə* and in poetry for reasons of rhyme.

21.24. Consonant clusters

A consonant cluster is a succession of two consonants not separated by a vowel. Treatment of a consonant cluster is different in nouns and verbs.

21.24.1. Initial consonant clusters

Amharic has no initial consonant clusters. A word such as ንጉሥ is to be read *nəgus*; ከቡር is *kəbur*. If, however, the 1st consonant is *k* or *g* and the 2nd consonant is *r*, and rarely *l*, or if the 1st consonant is *b* and the 2nd consonant is *l* or *r*, or if the 1st consonant is *f* and the 2nd consonant is *r*, there may or may not be a consonant cluster: thus, *krəstənna* 'Christianity', *krämt* 'rainy season', *krar* 'six-stringed lyre'; *grañ* 'left-handed'; *g(ə)rəmbiṭ* 'contrary (person)', *b(ə)latta*, honorific title, *b(ə)len* 'pupil of the eye', *b(ə)rəlle* 'small carafe', *b(ə)rät* 'iron', *b(ə)rəndo* 'meat eaten raw', but *bəlat* 'stratagem', *bələh* 'clever'; *frida* 'young gelded steer fattened for slaughter', but *fəre* 'fruit'.

Note that an initial consonant cluster in a foreign word is avoided by a prothetic *ə*: thus *əsport* for *sport*; *əspil* 'pin' from Italian *spillo*.

21.24.2. Final clusters

Amharic has final clusters of two consonants in verbal forms regardless of the nature of the consonants.

Only a few principles will be discussed here.

In the verbs with identical 2nd and 3rd radical, there is clustering: e.g. ሊወድድ *liwädd*.

If the 2nd radical is a liquid *l*, *r*, *n*, there is clustering: *liwäld*, *bəlṭ*, *liwärd*, *lizänb*.

If the 2nd radical is a labial, there is clustering: *linäfs*, *lilämd*, but if the 3rd radical is a liquid, there may or may not be clustering: *lisäbr* or *lisäbər*.

If the 2nd radical is a liquid and the 3rd radical is a labial, there is clustering: *likärm*.

If the 2d radical is a velar and the 3d radical is a labial, there is hesitation: *yərägm* and *yərägəm*.

If the last radical is a sibilant, there may or may not be clustering: *liläbs* or *liläbəs*.

If the last radical is a dental, there is clustering: *yəbälṭ*, *käbt*, *fərd*.

One would have to investigate whether there is a difference between nouns and verbs.

A geminated consonant is considered double. A word such as ልቅም, with geminated *q*, cannot, therefore, be read *ləqm*, with the final cluster -*qqm*. It has to be read *ləqqəm*.

There is no final cluster of three consonants: thus መንግሥት is to be pronounced *mängəst* and not *mängst*.

21.24.3. Medial clusters
When two consonants meet in the middle of a word, the 1st consonant closes the syllable and the 2nd consonant opens the next syllable. Thus, ይንጋር reads *yən-gär*, መንግሥት *män-gəst*.

The excluded syllabic pattern mentioned above is helpful in reading words that have consonants in the 6th order.[9] Thus, for instance, ድንግል can be read only *dəngəl* and not *dənəgəl*, nor can it be read *dəngl* as no final cluster of three consonants exists (see above). A word such as መጥፎ can be read only *mäṭfo* and not *mäṭəfo*. A word such as ብርቱ can be read only *bərtu* and not *bərətu*.

This clustering in medial position is valid only for nouns; for verbs the clustering depends on the verb form. Thus, ይስማል 'he kisses' is to be read *yəsəmall* and not *yəsmall*; or አድርጎ 'he having done' is to be read either *adərgo* or *adrəgo*.

There are no clusters of three consonants in medial position. The word መንግሥት cannot, therefore, be read *mängsət*. For its reading *mängəst*, see above.

A consonant in the 6th order preceding a geminated consonant is to be followed by *ə*. Thus, ምልክት (where *k* is geminated) is to be read *mələkkət*. Indeed, a reading such as *məlkkət* would result in a medial cluster of three consonants.

There are no definite rules covering all the possibilities. Thus, for instance, while ለከስከስ is to be read *ləkəskəs*, there is no valid rule that it should not be read *ləksəks*.

21.24.4. Clustering in phrases
All the examples of syllabic structure have dealt with words in isolation. Modifications, however, occur when words constitute a phrase. For instance, ልብስ is pronounced *ləbs* in isolation, the last consonant having no vowel. In the phrase ልብስ፡ነው *ləbs näw*, however, a vowel *ə* is intercalated

---

9. The consonant in the so-called 6th order [vowel differentiation of the consonant letter] either has the vowel *ə* or is *zero*.

between the last consonant of *ləbs* and the initial *n* of *näw*, and the phrase is then read *ləbsə näw*; ነጭ፡ነው *näččə näw* 'it is white'; አንድ፡ብር *andə bərr* 'one dollar'. Indeed, these two words form a unit that would then have a medial cluster of three consonants, a clustering not found in Amharic.

21.25. Accent

21.25.1. Stress

In general Amharic has an almost even distribution of stress on each syllable. Bold type indicates a stressed syllable.

It is safe to state that the last syllable is not stressed: thus, **sə**ga 'flesh' (and not sə**ga**); **wäm**bär 'chair' (and not wäm**bär**).

In bisyllabic nouns the stress is on the 1st syllable: thus **säñ**ño 'Monday', **sən**de 'wheat'.

In trisyllabic nouns the stress seems to vary: thus, **sa**muna 'soap', but tä**rä**käz, zəng"**ər**g"ər 'variegated'.

In quadrisyllabic nouns the stress is on the penultimate syllable: thus, zänä**zä**na 'pestle', aräng"**a**de 'green'.

The syllable preceding a geminated syllable is likely to be stressed: thus, **fäl**lägä, fä**lal**lägä, yə**fäl**ləgal; mä**säk**kärä, yəmä**säk**kər.

The question of the accent in Amharic still awaits a thorough investigation.

21.25.2. Intonation

Intonation plays an important role in the language. A few examples will illustrate its occurrence. Thus, *lə* + imperfect with a rising tone may express surprise: e.g., *ləttəhed?* 'are you really going to leave?'

The gerund at the end of a sentence may be uttered with rising-falling tone: e.g., *käbbädä yät allä? hedo* 'where is Käbbädä? Why, he has already left'.

mən 'what?' or *yämən* 'of what?' followed by a noun has a wide variety of meanings depending on the intonation: e.g., *zare dägmo mən* (or *yämən*) *säw näw?* 'what kind of strange (unwanted, unexpected) person came today?'; *yəh yämən səra näw?* 'what sort of job is this?' (with a shade of contempt or mock amazement).

The *tä*-stem may have an overtone of irony or sarcasm. The utterance is then spoken with a rising intonation. Thus, *suf täläbbäsänna yəkk"ärrall* '(look at him,) he puts on a wool suit and is all vain'.

Bibliography

Afework, G. J. 1905. *Grammatica della lingua amarica*. Rome: Tipografia della R. Accademia dei Lincei.

Armbruster, C. H. 1908. *Initia amharica: An introduction to spoken Amharic*. Part I, *Grammar*. Cambridge: Cambridge University Press.

Cohen, Marcel. 1936. *Traité de langue amharique* (Travaux et mémoires de l'Institut d'ethnologie 24). Paris. Institut d'ethnologie.

———. 1939. *Nouvelles études d'éthiopien méridional*. Paris: Champion. [Amharic, pp. 1–371.]

Dawkins, C. H. 1969. *The Fundamentals of Amharic*, rev. ed. Addis Ababa: Sudan Interior Mission. (1st ed., 1960).

Guidi, Ignazio. 1889. *Grammatica elementare della lingua amarica*. Rome: Tipografia della R. Accademia dei Lincei.

Hartmann, J. 1980. *Amharische Grammatik*. (Aethiopistische Forschungen 3). Wiesbaden: Steiner.

Leslau, Wolf. 1995. *Reference Grammar of Amharic*. Wiesbaden: Harrassowitz.

Ludolf, Hiob. 1698. *Grammatica linguae amharicae*. Frankfurt am Main: Prostat apud Johannen David Zunnerum.

Podolsky, Baruch. 1991. *Historical Phonetics of Amharic*. Tel Aviv: author.

Praetorius, Franz. 1879. *Die amharische Sprache*. Halle: Waisenhaus.

Chapter 22
Egyptian and Coptic Phonology
Antonio Loprieno
University of California, Los Angeles

22.1. Introduction

At the present state of our knowledge, a discussion of Egyptian and Coptic phonology must be addressed primarily as an issue of *diachronic*, rather than synchronic linguistics. While it is possible to recognize regular patterns of sound change in the history of the Egyptian language as a whole, including in many cases its Afroasiatic antecedents, the synchronic systems of phonological oppositions at any given time in the four millennia of the productive history of this language often defy a clear analysis. Furthermore, the dynamic models of historical phonology tend to hide many uncertainties behind the regularity of a reconstructed paradigm, conveying the misleading impression that for each of the different phases of the language (Early Egyptian, Middle Egyptian, Late Egyptian, Coptic) we are indeed able to establish a discrete phonological system.

The phonetic realities underneath the abstract phonological reconstructions are even more elusive: the traditional pronunciation and transliteration of many hieroglyphic phonemes rest upon hardly anything more than scholarly conventions, and even for the relatively well-known Coptic, in which Egyptian sounds are rendered in a Greek-based alphabet, it is difficult to assess reliable phonetic values for some of the Greek signs and of the Demotic graphemes that were added to the Greek alphabetic set.

In fact, the main reason for the difficulties in reconstructing the phonology of Ancient Egyptian lies in the very nature of the writing systems: Hieroglyphs, Hieratic, and Demotic represent the mere consonantal skeleton of a word (and sometimes only a portion thereof), followed by indicators of lexical classes, the so-called "determinatives." Semivocalic phonemes are rarely indicated, vowels practically never. As for Coptic, in which vowels are indeed rendered, one should not underestimate the methodological difficulty inherent in the widespread assumption of a phonological or phonetic identity between a specific Coptic sign and its original value in the Greek system—an identity which is by no means unquestionable.

Therefore, the reconstruction of the phonological inventory and of the phonetic values in any period of the history of Egyptian is bound to remain highly hypothetical: it can only be approached through a heuristic procedure in which three dimensions are checked against each other and mutually verified (cf. § 22.2): the reconstruction of Afroasiatic prehistory,[1] the information drawn from contemporary sources in other (mostly Semitic) languages with a better investigated phonology (Hoch 1991), and the laws of phonological evolution leading from older Egyptian to Coptic.[2]

22.2. Heuristic criteria

In spite of these difficulties, the study of Egyptian phonology has achieved significant progress since the initial studies of the late 19th century, both in the assessment of consonantal values and in the reconstruction of vocalic phonemes and prosodic rules. To achieve this goal, scholars rely on four procedures of linguistic reconstruction.[3]

22.2.1. *Comparative Afroasiatic linguistics*
Egyptian is a language of the Afroasiatic phylum, and the presence of established etymological correspondences offers a fundamental source for the reconstruction of phonological values. E.g., since Eg. <qʒb> corresponds to Sem. *qrb* meaning 'interior part', one can confidently establish that Eg. <q> = /q/ and that <b> = /b/.

22.2.2. *Contemporary transcriptions in foreign languages*
Many Akkadian texts, especially from the archive of el-'Amarna (15th–14th c. B.C.E.), contain Egyptian words, names, and short phrases in cuneiform transcription. Although the phonology and the graphemics of Akkadian are themselves by no means fully decoded, these transcriptions provide a valuable insight into the contemporary pronunciation of Egyptian. E.g., Eg. <stpnrʿ> 'the-one-whom-(the-god-)Ra-has-chosen' (royal name of King Ramses II) appears in cuneiform as *šá-te-ep-na-ri/e-a*, a form on the basis of

---

[1]. Suggestions for the reconstruction of the phonological evolution from Afroasiatic to Egyptian are presented by Schenkel 1990: 48–57; Kammerzell 1992; and Zeidler 1992.
[2]. The most complete description of these rules and of the patterns of Egyptian vocalization is found in Osing 1976: 10–30.
[3]. Cf. Schenkel 1990: 23–28. This book presents the most up-to-date and compact picture of Egyptian phonology (pp. 24–93). I shall make specific references to it only in the rare cases in which my analysis differs from Schenkel's in a significant way.

which one can both posit the contemporary Egyptian pronunciation as */saˌtepnaˈriːʕa/ and observe the correspondence Eg. <s> // Akk. <š>, both of which were probably realized as [s] or as a sound very close to it (at least in some dialects).[4]

22.2.3. Egyptian renderings of foreign words, especially of Northwest Semitic origin

This criterion represents the symmetrical counterpart to the preceding one: it provides an insight into the phonology of contemporary Egyptian while at the same time offering the possibility of verifying scholarly assumptions on Semitic phonology. E.g., Northwest Sem. *sōpēr 'scribe' ⇒ Eg. <ṯu-pa-r>. The relevance of this piece of evidence is twofold: on the one hand, it raises questions about the phonological status and the phonetic realization of Eg. /c/, which is the palatal phoneme usually transcribed ṯ by Egyptologists, while on the other, it can also be used to shed some light on the value of the phoneme /s/ (samekh), which originally must have been an affricate [t͡s] in Semitic (cf. Faber 1990: 627; Hoch 1991: 484f.; Faber 1992).

22.2.4. The evidence provided by Coptic

The latest stage in the development of Egyptian provides the broadest basis for the study of the phonology of older periods of the language as well. E.g., Eg. <wʕb> 'pure', 'to be pure', 'priest' appears in Coptic in the lexemes ⲟⲩⲁⲁⲃ 'holy', ⲟⲩⲟⲡ 'to be pure', ⲟⲩⲏⲏⲃ 'priest'. This evidence enables us to reconstruct three different vocalization patterns underlying the same graphic reality of hieroglyphic Egyptian: the stative *wáʕbaw 'he is pure', the infinitive *waʕáb 'to become pure', and the noun *wīʕab 'priest'. At the same time, this piece of evidence raises questions of consonantism, i.e., the fate of the phoneme /ʕ/ and the reason for the alternance ⲃ vs. ⲡ in the Coptic forms as opposed to <b> in both cases in their Egyptian antecedents.

In the practice of Egyptian phonological reconstruction, these four aspects appear constantly combined: while each of them, if considered individually, proves largely inadequate in order to determine a synchronic stage, together they convey a relatively homogeneous picture of the fundamental laws of Egyptian phonological development. What follows in the next paragraphs (§§ 22.3–6) is a tentative historical phonology of Egyptian from its Afroasiatic roots to alphabetic Coptic. Transcriptions from Egyptian and

---

4. See Faber 1990: 627ff.; 1992. For dialectal differences in the case of Akk. š cf. von Soden 1969 § 30.

Semitic follow the established conventions in these respective fields and are rendered in *italics*; transliterations of graphemes without reference to their phonological status are indicated in angle brackets (<x>); phonemes (/x/) and tentative phonetic values ([x]) are represented according to IPA conventions.

At this point, a methodological warning is in order: in the case of Egyptian (and of many other 'philological' languages known only through written records), the distinction between the *phoneme* as the distinctive minimal unit of the language (/x/) and the often much larger inventory of *sounds* ([x]) representing its physical realizations is heuristically less practicable than for languages with a better-known phonological structure: while scholars can strive for the reconstruction of the "sound units" of the language, the technical assessment of their phonological status, which would require in each case the minimal pair test, often proves a very problematic endeavor: on the one hand, our only source of information is represented by a complex writing system which combines phonetic and semantic principles; on the other hand, because of the restrictiveness of cultural conventions governing the use of writing in Egyptian society,[5] our knowledge of the lexicon is doomed to remain far from exhaustive.

22.3. The prehistory of Egyptian phonology

Before the emergence of Egyptian as a written language, a few adjustments within the stock of phonemes inherited from "Afroasiatic"[6] seem to have taken place. Three major evolutions from the original phonological stock characterize the Egyptian domain as it begins its recorded history.[7]

(a) In the apical and interdental series, voiced **d*, **z*, and **ð* develop into the pharyngeal phoneme /ʕ/ (Rössler 1971: 275–77), probably going through an intermediate stage with pharyngealized lateral: **d*, **z*, **ð* (> **ɬ*) > /ʕ/.[8] E.g., Eg. *ʕ.t* 'portal', cf. Sem. **dalt* 'door'; Eg. *ʒʕ* 'to speak a foreign

---

5. What is often referred to as "rules of decorum": cf. Eyre and Baines 1989.
6. "Afroasiatic" is here used as a conventional term to indicate the set of linguistic features which Egyptian shares with a certain number of other language families (Semitic, Berber, Cushitic, Chadic), without implying the belief in the existence of an actual proto-language ancestral to these families. The different theoretical models are discussed in Loprieno 1986: 1–12, 187–90.
7. In the following transcriptions, *v̆* denotes an unidentified short vowel (*a*, *i*, or *u*), corresponding (for typographic reasons) to the Egyptological convention ˘.
8. Cf. the comparable evolution from Proto-Sem. **ḏ* to Aram. <q>, later <ʕ>: **ʔrḏ* > <ʔarqā> > <ʔarʕā> 'earth' (Brockelmann 1908: 134).

language', cf. Sem. *lġz (Ar. laġaza 'to speak enigmatically', Hebr. l'z 'to speak a foreign language'); AA *ðupṗ 'fly' > Eg. ʿffj */'ʕuffv̌j/ > Coptic ⲁϥ, cf. Sem. *ḏbb (Akk. dubbum, Ar. ḏubāb, Hebr. zəbûb).

(b) Among the liquids, the original opposition between nasal *n, lateral *l, and vibrant *r underwent a profound reorganization, not yet fully understood in its specific details, in which a role was also played by dialectal varieties. AA *n and *r were kept as Eg. /n/ and /ʀ/—the latter being the phoneme conventionally transcribed ꜣ by Egyptologists and traditionally taken to be a variety of glottal stop /ʔ/, but in early Egyptian probably a "uvular trill";[9] Eg. jnk */ja'nak/ (Kammerzell 1991b: 201), Sem. *ʔanāku, 1st sg. pronoun, or Eg. kꜣm */'kaʀmv̌w/ (Osing 1976: 857), Sem. *karm 'vineyard'. On the contrary, AA *l does not display uniform Egyptian correspondences nor is Eg. */l/ indicated by an independent grapheme, in spite of its almost certain presence in the phonological inventory of the language: AA *l corresponds to Eg. <n>, e.g., AA *lis 'tongue' > Eg. ns */lis/, cf. Coptic ⲗⲁⲥ, Sem. *liš-ān; to Eg. <r>, e.g., jzr */'jaθrv̌w/ 'tamarisk', cf. Sem. *ʔatl; to Eg. <ꜣ>, e.g., ꜣ" 'to speak foreign languages', cf. Sem. *lġz (see above); and to Eg. <j>, e.g., AA *lib 'heart' > Eg. jb */jib/, cf. Sem. *libb or AA *lwn 'color' > Eg. jwn */ja'win/ (Osing 1976: 316), cf. Sem. *lawn. Presumably, proto-Eg. *l merged with other sonorants in the dialect which eventually led to the written language, while still being kept in less normative varieties of the language: in the New Kingdom, when Later Egyptian became the written form of the language for the domain of administration and literature, a specific grapheme <n>+<r> was created in order to express the phoneme /l/. In Demotic, /l/ is autonomously indicated by a grapheme <l>, a diacritic variety of <r> = /r/.

(c) The AA velar plosives *k, *g, and *ḳ display two outcomes in Eg.: either they are maintained as k /k/, g /g/, and q /q/, or they are palatalized into ṯ /c/, j /ɟ/, and ḏ /ɟ/ respectively: cf. the 2nd person suffix pronoun masc. /k/ < *-ka/-ku vs. fem. /c/ < *-ki (Kammerzell 1991b: 198ff.) or the opposition between the two Eg. roots wꜣḏ (cf. wꜣḏ */'waːʀiɟ/ 'green') and jꜣq (cf. jꜣq.t */'jʉʀqat/ 'vegetables') from an identical AA root *wrḳ.

(d) The phonemes corresponding to the so-called "emphatic" series of other branches of the AA phylum lost their phonological status in Egyptian, merging either with the corresponding voiceless fricative, as in the labial

---

9. A possible remnant of the early pronunciation of this phoneme is perhaps its outcome as Coptic /r/ in specific phonetic surroundings: ᴮⲭⲣⲟⲃⲓ 'sickle' < ḫ b.t */ça'ʀabjv̌t/(?), with [çʀ] > [kʰr]. Cf. the references in Westendorf 1965: 67.

series, in which AA *pỉ develops into Eg. /f/: AA *spỉy 'seven' > Eg. sfḫw */ˈsafχaw/, cf. Sem. *šbʿ, or with the corresponding voiced plosive: (1) the AA emphatic dentals *ṭ and *ṣ merge into Eg. /d/: Eg. dwn 'to stretch' */ˈdaːwan/, cf. Sem. ṭwl 'to be long'; Eg. wdpw 'servant', cf. Ar. waṣīf; (2) in specific phonetic environments, the AA emphatic velars *ḵ and *x̣ merge into the voiced palatal stop /ɟ/, the phoneme conventionally transcribed ḏ by Egyptologists: AA *wrḵ > Eg. wꜣḏ */ˈwaːɾiɟ/ 'green', cf. Sem. *warq 'leaf'; AA *nx̣m > Eg. nḏm */ˈnaːɟim/ 'sweet', cf. Sem. *nʿm. As we just saw, in absence of palatalization, AA *ḵ is kept in Eg. as /q/, which was probably articulated as ejective [qʼ] (see § 22.6 for Coptic evidence of this articulation): from AA *ḵrb/ḵlb are derived both Eg. qꜣb 'interior' (cf. Akk. qerbum 'inside') and Eg. ḏnb 'to turn' (cf. Ar. qlb 'to turn around'). As for AA *x̣, when not subject to palatalization it merges into the voiceless pharyngeal fricative /ħ/: AA *x̣al > Eg. ḥr */ħar/ 'on', cf. Sem. *ʿal.

22.4. The phonological system of Early Egyptian (about 2500 B.C.E.)

At the beginning of its written history, i.e., during the historical period known as the "Old Kingdom" (2800–2150 B.C.E.), one can assume that the Egyptian language displayed the phonological inventory shown in Table 22-1. Here, *x* indicates the traditional Egyptological transcription, /x/ the posited phoneme, [x] a tentative phonetic reconstruction (if different from /x/).

Some contemporary scholars, following Rössler 1971 (among Egyptologists cf. primarily Schenkel 1990: 24–57; cf. also Kammerzell 1992: 169ff.; Zeidler 1992: 204ff.) and a long tradition going back to the 19th century, offer a partially different analysis of these phonemes: since Eg. <d> and <ḏ> represent, as we just saw, the heirs of AA "emphatics" (*ṭ/ṣ and *ḵ/x̣ respectively), these phonemes, rather than as "voiced" /d/ and /ɟ/, should be understood as "voiceless emphatic" <d> = /ṭ/ and <ḏ> = /c̣/, although the actual phonetic realization of the feature [+EMPHATIC], whether pharyngealization, velarization, or glottalization, cannot be determined with certainty (Kammerzell 1992: 169).

Yet, because of the presence of just *two*, rather than *three* phonemes in the respective Egyptian consonantal series, I prefer to analyze them as poles of the simpler binary opposition "voiceless" vs. "voiced".[10] However, an important discovery of the alternative approach to Egyptian phonology must

---

10. An excellent discussion of adequacy and advantages of this simpler solution is offered by Hoch 1991: 508 ff.

Table 22-1. Early Egyptian Consonants

	Bilabial	Labio-dental	Inter-dental	Dental	Alveo-palatal	Palatal	Velar	Uvular	Pharyn-geal	Glottal
Plosive										
Voiceless	p /p/ [p(ʰ)]			t /t/ [(tʰ)]		ṯ /c/ [c(ʰ)]	k /k/ [k(ʰ)]	q /q/ [q']		ʔ /ʔ/ [a]
Voiced	b /b/			d /d/ [t']		ḏ /ɟ/ [c']	g /g/ [k']			
Fricative										
Voiceless		f /f/	z /θ/	s /s/ [s]	š /ʃ/	ẖ /ç/		ḫ /χ/	ḥ /ħ/	h /h/
Voiced									ʕ /ʕ/	
Nasal	m /m/			n /n/						
Vibrant				r /r/ [ɾ]				ꜣ /ʀ/ [b]		
Lateral				/l/ [c]						
Glide	w /w/					j /j/ [d]				

[a] The glottal stop [ʔ] was probably not a phoneme in Egyptian in its earliest phase; later on, presumably during the Middle Kingdom (2000–1750 B.C.E.), /ʔ/ represents on the one hand the result of the evolution /k/ > /ʔ/ (cf. note b), on the other hand the outcome of /j/ > /ʔ/ between two vowels in posttonic position (*/baːjin/ > */baːʔən/ 'bad') and before an unstressed vowel in initial poosition (*/jaʔnak/ > */ʔaʔnak/ 'I'). Kammerzell (1991b: 186–87; 1992: 168–69) prefers a consistent interpretation of ꜣ as palatal glide rather than as glottal stop /ʔ/.

[b] In the later phases of Early Egyptian (i.e., probably during the Middle Kingdom), the uvular trill /ʀ/, which is the Eg. heir of AA *r, progressively tends to acquire the realization as glottal stop [ʔ]—an evolution which appears almost completed in the New Kingdom (1550–1050 B.C.E.); cf., however, n. 9.

[c] In the hieroglyphic system, the phoneme /l/ is not indicated unambiguously: it is frequently conveyed by ⟨n⟩ and ⟨r⟩, more rarely by ⟨ ⟩ and ⟨j⟩; cf. above.

[d] For the writing of this phoneme, the following general rules apply (with many exceptions): /j/ is rendered by ⟨j⟩ in initial position: ⟨jt⟩ = */jaːtvj/ 'father', and immediately following a stressed vowel: ⟨bjn⟩ = */baːjin/ 'bad'; by ⟨jj⟩ within a word, if /j/ immediately precedes the stressed vowel: ⟨ḫjjk⟩ = */χaʕjak/ 'you will appear'; by ⟨∅⟩ at the end of a word: ⟨jt⟩ = */jaːtvj/ 'father'.

be borne in mind and accounted for: on the basis of both comparative evidence[11] and diachronic signals,[12] Egyptian *mediae* often appear to have neutralized the feature [+VOICED] and to have been realized—together with the uvular plosive /q/—as ejective stops.[13] Ejectivity, the existence of which can also be inferred through indirect Coptic evidence (cf. § 22.6), brought these phonemes into the phonetic proximity of Semitic (and Afroasiatic) "emphatics": most likely /ḏ/ = [t'], probably also /ǯ/ = [c'], /g/ = [k'], and /q/ = /q'/. A possible explanation of this phenomenon of especially initial devoicing[14] is that the feature [+VOICED] must have progressively become redundant under the competition of the optional aspiration which, at least in some varieties of the language and specific environments, characterized Egyptian voiceless stops: /p/ = [pʰ] and /t/ = [tʰ], probably also /c/ = [cʰ] and /k/ = [kʰ].[15] This is shown by the fact that Eg. /p/ and /t/ are rendered in the Greek transcriptions by φ and θ respectively: *ptḥ* */pi'taḥ/ '(the god) Ptah' > Φθα, and Eg. /c/ and /k/ often by σ and χ respectively: *tb-nṯr* */ˌcab'naːcar/ > */ˌcəb'nuːtə/ '(the city of) Sebennytos' > Σεβεννυτος, *bꜣk-n-rn=f* */ˌbaːʀak-v̆n-'riːnv̆f/ > */bokko'riː(nv̆)/ 'Bocchoris' (p.n., lit. 'servant-of-his-name') > Βοχχορις,

11. Schenkel 1990: 33–41. In loanwords from Egyptian to Semitic, Eg. *d* is always rendered by Sem. *ṭ*: Eg. *jdmj* */jv̆'duːmv̆j/ [jv̆'tˀuːm(v̆j)] > Hebr. *ʔēṭûn* 'red linen'. The same holds true for Babylonian transcriptions of Eg. words: *jfdw* */jaf'daw/ [jəfˀt'aw] 'four' = Middle Bab. *ipṭau* (Lambdin 1952: 136–37); Sem. *ṭ*, on the other hand, is rendered both by Eg. *d* (with which it shared "markedness," whatever the phonetic realization of this feature may have been) and by Eg. *t* (with which it shared "voicelessness"). Also, /g/ and /q/ were articulated in a very similar way, i.e., [k'] and [q'] respectively, a fact which explains why Eg. *g* (= [k']) is always rendered by Sem. *q* (= [q]): Eg. *gstj* */ˈgastv̆j/ ['kˀast(v̆j)] 'palette' > Hebr. *qešet* (< *qašt) 'bow' (Lambdin 1952: 148), whereas both Sem. *q* (= [q]) and *g* (= [g]) can be rendered by Eg. *g*. As for Eg. *ḏ* ("ejective"), it regularly corresponds to Sem. *ṣ* ("emphatic"): *ḏꜥn.t* */ˈjuʕnv̆t/ ['cˀuʕn(v̆t)] '(the city of) Tanis' > Hebr. *ṣōʕan* (< *ṣuʕn). Cf. Hoch 1991: 512 ff.
12. Cf. the consistency displayed by the evolutions Eg. /d/ > Coptic ⲧ, Eg. /ǯ/ > Coptic ϫ, Eg. /g/ > Coptic ⲕ or ϭ: see Worrell 1934: 17–30.
13. For the discussion of similar "glottalic" approaches to the phonology of Indo-European and of the proximity of voiced phonemes to ejectives see Schmalstieg 1990: 362–65. An exception is represented by /b/ = [b], in which the feature [+VOICED] was probably kept because of the difficulty of maintaining in a linguistic system a glottalized [pˀ], due to the distance between glottis and lips: cf. the discussion by Schmalstieg (pp. 363 f.).
14. This pattern of devoicing represents a form of "initial strengthening" (Hock 1991: 162–64).
15. An excellent analysis of the relation between three different types of stops (voiced-unaspirated, voiceless-aspirated, and voiceless-unaspirated) is provided by Worrell 1934: 17ff.: while Egyptian "voiceless" plosives are aspirated, their "voiced" counterparts, which were probably articulated as ejectives, correspond rather to Worrell's "half-voiced" (i.e., voiceless-unaspirated) stops.

Βοκχορις, Βοχορινις. This aspiration is still exhibited by some Coptic dialects such as Bohairic (cf. § 22.6).

As for the sibilants, Old Kingdom Egyptian displays three phonemes, conventionally transcribed z (or s̄), s (or ś), and š. When subject to palatalization, this last phoneme corresponds etymologically to AA *x (which, as a rule, evolves to Eg. ḫ = /ç/): Eg. ḫmm, šmm 'to become hot', cf. Sem. *ḥmm. This phenomenon seems indeed to indicate an articulation /ʃ/ for Eg. š, although both AA *š and *ś are continued by Eg. s (ś), i.e., by the second phoneme listed above: cf. AA *šuː 'he' > Eg. sw */suw/ (cf. Kammerzell 1991b: 190ff.), Sem. *šuwa; AA *śapat 'lip' > Eg. sp.t */ˈsaːpat/ (Osing 1976: 870f.), Sem. *śapat. It is quite possible, therefore, that Eg. s /s/ was characterized by a supplementary articulatory feature, whose precise phonic nature (perhaps of lateral or palatal type) is impossible to determine. Eg. z, on the other hand, is the heir of AA *θ and *s, as is shown by such correspondences as the already mentioned Eg. jzr */ˈjaθrv̆w/ 'tamarisk', cf. Sem. *ʔatl or AA *sulxam 'locust' > Eg. znḥmw */θanˈḥuːmv̆w/ (Osing 1976: 454), cf. Hebr. sol'ām. Here I reconstruct z as /θ/,[16] but it needs to be stressed that the phonological opposition between /θ/ and /s/ was neutralized by the beginning of the Middle Kingdom, at which time <z> and <s> had become graphic variants of the same phoneme /s/. However, the articulation and the phonological status of sibilants in the whole phylum remains a thorny issue of AA linguistics.

The Eg. phoneme /j/ represents the outcome of AA *j (Eg. jmn 'right side', therefore 'West', the point of reference being represented by the sources of the Nile, i.e., the South, vs. Sem. *ymn 'right side', therefore 'South', the point of reference being the place where the sun rises, i.e., the East) and of AA *l (Eg. jwn 'color', cf. Sem. *lawn, see also § 22.3) when subject to palatalization. Probably by the beginning of the Middle Kingdom, as part of the global reorganization of liquid phonemes which took place in Egyptian (with /ʀ/ > /ʔ/ and the neutralization of the opposition between /l/ and other sonorants, cf. Table 22-1), /j/ turned into /ʔ/ before an unstressed vowel in

---

16. Schenkel 1986 suggests the interpretation of z as affricate [t͡s], because it stands for /t/ + /s/ in the word nzw 'king', whose more traditional writing is ntsw. Whether an affricate (as suggested by Schenkel and by the equation with AA *s) or a fricative (as suggested by the correspondence with AA *θ), it is not surprising that this phoneme should be used to indicate a sibilant immediately following a nasal, a phonetic surrounding which often tends to generate affrication: /ns/ < <nts>, <nz> = [˘nt͡s] (à la Schenkel) or <nz> = [˘nθ] > <nts> = /ns/ [˘nt͡s] (as defended here): for "consonantal epenthesis" (as in the case of [ns] > [nt͡s]) cf. Hock 1991: 117 ff.

initial position (e.g., *jwn* */ja'win/ > */ʔa'win/ 'color') and in postvocalic position following the stress (e.g., *ḥjpw* */'hujpŭw/ > /'heʔpŭw/ '[the god] Apis').

Among the guttural fricatives, \<ẖ> = /ç/ continues AA *x (AA *xanam > Eg. *ẖnmw* '[the ram-god] Khnum', Ar. *ġanam* 'sheep'), \<ḫ> = /χ/ is the outcome of AA *γ (AA *wsγ 'wide' > Eg. *wsḫ*, Ar. *wsʿ*), and \<ḥ> = /ħ/ derives from AA **x̱* when not subject to palatalization (AA **sulx̱am* 'locust' > Eg. *znḥmw*, Hebr. *solʿām*). The phoneme \<h> = /h/ does not display any unequivocal AA cognate.

22.4.1. Vowels
The vocalic system of early Egyptian can be reconstructed as in Table 22-2.

Table 22-2. Early Egyptian Vowels

	Short	Long
Front	/i/	/iː/
Central	/a/	/aː/
Back	/u/	/uː/

The three vocalic qualities posited for early Egyptian are inherited directly from the AA prehistory of the language. While never spelled out in writing, vocalic phonemes can be reconstructed with a sufficient degree of systematic reliability on the basis of the four criteria formulated in § 22.2. For the earliest phase in the development of the Egyptian phonological system we do not posit the existence of a phoneme shwa.

Unlike stressed vocalic phonemes, unstressed vowels cannot be reconstructed with any degree of reliability. E.g., in *nṯr* */'naːcar/ 'god', while the stressed vowel can be reconstructed directly from Coptic ⲛⲟⲩⲧⲉ (with */naː/ > /nuː/, cf. § 22.6), the quality of the unstressed vowel in *-*car* can only be inferred indirectly through the feminine form *nṯr.t* */na'caːrat/ > Coptic -ⲛⲧⲱⲣⲉ (with */caː/ > /toː/, cf. § 22.6). The extent to which a whole paradigmatic class should be posited on the basis of analogy is still a matter of intense scholarly debate.

22.4.2. Syllabic structures
As a general rule, the opposition between short and long vowel is not phonological, but determined by the respective syllabic structure: long vowels appear in open stressed syllables, short vowels in closed and in open

unstressed syllables. Major exceptions are represented by the presence of a long vowel in closed stressed syllable in the infinitive of biconsonantal verbal roots and, at least according to some scholars, the possibility of long or doubly-closed syllables in final position. Accordingly, the following five or seven patterns of syllabic distribution (patterns 6–7 are not universally accepted) are characteristic for early Egyptian (C = consonant, V = vowel, # = word boundaries):

1. 'CVC   *jnn* */ja'**nan**/ 'we'
2. (_)CVC(_)   *rmṯ* */'ra:**mac**/ 'man'
3. 'CV: *ḥtp* */'**ḥa**:tip/ 'pleasing'
4. #CV'_   *tpj* */**ta**'pij/ 'first'
5. #CV:C#   *mn* */**ma:n**/ 'to stay'
6. _'CVCC#, _'CV:C# *mdw.w* */ma'**duww**/ 'words'[17]
7. '_CV#, '_CV:#   *stp.k(w)* */sv̌t'pa:**ku**/ 'I chose'[18]

Table 22-3 shows the syllabic paradigms admissible in early Egyptian. Parentheses signify that the presence of the corresponding syllabic structure is not universally accepted. This is the case of the doubly-closed stressed syllable, which characterizes a certain number of plural forms of bisyllabic nouns, and of the open unstressed syllable in final position, typical for the endings of specific verbal forms (pattern -CV#) and personal pronouns (pattern -CV:#).

Table 22-3. Early Egyptian Syllabic Structures

	Pretonic	Tonic	Posttonic
Open	#CV'_	#CV:_	('_CV#)
Closed	#CVC'_	'CVC	'_CVC#
Doubly-closed		('CVCC#)	
Long		'CV:C#	

In historical Egyptian, the stress falls either on the ultimate (oxytone) or on

---

17. Schenkel 1983a: 171–230; 1990: 63–78.
18. Kammerzell 1991a: 189–92; 1991b: 198 ff. In the more traditional interpretation, the fall of final vowels is seen in connection with the transition from the *Dreisilbengesetz* to the *Zweisilbengesetz* in the prehistory of Egyptian: cf. Fecht 1960 §§ 392–406; Schenkel 1990: 78–86.

the penultimate (paroxytone) syllable of a word. Oxytone patterns[19] are #CV'CVC# (*wbḫ* */waˈbaχ/ 'to become white', Coptic ⲟⲩⲃⲁϣ), #cvcˈcvc# (*jfdw* */jafˈdaw/ 'four', Coptic ϥⲧⲟⲟⲩ), #cv:c# (*dd* */ja:d/ 'to say', Coptic ϫⲱ), #cvˈcvcc# (*mdw.w* */maˈduww/ 'words', Coptic ᴮ-ⲙⲧⲁⲩ).[20] Paroxytone patterns are #ˈcvccvc# (*stp.w* */ˈsatpaw/ 'is chosen', Coptic ⲥⲟⲧⲡ), #ˈcv:cvc# (*stp* */ˈsa:tap/ 'to choose', Coptic ⲥⲱⲧⲡ), #cvˈcvccvc# (*ḫprw.w* */χuˈpirwaw/ 'transformations', Akk. transcription *(a)ḫ-pí/é-ia*; Osing 1976: 558ff.), #CV'CV:CVC# (*psḏw* */piˈsi:jv̆w/ 'nine', Coptic ⲯⲓⲧ), #CVCˈCVCCVC# (*wpw.tjw* */wapˈwutjv̆w/ 'messengers', Akk. *ú-pu-ti/ú-pu-ut*), #cvcˈcv:cvc# (*wpw.tj* */wapˈwu:tv̆j/ 'messenger', Meroitic *apote*; Osing 1976: 532–33).

Since the stress can only affect the last two syllables of an Egyptian word, the governing rule of syllabic patterns is known with the German term *Zweisilbengesetz* ('law of the two syllables'). For the prehistory of the Egyptian language, some scholars posit a situation in which, as in the related Semitic languages, the stress could also affect the antepenultimate syllable (*Dreisilbengesetz*, i.e., 'law of the three syllables'; Fecht 1960 §§ 325–47). Following the loss of the short vowel in the open posttonic syllable, words displaying this syllabic pattern were subsequently integrated into the regular patterns with penultimate stress: **/ˈχupiraw/ > */ˈχupraw/ 'transformation'.

22.4.3. Text sample (CT II 209c–210c)

Here is a short text sample of Early Egyptian. The conventional Egyptological transliteration of the original hieroglyphic text (drawn from the funerary corpus of the Coffin Texts, about 2000 B.C.E.) is followed by a translation and a tentative phonological reconstruction.

> *jr.t ḫprw.w m bjk   qj sšd snḏ nṯr.w*
> *rs ꜣs.t bkꜣ.tj ḥr mtw.t sn=s wsjr*
> *ṯz=s ḥjm.t wn.t jb=s nḏm.w m mtw.t sn=s wsjr*

'To make transformations as falcon. The lightning flash will strike, the gods will be afraid.
Isis will wake up pregnant from the seed of her brother Osiris.

19. In the following examples, the reconstruction of the phonological structure of a specific word in early Egyptian is accompanied by the later evidence (Akkadian transcriptions from the New Kingdom, Meroitic borrowings, or the Coptic form of the word) on which this reconstruction is based.
20. Superscript letters are abbreviations of Coptic dialects represented by the forms they precede: B, Bohairic; S, Sahidic; A, Akhmimic; L, Lycopolitan (or Subakhmimic); F, Fayyumic.

She will stand up—the hastening woman —with her heart rejoicing over the seed of her brother Osiris.'

*/ˈjiːrit χuˈpirwaw ʔv̆m ˈbaːjv̆k   qaj ˈsaːʃv̆d   ˌsanɟa naˈcuːruw ras ˈʀuːsat baˈkaʀtv̆j çur ˌmitwat ˈsaːnv̆s wv̆ˈsuːrv̆t caˈθas ˈhiːmat ˈwanjat ˈjiːbv̆s ˈnaɟmaw ʔv̆m ˌmitwat ˈsaːnv̆s wv̆ˈsuːrv̆t/

22.5. The phonological system of Later Egyptian (about 1000 B.C.E.)

By the end of the New Kingdom (1550–1000 B.C.E.), the phonological system described in the preceding section had undergone a certain number of developments which profoundly modified all its components. The phonology of later Egyptian is better known to us than the hypothetical reconstruction of older Egyptian thanks primarily to the cuneiform transcriptions of Egyptian words and phrases.

The major changes can be indicated as follows.

22.5.1. Consonants

(a) From the velar to the dental series, oppositions between voiced and voiceless phonemes become progressively neutralized: *t3.wj* */ˈtaʀwv̆j/ > Akk. transcription -*ta-a-wa* 'the Two Lands' ~ *dbn* */ˈdiːban/ > Akk. transcription *ti-ba-an* '*dbn*-weight' (Osing 1976: 420, 619–20). (b) While palatal phonemes are regularly kept in a number of lexemes, they often tend to acquire a dental realization: *psḏw* */piˈsiːjaw/ > Akk. transcription *pi/e-ši-it* 'nine' (Schenkel 1990: 89). (c) The dental phonemes /t/ and /r/ and the glides /j/ and /w/ undergo a process of lenition to /ʔ/ at the end of a syllable, and eventually to /ø/ at the end of a word: *pḏ.t* */ˈpiːjat/ > Akk. *-pi-ta* 'bow'; *hnw* */ˈhiːnaw/ > Akk. transcription *ḥi-na* 'jar'; */ˈmarjv̆w/ > Akk. transcription *ma-aʼ-ia-*, *ma-a-i-* 'beloved' (Osing 1976: 463, 809–10). (d) The uvular trill /ʀ/ completes its evolution to glottal stop /ʔ/ and eventually /ø/, merging with /ʔ/ < /j/ (cf. § 22.4): while in the execration texts of the Middle Kingdom the writing <jjjɜmt> renders the Sem. toponym *yarmuta* (Hoch 1991: 590), in the group writing of the New Kingdom <ɜ> has come to indicate the *a*-vowel (ibid. 599).

22.5.2. Vowels

A series of major developments alters the vocalic system of Egyptian during the late New Kingdom, after the reign of Ramses II, i.e., from around 1200 B.C.E. onward: (a) Parallel to the so-called 'Canaanite vowel shift' in contemporary Northwest Semitic languages, long stressed */ˈaː/ becomes */ˈoː/: *ḥrw* '(the god) Horus' */'ħa:ruw/ > */'ħo:rə/ (cf. the Akk. transcription of the Neo-Assyrian period -*ḫuru*-; Fecht 1960 § 172). (b) This sound change provokes other adjustments within the system, most importantly the change of long stressed */'u:/ into */'e:/: *šnj* 'tree' */'ʃu:nv̌j/ > */'ʃe:nə/ (cf. the Akk. transcription of the Neo-Assyrian period -*sini*; Fecht 1960 § 172; Osing 1976: 148). (c) Already in the early New Kingdom, short stressed */'i/ had become */'e/: cf. the Eg. anthroponym *mnj* 'Menes' */'ma'nij/ > */'ma'neʔ/ (cf. the Akk. transcription *ma-né-e*); at a later date, probably around 1000–800 B.C.E., short stressed */e/ < */i/ and */u/ merged into the realization */'e/: cf. the Eg. toponym *ḏ'n.t* 'Tanis' */'ʝuʕnv̌t/, borrowed in Hebrew at a time when the original vocalization was clearly productive (*ṣuʿn* > *ṣōʿan*), but transcribed as *ṣe-eʾ-nu/ṣa-aʾ-nu* in the Neo-Assyrian period (Schenkel 1990: 87–88; Osing 1976: 377. (d) Unstressed vowels, especially in posttonic position, merged into the mid central */ə/ (the so-called shwa): *rʿw* '(the god) Reʿ' */'riʕuw/ > */'reʕə/ (Akk. transcriptions -*ri-ia*, -*re-e*) ~ *nfr* 'good' */'na:fir/ > */'na:fə/ (Akk. transcription -*na-a-pa*) ~ *mȝʿ.t* */'muʀʕat/ > */'muʔə/ (Akk. transcription -*mu-a*; Osing 1976: 20, 605–6, 149). (e) A merely phonetic evolution which probably did not affect the phonological level is */i:/ > *[e:] in proximity of /ʕ/ and /j/: *wʿw* 'soldier' */'wiʕiw/ (cf. the Akk. transcription from el-Amarna *ú-i-ú*) > *['weʕə] (cf. later transcriptions *ú-e-eḫ*, *ú-e-e*, *ú-e-ú*); *mḥj.t* 'Northwind' */'ma'ħi:jv̌t/ > *[mə'ħe:ʔ] (cf. the Akk. transcription -*ma-ḫe-e*; Osing 1976: 20–21).

Thus, we can posit the vocalic system in Table 22-4 for later Egyptian around 1000 B.C.E. While at the phonetic level the vocalic sounds have indeed evolved from the earlier system presented in § 22.4, the number of vocalic phonemes (six) remains unchanged.

Table 22-4. Later Egyptian Vowels

	Unstressed	Stressed Short	Stressed Long
Front			/i:/
		/e/	
Central	/ə/		/e:/
		/a/	
Back			/o:/

22.5.3. Syllabic structures

Because of the loss of the final dentals and of the semivocalic glides caused by the strong tonic stress, the system of syllabic structures undergoes a partial reorganization, with the emergence of previously unknown or poorly documented syllabic patterns: (a) The development of -'CV:C# in plurisyllabic words (in early Egyptian, the pattern #CV:C# had a reduced functional yield, being limited to the infinitive of biradical verbs): *mḥj.t* '(the goddess) Mehit' */ma'ħu:jv̆t/ > */mə'ħu:ʔ/, cf. the Akk. transcription *-ma-ḫu-ú*, Greek -μχης (with */u:/ > η); *ḫmnw* 'eight' */χa'ma:nv̆w/ > */χa'ma:n/, cf. el-Amarna *ḫa-ma-an* (Osing 1976: 730, 476). (b) The same development affects the pattern -'CVCC#, previously limited to some plurals of the type *maduww*: *zꜣjw.tj* '(the city of) Asyut' */θv̆R'jawtv̆j/ > */sə'jawt/, cf. Neo-Assyrian cuneiform *ši-ia-a-u-ut* (Schenkel 1990: 87). (c) The fall of final consonants increases the presence of unstressed open syllables of the pattern '_CV#, which in the earlier phase of the language were limited to the endings of specific verbal forms (pattern -CV̆#) and personal pronouns (pattern -CV:#): *ḥrj-pd.t* 'overseer of the troop' */ħa,rij'pi:ʝat/ > */ħəri'pi:də/, cf. cuneiform *a/i/uḫ-ri-pí-ta* (ibid. 463).

Table 22-5. Later Egyptian Syllabic Structures

	Pretonic	Tonic	Posttonic
Open	(#)CV'_	'CV:_	'_CV#
Closed	(#)CVC'_	'CVC(#)	'_CVC#
Doubly-closed		'CVCC#	
Long		'CV:C#	

22.5.4. Text Sample (Wenamun 1,47–1,48)

Here is a short text sample of later Egyptian. The conventional Egyptological transliteration of the original hieratic text from the literary tale of Wenamun (about 1000 B.C.E.) is followed by the translation and a tentative phonological reconstruction.

jw dwꜣw ḫpr.w   jw=f hꜣb jw=f jtꜣy=j r-ḥrj
jw pꜣ nṯr ḥtp.w m pꜣ jmw ntj-sw jm=f sp.t pꜣ ym

'Then morning came, and he sent and brought me up,
while the god was resting in the tent in which he was, on the shore of the sea.'

*/ʔew'dawʔə χaʔp ʔewfʰoːʔəb ʔewfʔa'cajjv̆j ʔərħa'rej
ʔewpəʔ'noːtə ħatp ʔəmpəʔʔa'mew ʔəntejsuʔa'mef ˌsoːpəpəʔ'jam/

22.6. The phonological system of Coptic (about 400 C.E.)

Unlike ealier stages of the language, Coptic, which is written in an alphabetic system derived from Greek, is documented in a number of closely related "dialects."[21] These dialects, however, do not necessarily reproduce local varieties of the language: they represent, to a large extent, discrete sets of mainly graphic conventions for rendering Egyptian in an inadequate foreign script (cf. Loprieno 1981). The two major poles of the continuum of Coptic dialects are *Sahidic*, normally considered to reflect the Theban, upper Egyptian variety of the language, documented from the 4th century C.E. and representing the language of classical Coptic literature, and *Bohairic*, the dialect of the Nile delta, documented from the 5th century C.E. and progressively established as the dialect of the liturgy of the Coptic church. Since Sahidic represents classical Coptic, it has been chosen here for the basic presentation of Coptic phonology.[22] However, I shall refer to other dialects, especially Bohairic, whenever such references become necessary for the purpose of an historical or a typological analysis.

During the first millennium B.C.E. and the first centuries C.E., Egyptian continued to undergo a number of phonological changes. In the consonantal system, the tendencies described in § 22.5(a) developed further, leading to a complete neutralization of voiced plosives in the dental, palatal, and velar series: the phonemes /d/, /g/, and /z/ are present only in Greek borrowings, the rare exceptions to this rule being the result of sonorization in proximity of /n/ (e.g., ⲀⲚⲄ vs. ⲀⲚⲞⲔ < *jnk* 'I', ⲀⲚⲌⲎⲂⲈ vs. ⲀⲚⲤⲎⲂⲈ < *ꜥ.t n.t sbꜣ.w* 'school').

In the labial series, the situation is more complex: the voiced phoneme /b/, which by this time was probably articulated as a fricative [β],[23] is kept in all initial and medial positions (^BF ⲂⲰⲔ 'servant', ϨⲒⲂⲰⲒ 'ibis', ⲦⲂⲀ 'ten thousand'), and in final position whenever it did not immediately follow the tonic vowel of a closed syllable in the earlier stages of the language, although this

---

21. For recent accounts and literature on Coptic dialectology cf. the corresponding entries in Atiya 1991 on Akhmimic (Nagel 1991a), Bohairic (Shisha-Halevy 1991a), Fayyumic (Kasser 1991b), Lycopolitan (Nagel 1991b), and Sahidic (Shisha-Halevy 1991b).
22. Two insightful presentations of the problems faced by linguists in the reconstruction of Coptic phonology are Satzinger 1979 and Hintze 1980.
23. Cf. its frequent alternation with <ϥ> /f/ and <ⲞⲨ> /w/: ^SF ⲚⲞⲨⲂ ~ ⲚⲞⲨϤ < *nbw* /'naːbaw/ 'gold', ^S ⲂⲞⲒⲚⲈ ~ ^B ⲞⲨⲰⲒⲚⲒ < *bjn.t* /'bajnv̆t/ 'harp'.

Table 22-6. Coptic Consonants

	Bilabial	Labio-dental	Dental	Alveo-palatal	Prepalatal	Postpalatal	Velar	Pharyn-geal	Glottal
Plosive									
Voiceless[a]	ⲡ /p/ [p⁽ʰ⁾]		ⲧ /t/ [(tʰ)]		ϫ /c/ [c⁽ʰ⁾]	ϭ /kʲ/	ⲕ /k/ [k⁽ʰ⁾]		/ʔ/[b]
Ejective			ⲧ /d/ [t']		ϫ /ɟ/ [c']		ⲕ /g/ [k']		
[Voiced]	ⲃ /b/ [β]		ⲇ /d/ [d]				ⲅ /g/ [g]		
Fricative									
Voiceless		ϥ /f/	ⲥ /s/	ϣ /ʃ/			/χ/[c]		ϩ /h/
[Voiced]			ⲍ /z/					ʕ/[d]	
Nasal	ⲙ /m/		ⲛ /n/						
Vibrant			ⲣ /r/[e]						
Lateral			ⲗ /l/						
Glide	(ⲟ)ⲩ /w/				(ⲉ)ⲓ /j/				

[a] "Voiceless" stops were articulated with aspiration in specific phonetic environments. This feature was probably common to the entire Coptic domain: while most dialects do not indicate this feature in their graphic conventions, Bohairic uses the corresponding Greek *aspiratae* ϕ, θ, χ (for π, τ, κ) and the Coptic sign ϭ (for ϫ). The "voiced" phonemes (plosives ⲇ /d/ and ⲅ /g/ and fricative ⲍ /z/) are limited to Greek borrowings and are realized as voiced stops. "Ejective" phonemes, on the contrary, are characteristic for the vocabulary of Egyptian stock and are realized as ejective stops. They are written with the corresponding Greek *tenuis*.

[b] In Sahidic and in most other dialects, the phoneme /ʔ/ is rendered by <ⲱ> in initial and final position, and by the reduplication of the vocalic morpheme (<ⲾⲾ> = <Ⲿʔ>) when immediately following the stressed vowel of a word. In Akhmimic and Lycopolitan, /ʔ/ in final position of monosyllabic words is rendered by <ⲉ>. In Bohairic, /ʔ/ is expressed by <ⲟ> in any nonfinal position; at the end of a monosyllabic word, etymological /ʔ/ (primary or secondary) has evolved into <ⲥ> (this feature being shared by Fayyumic). Cf. the discussion below.

[c] The phoneme /χ/ is rendered by an independent grapheme in Akhmimic (ⳉ) and in Bohairic (ϧ), but in Sahidic it merged with /ʃ/ or /h/.

[d] The existence of the phoneme /ʕ/ in Coptic is very doubtful: most probably it merged with /ʔ/ already in later Egyptian; cf. below.

[e] Fayyumic is known for its "lambdacism": <ⲗ> appears in many words in which the other dialects display <ⲣ>. The ratio between the two phonemes in all other Coptic dialects is 70% to 30% in favor of <ⲣ>, whereas Fayyumic has a proportion of 80% to 20% in favor of <ⲗ> (Kasser 1991b: 125).

may indeed be synchronically the case in Coptic: ⲛⲟⲩⲃ < */naːbaw/ 'gold'. If final /b/ did follow the tonic vowel of an etymological closed syllable, whether in monosyllabic or plurisyllabic words, it became in Coptic voiceless /p/: ⲟⲩⲟⲡ < */waˈʕab/ 'to be pure', ⲧⲁⲡ < */dib/ 'horn'.

Guttural fricatives of earlier Egyptian merge in Sahidic either into ϣ /ʃ/ (especially /χ/: e.g., ḫꜣ 'thousand' */χaʀ/ > */χaʔ/ > ϣⲟ), or into ϩ /h/ (especially /ḥ/ and /ç/, sometimes also /χ/: e.g., ḥꜣ.t 'beginning' */ˈḥuːʀit/ > ϩⲏ, ẖ(w).t 'body' */ˈçuːwat/ > ϩⲏ, ẖrw 'voice' */χiˈraw/ > ϩⲣⲟⲟⲩ). Other dialects appear more conservative: Bohairic and Akhmimic keep the uvular fricative /χ/ (written ϧ in Bohairic, e.g. ᴮϧⲣⲱⲟⲩ, and ϩ in Akhmimic, e.g., ᴬϩⲣⲁⲩ 'voice'). Finally, the glottal stop /ʔ/, which represents the development of */ʔ/ and */ʕ/, on the one hand, and of the fall of final /t/ and /r/ on the other, is not expressed by an independent grapheme, but is rendered in Sahidic by <∅> at the beginning and the end of a word (e.g., ⲁⲛⲟⲕ /ʔaˈnok/ 'I' < */jaˈnak/, ⲧⲟ /toʔ/ 'land' < */taʔ/) and, except in Bohairic, by the reduplication of the vocalic grapheme when immediately following the stressed vowel of a word (e.g., ᴬϩⲟⲟⲡ /χoʔp/, ˢᴸϣⲟⲟⲡ, ᴮϣⲟⲡ /ʃoʔp/ 'to be' < ḫpr.w */ˈχapraw/ 'has become').[24]

Bohairic spelling conveys a traditional feature of Egyptian phonetics, namely the aspirated realization of stops, which are expressed by the corresponding *aspiratae* of the Greek alphabet: voiceless stops become aspirated when immediately preceding a tonic vowel, semivowels, and sonorant consonants (including ⲃ):

ⲡ /p/, ⲧ /t/, ϫ /c/, ⲕ /k/ → ⲫ [pʰ], ⲑ [tʰ], ϭ [cʰ], ⲭ [kʰ]
/_ˈV, /b/, /m/, /n/, /l/, /r/, /w/, /j/

Examples: ˢⲡⲣⲏ vs. ᴮⲫⲣⲏ 'the sun', ˢⲧⲁⲓ vs. ᴮⲑⲁⲓ 'this (fem.)', ˢϫⲟⲉⲓⲥ vs. ᴮϭⲱⲓⲥ 'lord', ˢⲕⲟⲩⲁⲁⲃ vs. ᴮⲭⲟⲩⲁⲃ 'you are holy'. This phonetic rule proves that ϭ [cʰ] represents in Bohairic the aspirated variety of the palatal plosive ϫ /c/; the value of the sign ϭ in this dialect, therefore, differs from its function in all other Coptic traditions, where it indicates the postpalatal plosive /kʲ/, a phoneme absent from the phonological inventory of Bohairic, where it has merged with ϫ /c/.

The rule of aspiration in Bohairic, however, exhibits an extremely interesting property: when /t/, /c/, and /k/ represent the outcome of older *d* /d/, *ḏ* /ɟ/, *g* /g/, and *q* /q/ respectively, no aspiration immediately preceding the tonic

---

24. However, final /ʔ/ is expressed by <ⲉ> in Sahidic and <ⲓ> in Bohairic in doubly closed syllables, cf. below.

vowel takes place: ˢᴮⲦⲀⲠ 'horn' < Eg. *db* */dib/, ᴮⲦⲰⲠⲒ parallel to ˢⲦⲰⲢⲈ 'hand' < Eg. *dr.t* */'ʒaːrat/, ᴮⲬⲒⲘⲒ ~ ˢϬⲒⲚⲈ 'to find' < Eg. *gmj.t* */'giːmit/, ˢᴮⲔⲀⲤ 'bone' < Eg. *qs* */qes/; in pre-sonorant environments, on the other hand, the rule of aspiration is upheld: ᴮⲈⲢⲈϤ- < *dj-jrj=f-*, ᴮⲐⲂⲀ 'ten thousand' < *dbʿ* /ʒa'baʕ/, ᴮⲞⲢⲎⲬⲒ 'dowry' < *grg.t* /ga'ruːgv̆t/, ᴮⲬⲂⲞⲂ 'to become cool' < *qbb* /qa'bab/ (Worrell 1934: 17–23).

This phenomenon can be conveniently interpreted by assuming that in spite of the forward movement of their point of articulation which took place in later Egyptian (cf. § 22.5) from the palatal to the dental (*d* > /d/), from the velar to the palatal (*g* > /ʒ/), and from the uvular to the velar region (*q* > /k/), these three phonemes of older Egyptian did in fact preserve their prevocalic ejective articulation down to Coptic (/ʒ/ = [c'] > /d/ = [t'], /g/ = [k'] > /ʒ/ = [c'], /q/ = [q'] > /k/ = [k']); hence the use of the Greek *tenues* rather than of the Greek *mediae* to indicate them in the writing: Ⲧ for /d/ = [t'], Ϫ for /ʒ/ = [c'], Ⲕ for /k/ = [k'].²⁵ On the contrary, etymological *t* /t/, *ṯ* /c/ and *k* /k/, which were not ejective but aspirated stops, maintained the aspiration under the phonetic contexts described above. Again, we can consider this aspiration graphically rendered only in Bohairic, but phonetically present in Coptic as a whole:²⁶ ˢⲦⲀϤ vs. ᴮⲐⲀϤ 'spittle' /taf/ = [t⁽ʰ⁾af] < Eg. *tf* */tif/ = [t⁽ʰ⁾if], ˢⲦⲰⲢⲈ vs. ᴮⲐⲰⲢⲒ 'willow' /'toːrə/ = [t⁽ʰ⁾oːrə] < Eg. *trj* */'caːrv̆j/ = ['c⁽ʰ⁾aːrv̆j], ˢⲬⲒ vs. ᴮϬⲒ 'to take' /ciː/ = [c⁽ʰ⁾iː] < Eg. *ṯ3j.t* /'ciʀjit/ > ['c⁽ʰ⁾iːʔət], ˢⲔⲎⲘⲈ vs. ᴮⲬⲎⲘⲒ 'Egypt' /'keːmə/ = ['k⁽ʰ⁾eːmə] < Eg. *km.t* */'kuːmat/ = ['k⁽ʰ⁾uːmat]. This would point to a phonological, rather than phonetic status of the underlying opposition "voiceless : ejective,"²⁷ an opposition graphically conveyed only by Bohairic and displayed by the presence of minimal pairs such as ᴮⲦⲰⲠⲒ 'hand' < *dr.t* : ᴮⲐⲰⲢⲒ 'willow' < *trj* or ᴮⲬⲎ 'dish' < *ḏ3.t* : ᴮϬⲎ 'quince', of uncertain etymology.

Therefore, as in the case of its Egyptian antecedents, the phonology of Coptic dialects may actually exhibit a higher degree of complexity than is

---

25. Indirect evidence of the ejective character of voiceless stops in Bohairic is provided by the 13th century Arabic version of the 'Apophthegmata Patrum' in Coptic script: cf. Satzinger 1971: 40–65; 1991. As a rule, <Ⲧ> and <Ⲕ> are used in this text to render Ar. /t/ and /q/, and <Ⲑ> and <Ⲭ> for Ar. /t/ and /k/ respectively (in final position Ar. /t/ is sometimes rendered by <Ⲧ>, and Ar. /k/ always by <Ⲕ>).
26. The reason for rendering aspirated stops in dialects other than Bohairic with the corresponding Greek *tenuis* would be that Greek *aspiratae* generally represent in Coptic the combination of the corresponding voiceless phoneme followed by the glottal fricative: Ⲫ = /ph/ (rather than /pʰ/), Ⲑ = /th/ (rather than /tʰ/), Ⲭ = /kh/ (rather than /kʰ/).
27. As generally assumed by scholars (see Kasser 1991c), except for Bohairic Ϭ, which some linguists consider phonemically distinct from Ϫ: cf. Shisha-Halevy 1991a: 54.

betrayed by a superficial graphemic analysis:[28] in our concrete example, we probably have to posit for the entire Coptic domain (although graphemically mirrored only in Bohairic) the presence of *three* stops in the dental, prepalatal, and velar region: (a) a voiceless series, characterized by an optional aspiration; (b) a voiced series, limited to Greek borrowings (with a few exceptions due to sonorization in proximity to /n/, cf. above); (c) an ejective series, the heir of the old voiced stops, which never exhibit aspiration and therefore resist a total fusion with the corresponding voiceless phonemes. Graphemically, the voiceless series is conveyed by the Greek *tenues* and Coptic ⲧ (or by the *aspiratae* or ⲑ in Bohairic in stressed pre-vocalic or pre-sonorant phonetic context),[29] the voiced series—limited to the Greek component of the lexicon—by the Greek *mediae*, and the ejective series—limited to the Egyptian vocabulary—again by the Greek *tenues*, but this time without the Bohairic change to the corresponding *aspirata* in stressed pre-vocalic or pre-sonorant environment.

The treatment of the glottal stop /ʔ/ also deserves particular attention. As pointed out in § 22.5, in later Egyptian /t/, /r/, /j/, and /w/ are dropped in final unstressed position, but become /ʔ/ when closing a stressed syllable, often representing the only remnant of an unstressed final syllable of older Egyptian that has been dropped in the later phase of the language. However, especially in final position after stressed vowels, glottal stops deriving from the development of final /t/, /r/, /j/, and /w/ are not treated exactly like etymological /ʔ/; in these cases one also finds slight differences in the treatment of /'eʔ/ < */'uʔ/ as opposed to /'eʔ/ < */'iʔ/.[30]

In the various Coptic dialects, different graphic solutions for /ʔ/ are adopted. All varieties display /ʔ/ = <ø> in initial position (cf. ⁽ᔆᴮ⁾ⲁⲛⲟⲕ /ʔa'nok/, ᴬᴸᶠⲁⲛⲁⲕ /ʔa'nak/ < */ja'nak/ 'I'). To express a glottal stop following the tonic vowel in words of more than one syllable, all dialects except Bohairic exhibit the reduplication of the vowel's grapheme, whether the glottal stop belongs to the same syllable (the vowel being in this case short: /'CVʔ/ = <CVV>, e.g. ᔆⲧⲟⲟⲧϥ, ᴮⲧⲟⲧϥ /'toʔtəf/, ᶠⲧⲁⲁⲧϥ /'taʔtəf/ < */'jartv̆f/ 'his hand', ᔆⲙⲟⲟϣⲉ, ᴮⲙⲟϣⲓ /'moʔʃə/ < */'maʃv̆j/ 'to walk') or to the following

---

28. For the traditional assumption that Coptic, unlike any other language, displays an exact correspondence between graphemic appearance and phonological structure, cf. Kasser 1991d: 207 ff.
29. This is a general context for the development of aspiration, technically called "delayed voicing onset," also shown, e.g., in Modern English and German; cf. Hock 1991: 121.
30. Cf. background information, discussion and examples in Osing 1976: 15–17, 403–48.

syllable (the tonic vowel being here long: /'CV:ʔ/ = <CV̄V̄>, cf. ⲟⲩⲏⲏⲃ /'weːʔəb/ < */'wiːʕvb/ 'priest'). In this last case, i.e., if /ʔ/ is the first phoneme of a final syllable of the type -ʔVC# following a stressed syllable of the type #'CV:,[31] it is conveyed in most dialects by the reduplication of the tonic vowel, and in Bohairic by <ø>: ⁵ϫⲱⲱⲙⲉ, ᴮϫⲱⲙ /'ʧoːʔəm/ < */'ʤaːmiʕ/ 'book'. That the interpretation of the phonological structure presented here is plausible is shown by two facts: (a) The interesting graphemic opposition found in Bohairic between the writing <-Cɪ> to express final /-Cə/, as in ᴮⲣⲱⲙⲓ /'roːmə/ 'man' or ᴮⲙⲟϣⲓ /'moʔʃə/ 'to walk', and the writing <-øC> to express final /-ʔəC/, as in ᴮⲙⲏϣ 'crowd', whereas in Sahidic both environments are graphically rendered by <-Cɛ>: ⁵ⲣⲱⲙⲉ, ⁵ⲙⲟⲟϣⲉ, ⁵ⲙⲏⲏϣⲉ. (b) The two graphic renditions exhibited by the unstressed syllabic structure /-ʔəC#/ in Sahidic, namely <-VVCɛ> as in ϫⲱⲱⲙⲉ /'ʧoːʔəm/, but also <-VVC> as in ⲃⲱⲱⲛ /'boːʔən/. There can be no doubt that these two patterns are phonologically identical: cf. on the one hand the Sahidic variant with final -ⲉ (⁵ⲃⲱⲱⲛⲉ), on the other hand the identical treatment of these two structures in the other dialects: cf. ᴬⲭⲟⲩⲟⲩⲙⲉ, ⲃⲟⲩⲟⲩⲛⲉ, ᴮϫⲱⲙ, ⲃⲱⲛ.

If /ʔ/ represents the last phoneme of a doubly-closed final syllable, it is expressed in the writing by <ⲉ> in the dialects of Upper Egypt and by <ɪ> in those of Lower Egypt: ⁵ⲉⲓⲟⲧⲉ, ᴮⲓⲟϯ /jotʔ/, ᴬᴸⲉⲓⲁⲧⲉ, ᴬᴸᶠⲉⲓⲁϯ /jatʔ/ < */'jatjaw/ 'fathers', ⁵ϩⲓⲟⲙⲉ, ᴮϩⲓⲟⲙⲓ /hjomʔ/, ᴬᴸϩⲓⲁⲙⲉ, ᶠϩⲓⲁⲙⲓ /hjamʔ/ < */hiˈjamwvt/ 'women'.[32]

A last problem is represented by the fate of the phoneme /ʕ/. Its existence, although not excluded, is in fact very doubtful. The graphic distribution of etymological /ʕ/ is identical with that of etymological /ʔ/, including /ʔ/ < /j/, /w/, /r/, and /t/, and scholars generally maintain[33] that it had already merged with the glottal stop /ʔ/ in later pre-Coptic Egyptian, but left traces in Coptic vocalism, especially in the anteriorization of its vocalic surrounding: unstressed ⲁ instead of ⲉ or <ø> (as in ⲁϣⲁⲓ < ꜥšꜣ */ʕiˈʃiʀ/ > */ʕəˈʃiʔ/ 'to become numerous' vs. ⲥϩⲁⲓ < zḫꜣ */θiˈçiʀ/ > */səˈçiʔ/ 'to write'), stressed ⲁ instead of

---

31. In most of these words, the /ʔ/ derives from an etymological /ʕ/ via metathesis: ⁵ⲧⲱⲱⲃⲉ, ᴮⲧⲱⲃ/ⲧⲱⲡ /'toːʔəb/ < */'jaːbaʕ/ 'to seal'.
32. Many scholars would interpret the syllabic structure of these words somewhat differently, namely as ⁵ⲉⲓⲟⲧⲉ, ᴮⲓⲟϯ = /'jotə/. From the point of view of the economy of a linguistic system, however, this phonological analysis presents the drawback of positing the existence of a stressed open syllable /'CV-/ in a polysyllabic word, which is not documented throughout the history of the Egyptian language and is wholly unnecessary at the purely synchronic level as well: cf. § 22.6.2 and n. 37.
33. Cf. the bibliographical information in Kasser 1991a.

452   Antonio Loprieno

ⲟ (as in ⲧⲃⲁ < ḏbꜥ */ɟa'baʕ/ > */tə'baʔ/ 'ten thousand' vs. ⲕⲣⲟϥ < qrf */qa'raf/ > */qə'raf/ 'ambush').³⁴

22.6.1. Vowels

Table 22-7 presents the vocalic system of Sahidic Coptic around 400 C.E.

Table 22-7. Sahidic Coptic Vowels

	Unstressed	Stressed Short	Stressed Long
Front	<ⲓ> /i/	<ⲉ>, <ø> /e/ᵃ	<(ⲉ)ⲓ> /iː/
			<ⲏ> /eː/
Central	<ⲉ>, <ø> /ə/	<ⲁ> /a/	
			<ⲱ> /oː/
Back	<ⲁ> /a/	<ⲟ> /o/	
			<ⲟⲩ> /uː/

ᵃAs we saw above, /e/ = <ø> in Sahidic, Akhmimic, and Lycopolitan, <ⲉ> in Bohairic, and <ⲏ> or <ⲩ> in Fayyumic before sonorant phonemes (including ⲃ).

When compared with the preceding phases in the history of Egyptian, the vocalic system of Coptic exhibits the continuation of the later Egyptian *Lautverschiebung*. Later Eg. stressed */'a/ becomes /'o/ in the two major dialects (Eg. *sn* */san/ 'brother' > ᴿᴮⲥⲟⲛ, ᴬᴸϥⲁⲛ), following the pattern of the evolution */'aː/ > /'oː/ (Eg. *rmṯ* */'raːmac/ 'man' > */'roːmə/ > ⲣⲱⲙⲉ) which had already taken place around 1000 B.C.E. (cf. § 22.5). Moreover, Later Eg. stressed */'e/, whether deriving from original */'i/ (as in *rn* */'rin/ > */'ren/ 'name') or from original */'u/ (as in *ḫrw* */'χurraw/ 'Hurrian' > */χel/ 'servant'), becomes /'a/ in Sahidic and Bohairic, whereas it is kept as /'e/ in the minor dialects: ᴿᴮⲡⲁⲛ, ᴬᴸⲡⲉⲛ, ᶠⲗⲉⲛ; ᔆᴸϩⲁⲗ, ᴬϩⲉⲗ, ᶠϩⲉⲗ.

These two developments in the quality of the short stressed vowels display a certain number of exceptions, of phonetic (if not purely graphemic) rather than phonological character and generally motivated by specific consonantal surroundings. Thus, */'a/ is kept as /'a/ in the two major dialects and is

---

34. For other possible signals of a preservation of the phoneme /ꜥ/ in final position cf. the discussion on the glottal stop /ʔ/ in § 22.6.2.

rendered as <ⲉ> in Fayyumic before etymological guttural fricatives (^(SAL)ⲧⲃⲁ, ^Bⲑⲃⲁ, ^Fⲧⲃⲉ < ḏbʿ */ʝaˈbaʕ/ 'ten thousand'); conversely, */ˈa/ becomes /ˈo/ also in Akhmimic and Lycopolitan before etymological /ʔ/ and /ʕ/ (^Sⲉⲓⲟⲟⲣ(ⲉ), ^Bⲓⲟⲣ, ^Aⲓⲟⲟⲣⲉ, ⲓⲱⲱⲣⲉ, ^Fⲓⲁⲁⲗ, ⲓⲁⲁⲣ < jtrw */ˈʝatraw/ > */ʝaʔr(ə)/ 'river'). Also, the diphthongs */ˈaj/ and */ˈaw/, which regularly yield /ˈoj/, /ˈow/ in Sahidic and /ˈaj/, /ˈaw/ in the minor dialects, appear written in Bohairic as <ⲱⲓ-> (except in final position) and <ⲱⲟⲩ> (in all positions) respectively: ^Sⲉⲣⲟⲓ, ⲉⲣⲟⲟⲩ, ^(AL)ⲁⲣⲁⲓ, ⲁⲣⲁⲩ, ^Fⲉⲗⲁⲓ, ⲉⲗⲁⲩ, ^Bⲉⲣⲟⲓ, ⲉⲣⲱⲟⲩ 'to me, to them'.

As for */ˈe/, which, as we saw, regularly turns into ^(SB)ⲁ and ^(ALF)ⲉ, its main phonetic (or graphemic) exception is represented by its being written as <ⲱ>[35] in Sahidic, Akhmimic, and Lycopolitan, as <ⲉ> in Bohairic, and as <ⲏ> or <ⲩ> in Fayyumic, before sonorant phonemes (including ⲃ): šmsj */ˈʃimsij/ > ^(SAL)ϣⲙ̄ϣⲉ, ^Bϣⲉⲙϣⲓ, ^Fϣⲏⲙϣⲓ /ˈʃemʃə/ 'to worship'. In all dialects except Bohairic, if the following sonorant is not followed by another consonant, it is subject to reduplication: qnj.t */ˈqinjit/ > ^Sⲕⲛ̄ⲛⲉ, ^Aⲕⲛ̄ⲛⲓⲉ, ^Bⲕⲉⲛⲓ, ^Fⲕϩⲛⲛⲓ 'to become fat'. Also, in proximity of sibilants one may find the outcome */ˈe/ > ^(SB)ⲉ or even ^(SBAF)ⲓ: e.g., wsḫ.t */ˈwisχat/ > ^Sⲟⲩⲉϣⲥⲉ, ^Sⲟⲩⲟϣⲥⲉ, ^Bⲟⲩⲉ/ⲏϣⲥⲓ 'breadth', pšs.t */ˈpuʃsat/ > ^Sⲡⲓϣⲉ, ⲡⲁϣⲉ 'half'. The diphthongs display slight irregularities as well: instead of the paradigmatic form <ⲁⲩ> (as in snwj */siˈnewwvj/ > ^Sⲥⲛⲁⲩ 'two', ḥnw */ħṽˈnew/ > ^Sϩⲛⲁⲩ 'jar'), */ˈew/ occasionally yields <ⲟⲩ>, and <ⲟ> in Akhmimic in final position: ^Sⲥⲛⲟⲩ, ^Aⲥⲛⲟ, ^Sϩⲛⲟⲩ. The outcome of */ˈej/ is even more complex: it develops as expected into ^(SL)ⲁ(ⲉ)ⲓ, but it keeps a vocalization closer to the original in ^Aⲉ(ⲉ)ⲓ, ^Fⲏⲓ; Bohairic exhibits a difference in treatment, depending on whether the original vowel was *u (i.e., */ˈej/ < */ˈuj/), in which case it goes with Sahidic ⲁⲓ, or *i (i.e., */ˈej/ < */ˈij/), in which case it goes with Fayyumic ⲏⲓ: e.g., zjnw */ˈθijnṽw/ > ^Sⲥⲁⲉⲓⲛ, ^Aⲥⲉ(ⲉ)ⲓⲛⲉ, ^(BF)ⲭⲏⲛⲓ 'physician', ʿjqy */ˈʕujqv̌j/ > ^(SL)ⲁⲉⲓⲕ, ^Bⲁⲓⲕ 'consecration'.

Moving on to the long vowels, Coptic displays no major phonological development from the later Egyptian system. At the phonetic level, the following phenomena take place: (a) All dialects exhibit an evolution */ˈaː/ > <ⲟⲩ> [uː] (instead of */ˈaː/ > /oː/), regularly after nasal consonants, and occasionally following other consonants as well: nṯr */ˈnaːcar/ > ⲛⲟⲩⲧⲉ /ˈnuːte/ 'god'. Akhmimic also displays <ⲟⲩ> in final position or if the vowel is followed by the glottal stop, i.e., by a reduplication of the vocalic grapheme: ^Sϫⲱⲱⲙⲉ,

---

35. The presence of a short, non-phonemic vowel [ə] is indicated in most dialects by a supralinear stroke (called in German *Vokalstrich*) over the following consonant.

ᴬⲭⲟⲩⲟⲩⲙⲉ. That /uː/, nonetheless, has acquired phonemic character in Coptic is shown by the presence of minimal pairs such as ϩⲱⲛ /hoːn/ < ḥnn */'çaːnan/ 'to approach' vs. ϩⲟⲩⲛ /huːn/ < ḥnw */'çaːnaw/ 'inside'. (b) Widespread is also the outcome <(ⲉ)ⲓ> [iː] instead of /eː/ from etymological */uː/ > */eː/ (cf. § 22.5) in proximity of /r/ and after etymological pharyngeals: ˢᴸϩⲓⲣ, ᴮϥⲓⲣ, ᴬϩⲓⲣ, ᶠϩⲓⲗ < */'χuːr/ 'street' (Sem. loanword). As in the case of */'aː/ > <ⲟⲩ> [uː], here too Akhmimic displays <ⲉⲓ> in final position or if the vowel is followed by /ʔ/: ˢⲧⲏⲏⲃⲉ, ᴬⲧⲉⲓⲃⲉ 'finger'. This same */uː/ > /eː/ occasionally appears as <ⲉ> before pharyngeal phonemes: ˢⲭⲙ̄ⲡⲉϩ < */tap'puːħ/ 'apple' (Sem. loanword). (c) We had already observed in later Egyptian the phonetic outcome */iː/ > *[eː] in proximity of /ʕ/ or /j/ (cf. § 22.5).

Most Coptic dialects have three unstressed vocalic phonemes (cf. Osing 1976: 27–30, 475–500), depending on the phonetic context of the original structure of the word: as a general rule, pretonic and posttonic vowels have developed into /ə/,[36] graphically rendered as <ⲉ> or <ø> (<ⲓ> in the northern dialects Bohairic and Fayyumic in final position); pretonic unstressed /i/, which often alternates with <ø>, derives from a pretonic unstressed syllable of the type */CVj-/ (ˢϩⲓⲃⲱⲓ 'ibis' < ḥ(j)bj.w */hij'baːjv̆w/, originally the plural of ḥ(j)bw */'hijbaw/ > */hiːb/, cf. ᴮϩⲓⲡ), whereas pretonic unstressed /a/ owes its origin to an earlier Egyptian unstressed */a/ (original or resulting from assimilation of */e/ < */i/ or */u/ in proximity of an etymological pharyngeal or velar phoneme: ⲁϣⲁⲓ 'to become numerous' < ʕš₃ */ʕi'ʃiʀ/), or to an unstressed sonorant phonetic surrounding (ⲁⲙⲣⲏϩⲉ 'asphalt' < */mv̆'riħjat/).

22.6.2. Syllabic structures

Coptic syllabic patterns are very similar to those of later Egyptian, the only major difference being represented by the emergence of new patterns from the reduction to shwa and eventually to zero of the short vowel of pretonic open syllables: *#CV-CV(C) > #C-CV(C). As in the earlier stages of the language, long and doubly-closed syllables are documented only in stressed final position.

These rules of syllabic distribution and the following comments apply to the vocabulary of Egyptian stock, not to the Greek words which entered the language especially in the religious sphere of vocabulary.

---

36. If the stressed syllable of earlier Egyptian was of the type CV:- and the first consonant of the posttonic syllable was /w/, /j/, or /ʔ/, Egyptian posttonic vowels in syllables of the type -CVw, -CVj, and -CVʔ have left different traces in the final long vowels or diphthongs of Coptic (Schenkel 1990: 91f.).

Egyptian and Coptic Phonology 455

Table 22-8. Sahidic Coptic Syllabic Structures

	Pretonic	Tonic	Posttonic
Open	(#)CV'_	'CV:(#)	'_CV#
	#CCV'_	'CCV:(#)	
Closed	(#)CVC'_	'CVC(#)	'_CVC#
	#CCVC'_	'CCVC(#)	
Doubly-closed	(#)CVCC'_	'CVCC#	
	#CCVCC'_	'CCVCC#	
Long		'CV:C#	
		'CCV:C#	

A pattern of tonic open syllable with short vowel ('CV) is apparently documented in words such as ⲡⲉ 'heaven' < *p.t* */pit/, ⲧⲟ 'land' < *tꜣ* */taʀ/, ϣⲁϫⲉ 'to tell' < *sḏd.t* */'siɟdit/, or ⲉⲓⲟⲡⲉ 'occupation' < *wpw.t* */'japwat/. However, I adopt here a more economic approach to Coptic phonology, which displays the supplementary advantage of establishing a continuity between earlier Egyptian and Coptic. It consists in analyzing this syllabic pattern as closed ('CVC) or doubly closed ('CVCC), by positing the existence of a final glottal stop /ʔ/: thus ⲡⲉ = /peʔ/, ⲧⲟ = /toʔ/, ϣⲁϫⲉ = /ʃaɟʔ/, and ⲉⲓⲟⲡⲉ = /jopʔ/, parallel to the pattern ⲣⲁⲛ = /ran/ or ⲥⲟⲧⲡ = /sotp/ 'chosen'.[37]

Two important elements in favor of this analysis are: (a) the graphic rendering of this glottal phoneme as final <-ⲉ> (in Akhmimic and Lycopolitan) or <-ⲓ> (in Bohairic and Fayyumic) in dialects other than Sahidic, and occasionally in Sahidic itself: cf. ˢⲙⲉ, ⲙⲉⲉ, ˢᴬᴸⲙⲏⲉ, ᴬⲙⲓⲉ, ᴮⲙⲏⲓ, ⲙⲉⲓ, ᶠⲙⲉⲓ, ⲙⲉⲉⲓ, ⲙⲏⲓ 'truth' = in all cases /mVʔ/; (b) the Akhmimic (and partially Lycopolitan) treatment of etymological */'a/ as <ⲟ> (or sometimes <ⲉ>) rather than <ⲁ> and of etymological */'aː/ as <ⲟⲩ> rather than <ⲱ> in final position and before reduplication of the vowel (ˢᴬᴸⲧⲟⲟⲧϥ̄, ᴮⲧⲟⲧϥ, ᶠⲧⲁⲁⲧϥ̄ 'his hand'; ˢᴮᴬᴸⲛ̄ⲧⲟ, ᶠⲛ̄ⲧⲁ 'you (fem.)', ˢᶠⲕⲱ, ᴮⲭⲱ, ᴸⲕⲱ(ⲉ), ᴬᴸⲕⲟⲩ 'to lay'; ˢⲭⲱⲱⲙⲉ, ᴬⲭⲟⲩⲟⲩⲙⲉ 'book'), two environments which were evidently perceived to share common features. This phenomenon points to the fact that what appears here graphically to be a final vowel is in fact a phonological /ʔ/. It also needs to be stressed that this glottal stop is always justified at the

---

37. Needless to say, the phonetic realization of these phonological strings may very well have been ['ʃajə], ['jopə], or ['sotəp], but in this instance the phonetic dimension is both impossible to reconstruct and irrelevant within the context of our discussion.

etymological level (coming from the lenition and eventually the fall of an earlier consonant, cf. § 22.5).

That this final glottal stop is not expressed in the writing should hardly be surprising, since this is the regular fate of /ʔ/ in Coptic in all initial and final positions, unless it represents the last phoneme of a doubly-closed syllable of the type we considered above (ⲉⲓⲟⲡⲉ = /joṗʔ/). Accordingly, a structure such as ⲧⲟⲉ 'part' < *dnj.t* */'danjut/ (cf. Osing 1976: 440) should probably be analyzed as /toʔʔ/, the sequence of two glottal stops at the end of the doubly-closed syllable being the reason for the variety of writings of this word (ⲧⲟⲓⲉ, ⲧⲁ(ⲉ), ⲧⲟ, to mention just the Sahidic forms).

Conversely, the apparent and utterly un-Egyptian presence of patterns with long unstressed vowel (CV:'_ as in ⲟⲩⲧⲁϩ 'fruit' or '_CV: as in ⲧⲏⲣⲟⲩ 'all of them') is easily removed from the phonological system of Coptic by interpreting <ⲟⲩ> in these cases as /w/: ⲟⲩⲧⲁϩ = /wtah/, pattern 'CCVC and ⲧⲏⲣⲟⲩ = /'te:rəw/, stressed pattern 'CV: and posttonic pattern '_CVC#. In both cases, the hypothetical [u:] in *[u:'tah] or *[te:ru:] represents the realization of /w-/ and /-əw/ respectively in these specific phonetic contexts.

22.6.3. *Text sample*

Here is a short passage from the works of Shenute (4th century C.E.), one of the main figures of the Coptic church and one of the classical authors of Coptic literature, after Till 1970: 293–94. The Coptic text is followed by the conventional scholarly transliteration. Greek borrowings are transliterated and transcribed in italics.

ⲚϢⲰϪⲠ ⲚⲚϢⲀϪⲈ ⲘⲠⲈⲒϪⲰⲰⲘⲈ Ⲏ ⲠⲔⲈⲤⲈⲈⲠⲈ ⲈⲚⲦⲀⲚϪⲞⲞⲨ ⲀⲨⲰ ⲀⲚⲤⲀϨⲞⲨ ϨⲚⲦⲘⲈϨⲢⲞⲘⲠⲈ ⲤⲚⲦⲈ ⲘⲚⲚⲤⲀ ⲦⲢⲈⲚⲔⲰⲦ ⲘⲠⲒⲎⲒ ϨⲘⲠⲔⲀⲒⲢⲞⲤ ⲈⲚⲦⲀⲚⲂⲀⲢⲂⲀⲢⲞⲤ ϢⲰⲖ ϢⲀⲚⲦⲞⲨⲂⲰⲔ ⲈϨⲞⲨⲚ ⲈⲦⲠⲞⲖⲒⲤ ⲈⲦⲞⲨⲘⲞⲨⲦⲈ ⲈⲢⲞⲤ ϪⲈ ⲔⲞⲈⲒⲤ ϨⲘⲠⲤⲎⲨ ⲈⲚⲦⲀⲠⲈⲒⲚⲞϬ ⲘⲘⲎⲎϢⲈ ϬⲞⲈⲒⲖⲈ ⲈⲢⲞⲚ

> <nšōjp nnšaje mpeijōōme ē pkeseepe entanjoou auō ansahou hntmehrompe snte mnnsa trenkōt mpiēi hmp*kairos* entan*barbaros* šōl šantoubōk ehoun et*polis* etoumoute eros je koeis hmpsēu entapeinoc mmēēše coeile eron>

/ʔənˈʃo:cəp ʔənʔənˈʃacʔ ʔəmpəjˈjo:ʔəm e: pkəˈseʔpə ˌʔentanˈjoʔw ʔaˈwo: ʔanˈsahw həntməhˈrompə ˈsentə mənʔənˈsaʔ trənˈko:t ʔəmpiˈʔe:j həmp ˈka*jros* ˌʔentaʔən ˈ*barbaros* ʃo:l ʃantəwˈbo:k ʔəˈhu:n ˌʔet ˈ*polis* ˌʔetəwˈmu:tə ʔəˈros jəˈkojs həmpˈse:w ˌʔentapəjˈnokʲ ʔəmˈmeːʔəʃ ˈkʲojlə ʔəˈron/

'The rest of the words of this book, i.e., the remaining (of the things) which we said and wrote in the second year after we built this house, at the time when the Barbarians plundered, until they reached the city called Qus, at the time when this huge crowd stayed with us.'

22.7. Further reading

The most accessible introduction to the study of Egyptian phonology is offered by Schenkel 1990, where the reader will find a history of the scholarly endeavors involving Egyptian phonological reconstruction, a description of the different methodological approaches, and a presentation of the contemporary state of the art, covering the Afroasiatic background, pre-Coptic phonology, and the fundamental rules of phonological development from older Egyptian to Coptic.

The most complete reference book for the study of vocalism throughout the history of Egyptian is Osing 1976, which systematizes the approach inaugurated by Fecht 1960. Two works by Schenkel were conceived on the footsteps of Osing's treatise, completing it and revising some of its assumptions: 1983a, 1983b. Of major significance for the study of Egyptian syllabic orthography and of the phonological correspondences between Egyptian and Semitic is the doctoral dissertation by J. E. Hoch (1991).

A radically different paradigm from the one followed by Fecht, Osing, and Schenkel has been pursued by scholars who assumed a much higher degree of correspondences between Egyptian and Semitic phonology and especially morphology: in this tradition cf. Vergote 1973–83 and Vycichl 1990.

A detailed bibliography on Egyptian and Coptic phonology can be derived from Osing 1976, Schenkel 1990, and Hoch 1991.

References

Atiya, Aziz S., ed. 1991. *The Coptic Encyclopedia*, vol. 8. New York: Macmillan.

Baldi, Philip, ed. 1990. *Linguistic Change and Reconstruction Methodology* (Trends in Linguistics, Studies and Monographs 45). Berlin: Mouton de Gruyter.

Brockelmann, Carl. 1908. *Grundriß der vergleichenden Grammatik der semitischen Sprachen*, vol. 1. Berlin: Reuther & Reichard.

Eyre, Christopher, and John Baines. 1989. "Interactions between Orality and Literacy in Ancient Egypt." In *Literacy and Society*, ed. Karen Schousboe and M. T. Larsen, pp. 91–119. Copenhagen: Akademisk Forlag.

Faber, Alice. 1990. "Interpretation of Orthographic Forms." In Baldi 1990: 619–37.

———. 1992. "Second Harvest: *šibbōleθ* Revisited (Yet Again)." *Journal of Semitic Studies* 37: 1–10.

Fecht, Gerhard. 1960. *Wortakzent und Silbenstruktur: Untersuchungen zur Geschichte der ägyptischen Sprache* (Ägyptologische Forschungen 21). Glückstadt: Augustin.

Hintze, Fritz. 1980. "Zur koptischen Phonologie." *Enchoria* 10: 23–91.

Hoch, James E. 1991. "Semitic Words in Egyptian Texts of the New Kingdom and Third Intermediate Period." Ph.D. dissertation, University of Toronto.

Hock, Hans Heinrich. 1991. *Principles of Historical Linguistics*, 2nd ed. Berlin: de Gruyter.

Kammerzell, Frank. 1991a. "Augment, Stamm und Endung: Zur morphologischen Entwicklung der Stativkonjugation." *Lingua Aegyptia* 1: 165–99.

———. 1991b. "Personalpronomina und Personalendungen im Altägyptischen." In *Ägypten im afro-orientalischen Kontext: Gedenkschrift Peter Behrens*, ed. Daniela Mendel and Ulrike Claudi, pp. 177–203 (Afrikanistische Arbeitspapiere, Sondernummer). Cologne: Institut für Afrikanistik.

———. 1992. Review of *Les langues dans le monde ancien et moderne*, troisième partie, *Les langues chamito-sémitiques*. *Lingua Aegyptia* 2: 157–75.

Kasser, Rodolphe. 1991a. "'Ayin." In Atiya 1991: 45–47.

———. 1991b. "Fayyumic." In Atiya 1991: 124–31.

———. 1991c. "Phonology." In Atiya 1991: 184–86.

———. 1991d. "Syllabication." In Atiya 1991: 207–14.

Lambdin, Thomas O. 1952. *Egyptian Loanwords and Transcriptions in the Ancient Semitic Languages*. Baltimore: Johns Hopkins University Press.

Loprieno, Antonio. 1981. "Methodologische Anmerkungen zur Rolle der Dialekte in der ägyptischen Sprachentwicklung." *Göttinger Miszellen* 53: 55–75.

———. 1986. *Das Verbalsystem im Ägyptischen und im Semitischen: Zur Grundlegung einer Aspekttheorie* (Göttinger Orientforschungen 4/17). Wiesbaden: Harrassowitz.
Nagel, Peter. 1991a. "Akhmimic." In Atiya 1991: 19–27.
———. 1991b. "Lycopolitan." In Atiya 1991: 151–59.
Osing, Jürgen. 1976. *Die Nominalbildung des Ägyptischen*, 2 vols. Mainz: von Zabern.
Rössler, Otto. 1971. "Das Ägyptische als semitische Sprache." In *Christentum am Roten Meer*, ed. Franz Altheim and Ruth Stiehl, vol. 1, pp. 263–326. Berlin: de Gruyter.
Satzinger, Helmut. 1971. "Zur Phonetik des Bohairischen und des Ägyptisch-Arabischen im Mittelalter." *Wiener Zeitschrift für die Kunde des Morgenlandes* 63–64: 40–65.
———. 1979. "Phonologie des koptischen Verbs (sa'idischer Dialekt)." In *Festschrift Elmar Edel*, ed. Manfred Görg, pp. 343–68 (Ägypten und Altes Testament 1). Wiesbaden: Harrassowitz.
———1991. "Pronunciation of Late Bohairic." In Atiya 1991: 60–65.
Schenkel, Wolfgang. 1983a. *Aus der Arbeit an einer Konkordanz zu den altägyptischen Sargtexten*, vol. 2: *Zur Pluralbildung des Ägyptischen* (Göttinger Orientforschungen 4/12). Wiesbaden: Harrassowitz.
———. 1983b. *Zur Rekonstruktion der deverbalen Nominalbildung des Ägyptischen* (Göttinger Orientforschungen 4/13). Wiesbaden: Harrassowitz.
———. 1986. "Das Wort für 'König (von Oberägypten)'." *Göttinger Miszellen* 94: 57–73.
———. 1990. *Einführung in die altägyptische Sprachwissenschaft* (Orientalistische Einführungen). Darmstadt: Wissenschaftliche Buchgesellschaft.
Schmalstieg, William R. 1990. "A Few Issues of Contemporary Indo-European Linguistics." In Baldi 1990: 359–74.
Shisha-Halevy, Ariel. 1991a. "Bohairic." In Atiya 1991: 53–60.
———. 1991b. "Sahidic." In Atiya 1991: 194–202.
Till, W. C. 1970. *Koptische Grammatik (Saïdischer Dialekt)*, 2nd ed. Leipzig: Verlag Enzyklopädie.
Vergote, Jozef. 1973–83. *Grammaire copte*, 2 vols. Louvain: Peeters.
von Soden, Wolfram. 1969. *Grundriss der akkadischen Grammatik* (Analecta Orientalia 33/47). Rome: Pontifical Biblical Institute.

Vycichl, Werner. 1990. *La vocalisation de la langue égyptienne*, vol. 1: *La phonétique* (Bibliothèque d'Étude 16). Cairo: Institut Français d'Archéologie Orientale.

Westendorf, Wolfhart. 1965. *Koptisches Handwörterbuch*. Heidelberg: Carl Winter Universitätsverlag.

Worrell, William H. 1934. *Coptic Sounds* (University of Michigan Studies, Humanistic Series 26). Ann Arbor: University of Michigan Press.

Zeidler, Jürgen. 1992. Review of Petráček, *Vergleichende Studien*. *Lingua Aegyptia* 2: 189–222.

Chapter 23
Berber Phonology
Maarten G. Kossmann and Harry J. Stroomer
Rijksuniversiteit te Leiden, The Netherlands

23.1. Berber languages

The Berber languages, spoken in North Africa by some 15 to 20 million people, are a branch of the Afro-Asiatic phylum.

The largest population of Berberophones can be found in Morocco. Approximately 45% of the total Moroccan population (26 million) speaks a Berber language as a mother tongue. People of the High Atlas and the Anti-Atlas mountains and the Sous valley speak Tashelhit (*tašlḥiyt*), also called Sous Berber (*tasusit*). This language is spoken by some 7 million. It is, together with Kabyle in Algeria, the most important Berber language in terms of number of speakers. Tashelhit Berber has some dialect variation, but not so strong as the Berber language spoken in the Middle Atlas mountains. This language, often called Tamazight (*tamaziɣt*), is spoken by some 3 million people in various dialects. Strong dialect variation can also be found in the Moroccan Rif mountains. The Riffian language (*θarifəçθ*) has some 2 million speakers.

In Algeria, 25% of the total population (about 26 million) speaks a Berber language. In a densely populated area in the north of Algeria, Kabyle Berber (*θaqβayliθ*) is spoken by approximately 7 million. In Algeria, Berber is also spoken in the Aurès mountains, the Mzab region, the Ouargla oasis, and by the sedentary population of the Sud Oranais area. Touareg, a Berber language spoken by a million, is found not only in the Algerian Sahara but also in neighboring areas of the Sahel republics of Mali and Niger. The Tamahaq (*tamaahaq*) dialect is spoken in the Ahaggar region in southern Algeria. The Tamajaq (*tamaažaq*) dialect is spoken in the Ayr region of Niger. The Tamashek dialect (*tamašəq*) is spoken in the Adrar des Ifoghas region in Mali. The Tawlemmet dialect (*tawləmmət*) is spoken by the Iwlemmeden Touaregs of the Mali–Niger borderland.

In Tunisia, Berber is spoken by the population of fewer than six villages on the Tunisian mainland. On the island of Djerba one finds some five

Berberophone villages. All together, Berber represents only 1% of the total population.

In Libya, some 25% of the total population of 4 million is Berberophone. In this country Berber is spoken in Zouara on the western Libyan coast, in the western Djebel Nefousa region, and in a number of oases.

As far east as Egypt we find a very small community of Berberophone people in the famous oasis of Siwa. In Mauritania a small group (say, around 3,000) of Zenaga Berber speakers still exists south of the capital Nouakchott.

Berbers emigrated from their North African homelands in all directions. One finds a considerable number of speakers not only in the big cities of Morocco and Algeria but also in several European countries.

23.2. Writing

The oldest epigraphic records that perhaps represent a form of Berber are the so-called Libyco-Berber inscriptions. They stem from the pre-Islamic period and are found mainly in Tunisia and Algeria, but also in Morocco. These inscriptions are undated and difficult to interpret. The script in which they were written resembles the so-called Tifinagh script, still in use among the Touaregs. There is some regional variety in the shape of the characters. The Arabic script is also used for writing Berber. There is a longstanding tradition of writing Tashelhit in Arabic characters. The Roman script is used for scientific and practical purposes.

23.3. Classification of Berber languages

Berber languages may be tentatively classified according to morphological criteria as follows:

    Group 1. Tashelhit and Middle Atlas Berber (with exception of the Beni Ouarayn Berber and Ayt Seghrouchen of the Eastern Middle Atlas)

    Group 2. Zenati languages: Beni Ouarayn, Ayt Seghrouchen, Rif, Chawia, the dialects of the Sud-Oranais (including Figuig), Mzab, Ouargli

    Group 3. Kabyle

    Group 4. Touareg, Ghadamsi

    Group 5. Zenaga of Mauritania

23.4. Phonology

Most grammars and textbooks pay but little attention to phonology. However, during the last two decades under the influence of modern trends in theoretical phonology, scholarly interest in the phonology of Berber languages has increased.

The variation in Berber phonological systems is large. Therefore, it is not possible to give an overview of Berber phonology without referring to particular languages (see §§ 23.6–8).

23.4.1. Vowels

Most Berber languages have *a, i,* and *u*. According to the context, the phonetic realizations of these three vowels may be quite different, *a* ranging from [ɑ] to [æ], *i* from [e] to [i], *u* from [o] to [u]. There are no diphthongs or vowel clusters. In some languages (Touareg, Ghadamsi, Zenaga), the vowel system is more complicated. The Touareg system is given in § 23.8.

23.4.2. The shwa

A problem in Berber phonology is the status of shwa or ə. Most Berber words contain ə or one or more syllabic consonants.

For some dialects, the leading principle for the placement of ə is the structure of the word. The principle of ə-placement is simple: If there is a cluster of two consonants, ə is placed between them, unless this would lead to ə in an open syllable (i.e., it would be followed by a single consonant followed by ə or a plain vowel). The rule operates from right to left. E.g.:

ilm → *iləm* 'skin' (Figuig)
išrz → *išrəz* 'he cultivated' (Figuig)

In *išrz*, the cluster *šr* cannot be broken by ə, as this would lead to ə in an open syllable: **išərəz* is an impossible string.

For other dialects, the leading principle for the placement of ə is the intrinsic sonority of the consonant. Consonants are ranked on a sonority scale, in which some consonants are more apt to be preceded by ə than others. The placement of ə in a string of consonants follows this scale. First, ə is placed before the consonants which are highest on the sonority scale, then before the second-highest consonants, etc. Again, ə in an open syllable is impossible. For instance, in Tashelhit, *r* ranks higher on the sonority scale than *k, s,* or *z*:

ikrz → *ikərz* 'he plowed'
iskr → *iskər* 'he did'

The prohibition of ə in an open syllable renders *ikərəz or *isəkər impossible.

These two principles account for the majority of cases where ə is found. However, almost all Berber languages have words or morphological contexts where the rules are violated. This fact has led to positing two types of ə: one inserted by phonetic rule, the other as a part of the underlying structure. This underlying ə is phonemic. It remains to be seen which of the Berber languages require an underlying ə. Its existence is certain in some of them, for instance in Figuig Berber.

23.4.3. Consonants

Almost every Berber language has bilabial, dental, palatal, velar, uvular, pharyngeal, and laryngeal consonants, and many have interdentals as well. A large number of consonants have been borrowed from Arabic or European languages, e.g., ṣ, ṭ, q, ḥ, and ʕ from Arabic and p from Spanish or French. Due to the massive influx of foreign vocabulary in some Berber languages, these borrowed consonants can be frequent.

Berber consonant systems can be described by a number of correlations. The Berber languages have voiced and voiceless consonants and fricatives, plosives, and approximants. Two correlations will be treated here: the contrast between pharyngealized and non-pharyngealized consonants, and that between lax and tense ones.

23.4.3.1. Pharyngealization

Berber languages contrast non-pharyngealized and pharyngealized consonants. They may be voiced or voiceless (e.g., ḍ and ṭ) and fricative or plosive (e.g., ḍ and ẓ). With the exception of some dialectal phonemes of marginal functionality, all pharyngealized phonemes are dental or interdental. Parallel to the situation in many Arabic dialects, pharyngealization is a spreading feature. Under the influence of a pharyngealized phoneme, other sounds may become pharyngealized. This process is automatic, and the pharyngealization of the other sounds is not phonemic. The domain of spreading is not the same in all varieties of Berber. Some languages seem to have the syllable or the word as a domain, while others have more complicated rules.

Proto-Berber had only two pharyngealized phonemes, ḍ and ẓ. The other pharyngealized phonemes were borrowed from Arabic. Assimilations may sometimes lead to new pharyngealized phonemes. For example, in Figuig Berber the cluster lḍ becomes the tense pharyngealized consonant ḷḷ, *tayəlḍimt gives tayəḷḷimt 'little ball of couscous'.

23.4.3.2. The opposition lax versus tense

In Berber morphology, consonants can alternate from lax to tense or vice versa. This is the case, e.g., in the verbal system, when we compare aorist forms with intensive aorist forms, or, in stative verb paradigms, the aorist forms with preterite forms. In the nominal system lax versus tense alternation can be found when one compares singular nouns with their plurals. The phonetic realization of the opposition lax versus tense varies from dialect to dialect and from consonant to consonant. Lax consonants are always realized shorter than their tense counterparts.

For some consonants the opposition is expressed in a difference in length, for example:

iləm 'skin' (Figuig)
illəm 'he has spun'

In other cases, the difference in length is supplemented by other phonetic features. Voiced lax consonants may have voiceless tense counterparts, e.g.:

mədl-əɣ 'I buried' (Figuig)
məṭṭl-əɣ 'I always bury'
ʕəbr-əɣ 'I measured' (Figuig)
ʕəppr-əɣ 'I always measure'

Fricative lax consonants may have affricate tense counterparts, e.g.:

ḥəsb-əɣ 'I counted' (Figuig)
ḥəttsb-əɣ 'I always count'

Lax approximants may have tense plosive counterparts:

ṛəwl-əɣ 'I flee' (Figuig)
ṛəggʷl-əɣ 'I always flee'

A spirantized lax consonant may have a plosive tense counterpart, e.g.:

βði-ɣ 'I began' (Riffian)
βəddi-ɣ 'I always begin'

A lax voiced dorso-velar fricative may have a tense voiceless uvular counterpart:

ad i-nəɣ 'he will kill' (Figuig)
ad i-nəqq 'he will continuously kill'

Some languages use the length opposition almost exclusively. For example, Tashelhit has only three cases where the length opposition is supplemented by some other change, viz., *ḍ* : *ṭṭ*, *ɣ* : *qq*, and *w* : *ggʷ*. On the other hand, in some Berber languages only *n*, *m*, *l*, *r*, *ḥ*, and *ʕ* express the lax : tense opposition exclusively by length.

There has been considerable discussion about the status of tense consonants. Generative linguists consider them to be geminates, i.e., clusters of two identical consonants. Most French scholars consider them to be monophonemic consonants. This problem is related to the insertion of ə. On the one hand, it is rare for a tense consonant to become divided into two parts by ə insertion. On the other hand, tense consonants behave differently from lax ones concerning open syllables. While ə insertion is impossible before a lax consonant followed by ə or a plain vowel, there is no impediment when a tense consonant is followed by ə or a plain vowel, e.g., Figuig Berber:

išrz → *išrəz* 'he cultivated' (*išərəz is impossible)

išrrz → *išərrəz* 'he always cultivates'

The issue is further complicated by the existence of a small number of words where two identical consonants may be separated by ə, e.g., Figuig Berber *imləl* 'it is white' (as opposed to *imall* 'he became bored with'). This form suggests an opposition between a sequence of two identical consonants and a monophonemic tense consonant. Another possibility, however, would be to analyse ə in *imləl* as a structural, i.e. underlying, ə.

23.5. Some dialectal developments

Two developments have affected the phonological systems of many Berber languages. The first of these developments is spirantization, the development of lax stops into fricatives. The second is the gradual confusion of *w* and *y* with *u* and *i*.

23.5.1. Spirantization

Spirantization is a common feature in the northern part of the Berberophone territory. It reaches its culminating points in Riffian and Kabyle. Spirantization implies the development of lax stops into fricatives, e.g., *b* becoming *β*. In some cases spirantization is accompanied by a change of place of articulation. Spirantized *d*, for example, is *ð*.

Spirantization never affects tense consonants. Moreover, it may be prevented in certain contexts. There is, for example, no dialect in which *t* in the cluster *nt* can be spirantized. Spirantized and unspirantized lax stops are in complementary distribution. In many cases subsequent laxification of some tense stops or borrowing has blurred this situation. This leads to a system with spirantized lax consonants, non-spirantized lax ones, and non-spirantized tense stops, each with phonemic status.

23.5.2. The development of w and y

An important phonological development is the confusion of *w* and *y* with *u* and *i* respectively. In some Berber languages, *w* and *y* can be opposed to *u* and *i* in any position, e.g., in Figuig Berber. In most languages, however, there is a neutralization of this opposition in certain environments. This tendency towards neutralization may lead to a situation in which *w* and *u* and *y* and *i* are virtually allophones of each other, as for example in Tashelhit.

23.6. Tashelhit

The consonants of Tashelhit are given in Table 23-1.

Table 23-1. Tashelhit Consonant Inventory

	lab	dent	dent phar	pal	vel	vel lab	uvu	uvu lab	phar	glot
stops		t	ṭ		k	k°	q	q°		
	b	d	ḍ		g	g°				
fricatives	f	s	ṣ	š	x	x°			ḥ	
		z	ẓ	ž	ɣ	ɣ°			ʕ	
nasals	m	n								
trill		r	ṛ							
lateral		l	ḷ							
approximant				y		w				h

23.6.1. Lax versus tense

As stated in § 23.4, the intensification of a consonant coincides in many cases with length. In Tashelhit, this is valid for all consonants, except *w*, *ḍ*, and *ɣ*, where the process of intensification leads to a phonetically unexpected result:

(1) lax *w* corresponding to tense *gg°*:
   aorist: *izwiɣ*, preterite: *zgg°aɣ* 'to be red' (a stative verb)
   singular: *adgg°al*, plural: *idulan* 'in-law'
(2) lax *ḍ* corresponding to tense *ṭṭ*:
   aorist: *fḍr*, intensive aorist: *fṭṭr* 'to have breakfast'

(3) lax *ɣ* corresponding to tense *qq*:
aorist: *ɣrs*, intensive aorist: *qqrs* 'to slaughter'
aorist: *ɣr*, intensive aorist: *aqqra* 'to read'
aorist: *imɣur*, preterite: *mqqur* 'to be great' (a stative verb)

Lax–tense differences can play a role in Tashelhit dialectology. One dialect may have a lax variant of a lexical item, where another dialect has a tense variant, e.g., 'flour' is *aggʷrn* in the Aštukn dialect corresponding to *awwrn* in Igdmiwn.

23.6.2. Labialized consonants

Besides the phonemes *k*, *g*, *x*, *ɣ*, and *q* one finds the labialized forms *kʷ*, *gʷ*, *xʷ*, *ɣʷ*, and *qʷ*. There are no minimal pairs of labialized versus unlabialized phonemes. In general we observe that some forms are more frequent than others. One finds more frequently: *akʷr* 'to steal', but the unlabialized variant exists also. On the other hand, we would never find *imikʷr 'thief' or *argʷaz 'man', but only *imikr* and *argaz*.

23.6.3. Vowels, syllabification, shwa-insertion

The vowels are *i*, *a*, and *u*. One finds [ə] on the phonetic level; it is, however, not a phoneme. The main preoccupation of recent phonological studies is the search for syllable build-up. None of the existing proposals is fully convincing. When one starts to apply proposed syllable structures to actually existing words, one sees that they do not give the expected surface result. An interesting analysis of Tashelhit syllabification and ə-insertion was presented by Dell and Elmedlaoui (1988) for the Imdlawn dialect, in which a simple system for syllabification is attached to a sonority scale for the units that form the nucleus of the syllable.

23.7. Riffian

23.7.1. Spirantization

Riffian includes many spirantized consonants. In most Riffian dialects all lax stops except *q* have become fricatives, e.g., in the dialect of the Beni Said tribe:

$b \rightarrow \beta$
$d \rightarrow \eth$
$ḍ \rightarrow \etḥ$
$t \rightarrow \theta$

g → *y* or *j*
k → *š* or *ç*

In other dialects, *g* has become *ž*, while in some western variants *g* and *k* are stops. Moreover, in a number of dialects *b* has remained a stop.

Spirantization occurs everywhere, except when the consonant is preceded by a homorganic nasal:

θβambəsθ 'darkness'
θanda 'pool'
nḍu 'jump!'
antun 'yeast'

In these four examples, spirantization does not occur in the clusters *mb*, *nd*, *nḍ*, and *nt*.

There are some cases of lax stops outside this environment. They are either recent loans (e.g., *dijaž* 'loosen' from French *dégager* with *d* instead of *ð*) or the result of a change of tense consonants to lax consonants. The precise conditions under which some tense stops have become lax stops are not clear.

The introduction of phonemic non-spirantized stops has lead to a tripartite system. First, we find a series of spirantized consonants. Second, we find the marginal series of non-spirantized stops. Third, we find the series of tense stops (which are never spirantized). On morphological grounds, it can be shown that the spirantized consonants are the lax counterparts of the tense stops, e.g.:

ddaa 'live!'
θuðaaθ 'life'

Here, *dd* in the verbal form corresponds to *ð* in the noun.

23.7.2. Shwa insertion

The insertion of *ə* is conditioned by the structure of the word, according to the rules given in § 23.4. Some words do not follow the rules, and should be analyzed as containing phonemic *ə*, e.g., *žžəhð* 'strength' instead of the expected **žžhəð*. Only in the case of *r* does sonority seem to play a role in the rules for *ə*-insertion. The development of *r* is complicated; it will be treated below.

23.7.3. Particular developments

Some phonemes have undergone developments which are typical for Rif Berber. Most important are the developments of *l*, *ll*, *r* and *rr*.

Except for some variants on the periphery of the Riffian territory, *l* has developed into an *r*-like sound, which is transcribed here as *ř*. Its phonetic realization varies from region to region. One may hear tap-like sounds, but also sounds similar to Czech *ř*. In most dialects *ř* is different from *r*, e.g.

θisiřa 'sandals' (← θisila)
θisira 'mills' (← θisira)

However, in some variants these two words are pronounced identically.

The tense counterpart of *l* has developed into the affricate *ddž*:

addži 'brains' (← alli)
ddžiřəθ 'night' (← lliləθ, a loan from Moroccan Arabic *l-lila*).

In a number of loans *l* and *ll* occur:

liṣanəṣ 'petrol' (← French *l'essence*)
βəlləʕ 'close!' (← Eastern Moroccan Arabic *bəlləʕ*)

However, in many loanwords *l* and *ll* have become *ř* and *ddž*.

The development of *r* and *rr* is more complicated. In Riffian, *r* is the only consonant which forces *ə* to be inserted before it. In most Riffian dialects, *r* and *rr* have had particular developments that can be summarized in stages as follows (we use V for *a*, *i*, or *u* and C for a consonant or a morpheme boundary):

stage 1:
    ər → ar   içərz → içarz 'he plowed'
    ərr → arr   içərrəz → içarrəz 'he plows'

stage 2:
    arC → aaC   içarz → içaaz 'he plowed'
    arr → aař   içarrez → içaařəz 'he plows'
    urC → oaC   θamurθ → θamoaθ 'land'
    urr → oař   ahurri → ahoaři 'free man'
    irC → eaC   aðβir → aðβea 'pigeon'
    rV → rV   ari → ari 'write!'

stage 3:
    aa → a   içaaz → içaz 'he plowed'
    ř → r   içaařəz → içarəz 'he plows'
                               aři (← ali) → ari 'go up!'

In the first stage of the development, the opposition between *ə* and *a* is neutralized before *r*. In the second stage, *r* becomes a (rather short) *a*-like sound if not followed by a vowel. When preceded by *a*, this sound merges into a long vowel; when preceded by *u* or *i*, the diphthongs *oa* and *ea* emerge.

These two diphthongs may eventually develop into *wa* and *ya*. In the third stage of the development, the long *a* is shortened and at the same time *ř* (as found in the reflexes of *rr* and of *l*) merges with *r*. The importance of the mergers in the last stage may be exemplified by the word *ira* 'play!'. From the form in the third stage of the development it is not possible to predict whether the original form was *irar, *irər, *ira, *ilar, *ilər, or *ila. If we look at the form of the word in the second stage, *iraa*, only *irar and *irər are possibilities. From evidence of dialects where *r* has not undergone any change, we know that the proto-form was *irar.

The three stages described above are not only historical stages, but are actually represented in the different dialects. The original situation can be found in Beni Iznassen (East), the first stage in Gueznaia (South), the second stage in Ait Said (Center), and the third stage in Ait Sidhar (North).

The question is whether *r* remains as an underlying phoneme in the three stages mentioned above or not. The answer is largely a theoretical choice. It should be noted, however, that these developments have not affected the morphology of the dialects. There has not been any analogical restructuring as a result of the phonetic developments.

23.7.4. Assimilations

The most important assimilations are:

A voiced non-liquid consonant becomes voiceless when immediately followed by *θ*:

aʕraβ 'Arab man'
θaʕrafθ 'Arab woman'

The consonant cluster *ř* + *θ* becomes *tš*:

ðwəř 'return!'
θaməðwətš 'return (noun)'

The consonant cluster *mð* becomes *nd*:

θandint 'town' (← Arabic *mdina*)

Two identical lax consonants merge into their tense counterpart when in immediate contact:

nyəθ θ → *nyətt* 'kill (pl.) him!'

The consonants *ð* or *d* followed by *θ* or *t* result in *tt*:

ð θandint → *ttandint* 'it's a town'

Similarly *ḍ* or *ḍ* followed by *θ* or *t* result in *ṭṭ*:

θaɣruḍθ → *θaɣruṭṭ* 'shoulder'

23.7.5. *w* and *y*

w and *y* are opposed to *u* and *i* in all environments except at the end of a word. Here *w* becomes *u* and *y* becomes *i*:

nəḍwəy 'I jumped' (stem: nḍw)
yənḍu 'he jumped'
ulyəy 'I went up'
yuli 'he went up'

23.8. Touareg

The phonological system of Touareg is quite different from that of the other Berber languages. It should be noted that especially in the field of the Touareg vowel system there is great uncertainty about the status of the different elements. This uncertainty is partly caused by internal complications of the system, partly by the variation across the different dialects and, last but not least, partly by the fact that much of the discussion is based on data collected at the beginning of this century.

23.8.1. *Vowels*

There are at least six vowels: *i, e, ə, a, o, u*. The vowel *ə* occurs in open syllables and is phonemic. There has been considerable discussion about the existence of a second short central vowel, transcribed here as *ä*, in opposition to *ə*. Recently, the existence of this phoneme has been shown with the help of phonetic instruments in Abalagh Touareg (Niger) by Naima Louali, featuring the following minimal pairs (1990: 138):

ägru 'understand!'
əgru 'find!'
älu 'weep!'
alu 'be like!'

This distinction is, however, not common to all dialects.

23.8.2. *Vowel quantity*

Most scholars distinguish long and short vowels. All vowels except *ə* and *ä* have a long variant. Length is said to play a role especially in the verbal system, where a number of tenses are distinguished by length. The study by Louali of the Abalagh Touareg system does not find any difference between short and long vowels. According to her, the tense differences which are said to be expressed by vowel length are expressed in reality by qualitative distinctions. Whether this situation pertains only to Abalagh or also for other dialects remains to be studied.

23.8.3. Consonants

In general, the Touareg consonant system is less rich than the systems of the northern dialects, due to the fact that Arabic has had less impact on Touareg and that most Arabic loans have been phonetically integrated into the Touareg system. Therefore, consonants like *ḥ*, *ʕ*, and *ṣ* and their tense counterparts are absent. For the same reason, simple *q* and *ṭ* are rare, though *ṭ* may be the result of assimilation of *ḍ* to a following voiceless consonant. Cf. Ayr *eḍəs* 'sleep' corresponds to Iwlemmeden *eṭəs* 'sleep'. Resulting from the influence of Songhay and Hausa, some southern Touareg dialects feature *ŋ* as a borrowed phoneme. Special mention is warranted for two consonants: *z* and *h*. In Touareg, simple *⋆z* has undergone various developments. In the north (Ahaggar), it has become *h*. In Mali one finds *š* and in Niger *ž*. This can be illustrated by the name of the language in the different dialects. In Algeria Touareg is called *tamaahaq*, in Mali *tamašəq*, in Niger *tamaažaq*. These terms correspond to *tamaziɣt* in other Berber languages. The tense *zz* is always retained. By analogical formation, simple *z* has been reintroduced in a number of lexical items.

The consonant *h* is frequent in Touareg. In the Algerian variants it may be the correspondent of *⋆z*, but it also occurs in words without *⋆z*. This second *h*, which is also found in the other dialects, corresponds generally with zero in the Berber languages of the north and *β* in Ghadamsi:

  ar 'lion' (Ouargla, Zenatic)
  ähär 'lion' (Ayr)
  aβor 'lion' (Ghadamsi)

There are a number of instances of palatalization. The consonants *g* and *k* become palatalized *gʲ* and *kʲ* and eventually develop into *ǧ* and *č*. These may become *ž* and *š*. Before *i*, *t* may become *š* in dialects of Niger.

Selected Bibliography

There are some good bibliographies concerning Berber linguistics. For the period until 1954 one can use the bibliography contained in Basset 1969. For the period 1954–1977, see Galand 1979. For the period after 1977, see Chaker 1991. The most readily available bibliography for American readers is Applegate 1970. Other titles given in the bibliography below all explicitly concern phonological subjects.

Alojali, Ghoubeïd. 1980. *Lexique Touareg–Français*. Copenhagen: Akademisk Forlag.

Applegate, Joseph R. 1970. "The Berber Languages." In *Current Trends in Linguistics*, ed. Thomas A. Sebeok, vol. 6: *Linguistics in South West Asia and North Africa*, pp. 586–661. The Hague: Mouton.

Bader, Yusuf. 1985. "Schwa in Berber: A Non Linear Analysis." *Lingua* 67: 225–49.

Basset, André. 1969. *La langue berbère*. London: Dawsons.

Boukous, Ahmad. 1982. "Les contraintes de structure segmentale en berbère (dialecte tachelhit)." *Langues et Litteratures* 2: 9–27.

———. 1987. "Syllabe et syllabation en berbère." *Awal: Cahiers d'Etudes Berbères* 3: 67–82.

———. 1990. "Pharyngalisation et domaines prosodiques." *Etudes et Documents Berbères* 7: 68–91.

Chaker, Salem. 1984. *Textes en linguistique berbère*. Paris: CNRS.

———. 1991. *Une décennie d'études berbères (1980–1990), bibliographie critique*. Algiers: Bouchene.

Cortade, Jean-Marie. 1969. *Essai de grammaire touareg*. Algiers: Institut de Recherches Sahariennes.

Dell, François, and Elmedlaoui, Muhammad. 1985. "Syllabic Consonants and Syllabification in Imdlawn Tashlhiyt Berber." *Journal of African Languages and Linguistics* 7: 105–25.

———. 1988. "Syllabic Consonants in Berber: Some New Evidence." *Journal of African Languages and Linguistics* 10: 105–25.

Dell, François, and Tangi, Oufae. 1992. "Syllabification and Empty Nuclei in Ath Sidhar Rifian Berber." *Journal of African Languages and Linguistics* 13: 125–62.

Galand, Lionel. 1953. "La phonétique en dialectologie berbère." *Orbis* 2: 225–33.

———. 1979. *Langue et littérature berbères, Vingt cinq ans d'études*. Paris: CNRS.

———. 1988. "Le berbère." In *Les langues dans le monde ancien et moderne*, ed. Jean Perrot, pt. 3, *Les langues chamito-sémitiques*, ed. David Cohen, pp. 207–42, 303–6. Paris: CNRS.

Guerssel, Mohammed. 1983. "A Phonological Analysis of the Construct State in Berber." *Linguistic Analysis* 11: 309–30.

———. 1985. "The Role of Sonority in Berber Syllabification." *Awal: Cahiers d'Etudes Berbères* 1: 81–110.

———. 1986. "Glides in Berber and Syllabicity." *Linguistic Inquiry* 17: 1–12.
Kossmann, Maarten G. forthcoming a. "Schwa en berbère."
———. forthcoming b. *Grammaire du Berbère de Figuig (Maroc Oriental)*.
Lanfry, Jacques. 1968. *Ghadamès, étude linguistique et ethnographique*. Fort-National, Algeria: Fichier de Documentation Berbère.
Leguil, Alphonse. 1981. "Remarques sur la labio-vélarité en berbère." *Bulletin de la Société de Linguistique de Paris* 76: 20–23.
———. 1982. "La phonologie au secours de la grammaire en Touareg." *Bulletin de la Société de Linguistique de Paris* 77: 341–63.
———. 1983. "La corrélation de concomitance en touareg." *Bulletin des Etudes Africaines de l'INALCO* 6: 77–123.
Louali, Naïma. 1990. "L'emphase en berbère, étude phonétique, phonologique et comparative." Thèse pour le Doctorat en Sciences du Langage, Université Lumière Lyon 2.
Petites Sœurs de Jésus, Agadez, Niger. 1968. *Initiation à la langue des Touaregs de l'Aïr*. Paris: Société d'Etudes Linguistiques et Anthropologiques de France (SELAF).
———. 1974. *Contes Touaregs de l'Aïr* (with a grammatical introduction by L. Galand). Paris: Publié avec le concours du CNRS.
Prasse, Karl G. 1972–74. *Manuel de grammaire touarègue (tahaggart)*, 3 vols. Copenhagen: University of Copenhagen.
———. 1984. "The Origin of the Vowels o and e in Twareg and Ghadamsi." In *Current Progress in Afro-Asiatic Linguistics (Proceedings of the Third International Hamito-Semitic Congress, March 1978)*, pp. 317–26. Amsterdam: Benjamins.
Saib, Jilali. 1976. "Schwa Insertion in Berber: Un Problème de Choix." *Afroasiatic Linguistics* 3/4: 71–83.
———. 1978. "Segment Organization and the Syllable in Tamazight Berber." In *Syllables and Segments*, ed. Alan Bell and Joan Bybee Hooper, pp. 93–103. Amsterdam: North-Holland.
Stroomer, Harry J. forthcoming. *Dictionnaire Tachelhit–Français*.
Willms, Alfred. 1972. *Grammatik der südlichen Beraberdialekte (Südmarokko)*. Glückstadt: Augustin.

Chapter 24
Awngi Phonology
Robert Hetzron
University of California, Santa Barbara

24.1. Introduction

Awngi is the southernmost representative of Central Cushitic, or Agaw, the language cluster that is the most important substratum of Ethiopian Semitic and has survived in scattered pockets in Ethiopia and Eritrea. It is spoken today in the Province of Agawmeder, Goǧǧam Governorate General in Ethiopia. When I visited the location in 1965–66, I was told that the number of speakers may be around 50,000. Unfortunately, this figure is completely unreliable. It is only an estimate given by local tax-collectors.

I had the opportunity to talk briefly with Awngi speakers of other areas within the same province and detected dialectal differences. This contact was too brief to yield any publishable information.

In general presentations of Ethiopian languages, one often sees reference to an Agaw "language." This is decidedly incorrect. The difference between the various Agaw tongues—the northern Bilin, the eastern Xamir, the western Kemant, and the southern Awngi—is greater than the diversity of the Romance languages.

In the older literature, Awngi was referred to as "Awiya," a term introduced by Conti Rossini (1905). This important Italian scholar apparently had relatively little time to work on Awngi, and did not realize that the term *awíya* actually means 'Agaw person', lit., 'son of Agaw', fem. *awíja*, pl. *awayírí*. I introduced the term "Southern Agaw" (Hetzron 1969), but my colleagues preferred the name used by the speakers themselves, *awŋi*, with the derivative *-ŋi* used for names of languages (equivalent to, and indubitably the etymon of, Amharic *-ñña*). The *aw*(V) portion of these words was demonstrably *ay^w- in the older language, the source of the Amharic name *agäw*.

My fieldwork[1] on Awngi was carried out in 1965–66 in Ethiopia, mainly in Addis Ababa, with a field trip to and a stint of ten days at the home of my

---

1. Sponsored by the Ford Foundation via the Near Eastern Center and the African Studies Center of the University of California, Los Angeles.

main informant, Mr. Asmare Tegenye, then a 22-year-old student, from the village of Bərcí (Amharic *Bərṭa Abbo*), subdistrict of Fafa, district of Ankäša, province of Agawmeder.

The oldest Southern Agaw document comes from the 1770s, a translation from Amharic of the Song of Solomon (Ms. 33, Ethiopian Collection, Bodleian Library, Oxford, "Damot Agaw," fols. 18–20), commissioned by the Scottish traveler James Bruce. This text is still unpublished. It is of mediocre quality. Basically, the translator applied a word-by-word translation from an Amharic version (which, also commissioned by Bruce, was translated from Geʻez) without much adjustment for style and grammatical continuity. He used the Amharic script (with inconsistencies), yet it is valuable for purposes of historical morphology.

24.2. The phonemes

24.2.1. *The consonants*

Length is in principle relevant for consonants, but geminate consonants are rare. Minimal pairs are few, either in some Amharic borrowings: *fetenəŋ* 'do quickly' (Amh. √*fṭn*[2] vs. *fettenəŋ* 'give an exam' (Amh. √*ftn*), or involve morpheme boundaries: *dadá* 'path' (diminutive-feminine of *dad* 'road') vs. *daddá* 'on the road'. Yet geminates occur in genuine Awngi words as well: *əttiŋ* 'to fall', *əttíní* 'flour' (the "fall-out" of milling), *cəllí* 'little', *kuppi* 'fruit', *angučča* 'cat', etc.

Table 24-1. Awngi Consonants

p	f	t	c	s	š	č	k	k^w	q	q^w
b		d	ʒ	z	ž		g	g^w	γ	γ^w
m		n					ŋ	ŋ^w		
w					y					

The symbols *c/ʒ* stand for the affricates *ts/dz*.

As in Amharic, *b* is [β] in intervocalic and word-final positions. There is no *v*. The *d* is slightly retroflex. Even though Awngi has *ʒ* (which only occurs in the numeral *seʒa* '4' and its derivatives), in morphophonemic alternations

---

2. This may be a recent borrowing. Amharic *ṭ* is usually rendered by *c* in Awngi, e.g., *kecer-* 'make an appointment', Amh. √*qṭr*. In the following, glottalization is marked by an underdot, except for *ḍ*, which stands for a retroflex.

the voiced counterpart of *c* is *z* (most certainly reflecting older articulations).³ Unless geminated, *r* is realized with only one flap. It does not occur in absolute initial position. Both *q* and *γ* are lax, but not fricative. Labiovelars and labio-uvulars are distinct from the homologous velars and uvulars only before *-a*, *-e*, *-i* and word-finally. In morphophonemic alternations, both semivowels, *w* and *y*, assume the status of the voiced member of the pair.

24.2.1.1. Some consonantal changes
Not less surprising than the etymological relatedness of French [fis] and Spanish [ixo] 'son' is the fact that Awngi ŋárí and Somali *madaħ* (< *matħ), both meaning 'head', are perfect cognates. (The final *í* of Awngi represents the palatalization caused by the final pharyngeal). Two historical changes explain this.

I wish to point out that at the present stage of research, hardly any work has been done on historical phonology of Agaw. The contexts in which the changes took places, as against those in which the phoneme kept its phonetic character, are unclear.

24.2.1.1.1. *m > γ*
Awngi *ŋ* often corresponds to *m* in other Cushitic languages, but to *ŋ* or *n* elsewhere in Agaw. Unlikely as it looks, surmising a *m > ŋ* change for Proto-Agaw is inevitable.⁴

The root *γu-* 'eat' corresponds to *ḳom in East Cushitic, suggesting that in some positions different types of changes took place as well.

The Agaw languages also have /m/. The only clear attestation of a *m* that comes from Afroasiatic is in the question particle *-mà*. For the rest, most of them are obvious borrowings from Ethiopian Semitic. A number of them cannot be accounted for, and the only significant statement is that they seem to have no Cushitic etymology.

24.2.1.1.2. **t > r > y*
Let me illustrate the changes through the borrowing from Semitic *(')amät* 'year' which follows the behavior of native words. Bilin regularly has *r* where Proto-Cushitic *t must be posited: *amära*. On the other hand, -*r* → -*t* change is one of the plural-forming devices: *šəmár* → *šəmát* 'tail' (Palmer

---

3. In Palmer's 1957 material, there are several occurrences of *ʒ* where my informants had *z*, a clear case of age-dialect (his informant was from the same area as mine).
4. Diakonoff's (1992: 33) suggestion that *ŋ* arose through merger with the next phoneme is untenable.

1958: 385, cf. Xamir ṣə́mər, Awngi cə́már),[5] though 'year' keeps its r. Kemant has y: amäy. As in Bilin, one of the nominal plural-forming devices is r → t, and it also applies to ámra → amə́ṭ or ə́mə́ṭ 'year' (Appleyard 1984: 41, 1987: 255). Awngi has amet (which may also be a recent borrowing), but the overall situation is more complicated.

Albeit rarely, r < *t is indeed found in Awngi, as in -rŋa, the ending that makes '20' out of '2' (elsewhere it is the 10-formative in general: Bilin -räŋan, Kemant -yəŋ), coming from Cushitic *tVmVn 'ten'. The verb for 'die' has the alterating stems kət/kə/kər- where the final consonant may ultimately represent the "autobenefactive" ending, Cushitic *ḍ.

More frequently, *t may either remain t or become y, as in Kemant. One important case in point is the onset of the Sg./Pl.2/Sg.3f. ending of the verbs that comes from Proto-Cushitic/Afroasiatic *t- (the suffixes come from prefix-conjugated auxiliaries). Bilin has -r- for Sg.2/3f. and -d- for Pl.2, Kemant only -y-.[6] Xamir has the alternation -r- ~ -d- or -dr-(?) for the entire domain of this person-marker, -d- after l, n, r, and -r- everywhere else (Appleyard 1987: 478). Appleyard (1987: 472–73, 476) also mentions the alternation -t- ~ -r- for the autobenefactive ending: Pl.1/3 and the indicative Sg.3f. exhibit -r-, the rest -t-, including subordinate Sg.3f.

Let me first mention the root bay- 'leave', cf. Bilin bár-, Xamit bär-, Kemant be-. This type of correspondence suggests an original *bat-, which does show up in the conjugation as bay- as well.[7] Moreover, the person-marker *t does have palatal manifestations in Awngi (§ 24.4.3). Let us consider the following comparative table of some persons of the Indefinite Nonpast in three verb classes where classification is based on the choice of suffixes:[8]

---

5. Reinisch (1887: 325) compares this word with Hebrew √smr 'bristle, stiffen', particularly såmår 'wiry-haired' and Aramaic 'mr 'wool' (also qmr) and to Geʻez ḏämr 'wool' (Hebrew also has ṣmr for 'wool'). It does not seem to be a borrowing, but rather common Afroasiatic heritage, starting with the phoneme that Diakonoff (1992: 15–16) reconstruct s as *ŝ. The Aramaic root does not fit into the picture, since it has what Diakonoff (1992: 20–21) reconstructed as *ĉ. Geʻez also has the verbal root √dmr for 'attach', so that the semantic feature connecting all of this may be "appendage."

6. Archaic -t- is still used in four verbs, all of which ending in -y, which blocked the change t > y (Appleyard 1975: 332).

7. Appleyard (1987: 473 n. 38) compares this to East Cushitic *baḥ 'go out' + autobenefactive *ḍ, a retroflex.

8. Only the first hyphens are to be taken as clear morpheme boundaries. The later hyphens are added to facilitate the explanation; cf. note 9. There are two more verb classes which do indeed involve t's and y's (the latter even in the Sg.3m.) and combinations of both (second

		A	B	C
I:	Sg.1	des-é	qúc-é	bá-t-é
II:	Sg.2=Sg.3f.	des-té	qúc-í	bá-t-é
III:	Sg.3m.	des-é	qúc-é	báy-é
IV:	Pl.1	des-né	qúc-né	bá-né
		'study'	'wash'	'leave'

A glance at this comparative table suggests the following. Class A exhibits the relatively most archaic features. Class B uses a II form where the person-marker *t* > *y*. Class C must have had a root ending in **-t* which became *-y*, except in I.[9] The *-y-* disappeared in IV.

24.2.1.1.3. THE SG.3F. INDEPENDENT PRONOUN

Here is a manifestation of *t* > *y* that has typological interest. The fact that Awngi, a language that has grammatical (though semantically determined) gender, does not have it in its Sg.3 pronoun, is in contradiction to one of Greenberg's (1966: 96) universals (43): "If a language has gender categories in the noun, it has gender categories in the pronoun." The explanation is historical. On the basis of comparison with other Agaw languages one may reconstruct *ŋi for 'he' and *ŋit for 'she'. The latter underwent a series of changes: *ŋit > *ŋir > *ŋiy (> **ŋi:*) > *ŋi*, each stage of which, other than the starting point, is attested in various Agaw languages (Bilin *nirí*, Xamir *ŋír* or *ŋí*, Kemant *niy*). Thus, in the last reconstructed stage there may have been an opposition **ŋi/ŋi:* or *ŋiy for 'he/she', and with the loss of length or reduction of the diphthong, the two collapsed.

24.2.2. The vowels

Vocalic length is not relevant in Awngi. Table 24.2 presents the vowels.

---

persons+Sg.3f.) for which I have no explanation except for the assumption that the palatal element may have been part of the root.

It should be mentioned that proto-Cushitic may have had *d, *t, glottalized **d'*, **t'*, and retroflex *ḍ, as against a poorer system in Agaw. Our *t > *r* > *y* may come from *t, as in the person marker, and from *ḍ as in the root final assimilated autobenefactive. In Xamir, however, there is *r ~ t* for the autobenefactive, but *r ~ d/dr* for the person marker. In both Bilin and Xamir, the plural shows an alternation *r ~ t/ṭ*, whereas the person marker has a voiced consonant as the second member.

9. Palmer (1959: 283) considers this a voice-pairing *y/t* in the sense of my § 24.4.2. Two objections may be raised. Historically, the first members of the pair are more archaic in § 24.4.2, whereas here *t* is the relic. Descriptively, one ought to set up a *y*-deletion rule for II and IV (the clusters *-yt-*, *-yn-* are otherwise allowed), and the situation in C would be even more complicated.

Table 24-2. Awngi Vowels

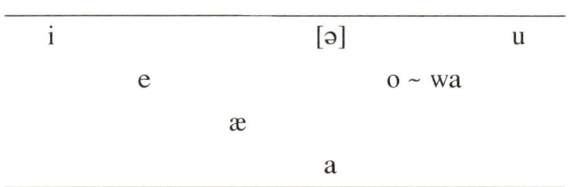

i	[ə]	u
e		o ~ wa
	æ	
	a	

REMARKS: æ occurs only at a morpheme boundary, the result of a contraction of a preceding palatal element and a subsequent *a*, thus *ŋi-* 'his/her/its' + *-ará* 'husband' yields *ŋærá* 'her husband'. Most occurrences of [ə] are predictable on the basis of syllabic and phonetic structure: the avoidance of triple clusters within the word, of double clusters word-initially, and of word-initial *r*, but they are relevant in the tonal rules (which are then ordered after the shwa-introduction), e.g., *ə́rí* 'rain'. Yet, there are a handful of words beginning with *əCV-*: the verbs *əŋəŋ* 'bite', *əqʷiŋ* 'call', *əšiŋ* 'spend the day', *əyəŋ* 'give', *əγaγerəŋ* 'curse', and *əγoγiŋ* 'laugh', where the post-*ə* consonants have no positional constraints, cf., *yiməŋ* 'beg', *γasəŋ* 'have on/with oneself', etc.

The close vowels *i*, *ə*, *u* sound somewhat more open before uvulars and labio-uvulars. In a sequence /iγ/, one hears something like [iᵃγ], comparable to the phenomenon of furtive *pataḥ* in Hebrew.

Amharic *ä* is rendered by the palatal vowel *e* in loanwords.

24.3. The tone system

The fact that Awngi is a tone language was first recognized by Palmer (1959). More and more tonal systems have been found in the Cushitic area, which inevitably leads to the conclusion that Proto-Cushitic must have been tonal. The northern Agaw language Bilin was described by Palmer (1960: 111) noncommittally as to tone. First of all, whatever the descriptive device, historically speaking in languages where a major word may have no stress at all (like Japanese and Bilin), one must suspect an earlier tonal stage where the now stressless word had no High tone. In Bilin the stressed syllable, with a high pitch, is followed by syllables carrying the same pitch, not unlike the case in Awngi (§ 24.3.4); but in absolute final position, the high tone is not realized. Thus the distinction between the minimal pairs *bəta* 'dust' and *bətá* 'louse' is perceivable only if they are followed by some other word (Palmer 1960: 113). In Awngi, indeed, tones play a greater role than in Bilin.

24.3.1. The tonemes

Awngi has four tonemes arranged on three levels: High *á*, Mid *a* (unmarked in this notation), Low *à*, and Falling *â* (a fall from High to Mid). The last two are quite rare. Low tone *à* (only with this vowel) occurs only in the past tense ending -*y"à* and the sentence-question particle -*mà*.[10] The Falling tone always occurs in word-final, but not necessarily absolute final, position. Some minimal oppositions: *aqê* 'man (accusative)', *áqé* 'I am/know', *aqé* 'don't be!'; *kur* 'hill', *kúr* 'saddle'; *yuna* 'woman', *yúna* 'we have eaten', *yúnà* 'they ate'.

Since Awngi has no expressive intonation or downdrift to speak of, from a distance Awngi speech sounds like a sort of "twittering," a succession of equitonal High and Mid pitches, with occasional Low tones. Tones may be recognized even out of context, when a single word is pronounced. Mid represents the normal "tessitura," or level of voice, High is shriller, more elevated, though not falsetto, and a Low is creaky.

24.3.2. Tonemic rules

Before an added syllable, the Falling tone becomes High and the Low one Mid: *desûs* 'while he studies' has a variant *desúsi*, and it is *desúskí* before the multifunctional (connective-topical) particle -*kí*. The past tense form *desy"à* 'he studied' becomes *desy"amà* in interrogation: 'Did he study?'.

24.3.3. Stress

Somewhat surprisingly, Awngi has some stress phenomena that operate independently of the tone system. Accompanied by a slight rise of the pitch, it normally falls on the penultimate syllable.[11] Yet it does play a role in two situations. Unlike other suffixes, the referential article -*ká* and the connective-topic marker -*kí* do not change the position of the stress (while the plural ending -*ka/ká* does).

---

10. While the former is always sentence-final, the question particle may also be placed after a focus-element, if any, which keeps it original position. In the absence of focus, it is the sentence-final verb that will carry it.

11. For example, for the postposition *falengá* 'after', I first transcribed a Mid-High-High tone pattern. My informant was linguistically sophisticated enough by that time to understand it and to object, suggesting Mid-Mid-High. When I asked him to whistle the word (a technique that I learned from the late A. N. Tucker), he unmistakably produced a Mid-Mid-High melody. Further familiarization with the Awngi sound system under the guidance of Mr. Asmare later allowed me to hear that the rise on the middle syllable was slighter than of the final one, as an exponent of stress.

There is a small class of nouns where the stress is not penultimate in that it may not leave the stem even if it is followed by more than one syllable (see § 24.4.5.2), e.g., g'uzg$_i$-u$_j$-des$_k$ 'from$_k$ that of$_{j, \text{masc. gen.}}$ the stomach$_i$,' vs. "normal" giz-'u-des 'from that of time' (i.e., genitives combined with another case-marker). The first type with stress restriction is very rare. Its origin is likely to be somehow connected with the fact that these nouns only have Mid tone syllables.

24.3.4. The origin of tonemes

In roots, i.e. words without suffixes, there may be Mid-High sequences, but not High-Mid ones (cf. the beginnings of §§ 24.4.5 and 24.4.6.1). Thus, once High tone is assumed, it remains High for the rest of the root, as is probably the case in Bilin. This may have been the Proto-Agaw situation, though not the Proto-Cushitic one. Descriptively, however, this is no longer true in view of the complications involving suffixes.

While I am not sure of the origin of the Low tone in the sentence question particle (language universals would have rising in interrogation),[12] plausible justification for it may be advanced in the case of the past tense suffix. One may reconstruct *-uya with a principle of equitonality for the two vowels. When u was reduced to ʷ, i.e. lost its syllabicity and capability of carrying tone, the closest the originally equitonal a could do was to become Low, which thus properly stands for lack of tone.

The Falling tone always occurs in word-final position and comes from the contraction of two syllables (with no intervening consonant, thus *-iá → ê, still so in Bruce's unpublished document).

24.4. Morphoph/tonemic rules

24.4.1. Regressive vowel height assimilation

See (Palmer 1959: 273, Johnson 1972: 74–5). Given a word where the last syllable of a word has e, when a suffix with i is added, e → i. This assimilation spreads regressively in a chain onto immediately preceding syllables. If they also have e, it also becomes i. While only stem-final e can trigger this assimilation, farther back in the chain o → u also takes place. All other

---

12. As the native speaker of a language (Hungarian) that has High-Mid melody at the end of a sentence question, I cannot help suggesting that the Low tone in -mà reflects the possibility that this particle started out as a sort of tag-question marker, "…?, or what," which does go down.

vowels stop the spread. Thus, with the masculine suffix -*í*, the root *moleqés- 'monastic' (from Greek μοναχός via Amharic) yields *muliqísí* 'monk', whereas the feminine exhibits the original underlying vowels: *moleqésá* 'nun'. By itself, *o* cannot start this process. The word *goryí* 'spade' has no raising. In my material there is no sequence of two *o*'s or *o* → *u* preceded by underlying *e*.

A few words, mainly Amharic borrowings, such as *šererití* 'spider', but also the indigenous *əyáγérí* 'curse', are exempt from this rule.

24.4.2. The root-final voice alternation
In the verbal system, the following alternations of root-final consonants are observed:

$b \rightarrow p, w \rightarrow p, d \rightarrow t, z \rightarrow c, ž \rightarrow č, g \rightarrow k, γ \rightarrow k, g^w \rightarrow k^w, γ \rightarrow q, γ^w \rightarrow q^w$

The first members of the pair are the unmarked ones, as is illustrated by the fact that two different consonants lead to *p* or *k*. The second ones occur (i) in the imperative, (ii) before a Sg.1 suffix. Examples: *cép-é* 'I do' vs. *céw-é* 'he does' and *cíp* or *cipí* 'do$_{sg.}$'. Naturally, roots may end in voiceless consonants, in which case no alternation takes place.

The following explanation may be appropriate for the alternation in question. The singular imperative is the only form of the verb where the root-final consonant is in absolute word-final position, actually in sentence-final position because of strict verb-final syntax of Awngi from Proto-Cushitic on. This may have led to devoicing, a phenomenon that is well attested elsewhere. The plural imperative (and the imperative of verbs ending in a vowel) and the prohibitive may have adopted the devoicing by solidarity. Now, Cushitic verbal suffixes are known to have been independent prefix-conjugated auxiliaries based on the general Afroasiatic pattern (as in Semitic): *t-* for second persons and Sg.3f., *y-* for the rest of the third persons and *n-* for Pl.1. For Sg.1 we find *a-* in Cushitic prefix-conjugations, and 'V- in Semitic.[13] If we take 'V- to be the original prefix (in proto-Agaw at least), the addition of -'V- to the verbal stem as part of the prefix of the auxiliary-to-become-suffix, this 'created an environment comparable to absolute final position, hence the devoicing.

---

13. The glottal stop is not automatic, as shown in Classical Arabic where automatic glottal stops drop after a prefix (*waṣla*), but not in Sg.1, e.g., *'al-malik-* 'the king', but *wa-l-malik-* 'and the king' with the glottal stop dropped, vs. *'asma'-* 'I hear' and *wa-'asma'-* 'and I hear'.

24.4.3. The palatal -y- (< *t) suffix-person-marker (see § 24.2.1.1.2)

In several verb classes, Sg.3f. and Sg./Pl.2 have a palatal person-marker[14] followed by the rest of the suffix expressing tense, mood and/or type of subordination.[15] Before a consonant, it manifests itself as *i* or *í*: *kantiy"à* 'she saw'. It palatalizes through merger with the subsequent vowel in the following manners. (i) with a nonfinal *-a-* it merges into *-e-*: **kanti-ání → kanténí* 'when she sees/saw'. (ii) With a word-final *-a* it yields *-æ*: **kanti-a → kantæ* 'she has seen'; yet when this becomes nonfinal through the addition of a further suffix *-æ- → -i-*: **kantæ-štíy"à → kantištiy"à* 'she was seeing'. (iii) It blends with a subsequent *-u*, *-e*, *-ə* (and vacuously with an *-i*) into *-í-*: **kanti-ûs → kantís* 'while she is/was seeing' (note the change of tone).

24.4.4. Tonal dissimilation and assimilation

Two case-suffixes, the locative *-da* and the ablative *-des*, have the tone opposite to that of the preceding syllable: Mid after High and High after Mid, e.g. *murí-des* 'from (a/the) village' vs. *múri-dés* 'from (a/the) snake'. Yet the tone is always Mid when the preceding syllable is a genitive ending (in Awngi, genitives agree in sentence-case with their headnouns, see Hetzron 1994, and § 24.4.5.2 for an example).

The adverbial ending *-ŋa* 'in the manner of, like', on the other hand, always has the same tone as the preceding syllable (final vowels of stems drop): *mur-ŋa* 'like a village' and *múr-ŋá* 'like a snake'.

The other case-endings have their own tones.

24.4.5. Tonal phenomena in nominals

Nominals possess a lexically determined tone pattern which is constant except for the few illustrated in § 24.4.5.1. High-Mid sequences within a stem are very rare; I only found a reduplicative *bádbaday* 'dove', *óyay-i* 'ice', and *cəmark"-í* 'eyelash'.[16]

Five parameters are to be used to determine the nominal classes (also including adjectives). Two of them apply only to a handful of nouns.

---

14. Other verb-classes still have the original *-t-*. Second persons and Sg.3f. having the same morphological marking is a feature of Afroasiatic prefix-conjugations. The Cushitic conjugational suffixes come from original prefix-conjugated auxiliaries.

15. In Awngi suffix-conjugations the person-marker never stands alone.

16. Could this be a compound (cf. *ərk"-í* 'tooth')? The interrogative pronoun *wóšiní* 'which' is clearly composite: with an adjectival derivative *-in-í*.

24.4.5.1. Tone Lowering
Most nominals have a consistent tone pattern, the same all through the inflections. However, a few have a Mid-(Mid-)High tone pattern with the last High lowered before the plural ending or before the adverbial case-suffix (the first one is an Amharic borrowing, the third comes from Arabic):
   agér 'country', ager-ká 'countries', ager-ŋa 'as a country'
   areméc 'embers', pl.: aremec-ká
   firísí 'horse', pl.: feres-ka
Note that the last noun has Mid tone on the plural ending.

24.4.5.2. Stem stress (see end of § 24.3.3)
For a few nominals that have only Mid tones, High plural ending and Mid accusative suffix, the stress may not leave the stem: g'uzg-u-des 'from that$_{masc.}$ of the stomach', as against gurgóm-'u-des 'from that of the neck', which exhibits the majority behavior.

24.4.5.3. Post-stem vowel
The feminine ending may be -a or -á, according to the class. The corresponding masculine may end in -i/-í with the same tone or in a consonant.

24.4.5.4. Plural
The plural ending may be -ka or -ká, a further criterion for classification (cf. § 24.4.5.1).

24.4.5.5. Accusative
The accusative ending is -o/-ô after consonant, where the tone is as a classificatory factor. After masculine -i/-í, it merges with it yielding -e/-é, after another vowel it is -wa. These latter are thus not relevant for classification.

24.4.6. Tone in verbs
24.4.6.1. Tone patterns of stems
With only a few exceptions, no matter what the tone-pattern of the verb stem is, infinitives only have Mid tones. They end in -əŋ, most probably from Afroasiatic *m-.

As for the finite forms, most verbs have a constant tone-pattern for all the conjugations (I Mid and II High below). However, there are a few monosyllabic verbs, mainly prefix-conjugated ones and one suffix-conjugated (cewŋ) that have High tone in the Nonpast and forms derived therefrom, and a Mid one in the Past and its derivatives (III and IV below both have the Raising feature (§ 24.4.6.2), hence the *-ú-*). Moreover, a handful of verbs[17] have different tone-patterns according to the person within the conjugation (group V below):

	I	II	III	IV
Sg.3m.				
Indef.Nonpast	*des-é*	*tás-é*	*céw-é*	*y-ínt-é*
Def.Past	*des-y"à*	*tás-y"à*	*cew-úyà*	*y-int-úyà*
	'study'	'hit'	'do'	'come'

but

	V	
	Indef. Nonpast	Imperative
Sg.1/3m.	*gemé*	sg. *gém*
Sg.2/3f.	*gembé*	pl. *gemán*
Pl.1	*gémné*	
	'go down'	

24.4.6.2. Tonal influence on suffixes

Many verbs have the quirk of exerting a tonal influence on the first syllable of the subsequent suffix, doubtless the remnant of a dropped stem-final syllable, probably a vowel (a connective vowel in Bilin). Indeed, when there is no suffix, in the Sg.m. Imperative, a final *-i* carrying the tone projected from the root is added. When that syllable has the vowel required by the root anyhow, the rule applies vacuously. This allows a fivefold classification of the verbal roots:

(I) **Neutral**: roots that exert no influence on the subsequent syllable and thus allow the establishment of the basic tone of the suffixes.

(II) **Raising**: roots that require a Falling tone on the subsequent syllable if it is final (#), otherwise it will be High.

In the rest of the verb classes, the second persons and Sg.3f. are marked by a palatal element (§ 24.4.3):

(III) **Lowering**: roots that, except for Pl.1, require a Mid tone on the subsequent syllable. This is all monosyllabic verbs or reduplicative bisyllabic ones.

(IV) **3-Lowering**: roots that require a Mid tone on the subsequent syllable in the second persons and Sg.3f. only. Along with (I) and (II), this is a class with wide membership.

17. There are seven of them, all monosyllabic, four end in *-ŋ*, two in *-m*, and one in *-y* (*əyəŋ* 'give') where etymology would suggest a final **-w* [Kemant *iw-*, Xamir *yəw-*].

(V) **Raising-Lowering**: a root that require Mid tone on the subsequent syllable in the second persons and Sg.3f., and a Falling#/High one in all other persons. One verb only.

(VI) **Lowering-Raising**: a root where the Sg.3m./Pl.3 marker is palatal with Lowering, all the rest have Raising. One verb only.

(VII) **Partial Raising**: Raising in Sg.1 and in the second persons and Sg.3f. One verb only.

(VIII) **Partial Lowering**: Lowering in all second and third persons, but not in the first persons. Four verbs.

	I	II (R)	III (L)	IV (y-L)
Past Sg.3m.	des-ɣʷà	cew-úyà	zum-uyà	kantyʷà
Sg.3f.	des-tóɣʷà	cew-túyà	zum-iɣʷà	kant-iɣʷà
Nonpast Sg.3m.	des-é	céw-é	zum-e	kant-é
Sg.3f.	des-té	céw-té	zum-i	kant-i
Pl.1	des-né	céw-né	zum-né	kant-né
	'study'	'do'	'talk'	'see'

	V (RL)	VI (RL)	VII (PR)	VIII (PL)
Past Sg.3m.	beft-úyà	əs-iɣʷà	kəmbabl-iɣʷà	fəč-iyà
Sg.3f.	bift-iyà	əst-úyà	kəmbabəl-túyà	fəčt-iyà
Nonpast Sg.3m.	beft-é	əs-i	kəmbabl-i	fəč-i
Sg.3f.	bift-i	əst-é	kəmbabəl-tí	fəčt-i
Pl.1	bəftə-né	əsn-é	kəmbabəl-né	fəč-né
	'be hidden'	'weep'	'roll about'	'hate'

As we can see, Pl.1 is never affected by Lowering; in fact it is never affected at all. Not all instances of palatal second person/Sg.3f. marker have Lowering, but there is no Lowering without at least one palatal element at the end of the root. When this one is in the Sg.3m./Pl.3 form, there is always Lowering. Thus, as in the case of the Low tone (§ 24.3.3), Lowering must have something to do with the palatal element *i losing its segmental character in several contexts. As for Raising, it has its parallel in Bilin, in the verb class where the connective vowel carries the stress (Palmer 1957: 138 [ii]).

The causative verb *yigʷcəŋ* 'save (for later)', the causative of the prefix-verb *yiguŋ* 'remain' represents a mixed type: Mid tone and Raising-Lowering for the past, and High tone with neutral suffix s for the Nonpast. Finally, Awngi has 13 short roots consisting of one consonant (in half the cases with a labial appendix ʷ). They are idiosyncratic and need no analysis in a general study.

Bibliography

Appleyard. D. L. 1975. "A Descriptive Outline of Kemant." *Bulletin of the School of Oriental and African Studies* 38: 316–50.

———. 1984. "The Internal Classification of the Agaw Languages: A Comparative and Historical Phonology." In *Current Progress in Afro-Asiatic Linguistics: Proceedings of the Third International Hamito-Semitic Congress*, ed. James Bynon (Current Issues in L inguistic Theory 28). Amsterdam: Benjamins.

———. 1987. "A Grammatical Sketch of Khamtanga, I–II." *Bulletin of the School of Oriental and African Studies* 50: 241–66, 470–507.

———. 1992. "Vocalic Ablaut and Aspect Marking in the Verb in Agaw." *Journal of Afroasiatic Languages* 3: 126–50.

Conti Rossini, Carlo. 1905. "Noti sugli agaw, II. Appunti sulla lingua Awiya del Danghela." *Giornale della Società Asiatica Italiana* 18: 103–94.

———. 1912. *La langue des Kemant en Abyssinie* (Sprachkommission der Kaiserl. Akademie der Wissenschaften 4). Vienna: Alfred Hölder.

Dolgopolski, Aron B. 1973. *Сравнительно-Историческая Фонетика Кушитских Языков.* Moscow: Nauka.

Diakonoff, Igor M. 1992. "Proto-Afrasian and Old Akkadian: A Study in Historical Phonetics." *Journal of Afroasiatic Languages* 4: 1–133.

Greenberg, Joseph H. 1966. "Some Universals of Grammar with Particular Reference to the Order of Meaningful Elements." In *Universals of Language*, ed. J. H. Greenberg, pp. 73–113. Cambridge: MIT Press.

Hetzron, Robert. 1969. *The Verbal System of Southern Agaw* (University of California Publications, Near Eastern Studies 12). Berkeley and Los Angeles: University of California Press.

———. 1976. "The Agaw Languages." *Afroasiatic Linguistics* 3/3: 31–75.

———. 1978. "The Nominal System of Awngi (Southern Agaw)." *Bulletin of the School of Oriental and African Studies* 41: 121–41.

———. 1994. "A Note on Genitival Agreement in Awngi." In *Double Case*, ed. Frans Plank. New York: Oxford University Press.

Johnson, C. Douglas. 1972. *Formal Aspects of Phonological Description* (Monographs on Linguistic Analysis 3). The Hague: Mouton.

Palmer, F. R. 1957. "The Verb in Bilin." *Bulletin of the School of Oriental and African Studies* 19: 131–59.

———. 1958. "The Noun in Bilin." *Bulletin of the School of Oriental and African Studies* 21: 376–91.

———. 1959. "The Verb Classes of Agaw (Awiya)." *Mitteilungen des Instituts für Orientforschung* 7: 270–97.

———. 1960. "An Outline of Bilin Phonology." *Atti del Convegno Internazionale de Studi Etiopici, Roma, 2–4 Aprile 1959*, pp. 109–15 (Problemi attuali di scienza e di cultura 48). Rome: Accademia Nazionale dei Lincei.

Reinisch, Leo. 1887. *Die Bilin-Sprache*, II. *Wörterbuch der Bilin-Sprache*. Vienna: Alfred Hölder.

Sasse, Hans-Jürgen. 1979. "The Consonant Phonemes of Proto-East Cushitic (PEC): A first approximation." *Afroasiatic Linguistics* 7/1: 1–67.

Chapter 25
Oromo Phonology
Maria-Rosa Lloret
Universitat de Barcelona

25.1. Introduction

Oromo, formerly known as Galla, is a Cushitic language of the Afroasiatic family. Within Cushitic, Oromo, as well as Somali, Saho-Afar, Arbore-Dasenech, Burji-Deleba, Boni, and Rendille, belongs to the Lowland East Cushitic group. It is spoken in the southern part of Ethiopia (where together with Amharic it is the most important language) and northern Kenya, with native speakers living in Somalia and Sudan, too. Though it is one of the most widely spoken languages of Africa with upwards of seven million speakers (Heine et al. 1981), some figures mentioning more than ten (Gragg 1976) and up to twenty (Ali & Zaborski 1990) million speakers are consired high (Bender & Eteffa 1976).

25.2. Characteristics of the present study

The present study sets out a description of the phonological system of Oromo. It includes a presentation of the sounds and phonemes of the language and the way they tend to combine, as well as a description and classification of regular and contextually well-defined processes of sound change. Suprasegmental patterns are described in less detail, since this is a field which deserves further investigation. Issues strictly related to specific morphological processes, such as reduplication and lengthening/shortening of final segments concomitant with certain morphemes (i.e., length as a component of a specific morpheme), will not be described. The work benefits from previous descriptions of Oromo (see *References*, among others) and tries to systematically put together their findings, especially on issues about which scholars are most at variance.

On the subject of dialect differentiation, Oromo scholars agree on the mutual intelligibility between them, though, with the only exception of Stroomer's (1987) major dialectal study on the Southern area, the status and boundaries among the various dialects have not been clearly established.

Oromo studies usually refer to three major groups, namely Western, Eastern, and Southern. The Western group roughly includes Northern, Western, and Central dialects (cf. Heine 1981: 15); however, sometimes a large transitional area (cf. Gragg 1976: 172) or even a further Northern group (cf. Bryan 1948: 21–22) are distinguished. In this study, the description is based on the Western dialects, among which Mechaa (spoken in the Wellegga area) is the major representative. Dialectal variation will be pointed out whenever significant correspondences can be established through the descriptions of previous works.[1]

Since the present study is descriptive, the reader will not find methodologically sophisticated analyses of the phonological processes. During the description, a distinction will be made between phonetics and phonemics. Phonemic notation will only include those sounds which are distinctive in the language, i.e., may cause differences in the meaning. The characterization of the phonological processes will be done on the grounds of the regularities observed from the phonetic data. Abstract representations will be disregarded. Nevertheless, whenever Oromo provides interesting data for linguistic research on the nature of phonological representations, it will be pointed out.

25.3. Segmental phonology

Oromo has the vowels and consonants shown in Tables 25-1 and 25-2.

Table 25-1. Oromo Vowels

i, ii		u, uu
	e, ee	o, oo
	a, aa	

In order to facilitate the exposition some simplified symbols are used. A list of the corresponding IPA phonetic symbols and the corresponding symbols in Latin script as used by most of the Oromo is presented in Table 25-3.

---

1. Throughout this work, the description of the Western dialect is based on the Mechaa variety as described in Gragg (1976, 1982) and Lloret (1988, 1989); the description of Eastern is based on the Harar variety as described in Owens (1980, 1985) and Ali & Zaborski (1990), and the description of Southern is based on the Orma, Waata, and Boraana varieties as described in Owens (1980), Heine (1981), and Stroomer (1987).

Table 25-2. Oromo Consonants

	Labial	Dento-Alveolar	Palatal	Velar	Laryngeal
Stops					
Voiceless		t	č	k	
Voiced	b	d	ǰ	g	
Ejective	p'	t'	č'	k'	'
Implosive		d'			
Fricatives					
Voiceless	f	s	š	(x)[a]	h
Sonorants					
Nasal	m	n	ñ		
Liquid		l r			
Glide	w		y		

[a] /x/ occurs as a phoneme in Eastern Oromo, which corresponds to /k/ in other dialects. It might also occur as allophone of /k/ in other varieties (see the description of /k/ in § 25.3.2).

Table 25-3. Oromo Transcriptions

	IPA	Latin Script
c corresponds to	t͡ʃ	c
p'	p'	ph
č'	t͡ʃ'	ch
'	ʔ	'
š	ʃ	sh
ǰ	d͡ʒ	j
t'	t'	th
k'	k'	kh
d'	ɗ	dh
ñ	ɲ	ny

Geminate ejectives and implosives are transcribed with glottalization in the second consonant only, e.g. /tt'/ or /dd'/. The same holds of heterorganic ejective clusters, e.g. /pt'/.

25.3.1. Vowels

Oromo makes a phonemic distinction between five short and five long vowels, which occur either within the word or at the end of the word. The minimal pairs in (1) exemplify this two-way distinction. Sequences of non-identical vowels do not occur.[2]

(1)   d'aba   'I am unable'   d'aaba   'I plant'
      egaa   'then'   eegaa   'watch! (pl.)'
      d'isa   'I stretch skin'   d'iisa   'I leave'
      boruu   'east'   booruu   'muddy'
      d'ufii 'coming'   d'uufii 'fart'

Unstressed short vowels tend to be laxer and more centralized than their longer counterparts. This distinction is especially clear for the non-rounded series /a, e, i/, while the phonetic difference for the rounded vowels /o, u/ tends to be purely quantitative.[3]

(2)   nama   [námə]'man'   namni   [námnɨ]   'man+NOM'
      boruu [borúu]'east'   d'ufii [d'ufíi] 'coming'

This short/long vowel contrast is phonetically realized both within a word and at the end of a word when it is not followed by a pause. In pre-pausal position there is also a two-way vowel contrast, but this has generally been described as a contrast between voiceless vowels vs. short vowels with final glottal stop. There is, however, a lot of variation in the realization of these final vowels among speakers and dialects, especially in relation to short vowels, which are better described as phonetic tendencies.

---

2. Although this is true for all dialects morpheme-internally, non-identical abutting vowels exceptionally arise through morphophonemic changes in some dialects. Western dialects never show sequences of non-identical vowels. Eastern dialects, though, show diphthongs originated by morphophonemic changes (e.g. *hak'+sis+a* → *haisisa* or *heesisa* 'I make wipe'). Southern dialects show bisyllabic vocalic sequences also originated across morpheme boundaries (e.g. *mač'aw+e* → *mač'ae* 'he was drunk'). (These issues are further discussed in §§ 25.3.4 and 25.3.5.)
3. Stroomer (1987: 27) reports that this lax realization also holds of /o/ for the Southern dialects.

In pre-pausal position, long vowels are phonetically shortened and usually closed by a glottal stop,[4] except original long vowels that should be lengthened through grammatical marking (3a).[5]

(3) a. *gogaa* [goga'], pre-pausally 'skin'
      [gogaa], elsewhere
      (Cf. *gogaa* [gogaa], always 'skin+GEN')
   b. *namaa* [nama'], pre-pausally 'man+GEN'
      [namaa], elsewhere
      (Cf. *nama* 'man')

The realization of pre-pausal short vowels shows a larger number of phonetic surface contrasts, though the following tendencies have been observed:

(i) Short vowels tend to be pronounced as reduced, i.e. less audible, unless they bear a grammatical low tone (4a).[6] (Reduced vowels are indicated by superscript in the phonetic transcription.)

(ii) /i/ goes a step further in the reduction and may be completely deleted at the end of a word, unless it is preceded by two consonants or it carries a low tone. In this case, it generally reduces (4b).

(iii) All short vowels may be pronounced with different degree of voicing according to the previous consonant: they tend to be voiced or partially devoiced when the preceding consonant is voiced but fully devoiced when the preceding consonant is voiceless (4c).[7]

(iv) Reduced vowels tend to be pronounced as voiceless, while full short vowels are not (4d).

---

4. In Southern Oromo, these pre-pausal long vowels may be realized as short or as vowel plus laryngeal consonant plus (reduced) voiceless vowel, e.g. *garaa* [gara], [gara'a], [garaha] 'belly' (cf. Stroomer 1987: 28).
5. On the possible interactions between the realization of final vowels and grammatical marking, see Stroomer (1987) for Southern Oromo and Lloret (1988, 1989) for Western Oromo. In the Orma and Waata Southern dialects, these grammatically lengthened long vowels may dissimilate, e.g., *hattuu* 'thief', *hattua* 'thief+GEN', originating one of the exceptional cases of non-identical vocalic sequences that occur in the language.
6. This does not always hold of the Harar Eastern variety, where pre-pausal short vowels are usually pronounced like long vowels, i.e. with a final glottal stop (cf. Owens 1985: 10, Ali & Zaborski 1990: xxii).
7. Though Harar tends to pronounce pre-pausal short vowels with a final glottal stop (see previous footnote), devoiced realizations also occur (cf. Owens 1985: 23).

(v) Reduced vowels, especially if they are devoiced, tend to be dropped in normal connected speech (4e).[8]

(4) a. *mana* [manᵃ] 'house', *mana* [manà] 'it's a house'
 b. *ilkaani* [ilkaan] 'tooth', *inni* [innⁱ] 'he', *ilkaani* [ilkaanⁱ] 'it's a tooth'
 c. *mana* [manᵃ], [manᵃ̥] 'house'; *bofa* [bofᵃ] 'snake'
 d. *mana* [manᵃ] 'house', *mana* [maná] 'it's a house'
 e. *man(a) guddaa sadii arge* 'he saw three big houses'

In sum, the phonemic distinction that Oromo makes between short and long vowels is phonetically realized in a number of different ways, though in any case none of these allophones are to be considered phonemes, neither is there any reason to recognize a larger phonemic length contrast. The only change that systematically occurs is shortening of pre-pausal long vowels. The strongest tendency that has been observed is reduction of final /i/, which may or may not be completely dropped, depending on the dialect and the context in which it occurs.

25.3.2. *Consonants*

In general, consonants occur single in initial position while intervocalically they may occur single, geminated, or as members of biconsonantal clusters. Phonemically, all Oromo words end in a vowel, though, as previously mentioned, this vowel may be phonetically dropped under certain conditions. Restrictions on the distribution of some consonants as well as their allophonic variation are presented below.

All consonants occur initially and medially, except /'/ which never occurs initially (although it is true that a prothetic ['] is added to vowel-initial words in absolute initial position) and /h/ which, except in Eastern Oromo, only occurs initially.[9] /h/ also has the peculiarity that in some, but not all, words it can be dropped and, according to Oromo scholars, under no clear conditioning (5a) (cf. Gragg 1976: 174, Stroomer 1987: 16). The interchangeability of /h/ with zero seems to be a matter of idiolect (cf. Stroomer 1987: 16).

---

8. In this respect, there is also quite a big amount of dialectal variation, i.e. final unstressed non-low-toned /a/ tends to be deleted in the Arussi Eastern dialect but maintained in the Harar Eastern variety (cf. Owens 1985). It also usually drops in the Boraana and Waata Southern varieties (cf. Owens 1980, Heine 1981), and less frequently in the Western dialects.
9. The phonemic status of the glottal stop has been questioned, since in some dialects the two laryngeal consonants are in total complementary distribution and thus their occurrences are fully predictable (cf. Stroomer 1987: 52). This does not seem to be the case of Western and Eastern dialects, though it is true that its full phonemic status is at least problematic and deserves further research.

Thus, it is attributed to the lexicon, not to the phonemic inventory of the language. Only one minimal pair of initial /h/ versus initial vowel has been found (5b) (cf. Stroomer 1987: 16).

(5) a. *harree*, *arree 'donkey'   *harka*, *arka* 'hand'
       hima, *ima 'I tell'   *hirkoo*, *irkoo* 'back'
    b. *hafa* 'I remain behind'   *afa* 'I spread out
                                         (to dry in the sun)'

All consonants except /h/ can occur single or geminate. In the Western and Southern dialects, this follows from the fact that geminate consonants only occur in medial position and /h/ only occurs initially. Geminate /'/ only occurs in one instance and only in Western Oromo, i.e. *(h)o''uu* 'to be warm', which corresponds to geminate /w/ in other dialects, i.e. *owwuu*. In Southern Oromo, there are no instances of geminate /š/, /ñ/, and /p'/ either (cf. Stroomer 1987: 11). The following list of minimal pairs illustrates the opposition of short versus long consonants.

(6)   *badaa* 'red soil under fire'   *baddaa* 'highland'
       butaa 'snatcher'   *buttaa* 'period of time
                                                   of the Gada system'
       hod'a 'I suck'   *hodd'a* 'I sew'
       diree 'necklace'   *dirree* 'hill'
       kalee 'kidney'   *kallee* 'child's garment'
       d'owa 'valley'   *d'owwa* 'I avoid'

In addition to the consonant phonemes presented at the beginning of § 25.3, some Oromo words contain /z/ and /p/, but they clearly are loans. In general, loanwords which have /z/ tend to be assimilated in the language as /s/ (occasionally also as /ǰ/) (7a), while /p/ tends to be assimilated as /f/ (occasionally also as /p'/ or /b/) (7b). More recently, some loans with /v/ have been introduced in the language, which also tend to be assimilated as /f/ (7c).

(7) a. *muuza*, *muusa* 'banana' (from Arabic, Amharic *muz*)
       Cf. *aǰaǰa* 'I command' (Western) (from Amharic *azzázä*)
    b. *poolisii*, *foolisii* 'police' (from Amharic *polis*, ultimately of European origin)
       Cf. *p'eesaa*, *beesee* 'money' (Southern) (from Swahili *pesa*)
    c. *vitaamini*, *fitaamini* 'vitamin' (from English)

[p] also occurs as an allophone of /b/ when it is followed by a voiceless consonant (see § 25.3.7).

(8) *obs₊a* [opsa] (Western) 'I endure', *obsa* [opsa] (Southern: Boraana) 'patience'

č'ab₊sa [č'apsa] (Western, Southern) 'I break' (transitive)

Cf. *č'ab₊a* [č'aba] (Western, Southern) 'I break' (intransitive)

č'ap'₊a [č'ap'a] (Eastern, occasionally in Southern) 'I break' (intransitive)

/p'/ never occurs in initial position, except in some loans which show /p/ in the original language. It may appear as /b/, too.

(9) *p'eesaa* (Southern: Orma), *beesee* (Southern: Boraana, Waata) 'money' (from Swahili *pesa*) (cf. Stroomer 1987: 20)

Oromo shows the peculiarity of displaying a stop system which has /p'/ and /b/, but a gap for /p/. According to universal typologies, this is a rare occurrence since glottalized segments are functionally the weaker members of the stop series and thus one would expect a system with a gap in the ejective series but a complete simple series (cf. Gamkrelidze 1978: 17). Oromo does follow universal claims in that among voiceless stops a gap in the labial position is natural because /p/ is the marked member of the series (cf. Gamkrelidze 1978: 15). Oromo also patterns with other Afroasiatic languages in having the absence of /p/ but the presence of the corresponding voiceless fricative /f/. Thus, one can look at this peculiarity of the labial series from a comparative point of view and claim that /f/ fills the labial gap, so that one ends with a three-way contrast *f/b/p'*. Under this interpretation, the absence of /p/ is no longer to be considered such a rarity.

/d'/ is more or less retroflex in most dialects.[10] In some lexical items, /d'/ alternates with zero. This alternation is lexically restricted and may vary according to the dialect, e.g.

(10) a. *d'uumma, uumma* (Western) 'peninsula' (cf. Gragg 1982: 132)
 b. *d'agamsa, agamsa* (Southern: Boraana) '*Carissa edulis*' (cf. Stroomer 1987: 16)
 c. *d'arga* (Southern: Orma, Waata), *arga* (Western and Southern: Boorana), *arka* (Eastern) 'I see' (cf. Stroomer 1987: 15, Gragg 1982: 19, Owens 1985: 254)
 d. *d'ameelaa* (Southern: Boraana), *ameeloo* (Southern: Orma) 'milk container' (cf. Stroomer 1987: 16)

10. In Andrzejewski's (1957: 355–56) study on the Boraana Southern dialect, /d'/ is described as fully implosive without retroflexion. Stroomer (1987: 15), however, emphasizes its retroflex articulation in all the Southern varieties and even doubts of its glottalized character. He also points out that it may have a flap pronunciation between vowels.

The fact that Oromo has /t'/ as well as /ɗ/ is another rarity, because if a language displays an ejective series it usually does not have implosives at the same point of articulation. In fact, most other Cushitic languages only present either the implosive/retroflex segment (e.g. Saho-Afar, Somali, Konso) or the ejective one (e.g. Hadiyya). Only one other Cushitic language presents both segments, namely Dullay (Gawwada and Gollango). (Cf. Sasse 1979.)[11]

/š/ is not widely distributed. It alternates with [s] in a good number of words (11a).[12] In some lexical items, this alternation is dialectally determined (11b).

(11) a. *išeeni, iseeni* (Western) 'she'
bišaani, bisaani (Western) 'water'
b. *išiini* (Southern: Orma, Waata), *isiini* (Southern: Boraana) 'she'
šeeftii (Southern: Boraana), *seeftii* (Southern: Orma) 'knife' (cf. Stroomer 1987:20)

/š/ is found in initial and intervocalic position. It occurs initially in relatively few words. It does not occur in syllable-final position except in exceptional cases, i.e., in some loans and interjections where it always occurs geminated (12a) or as a result of lexical reduplication (12b).

(12) a. *aššabo* 'salt' (from Amharic)
iššoo 'bravo!'
aššaami 'hello!'
b. *bušbušii* 'very thick beer' (Western)

/ñ/ and /y/ are not very frequent either. They also occur initially in few words, especially the nasal. Neither of them, unless geminated, phonetically occurs in syllable final position. Moreover, there are relatively few cases of geminate /ñ/ or /y/. /č/ is not found in initial position except in one interjection (i.e., *čee* 'command to donkeys') and in some loans (e.g., *čiifa* 'chief', *čaačii* 'church', both from English). Unlike these palatals, /j/ and /č'/ are widely distributed and occur in a large number of words. /čč/ is fairly common, though in nearly all cases it arises from morphophonological alternations (see § 25.3.4.8).

---

11. Within the Chadic family, implosives and ejectives at the same point of articulation are attested in Goemai and related languages.
12. The shift from /š/ to /s/ is a general tendency of the total Ethiopian area (cf. Sasse 1975: 261–62). In some dialects, e.g. Boraana, /š/ has been almost eradicated in native words. In the peripheral dialects it remains here and there vacillating with [s]. This has led to the replacement of /š/ by /s/ in individual dialects during the last few centuries.

/k/ sometimes spirantizes into [x]. In Western Oromo, it is never spirantized. Within the Southern dialects, /k/ becomes [x] in initial and intervocalic position commonly in the Boraana variety but rarely in Orma and Waata (cf. Stroomer 1987: 17). In Eastern Oromo, however, /k/, with very few exceptions, occurs only geminate or as the second consonant of a cluster. In all other contexts [x] occurs, which has phonemic status in this dialect (cf. Owens 1985: 15).

(13) *muka* 'tree': *mu*[k]*a*, always in Western, commonly in Orma and Waata, occasionally in Boraana
mu[x]*a*, commonly in Boraana, occasionally in Orma and Waata
muxa 'tree': *mu*[x]*a*, always in Eastern

25.3.3. Consonant clusters

Oromo has abutting consonants in medial position. All the sequences are biconsonantal, because the language does not allow sequences of more than two consonants. The syllable break is almost always between the two consonants. In Western Oromo and in the Waata Southern variety there are few exceptions and they all occur in loanwords (14a). Harar Eastern and Boraana and Orma Southern varieties also show occurrences of monosyllabic /br/ clusters, which correspond to bisyllabic /rb/ and /rf/ clusters in Western and Waata Southern dialects, respectively; in Western Oromo monosyllabic [br] occasionally occurs in free variation with [rb] (14b). Other instances of /l/ occurring after labials /b, f/ are reported for Eastern and Southern dialects. These sequences are pronounced with a syllable break between the two consonants in careful speech but this break is fairly maintained in connected normal speech; Western dialects occasionally show /lb/ sequences in free variation with [bl] (14c).

(14) a. *kristaana* 'Christian' (European origin)
kabriitii 'match' (from Amharic)
b. *dubra* (Eastern; Southern: Boraana, Orma; occasionally in Western) 'girl'
Cf. *durba* (usually in Western), *durfa* (Southern: Waata)
c. *kofla* (Southern), *xofla* (Eastern) 'I laugh'
ablee (Eastern, Southern, occasionally in Western) 'knife'
Cf. *kolfa* (Western), *albee* (usually in Western)

Most of the consonant clusters that appear within a morpheme in non-loanwords involve at least a liquid or a nasal in first position. Clusters where the first consonant is /n/ are phonetically homorganic (see § 25.3.7.1).

(15) *leenč'a* [leeñč'a] 'lion'
danfa [daɱfa] 'it boils'

/ñ/ shows a strong restriction on its distribution: it only exceptionally occurs in some Western items, where it exclusively combines with a following glottal stop and alternates in free variation with a geminate palatal sequence (e.g., *mañ'ee, maññee* 'lower part of leg'). The restricted distribution of /ñ/ follows from a strong restriction that holds of all palatal consonants, namely a palatal consonant cannot be followed by a consonant: /š, č, č'/ never occur as the first element of a non-geminate consonantal cluster;[13] /y/, like /ñ/, exceptionally occurs in few Western items combining with a glottal stop and aternating with geminate sequences, e.g. *bay'ee, bayyee* 'much, many'); /y/ also exceptionally occurs in the Waata Southern variety, e.g. *toyba* 'seven' (cf. *torba* in Western, Eastern, and Boraana Southern, and *tolba* or *tolp'a* in Orma Southern) (cf. Stroomer 1987: 25).

Among other possible consonant clusters, it is important to note the frequent occurrence of the sequence /f/ plus consonant. This has a straightforward explanation in Oromo, since /s/ regularly changed into /f/ when immediately preceded by another consonant. This labialization morphophonemically still applies in most dialects (see § 25.3.4.1). The sequence /s/ plus consonant is only found in loanwords, e.g.

(16) *maskootii* 'window' (from Amharic)
masgiida (Western), *meskitii* (Southern) 'mosque' (from Arabic)
misraaččoo (Western) 'good news' (from Amharic)

Other possible combinations do not occur often and very few examples are found, some of which just occur in one of the varieties: /kt/, /ks/, /k's/, /kn/, /bs/, /bd/, /bǰ/, /gd/, and /gn/ in Western Oromo (cf. Lloret 1988: 22–23); /bs/ and /bǰ/ in Boraana, /dy/ in Waata, and /n/ plus /y/ in all Southern dialects (cf. Stroomer 1987: 25).

25.3.4. *Morphophonemic changes involving consonant clusters*
Consonant clusters accross morpheme boundaries arise only between the final consonant of a stem and /n/, /t/, or /s/, or between /n/ and a consonant-initial stem. The first two cases originate within both verbal and nominal morphology while the last two only originate within verbal morphology.

---

13. /š/ exceptionally occurs in preconsonantal position in one lexically reduplicated word, i.e., *bušbušii* 'very thick beer' (Western).

Some changes are grammatically restricted since they only occur in isolated morphemes; others are unrestricted, i.e., the morphophonological changes involved are independent of the grammatical status of the forms. Changes involving stems ending in a glide or in a laryngeal consonant will be independently treated (see § 25.3.5), because they are quite complex and show a large amount of dialectal variation.

Oromo has two changes that specifically occur in nominative forms. In Oromo, nouns and descriptive adjectives have distinct nominative forms, which are formed by suffixation of a marker /ni/ (/ti/ in some feminine forms ending in a short vowel).[14] When this suffix is attached to a form ending in a long vowel, no change occurs (17a); however, nouns and adjectives ending in a short /a/ drop this vowel (17b).

(17) a. *saree+ni* → *sareen(i)*[15]   'dog+NOM'
       adii+ni → *adiin(i)*   'white+NOM'
   b. *nama+ni* → *namni*   'man+NOM'
       lafa+ti → *lafti*   'earth+NOM'

The nasal of the nominative suffix may optionally assimilate to the point of articulation of a preceding /m/.

(18) *nam(a)+ni* → *namni, nammi*   'man+NOM'
     č'oom(a)+ni → *č'oomni, č'oommi*   'fat+NOM'
     Cf. *tum+na* → *tumna*, *tumma   'we beat'

Unlike these two changes, which are restricted to the nominative suffix,[16] other morphophonological changes are unrestricted, though some are only found within verbal morphology because, as previously mentioned, some environments do not originate within nominal morphology. Only changes which can be ascertained not to occur in nominal morphology will be considered to be restricted to verbal forms.

---

14. In order to facilitate the exposition, /ni/ and /ti/ are considered the basic nominative suffixes, though variation in vowel length and combinations of both (e.g. *ti(i)ni*) are reported for specific varieties (cf. Owens 1985: 100–2, Stroomer 1987: 167, Lloret 1988: 116–18).

15. On the phonetic realization of this final /i/, which bears a high tone, see § 25.3.1. In the examples, this vowel is given between parentheses when it usually drops.

16. A further morphophonemic restricted change could be considered to occur in nominative forms, namely /n/ drops after an abutting consonantal cluster, e.g. *harka+ni* → *hark+ni* → *harki* 'hand+NOM', *duumessa+ni* → *duumess+ni* → *duumessi* 'cloud+NOM' (cf. Gragg 1976: 183, Lloret 1988: 118). This analysis, though, presupposes a certain degree of abstraction, since these cases can also be interpreted as forms that merely attach a separate nominative suffix /i/ (cf. Owens 1985: 101, Stroomer 1987: 167, Banti 1988: 47).

25.3.4.1. s-Labialization

/s/ becomes [f] when it is followed by a consonant. This change always takes place in Western and Eastern Oromo and in the Boraana and Orma Southern varieties, though the alternation with [s] is optional (19a). In the Waata Southern dialect, however, /s/ tends to be either maintained or (partially) assimilated to the following consonant (19b).

(19) a. **Western, Eastern, and Boraana and Orma Southern varieties:**
    ajjees+na → *ajjeefna* (occasionally: *ajjeesna*) 'we kill'
    čiis+ta → *čiifta* (occasionally: *čiista*) 'you lie down'
  b. **Waata Southern variety:**
    huk'+s+ta → *huk'ista, huk'ibta, huk'itta* 'you make thin'
    gudd+s+na → *guddisna, guddimna* 'we raise children'

25.3.4.2. Nasal Total Assimilation

/n/ completely assimilates to a preceding liquid (20a) and to a following liquid or glide (20b).[17] In Southern Oromo, /n/ also assimilates to a following /s/ (20c).

(20) a. *gaal(a)+ni* → *gaalli* 'camel+NOM'
    gal+na → *galla* 'we enter'
    moor(a)+ni → *moorri* 'fat+NOM'
    mur+na → *murra* 'we cut'
  b. *hin+latu* → *hillatu* 'it does not sprout'
    hin+rafu → *hirrafu* 'he does not sleep'
    hin+wareegu → *hiwwareegu* 'he does not promise'
    hin+yaadu → *hiyyaadu* 'he does not think'
  c. *hin+sirba* → *hissirba* 'he does not dance' (Southern dialects only)

25.3.4.3. Glottalization

/t/ assimilates in ejection to a preceding consonant. In the case of a preceding velar, other changes may occur (see § 25.3.4.6) (21a). In the Southern varieties, the ejection is occasionaly lost (21b).

(21) a. *čap'+ta* → *čapt'a* (Eastern, occasionally in Southern) 'it breaks'
    Cf. *čab+ta* → *čabda* (Western, usually in Southern)
    fit'+ta → *fitt'a* (Eastern, Western)[18] 'you enter'
    hiik'+ta → *hiikt'a* (Western) 'you go'; *hiitt'a* (Eastern)

---

17. It should be pointed out that Stroomer (1987: 41) does not mention assimilation of /n/ to a following glide for the Boraana Southern dialect.
18. In the Southern varieties /t'/ is treated as a double consonant (see § 25.3.4.9).

b. *d'ek'+ta → d'ett'a, d'etta* (Southern: Boraana, Orma) 'you go'; *d'eča* (Southern: Waata)

In Western Oromo, ejection also spreads over the second consonant in the case of an original /t'+s/ sequence, which becomes [čč'] through a palato-affrication process described below.

(22) *lit'+siis+a → fičč'iisa* (Western) 'I make enter'
   Cf. *t'ut'+siis+a → t'usiisa* (Eastern) 'I make suck'

25.3.4.4. Voice assimilation between stops

/t/ assimilates in voicing to a preceding stop. In the case of a preceding velar, other changes may occur (see § 25.3.4.6) (23a). This change does not affect /d'/, which behaves like a voiceless consonant and does not induce voice assimilation (see § 25.3.4.6). In the Southern varieties, the voiceless character of /t/ is sometimes optionally maintained: it is never maintained when it is preceded by a coronal, but it may be maintained in all dialects after a labial stop, [bt], and in Orma and Waata after a velar stop (23b) (cf. Stroomer 1987: 46).

(23) a. *did+ta →*   *didda* 'you refuse'
     k'ab+ta →   *k'abda* 'you have'
              k'adda (occasionally in Waata Southern variety)
     ǰab+tuu →   *ǰabduu* 'strong (fem.)'
              ǰadduu (occasionally in Waata Southern variety)
     d'iig+ta → *d'iigda* (Western) 'you bleed'
              d'iidda (Southern: Boraana, Orma)
              d'iiydda (Eastern)
              d'iiǰa (Southern: Waata)
     mid'aag+tuu →mid'aadduu (Southern: Boraana, Orma) 'nice (fem.)'
              mid'aaǰuu (Southern: Waata)
     ǰaǰ+ta →   *ǰaǰǰa* (Western) 'you boast' (no examples reported in other dialects)
   b. *did+ta →*   *didta
     k'ab+ta →   *k'abta* (occasionally in Southern)
     d'iig+ta → *d'iitta* (occasionally in Orma Southern variety)
              d'iiča (occasionally in Waata Southern variety)[19]

---

19. Stroomer (1987: 44) points out that /g+t/ becoming [č] instead of [ǰ] might be explained in terms of analogy to other verbs. In general, no example with voiceless alternant is reported within nominal morphology (e.g. *deg(a)+ti → deǰi*, *deči 'people+NOM', in Waata).

25.3.4.5. Palatal assimilation

A consonant preceded by a stem ending in a palatal consonant becomes palatal, too (24a). It may undergo further changes, i.e., a coronal totally assimilates to a following nasal (24b) while /t/ completely assimilates to a preceding palatal (24c). Very few examples are found because of the limited distribution of palatals.

(24) a. d'eereeñ(a)+ni → d'eereeññi (Eastern) 'tallness+NOM'
b. ǰaǰ+na → ǰañña (Western) 'we boast'
c. ǰaǰ+ta → ǰaǰǰa (Western) 'you boast'

In the Waata Southern variety, a velar stop plus /n/ becomes [ñ]. This process is probably related to the palatalization induced by a velar stop over a preceding vowel in Eastern Oromo. (See § 25.3.4.6.)

(25) beek+na → beeña (Southern: Waata) 'we know'
d'ek'+na → d'eña (Southern: Waata) 'we go'
neek'(a)+ni → neeñi (Southern: Waata) 'lion+NOM'
d'ug+na → d'uña (Southern: Waata) 'we drink'
lag(a)+ni → lañi (Southern: Waata) 'river+NOM'

25.3.4.6. Stop consonant assimilation

There is a large amount of variation among dialects with respect to the degree of assimilation allowed between a stop and a following /t/ or /n/. The only change that systematically occurs in all dialects is total assimilation of a non-glottalized coronal stop to a following nasal, though examples with final /ǰ/ are only reported for Western Oromo (26). If a stop is followed by /t/, voice assimilation applies as previously described, cf. (23).

(26) fid+na → finna 'we bring', haad(a)+ni → haanni 'rope+NOM'
bit+na → binna 'we buy', hantuut(a)+ni → hantuunni 'rat+NOM'
ǰaǰ+na → ǰañña (Western) 'we boast'

/d'/ completely assimilates to /t/ and /n/ in Eastern and Southern Oromo; in the latter, the previous vowel may be short, in which case it lengthens (27a). /t'/ only assimilates in the Eastern varieties (27b).

(27) a. fuud'+ta → fuutta 'you take', haad'+ti → haatti 'mother+NOM'
(Eastern, Southern)
fed'+na → feenna (Southern) 'we want'
feed'+na → feenna (Eastern)
Cf. fuud'+ta → fuuta, haad'+ti → haati, fed'+na → feena (Western)

b. *fiit'+na* → *fiinna* (Eastern) 'we finish'
Cf. *fit'+na* → *find'a* (Western), *fit'ina* (Southern)

If a velar stop precedes /t/ or /n/ no change other than voice assimilation and glottalization occurs in Western Oromo. However, in Eastern and in Boraana and Orma Southern, the stop completely assimilates to the following consonant. (Voice assimilation and glottalization take place as previously described.) In the case of the Eastern dialects, assimilation of the velar consonant induces a strong palatalization of the preceding vowel, except in the case of /ee/ (cf. Owens 1985: 24). In the Orma Southern variety, /k+t/ may voice into [dd] while [gd] is occasionally maintained (cf. Stroomer 1987: 41). In Boraana, /k'+n/ exceptionally changes into [nd'][20] (cf. Stroomer 1987: 39).

(28) *beex+ta* → *beetta* (Eastern) 'you know'
beex+na → *beenna* (Eastern) 'we know'
mux+ni → *muynni* (but also: *muxni*) (Eastern) 'tree+NOM'
beek+ta → *beetta* (Southern: Boraana, Orma), *beedda* (Orma) 'you know'
beek+na → *beenna* (Southern: Boraana, Orma) 'we know'
muk(a)+ni → *munni* (Southern: Boraana, Orma) 'tree+NOM'
d'uug+ta → *d'uuydda* (Eastern) 'you drink'
d'uug+na → *d'uuynna* (Eastern) 'we drink'
lag(a)+ni → *laynni, leenni* (Eastern) 'river+NOM'
d'ug+ta → *d'udda* (Southern: Boraana, Orma); *d'utta, d'ugda* (Orma) 'you drink'
d'ug+na → *d'unna* (Southern: Boraana, Orma) 'we drink'
lag(a)+ni → *lanni* (Southern: Boraan, Orma) 'river+NOM'
d'ak'+ta → *d'aytt'a, d'eett'a* (Eastern) 'you arrive'
d'ak'+na → *d'aynna, d'eenna* (Eastern) 'we arrive'
warak'(a)+ni → *waraynna, wareenna* (Eastern) 'paper+NOM'
d'ak'+ta → *d'att'a, d'atta* (Southern: Boraana) 'you go'
d'ek'+ta → *d'ett'a, d'etta* (Southern: Orma) 'you go'
d'ak'+na → *d'anna, d'and'a* (Southern: Boraana) 'we go'
d'ek'+na → *d'enna* (Southern: Orma) 'we go'
waak'(a)+ni → *waanni* (Southern: Boraana, Orma) 'god+NOM'

In Southern Oromo, /b/ and /f/ may optionally assimilate, either completely or partially, to a following /n/.

---

20. This chage to [nd'] is only found in verbal forms in Stroomer (1987).

(29) k'ab+na → k'abna (Orma) 'we have'
k'amna (Boraana, Orma, Waata)
k'anna (occasionally in Waata)
arrab(a)+ni → arrabni (Orma) 'tongue+NOM'
arramni (Boraana, Orma, Waata)
arranni (occasionally in Waata)
d'uf+na → d'ufna (Boraana, Orma) 'we go'
d'umna (Boraana, Waata)
d'unna (occasionally in Waata)
bof(a)+ni → bofni (Boraana, Orma) 'snake+NOM'
bomni (Boraana, Waata)
bonni (occasionally in Waata)

In the case where a stop precedes /s/, which can be only (part of) the causative verb extension, total assimilation only occurs with a velar stop and only in the Southern varieties, though in Waata /k'+s/ usually reduces to [s] (see § 25.3.4.7).

(30) beek+s+a → beessa (Southern) 'I make know'
d'ug+siis+a → d'us(s)iisa (Southern) 'I make drink'
fiik'+sa → fiissa (Boraana, Orma) 'I whistle'
fiinsa (rarely in Boraana)
fiisa (Waata)

25.3.4.7. Stop deletion

In Western Oromo, /d'/ is systematically dropped before a consonant. If the preceding vowel is short, it obligatorily lengthens (31a). This deletion occurs in all dialects when the following consonant is /s/ (31b). In Eastern Oromo, /t'/ also drops before /s/ (31b).

(31) a. fuud'+ta → fuuta (Western) 'you take'
haad'(a)+ti → haati (Western) 'mother+NOM'
fed'+na → feena (Western) 'we wish'
b. fuud'+sis+a → fuusisa 'I cause to take'
c. t'ut'+siis+a → tusiisa (Eastern) 'I make suck'

In Eastern Oromo, a velar stop, which induces palatalization of the previous vowel, is dropped before /s/; in the Waata Southern variety /k'+s/ also reduces to [s], though some exceptions are found (see § 25.3.4.9) (32a). In all Southern varieties, /g+s/ may optionally reduce to [s] (32b).

(32) a. beex+sis+a → beesisa (Eastern) 'I make know'
d'uug+sis+a → d'uuysisa (Eastern) 'I make drink'
hook'+s+a → hooysa (Eastern) 'I make scratch'
hoosa (Southern: Waata)
b. d'ug+siis+a → d'ussiisa 'I make drink'
d'usiisa (Southern)

25.3.4.8. Palato-affrication

In all dialects, a non-glottalized coronal plus /s/, which can only be (part of) the causative verb extension, becomes [čč] (Western, Eastern) or [č] (Southern). In Western Oromo, this also holds of /t'/ (33a). In all dialects, /s/ becomes [č] after /l/ (33b).

(33) a. k'ot+sisiis+a → k'oččisiisa (Western, Eastern) 'I make dig'
k'očisiisa (Southern)
did+sisiiis+a → diččisiisa (Western, Eastern) 'I make refuse'
dičisiisa (Southern)
aǰaǰ+siis+a → aǰaččisiisa (Western) 'I make command'
lit'+siis+a → liččiisa (Western) 'I make enter'
b. gal+s+a → galča 'I bring home'
bul+s+a → bulča 'I spend the night'

In the Waata Southern dialect, a velar plus /t/ becomes affricate too. (The palatalization is probably related to the palatalization induced by a velar stop over the preceding vowel in Eastern Oromo, see § 25.3.4.6.)

(34) beek+ta → beeča (Southern: Waata) 'you know'
d'ek'+ta → d'eča (Southern: Waata) 'you go to'
d'ug+ta → d'uǰa, d'uča[21] (Southern: Waata) 'you drink'
deg(a)+ti → deǰi (Southern: Waata) 'people+NOM'

25.3.4.9. Vowel epenthesis

Oromo does not allow sequences of more than two non-syllabic segments. When such a sequence would arise, [i] is inserted between the second and third consonants.

(35) elm+ta → elmita 'you milk'
fayy+na → fayyina 'we are well'
gudd+s+a → guddisa 'I raise (children)'
add(a)+ti → additi (Southern: Boraana) 'forehead+NOM' (addi, in other dialects)

---

21. See footnote 19.

In Southern Oromo, this also holds of stems ending in /č/, /č'/, /t'/, and optionally /d'/, even if the affricate is derived, i.e., [č] originated through palato-affrication (36a) (cf. Stroomer 1987: 54). In all dialects, there are exceptional forms in which [i] appears between the stem and the causative morpheme (36b).

(36) a. *boč'+ta* → *boč'ita* (Southern) 'you carve wood'
t'uut'+na → *t'uut'ina* (Southern) 'we suck'
hod'+s+a → *hod'isa* (Southern) 'I make suck'
duud+s+ta → *duučita* (Southern) 'you fill up a hole'
b. *damač'+siisa* → *damač'isiisa* (Western) 'I make crush'
huk'+s+ta → *huk'ista, huk'ibta, huk'itta* (Southern: Waata) 'you make thin'

In Eastern Oromo, [a] is inserted between the first and second consonants if the second consonant is a liquid (37a) (cf. Owens 1985: 21). This also occasionally occurs in Southern Oromo, where the epenthetic vowel may further copy the preceding vowel (37b) (cf. Stroomer 1987: 55).

(37) a. *k'ofl+ta* → *k'ofalta* (Eastern) 'you laugh'
dabr+ta → *dabarta* (Eastern) 'you pass'
b. *kofl+ta* → *kofalta* (Southern: Boraana, Waata)
kofl+ta → *kofolta* (Southern: Orma)

25.3.4.10. Special changes

A group of verbs, which are very frequent because of the middle voice extension, show unusual conjugated forms. The changes they involve are thus restricted to specific verbal morphemes. In prevocalic position, they show a geminate [dd'] in the first person singular and in the imperative (38a) and a geminate [čč] in the infinitive form[22] (38b), while [t] occurs in the remaining prevocalic forms (38c). In preconsonantal position, this segment alternates like /t/ (38d).[23]

(38) a. *bit+a(a)dd'+a* 'I buy for myself'
bit+a(a)dd'+uu 'buy for yourselves!'
b. *bit+a(a)čč+uu* 'to buy for one self'

---

22. Other [cc(')] forms have been reported as alternative infinitive forms for some verbs ending in alveolar obstruent, e.g. *fit'uu, fičč'uu* 'to finish', *gammaduu, gammaččuu* 'to want', *god'uu, goččuu* 'to make' (cf. Moreno 1939: 73).
23. Oromo scholars have provided different analyses of these verbs, assuming either an original /dd'/ form (cf. Gragg 1976: 186, Stroomer 1987: 153) or an original /t/ form (cf. Owens 1985: 64). For a more abstract analysis see Lloret (1988: 187–99).

c. *bit+a(a)t+a* 'he buys for himself'
   bit+a(a)t+an(i) 'they buy for themselves'
d. *bit+a(a)t+ta* 'you buy for yourself'
   bit+a(a)n+na 'we buy for ourselves' (cf. *bit+na* → *binna* 'we buy')
   bit+a(a)č+čisiis+a 'I make buy for myself' (cf. *bit+sisiis+a* → *biččisiisa* 'I make buy')

There is only one attested case where the long implosive behaves like a geminate, namely the verb *hodd'-* 'sew' (e.g. *hodd'ita* 'you sew', *hodd'a* 'he sews', *hodd'uu* 'to sew').

25.3.5. Morphophonemic changes involving glides and laryngeal segments
Stems ending in /w, y, ', h/[24] undergo changes that involve these segments as well as the preceding vowels. In Western and Southern Oromo, a glide becomes ['] if it is followed by a vowel-initial suffix. In the Southern varieties, the glide may also completely delete, which may originate heterorganic vocalic sequences.

(39) *d'aw+a* → *d'a'a* (Western, Southern), *d'aa* (Southern) 'I weave'
    Cf. *d'ow+a* → *d'owa* (Eastern) 'I hit'
    d'agay+e → *d'aga'e* (Western, Southern), *d'agae* (Southern) 'I heard'
    Cf. *d'agay+e* → *d'ageye* (Eastern)

In Western and Southern Oromo, stems ending in /', w, d'/ lengthen the previous vowel, if it is short, when they are followed by a consonant-initial suffix. The glottal stop further drops; the glide and the implosive may undergo and entail other changes. (See § 25.3.4.6 and § 25.3.4.7 for the behavior of /d'/.)

(40) *ta'+ta* → *taata* (Western, Southern) 'you become'
    d'aw+sis+a → *d'oofsisa* (Western), *d'ees(s)isa* (Southern) 'I make weave'
    fed'+na → *feena* (Western), *feenna* (Southern) 'we want'

In Western Oromo, lengthening of the preceding vowel in pre-consonantal position also occurs if the stem ends in /y/ (41a). In Eastern Oromo, it does occur when the stem ends in a laryngeal consonant, which further deletes, and when /y/ is followed by /t/ or /n/, which undergo other changes (41b).

24. In medial position, /h/ only occurs in Eastern Oromo, which appears as /'/ or zero in other dialects, e.g., *taha* (Eastern), *ta'a* (Western), *taa* (Southern) 'I become'. Stems ending in /V'/ are considered to end in /VV/ in Stroomer (1987: 51–2).

(41) a. d'agay+ta → d'ageessa (Western) 'you hear'
     d'agay+na → d'ageeñña (Western) 'we hear'
     d'agay+sis+a → d'ageessisa (Western) 'I make hear'
  b. tah+ta → taata (Eastern) 'you become'
     deebi'+sis+a → deebiisisa (Eastern) 'I make return'
     d'agay+ta → d'ageessa (Eastern) 'you hear'
     d'agay+na → d'ageeñña (Eastern) 'we hear'
     dallay(a)+ni → dalleeni (Eastern) 'fence+NOM'

In Eastern Oromo, short /a/ may be affected by vowel harmony. It becomes [e] if the stem ends in a laryngeal consonant or in /y/ and the suffix begins in /e/ (42a). It becomes [o] if the stem ends in a laryngeal consonant and the suffix begins in /u(u)/; if the suffix has short /u/, it may further become [o] (42b). (Cf. Owens 1985: 21.)

(42) a. tah+e → tehe (Eastern) 'he became'
     ǰa'+e → ǰe'e (Eastern) 'he said'
     d'agay+e → d'ageye (Eastern) 'he heard'
  b. bah+uu → bohuu (Eastern) 'leaving (noun)'
     ǰa'+u → ǰo'u (Eastern) 'let him say'
     tah+u → tohu, toho (Eastern) 'he becomes (in subordinate clause)'

In preconsonantal position, /w/ systematically becomes [f] in Western Oromo (43a). In Eastern, preconsonantal /w/ assimilates to a preceding /o/; it optionally becomes [y] if the preceding vowel is /a/ and the next consonant is /t, n/; it deletes when it is followed by /s/ (43b). In the Boraana Southern variety, /w/ becomes [f] before /t/, [m] before /n/, and [s] before /s/, which may be optionally dropped; in the Orma Southern variety, /w/ assimilates in different degrees to the following consonant, which may be optionally dropped after /s/; in the Waata Southern variety, /w+t/ becomes [č], /w+n/ becomes [ñ], and /w+t/ becomes [s] (43c). In Southern and Eastern Oromo, /w/ after /s/ raises and fronts a preceding /a(a)/ into [e(e)], see (43b) and (43c).

(43) a. **Western:**
     d'aw+ta/na/sisa → d'oofta/d'oofna/d'oofsisa 'you/we/I make weave'
  b. **Eastern:**
     d'ow+ta/na/sisa → d'oota/d'oona/d'oosisa 'you/we/I make hit'
     beelaw+ta/na → beeloyta/beeloyna 'you/we become hungry'
       (optional)
     beelaw+sa → beelesa 'I make hungry'

c. **Southern:**

d'aw+ta/na/sisa → *d'oofta/d'oomna/d'ees(s)isa* (Boraana) 'you/we/I make hit'
d'oot(t)a/d'oon(n)a/d'ees(s)isa (Orma)
d'ooča/d'ooña/d'eesisa (Waata)

In preconsonantal position, /y/ always palatalizes a preceding /a(a)/ vowel, which becomes [e(e)]. In Western Oromo, /y+t/ further becomes [ss] and /y+n/ becomes [ññ] (44a). In Eastern, the same changes occur, which also affect final /aa'/ stems,[25] though in the Harar variety [ññ] only appears within verbal morphology (cf. Owens 1985: 20, Banti 1988: 47). The sequence /y+s/ becomes [ss] in Western while it simplifies into [s] in Eastern and Southern (44a–c). In the Boraana and Orma Southern varieties, /y/ always deletes before a consonant; in Waata, /y+t/ becomes [č] and /y+n/ becomes [ñ] (44c).

(44) a. **Western:**

d'agay+ta/na → *d'ageessa/d'ageeñña* 'you/we hear'
d'agay+sisa → *d'ageessisa* 'I make hear'
nagay(a)+ni → *nageeññi* 'peace+NOM'

b. **Eastern:**

d'agay+ta/na → *d'ageessa/d'ageeñña* 'you/we hear'
taa'+ta/na → *teessa/teeñña* 'you/we sit'
d'agay+sisa → *d'ageesisa* 'I make hear'
nagay(a)+ni → *nageeññi* (Arussi) 'peace+NOM'
Cf. *nagay(a)+ni* → *nageeni* (Harar) 'peace+NOM'

c. **Southern:**

d'agay+ta/na → *d'ageeta/d'ageena* (Boraana, Orma) 'you/we hear'
d'agay+ta/na → *d'ageeča/d'ageeña* (Waata)
d'agay+sis+a → *d'ageesisa* (Boraana, Orma, Waata) 'I make hear'
nagay(a)+ni → *nageeni* (Boraana, Orma), *nageeñi* (Waata) 'peace+NOM'

25.3.6. Vowel length alternation

In Oromo, some inflectional and derivational suffixes exhibit alternation in vowel length depending on the length of the preceding vowel, namely the suffix has a long vowel if the vowel of the preceding syllable is short, and a short vowel if the vowel of the preceding syllable is long. This morpho-

---

25. These final /aa'/ Eastern stems significantly correspond to final /aay/ stems in other dialects, e.g., *taa'+ta* → *teessa* (Eastern), *taay+ta* → *teessa* (Western), *teeta* (Southern: Boraana, Orma), *teeča* (Southern: Waata) 'you sit'.

phonemic vowel alternation is mainly differentiative of Western Oromo (cf. Gragg 1976: 177, Lloret 1988: 77–81). In Eastern and Southern Oromo, it does not systematically apply though some cases are found, especially within the causative forms (cf. Owens 1985: 63, Stroomer 1987: 424).

(45)   *ul+oota*   'sticks'   *gaal+ota*   'camels' (Western)
      lugn+ooma   'I am coward' *afčaal+oma*   'I am kind' (Western)
      tee(s)+sis+a 'I make sit'   *k'oč(č)i+siis+a* 'I make dig' (all dials.)

25.3.7. Unrestricted consonantal changes
Some changes that Oromo consonants undergo do not exclusively apply accross morphemes but whenever the phonetic context is satisfied.

25.3.7.1. Nasal Place Assimilation
/n/ assimilates to the point of articulation of a following consonant.

(46)   *leenč'a* [leeñč'a] 'lion'
      danfa [daɱfa] 'it boils'
      hinbaru [himbaru] 'he does not learn'
      hinkennu [hiŋkennu] 'he does not give'

25.3.7.2. Glottal Stop Assimilation
A glottal stop may optionally assimilate to a preceding sonorant consonant or to a following vowel, e.g.

(47)   *bal'aa* [bal'aa], [ballaa] 'wide'
      bay'ee [bay'ee], [bayyee] 'much'
      (*ka'+uu* →) *ka'uu* [ka'uu], [kawuu] 'to rise'
      (*d'agay+uu* →) *d'aga'uu* [d'aga'uu], [d'agawuu] 'to hear'

25.3.7.3. Stop Devoicing
A stop tends to devoice when it is followed by a voiceless consonant (48a). It also devoices before pause, when the final vowel is phonetically realized as voiceless (48b) (cf. Owens 1985: 23).

(48)   a.   *obs+a* [opsa] (Western) 'I endure'
         obsa [opsa] (Southern: Boraana) 'patience'
         obsaa [opsaa] (Southern: Boraana) 'officer' (from English)
         č'ab+sa [č'apsa] (Western, Southern) 'I break'
         k'ab+ta [k'apta] (occasionally in Southern) 'you have'
         Cf. *k'ab+ta* → *k'abda, k'adda* (usually in Southern)

fiig+sisa [fiiksisa] (all dialects) 'I make run'
b. k'ab+ta → k'abda [k'apta] (in pre-pausal position) 'you have'
gub+ta → gubda [guptḁ] (in pre-pausal position) 'you burn'

25.4. Suprasegmentals

Phonetically, Oromo contrasts high and low tones as well as different stress levels. Pitch and stress are assigned according to the phonological shape of a word in isolation and as a result of the grammatical information it encodes. Although there is general agreement on the tonal character of the language, as for almost all Cushitic languages (cf. Sasse 1981: 205), the exact status of tone is far from being clearly established. The large amount of dialectal variation that the language presents on this topic and the fact that tone on a word shows considerable variation according to the context in which the word occurs are the main problems for the description of the prosodic system of Oromo.

It is generally accepted that in Oromo tone is determined primarily morphosyntactically, and that its prosodic system conforms to pitch-accent systems, in the sense that tone is specified on a single syllable (usually on the penultimate) and from it the overall tonal pattern is identified on the morpheme. However, since in Oromo each morpheme contributes to the tonal pattern of the word, it differs significantly from other paradigmatic cases of pitch-accent languages, such as Japanese (cf. Owens 1985: 35–36). One further point to be mentioned is the correlation between tone and stress. In general, the stressed syllable is perceived as the first syllable of a word with high pitch (cf. Owens 1985: 37). Their complex relationship, though, seems to be more adequately established within the autosegmental framework, as Banti (1988) has done for the Arussi Eastern variety.[26] The following assumptions are fairly well accepted.

Verbal stems are toneless. They acquire tone by tonal patterns of the verbal affixes or by other tonal patterns of specific grammatical information. For instance, the affirmative imperative forms have a high–low tonal pattern in the singular, high being associated with the penultimate syllable, while a low–high pattern in the negative, high being associated with the penultimate syllable.

---

26. Banti (1988: 43) points out that the Oromo prosodic system involves a somewhat elaborate set of stress rules and a very simple set of tone rules. This statement presumably holds for other Cushitic languages, too.

(49) *rafi* [ráfì] 'sleep!' (*hin+rafini* → *hirràfini* [hìrráfín(í)] 'don't sleep!'
taa'i [táa'ì] 'sit!' *hintaa'ini* [hìntàa'ín(í)] 'don't sit!'

Most nouns (and adjectives) in isolation have a predictable tonal pattern according to their segmental shape, which may vary among dialects. Some of them, however, seem to be lexically marked. For instance, in Western and Eastern Oromo nouns ending in a long vowel have a low–high tonal pattern, low being associated with the penultimate syllable, though there are some exceptions, e.g.

(50) *lafee* [làfée] 'bone', *mataa* [màtáa] 'head'; but *harree* [hárrée] 'donkey' (Cf. Southern: *lafee* [láfèe]; *mataa* [mátàa], [màtáa])

All bound morphemes, except the ones that create extended verbal stems, have their own tonal specification, which contributes to the tonal pattern of the word. For instance, the genitive construction consists of the thing possessed followed by the possessor with lengthening of the last vowel and assignment of high tone, e.g.

(51) *fira   intala   kan   d'ufte+e* [d'úftée] 'the friend of the girl who came'
    friend   girl   that   came+GEN
    Cf. *d'ufte* [d'úftè] 'she came' (in isolation)

Western Oromo is characterized by displaying a simplified tonal system (cf. Gragg 1976: 173).[27] For example, in the Harar Eastern variety, almost all suffixes ending in a long vowel induce a high tone on the syllable preceding them (cf. Owens 1985: 29); however, in Western Oromo they tend to follow the general low–high pattern, though some words escape to this generalization, e.g.

(52) *gudd+aa* [gúddáa] (Harar Eastern), [gùddáa] (Western) 'big (masc.)'
    gudd+oo [gúddóo] (Harar Eastern), [gùddóo] (Western) 'big (fem.)'
    Cf. *gog+aa* [gógáa] (Harar Eastern, Western) 'dry'

Tonal patterns that bear grammatical information cannot vary. Words in variable tone contexts, i.e., in grammatical contexts that do not require a fixed tonal pattern, may vary their basic tonal pattern. Owens (1985: 49) points out that other relatively independent factors may govern variability

---

27. Significantly, only in this variety some individual words have been found to be distinguished by tone alone, e.g., *gogaa* [gógáa] 'dry', *gogaa* [gògáa] 'skin'. The negative verbal prefix and the focus verbal prefix are also differentiated by means of tone, e.g., *hin* [hín] (focus), [hìn] (negation): *hirrafa* [hírràfà] 'he sleeps (focus)', *hirrafu* [hìrráfù] 'he does not sleep'.

of tonal patterns in Oromo, namely factors of meaning, according to which certain tonal patterns occur in order to minimize ambiguity, and factors of information, having to do with the distribution of old and new information.

References

Ali, Mohammed, & Andrzej Zaborski. 1990. *Handbook of the Oromo Language*. Cracow: Polska Akademia Nauk—Oddzial W. Krakowie.

Andrzejewski, B. W. 1957. "Some Preliminary Observations on the Borana Dialect of Galla." *Bulletin of the School of Oriental and African Studies* 19: 354–74.

Banti, Giorgio. 1988. "Two Cushitic Systems: Somali and Oromo Nouns." In *Autosegmental Studies on Pitch Accent*, ed. H. van der Hulst and N. Smith, pp. 11–49. Dordrecht: Foris.

Bender, M. Lionel, & Mulugeta Eteffa. 1976. "Galla." In *Language in Ethiopia*, ed. M. L. Bender, J. D. Bowen, R. L. Cooper, & C. A. Ferguson, pp. 130–48. London: Oxford University Press.

Bryan, Margaret A. 1948. *The Distribution of Semitic and Cushitic Languages of Africa*. London: Oxford University Press.

Gamkrelidze, Thomas V. 1978. "On the Correlation of Stops and Fricatives in a Phonological System." In *Universals of Human Language*, ed. Joseph H. Greenberg, vol. 2, pp. 9–46. Stanford: Stanford University Press.

Gragg, Gene B. 1976. "Oromo of Wellegga." In *The Non-Semitic Languages of Ethiopia*, ed. M. L. Bender, pp. 166–95. East Lansing: Michigan State University Press.

———. 1982. *Oromo Dictionary*. East Lansing: Michigan State University, African Studies Center.

Heine, Bernd. 1981. *The Waata Dialect of Oromo: Grammatical Sketch and Vocabulary*. Berlin: Reimer.

Heine, Bernd, Thilo C. Schadeberg, & Ekkehard Wolff (eds.). 1981. *Die Sprachen Afrikas*. Hamburg: Helmut Buske.

Lloret, Maria-Rosa. 1988. "Gemination and Vowel Length in Oromo Morphophonology." Ph.D. dissertation, Indiana University.

———. 1989. "Final Vowels and Grammatical Marking in Oromo." In *Current Approaches to African Linguistics*, vol. 5, ed. Paul Newman and R. B. Botne, pp. 73–83. Dordrecht: Foris.

Moreno, M. M. 1939. *Grammatica teorico-pratica della lingua galla con essercizi*. Milan: Mondadori.

Owens, Jonathan. 1980. "Observations on Tone in the Booran Dialect of Oromo." *African Language Studies* 17: 141–96.
———. 1985. *A Grammar of Harar Oromo (Northeastern Ethiopia)*. Hamburg: Buske.
Sasse, Hans-Jürgen. 1975. "Galla /s/, /š/, und /f/." *Afrika und Übersee* 58: 244–63.
———. 1979. "The Consonants Phonemes of Proto-East-Cushitic (PEC): A First Approximation." *Afroasiatic Linguistics* 7/1.
———. 1981. "Die Kuschitischen Sprachen." In Heine, Schadeberg, & Wolff 1981: 187–215.
Stroomer, Harry. 1987. *A Comparative Study of Three Southern Oromo Dialects in Kenya: Phonology, Morphology, and Vocabulary*. Hamburg: Buske.

Chapter 26
Somali Phonology
Annarita Puglielli
Terza Università degli Studi di Roma

26.1. Introduction

Somali belongs to the Cushitic subgroup of the Afroasiatic family. The term Afroasiatic, which was made famous by Greenberg (1955), refers to a large number of languages spoken in northeastern Africa that were previously identified by the term Hamito-Semitic. It includes Semitic, Berber, Egyptian, Chadic, and the controversial Omotic.

The Cushitic branch consists of a large number of languages and can in turn be subdivided into two groups: Highland East Cushitic and Lowland East Cushitic. The first includes such languages as Sidamo, Hadiyya, Kambata, and Burji, spoken by about 2 million people in southwestern Ethiopia, along the Rift Valley. Among the major members of the second group are the Oromoid languages (which include Oromo, Konso, Gidole), and the Somaloid languages. The latter include Rendille, Boni, etc., as well as Somali, which is spoken by about 5 million people in the territory of the Republic of Somalia, the Ogaden (southern part of Ethiopia), Djibouti, and some northeastern territories of Kenya. There are still some problems of classification for several languages in the Cushitic group. This is not, however, the case of Somali, certainly one of the most well described African languages. Somali has been the object of study since the end of last century and scholars like Berghold (1897, 1899), Schleicher (1892), Reinisch (1903), and Cerulli (1957–59) have contributed to its scientific description (the variance in the description is due to the fact that different authors worked on different regional and/or ethnic varieties of the language).

Although characterized by overall linguistic uniformity, the language that we call Somali does contain dialects, even if they are usually mutually comprehensible ones. We will not go into them here; readers may refer to Cerulli (1957–59), Moreno (1955), and Lamberti (1983). The relevant fact about Somali, though, is that linguistic standardization has been going on for several decades, and that the variety spoken in the Mudug area (central-northern region) has been regularly used since 1943 for radio broadcasting.

522   Annarita Puglielli

This variety was adopted as the national language and officially transcribed in 1972. As for which script to use, a long debate ensued between supporters of Arabic, Latin, and Osmanian (a modified version of the Arabic script created by a Somali scholar, Osman Keenadid). The final decision was in favour of the Latin script. The phonemic notation by Andrzejewski (1955) was chosen for transcriptions, and all special characters or diacritics that had been used in the past were replaced with unused characters in the Latin alphabet (in particular c = ʕ, x = ħ, dh = ɖ).

26.2. The sound pattern of Somali

26.2.1. Consonants

Somali has a system of 21 consonant phonemes, each of which has important positional variants (Armstrong 1934, Cardona 1981). This produces a rich and varied consonant system as follows:

Table 26-1. Somali Consonants

	Labial (Dental)	Dental (Alveloar)	Postalveolar	Palatoalveolar	Palatal	Velar	Uvular	Pharyngeal	Glottal
stops	b	t d	ɖ			k g	q		ʔ
affrivate				ʤ					
nasal	m	n							
lateral		(l)							
rolled		(r)							
fricative	(f)	s		ʃ			χ	ħ ʕ	h
approximant	w				j				

/b/   is almost devoiced in initial position [b̥ʌd] 'sea'; [β] (affricate without complete closure) between vowels, especially after a stressed syllable [ˈlʌβʌ] 'two'; a voiced stop when geminate in intervocalic position [gabbal] 'twilight'; devoiced and unreleased [laab̥ʼ] 'chest' or as [pʼ] with glottal closure and release [sapʼ] 'outcast' in final position.

/t/ can occur only initially or in intervocalic position; it never occurs in final position, where it neutralizes with /d/. It is strongly aspirated.

/d/ has the same phonetic variation as /b/ with the same distribution.

/ḍ/ is postalveolar, pharyngalized, and voiced; it occurs in initial position (although only in Isaaq, a variety spoken in northern Somalia) as well as in syllable-final position. In common Somali, when in final position, it has become [r]: /bʌd/ → [bʌr].

/k/ is aspirated like /t/ and is a voiceless velar; it cannot occur in final position, where it neutralizes with /g/.

/g/ has the same realization as /b/. It can be double in intervocalic position [haggee] 'where'.

/q/ in initial position is [ɢ] with little voicing; it becomes a voiced fricative in intervocalic position, especially after a stressed syllable. In final position it can be either unexploded and voiceless or more frequently a voiceless fricative uvular.

/dʒ/ occurs only at the beginning of a syllable and is [d̥ʒ̊] with little voicing; for some speakers it is [tʃ].

/ʔ/ is a glottal stop both in initial and final position. It is often optional in final position but if it is present, it necessarily appears in the presence of suffixes.

/m/ is normally articulated and it occurs only in syllable-initial position. In syllable-final it neutralizes. So we have *nin* 'man' whose underlying form is /nim/ so that we have [nin] or [ninka], but [niman] 'men'.

/n/ appears in all positions.

/l/ its pronunciation varies according to the quality of the vowel that follows it in all positions.

/r/ is [r] in all positions; it can be doubled in middle position [ʕarʌb] 'Arabic' [ʕarrʌb] 'tongue'.

Fricatives and approximants are always pronounced according to the description given in the general table and do not show positional variants with the exception of /ħ/ and /h/, which can be voiced in intervocalic position.

26.2.2. *The vowel system*

The vowel system of Somali was first described by Armstrong (1934), who recognized 18 vowel phonemes, and subsequently by Andrzejewski (1955), who described a system of 20 vowels. There is an opposition between "retracting vowels" and "fronting vowels," and an opposition between short and long vowels. Official orthography does not note the first of these two oppositions, whereas it makes use of two letters (*aa*, etc.) to signal long vowels. The following is therefore a comprehensive table of the Somali vowel system, with "fronting" or advanced vowels marked with a comma.

Table 26-2. Somali Vowels

Short Vowels			
Fronting		Retracting	
i̦ [i]	u̦ [u]	i [ɪ]	u [ʊ]
e̦ [e]	o̦ [o]	e [ɛ]	o [ɔ]
	a̦ [æ]	a [ʌ, a]	
Long Vowels			
Fronting		Retracting	
i̦i [i:]	u̦u [i:]	ii [i:]	uu [ʊ:]
e̦e [e:]	o̦o [o:]	ee [ɛ:]	oo [ɔ:]
	a̦a [æ:]	aa [a:]	

One of the peculiarities of the Somali system is that within the same phonological unit only one of the two series of vowels can be present, i.e., there exists a system of vowel harmony. Thus a single word can contain only vowels that belong to the "advanced" set or to the "retracted" one. In addition, this opposition impacts not only on phonology, but also on morphology. In fact, monosyllabic nouns such as ga̦r "beard' ~ gar 'will', du̦b 'skin' ~ dub 'tail', ca̦d 'piece' ~ cad 'white', which are respectively masculine and feminine, are differentiated on the basis of the vowel quality.

There are also verbs in which the difference between the imperative and the past is marked by fronting vs. retracting vowels: tu̦n [tʉn] 'hit it' ~ tun [tʊn] 'he hit', e̦eg [eeg] 'look' ~ eeg [ɛɛg] 'he looked'.

Finally, the interaction of the vowel quality (fronting vs. retracting) and tonal stress—one extremely important feature of Somali grammar—also has consequences on the final consonant sound in a bisyllabic word. The stops (b, d, g) are devoiced in final position (see § 2.1) as in many other languages, but devoicing goes together with releasing or unreleasing according to the position of stress and the quality of the vowel. If the tonal stress is on the last vowel, the stop will be released except where the vowel is fronted. In all other cases—words with stress on the penultimate vowel and/or words with fronted vowels—the stops will not be released (Angoujard & Mohamed 1991).

Somali vowels pose some problems since more parameters are involved in the differentiation of minimal pairs. In addition, only long vowels have a rather constant realization while short vowels vary considerably according to context and different speakers.

26.2.3. Tonal accent

The description of this aspect of the phonological system of Somali has been highly discussed and the debate whether Somali is a tone language or not has been going on for decades.

The first descriptions of Somali do not mention tone at all, and some of the grammars mention that accent in Somali falls mainly on the penultimate syllable (Hunter 1880: 6; Reinisch 1903: 28–29). The first to notice the tonal nature of this accent was Armstrong (1934), who distinguishes 4 different tonal levels and notices a strict relationship between tone and accent. In 1949 Klingenheben considers accent to be the primary aspect of Somali and tone to be secondary or derived; thus, on the basis of phonological criteria, he does not consider Somali a tone language but rather something approaching a system with "Starktonsprachen" ("accent of intensity") like English or German. More recently Somali has still been considered a tone language characterized by tonal accent without an explicit consideration of the accentual nature of these tonal accents (Jones 1950, Abraham 1964, Andrzejewski 1956).

It is only in recent years that Hyman (1981) proposed a formal description of Somali as a system with tonal accent. From a phonetic point of view Somali shows a contrast between a high tone (A) and a low tone (B). The first has a very limited distribution; each word can have only one A tone and this has to be either on the last vowel or on the penultimate one. The superficial distribution of different surface tonal patterns may be seen in the following examples:

(1) a. *ínan*   'boy'   b. *inán*   'girl'
     qaálin   'little'   *qaalín*   'little' (female)
     daméer   'donkey'   *dameér*   'donkey' (female)

(2) a. *túug*   'thief'   b. *tuúg*   'thieves'
     doofáar 'pig'   *doofaár*   'pigs'
     Soomaáli 'Somali'   *Soomaalí* 'Somalis'

The words in (1) and (2) are all nouns. In (1) the tonal alternation in (a) and (b) shows the opposition between masculine nouns (in [a]) and feminine nouns (in [b]). The masculine nouns are characterized by tone A on the penultimate vowel, while the feminine nouns are characterized by tone A on the last vowel. The alternance shown in (2a) and (2b) is used to mark number. The nouns in (2a) are singular while those in (2b) are plural. One notes that nouns in (2b) are also feminine and their tone A falls on the last vowel as in (1b). The consideration of the long vowel as a unit made up of two units allows us to give a general rule for cases like *ínan/inán* and *daméer/dameér*. The possible generalization is therefore that masculine nouns are characterized by an A tone on the penultimate vowel and feminine nouns by an A tone on the last vowel. As for verbs, the situation parallels that described for nouns (i.e., tone A appears either on the last or on the penultimate vowel). Of course the morphological features relevant here will not be gender and number but rather the mode, the conjugation, or the construction in which the verb occurs (main vs. relative/subordinate clause). Here are some examples of A tone distribution in imperatives and infinitives (the two possible citation forms of verbs) for verbs of different conjugations:

(3) | Conjugation | Imperative | Infinitive |
| --- | --- | --- |
| 1 | *cún* | *cuní* |
| 2 | *joóji* | *joojín* |
| 3 | *dháqso* | *dhaqsán* |

All other word classes fall in one of the two tonal patterns described for nouns and verbs: adjectives are normally considered a separate class of verbs and share the tone patterns of verbs; numerals are nouns and have the same patterns as nouns. Particles normally do not show an A tone. These include prepositions, clitic pronouns for subject and object, impersonal subject pronouns, and focus markers which, from a distributional point of view, all occur in pre-verbal position with fixed relative order.

As shown by the data just examined, an A tone must be present in all nouns, verbs, and other words except particles. It therefore has the same culminative properties we find in languages characterized by stress. A description of the tone in Somali has to explain both its superficial phonetic tonal nature and its underlying accentual identity. Hyman therefore proposes to consider this system, at an abstract level, as an accentual one rather than a tonal one. It is not possible to give here the full description of the whole system and the rules he proposes, but we will try to outline the main points he makes.

First of all accents (and related tone realizations) are not determined by lexical features but rather by grammatical features. Hence underlying forms are registered in the lexicon without prosodic information. Accents are introduced by morphological rules and then, after the application of reduction rules, their tonal realization is specified by means of phonetic rules. The rules for accent assignment are determined by grammatical features. Stress pattern is predictable: for nouns, on the basis of grammatical gender, declension, and type of construction; for verbs, on the basis of modality, conjugation, and type of construction. From a typological point of view, therefore, the system of Somali is of particular interest: it differs from tone systems in that the occurrence of tone A is limited to the last two vowels of a word and only one tone A can occur in a single word. It is also different from languages characterized by an accentual system, since the accent is assigned to a single vowel rather than to the syllable (as in English).

26.3. Phonological rules

Before going into the description of the main phonological rules of Somali, it is important to establish the following facts the relevance of which will be evident in the succeding description.

First of all, Somali is more accurately described in terms of syllable structure than in terms of morpheme structure. The syllable has the following structure:

(4) $(C_1)V(V)(C_2)$

In the underlying form there is no constraint on C_2, whereas in the surface form the sounds [k, t, ɖ, m] cannot occur syllable final ([ɖ] can occur in this position in Isaaq).

Given this syllable structure, a contoid which is phonetically long cannot be considered a single consonant, but rather a sequence of two consonants which are identical but belong to two contiguous syllables. On the basis of the restrictions on the possibility of occurrence of contoids in syllable final position, we deduce that geminates can only be consonants occurring in that position; thus [-tt-, -kk-, -mm-] are not possible. It follows that two consonants can meet only at the boundary of two syllables or at the boundary of two morphemes. When two consonants occur in a single morpheme (for example, in borrowings from Arabic) an epenthetic vowel is introduced, producing two syllables: *labis*-from Ar. *labs* 'uniform', *rodol* from Ar. *ratl* 'unit of measure'.

An opposite and very general rule of syllable reduction applies instead when we have a sequence of three syllables where the first and second syllable are open and have a short vowel. In this context the middle vowel is generally canceled and we obtain a two-syllable word rather than a three-syllable one. The corresponding rule is:

(5)   (C)VCVCV → (C)VCCV

For this rule to apply, the middle vowel must be unstressed. A syllable structure like the one in (5) is often obtained when we add a suffix—either derivational or inflectional—to a root or base, and the rule of syllable reduction applies systematically with very few exceptions (Puglielli 1984a, Puglielli & Ciise 1984). Here are some examples:

(6)
Underlying	Surface	
orod+ay run+1st past	*orday*	'I ran'
hadal+ay talk+1st past	*hadlay*	'I talked'
fur+am+ayaa open+pass.+3rd progr.	*furmayaa*	'it is getting opened'
hílib+o meat+plural	*hilbó*	'meats'
xárig+o rope+plural	*xargó*	'ropes'
qósol+e laugh+agentive	*qoslé*	'the one who laughs'
qósol+id laugh+nominalizer	*qoslíd*	'laugh (noun)'

The second general statement to be made is that most of the rules involving sound modification are grammatically conditioned, i.e. the grammatical status of morphemes determines the sound change they undergo. Consider for example the following rule:

(7)   /l + t/ → /ʃ/ (sh)

This happens in examples like:

(8)   *qosol + ta* → *qososho* 'the one who laughs'

where *t* is the initial consonant of the definite feminine article, or the initial consonant of the person agreement suffix in the verb. But in a case like

(9)   *ul+tan* → *ultan* 'stick'

where *-tan* is a derivational morpheme that permits the derivation of a verb from a noun, and therefore has the status of a lexical affix, the sequence /l+t/ does not change into /ʃ/. Another example of the same phenomenon is present in what follows. In words like

(10)   *badda* 'the sea'
        qaadday 'you (sing.)/she took (it)'

the noun *bad* plus the feminine definite article *ta* results in *badda* with the assimilation of [t] to [d]. In *qaadday*, to the base *qaad* is added the inflection *-tay* (which is the form of the second singular or the third feminine singular ending for the past tense) which gives *qaadday* where [t] assimilates to the preceeding [d]. But in a word like *qaatay* 'I/he took it for myself/himself' (formed by the base *qaad-* plus the root extension for autobenefactive *-at* and the person inflection *-ay*), the result of combining these elements is not the assimilation of the [t] of the lexical extension of the verb to the preceding [d], but rather the simplification of the cluster obtained through the application of the syllable reduction rule described earlier. In other words the stages of the derivation of this word are:

(11)   *qaad+at+ay* → *qaadatay* → *qaadtay* → *qaatay*

Even in this case the fact seems to be due to the lexical nature of the affix *-at*. It seems therefore reasonable to conclude that in general morphophonological rules are grammatically conditioned.

26.3.1. Juncture phenomena

In the Somali lexicon, morphemes are mostly monosyllabic but there is a rich system of both verbal and nominal derivation; as a consequence, affixes are added to roots and the final sound of the root joins with the initial sound of the affix. Furthermore, this language has a rich inflectional system both for nouns and for verbs: nouns are marked for gender and number, and verbs for tense/aspect, mood, and person. Finally determiners (i.e., definite articles, demonstratives, possessives, etc.) are all affixed to the noun. Hence juncture phenomena occur in many contexts. We will limit our description to the most common phonological rules determined by this situation for two good reasons: first, because the existing descriptions are still not exhaustive and there are several aspects that need further investigation, and secondly, because of the introductory nature of this work.

We may start by examining the phenomena connected with the co-occurrence of definite articles with nouns. These articles are respectively *-kV* (where V stands for any of the following: *a, u, ii*) for masculine nouns and *-tV* (*-ta, -tu, -tii*) for feminine nouns. Notice that *-k-* as marker of masculine and *-t-* as marker of feminine is used in other contexts in Somali and is characteristic of other Cushitic languages as well.

When *-kV* is added to masculine nouns we have the following situation:

(12) /k/ → /g/ when preceded by /g, w, y, i/
 buug+ka → *buugga* 'the book'
 rag+ka → *ragga* 'the men'
 bari+ka → *bariga* 'the East'

(13) /k/ → ø when preceded by /h, ħ, ʕ, q, χ/
 rah+ka → *raha* 'the frog'
 madax+ka → *madaha* 'the head'

(14) /k/ → /h/ when preceded by a V except /i/
 bare+ka → *baraha* 'the teacher'
 aabbe+ka → *aabbaha* 'the father'
 biyo+ka → *biyaha* 'the water'

In (12) there is a case of progressive assimilation which is determined by the feature [+back]. In (13) the derivation takes place in two steps: first assimilation and then simplification of the double consonant:

(15) *rah+ka* → *rah - ha* → /raha/

The same derivation applies to all the other consonants given in (13) that are all uvular and either fricatives or stops.

In (14) /k/ becomes /h/ when preceeded by a vowel except /i/. This form can only be described synchronically by an ad hoc rule and furthermore, if one looks at the examples, there is more going on than the shift from /k/ to /h/. In order to explain these forms Cardona (1981: 19–20) hypothesizes that the underlying form is /aabbah/, /biyah/ to which the following rules apply:

(16) /aabbah+ø/→ /aabbe/
 /aabbah+ha/→ /aabbah - ha/→ /aabbaha/

He says that there is no superficial manifestation of this underlying form in today's Somali, but Abraham (1964: 329) makes the assertion that there are some speakers that pronounce nouns ending in /-o/ and /-a/ as [-oh] and [-ah]; this seems to be confirmed by an instrumental analysis conducted by Farnetani (1981), whose data do not show an abrupt closure of the glottis at the end of the final vowel.

A parallel situation occurs for *-tV* when added to a feminine noun. When preceded by a vowel, /j/, /w/, or /d/, the initial /t/ becomes /d/:

(17) kaneeco+ta→   kaneecada   'the mosquito'
      dulmadow+ta→   dulmadowda   'the jackal'
      mindi+ta →   mindida   'the knife'
      bad+ta   →   badda   'the sea'

/t/ becomes voiced when the preceeding noun ends in /q/, /h/, /χ/, /ʕ/, /ʔ/. This is obvious for /ʕ/ that is voiced, but not for the other consonants that are voiceless. This fact can be explained in terms of articulatory mechanisms, since a short vocoid seems to be realized at the end of voiceless fricatives by the vibration of the vocal cords, and the same thing happens for /q/ (Cardona 1981: 20).

Finally, when *-tV* follows an /l/ the two sounds become /ʃ/ through assimilation:

(18) ul+ta → usha /uʃa/ 'the stick'

It is rather complex to explain this change: the only proposed explanation is the one by Cardona (1981: 20) based on the fact that /l/ assimilates /n/ in verbal endings and produces /ʃ/ even when followed by /s/ (see *fuul* 'to climb' ~ *fuushan* 'to be on top'), but it can co-occur with /k/ (*wiilkii* 'the boy') and /ʃ/ (*bulsho* 'society').

The reason for the assimilation of /l+t/ to /ʃ/ has to be attributed to some peculiarity of /l/ when it occurs at the end of a morpheme; it seems to have a fricative component (cf. Armstrong 1934: 126). On these bases Cardona (1981) suggests the following steps:

(19) [lˡt] → [lˡθ] → [lʃ] → [ʃ]

The last to be taken into consideration is when /t/ follows /ɖ/. Here /t/ assimilates to the preceeding sound:

(20) gabadh+ta → gabadha [gabaɖɖa]

The following table taken from Cardona (1981) will give an overall picture of the phonological rules that operate between a base ending in a consonant and a suffix beginning with a consonant. The table covers the majority of the existing cases, since /k, t/ are normally the possible initial consonants of nominal suffixes and /t, s, n/ those for verbal suffixes.

Table 26-3. Somali Sandhi

	k	t	n	s
b	bk	bt		
d	dk	dd		
g	gg	gt		gs
t			nn	
q	q	qd		
ʔ	ʔ	ʔd	nn	
f	fk	ft		
s	sk	st		
ʃ		ʃt		
ħ	ħ	ħd	nn	
χ	χ	χd		
ʕ	ʕ	ʕd		
h	h	hd	hn	
r	rk	rt	rr	
l	lk	ʃ	ll	
n	nk	nt		
j	jg	jd		
w	wg	wd		
V	Vg	Vd		

Before concluding this section we must consider those cases where two vowels meet, one being the last sound of the base and the other the initial sound of the suffix. Here are some examples:

(21) a. *gudi+id* → *gudiyid* 'the dangling of the head'
    b. *dibi+o* → *dibiyo* 'bulls'
    c. *aabbe+aal* → *aabbayaal* 'fathers'
    d. *mindi+o* → *mindiyo* 'knives'

The phonological rule prescribing the insertion of /y/ between two vowels is the same in all cases—whether the root is a verb (as in [21a]) or a noun (as in [21b–d]), and whether the affix is derivational (as in [21a]) or inflectional (as in [21b–d]).

26.3.2. Palatalization
This phenomenon is very general in Somali so that we have for example:

(22)   *jilib* /dʒilib/ 'knee'

while the initial sound for the same word in other Cushitic languages is /g/ (Bayso *gilib*, Konso-Gidole and Gato *kilba*, Burgi *gilba*, etc.).

In this respect, Somali itself still shows an allomorphic variation /dʒ~g̣/ as in *joog* 'to stop', *jooji* 'to cause to stop', *dhergan* 'to be satisfied', *dherjin* 'to satisfy'.

As shown in the example, palatalization occurs frequently in causative verbs where the final consonant of the root is followed by /-i/, part of the causative suffix.

Palatalization occurs also in other cases, like *shimbir* /ʃimbir/, 'bird' (Bayso *kimbir*, Afar *kimmiro*), *shan* 'five' (Bayso *kɛni*, Konso *keni*).

26.3.3. Epenthesis
The epenthesis of [n] in front of any consonant—not deriving from dissimilation of a geminate consonant or influence of neighboring sounds—is present in Common Somali and even more frequently in varieties such as Benadir and Digil. Examples are: *ca(n)shuur* 'tax', *ma(n)qas* 'scissors'.

26.3.4. Coalescence
Morphemes and words very often combine so that one obtains a word shorter than its independent parts, as shown in the following examples.

The focus particle *baa*, which necessarily marks an NP, is added to the noun or to the last word of the NP ending in a short vowel or diphthong and we obtain:

(23)   *ninka+baa = ninkaa* 'the man'
        maxay+baa = maxaa 'what?'

The presence of the focus particle in words like *ninkaa* is revealed by the long vowel and the tone pattern (Saeed 1987: 25).

When the focus particle *baa* is followed by a clitic subject pronoun, the two will coalesce. See:

(24)   *Axmed baan arkay* 'I saw Axmed'

where *baan* is the fusion of *baa* (focus particle) plus *aan* 'subject clitic pronoun 1st person singular'. Coalescence can be even more complex:

(25)   *Maxaad doonaysaa?* 'What do you want?'

In (25), *maxaad* is the result of the fusion of three words: *maxay* 'what' + *baa* 'focus'+ *aad* 'you'.

26.3.5. Reduplication

This mechanism is widespread in Somali morphology, showing a certain amount of correspondence between form and meaning. All reduplicated forms express the meaning 'more' in terms of intensity or number.

Reduplication can be used both with verbs and nouns: when used with nouns the result is a plural and can be used only with monosyllabic masculine nouns:

(26)   af   afaf   'mouth, tongue'
       nin   niman   'man'
       buug   buugag   'book'

Notice that the plural formation operates on the noun's underlying form (see *nin/niman*).

As for verbs, reduplicated forms have an intensive meaning of repeated action:

(27)   *fur* 'to open' *furfur* 'to open more than once'

References

Abraham, R. C. 1964. *Somali-English Dictionary*. London: University of London Press (repr. 1968).

Andrzejewski, B. W. 1955. "The Problem of Vowel Representation in the Isaaq Dialect of Somali." *Bulletin of the School of Oriental and African Studies* 17: 567–80.

———. 1956. "Accentual Patterns in the Isaaq Dialect of Somali." *Bulletin of the School of Oriental and African Studies* 18: 103–29.

Angoujard, Jean, & Mohamed M. Hassan. 1991. "Qualité vocalique, rhythme et genre grammatical en Somali." *Linguistique Africaine* 6: 11–49.

Armstrong, Lilias E. 1934. "The Phonetic Structure of Somali." *Mitteilungen des Seminars für orientalischen Sprachen zu Berlin* 37–38: 116–61 (repr. Westmead Farnborough: Gregg, 1964).

Berghold, K. 1897. "Somali-Studien." *Zeitschrift für afrikanische und ozeanische Sprachen* 3: 116–98.

———. 1899. "Somali-Studien." *Wiener Zeitschrift für die Kunde des Morgenlandes* 13: 123–98.

Cardona, Giorgio R. 1981. "Profilo fonologico del Somalo." In Cardona & Agostini 1981: 5–26.

Cardona, Giorgio R., & Francesco Agostini (eds.). 1981. *Fonologia e Lessico*. Studi Somali 1. Rome: Ministero Afferi Esteri.

Cerulli, Enrico. 1957–59. *Somalia: scritti vari editi e inediti*. Rome: Istituto Poligrafico dello Stato.

Farnetani, Edda. 1981. "Dai tratti ai parametri: introduzione all'analisi strumentale della lingua somala." in Cardona & Agostini 1981: 27–107.

Greenberg, Joseph H. 1955. *Studies in African Linguistic Classification*. New Haven: Compass.

Hunter, F. M. 1880. *A Grammar of the Somali Language*. Bombay.

Hyman, Larry M. 1981. "L'accento tonale in somalo." In Cardona & Agostini 1981: 109–41.

Jones, Daniel. 1950. *The Phoneme: Its Nature and Use*. Cambridge: Heffer.

Klingenheben, A. 1949. "Ist das Somali eine Tonsprache?" *Zeitschrift für Phonetik und allgemeine Sprachwissenschaft* 3: 289–303.

Lamberti, Marcello. 1983. "The Linguistic Situation in the Somali Democratic Republic." In *Proceedings of the Second International Congress of Somali Studies, University of Hamburg, August 1–6*, 4 vols., ed. T. Labahn, vol. , pp.155–200. Hamburg: Buske.

Moreno, Martino M. 1955. *Il somalo della Somalia. Grammatica e testi del benadir, darod e dighil*. Rome: Istituto Poligrafico dello Stato.

Puglielli, Annarita. 1984a. "La derivazione nominale in somalo." In Puglielli 1984b: 1–52.

——— (ed.). 1984b. *Aspetti morfologici, lessicali e della focalizzazione*. Studi Somali 5. Rome: MAE.

Puglielli, Annarita, & Ciise M. Siyaad. 1984. "La flessione del nome." In Puglielli 1984b: 53–112.

Reinisch, Leo. 1903. *Die Somali-Sprache: Grammatik*. Vienna: Holder.

Saeed, John H. 1987. *Somali Reference Grammar*. Wheaton, Md.: Dunwoody.

Schleicher, A. W. 1892. *Die Somali-Sprache*, part 1: *Texte, Lautlehre, Formenlehere und Syntax*. Berlin: Frohlich.

Chapter 27
Hausa Phonology
Paul Newman
Indiana University

27.1. Introduction

Hausa has the largest number of speakers of any language in sub-Saharan Africa.[1] It is the first language of some 30 million people in northern Nigeria, the Niger Republic, and in scattered communities of settlers and traders in large towns throughout West Africa. In addition, there is also a Hausa-speaking community in the Blue Nile area of the Sudan dating from the beginning of the 20th century.

Hausa is also widely spoken as a second language and is spreading rapidly in its role as a lingua franca. It is extensively used for governmental, educational, and commercial purposes and is employed in the mass media. Hausa language broadcasting, for example, is done not only within Nigeria and Niger, but also by international stations such as the BBC, Voice of America, Radio Deutsche Welle, and Radio Moscow. A number of newspapers appear in Hausa and book publishing is active. Both the Bible and the Koran have been translated into Hausa.

The predominant writing system now employed, which was introduced by the British colonial administration at the beginning of the 20th century, is a modified Roman alphabet, with neither tone nor vowel length represented.[2] Many Hausas, however, still prefer the Arabic script (called *àjàmi*), in which the language had been written a century earlier.

Hausa belongs to the Chadic language family, itself a constituent part of the Afroasiatic phylum. In Chadic, Hausa effectively constitutes a group by itself within the West branch. The only other member of the group, Gwandara, which is spoken some 300 kilometers to the south of Hausaland proper, is a creolized offshoot of Hausa rather than a true sister language.

1. This description is part of a Hausa Reference Grammar being prepared with the support of grants from the U.S. Department of Education (PO-17A10037), the National Endowment for the Humanities (RT-21236), and the National Science Foundation (DBS-9107103).
2. An attempt in Niger to promote an orthography in which long vowels were written with double letters proved to be a failure and was eventually dropped.

Lexically, Hausa has borrowed extensively from other languages. Most of its loanwords have come from Arabic, but it has also taken words from Mande, Tuareg, Kanuri, and other neighboring African languages. In this century, vocabulary development has been due primarily to loanwords from English (in Nigeria) and French (in Niger).

Considering the size and geographical extent of Hausa, it exhibits relatively modest dialect variation. The dialect regarded as Standard Hausa is that spoken in Kano State and adjacent areas to the north and south. The dialects spoken to the west in Sokoto and northwest into Niger can be roughly grouped together as Western Hausa.

Some of the most important sources of information on Hausa phonology are Abraham (1959), Greenberg (1941), Klingenheben (1927/28), and Parsons (1970). A comprehensive bibliography of works on the language is Baldi (1977), to which an update has been provided by Awde (1988).

27.2. Phonological inventory

27.2.1. Consonants

The consonant phonemes of Standard Hausa (SH) are presented in Table 27-1.

Table 27-1. Hausa Consonants

vl	f	fy	t	c	k	kw	ky
vd		b		d	j	g	gw	gy
gl		ɓ		ɗ	'y	ƙ	ƙw	ƙy
vl				s	sh			
vd				z	(j)			
gl				ts				
		m		n				
				l				
				r				
				r̃				
				y		w		h	ʔ

The letters *c* and *j* represent the affricates [tʃ] and [dʒ] respectively. (In the Hausa of Niger, /j/ is usually pronounced [ʒ].) The /f/ phoneme is variably pronounced as [p], [f], or [ɸ]. In Western Hausa (WH), it is usually [hw] before /a(a)/ and [h] before other vowels, e.g. WH *hwaadì* 'fall' (= SH *faadì*), WH *tàhi* 'go' (= SH *tàfi*). Before back rounded vowels it is often pronounced (and, if so, written) as [h], e.g. *dafàa* 'cook', *dàfuwaa* = *dàhuwaa* 'cooking'. The glottalized series includes both laryngealized, implosive stops, indicated by the "hooked" letters ɓ and ɗ, and glottalized ejectives, indicated by the hooked letter symbol ƙ and the digraph *ts*. The non-glottalized counterparts of these consonants are /b/, /d/, /k/, and /s/, respectively. In Katsina and other WH dialects, there is also a palatal ejective /cʼ/, which contrasts with /ts/ before /a(a)/, e.g. WH *c'àaki* 'chicks' vs. *tsàaki* 'clicking sound in the throat', both of which are pronounced /tsàaki/ in SH. The glottalized approximant /ʼy/, which occurs in only a few very high frequency words, is a historically recent phoneme, having developed from the sequence /ɗiy-/ via /ɗy/, cf. SH *ʼyaa* with WH *ɗìyaa* 'daughter'.

The palatalized and labialized velars contrast with their plain counterparts before the vowel /a(a)/, e.g. *gàdaa* 'duiker', *gwàdaa* 'test!', *gyàdaa* 'peanuts'. Before the back/rounded vowels, the velars are all redundantly labialized and before front vowels they are automatically palatalized. These features are not shown in standard orthography, i.e. *doogoo* 'tall' = [doogwoo], cf. the pl. *doogwàayee*; *geefèe* 'side' = [gyeefèe], cf. the pl. *gyâffaa*. The exceptional words with a labialized velar followed by /i(i)/, e.g. *gwiiɓàa* 'sediment', *kwiikwiyòo* 'puppy', are due to historically recent changes of /u/ to /i/, especially in connection with the monophthongization of the */ui/ diphthong to /ii/, i.e. *gwiiɓàa* < *gwuiɓàa*; *kwiikwiyòo* < *kwuikwuyòo*.

The palatalized labial /fy/ is lexically infrequent and is often replaced by its plain counterpart, e.g. *fyaacèe* = *faacèe* 'blow one's nose'. Some WH dialects—the exact distribution is not clear—also have a set of labialized alveolars as part of their consonant inventory, e.g. WH *twàarii* = SH *tàarii* 'cough'; WH *dwai* = SH *dòoyii* 'stench'.

In word final position /n/ is pronounced [ŋ], e.g. *cân* 'there' = [câŋ]. Speakers of Standard Hausa also commonly pronounce final /m/ as [ŋ], thereby resulting in a merger of the two phonemic nasals, e.g. *maalàm* 'teacher' = [maalàm] or [maalàŋ].

The symbol r̃ is used to distinguish the apical tap or roll from the retroflex flap *r* with which it contrasts, e.g. *r̃ahàa* 'pleasant chatting', *raanii* 'dry season', *màr̃gaa* 'a cassia tree', *sarkii* 'emir'. In word-final position, only r̃ occurs, e.g. *'àshâr̃* 'obscene language', *teebùr̃* 'table', *bar̃* pre-object form of *barìi* 'leave, let'. The difference between the two rhotics is not indicated in orthography. In syllable-final position, many speakers, especially in WH dialects, commonly substitute /l/ for either or both R's. The flap is the native Hausa R; the roll has come in through loanwords, primarily from Arabic, Kanuri, and English, from the phonemicization of expressive pronunciation used with ideophones and intensive forms, e.g. ȓagaȓgàzaa 'shatter', ȓamas 'emphasizes dryness', and from the rhotacization of alveolar obstruents in syllable-final position, e.g. faȓkàa 'wake up' (< *faɗkàa), cf. fàrkaa 'paramour'.

Glottal stop and /h/ are also historically recent phonemes in Hausa, having developed in a similar manner. They both probably existed in the language for some time, in the case of ['] as a phonetic marker of vowel-initial words and, with short vowels, of prepausal position, and in the case of [h] as an allophone of /f/ as well as also being an alternative means of attack for vowel-initial words. Their phonemicization was due to a combination of language-internal sound changes reinforced and/or stimulated by their introduction in medial and initial position in Arabic loanwords, e.g. àddu'àa 'prayer', sàbà'in 'seventy', 'azùmii 'fasting', haajàa 'merchandise', hàmsin 'fifty', jaahìlii 'ignorance', shàhaadàa 'martyrdom'.

The semivowels /y/ and /w/ only occur in syllable onset position. If they are shifted to the coda because of vowel apocope or morphological processes, they automatically alternate with their corresponding vowels, /i/ and /u/, e.g. màraayaa 'orphan', màrainìyaa 'female orphan'; maayèe 'sorcerer', mâitaa 'sorcery'; sàyi 'buy' = sai (optional clipped form); ɓàraawòo 'thief', ɓàraunìyaa 'female thief', baawàa 'slave', bàutaa 'slavery', 'awoo 'weighing', 'aunàa 'to weigh'.

All Hausa consonants can be geminated. (With consonants indicated by a diagraph, only the first letter is written doubled, e.g. /gàsaššee/ 'roasted' is indicated here and in standard orthography as gàsasshee.) At an analytical level, geminates can be viewed as a sequence of identical consonants abutting across a syllable boundary, i.e. baccii 'sleep' has the canonical form $C_1VC_2.C_3VV$, where C_2 and C_3 happen to be identical. In underived words, only geminate nasals and liquids are common, e.g. dannèe 'suppress', hannuu 'hand' (cf. hanuu 'frankincense tree'), tallee 'soup pot'; but others do occur sporadically in native words, e.g. tukkuu 'bird's crop' and more frequently in loanwords from Arabic, e.g. hajjì 'the Hajj', jabbàa 'sleeveless robe'. In morphologicially derived forms, however, geminates are extremely common, e.g. râssaa 'branches', pl. of reeshèe, hahhau 'mount many or often', pluractional[3] of *hau*; *fàffaaɗaa* 'broad', derived adjective from *faaɗii* 'breadth', and *zàaɓaɓɓee* 'chosen, adjectival past participle of *zàaɓaa* 'choose'.

27.2.2. Vowels
The vowel phonemes (which are the same for all dialects) are presented in Table 27-2.

Table 27-2. Hausa Vowels

Short			Long		Diphthongs	
i		u	ii		uu	
	e	o		ee	oo	
	a			aa	ai	au

Hausa has five basic vowels, all of which have long and short counterparts. The long vowels have typical IPA values, while the corresponding short vowels are more lax and centralized. In prepausal position, the qualitative difference between the vowels is less pronounced, but the short vowels are easily recognizable as such because they are automatically checked by a glottal closure. The length contrast is only found in open syllables: in closed syllables all vowels are short.

In word-medial position, vowel length functions lexically, e.g. *fiitòo* 'whistling' vs. *fitòo* 'ferrying'; *faasàa* 'postpone' vs. *fasàa* 'smash'; *duukàa* 'beating' vs. *dukà* 'all'. In final position, however, its function is to a great extent morphological and grammatical, e.g. *hannuu* 'hand' vs. *'à hannu* 'in the hand'; *fitaa* 'going out' vs. *fita* 'go out'; *shi* 'him (direct object form)' vs. *shii* 'him (independent form)'; *saaboo* 'new' vs. *Saabo* 'proper name'.

The present balanced vowel system derives historically from a skewed system in which the number of contrasts varied depending on the position within the word. In final position, all five vowels occurred, but with a minimal length contrast, if at all. The rule seems to have been that apart from monosyllabic content words (nouns and verbs) ending in /aa/, all final vowels were

---

3. The term "pluractional" refers to a verbal derivation, traditionally called "intensive" in Hausa and other languages, which is used to indicate the plurality of the action and/or of the patient (either object of a transitive verb or subject of an intransitive), see Newman (1990).

short. In word-initial position—and Hausa did have vowel-initial words—only short /a/ and /i/ were used. (If [u] occurred, it would have been a conditioned variant of /i/.) Otherwise, the language had three vowels (/i(i)/, /a(a)/, and /u(u)/), which could occur long or short.

The vowels /i/ and /u/ exhibit special restrictions in relation to their semivowel counterparts. The first is the fact that /i/ before /y/ and /u/ before /w/ are always short.[4] The second is the fact that whereas the sequences /yi/ and /wu/ occur, */yu/ and */wi/ normally do not.[5] (Surface exceptions result from the fact that /u/ before /y/ is pronounced [i], i.e. *wuyàa* 'neck' → [wiyàa].)

The vowels /e(e)/ and /o(o)/, which underlyingly are always long in medial position, only occur in in open syllables. If the syllable becomes closed, due to any number of morphophonological processes, the vowel invariably shortens and generally merges with short /a/, e.g. *gyeefèe* 'side', pl. *gyâffaa* (< *gyêffaa < *gyêeffaa < *gyeefàfaa), *toonàa* 'dig up', pluractional *tantòonaa* (< *tontòonaa < *toontòonaa).

Synchronically there are two diphthongs /ai/ and /au/, which function as long vocalic nuclei, e.g. *mâi* 'oil', *kaifii* 'sharpness', *sàu* 'times', *ɓaunaa* 'buffalo'. In the not so distant past, there were two other diphthongs: */ui/, which monophthongized to /ii/, e.g. *gwuiɓàa > gwiiɓàa 'sediment', and */iu/, which monophthongized to /uu/, e.g. *shiukàa (< *shibkàa) > shuukàa 'to sow'. (Note the instructive doublet meaning 'illness': *cùutaa (< *cìutaa < *cìiw-taa (with the -taa abstract suffix) = *ciiwòo.) The /ai/ diphthong is pronounced [ai] or [əi] when occurring in a monosyllabic word with falling tone or when preceded by /'/ or /h/. Elsewere it is pronounced as [ei] or often even [ee], thereby merging with long /ee/. The back diphthong /au/ varies in the [au] to [ou] range, but usually remains distinct from /oo/.

27.2.3. Tone

Hausa has two level tones, Hi (unmarked in transcription) and Lo (indicated by a grave accent), e.g. *raanaa* 'sun, day', *dàgà* 'from', *taagàa* 'window', *bàara* 'last year', *gooràa* 'bamboo', *gòoraa* 'large gourd'. (With long vowels, the tone mark is only placed on the first of the two vowels.) It also has a Falling contour (indicated by a circumflex), which only occurs on heavy syl-

---

4. As pointed out by Gouffé (1965: 195n), the usually reliable dictionary by Abraham (1962) is systematically wrong in this regard: Abraham invariably transcribes long /ii/ and /uu/ before /y/ and /w/ respectively.

5. This asymmetry is contrary to the supposed norm, discussed by Ohala and Kawasaki (1984: 122–24), which is that /yi/ and /wu/ lack acoustic salience and thus are marked in relation to /yu/ and /wi/ and would be expected to occur less commonly than the latter pair.

lables. This Falling tone can be analyzed as Hi plus Lo on a single syllable, e.g, *yâaraa* (HiLo-Hi) 'children', *mântaa* (HiLo-Hi) 'forget', *mîn* (HiLo) = *minì* 'to me'.[6] There is no Rising tone. Presumed Lo-Hi sequences on a single syllable, which would be expected to result from apocopation and such, do not surface. They are simplified to Lo if immediately preceded by Hi, and Hi elsewhere, e.g. *gawàyii* = *gawài* (< *gáwàî) 'charcoal', *mukà yi* = *mukài* (< *múkàî) 'we did'; *tàawa* = *tau* (< *tàû) 'mine'; *tàusàyii* = *tàusai* (< *tàusàî) 'pity'.

27.3. Syllable structure

Only three syllable types occur in the language: CV, CVV (where VV can be a long vowel or a diphthong), and CVC. (In a few instances, a syllabic nasal serves as the vocalic nucleus of a syllable or as a syllable by itself, e.g. *ǹgùlu* or *ňgùlu* = *ùngùlu* 'vulture'; *ǹ zoo?* or *ň zoo?* = *'ìn zoo?* 'Should I come?') The CV syllable type is light; the other two are heavy. Syllables may not contain both a long vowel (whether monophthongal or diphthongal) and a final consonant. Such overheavy syllables, which commonly result from morphological processes, are automatically pared down by nucleus reduction rules, e.g. *râi-n-sà (lit. life-of-him) → *rânsà* 'his life' ; *faar-koo → *farkoo* 'beginning' (cf. *faaràa* 'begin'); *cuus-cùusaa* → *cuccùusaa* 'stuff repeatedly'.

All Hausa syllables (and thus all Hausa words) begin with a consonant. Words that appear in the orthography with an initial vowel begin phonemically with a glottal stop, e.g. *aure* 'marriage' = /*'auree*/. This restriction against vowel-intial words is *not* an inherited Afroasiatic feature as it might first appear. Rather it is due to a historically shallow change whereby a prothetic, originally sub-phonemic, consonant, /'/ or /h/, was added to vowel-initial words, e.g. *askìi > *'askìi* 'shaving', *aɓàa > *haɓàa* 'chin'. True consonant clusters are not allowed, although two consonants may abut across a syllable boundary, e.g. *han.tàa* 'liver'. Most words end in a vowel, the exceptions being ideophones, e.g. *wulik* 'emphasizing blackness', recent loanwords, e.g. *kyât* 'cake', or the result of vowel apocopation, e.g. *kâr̃* = *kadà* 'don't'.

Hausa words tend to be disyllabic, trisyllabic, or even quadrisyllabic. Monosyllabic words occur, but with a more restricted distribution. They are the norm for pronouns, connectors, and other function words and they are

---

6. Although structurally the Falling tone is easily analyzed as a combination of Hi + Lo, there is evidence that at the level of *Sprachgefühl* it exists as a unitary contour.

also common with ideophones. On the other hand, there are only some twelve monosyllabic verbs, mostly C*i* or C*aa* with Hi tone (e.g. *bi* 'follow', *jaa* 'pull') and a small number of CVV nouns with Hi or Falling tone, e.g. *faa* 'flat rock', *mâi* 'oil', *sau* 'foot'.

27.4. Phonotactic restrictions

27.4.1. Sonorants

In normal CVCV sequences, /l/ and /n/, and /l/ and /r/ cannot co-occur. (As a result, the rendition of the English loanwords 'linen', /lilìn/ and 'nylon' /liilìn/ end up almost being identical.)[7] The restriction does not, however, apply to the plural suffix -*unàa*, e.g. *tùuluu* 'waterpot', pl. *tuulunàa*, or to other cliticized elements, e.g. *tùuluunaa* 'my waterpot'. The l/r restriction only applies to the flap /r/; words with the sequence /r̃/ – /l/ and /l/ – /r̃/ do occur, e.g. *lùur̃a* 'look after', *r̃uulàa* 'ruler'. In the case of flap /r/ and /n/, there is a one-directional restriction: /r/ – /n/ occurs readily, e.g. *rinàa* 'dye', *raanii* 'dry season', but /n/ – /r/ does not, the word *narkèe* 'melt' being an exception.

27.4.2. Glottalized segments

There are two restrictions that affect the glottalized consonants.

(a) One cannot have two different glottalized consonants in the same word, i.e. /ɓ/ – /ts/ or /ƙ/ – /ɗ/ do not co-occur in the same word, whether in immediate sequence or separated by other elements. The Arabic loanword *ɗar̃iiƙàa* 'religious sect' is an exception. One can, however, have multiple instances of the same consonant, e.g. *ɓaaɓèe* 'quarrel', *ɗàaɗumàa* 'drive away', *tsaatsàa* 'rust', *ƙuuƙùutaa* 'try hard'.

(b) Generally speaking, glottalized consonants and their non-glottalized counterparts cannot co-occur in the same word, i.e. sequences of /b/ – /ɓ/ or /k/ – /ƙ/ do not occur in either order. On the other hand, whereas the sequence /ɗ/ – /d/ does not occur in that order, /d/ – /ɗ/ is quite normal, e.g. *daaɗii* 'pleasantness', *daɗèe* 'last long'. Similarly, /ts/ – /s/ does not occur, although there are a few examples of /s/ – /ts/ with an intervening consonant, e.g. *santsii*, 'slipperiness', *sartsèe* 'splinter'. Instances of words containing /ƙ/ and a suffix with /k/, e.g. *ƙauy-ukàa* 'villages', *ƙar-koo* 'durability', suggest that the glottalization restriction is perhaps a property of roots rather than full words.

---

7. Syllable-final nasals have an ambiguous status in Hausa (behaving in many respects like components of the vocalic nucleus) and thus would not be expected to obey the same principles.

27.4.3. Tone and vowel length

With some exceptions (e.g. recent loanwords and ideophonic reduplicatives) there are no words ending in a Lo-Lo tone sequence and a long final vowel. Thus, *màcè* 'woman', *gwàdò* 'blanket', and *kaaɽùwà* 'prostitute' occur, but words such as **kàrèe* or **zòomòo* or **tunkìyàa* do not.[8]

27.5. Syllable weight

Syllable weight plays an essential role in Hausa phonology and morphology in a number of different areas, of which the following are only some selected examples (see Newman 1972, 1981).

27.5.1. Canonical shape

(a) Different pronoun paradigms are generally marked by a fixed weight pattern. For example, direct object and subjunctive subject pronouns are all characterized by a light syllable, whereas disjunctive and perfective pronouns are characterized by a heavy syllable, e.g. ('1, 2m., 2f., 3m., 3f., 1pl., 2pl., 3pl.'):

direct object (Hi tone set): *ni, ka, ki, shi, ta, mu, ku, su*
subjunctive: *ǹ, kà, kì, yà, tà, mù, kù, sù*
disjunctive: *nii, kai, kee, shii, 'ita, muu, kuu, suu*[9]
perfective: *naa, kaa, kin, yaa, taa, mun, kun, sun*

(b) Abstract nouns of sensory quality, a group of semantically related nouns ending in *-ii*, all have a heavy first syllable, e.g. *zaafii* 'heat', *nauyii* 'heaviness', *ƙarfii* 'strength'.

(c) Verb + noun compounds in which the first element is monosyllabic invariably have a heavy first syllable, even if the verb would normally have a short vowel, e.g. *shàa-zumaamì* 'sugar ant' (lit. drink honey); *cìi-raani* 'dry season work' (lit. eat dry season < *ci* 'to eat'); *bìi-bango* 'water dripping along the wall' (lit. follow the wall < *bi* 'to follow'); *kàs-dafî* 'a poison antidote' (lit. kill poison).

27.5.2. Rhythmic weight polarity

(a) With the verbalizing suffix *-a(a)ta*, the length of the /a(a)/ is determined by the weight of the preceding syllable to produce either a Heavy–Light

---

8. This phonotactic restriction was first pointed out explicitly by Leben (1971). For a reinterpretation of various synchronic tone rules postulated in connection with this restriction, see Newman and Jaggar (1989).

9. The feminine pronoun *'ita* illustrates the metrical equivalence of a heavy syllable to two light syllables.

pattern or a Light–Heavy alternation, e.g. *tsooràtaa* 'frighten' < *tsòoroo* 'fear'; *ƙàunatàa* 'love s.o.' < *ƙàunaa* 'love'; *ɗanyàtaa* 'moisten' < *ɗanyee* 'fresh, moist'; cf. *fùsaatà* 'be angry' < *fushii* 'anger'; *wàdaatàa* 'enrich' < *wàdaa* 'wealth'.

(b) The reduplicative verbalizer also exhibits weight polarity, e.g. *zaafàfaa* 'to make hot' < *zaafii* 'heat', *kaifàfaa* 'sharpen' < *kaifii* 'sharpness'; cf. *ɗumàamaa* 'warm up' < *ɗùmii* 'warmth'.

27.5.3. Syllable weight and tone

(a) Basic disyllabic intransitive verbs ending in -*a* (the so-called "grade 3" verbs) normally have Lo-Hi tone and a light first syllable, e.g. *tùma* 'jump', *shìga* 'enter', *tsìra* 'germinate'. Grade 3 verbs with a heavy first syllable generally have Hi-Hi tone, e.g. *girma* 'grow up', *ƙaura* 'migrate', *tsiira* 'escape'.

(b) Plurals of "ethnonyms" (which includes occupations and such) are formed by means of a suffix -*aawaa*. Those which are built on disyllabic stems with a heavy first syllable often have a Lo-Lo-Hi tone pattern; ethnonyms with all other syllabic shapes have all Hi tones, e.g. *Hàusàawaa* 'Hausa people', *Gwàaràawaa* 'Gwari people', *dùukàawaa* 'leather workers'; cf. *Badaawaa* 'Bade people', *Kanaawaa* 'people from Kano', *Zazzagaawaa* 'people from Zaria'.

(c) Hypocoristics formed by final syllable reduplication have Lo-Hi-Hi tone if the initial syllable is heavy. If the initial syllable is light, the word has an initial Hi tone, the other tones being unpredictable, e.g. *Làadiidi* < *Laadì* 'fem. name'; *Àuduudu* < *Audù* 'masc. name'; *Mùɗɗeeɗe* < *Mùɗɗe* 'masc. name'; cf. *Inuunu* < *Inuu* 'masc. name', *Kulùulu* < *Kulù* 'fem. name'.

27.6. Functioning and operation of tone

27.6.1. Lexical and grammatical tone

Tone functions both lexically and grammatically. Although lexically tone does not have a functional load comparable to a West African language such as Igbo, it does serve to distinguish a number of lexical items from one another, e.g. *kai* 'you (m.)', *kâi* 'head'; *gòoraa* 'large gourd', *gooràa* 'bamboo'; *kuukàa* 'baobab tree', *kuukaa* 'crying'; *wuyàa* 'neck', *wùyaa* 'trouble'; *suntàa* 'untie, loosen', *sùntaa* 'catch fish'. Grammatically, tone serves to mark tense/aspects, verb derivations, nominalizations, adverbializations, etc. This is sometimes done by tone itself but more often in conjunction with changes in vowel length, e.g.

taa 'she (past tense)', *tâa* 'she (future tense)'
dafàa 'to cook', *dàfaa* 'cook! (imperative)'
shaa 'to drink', *shâa* 'drinking'; *ci* 'to eat', *cîi* 'eating'
'idòo 'eye', *'ido* 'in the eye'; *ƙasaa* 'ground', *ƙasà* 'on the ground'

27.6.2. Fixed tone patterns

Inflectional and derivational constructions in Hausa tend to have associated with them set tone patterns which override the lexical tone of the underlying items. For example, agentives with the prefix *ma-* have the tone pattern Hi-(Lo-)Lo-Hi; language names and locative nouns with the prefix *ma-* are all Hi; abstracts with the ending *-(n)takaa* have the pattern Lo-Lo-Hi-Lo; plurals with the suffix *-unaa* have a ...Hi-Lo pattern; and plurals with the suffix *-ai* have a ...Lo-Hi pattern.

manòomii 'farmer', *maròowàcii* 'miser', *majèemii* 'tanner'
Laaȓabcii 'Arabic', *Jaamusancii* 'German'
makaȓantaa 'school', *majeemaa* 'tannery'
jàaȓùntakàa 'bravery', *yàaràntakàa* 'youthfulness'
tùddai 'hills', *bàalìgai* 'adults', *'àlmùbàzzàȓai* 'spendthrifts'
huununàa 'caps', *agoogunàa* 'clocks'; *bakunkunàa* 'bows'

27.7. Phonological processes

Understanding of Hausa phonology and morphology requires the recognition of a number of phonological processes. Some of these processes are essentially historical in nature, although their existence is still evident in morphological alternations; whereas others still function as synchronic rules, although not necessarilty in a totally productive, exceptionless manner. For convenience, one can divide the changes into two groups, those affecting coda (i.e. syllable-final) consonants,[10] and those showing the influence of vowels on syllable initial consonants.

27.7.1. Assimilation of nasals

In prevocalic position, there are two distinct nasals, the bilabial /m/ and the alveolar /n/. When followed immediately by another consonant, whether within the same word or across word boundaries, /n/ always undergoes anticipatory assimilation to the position of that abutting consonant, e.g.

---

10. A number of these changes were described over a half century ago by Klingenheben (1927/28). Some of these, especially the weakening of velar and labial stops to /u/, have now come to be called "Klingenheben's laws."

sun bi 'they followed' → [sumbi]
gidankù 'your house' → [gidaŋkù] (cf. [gidansù]/[gidammù] 'their/our house')

In Standard Hausa, but not in WH dialects, /m/ codas also undergo place assimilation, e.g.

ɗinkàa [ɗiŋkàa] 'sew' = WH *ɗumkàa*
ƙàzântaa 'filthiness', cf. *ƙàzaamii* 'filth'.

27.7.2. Syllable-final velars

Syllable-final velars historically weakened to /u/, e.g.

talaucìi 'poverty' < **talakcìi*, cf. *talàkà* 'common man'
sàraunìyaa 'queen' < **sàraknìyaa*, cf. *sarkii* 'king'
haurèe 'tooth' < **haƙrèe*, cf. *haƙoorii* 'tooth/teeth' (originally a plural form)

27.7.3. Syllable-final labials

Syllable-final labial obstruents historically weakened to /u/, but in Standard Hausa only. The change also affected /m/, but only when abutting with a following /n/ or /r/. In WH dialects, the original consonant remained.

sàuka 'get down' = WH *sàpka*
Audù 'proper name' = WH *Abdù*[11]
'audùgaa 'cotton' = WH *'abdùgaa*
shuukàa 'to sow' (< **shiukàa*) = WH *shipkàa*
taushii 'type of drum', (pl. *tafàashee*) = WH *tafshii*
zaunàa 'sit' (cf. *zamaa* 'sitting') = WH *zamnàa*
'auree 'marriage' (cf. *'amaryaa* 'bride') = WH *'amree*

27.7.4. Rhotacization

Syllable-final coronal stops and the ejective /ts/ undergo rhotacization to the rolled /r̃/ as an active process.

kar̃kàɗaa 'beat repeatedly' < **kaɗkàɗaa*, cf. *kaɗàa* 'beat'
mar̃màtsaa 'push, pester repeatedly', cf. *matsàa* 'push, pester'
hur̃huɗu 'four each', cf. *huɗu* 'four'
'yar̃sà = *'yaatasà* 'his daughter'
far̃kee 'trader' (< **fatkee*), cf. pl. *fatàakee*
kar̃ apocopated form of *kadà* 'do not!'

---

11. Interestingly, names such as *Àbdùllaahì*, *Àbdùlsàlâm*, and *Àbdùlmaalìk* are pronounced with /b/ rather than /u/ even by Standard Hausa speakers who say *Audù* rather than *Abdù*.

The rule also applies to /s/ and /z/, but in a more sporadic, unpredictable fashion, e.g.

> marár̃ = marás 'lacking', cf. pl. marásaa
> fitar̃ = fitas (WH) 'take out' (from fìta 'go out')
> gìr̃gijèe (< *gìzgizèe) 'raincloud', cf. pl. gìzàagìzai
> mar̃maza 'very quickly', cf. maza 'quickly'
> cf. kaskoo 'bowl' (not *kar̃koo); fìzgaa 'grab' (not *fìr̃gaa)

27.7.5. Gemination

Coda consonants in Hausa commonly assimilate fully to an abutting consonant to form a geminate, e.g.

> *fit-shee → fisshee 'take out (pre-pronoun form)'
> *kwan laafiyàa → kwal laafiyàa 'rest well!'
> fuskàr̃kà = fuskàkkà 'your face'

The gemination particularly shows up in reduplicative constructions such as pluractional verbs or adjectives derived from sensory quality nouns. In these cases, gemination occurs instead of the rules changing velars and bilabials to /u/ and alveolars to /r̃/, the latter usually being a possible option.

> daddàkaa pluractional of dakàa 'pound' (not *daudàkaa)
> kakkàfaa pluractional of kafàa 'affix' (not *kaukàfaa)
> fìffìta (= fìr̃fìta) pluractional of fìta 'go out'
> mammàtsaa (= mar̃màtsaa) pluractional of matsàa 'push, pester'
> kakkaawoo pluractional of kaawoo 'bring'
> gwàggwaaɓaa 'thick' < gwaaɓii 'thickness'
> zàzzaafaa 'hot' < zaafii 'heat'
> wàwwaaraa 'smelly' < waarii 'stench'
> kàkkauraa 'stout' < kaurii 'stoutness'

27.7.6. Palatalization

(a) When followed by a front vowel, either i(i) or e(e), the alveolars s, z, and t palatalize to sh, j, and c, respectively, e.g.

> gàshe stative form of gasàa 'roast'
> kàajii pl. of kàazaa 'hen'
> sàacee pre-pronoun form of sàataa 'steal'

The voiced stop d also palatalizes to j, with resultant neutralization of the z/d contrast, but less regularly than with the above consonants. It generally is blocked by a preceding /n/ and in other environments the palatalization is either optional or lexically determined, e.g.

> *gìndii* 'base', *kundii* 'pad of paper', cf. *hanjìi* (< *hanzìi) 'intestines'
> *jìdee* pre-pronoun form of *jìdaa* 'transport'
> *bidoodii* pl. of *bidàa* 'thatching needle'
> *kadoodii* = *kadoojii* pl. of *kadàa* 'crocodile'
> *gàajee* (not *gàadee) pre-pronoun form of *gàadaa* 'inherit'

The sonorants *n, l, r̃,* and *r̃* do not undergo palatalization, nor does *d*. The ejective sibilant *ts* palatalizes to *c'* (an ejective affricate) in WH dialects, but not in Standard Hausa, e.g. SH *duutsèe* = WH *duuc'ìi* 'stone', SH *tsiilaa* = WH *c'iilaa* 'tapeworm'.

The palatalization process shows up readily in morphological constructions. Because of the introduction of loanwords and the operation of various sound changes, non-palatalized alveolars before front vowels are now very common, e.g.

> *sillee* (= *sullee*) 'top of corn stalk'
> *ƙoosee* (= *ƙoosai*) 'fried beancake'
> *zîi* 'diamonds' (card suit), *ziinaar̃ìi* 'gold'
> *teebùr̃* 'table', *'asìbitì* 'hospital' (pl. *'asibitoocii*, with palatalization!)

Because the palatalization rule was presumably fully regular at an earlier historical stage, one now finds words with the palatalized consonant in the underlying, lexical form and the non-palatalized counterpart in the derived form, e.g.

> *gaashìi* 'hair', *gàr̃gaasaa* (< *gàsgaasaa) 'hairy'
> *dùƙushii* 'colt', *dùƙusaa* 'female colt'
> *mijìi* 'husband', pl. *mazaa* 'males'
> *ƙuncii* 'restricted', *ƙuntàtaa* 'restrict'

As was mentioned earlier, /e/ normally changes to /a/ in closed syllables. It should be pointed out that the application of the rules must be ordered so that the palatalization takes place before the /e/ → /a/ change, e.g.

> *jeenèe* (< *zeenèe) 'row of reaped corn' pl. *jânnaa* (not *zânnaa)
> *sàataccân* 'the stolen one' (< **sàatattee-n̄*)

(b) The semivowel *w* also palatalizes regularly to *y*, e.g.

> *kàasuwaa* 'market', pl. *kaasuwooyii*
> *ɓàraawòo* 'thief', pl. *ɓàràayii*
> *rawaa* 'dancing', pl. *ràye-ràye*

Viewed in the context of the palatalization rule affecting alveolar obstruents, the *w* → *y* change seems totally ad hoc, but this is not so. The velars *k, g, ƙ* (and their labialized counterparts) also undergo palatalization, e.g. *taagàa* 'window', pl. [taagwooyii] (orthographically *tagogi*), *ràkee* [ràkyee], 'sugarcane', cf. *ràkensà* [ràkyansà] 'his sugarcane'. This change, unlike the palatalization of alveolars, is not, however, noted in the orthography and thus it has tended to be neglected by Hausaists. Recognizing it, however, allows one to view the *w* → *y* rule as part of a more general pattern.

27.7.7. Alternation of *f* and *h*
Much less active synchronically than palatalization is the change of /f/ to /h/ when followed by one of the back rounded vowels /u(u)/ or /o(o)/, e.g. *tàfī* 'go', *tahoo* 'come'; *dafàa* 'cook', *dàhuwaa* 'cooking'. It is evident not only in morphological alternations and dialect variants, but also in the realization of a number of English loanwords, e.g.

hudu = *fudu* 'four'
mahuucii = *mafiicii* 'fan'
mahòo 'a patch', cf. *mafèe* 'to patch'
tsoohoo 'old', cf. pl. *tsòofàffii*
hòotoo 'photo' (< Eng.)
hòoloo 'polo' (< Eng.)

The following two examples with "irregular" morpheme alternants illustrate the interaction of the various phonological processes that have been described.

(i) *màkaahòo* 'blind person' (**f* > /h/ before /oo/); *màkàafii* 'pl.' (set ...Lo-Hi tone pattern; surfacing of the underlying /f/); *màkaunìyaa* 'blind woman' < **màkaaf-nìyaa* (syllable final **f* > *u*; shortening of /aa/ to /a/ to avoid an overheavy syllable)

(ii) *zuucìyaa* 'heart' < **zuktì-yaa* (syllable final **k* > *u*; palatalization of /t/); *zukàataa* 'pl.' (set Hi-Lo-Hi tone pattern, surfacing of underlying /k/ and /t/).

References

Abraham, R. C. 1959. *Hausa Literature and the Hausa Sound System*. London: University of London Press.

———. 1962. *Dictionary of the Hausa Language*, 2nd ed. London: University of London Press.

Awde, Nicholas. 1988. "A Hausa Language and Linguistics Bibliography 1976–86 (including supplementary material for other years)." In *Studies in Hausa Language and Linguistics in Honour of F. W. Parsons*, ed. by Graham Furniss and Philip J. Jaggar, pp. 253–78. London: Kegan Paul International.

Baldi, Sergio. 1977. *Systematic Hausa Bibliography* (Istituto Italo-Africano, Collana di Studi Africani 3). Rome: Tip. Pioda.

Gouffé, Claude. 1965. "La lexicographie du haoussa et le préalable phonologique." *Journal of African Languages* 4: 191–210.

Greenberg, Joseph H. 1941. "Some Problems in Hausa Phonology." *Language* 17: 316–23.

Klingenheben, August. 1927/28. "Die Silbenauslautgesetze des Hausa." *Zeitschrift für Eingeborenen-Sprachen* 18: 272–97.

Leben, William R. 1971. "The Morphophonemics of Tone in Hausa." In *Papers in African Linguistics*, ed. by C.-W. Kim and Herbert Stahlke, pp. 201–18. Edmonton: Linguistic Research.

Newman, Paul. 1972. "Syllable Weight as a Phonological Variable." *Studies in African Linguistics* 3: 301–23.

———. 1981. "Syllable Weight and Tone." *Linguistic Inquiry* 12: 670–73.

———. 1990. *Nominal and Verbal Plurality in Chadic* (Publications in African Languages and Linguistics, 12). Dordrecht: Foris.

Newman, Paul, and Philip J. Jaggar. 1989. "Low Tone Raising in Hausa: A Critical Assessment." *Studies in African Linguistics* 20: 227–51.

Ohala, John J., and Haruko Kawasai. 1984. "Prosodic Phonology and Phonetics." *Phonology Yearbook* 1: 113–27.

Parsons, F. W. 1970. "Is Hausa Really a Chadic Language? Some Problems of Comparative Phonology." *African Language Studies* 11: 272–88.